Political Prisoners and Trials

Political Prisoners and Trials

A Worldwide Annotated Bibliography, 1900 through 1993

by

JAMES R. BENNETT

McFarland & Company, Inc., Publishers
Jefferson, North Carolina, and London

British Library Cataloguing-in-Publication data are available

Library of Congress Cataloguing-in-Publication Data

Bennett, James R., 1932–
Political prisoners and trials : a worldwide annotated bibliography, 1900 through 1993 / by James R. Bennett.
p. cm.
Includes bibliographical references and index.
ISBN 0-7864-0023-4 (lib. bdg. : 50# alk. paper)
1. Political prisoners—Bibliography. 2. Human rights—Bibliography. I. Title.
Z7164.L6B46 1995
[JC571]
016.3641'31'0922—dc20 95-6232
CIP

Manufactured in the United States of America

McFarland & Company, Inc., Publishers
Box 611, Jefferson, North Carolina 28640

TABLE OF CONTENTS

Introduction 1

General 29
Afghanistan 53
Albania 53
Algeria 54
Angola 54
Argentina 55
Armenians (*see* Turkey [Armenian persecution])
Australia 61
Austria 62
Bahrain 62
Bangladesh 62
Benin 63
Bhutan 63
Bolivia 64
Brazil 64
Brunei Darussalam 66
Bulgaria 66
Burkino Faso 67
Burma (*see* Myanmar)
Burundi 67
Cambodia (*see* Kampuchea)
Cameroon 67
Canada 67
Central African Republic 68
Chad 68
Chile 69
China, Nationalist 75
China, People's Republic of 76
China, Republic of (*see* Taiwan)
Colombia 84
Comoros 85
Congo 85
Costa Rica 85
Côte d'Ivoire (Ivory Coast) 85
Croatia 86
Cuba 86
Cyprus 90
Czechoslovakia 90
Djibouti 94
Dominican Republic 94
Ecuador 95
Egypt 95
El Salvador 97
Equatorial Guinea 99
Ethiopia 100
Fiji 101
Finland 101
France 101
Gabon 102
Gambia 102
Germany 102
Germany, German Democratic Republic (East) 103
Germany, Federal Republic of Germany (West) 104
Germany, Nazi 105
Ghana 124
Greece 125
Grenada 128
Guatemala 128
Guinea 131
Guinea-Bissau 132
Guyana 132
Haiti 132
Honduras 133

Hong Kong 134
Hungary 134
India 135
Indonesia 139
Iran 141
Iraq 146
Ireland 147
Israel 147
Italy 152
Ivory Coast (*see* Côte d'Ivoire)
Jamaica 153
Japan 154
Jordan 154
Kampuchea (Cambodia) 154
Kenya 156
Korea, North 158
Korea, South 158
Kuwait 161
Laos 161
Lebanon 162
Lesotho 162
Liberia 162
Libya 163
Madagascar 163
Malawi 164
Malaysia 164
Maldives 165
Mali 165
Mauritania 166
Mauritius 166
Mexico 166
Morocco 168
Mozambique 169
Myanmar (Burma) 169
Namibia 171
Nepal 171
Nicaragua 172
Niger 173
Nigeria 173
Pakistan 174
Panama 175
Papua New Guinea 175
Paraguay 176
Peru 177
Philippines 178
Poland 184
Portugal 187
Rhodesia (**also see** Zimbabwe) 188
Romania 189
Russia (Pre-Revolution) 191
Rwanda 191
São Tomé and Principe 192
Saudi Arabia 192
Senegal 192
Serbia 192
Seychelles 192
Sierra Leone 193
Singapore 193
Slovakia (*see* Czechoslovakia)
Somalia 194
South Africa 195
Spain 211
Sri Lanka 213
Sudan 214
Suriname 215
Swaziland 215
Sweden 215
Switzerland 215
Syria 215
Taiwan 216
Tanzania 217
Thailand 217
Tibet (*see* China, People's Republic of)
Togo 218
Tunisia 218
Turkey 219
Turkey (Armenian persecution) 221
Uganda 223
Union of Soviet Socialist Republics 224
United Arab Emirates 257
United Kingdom 257
United States of America 267
Uruguay 305

Uzbekistan 307
Venezuela 307
Vietnam (Socialist Republic of) 308
Vietnam, North (Democratic Republic of Vietnam) 310
Vietnam, South (Republic of South Vietnam) 310
Yemen Arab Republic (North) 313
Yemen (People's Democratic Republic of) 313
Yugoslavia 313
Zaire 315
Zambia 315
Zimbabwe (**also see** Rhodesia) 316

Index 321

"The life you face shall be precarious; you shall live in terror, night and day, with no assurance of survival."

Deuteronomy 28:66

Khhong, danh cho co
"If they are innocent, beat them until they become guilty."

Saying popular among South Vietnam police.

"The thousands degraded in prisons,
whose innocence, like mine, has made them guilty;
the thousands tortured and persecuted
with neither trial nor verdict in an honorable court.
the countless ones
who have been victimized
in fields and villages, in cities and in towns;
in hovels and tenements gutted by fire
how many living souls were buried without names,
without a cross?
We will not forget, they will not be forgotten,
their voices reach the ears of tomorrow's avengers."

Amado V. Hernandez, "Panata ng Kalayaan"
(Vow for Freedom) written in prison, October 1951
(tr. E. San Juan, Jr.)

"...Dr. Rieux resolved to compile this chronicle, so that he should not be one of those who hold their peace but should bear witness in favor of those plague-stricken people; so that some memorial of the injustice and outrage done to them might endure; and to state quite simply what we learn in a time of pestilence: that there are more things to admire in men than to despise."

Albert Camus, The Plague

"Upon the plain of blood roses and iron stalks
I will not stay silent
So hear my voice
As it sings in the slaughterhouse."

Iranian poet and playwright, Saeed Soltanpour, imprisoned many times by the Shah for his writings and then executed by the new Islamic government after accusing the authorities of torturing people and suppressing freedom.

POLITICAL TRIALS AND PRISONERS IN THE TWENTIETH CENTURY: INTRODUCTION

"The inability of most people to feel the pain of others as if it were their own is what makes evil possible."

Andrei Amalrik, Notes of a Revolutionary

"What unites the members of the [Soviet] Democratic Movement....is illustrated by a legend about the Indian mystic Ramakrishna, who saw a peasant being flogged so severely that bloody lines were left on his back. Identical lashmarks appeared on Ramakrishna's back."

Leonid Plyushch, History's Carnival

History[1]

It is appropriate to begin this bibliography with a tribute to the people who have felt the pain of others--the people who created the United Nations and its Universal Declaration of Human Rights and other rights conventions, and the dedicated members of Amnesty International, two of the noblest enterprises in the history of humankind.

On December 10, 1948, the United Nations declared for the first time in history that every human being has inalienable rights, and the member countries pledged themselves to protect and promote those rights not only in their own countries but throughout the world. Before World War II the international community and international law were concerned primarily with national relations, with little protection to individuals. A government's mistreatment of its own citizens was its own business. The Charter of the United Nations and the Universal Declaration established the revolutionary principle that individuals have the right to be protected by the international community.

Amnesty International originated from the foundation of the Universal Declaration with a newspaper article by Peter Benenson, "The Forgotten Prisoners," in May 1961, calling for the freedom of women and men from imprisonment for their beliefs--the prisoners of conscience. At that time trade unionists and teachers were being arrested around the world, detainees in many countries were treated cruelly in jails, unfair political trials were widespread, and in some countries people were tortured and executed for their opinions. Thousands immediately responded to Benenson's appeal, and within six months an international movement had begun. In 1992 there were AI sections in forty-seven countries overseeing 6000 local groups in over 70 countries, and more than 1,100,000 members, subscribers and regular donors in over 150 countries. At the end of 1991 AI was working on more than 2,400 cases involving over 3,300 individuals, and during that year it began 975 new cases involving more than 1,100, and 1,338 cases involved release (A.I. Report: 1992 311).

Yet the annual report and the numerous special country reports announce emphatically how much work there is yet to do. In more than half the countries of the world people are jailed for expression and association, often without trial or after sham trials. In perhaps a third of the nations of the world, men, women and children are tortured. In dozens of countries governments perpetrate abductions and murders of their own citizens. More than 120 states execute by law people convicted of certain crimes, and more than a third carry out such killings each year. In 1991, in Sri Lanka hundreds of people were extrajudicially executed, hundreds more disappeared, and thousands were detained without trial; in Israel, about 18,000 Palestinians were arrested in the context of the intifada (uprising) and around 2,000 detained without charge or trial; in India, at least 25,000 political prisoners were held without charge or trial with ill-treatment widespread. "The number of people in administrative detention without charge in 1991 was believed to be in the millions....and thousands of people were executed, often after the most perfunctory of trials" (AI Report: 1992 2).

The degradations and atrocities done to people by their own governments--called state terrorism--almost defy imagining. Yet gains have been achieved. There is a worldwide human rights movement. Abusive nations are exposed to the light of international investigation and publicity. Whereas in 1934 the massacre of possibly 30,000 peasants by the El Salvadoran army elicited virtually no coverage or interest outside the country, in 1987 the international outcry over the death by torture of student Park Chong-chol in South Korea led to the arrest of police officers and the resignation of government officials.

The recognition of international responsibility for crimes against individuals has been extended into international law and practice. Apart from the Geneva Conventions that apply in time of war, until after WWII there was not a single universal treaty obliging states to give fair trials or prohibit torture. Since then, protections available under international law have increased significantly. The Universal Declaration was followed by the International Convention on Genocide, International Covenants on Human Rights, the UN Convention Against Torture and Other Cruel, Inhuman or Degrading Treatment or Punishment, the Principles on the Effective Prevention and Investigation of Extra-Legal, Arbitrary and Summary Executions, the Convention on the Rights of the Child, and other agreements.

The "International Bill of Human Rights" (Forsythe 265-305) is composed of four separate UN resolutions: 1) the Universal Declaration of Human Rights (General Assembly Resolution 217 A [III], Dec. 10, 1948); 2) the International Covenant on Economic, Social and Cultural Rights (General Assembly Resolution 2200 A [XXI], Dec. 16, 1966, in force Jan. 3, 1976); 3) the International Covenant on Civil and Political Rights (General Assembly Resolution 2200 A [XXI], Dec. 16, 1966, in force March 26, 1976; 4) the Optional Protocol to the International Covenant on Civil and Political Rights (General Assembly Resolution 2200 A [XXI], Dec. 16, 1966, in force March 26, 1976.

Since its creation in 1980 by the UN, the Working Group on Enforced or Involuntary Disappearances has acted on many cases of disappearances throughout the world. The UN's Special Rapporteur on summary executions has confronted numerous countries to prevent threatened executions and torture, sometimes unsuccessfully, but a beginning.

But as this bibliography attests, violations of human rights continue throughout most of the world. Although all members of the UN subscribe to the Universal Declaration, many of them disregard its principles, and some have not signed various specific conventions. Insurgencies and opposition movements or parties are often used to rationalize state terror--arbitrary arrest, torture, murder. "National security" is a chief pretext for suppressing opposition. In the name of protecting national prerogatives and "rights," ruling elites in many countries grossly violate citizens' rights. The four men who led a march in Colombia to support the right to life were assassinated by "security" forces death squads; the coordinator of the El Salvadoran human rights commission was assassinated for "national" security; in Haiti a prominent lawyer was assassinated by police while he conversed with journalists with a copy of the Haitian Constitution in his hand outside a prison; the president of the farmers' association in Turkey was jailed for a year as a threat to public security; Breyten Breytenbach, a black South African poet, was sentenced to nine years in prison in 1975 for criticizing apartheid, but charged with trying to establish a revolutionary organization; 'Ali 'Abdul-Fattah Hashim, Yemen writer and teacher, is being held in prison charged with heresy and apostasy, and faces possible execution; Jigme Sangpo, 65-year-old former teacher, has spent more than 23 of the last 29 years in a Chinese (Tibet) prison for various "counter-revolutionary" dissent; and on and on as this bibliography sadly demonstrates. These atrocities are perpetrated on the basis of a panoply of laws and bureaucracies of "Internal Security"--the Internal Security Act, the Subcommittee on State Security, the Quick Action Security Force, etc.

The list and the bibliography would be longer were it not for the secrecy that prevails in so many cases of political imprisonment or murder and for the sheer quantity of abuses throughout the world that exhaust the best efforts of human rights groups to record the prisoners. Newsweek in 1983 estimated "at least 10,000 in the Soviet Union, perhaps 2,000 in Poland, 15,000 in Turkey, a minimum of 10,000 scattered across Africa, 5,000 in South America, Cuba and Haiti and as many as 100,000 strewn from Pakistan and Afghanistan, Iran and Iraq to South Korea, the Philippines, China and Taiwan." And "nearly one-half of the 157 members of the United Nations hold political prisoners." And some countries, like the United States, support major human rights violators ("The Salvadoran").

Definition

Amnesty International originally followed a mandate and definition restricted to "prisoners of conscience": "to seek the release of men, women and children detained for their beliefs, colour, sex, ethnic origin, language or religion, provided they have not used or advocated violence" (1988 Report, 1). But this orientation has expanded in recent years.

Some commentators emphasize the motivation of political prisoners, particularly their idealism. Ward Churchill defines them as people "motivated by a desire. . .to transform the social order into something more positive for the oppressed, less profitable for the oppressor," and who deliberately or inadvertently violate laws in the process. The magazine Philippine Human Rights Update agrees: "Persons espousing an alternative form of society from an existing decrepit government could not be equated with those who steal or kill for other reasons. The 'noble' vision of changing oppressive structures to pave the way for a better society is the motivation of those charged with political offenses" ("Hernandez" 14). The Prisoners of Conscience Project, sponsored by the Racial Justice Working Group of the National Council of the Churches of Christ in the U.S. (32 denominations and 40 million members) employs the terms prisoner of conscience and political prisoner interchangeably, defined as "a person imprisoned--awaiting trial, serving a sentence, or held without trial (such as on grand jury contempt charge)--for reason of acts, associations or beliefs based on a concern for justice and human rights." Here the crucial factor is motive: the desire and effort to effect change for the better. Thus Martin Luther King, Jr., Bobby Seale in the Chicago conspiracy trial, the Berrigan brothers, and Dr. Benjamin Spock in the US were political prisoners from their perspective of individual citizens desiring to change society. The problem, of course, is that the prosecutors did not recognize motive but only the breaking of specific statutes.

Some writers attempt to combine both the state's and the dissident's perspectives. In another number of Philippine Human Rights Update the magazine quoted the definition employed by the Presidential Committee on Political Prisoners established by Pres. Aquino: "'a person who has been arrested or detained by reason of the commission of an act penalized by existing law as a political crime (crime against national security or public order), or by reason of any other act which is complexed with, or connected to such crimes, or impelled by a political reason or motive'" ("Political" 10). In its dual nature this is a more complex definition: a political crime is identified both as its perception as such by authorities (a violation of a law) and as a motive that distinguishes the perpetrator from ordinary criminals.

(The definition by a writer in Time, although it recognizes both individual motive and state response by emphasizing antagonistic views--"Classically," a political crime "refers to someone who is prosecuted or jailed, not for crimes in the ordinary sense of the word, but for harboring or expressing opinions antagonistic to the established order of government" (Morrow 18)--is insufficient because it omits the criminality assigned to opinions by repressive states through conspiracy, subversion, security, slander, and other statutes effectively removing antagonism from the realm of opinion.)

Other theoreticians place the emphasis upon the state's perspective. "Political crime is a slippery term, but it may be defined as any action 'intended to disrupt or destroy the integrity of a governmental system.' Political offenses in one way or another strike at the roots of state power and 'affect the structure or stability of the existing regime.'" Motive--intention--is retained, but refocused from the ethics of the Churches of Christ definition to one of challenge to power. Immediately following this apparent acknowledgment of state and individual, however, the author wholly emphasizes the state's perspective: "Actually, what makes a crime political is the legal response the criminal's action evokes from the state" (Mitchell xi).

In his closely reasoned analytical and historical study of political crime, Barton Ingraham also supports the restriction of the definition to how a crime is perceived and reacted to by those possessing ruling power. He comments on Stephen Schafer's definition which distinguishes the "convictional" criminal who commits a crime from altruistic motives and whom Schafer classifies as political from the "conventional" criminal who acts from selfish motives: Schafer never explains "why a government or a people should react differently (and thus make a distinction) to crime which threatens their vital interests according to whether or not the offender's motives were altruistic or selfish" (Ingraham 3-4). Ingraham reduces a list of twelve kinds of political offenses (earlier called treason) to four basic types as historically perceived by rulers in European law: 1) acts of betrayal with regard to a foreign enemy, 2) challenges to political authority, legitimacy, and the right to rule, 3) hindrance of official function, such as taxation or the waging of war, and 4) usurpations of granted powers (21-22). These first three--betrayal, challenge, hindrance to the authority and legitimacy of those holding the powers of government--provide the definition of political criminals as "perceived during most of human history" (22). The Time definition seems to follow a similar constraint: "harboring or expressing opinions antagonistic" to (as perceived by) the government is a political crime. Ingraham's fourth category, concerning the protection of the people from tyrannical rulers, provides a partial explanation of why an individual might oppose a government, but it is not essential to the definition. What matters is "the kind of legal response the act evokes from those in authority" (19); that is, what those in command of the agencies of government decide is threatening (betraying, challenging, hindering) to their security and safety and to the nation and society which they identify with themselves.

But although this "response" formulation provides a principled and objective foundation, it contains two apparent liabilities. First, governments sometimes cover up their political response by accusing opponents of common criminal acts. King, Seale, the Berrigans, and Dr. Spock would not be political criminals. Morrow denies political status to George Jackson and Angela Davis because they were specifically detained for criminal acts--Jackson given eleven years for robbing a gas station of $70 at the age of 19 (following two other armed robberies) and Davis refused bail because she was accused of supplying weapons for an escape which resulted in the deaths of four people, including a judge (a crime of which she was judged innocent). But although Morrow admits that Jackson's crime "scarcely warranted an eleven-year sentence," condemns the seven years he spent in solitary confinement, and acknowledges that parole boards refused his release because they feared his radical Marxist views acquired while in solitary, he requires a person to be jailed "solely for his ideological opinions" in order to be defined as political. To the contrary, his own definition and arguments could lead us to pinpoint the actual political response underlying Jackson's and Davis's prolonged incarceration.

The second liability pertains to the question of what is human rights. If we argue that the notion of rights is inseparable from the notion of law, a dictatorship has the right to punish an accused citizen without due process, when no law forbids it to do so. This can be answered in two ways. First, many of the countries which subject their citizens to incommunicado detention, unfair trials, and torture violate their own constitutions. Second, to return to the opening section on history, a body of international conventions and laws has developed that supersede national legalities or the absence of them. So-called "natural rights" or "human rights" are being codified and agreed to by nations under the United Nations and the World Court. So that a nation which does not have constitutional safeguards or which violates its own constitution and statutes may be judged from an international legal foundation, as does Amnesty International following United Nations conventions. Although rights are artificial, depending upon socially established rules of conduct or legislative substance, certain rights have been recognized as prior to any individual government, and these principles are now embodied in the Universal Declaration and other international agreements.

The AI definition thus seems to offer a practical definition: a prisoner of conscience is one who is detained (and often ill-treated, tortured, and killed) because of her or his belief, color, sex, sexuality, ethnic origin, language, or religion (and has not employed or advocated violence), and this condition they oppose on the grounds of established international ethical principles.

But although AI emphasizes nonviolence (and avoids prisoners accused of espionage), the organization now defends all prisoners, including those who have used or advocated violence in their defence against state violence, when they have been denied trial within a reasonable time, when trial procedures do not conform to recognized international norms, when prison conditions are cruel, degrading, and inhuman, specifically when they do not meet the UN's 94 basic requirements set forth in the "Standard Minimum Rules for the Treatment of Prisoners," particularly in regard to torture, and when they have been condemned to death (Amnesty International Handbook [1977] 9-10; "Amnesty International and the Use of Violence: An Explanatory Note"[1976]). AI thus defends members of the Plowshares movement, who destroyed government property to oppose the Vietnam War and nuclear missiles, and Leonid Gromov, who destroyed Soviet property to oppose the Afghanistan War (he sabotaged the Ulyanov Automobile Factory where armored vehicles were produced).

At their International Council Meeting in Yokohama in 1991, AI extended their mandate in several ways. Now people imprisoned because of their homosexuality are prisoners of conscience. And the organization resolved to oppose forcible exile or relocation, where it is imposed for political reasons (ethnic origin, sex, color, language, or religion). Opposition to killings and hostage taking by rebel groups was emphasized. AI's definition of political prisoner does not include prisoners of war.

State Crime/State Terrorism

Political prisoners are the victims of state crime and terrorism, defined as criminality organized by the state consisting of acts defined by national laws or international codes as criminal and committed by state officials in the pursuit of their job as representatives of the state--for example, piracy, smuggling, assassination, criminal conspiracy, spying on citizens, selling arms, extracting confessions by torture, kidnapping, murder. Criminal acts that benefit only individual officeholders (bribes, individual police violence) are not included.

Hitler's "Night and Fog" decree covering offenses against the German state in the occupied countries is unmatchable in its inhumanity. In those cases where guilt was established the death sentence would be pronounced within eight days of arrest. But in doubtful cases, the majority (usually entirely innocent people unconnected to acts of war), the prisoners were to be shrouded in "night and fog"--that is, transported secretly to Germany for execution or slave labor without a trace and with no information given to their family or friends. The intent of these combined measures--the public execution of the guilty and the disappearance of the innocent--was to create maximum fear and intimidation. Military leaders of Argentina's "dirty war" imitated the Nazis' "night and fog" terror campaign. Frank Graziano in Divine Violence treats the institution of "disappearance" (abduction, torture, execution) as "a blatant and grotesque breach of domestic Argentine law, of international human rights conventions, of ethics by any rendering, and of the fundamental values on which civilization is founded" (x). But these facts and arguments have been covered exhaustively elsewhere. His analysis delves into the deepest psychological sources of violence. The military rulers of the country following the March 24, 1976, coup exploited the "religion-violence-psychosexual nexus" of power. "The highly ritualized atrocity and symbolically freighted discourse of the 'dirty war'" make it "a model case for pursuing the source of political violence."

See Tunnell for a radically broader definition of state crime.

Trials

In its 1988 Report, Amnesty International declared that "in at least half the countries of the world, people are locked away for speaking their minds, often after trials that are no more than a sham" (2). The foundation for a right to a fair trial is set forth in Article 9 of the Universal Declaration of Human Rights: "No one shall be subject to arbitrary arrest, detention, or exile." The Council of Europe's Convention for the Protection of Human Rights and Fundamental Freedoms discusses trial principles in detail (see J.E.S. Fawcett). Donnelly and Howard focus on habeus corpus and an independent judiciary as keys to an assessment of a country's protection rights record.

The Human Rights and Peace Law Docket, 1945-1991 covers cases related to the Nuremberg Principles, Universal Declaration on Human Rights, the Constitution of the U.S., Charter of the U.N., and the International Covenant on Civil and Political Rights, mainly cases in the U.S. but many critical cases from other countries are also listed.

Theodore Becker in Political Trials examines judicial procedures and the issue of fair, impartial justice in cases from the U.S. (Chicago Conspiracy Trial), Cuba (charges arising from Castro's overthrow of the Batista regime), USSR (the Sinyavski-Daniel Trial), and from other countries.

AI opposes the detention of any prisoners "without trial within a reasonable time, or any trial procedures relating to such prisoners that do not conform to recognized norms to ensure a fair trial." All prisoners should be "given the full right to defend themselves in court." By "fair trial," "recognized norms," and internationally accepted standards, AI includes "the provision of defence lawyers of the prisoner's choosing, full prior consultation with defence counsel, open trial in the presence of outside observers, the testimony of defence witnesses and right of cross-examination, the repudiation of evidence extracted under duress or torture," and the rejection of military tribunals for civilians (AI Handbook 11).

Francis Boyle has written a manual to assist dissidents to defend themselves under international laws.

Prisons

Prison life degrades all prisoners. Not only hunger, illness, and physical punishment make imprisonment destructive, but the claustrophobic atmosphere and the everyday frustrations of psychological punishment wear away the identity and dignity of prisoners. Altogether, the damage is irreparable. And political prisoners are often treated more harshly than common criminals (in fact in some countries criminals are employed to harass and beat political prisoners).

Death in prison not only from torture but from starvation, illness, and harsh treatment is common. In South Africa prison deaths broke through the rigid secrecy to become a national scandal. For example, three prisoners died at Barberton, of heat exhaustion according to officials, which sent forty-four other prisoners to hospital. It was finally revealed that in addition to the temperature of 35 centigrade the three who died and thirty-four others had been beaten by the eight guards, and the thirty-four left alive had been threatened with death if they testified.

AI reports consistently examine prison conditions, and some reports focus exclusively on the subject. Human Rights Watch established its Prison Project in 1988 to focus on pretrial detainees, sentenced prisoners, and administrative detention (incommunicado and detention without charge or trial) of all prisoners. In 1991, HRW published reports on India, Mexico, Poland, and Israel.

In his comprehensive study of The Treatment of Prisoners Under International Law, Chapter 3, "What Constitutes Torture and Ill-Treatment?" Nigel Rodley discusses case-law related to the issue of ill-treatment of prisoners immediately following their arrest or abduction, preceding formal commitment of pre-trial or post-conviction incarceration. That is the period during which prisoners are most at risk because officials are seeking information and confession. In Chapter 9, "Conditions of Imprisonment or Detention," Rodley deals with conditions of imprisonment after the detained person has been formally committed to pre-trial or post-conviction imprisonment, or to formal administrative internment. He also continues the examination begun in Chapter 3 of "the scope of the prohibition of torture or other cruel, inhuman, or degrading treatment or punishment" (219), based upon United Nations Declarations and Conventions and the Standard Minimum Rules for the Treatment of Prisoners. He discusses the application of the SMR to Greece (1969) and to a variety of individual pre-trial and post-conviction cases, the problem of solitary confinement, issues pertaining to medical experimentation on prisoners, persons detained in psychiatric hospitals, forcible feeding, and separation of categories of prisoners.

Torture

Torture "has increasingly become illegitimate in the eyes of the world community," as Article 55 of the Charter of the United Nations (1945), the International Bill of Rights (particularly Article 5 of the Universal Declaration of Human Rights [1948]), the "Declaration of the Protection of All Persons from Being Subjected to Torture and other Cruel, Inhuman or Degrading Treatment or Punishment" (Resolution 3452(XXX) of the U. N. General Assembly, Dec. 9, 1975), the Convention against Torture and Other Cruel, Inhuman or Degrading Treatment or Punishment (Assembly 1984, in force 1987), and other U.N., regional, and professional declarations make clear. Nigel Rodley in his book on prisoners under international law "traces the development of international and regional legislation aimed at eliminating the practices of torture and other ill-treatment," such as extra-judicial execution, disappearance, and capital punishment. AI has published numerous investigations of torture; SOS Torture (now the World Organization Against Torture) and other organizations also send delegations to countries to expose the practice. Yet torture continues to be widespread and systematic in many countries, even among members of the U. N. Rita Maran, for example, analyzes the contradiction between France's official "civilizing mission" and its systematic use of torture throughout the Algerian war of liberation (1954-1962).

The definition of torture is complicated by the inclusion of psychological abuse. Sometimes the word is used so broadly as to make it meaningless. But the U.N. definition limits the meaning to an official context. Here is the definition according to Article 1 of the Annex to the 1975 Declaration:

> any act by which severe pain or suffering, whether physical or mental, is intentionally inflicted by or at the instigation of a public official on a person for such purposes as obtaining from him or a third person information or confession, punishing him for an act he has committed or is suspected of having committed, or intimidating him or other persons.

Edward Peters' Torture provides a history of torture that reveals its historical, political but not inevitable occurrence. He traces the use of torture in western Europe from the Greeks, through the Romans, through the Middle Ages, down to "the abolition of torture in criminal legal procedure virtually throughout western Europe by the first quarter of the nineteenth century." But it was re-instituted in much of Europe and in its colonial empires from the late nineteenth century on, and its use accelerated during the twentieth under the concept of the exceptional crime--the crimen exceptum--so dangerous to the state as to allow extraordinary methods. Peters observes the irony of the correlation between enormous state power and its leaders' sense of vulnerability which has resulted in such horrendous state terrorism against the rights of its citizens (5-7).

Now "torture is used, formally or informally, in one country out of every three" (5). As Amnesty International and other organizations, professional research, and the growing number of personal testimonies reveal, "medieval and early modern torture appears considerably more restricted in its application, purpose and technology" (161). Mary Costello gives three motives for torture: 1) to obtain confessions for prosecution, 2) to obtain information about others, and 3) to intimidate not only the victim and his associates but the public at large (729). Today, according to Peters, torture is increasingly scientifically applied primarily to spread a climate of terror and only secondarily to procure information (162). Orwell portrayed this in 1984, in which the hero Winston Smith is tortured to compel total submission, the relinquishment of all that was his subjective self, his "I." Elaine Scarry suggests a similar idea in her book The Body in Pain, where torture is explained as education in the futility of an object acting like a subject. This is not to say its other purpose, to compel confession or information, is not pervasive also.

So many victims, yet not until 1979 was the first clinic for their rehabilitation established in Copenhagen. The Rehabilitation Centre for Torture Victims was established by Dr. Inge Kemp Genefke, whose work for many years through Amnesty International for the release of prisoners gradually made her aware of how many victims of torture remained seriously physically and psychologically impaired after release. For many, perhaps for all victims, indvidual healing depends upon national accountability. The victims and their families desire truth and justice as essential to their healing, at least the public acknowledgment of the wrongs which have disabled their lives. But judges, lawyers, witnesses, and family members are killed or threatened with death. Nor does the change from state terror to democracy and free elections necessarily produce social rehabilitation, since the torturers usually still possess military power, demand amnesty, and usually manage to "enforce a total amnesia" regarding their crimes (Weschler 92). In Argentina, after more than 8,000 people were abducted, tortured, and murdered, a national commission exposed some of the truth and five of the responsible military commanders were convicted (1984-85), and then amnesty laws stopped further prosecutions. Even the population seems paralyzed: in Uruguay in 1989, a popular referendum to cancel an amnesty negotiated by the outgoing military government was defeated (A.I. Report: 1992, 6).

Even countries with seemingly civilized judicial systems find it impossible to bring their own torturers to justice. After more than ten years of torture in Egypt, the one trial of security forces on torture charges resulted in acquittal; in 1991 Turkey's Anti-Terror law made it more difficult to prosecute torturers; in India "torture remains routine" (7).

Some individual suits have been undertaken, a few successfully. In the U.S. it was possible to gain compensation judicially for torture abroad under the Torture

Victim Protection Act (March 1992). In 1992 the first legal judgment under the act was entered against the Estate of Ferdinand Marcos in behalf of some 10,000 victims of torture, "disappearance," and summary execution during his regime (1972-1986). In addition, the Alien Tort Claims Act allows foreigners to sue for human rights violations. Three Ethiopian women won their case in Atlanta against the man who tortured them in Ethiopia fourteen years ago and the court awarded each of them $500,000 in damages. The women have also asked for the man's deportation, so that torturers find no safe haven in the U.S., one purpose of these laws. In Filartiga v.Peña-Irala, Dr. Joel Filartiga, a citizen of Paraguay, successfully sued his son's torturer and murderer, while Peña was in the U.S., and was awarded $10 million. But in 1993 the Supreme Court ruled that U.S. citizens abused and tortured abroad cannot sue in U.S. courts.

A glaring gap in the scholarship of torture is the adequate study of torturers. Amnesty International has focused upon the victims of the torture. No book has yet been written on torturers worldwide, naming names, giving cases, exposing the torturers to public knowledge if not to punishment, comparing one to the other, exploring their lives and minds. Leonid Plyushch "exposed the identities of several scoundrels and cowards," but these are more informers than torturers. Pericles Korovessis names and individualizes his torturers in the Asphalia police torture center--their ruses to avoid identification, their insistence upon just carrying out orders.

The Nazi war crimes trials in Germany, Israel, and other countries attempted to do this, to restore some sense of reality, justice, and guardianship to a world torn by such savagery. Actions were recorded, names were named, books written, films made. Dr. Mengele is well known to the world. But there is no compilation of the torturers in Greece or Chile or El Salvador or the Soviet Union. Lifton and Markusen examine the mentality of those who have participated in projects of titanic destruction of various kinds. But other than those about the Nazis and a few biographies of major dictators, no books explore the policemen and military officers who beat and burned people and then went home to their wives and children in South Africa, Turkey, or Peru. A main explanation for this lack is that all attention and energy has properly been applied to saving the victims; the victimizers must be relegated to later. Our knowledge of the Nazi torturers has taken fifty years to accumulate. Perhaps a universal impediment is that such books lead to so many others complicit in the torture by their silence. As Tina Rosenberg argues in Children of Cain, the population of Chile, a country with a 150-year tradition of democracy and respect for human rights, made a "Faustian bargain" with the torturers, trading their rights and morality for comfort and tranquility. Pericles Korovessis ironically dedicates his book to the "peace-loving and fair-minded people all over the world, who by their silence and indifference have contributed to the continuation and spread of the tortures" (Postscript).

Health Personnel, Physicians

Nazi physicians experimented cruelly on concentration camp prisoners; Soviet psychiatrists supervised the forced incarceration and drugging of political prisoners; medical personnel around the world have engaged in and are participating in today dubious to reprehensible practices. In response, the United Nations General Assembly in Resolution 37/194 adopted the "Principles of Medical Ethics relevant to the role of health personnel, particularly physicians, in the protection of prisoners and detainees against torture and other cruel, inhuman or degrading treatment or punishment." Principle 1 of 6 Principles states: "Health personnel, particularly physicians, charged with the medical care of prisoners and detainees have a duty to provide them with protection of their physical and mental health and treatment of disease of the same quality and standard as is afforded to those who are not imprisoned or detained."

Secrecy and Censorship

The sheer difficulty of discovery in a terror state facilitates looking the other way by the majority. The secrecy is part of the torture: no one will ever know. And this is true. In Argentina between 1976 and 1983 more than 8,000 people disappeared after abduction--buried in mass graves, thrown in rivers, or dropped out of airplanes over the ocean. And of course the same message is essential to the well-being of the torturer. The masks and blindfolds, the kidnappings and incommunicado detention, the torture techniques which leave no marks, all thrive on this dual functionality to demoralize the victim and encourage the victimizer.

The combat is massively onesided, but the truth cannot be entirely contained; messages emerge; there are survivors. Some of the persecuted have written passages or poems on toilet paper, match covers, soap, sheets, between the lines of other books, in the dark, on any available surface, for smuggling out, determined to reveal the suffering to the world. Bonhoeffer found a friendly guard. Others left bits of paper to be picked up. Some have memorized what they would have written and put it on paper when released, or some certainly doomed dictated their thoughts or experiences to others to write when released, or they have told their recollections after release. Thus we know about the global gulags, and will know about those operating at this moment.

Disappearance

An especially sinister and repugnant aspect of political repression is the disappearance of an abducted person, for "'whereas grief has limits...apprehension has none'" (Disappeared! 19). AI uses the term "disappearance" "whenever there are reasonable grounds to believe that a person has been taken into custody by the authorities or with their connivance and the authorities deny that the victim is in their custody....Many political killings by governments have been concealed because the victims have 'disappeared'" (Sri Lanka 8). Disappearance "combines in itself violations of several fundamental rights: the right to freedom, the right to physical integrity, and usually the right to life. Disappearance also violates all rights of legal defence, since no warrant for arrest is issued; there is no trial, no defending advocate and no public announcement" (Disappeared! 13-14). Disappearances violate Articles 3, 8, and 9 of the Universal Declaration of Human Rights, Articles 2 and 9 of the International Covenant on Civil and Political Rights, and Rule 92 of the UN Standard Minimum Rules for the Treatment of Prisoners.

"The term 'disappeared' did not enter the international human rights vocabulary until relatively recently, translated from the Spanish desaparecido" ("Disappearances": A Workbook 75). (The new use of the verb "to be disappeared" originated in Argentina). Disappearances were first documented in the mid-70s. Beginning in Guatemala in 1966 and intensified in Chile in 1973 and Argentina in 1976, these military regimes practiced violent repression to maintain their power, including systematic abduction, incommunicado detention, torture, and murder, while authorities denied involvement. ("Denial of accountability by the authorities is the factor that makes a 'disappearance' unique among human rights violations" [78]). Despite thousands upon thousands of inquiries by families, mass habeus corpus petitions, mounting torment and despair in the minds of loved ones, the "disappeared" increased. These people had vanished from the face of the earth--until they were discovered in mass graves.

The impact on families is devastating. Constant search is met with lies, delays, uncertainty, perhaps threats, even arrest. And because the victims know their families do not know what happened to them, there is no hope. Children particularly suffer. (Disappeared! 19-29).

Disappearances concern the UN increasingly. In 1978 in resolution 33/173 the General Assembly expressed its abhorrence for the practice and exhorted all governments to ensure accountable police and to search for the missing and punish the guilty. In 1980 the UN established the Working Group on Disappearances.

Death Penalty

AI also opposes the death penalty for all prisoners on the grounds that "it constitutes a cruel, inhuman and degrading punishment, is irrevocable, is capable of being inflicted on the innocent, does not act as a deterrent to crime, and is a violation of the right to life provisions of the Universal Declaration of Human Rights and other international covenants" (10). Hugo Bedau and Michael Radelet reported that 350 people have been wrongfully sentenced to death in the U.S., twenty-three of whom were killed by the state before they were found to have been innocent. England abolished the death penalty after one person was executed who was later found to be innocent. The Council of Europe adopted Protocol No. 6 to the "Convention for the Protection of Human Rights and Fundamental Freedoms Concerning the Abolition of the Death Penalty." Article 1 states: "The death penalty shall be abolished. No one shall be condemned to such penalty or executed."

Although during 1991, "2,086 prisoners are known to have been executed in 32 countries and 2,703 people were sentenced to death in 62 cases" and "the true number is certainly higher," progress is indicated by the abolition of the death penalty by over 43 percent of the countries of the world by the end of 1991 (A.I. Report: 1992, 27).

Genocide

The history of political imprisonment and torture is often connected to the history of genocide. Genocide (from geno, tribe or race, and cide, to kill) means "the deliberate destruction or murder of a particular group of people," sometimes even millions, as in the Nazi effort to exterminate the Jews (Totten 91). "Destruction" is included in the definition to acknowledge actions such as the Soviet starvation of possibly ten million Ukrainians between 1932 and 1933. War is not included in the definition, unless it is part of the planned murder of a group of people. Political killings are not strictly included, if one follows the Genocide Convention, which specifies the destruction of a national, ethnic, racial, or religious group. Yet mass political killings are committed when the group in power wishes to eliminate its opposition (113).

Often during genocidal campaigns prisoners are taken, at least temporarily, sometimes on a mass scale, as in the Nazi concentration camps. With "over 119 million people" dead in genocidal acts since 1900 (93), the brutal confinement of prisoners as an aspect of genocide is massive. During the campaign to exterminate the Armenians, for example, the Turks first arrested and then executed their leaders. Then the men were rounded up and killed. And then the women, children, elderly, and sick were deported to the desert. Out of more than two million Armenians in the Ottoman Empire, by 1918 only about 100,000 remained. Very few of the murderers were punished, and to this day the Turkish government refuses to admit the slaughter took place and spends great sums of money to suppress its mention (99).

The massive killings during WW II motivated the nations under the U.N. to adopt the Genocide Convention on December 9, 1948. The convention makes genocide an international crime whether during war or peace. But genocide continues, in Kampuchea 1975-1979 (at least two million out of only seven million citizens) and apparently in Iran today against the Baha'is.

Exiles and Refugees

The number of refugees rose by one million in 1992, raising the total number in exile to 17.5 million. "One out of every 135 people in the world was in exile," from Somalia, Haiti, the republics of the former Soviet Union, Mozambique, Afghanistan, Palestine, Bosnia.

More than 24 million people were internally displaced--remaining within their country but driven from their homes. There are many causes attributedto such massive displacement--ecological disasters, famine, wars--but a major cause is oppression, as in Burma (Mollison).

Trade Unionists

Trade unions are frequent targets of state terrorism, because they can offer organized resistance, and they characteristically struggle for economic justice, which leads often to demands for political justice. Lawrence and Rita Ndzanga, South African trade unionists, were arrested in the early morning hours, forced to leave their three children unattended, and detained for seventeen months, tortured, tried and acquitted, re-detained without being allowed to leave the court, acquitted again, and said upon release: "What can we do about getting our people unemployment benefits?" Mr. Ndzanga was later detained again and died of "natural causes" in prison (Cosmas Desmond, 15).

Many nations control unions by creating legal unions, as in Poland, whose government outlawed the Solidarity union movement and imprisoned its leaders. In some countries, as in Chile and El Salvador, union leaders and members are detained without trial, tortured, murdered, and "disappeared." Often the repression is connected to allegations of communism in unions, another motive for government repression.

Communists

A repeated theme throughout this bibliography is anti-communism--from India to Latin America to the U.S. The fanatical opposition to communism, the basis upon which the system of National Security States has been erected, explains much of the political oppression throughout the world. Indonesia offers a particularly atrocious example. In October 1965 a small group of Army officers attempted a coup. In retaliation the Army carried out a massively violent purge of members of the Communist Party, left-wing organizations, and associated relatives and friends. Between a half-million and over a million people were killed during the period. "Of those who were arrested, but not killed, at least more than half a million were kept in prison" for long terms, and as late as 1977 "tens of thousands of political prisoners" were still held "without charge or trial" (Indonesia 12-13). In 1974 Indira Gandhi's government incarcerated from 15,000 to 40,000 opponents, many or most of whom were "Naxalites," members of the Communist Party of India-Marxist-Leninist and their families and friends. Philippine dictator Ferdinand Marcos waged violent war against communists and everyone he deemed a communist sympathizer. In the 1970s the military leaders of the Argentine torture state kidnapped, tortured, and "disappeared" thousands of alleged subversive communists. And the police and military of many of these nations received direct police training and equipment and money from the U.S. for their war against political opposition.

Women

The special problems confronting women prisoners make their lives often more painful than that of men. They are faced not only with the intense anguish of sexual humiliations (execrable epithets, torture while naked, electric shock to sexual organs) but with rape and group rape. Saida Botan Elmi was detained without charge, tortured with electric shock, and raped in 1976. A child she was carrying while pregnant miscarried after she was beaten. Finally she was admitted to a mental hospital in 1981 after suffering a mental breakdown and contracting tuberculosis. Seviye Koeprue of Turkey, a nurse, was arrested for alleged Communist party membership, tortured, sexually abused, and detained for over a year without charge. Pregnant women are imprisoned and tortured, and their babies are sometimes stolen from them for murder or adoption never to be seen again, as often happened in Argentina during the "dirty war." Some women have been sentenced to long terms for their political convictions. Dorothy Nyembe served fifteen years on the single charge of harbouring South African ANC freedom fighters.

The UN has twice notably asserted principles in support of women. In 1954 it issued the Convention on the Political Rights of Women, and in 1979 the General Assembly adopted the Convention on the Elimination of All Forms of Discrimination Against Women. More particularly for this bibliography are the denunciations against torture in the 1948 Universal Declaration of Human Rights (Article 5) and the 1975 Declaration to protect all persons from torture and "other Cruel, Inhuman or Degrading Treatment or Punishment."

Children

Children are imprisoned with their parents, for their own beliefs, or for no reason at all; some are tortured, some disappear, some die in prison, some languish in prison for many years. Some are forced to witness the torture of their parents. Some are born in prison and are taken from their mothers to be killed or for secret adoption. A child of 11, among a group of Haitian peasants when they were imprisoned for protesting economic conditions, reportedly died in prison (Children 6-7).

Otto Zoff considers the desire to protect children "far more compelling even than the instinct to save our own lives." Only the depraved would refuse to try to save a child from impending death from a train. "Yet when hundreds of thousands of children are in danger--they become statistics," "dimmed and blurred by the sheer horrible vastness of the tragedy" (vi). International awareness of the plight of children finally focused in 1989 when the U.N. General Assembly adopted the United Nations Bill of Rights for Children. Resolution 44.25, the Convention on the Rights of the Child contains 54 articles. By 1992 it had been signed by 109 countries and ratified by 40 (though not the U.S.).

Conscientious Objectors

Amnesty International recognizes conscientious objection to military service as a fundamental human right and anyone imprisoned for exercising this right is considered by AI to be a prisoner of conscience. The right includes selective objection (willingness to serve in some circumstances, and volunteers who develop conscientious objections at any stage). Alternative civilian service becomes imprisonment when provided in a punitive manner. For example, France's alternative civilian service available to recognized conscientious objectors is twice the length of ordinary military service. Because France imprisons everyone who refuses to conform to narrowly limited national service laws, some 500 Jehovah's Witnesses were imprisoned in 1992 alone for refusing military service. In contrast, Resolution 337 of the Parliamentary Assembly of 1967 of the Council of Europe declares that, with respect to Article 9 of the European Convention on Human Rights, individuals should be released from the obligation to perform armed service if they refuse to do so for "religious, ethical, moral, humanitarian, philosophical or similar motives."

Writers, Journalists

Writers are among the hardest hit by repressive regimes, who fear their revelatory skills, or, the best of them at least, their independent minds. For example, Pramoedya Ananta Toer is regarded by many as the finest Indonesian writer of his generation. But his views were disliked by successive governments, and he was imprisoned first by the Dutch, then by Sukarno, and finally by General Suharto. He has been a prisoner since 1965 although never charged nor tried by the military rulers. As special punishment, he has been denied pencil and paper (Indonesia 59). In Haiti in early 1993 a campaign of arrests, torture, and death threats against journalists intensified. For example, Colson Dorme disappeared after reporting for Radio Tropic FM on the right-wing protest at the Port-au-Prince airport against a U.N. peace-keeping mission. The Duvalierist Ton-ton Macoute confiscated film from one photographer, threatened two reporters with death, told another they would burn down his radio station. One radio reporter was beaten and jailed for "subversion" and tortured by the "twins" technique (slapped on both ears simultaneously). Filipina poet Mila Aguilar was arrested incommunicado, blindfolded and taken at gunpoint to a prison, forced into an isolation cell, endured beatings, kicking strangulation, electric shock, and sexual molestation, then charged with "illegal possession of subversive documents" by a military court, and later with "rebellion." She was still in prison, often in solitary confinement, a year later. These three examples can be multiplied by the thousands throughout the world, many of which are recorded by the magazine Index on Censorship.

In 1984 International PEN recorded 480 writers in prison, labor camps, psychiatric "hospitals," or who had disappeared after abduction. Many more were unrecorded. And thousands more were prevented from publishing by less violent methods. Writer (and artist, filmmaker, etc.) victims of state oppression are of two kinds: 1) those who suffer for their writings alone (or fear of what they might write) and 2) those who have actively and directly resisted repression.

Institutional Reporting

Human Rights statistics and analyses have become a major research enterprise around the world. Besides the prestigious annual report of every country in the world by Amnesty International, several individual countries survey world human rights, and many organizations provide special reports of individual countries. The annual AI reports are praised as "meticulously researched" (Brenner 319, who also blames AI for its civil libertarian ineffectuality). Supported by numerous special reports, they provide massive data about human rights conditions in the world.

The annual Country Reports on Human Rights Practice by the United States State Department is "widely known and respected." While there are serious criticisms of chapters on particular countries, "most critics...agree that on the whole the volume reflects a professional effort to report accurately and fairly," and it has "improved in coverage and consistency during the Reagan years" (Innes 235-36).

One of the critics of the Country Reports has been Human Rights Watch, a private monitoring group. For example, although in 1989 it found some improvements in the reports since President Bush came into office, it condemned the State Department's unverified acceptance of statements and data made by allied governments. Turkey is one example, which continued torturing even after ratifying the U. N. Convention Against Torturing, which the U. S. praised. And the reporting of El Salvador is "'nearly useless'" ("State").

Kathleen Pritchard's discovery of "serious differences" in the 1986 human rights reports of the U.S. and Norway causes her to recommend multiple sources in gathering human rights data and to exercise "extreme caution in utilizing these widely varying estimates" (269). But not only does she find conflicting statistics but "directly contradictory information on the same country" (270). Particularly contradictory are the reports on Nicaragua, with the Norwegian report praising Sandinista social progress despite the U.S.-organized and financed war against the country, and with the U.S. report riddled with omissions and exaggerations (271-72).

Media

Popular acceptance of official definitions and designations of the words "terrorist" and "political prisoner" are probably always ideological; they reflect the leaders and policies of the particular government. Popular acceptance of the official definitions depend upon the success or failure of their government's propaganda, which in turn derives from a concerted campaign by all relevant agencies of the government working together. In the US, the White House, the CIA, the State Department, the USIA, and other governmental institutions have foregrounded the political prisoners of the nation's official enemies and downplayed political prisoners in the US and in allied nations. And numerous non-governmental agencies--think tanks, foundations, religious groups--are drawn upon for ideological support and persuasion. Conformity is reinforced by complicit mainstream media and even by libraries (Bennett). Newsweek, Time, and U.S. News and World Report, as my survey of Reader's Guide Index from 1900 to the present revealed, perceived political prisoners overwhelmingly an eastern bloc problem (and see Lederer). Even when acknowledging allied misdeed, the bias is blatant. A revealing example is found in Newsweek's stories about the Soviet Union and Indonesia (Jan. 2, 1978, 28-29). Their correspondent from Moscow writes a moving account in three-and-a-half columns of the hardships suffered by the relatives of three imprisoned dissidents. On the facing page in two-and-a-half columns their correspondent (it does not give his location) gives an equally moving account of the sufferings endured by the tens of thousands of Indonesians imprisoned and tortured. Ten thousand, most of them over 50 and seriously ill, at their release are compelled to read an oath of allegiance to President Suharto, denounce Marxism, and vow not to sue the government for being held without trial (and they are subject to instant reincarceration at any time). The 100,000 remaining prisoners "faced an even bleaker future." Newsweek didn't see the irony of the discrepancy between their reporting of enemies and friends, and their functioning here as an extension of US Cold War policy. This blindness extends into the discipline of librarianship. The Reader's Guide from 1900 to the present seldom recognized political prisoners in the US. This is because it surveys mainly mainstream magazines which serve as a conduit of official views. Perhaps also librarians are simply average citizens first and are unaware of the bias in this great research tool. But also available in some libraries is the Alternative Press Index which surveys small, independent magazines, and many of them define political trials and prisoners in such a way that they can perceive the existence of political trials and prisoners in the US. Another example. Some libraries subscribe to an electronic database called UnCover, which provides access to the table of contents of journals received by the twelve libraries in the Colorado Alliance of Research Libraries. There were approximately 8,000 interdisciplinary journals available in this database when I checked it in 1992. It discovered not one piece of writing on "political prisoners/USA." I discuss the US because I am familiar with it; similar nationalistic, ideological biases will probably be found in the media and libraries of many other countries.

United States of America

The human rights record of the U.S. fails in two areas. If you ask the average U.S. citizen if the country has or had political prisoners, the reply is likely to be no. This is a free country, we have a Bill of Rights, we are a country of laws, might be the explanation. But the country has imprisoned thousands of its citizens for their beliefs--trade unionists, suffragettes, communists and socialists, conscientious objectors, anti-war demonstrators, civil rights protestors, and many more representatives of ideas.

On the international level also one finds a discrepancy between ideal and practice. Since 1945, "concern for morality and rights...collapsed" into anti-communism (Forsythe 104). Although at first the Truman Administration supported human rights language in the U.N. Charter and other documents, it soon turned to the Truman Doctrine of containment of communism, and the Eisenhower Administration followed suit. A consequence of this Sovietphobia was U.S. support for numerous repressive allies no matter how atrocious--the Greek junta (1967-1974), South Korea, Morocco, Nicaragua, S.Vietnam, too many to name. The rhetoric of rights remained, but the reality was containment of Soviet power.

Also, while proclaiming its support for human rights in all nations, the government has maintained a narrowly limited list of "terrorist" nations. Today these nations are Cuba, N. Korea, Libya, Iran, Iraq, Syria, and Sudan (added in 1993), the sponsors of "international terrorism." But this kind of terrorism--even the murderers and bombers supported by Iran--is insignificant compared to the massive state terrorism of countries like China and Turkey that enjoy trade with the U.S. despite their horrendous records of violent repression. Cuba's or Libya's "terrorism" is insignificant or virtually nonexistent compared to that of dozens of US allies. And this kind of peanuts terrorism is decreasing, reaching a 17-year low in 1992.

During the 1988 presidential campaign, Human Rights Watch petitioned the next president to adopt an International Human Rights Agenda on behalf of the millions of men, women, and children who because of their beliefs are wrongfully imprisoned, tortured, murdered, or otherwise deprived of their personal freedoms. Desiring the U.S. to maintain an even hand in their international human rights policy (sanctions against Cuba, favored nation status for China), Human Rights Watch called upon the U.S. to report fairly on human rights abuses by all nations, whether friend or foe, and to withhold military and economic aid from any nation guilty of gross human rights violations.

Research Methods

I began with a computer list of approximately 2000 books and pamphlets in English gathered from the OCLC data base using their EPIC system. More sources were gleaned from the bibliographies of individual books; for example, Totten and Kleg's Human Rights, Totten's Genocide, Harlow's Barred. The Reader's Guide from 1900 through 1991 and the Alternative Press Index (1975-1991) were surveyed for articles, and that process led me to advertisements and reviews of additional books. The API was particularly helpful, because it indexes more than 200 "underground" periodicals "which amplify the cry for social change and social justice." Every number of several magazines was scanned (Matchbox, Militant, Human Rights Internet Reporter, Human Rights Quarterly, The Nuclear Resister). Every country report in Amnesty International's 1980 and 1990 annual country reports was annotated.

Conclusion

I have tried to include both the necessary information of a bibliography and the urgency of the subject. The twentieth century is the century of slaughter and torture. Our heroes of conscience are dying in prisons:

Mala Zimetbaum escaped from Auschwitz-Birkenau. A young Polish Jewess fluent in many languages she enjoyed unusual freedom in the camp as an interpreter. Desiring to tell about the mass massacre occuring at Auschwitz, she and a Polish political prisoner managed to acquire two SS uniforms and to escape. They were caught. At her execution before all the women in the camp she slashed her wrist below the gallows and slapped the SS officer in the face with her bloodied hand (Primo Levi, 12).

Franz Jägerstätter refused to serve in Hitler's army. Against the arguments of his bishop, the recruiting officers, his villagers, his family, and his military tribunal, he chose his faith and death rather than serve the Nazis.

Romeo Legaspi, a 58-year-old Philippine journalist, in January 1993 exposed illegalities by the Philippine National Police intelligence unit in his area. He was threatened and then abducted by armed men, and has not been seen since.

Poet Irena Ratushinskaya was sentenced to seven years of hard labor followed by five years of internal exile, endured repeated incarcerations in filthy, unheated punishment isolation cells, beaten, and several times almost died, for writing poetry "independent of the Soviet state." But she never wavered from the motto of the women politicals at her camp: "Back to freedom with a clear conscience."

We yearn for a future that vindicates their courage. We yearn to find grounds for hope. Not until 1948 was what is now called human rights an established part of world politics. Now many international human rights conventions and laws are legally in force in many nations. International agencies exist to watch individual nations. Just as the Bill of Rights in the United States holds officials to high standards of respect for citizens, these international standards and organizations challenge nations to treat their citizens with dignity. Of course, like the US Bill of Rights, their strength depends upon the insistence for justice by the people. But in the history of mankind, the imagination of international rights is relatively new. Structures of international justice are coming and yet to come. A U.S. court convicted Argentine General Suarez-Mason of torture and extradited him to Argentina to stand trial for his part in the murder of 9,000 Argentinians. UNESCO proclaimed a World Day of Animal Rights. In 1979 Amnesty International cited nine countries for "an unblemished record": Austria, Iceland, Luxembourg, Norway, Fiji, Bahamas, Bermuda, Canada, and Costa Rica. The vision and rhetoric of rights, now widely established, will be followed someday, we must hope, by the reality of rights throughout the world.

Notes

[1]Data in this section derived mainly from the annual reports by Amnesty International.

[2]This view is not held by all. Cosmas Desmond's argument is two-pronged: first, "an abstract ideal is a barrier, rather than a spur, to the practical expression of an ideal"; instead of preconceived principles or legalistic formulations what is essential to reconstituting society is "experience and commitment" to radical change; second, "a radical transformation of human beings in society is not only an obvious necessity, but is also possible if, and only if, we abandon the Western individualist views and the attendant reformist practices" (10). He finds all of these limitations in Amnesty International. Not only does he believe that Western liberal, individualistic philosophy has not solved the "problem of oppression" but it cannot (11). He advocates a radical Christian socialism.

Works Cited

Amnesty International Handbook. London: AI, 1977.

Bedau, Hugo, and Michael Radelet. "Miscarriages of Justice in Potentially Capital Cases." Stanford Law Review 40: 21-179.

Bennett, James R. Control of the Media in the United States: An Annotated Bibliography. New York: Garland, 1992.

Bould, Geoffrey. Conscience Be My Guide: An Anthology of Prison Writings. London: Zed, 1991.

Brenner, Lenni. "White Hats vs. Black Hats." Nation (March 5, 1990) 19-20.

Bushnell, P. Timothy, et al., eds. State Organized Terror: The Case of Violent Internal Repression. Boulder, CO: Westview, 1991.

Children. London: Amnesty International, 1979.

Churchill, Ward. "The Third World at Home: Political Prisoners in the U.S." Z Magazine 3.6 (June 1990) 89-96.

Costello, Mary. Political Prisoners. Washington, DC: Editorial Research Reports, 1976.

Desmond, Cosmas. Persecution East and West. Harmondsworth, Eng.; New York: Penguin, 1983.

Disappeared! Technique of Terror. London: Zed, 1986.

Herman, Edward S. The "Real" Terror Network. Boston: South End, 1982.

"The Hernandez Doctrine: What Now?" Philippine Human Rights Update 5 (May 15-June 14, 1990) 10-14.

Indonesia. New York: Amnesty International, 1977.

Ingraham, Barton. Political Crime in Europe: A Comparative Study of France, Germany, and England. Berkeley: U of California P, 1979.

Innes, Judith. "Human Rights Reporting as a Policy Tool: An Examination of the State Department Country Reports." Human Rights and Statistics. Ed. Thomas Jabine and Richard Claude. Philadelphia: U of Pennsylvania P, 1992. 235-257.

Korovessis, Pericles. The Method: A Personal Account of the Tortures in Greece. London: Allison and Busby, 1969.

Lederer, Bob. "U.S. Political Prisoners Face Media Silence." Extra! 5.6 (Sept. 1992) 18-19.

Levi, Primo. "Beyond Judgment." New York Review (December 17, 1987) 10-14.

Lifton, Robert Jay, and Eric Markusen. The Genocidal Mentality. New York: Basic, 1990.

Middleton, Jean. "Murders in Gaol--The Case of Barberton." Sechaba (Jan. 1984) 22-29.

Mitchell, Richard. Janus Faced Justice: Political Criminals in Imperial Japan. Honolulu: U of Hawaii P, 1992.

Mollison, Andrew. "1 Million New Refugees Raise Total to 17.5 Million." Arkansas Democrat-Gazette (May 25, 1993) 4A.

Montenegro, Miguel, Joaquin Caceres, Herberth Sanabria, Rafael Ramos (The Human Rights Commission of El Salvador, Non-Governmental). Torture in El Salvador: From La Esperanza (Mariona) Prison. San Salvador: Comision de Derechos Humanos de El Salvador, Sept. 28, 1986.

Moore, Barrington, Jr. Injustice: The Social Bases of Obedience and Revolt. New York: Sharpe, 1978.

Morrow, Lance. "Who (and What) Is a Political Prisoner?" Time (September 6, 1971) 18-19.

Peters, Edward. Torture. Oxford: Blackwell, 1985.

Plyushch, Leonid. History's Carnival: A Dissident's Autobiography. New York: Harcourt Brace Jovanovich, 1979.

"Political Detention in the Country Today." Philippine Human Rights Update 4 (June 15-July 14, 1989) 10-13.

"The Prisoners of Conscience." Newsweek (February 14, 1983) 40-41.

Pritchard, Kathleen. "Human Rights Reporting in Two Nations: A Comparison of the United States and Norway." Human Rights and Statistics. Philadelphia: U of Pennsylvania P, 1992. 258-284.

Rodley, Nigel. The Treatment of Prisoners under International Law. Paris: UNESCO; New York: Oxford, 1987.

Rosenberg, Tina. Children of Cain. New York: Morrow, 1991.

Sri Lanka: Disappearances. New York: Amnesty International, 1986.

"State Department Fares Better in Rights Review." Arkansas Democrat-Gazette (July 2, 1989) 19A.

Totten, Samuel, and Milton Kleg. Human Rights. Hillside, NJ: Enslow, 1989.

Weschler, Lawrence. "Afterword." State Crimes: Punishment or Pardon. Queenstown, MD: Aspen Institute, 1989.

"Women Beaten in Ethiopia ID Bellhop, Get $500,000." Arkansas Democrat-Gazette (August 21, 1993) 11A.

"World Terrorism Hits 17-year Low." Arkansas Democrat-Gazette (May 1, 1993) 12A.

Zoff, Otto. They Shall Inherit the Earth. New York: Day, 1943.

GENERAL

1. "555 Forgotten Americans, Are They in Red Prisons?" U.S. News and World Report 41 (July 27, 1956) 33. "Evidence actually is conclusive that at least 70 U.S. citizens are being held."

2. Adilman, Mona Ed. Spirits of the Age : Poets of Conscience. Kingston, Ont., Canada; Clayton, NY; St. Paul, Minn.: Quarry, 1989. 169. Presents in translation the best work of poets from around the world who have been imprisoned, tortured, exiled, or otherwise oppressed because of their writing.

3. "Africa." Amnesty International Report 1980. London: Amnesty International, 1980. 27-29. During May 1, 1979 to April 30, 1980 human rights improved in Zimbabwe (end of civil war), Nigeria (return to civilian rule), Equatorial Guinea, and Central African Empire (brutal dictators overthrown). Many prisoners of conscience were released. But detention without trial continues in wide use, detainees are frequently treated harshly, incommunicado detention is notorious in some countries, disappearances are occurring, children and students are beaten and killed, and all countries retain the death penalty (though not all use it).

4. "Africa's Hidden Terror." Reader's Digest 127 (July 1985) 65-9. Compilation of quotations from diverse magazines about atrocities committed in black Africa--Uganda, Kenya, Nigeria, Zimbabwe, Guinea.

5. Africa Watch. New York: Human Rights Watch, 1988-. A publication by Human Rights Watch.

6. Agosin, Marjorie. "So We Will Not Forget: Literature and Human Rights in Latin America." Trans. Janice Molloy. Human Rights Quarterly 10 (1988): 177-92. Analyzes "prose texts [written in the 1970s and 1980s] where the theme of human rights is intrinsically linked to a literature that does not forget and that refuses to be silenced."

7. AIUSA : Companion to the Amnesty International Handbook. 2nd edition. Bloomfield, N.J.: AIUSA Publications, 1979. 37. A general introduction to the U.S. section of AI.

8. AIUSA Legal Support Network Newsletter. New York: Amnesty International U.S.A., 1985-.

9. Americas Watch. New York: Human Rights Watch, 1981-. Established to monitor and promote human rights in Latin America and the Caribbean. Issued irregularly.

10. "The Americas." Amnesty International Report 1980. London: Amnesty International, 1980. 101-102. Torture, disappearances, arbitrary arrests and extra judicial killings were reported in many countries, especially in Argentina, Chile, El Salvador, Guatemala, Uruguay, and Paraguay.

11. Amnesty Action. Vol. 1 1966. Journal published by Amnesty International USA.

12. Amnesty International and the Use of Violence: An Explanatory Note. London: Amnesty International, 1976. 4. AI will support political prisoners who employed violence if he or she has been tortured or not provided a fair trial within a reasonable time.

13. Amnesty International Bulletin. London: Amnesty International, 1963-1967. Nos. 1-18.

14. Amnesty International Country Dossiers, 1975- Africa. Zug, Switzerland: Inter Documentation, 1980. 16. Microfiches. Rights violations in the countries of Africa.

15. Amnesty International Country Reports: Asia. Zug, Switzerland: Inter Documentation, 1980. Microfiche. Rights violations in the countries of Asia.

16. Amnesty International Country Reports: Europe. Zug, Switzerland: Inter Documentation, 1980. Microfiche. Rights violations in the countries of Europe.

17. Amnesty International Country Reports: Middle East. Zug, Switzerland: Inter Documentation, 1980. Microfiche. Rights violations in Middle Eastern countries. Syria, Iraq, and Morocco are emphasized.

18. Amnesty International Cumulative Inventory. Zug, Switzerland: Inter Documentation, 1986-. Annual.

19. Amnesty International Handbook. Ed. Marie Staunton, Sally Fenn, and Amnesty International USA. Claremont, CA: Hunter House, 1991. 145. An introduction to Amnesty International and how it works to help political prisoners. Chapters on torture, disappearances, children, women, trials, refugees, the structure of Amnesty International, and more.

20. Amnesty International Handbook. 5th ed. London: Amnesty International, 1977. 71. The fifth edition of an AI publication previously titled Handbook for Groups; it is divided into three sections: the first section (ch. 1-6) gives a general introduction to AI; the second section, ch. 7-8.,"provides detailed suggestions and guidelines or group activities," and the final section, ch. 9-11, gives useful reference material. First, 3d, and 4th ed. published under title: Handbook for Groups; 2d ed. published under title: How to Help Prisoners of Conscience.

21. Amnesty International Handbook. New York: Amnesty International, 1991. 141. Updates the introduction to AI: discusses the mandate, prisoners of conscience, torture, death penalty, etc.

22. Amnesty International Newsletter. London: Amnesty International, 1971-. Quarterly.

23. Amnesty International Photo File, 1961-1981. London: Amnesty International, 1981. Photos indicate the range of Amnesty International's concerns since the 1960s.

24. Amnesty International Publications: Catalogue. New York: Clearwater, 1980-.

25. Amnesty International Report 1 June 1975 - 31 May 1976. London: Amnesty International, 1976. 220. Country reports covering the period June 1, 1975 - May 31, 1976.

26. Amnesty International Report 1977. London: Amnesty International, 1977. 352. Country reports covering the period July 1976 to June 1977 organized by geographical area. Focuses upon people detained for their beliefs, race, etc., who have not used or advocated violence (prisoners of conscience). It is not an exhaustive survey, for information is restricted by government censorship and secrecy. (Because these annual reports are immensely informative and fundamental to this biblio., yet impossible to describe adequately in one brief annotation, I have annotated each country report in the 1980 and 1990 reports.).

27. Amnesty International Report 1978. London: Amnesty International, 1979. 320. Country reports covering the period July 1, 1977, to June 30, 1978.

28. Amnesty International Report 1979. London: Amnesty International, 1979. 220. Country reports covering the period May 1, 1978 to April 30, 1979.

29. Amnesty International Report 1980. London: Amnesty International, 1980. 408. Country by country reports covering the period May 1, 1979 to April 30, 1980. (Each country report has been annotated separately.)

30. Amnesty International Report 1981. London: Amnesty International, 1981. 426. Country by country reports covering the period May 1980 to April 30, 1981.

31. Amnesty International Report 1982. London: Amnesty International, 1982. 367. Country by country reports covering the period January to December 1981.

32. Amnesty International Report 1983. London: Amnesty International, 1983. 351. Country by country reports covering the period January to December 1982.

33. Amnesty International Report 1984. London: Amnesty International, 1984. 382. Country by country reports covering the period January to December 1983.

34. Amnesty International Report 1985. London: Amnesty International, 1985. 359. Country by country reports covering the period Jan. to Dec. 1984.

35. Amnesty International Report 1986. London: Amnesty International, 1986. 386. Covers the period January to December 1985.

36. Amnesty International Report 1987. London: Amnesty International, 1987. 391. Country by country report covering the period January to December 1986.

37. Amnesty International Report 1988. New York: Amnesty International USA, 1988. 278. Surveys the year 1987.

38. Amnesty International Report 1989. New York: Amnesty International USA, 1989. 310. Surveys the year 1988. "The 1980s have been marked by an extraordinary level of mass killings and individual assassinations by government forces."

39. Amnesty International Report 1990. New York: Amnesty International USA, 1990. 298. Covers the year 1989, 143 countries in alphabetical order. (Each country report has been annotated separately.)

40. Amnesty International Report 1991. New York: Amnesty International USA, 1991. 290. Covers the year 1990.

41. Amnesty International Report 1992. New York: Amnesty International, 1992. 320. Covers the year 1991 and most of the countries of the world in alphabetical order. Reports on prisoners of conscience, political prisoners denied fair trials, victims of torture, "disappearance" and political killings, death sentences and execution, etc.

42. Amnesty International Reports on Topics. Microfiche. Zug, Switzerland: Inter Documentation, 1973. Description based on Vol. 27 (1986).

43. Amnesty International, 1961-1976: A Chronology. London: Amnesty International, 1976. 17. An instant review of AI's activities during these years.

44. Amnesty International, 1962-1990 : Guide to the Microfilm Collection. London; Leiden, The Netherlands: Amnesty International, 1991. 295.

45. Amnesty International: A Major Collection of Published and Unpublished Research Material. Zug, Switzerland: Inter Documentation, 1981.

46. Andersen, G.M. "Torture in Latin America." America 152 (June 8, 1985) 470-2. On Americas Watch and Amnesty International Reports on torture, which is not decreasing.

47. Andrews, J.A. and W.D. Hines. Keyguide to Information Sources On the International Protection of Human Rights. New York: Facts on File, 1987. 169. Part I provides an "overview of the international protection of human rights and its literature." Part II lists sources of information. Part III is a listing of selected human rights organizations.

48. Annual Report of the Inter-American Commission on Human Rights 1986-1987. Washington D.C.: Organization of American States, 1987. 284. Summary of the activities of the Inter-American Commission on Human Rights in countries throughout Latin America: on-site investigations of human rights situations, reports of fact-finding missions, individual case studies and individual country studies.

49. "Asia." Amnesty International Report 1980. London: Amnesty International, 1980. 173-175. Political imprisonment is on a "vast scale" in Asia. Special representations were made to the UN regarding Afghanistan and Indonesia. Indefinite detention without trial is widespread, for example as in Vietnam and Laos. Where prisoners are allowed a trial, it is usually unfair, as in Taiwan, Pakistan, and the Republic of Korea.

50. Asia Watch. New York: Human Rights Watch, 1985-. Established to monitor and promote human rights in Asia. Issued irregularly.

51. Association for International Cooperation and Disarmament. Political Prisoners: A World Report. Sydney: South-East Asia Committee, AICD, 1972. 64.

52. Aston, Clive C. A Contemporary Crisis: Political Hostage-Taking & the Experience of Western Europe. Westport, CT: Greenwood, 1982. 217. Discusses the constraints on host government response, using the siege of the 1972 Munich Olympics as illustration.

53. Background Papers on Czechoslovakia, Ghana, Greece, Iran, Namibia, Rhodesia, Spain, Zambia. London: Amnesty International Research Dept., 1971-1974. Separate reports by country: e.g., Spain 4-5 pp., Zambia 10 pp. All reports contain sections on political prisoners and trials. For example, data about repression in Czechoslovakia is given ("between 18-20 August, 1970, 6,217 people were detained, 829 of them imprisoned").

54. Bailey, George. Galileo's Children: Science, Sakharov & The Power of the State. New York: Arcade, 1990. 458. On Galileo, J. Robert Oppenheimer, and especially Andrei Sakharov and the conflict between science and the state.

55. Baker, Eric. Public Policy and the Use of Torture. London: Quaker Peace & Service with Amnesty International, 1980. 32. By one of the founders of Amnesty International.

56. Basisu, Mu'in. Descent into the Water: Palestinian Notes from Arab Exile. Tr. Saleh Omar. Wilmette, IL: Medina P, 1980. 102. On the persecution of the Palestinian Communist Party by several nations. The author, a native of Gaza, was imprisoned for his political activities, and much of this book is about that.

57. Becker, Theodore. Political Trials. Indianapolis: Bobbs-Merrill, 1971. 255. Examines judicial procedures and the issue of fair, impartial justice in the U.S. (Chicago Conspiracy), Cuba, Germany, India, Philippines, Soviet Union (Sinjavski-Daniel), and Africa.

58. Bedau, Hugo, ed. Civil Disobedience: Theory and Practice. Indianapolis: Pegasus, 1970 (1982 printing). 282. Includes essays on practice by H.D. Thoreau, M.L. King, Jr., Bertrand Russell, a "Two-Time Draft Card Burner," and on theory by John Rawls, N.B. Acton and others.

59. Beneson, Peter. "The Forgotten Prisoners." Matchbox: AIUSA Anniversary Supplement (May 1981) 1A-2A. "On May 28, 1961 an article by Peter Beneson appeared in the London Observer which launched Appeal for Amnesty 1961. Twenty years later, Amnesty International continues to work on behalf of 'forgotten prisoners' throughout the world. A major portion of Beneson's appeal is reprinted here in observance of 'Prisoner of Conscience Day,' May 28, 1981."

60. Birtles, Dorothy. Letters from Prison: 100 Political Prisoners Befriended by Quakers. London: Quaker Peace & Service, 1982. 19. British Quakers support prisoners around the world.

61. Blaustein, Albert P., et al., eds. Human Rights Sourcebook. New York: Paragon House for the Washington Institute for Values in Public Policy, 1987. 970. A "one-volume compilation of the official texts of all of the fundamental human rights documents."

62. Bould, Geoffrey, ed. Conscience Be My Guide: An Anthology of Prison Writings. London, Zed Books, 1991. 262. Selections drawn from throughout history, topically arranged. Contains a wide variety of 20th century political prisoners -- COs, psychiatric, whistleblowers, nuclear, Holocaust, etc.

63. Boulesbau, Ahcene. "The Nature of the Obligations Incurred by States Under Article 2 of the UN Convention Against Torture." Human Rights Quarterly 12 (1990) 53-93. Suggests means by which the objectives of the Convention_Against Torture (1987) may be attained.

64. Boyle, Francis. Defending Civil Resistance Under International Law. Dobbs Ferry, NY: Transnational, 1987. 378. A practical legal manual for use in preparing the defence of dissident citizens who wish to hold the U.S. accountable to international law.

65. The Breaking of Bodies and Minds: Torture, Psychiatric Abuse, and the Health Professions. New York: Freeman, 1985. 319. Essays on "the gross and pervasive violation of human rights" in the world and the participation by health professionals in physical and psychological torture.

66. Brenner, Lenni. "White Hats vs. Black Hats."" Nation (March 5, 1990) 319-320. Evaluates Amnesty International's 1989 annual report pointing out strengths and weaknesses.

67. Brownlie, Ian, ed. Basic Document on Human Rights. 3rd ed. London: Oxford UP, 1992. 600. "Completely revised and updated, this third edition...is designed to provide a useful collection of sources on human rights in the form of a handbook." Coverage is given to recent United Nations declarations and conventions, European institutions and conventions, the contribution of the International Labor Organization, and developments in Latin America, Africa and Asia in human rights. See Blaustein.

68. Bunster-Burotto, Ximena. "Surviving Beyond Fear: Women and Torture in Latin America." Women and Change in Latin America. Ed. Julie Nash and Helen Safa. South Hadley, MA: Bergin and Garvey, 1986. 372. On sexual sadism used by police and prison officials to compel political conformity in Argentina, Uruguay, and Chile.

69. Bushnell, P. Timothy, et al., eds. State Organized Terror: The Case of Violent Internal Repression. State Violence, State Terrorism, and Human Rights Series. Boulder, CO: Westview Press, 1991. 312. "In this century alone, tens of millions of people, living in most regions of the world...have been and continue to be victims of state organized repression and violence."

70. Cassese, Antonio, ed. The International Fight Against Torture, La Lutte International Contre La Torture. Baden-Baden: Nomos, 1991. 186. Evaluates the effectiveness of existing legal mechanisms for safeguarding human dignity against torture.

71. Center: The Magazine of PEN Center USA West. Los Angeles. Founded in 1952 as PEN Los Angeles, this center is one of two in the U.S. chartered by International

PEN, a worldwide association of writers. Part of their work is supporting writers victimized by repressive states. They name imprisoned writers honorary members.

72. Chalk, Frank, and Kurt Jonassohn. The History and Sociology of Genocide: Analyses and Case Studies. New Haven, CT.: Yale UP, 1990. 461. Part I surveys the literature and provides a definition and typology; Part II gives cases; and Part III is a topically organized bibliography.

73. The Challenge: Bulletin of the Association of Former Political Prisoners of Soviet Labor Camps. New York: 1950-.

74. Charney, Israel, ed. Genocide: A Critical Bibliographic Review. Vol I. London and New York: Mansell, Facts on File, 1988. 273. On first-person accounts.

75. Children. London: Amnesty International, 1979. 30. On the plight of children political prisoners.

76. Clare, Anthony, M.D. Medicine Betrayed: The Participation of Doctors in Human Rights Abuses. British Medical Association. London: Zed, 1992. 234. Assesses doctors' involvment in human rights violations, chapters on ethical standards, evidence of violations, torture, psychiatry, corporal and capital punishment, hunger strikes, etc.

77. Clayton, R.M. "A Burden Shared." Christian Century 93 (December 22, 1976) 1141-2. An account of the brutal treatment of a political prisoner just released.

78. Closet Land (film). Dir., screenplay, Radha Bharadwaj. Universal Studios, 1991. A writer of children's stories is tortured to compel her to confess that her latest story is "thinly veiled anti-government propaganda." Allusions to 1984, Brave New World, and Antigone.

79. Congress on International Solidarity and Humanitarian Actions. Geneva: United Nations High Commissioner For Refugees, 1980. 401. Section IX, "International Solidarity and the Protection of Political Detainees." On efforts to strengthen international conventions and procedures to protect political prisoners.

80. Conquest, Robert. Tyrants and Typewriters: Communiques for the Struggle for Truth. Lexington, MA: Lexington Books. 1989. 208. On writer dissenters--Sakharov, Koestler, Medeved, Solzhenitzyn.

81. Corradi, Juan et al., eds. Fear at the Edge : State Terror And Resistance in Latin America. Berkeley: U of California P, 1992. 260. The effects of systematic state terror in Chile, Argentina, Brazil, and Uruguay.

82. Costello, Mary. Political Prisoners. Washington: Editorial Research Reports/Congressional Quarterly 2.13 (1976) 723-744. United States perspective.

83. Country Reports on Human Rights Practices for 1977. Washington, DC: GPO, 1978. 426. U.S. State Department reports arranged by six regions. Not a worldwide study, but covers only those countries receiving U.S. economic assistance. Annually.

83a. Country Reports on Human Rights Practices for 1978. Washington, DC: GPO, 1979.

84. Country Reports on Human Rights Practices For 1979. Washington, D.C.: GPO, 1980. 854. Country reports arranged by five regions, not a world-wide report, but only covering those countries receiving U.S. economic assistance.

85. Country Reports on Human Rights Practices for 1980. Washington, D.C.: GPO, 1981. 1140. Country reports arranged by 5 regions, not a world-wide report but only those countries receiving U.S. economic assistance.

86. Country Reports on Human Rights Practices for 1981. Washington, D.C.: GPO, 1982. 1142. Country reports arranged by five regions, not a world-wide report, but only those countries receiving U.S. economic assistance.

87. Country Reports on Human Rights Practices for 1982. Washington, D.C.: GPO, 1983. 1323. Country reports arranged by five regions, not a world-wide report, but only those countries receiving U.S. economic assistance.

88. Country Reports on Human Rights Practices for 1983. Washington, D.C.: GPO, 1984. 1485. Country reports arranged by five regions, not a world-wide report, but only those countries receiving U.S. economic assistance.

89. Country Reports on Human Rights Practices for 1984. Washington, D.C.: GPO, 1985. 1453. Country reports arranged by five regions, not a world-wide report, but only those countries receiving U.S. economic assistance.

90. Country Reports on Human Rights Practices for 1985. Washington, D.C.: GPO, 1986. 1440. Country reports arranged by five regions, bot a world-wide report, but covering those countries receiving U.S. economic assistance.

91. Country Reports on Human Right Practices for 1986. Washington, D.C.: GPO, 1987. 1356. Country reports arranged by five regions, not a world-wide report, but only those countries receiving U.S. economic assistance.

92. Country Reports on Human Rights Practices for 1987. Washington, D.C.: GPO, 1988. 1358. Country reports arranged by five regions, not a world-wide report, but only covering those countries receiving U.S. economic assistance.

93. Country Reports on Human Rights Practices for 1988. Washington, D.C.: GPO, 1989. 1560. Country reports arranged by five regions, not a world-wide report, but only covering those countries receiving U.S. economic assistance.

94. Country Reports on Human Rights Practices for 1989. Washington, D.C.: GPO, 1990. 1641. Country reports arranged by five regions, not a world-wide report but only those countries receiving U.S. economic assistance.

95. Country Reports on Human Rights Practices for 1991. Washington, DC: GPO, 1992. 1196. The seventeenth (annual) report to Congress covering not only "countries that receive aid from the U.S. and countries that are members of the United Nations, as required by law," but also reports on additional countries.

96. Country Reports on Human Rights Practices for 1992. Washington, DC: G.P.O., 1993. 1216. U.S. State Department reports continue.

97. Cox, Larry. "The Death Penalty: Torture with a Respectable Face." Matchbox (Feb. 1981) 8. Compares torture by electric wires attached to genitals in Argentina to capital punishment by electric wires attached to the head in the United States.

98. "Crackdown." Time 100 (July 31, 1972) 27. Increasing repression throughout Eastern Europe.

99. Crawford, James, ed. The Rights of Peoples. London: Oxford UP, 1988. 248. "While the concepts of individual and collective human rights are well-known and have produced important changes in international law, there has emerged a 'third generation' of human rights claims calling for the 'rights of peoples.'" This work is the first full-length study of this controversial topic, discussing from a variety of viewpoints the claims made for a third generation of peoples' rights.

100. Crelinsten, Ronald, et al., eds. Terrorism and Criminal Justice: An International Perspective. Lexington, MA: Lexington, 1978. 131. Contains "Political Prisoners and Terrorists in American Correctional Institutions" by Edith Flynn, "The Facts on Internment in Northern Ireland" by Kevin Boyle, et al., and twelve other articles.

101. Curry, Jane L., ed. Dissent in Eastern Europe. New York: Praeger, 1983. 227. Country by country survey of dissent and repression.

102. Database on the Rights of a Child. New York: Children's Clarion, 1987. 350. Section one consists of a printout of three key pieces of international legislation relating to the rights of children. Section two contains over 1,000 abstracts from over 175 sources. Section three contains a geographic index to section two and a list of sources.

103. Davies, Miranda, ed. Third World--Second Sex: Women's Struggles and National Liberation. London: Zed, 1983. 257. Primary documents and interviews.

104. The Death Penalty. New York: Amnesty International, 1979. 209. A country by country survey of the Death Penalty covering 1973-1976.

105. The Death Penalty Briefing 1989. New York: Amnesty International, 1989. 16. A briefing that summarizes the more extensive When the State Kills.

106. Decalo, Samuel. Psychoses of Power: African Personal Dictatorships. Boulder, CO: Westview, 1989. 232. Explores the personal abuse of state power by three tyrannical regimes and their megalomaniac rulers: Idi Amin of Uganda, Jean-Bedel Bokassa of the Central African Republic, and Francisco Macias Nguema of Equatorial Guinea. Gives detailed analyses of the "systematic brutalizations of their populations."

107. Desmond, Cosmas. Persecution East and West : Human Rights, Political Prisoners, and Amnesty. Harmondsworth, Middlesex, England; New York: Penguin, 1983. 171. An attack by a Christian Marxist upon capitalism and the Soviet Union's socialism and their oppression and injustice, and a critique not only of Amnesty International but "of the whole Western approach to human rights."

108. Deutscher, Tamara. Political Prisoners in Czechoslovakia and the USSR: The Struggle for Socialist Democracy. Nottingham: The Spokesman, 1975. 19. Information on the four cases cited in the 1974 world appeal for solidarity with political prisoners in socialist countries: Pyotr Grigorenko, Jaroslav Sabata, Jiri Muller, and Vladmir Bukovsky.

109. Di Ciro, Giovanna. "NOW Joins Network to Free Women Prisoners." National NOW Times 21.4 (Oct. 1988) 13. NOW Action Center joins the Women's Urgent Action Network of thousands of volunteers from sixty countries who exert pressure to assist threatened prisoners.

110. Directory of Persecuted Scientists, Engineers, and Health Professionals. Washington, DC: American Association for the Advancement of Science, 1992. 121. 27 countries are surveyed, listing more than 300 people, plus an index of cases by discipline.

111. "Disappearances," A Workbook. New York: Amnesty International, 1981. 168. Based on discussion at a seminar on disappearances in Racine, WI., 1980, organized by AIUSA. Defines "disappearance," explains the people who became agents of disappearances, and discusses five countries: Argentina, Guatemala, Africa, Afghanistan, and the Philippines.

112. Disappeared! Technique of Terror: A Report for the Independent Commission on International Humanitarian Issues. London; Atlantic Highlands, N.J.: Zed Books, 1986. 107. Studies the people who have been made to disappear for political reasons in violation of all rights of legal defence (no warrant for arrest, no trial, no defending advocate, no public announcement), usually resulting in torture and often murder.

113. "'The Disappeared'- Where Are They?" New York: Amnesty International, 1981. 4. A special supplement to the November 1981 issue of Matchbox documenting cases of 'disappearances' all over the world.

114. Dobrin, Arthur. Convictions: Political Prisoners, Their Stories. Maryknoll, NY: Orbis, 1981. 100. Nine case studies from around the world.

115. Domínguez, Jorge I., et al., eds. Enhancing Global Human Rights. 1980's Project/Council on Foreign Relations. New York: McGraw-Hill, 1979. 270. Essays on assessing human rights norms and conditions, monitoring human rights violations, Latin America, and responding to severe violations.

116. Donnelly, Jack. Universal Human Rights in Theory and Practice. Ithaca: Cornell UP, 1989. 295. Chapter ten examines human rights, development rights, dictatorships, and repression.

117. Donnelly, Jack and Rhoda E. Howard. "Assessing National Human Rights Performance: A Theoretical Framework." Human Rights Quarterly 10 (1988) 214-248. Identifies ten essential rights in four categories that, carefully assessed, could "approximate a comprehensive assessment of a country's overall human rights record"--survival rights, protection rights, membership rights, and empowerment rights.

118. Dorfman, Ariel. "Fictionalizing the Truth in Latin America." Nation 236 (June 25, 1983) 794-6. On two films which tell about the "disappeared" in Latin America: Missing (Charles Horman murdered in Chile) and Jacobo Timerman (torture and survival in Argentina).

119. Dowty, Alan. Closed Borders: The Contemporary Assault on Freedom of Movement. New Haven, CT: Yale UP, 1987. 258. Focuses on the right to travel in its historical-political context.

120. Drinan, Robert F. Cry of the Oppressed: The History and Hope of the Human Rights Revolution. San Francisco: Harper and Row, 1987. 210. Surveys the struggle for human rights around the world, cites the dire needs in specific countries, and calls for an international court to protect human rights. Diverse subjects--e.g., Chap. 4 "International Efforts to Eradicate Torture," Chap. 8, "The Reagan Administration and Human Rights."

121. "Equality of Conscience: Women in Prison." Matchbox (Spring 1977) 4-5. A report on the special problems women political prisoners face: torture in the form of sexual brutality, low status, forced marriage, etc. Includes four case studies.

122. "Europe." Amnesty International Report 1980. London: Amnesty International, 1980. 247. During the year covered by this report -- May 1, 1979 to April 1980 -- numerous people were imprisoned in Eastern Europe for a variety of "crimes," ranging from peaceful dissent, to religious belief, to desiring to leave a country. Harsh prison conditions, unfair trials, misused psychiatry, and arbitrary arrests and detentions are widespread. In Western Europe most prisoners are objectors to military service, but some countries have imprisoned people solely for political expressions (Turkey, Spain).

123. Europe: Concerns in Europe November 1991 - April 1992. New York: Amnesty International, 1992. 99. This bulletin contains information about Amnesty International's main concerns in Europe during the period Nov. 1991 - April 1992.

124. "Excerpts From: A Guide to the United Nations Body of Principles For the Protection of All Persons Under Any Form of Detention or Imprisonment." Philippine Human Rights Update 5 (July 15-August 14, 1990) 19-21. U.N. principles designed to protect people against arbitrary detention, coercive interrogation, inhuman prison conditions, torture, disappearance, etc.

125. Falgiano, Lisa and Kerstin LeMaire. "A Review of Human Rights Watch Publications." Human Rights Quarterly 14 (1992) 623-52. Analyzes Human Rights Watch World Report (1990), three Africa Watch publications (1991), nine Americas Watch publications (1991), three Asia Watch publications (1991), two Middle East Watch publications (1991), four Prison Project publications (1991), and one Women's Rights Project publication (1991).

126. Fawcett, J.E.S. The Application of the European Convention on Human Rights. Oxford: Clarendon, 1987. 444. Article by article analysis.

127. Fein, Helen. Genocide: A Sociological Perspective. Newbury Park, CA: Sage, 1993. 144. Nature and history of genocide.

128. "Flaws in the Pattern": Human Rights in Literature. Ottawa: Amnesty International Canada, 1978. 79. Documents, essays, and poems on persecution, censorship, confinement, and related topics. "This book and its companion, Human Rights, Past and Present, have been prepared for the use of teachers and students in Canadian High Schools.

129. Forché, Carolyn. Against Forgetting: Twentieth-Century Poetry of Witness. New York: Norton, 1993. 812. Includes poetry on the Armenian genocide, the struggle for democracy in China, repression in the Soviet Union, the Holocaust, repression in Latin America, and repression in Africa.

130. Forsythe, David P. Human Rights and World Politics. 2nd Ed. Lincoln: U of Nebraska P, 1989. 316. On promoting and protecting human rights and U.S. foreign policies. Chapter five discusses rhetoric vs. reality: Kissinger, Carter, Reagan.

131. Franks, C.E.S., ed. Dissent and the State. Toronto: Oxford UP, 1989. 288. Explores the relationship between legitimate dissent and subversion as played out around the world.

132. Fraser, Antonia. "PEN's Work For Imprisoned Writers." Index On Censorship 17.1 (Jan 1988) 28. Focuses on Martha Kumsa of Ethiopia and Mart Niklus of Estonia. Niklus is serving a 10-year sentence in the USSR, to be followed by five years internal exile. Kumas had been held for seven years without charge or trial.

133. Free At Last. Amnesty International USA, 1986. 30 min. videocassette, VHS format. Video celebrating Amnesty International and its investigations and campaigns concerning torture and enforcement of human rights around the world.

134. Freedman-Apsel, Joyce, and Helen Fein, eds. Teaching About Genocide: A Guidebook For College and University Teachers: Critical Essays, Syllabi, and Assignments. Ottowa, Ont: Human Rights Internet; New York Institute for the Study of Genocide, 1992. 102. Essays with reading lists and syllabi on "Genocide in History," "Comparative Study of Genocide," "Literature of the Holocaust and Genocide," etc.

135. Freedom at Issue. New York: Freedom House. A bimonthly devoted to supporting free institutions.

136. Freedom from Arbitrary Arrest, Detention, and Exile. Yearbook on Human Rights, First Supplementary Volume. New York: United Nations, 1959. 249. Statements by 56 countries regarding their application of the right set forth in Article nine of the Universal Declaration of Human Rights--i.e., "No one shall be subject to arbitrary arrest, detention, or exile."

137. "Freedom to Write." A regular section of Center: The Magazine of PEN Center USA West devoted to imprisoned writers.

138. Friedman, Julian R. and Laurie S. Wiseberg. Teaching Human Rights. Washington D.C.: Human Rights Internet, 1981. 134. A collection of syllabi-outlines for courses taught in universities, law schools, and high schools that deal specifically with human rights. Includes a bibliography of human rights bibliographies.

139. Gara, Larry. "Prison Notes." WIN 15.38 (November 15, 1979) 19. On Canadian and U.S. unfair trials and imprisonment.

140. Gastil, Raymond D., et al. Freedom in the World: Political Rights and Civil Liberties 1988-1989. New York: Freedom House, 1989. 522. Comparative country and related territory summaries.

141. Gastil, Raymond D., et al. Freedom in the World: Political Rights and Civil Liberties 1987-1988. New York: Freedom House, 1988. 450. Contains chapters on geographical analysis of civil and political liberties in the world, a "scale of polyarchy," and other studies, and the annual country and related territory comparative summaries.

142. Gastil, Raymond D., et al. Freedom in the World: Political Rights and Civil Liberties 1986-1987. New York: Greenwood, 1987. 411. Comparative country reports.

143. Gastil, Raymond D., et al. Freedom in the World: Political Rights and Civil Liberties 1985-1986. New York: Greenwood, 1986. 432. Comparative country summaries.

144. Gastil, Raymond D., et al. Freedom in the World: Political Rights and Civil Liberties 1984-1985. London: Greenwood, 1985. 438. Country summaries and related territory summaries, comparative.

145. Gastil, Raymond D., et al. Freedom in the World: Political Rights and Civil Liberties 1983-1984. London: Greenwood, 1984. 474. Articles on information and democracy, long section on China, and the annual country summaries.

146. Gastil, Raymond D., et al. Freedom in the World: Political Rights and Civil Liberties 1982. London: Greenwood, 1982. 379. Mainly on economic, worker, media, and religious freedoms. One section compares the human rights records of the former governments of South Vietnam and North Vietnam while they were fighting each other until April 1975, concluding that North Vietnam was much worse. Annual country summaries.

147. Gastil, Raymond D., et al. Freedom in the World: Political Rights and Civil Liberties 1981. Westport, Conn.: Greenwood, 1981. 434. Part III, pp. 81-312 deals with Central Asia; Part IV gives country summaries and ratings based partly on "freedom from political imprisonment, torture, and other forms of government reprisal." In contrast to Amnesty International reports, comparisons of countries are made.

148. Gelman, Anne and Milos Stehlik, eds. Human Rights Film Guide. New York: Smyrna, 1993. 130. Discussion of 400 films and videos dealing with civil, political, human, and prisoner rights. Includes distributors' addresses.

149. George, Alexander, ed. Western State Terrorism. New York: Routledge, 1991. 264. Essays on the U.S. and counterinsurgency, Northern Ireland, Indonesia, etc.

150. Ginger, Ann Fagan, Beverly Wilson, Linton Hale, eds. Human Rights Organizations and Periodicals Directory. 7th ed. Berkeley, CA: Meiklejohn Civil Liberties Institute, 1990. 232.

151. "A Glimpse at Monitoring Human Rights Overseas: Three Monitors Honored in 1992 Tell Their Stories." Human Rights Watch 11.4 (Fall 1993) 6-9. Brave people from Thailand, Colombia, and Nigeria.

152. Graham-Yool, Andrew. "Nothing's Changed in the Wider World." Index on Censorship 18.10 (Nov. 1989) 2. Survey of world repression, focusing on Malawi, Chad, and Argentina.

153. Gruschow, Janet and Kari Hannibal. Health Services for the Treatment of Torture and Trauma Survivors. Washington D.C.: American Association for the Advancement of Science, 1990. 158. From symposia sponsored by the AAAS Committee on Scientific Freedom and Responsibility, Boston, Massachusetts, February 14, 1988, and San Francisco, California, January 16, 1989.

154. Hancock, Ian. The Pariah Syndrome: An Account of Gypsy Slavery and Persecution. Ann Arbor, MI: Karoma, 1987. 175. Little has changed since Hitler's attempt to exterminate the Gypsies: official statements calling for sterilization, deportation and extermination are still released in eastern and western European countries.

155. Hannum, Hurst. The Right to Leave and Return in International Law and Practice. Boston: Martinous Nijhoff, 1987. 134. Focuses on the right within a legal framework.

156. Harlow, Barbara. Barred: Women, Writing, and Political Detention. Hanover, N.H.; London: Wesleyan UP, 1992. 292. "Barred" refers to the policies that deny political and literary status to women and to their organized dissent, to writers and writings banned, and the strategies of control inside and outside prison. A book on the struggle against political detention by women through writing in Northern Ireland, Palestine, Egypt, South Africa, El Salvador, and the U.S.

157. Hayes, John. "Massive Canvasses Record 'Brute Facts and Brutal Events.'" Matchbox (Feb. 1983) 11. The art of Leon Golub on interrogations, "white" (death) squads, torture and murder.

158. Hoch, Nancy. "Children as Victims of Repression." Guardian 32.4 (October 31, 1979) 15. A report released by Amnesty International tells of the victimization and torture children of political prisoners go through when separated from their parents.

159. Holiday, David. "Disproving the 'Official' Story with Forensics." Human Rights Watch 10.2 (Spring 1992) 5. Forensic teams are conducting exhumations all over Latin America in the struggle for accountability by government forces.

160. Hooded Men. Video, 55 min. Canadian Broadcasting Corporation film on the use of torture against political prisoners in 65 countries, focusing particularly on N. Ireland, Argentina, and Nicaragua.

161. The Houses Are Full of Smoke. 16 mm film. Dir. Alan Francovich. Berkeley, CA, 1987. 180 min. Documentary on CIA activities in and relations with Guatemala, El Salvador, and Nicaragua since the 1950s, including human rights violations, death squads, plot to kill Archbishop Romero, secret cemetaries of the Contras, etc.

162. Human Rights and Peace Law Docket, 1945-1991. Berkeley, CA: The Meiklejohn Civil Liberties Institute, 1992. 300. Covers cases on topics from war crimes in the late 1940s to the Grenada Invasion, death penalty, nuclear power, immigrants' rights, political surveillance, war, tax refusal, and conscientious objection. Also, texts of the Nuremburg principles, Universal Declaration on Human Rights, the Constitution of the U.S., Charter of the U.N., and the International Covenant on Civil and Political Rights are reprinted here.

163. Human Rights and the Phenomenon of Disappearances: Hearings Before the Subcommittee on International Organizations, of the Committee on Foreign Affairs, House of Representatives, Ninety-sixth Congress, First Session, September 20, 25, and October 18, 1979. Washington: GPO, 1980. 636. A "compilation of several hearings," including reports from nongovernment organizations and individual testimonies. A "shocking picture of the violation of human rights on an unprecedented scale," especially in Latin America.

164. Human Rights Internet Reporter, 1980-. A quarterly journal that reports on key human rights developments in national and international law, and on individual human rights cases around the world. Each issue contains an extensive, thoroughly annotated bibliography divided into general topics and by region and country as well.

165. Human Rights Practices Countries Receiving U.S. Security Assistance. Washington, D.C.: GPO, 1977. 137. Eighty-two countries surveyed, current as of December 1976.

166. Human Rights Reports. Washington, D.C.: GPO, 1977. 143. Country reports arranged by five regions, not a world-wide report but covering only those countries receiving U.S. economic assistance.

167. "Human Rights Watch Honors International Human Rights Monitors." Human Rights Watch 11.4 (Fall 1993) 1, 4-5. Thirteen monitors have been invited to the U.S. Brief biographies are given.

168. "Human Rights Watch Looks Within." New Yorker (Dec. 13, 1993) 53-4. The new executive director of Human Rights Watch speculates about the future: "'monitoring abuses and then stigmatizing the responsible regimes...is not enough.'"

169. Human Rights Watch Quarterly Newsletter. New York: Human Rights Watch, 1991-. Membership newsletter.

170. Human Rights Watch World Report. New York: Human Rights Watch, 1990-. Annual. Focuses on U.S. record on human rights abroad.

171. Human Rights Watch World Report 1992: An Annual Review of Developments and the Bush Administration's Policy on Human Rights Worldwide. New York: Human Rights Watch, 1992. 912. Profiles fifty-seven nations.

172. Humana, Charles. World Human Rights Guide. 3rd ed. New York: Oxford UP, 1992. 416. Gives the human rights records of over 100 countries.

173. "If you want peace...defend life:" 10th Annual World Period of Peace, November, 1976. Washington, D.C.: United States Catholic Conference: Office of International Justice and Peace, 1977. 26. Indicts human rights abuses, especially torture, citing five countries (Argentina, Czechoslovakia, Indonesia, Iran, South Africa), and names victims.

174. Ingraham, Baron L. Political Crime in Europe : A Comparative Study of France, Germany, and England. Berkeley: U of California P, 1979. 380. Part I provides a theory and definition of political crime; Part II compares the laws of the three countries from 1770 to the present.

175. International Civil Liberties Report. Los Angeles: International Human Rights Task Force, ACLU Foundation of S. California. Especially interested in articles about the use of international human rights law in ACLU work. (The ACLU affiliates of Georgia and S. Calif. in 1993 won a suit for three Ethiopian women who had been tortured by a man now living in Atlanta.)

176. Jenkins, Lyll Becerra de. The Honorable Prison. New York: Puffin, 1988. 199. Novel about a journalist and his family jailed in a house in the Andes.

177. Joint Working Group for Refugees From Chile in Britain. Political Prisoners and Refugees in the Southern Cone of Latin America: A Report. London: The Working Group, 1977. 25.

178. Katsiaficas, George. The Imagination of the New Left: A Global Analysis of 1968. Boston: South End, 1987. 323. Two chapters on 1968, two on general strikes (May 1968 in France and May 1970 in the U.S.).

179. Kaufman, Edy. "Prisoners of Conscience: The Shaping of a New Human Rights Concept." Human Rights Quarterly 13 (1991) 339-367. Traces the development of the concept after 1961 when the founders of Amnesty International made it popular, and analyzes the many dilemmas--e.g. breaking laws, use of violence.

180. "Keeping Score." Common Cause (May\June 1988) 30-31. Evaluates the U.S. State Department's annual human rights country reports.

181. Kis, Danilo. A Tomb for Boris Davidovich. Trans. Duska Mikic-Mitchell. New York/London: Penguin, 1980. 135. (Orig. pub. in Yugoslavia 1976. Trans. Harcourt Brace Jovanovich 1978.) A novel about the fate of several people who perished during the Great Terror of the late 1930's, mainly in the Soviet Union.

182. Knoll, Erwin. "On the Confraternity of Power." Progressive 42 (September 1978) 21. Parallels the continued supression of dissent in the Soviet Union and the Eastern Block nations with repression in the United States.

183. Konrad, George, Peter Reddaway, and Barbara Sproul. "The East: Three Reports." New York Review of Books (November 5, 1981) 49-50. On Hungary, USSR, and Czechoslovakia.

184. Laffin, John. The Anatomy of Captivity. London, New York: Abelard-Schuman, 1968. 208. About the hundreds of thousands of people who have been imprisoned for political reasons. Focuses on Europe.

185. Lange, Martin and Reinhold Iblacker, eds. Witnesses of Hope: The Persecution of Christians in Latin America. Trans. William Jerman. Maryknoll, N.Y.: Orbis Books, 1981. 156. Documents the unjust imprisonment, torture, and murder of poor Christians and those who have championed their cause.

186. Langer, Lawrence. The Age of Atrocity: Death in Modern Literature. Boston: Beacon, 1978. 256. Discusses Sozhenitsyn's response to the Soviet labor camps and Charlotte Delbo's to the Nazi extermination camps.

187. Latin America : Human Rights Violations Against Trade Unionists. New York: Amnesty International, 1992. 39.
Trade unionists are still subject to illegal detention, torture and ill-treatment, "disappearance" and extrajudicial execution. (Brazil, Chile, Colombia, El Salvador, Guatemala, and Peru.)

188. Latin American Political Prisoners Report. Toronto: Canadian Committee for Justice to Latin American Political Prisoners, n.d.

189. Lernoux, Penny. Cry of the People: The Struggle for Human Rights in Latin America--The Catholic Church in Conflict with U.S. Policy. New York: Penguin, 1991. 560. Some chapter titles: "Be a Patriot (in El Salvador) and Kill a Priest!," "The Doctrine of National Security--Terror--The United States Teaches Latin America How," "Villains Afoot--The CIA," "Clockwork Orange--Torture, Murder, Repression, and Anti-Semitism in Brazil, Argentina, and Mexico."

190. Luttwak, Edward. Coup d'État: A Practical Handbook. New York: Fawcett, 1969; Cambridge, MA: Harvard UP, 1979. 215. Chapter 5 on "The Execution of the Coup d'État" and Appendix A on "The Economics of Repression."

191. Makiya, Kanan. Cruelty and Silence: War, Tyranny, Uprising and the Arab World. New York: Norton, 1993. 367. On the desperate state of human rights across the Middle East, focusing on Iraq before, during, and after the invasion of Kuwait.

192. Malamud-Goti, Jaime. "Transitional Government in the Breach: Why Punish State Criminals?" Human Rights Quarterly 12 (1990) 1-16. Discusses the issues involved in bringing military violators of human rights to trial. (The Argentine government pardoned all members of the security forces facing trial.)

193. Marange, Valerie. Doctors and Torture: Resistance or Collaboration? London: Bellew, 1991. 166. Describes a ten year battle to defend human rights against medical transgressions; record of 1989 conference organized by the French Medical Section of Amnesty International. Original title: "Doctors Who Torture, and Doctors Who Resist." "The central concern of the book is the involvement of doctors (and other health professionals) in human rights violations, the extreme form of which is torture."

194. Marrus, Michael R. The Unwanted: European Refugees in the Twentieth Century. New York; Oxford: Oxford UP, 1985. 414. Special attention to Jews, but also Armenians, Cold War refugees, etc., people everywhere fleeing persecution, torture, slaughter.

195. Matchbox. New York: Amnesty International. AI's journal which began Spring/Summer 1974 and ceased publication Oct. 1983. The following explanation of "Matchbox" is printed in every issue of the journal (here summarized): "After weeks of torture and torment, the prisoner was sure there was no hope...no one knew or cared." But that night the jailer "threw a loaf of bread onto the dirt floor" of the cell. The prisoner, ravenous, tore open the loaf and found a matchbox. The prisoner lit a match. On the paper there was a single word: Coraggio! Take courage. "Don't give up, don't give in. We are trying to help you. Coraggio!"

196. Mazian, Florence. Why Genocide? The Armenian and Jewish Experiences in Perspective. Ames, IA: Iowa State UP, 1990. 291. This examination of the Armenian genocide and the Holocaust searches for specific social factors that make such violence possible: creation of the "outsider" group, propaganda, war, etc.

197. McColm, R. Bruce, et. al. Freedom in the World: Political Rights and Civil Liberties 1990-1991. New York: Freedom House, 1991. 480. Regional essays, comparative survey, comparative map, country and related territories reports, etc.

198. McColm, R. Bruce, et. al. Freedom in the World: Political Rights and Civil Liberties 1989-1990. New York: Freedom House, 1990. 330. Contains a comparative map of freedom (1990), the annual comparative country and related territories reports, and other tables and ratings.

199. McLennan, Barbara N., ed. Political Opposition and Dissent. New York: Dunellen, 1973. 393. Essays on ten countries with two general chapters.

200. Méndez, Juan E. "New Center Seeks Justice in the Americas." Human Rights Watch 10.1 (Winter 1992) 5. Discussing judicial remedies to human rights abuses in Latin America.

201. Merton, Thomas. The Nonviolent Alternative. Ed. Gordon C. Zahn. New York: Farrar, Straus, Giroux; Toronto: McGraw-Hill Ryerson, 1980. 270. Essays on Franz Jägerstätter and Max Josef Metzger, imprisoned and executed for opposing Hitler peacefully; a chapter on Auschwitz.

202. "The Middle East and North Africa." Amnesty International Report 1980. London: Amnesty International, 1980. 319-321. Political trials are taking place in many countries: Iran, Egypt, Morocco, Libya, and others. Detention without trial is widespread, and allegations of torture and ill-treatment of prisoners are made in a dozen countries.

203. Mikes, George, ed. Prison, a Symposium. New York: Horizon, 1963. 215. A collection of memoirs on a wide range of prison experiences--penitentiaries, mental asylums, political prisons and concentration camps--marking the Age of Prison. "Never in the past have so many people been in prison--most of them innocent people in political captivity."

204. Moore, Barrington, Jr. Injustice: The Social Bases of Obedience and Revolt. New York: Sharpe, 1978. 540. Political philosophy on the paradoxical question of injustice: Why do people submit to injustice as a manifestation of a higher moral authority or an "inevitable edict of nature" yet also find a sense of injustice to be a source of liberating moral and political passion?

205. Moreillon, Jacques. The International Committee of the Red Cross and the Protection of Political Detainees. Geneva: The Committee, 1985. 24. Extracts from the Red Cross (Nov. 1974 and April 1975) regarding Red Cross efforts to succor political prisoners from Russia (1918) and Hungary (1919) to Colonial regimes 1958 to 1970.

206. Mss. 34, Amnesty International. Coventry, Eng: Modern Records Centre, U of Warwick Library, 1976. 13. The center became an official depository of all Amnesty publications in 1974.

207. National Academy of Sciences, Committee on Human Rights. Science and Human Rights. Washington, DC: National Academy Press, 1988. 92. Part I, "Torture, Psychiatric Abuse, and the Ethics of Medicine," focuses on Chile; Part II, "Human Rights, Human Needs, and Scientific Freedom," on South Africa; and Part III, "Human Rights and Human Survival," on the Soviet Union.

208. Neier, Aryeh. "Watching Rights." Nation (January 28, 1991) 79. On long-term prisoners in Singapore and South Korea who refuse to recant their beliefs.

209. Neier, Aryeh. "Watching Rights." Nation (October 19, 1992) 423. Human rights and economic development are compatible.

210. The New Conscientious Objection : The Secularization of Objection to Military Service. Ed. Charles C. Moskos and John W. Chambers. New York: Oxford, 1993. 320. Conscientious objection has grown rapidly; nearly 2,000 active-duty soldiers and mobilized reservists applied for CO status during the Gulf War. This study examines the history and practice of conscientious objection in the Western World and the state policies that have grown up in response to it.

211. "News Briefs." Matchbox. New York: Amnesty International. A survey of abuses around the world, a regular feature of AI's magazine (no longer published).

212. Niccolls, S. Thomas. "Human Rights: A Concern of the Righteous." Christianity Today 23 (May 25, 1979) 23-27. A plea to Christians to fight for human rights around the world.

213. Nickel, James W. Making Sense of Human Rights: Philosophical Reflections on the Universal Declaration of Human Rights. Berkeley: U of California P, 1987. 269. Argues that contemporary human rights standards as embodied in the bills of rights drafted since 1948 should guide both international and domestic politics.

214. Nino, Carlos Santiago. The Ethics of Human Rights. Oxford: Oxford UP, 1991. 336. Ethical, political, and legal theory by a writer noted also for his contribution to practical politics (the establishment of a system of human rights in his native Argentina).

215. Omaar, Rakiya. "African Academics Under Siege--and Many Flee." Human Rights Watch (Fall 1991) 6, 8. Academic freedom is "increasingly under attack" by university closure, denial of promotion and tenure, restrictions on travel and grants, arrest and torture (from Academic Freedom and Human Rights Abuses in Africa).

216. Orwell, George. Nineteen Eighty-four, a Novel. New York: Harcourt Brace, 1949. 314. In this novel Winston Smith is first subjected to isolation and sensory deprivation, then subjected to a complex technical device that apparently produces sophisticated electrical assaults upon his nervous system, and finally threatened with the single thing in the world which he fears most (an attack by rats), all not to elicit information (his torturers already know everything about him) but to break his will and compel absolute cooperation.

217. Patterson, Judy, and Austin Straus. "Whereas mankind owes the child the best it has to give..." Matchbox (Winter 1979) 1-3; (Spring 1979) 10; (November 1979) 1-2. A three-part report on human rights abuses which affect children: children born in prison and then separated from their mother to become wards of the state or sold, children raised in prison, illegitimate children born to women raped by prison guards, children who are imprisoned and tortured often as either retaliation or in order to extract confessions from their parents.

218. PEN International. Founded in 1921 by notable authors to foster understanding among people of letters in all countries. Works on behalf of censored and imprisoned writers.

219. Persecuted Writers Receive Grants: 36 Writers from 15 Countries Are Recognized with Funds from the Lillian Hellman/Dashiell Hammett Estates. New York: Human Rights Watch, 1993. 4. The Hellman and Hammett Estates recognize writers who have been victims of political persecution.

220. Peters, Edward. Torture. New York: Basil Blackwell, 1985. 202. A history of torture from Greece and Rome to Algeria and the 1980's.

221. Political Abuse of Psychiatry : A List of Victims, 30 November, 1985. London: Working Group on the Internment of Dissenters in Mental Hospitals, 1985. 44.

222. Political Killings By Governments. New York: Amnesty International, 1983. 127. This report is part of a global campaign to stop the killings and includes background studies of mass killings in countries ranging from Uganda to Kampuchea and of incidents reported from more than 20 countries in the 1980's.

223. Political Prisoners: A World Report. Sydney: Association for International Cooperation and Disarmament, South East Asia Committee, 1972. 64. Especially concerning Southeastern Asia and Sri Lanka.

224. Political Prisoners: A World Report. Ed. Lester Sobel. New York: Facts on File, 1978. 285.

225. Political Prisoners in the Oil States: Oman, Bahrein, Saudi Arabia, Iran. London: Gulf Committee, 1974. 32. These contries "deny their people many basic human rights" and conditions have worsened. Notes also the "silence of the world's press."

226. Power, Jonathan. Amnesty International, the Human Rights Story. Oxford; New York: Pergamon, 1981. 128. An account of Amnesty International's efforts for the past 20 years to diminish torture, false imprisonment, unfair trials, and other human rights abuses.

227. Prejean, Helen. Dead Man Walking: An Eyewitness Account of the Death Penalty in the United States. New York: Random House, 1993. 278. Notes the inherent racism, the arbitrary sentencing, the fact that execution does not deter crime but actually diverts millions away from effective crime fighting programs, that electrocution is far from painless, as well as focusing on the suffering of those left behind--the criminal justice system itself further assaults victims of crime.

228. "Price of Dissent."" Time 114 (December 24, 1979) 35. Discusses Amnesty International's annual report on 96 countries: torture nearly universal, disappearing and political murders on the rise. Nine countries had "an unblemished record": Austria, Iceland, Luxembourg, Norway, Fiji, Bahamas, Bermuda, Canada, and Costa Rica.

229. "Prisoners for Peace." Peace Notes 20.59 (December 16, 1977) 8. Addresses of people around the world who are imprisoned because of their refusal to be involved in the armed forces of their country.

230. Prisoners of Conscience. Houston: Amnesty International USA, Group 23, 1986. 72. Works by Houston artists dedicated to thirty-two men and women imprisoned around the world.

231. Prisoners of Conscience: An Amnesty International Report. London: Amnesty International, 1981. 43. Eighteen case histories from around the world.

232. Prisoners of Conscience: In Recognition of the 25th Anniversary of Amnesty International, September 6 through October 5, 1986. Arvada, Colo.: The Arvada Center for the Arts and Humanities, 1986. 62. Art and photo exhibition.

233. "Prisoners of the Month." Matchbox. New York: Amnesty International, 1974-. A regular feature of the magazine (no longer published) in which several individual prisoners are profiled.

234. Prisoners of War and Political Hostages: A Select Bibliography. Springfield, VA: Monroe Corporation, 1973. 46. Organized topically: historical, legal, military, behavioral, journalistic, personal experience, medical, and bibliographies. Several entries relate to political prisoners.

235. Puig, Manuel. Kiss of the Spider Woman. Trans. Thomas Colchie. New York: Knopf, 1979. 281. A novel about the experiences of a politically active journalist imprisoned with a homosexual in an unnamed South American country. A film was made from the novel with the same title in 1985, starring Raul Julia and William Hurt.

236. Quigley, John. "Government Vigilantes at Large: The Danger to Human Rights from Kidnapping of Suspected Terrorists." Human Rights Quarterly 10 (1988) 193-213. Examines the issue of prosecution on terrorism charges following forcible abduction.

237. Refugees and Political Prisoners in Latin America. London: Joint Working Group for Refugees from Latin America, 1979. 42. Separate chapters on Argentina, Uruguay, Brazil, and Chile; summaries of other countries.

238. Rejali, Darius. Torture and Modernity: Self, Society, and State in Modern Iran. Boulder: Westview, 1993. Explains the relationship between the practice of torture and the process of modernization, using Iran from the establishment of the Quajor dynasty in 1796 to the aftermath of the Gulf War for illustration. Tests current theories of the re-emergence of torture in the modern world, and shows a common past, one shared by Iranians and non-Iranians, that supports modern torture.

239. Remmer, Karen L. Military Rule in Latin America. Boulder, Colo.: Westview, 1989. 213. Four chapters on Latin America, three on Chile.

240. Report and Decisions of the 10th International Council Meeting of Amnesty International, Bad Honnef, Federal Republic of Germany, 16-18 September 1977. London: Amnesty International, International Secretariat, 1978. 126. A wide range of reports and resolutions.

241. Ridenour, Ron. "Healing Torture Victims: A Long and Lonely Task." Guardian 36.3 (Oct. 19, 1983) 18. About the new International Rehabilitation and Research Center for Torture Victims in the Copenhagen University Hospital.

242. Rivabella, Omar. Requiem for a Woman's Soul. Trans. Paul Riviera and Omar Rivabella. New York: Random House, 1986. 116. A fictional account of the sadistic, horrifying treatment of female political prisoners, via a diary by one prisoner.

243. Rocha, Ruth and Otavio Roth. The Universal Declaration of Human Rights: An Adaptation for Children. New York: Amnesty International, 1989. 45. Designed to familiarize children with the Declaration of Human Rights.

244. Rodley, Nigel S. The Treatment of Prisoners Under International Law. Paris: Unesco; Oxford: Clarendon P, 1987. 374. Traces "the development of international and regional legislation aimed at eliminating the practices of torture and other ill-treatment" (extra-judicial executions, disappearances, etc.), and examines "the problems of definition of torture" and of "implementing the newly developed legislation."

245. Rogge, O. John. Why Men Confess. New York: Thomas Nelson, 1959. 298. Chapters 6-8 describe the inquisitional techniques of Stalinism. Other chapters deal with ex-communists in the U.S., confessions of crimes by U.S. citizens in Chinese jails, the compulsion to confess, and other topics.

246. Rosenberg, Tina. Children of Cain: Violence and the Violent. New York: Penguin, 1991. 394. Surveys Colombia, Argentina, Chile, Peru, El Salvador, and Nicaragua, focusing on one individual in each country to illustrate the whole.

247. Ross, Irwin. "Rescuing the Forgotten Prisoners." Saturday Review 48 (January 16, 1965) 17-18+. Explains Amnesty International's strategy of success in freeing political prisoners.

248. Satchell, Michael. "The Greatest Evil Is Indifference." Parade (May 12, 1985) 4. Overview of the plight of political prisoners all over the world, examples of "selective morality" in U.S. foreign policy, and information on human rights organizations.

249. Sax, Boria. "With Blood and Indelible Ink." Commonweal 112 (May 17, 1985) 300-1. On imprisoned poets Gintas Iesmantis, Armando Valladares, and others.

250. Scheffler, Judith, ed. Wall Tappings: An Anthology of Writings by Women Prisoners. Boston: Northeastern UP, 1986. 375. Several selections are by political prisoners: Chilean women's poems and testimonies, civil rights worker Barbara Deming in the Albany, GA., jail, Joyce Sikakane in South Africa, etc.

251. Sharp, Gene. The Politics of Nonviolent Action. Boston: Porter Sargent, 1973. 902. Examines its view of power, its specific methods of action, its dynamics in conflict, and the conditions for success or failure. Chapter 10 "Challenge Brings Repression," Chapter 11 "Solidarity and Discipline to Fight Repression."

252. Sharp, Gene. Social Power and Political Freedom. Boston: Porter Sargent, 1980. 440. Focuses on "the criminal realities of centralized government" and its "institutionalized violence."

253. Shelton, Roberto. "The Geography of Disgrace: A World Survey of Political Prisoners." Saturday Review World 1 (June 15, 1974) 14-19. "Jailed and tortured solely for their beliefs, millions of people know the Seventies not as a golden Space Age, but rather as a new era of political barbarism."

254. Shernock, Stanley. "Conflict and Boundaries Between Political and Criminal Prisoners." Law and the Legal Process. Ed. Victoria Swigert. Beverly Hills, CA: Sage, 1982. 131-158. Challenges the anomie model of concentration camps (political prisoners became slaves of the system and collaborators in their own enslavement and demise) with evidence of resistance, and camps and individuals highly diverse. Focuses on differences between common criminals and political prisoners.

255. "Sisters Inside." Kinesis (June 1987) 15. Individual case studies of women around the world imprisoned and "targeted for especially vicious treatment" due to their political beliefs.

255a. Skloot, Robert. "Theatrical Images of Genocide." Human Rights Quarterly 12 (1990) 185-201. Analyzes four plays about genocides perpetrated to eliminate peoples who stood in the way of economic exploitation: Kopit's Indians, and the Canadian James Nichol's Sainte-Marie Among the Hurons, Christopher Hampton's Savages (Brazilian Indians), and Thomas Keneally's Bullie's House (indigenous people of Australia).

256. "Some Governments Are Getting Away with Murder." Matchbox (June 1983) 1-3. "Over the past decade, hundreds of thousands of people have been murdered by their own government."

257. "South America: Tales from the Southern Cone." Connexions 23 (Spring 1987) 8. Summarizes the gross and systematic violation of the human, civil, and legal rights of the people of Argentina, Chile, and Uruguay since 1973.

258. Spencer, Miranda. "Human Rights Reporting: Letting Nations Off the Hook." Deadline (January\February 1988) 6-7. Analyzes the extremely poor media coverage of Amnesty International's annual country reports.

259. Stackhouse, Max. Creeds, Society and Human Rights. Grand Rapids: Eerdmans, 1984. 315. Intellectual history of ethics, religions, and rights, with specific chapters on the U.S., GDR, and India.

260. State Crimes: Punishment or Pardon: Papers and Report of the Conference, November 4-6, 1988, Wye Center, Maryland. Queenstown, Md.: Justice and Society Program for the Aspen Institute, 1989. 96. About "how successor governments should deal with the human rights violations of a prior regime," what to do with brutal, murderous officials, and how victims might be rehabilitated.

261. Stock, A.G., and Reginald Reynolds, eds. Prison Anthology. London: Jarrolds, 1938. 292. A collection of writings by various political prisoners across the world and throughout history, from Boethius to Gandhi to the "burglar and the blackmailer" who challenge the social order as much as any anarchist, and defy its moral codes as vigorously as Nietzsche.

262. Stohl, Michael, and George A. Lopez. Government Violence and Repression: An Agenda for Research. Contributions in Political Science 148. New York: Greenwood, 1986. 278. Part of the growing scholarship and evidence of the enormous magnitude of state terrorism as compared to the relatively minor insurgent or revolutionary terror. Each chapter delineates "a particular aspect of government violence in our time."

263. Stohl, Michael, and George A. Lopez. The State as a Terrorist: The Dynamics of Governmental Violence and Repression. Contributions in Political Science 103. Westport, CT: Greenwood, 1984. 202. In contrast to insurgent and anti-state terrorism, the major massive terror comes from states using force and violence against their own and other populations in pursuit of their leaders' interests.

264. Storr, Anthony. Human Destructiveness: The Roots of Genocide and Human Cruelty. 2d ed. New York: Ballantine/Random House; London: Routledge, 1991. 183. Examines genocide, torture and other atrocities in today's societies.

265. "Support Peace Prisoners." Peace News 22.82 (November 28, 1986) 9. A selective list of imprisoned conscientious objectors around the world.

266. Swidler, Arlene, ed. Human Rights in Religious Traditions. New York: Pilgrim, 1982. 114. Explores the significance of human rights from the perspective of seven religious traditions.

267. Szasz, Thomas. Ideology and Insanity : Essays on the Psychiatric Dehumanization of Man. Harmondsworth: Penguin, 1974. 254; London: Calder and Boyars, 1973. 264. Chapter 9, "Involuntary Mental Hospitalization: A Crime Against Humanity."

268. Szent-Miklosy, Istvan. With the Hungarian Independence Movement, 1943-1947: An Eyewitness Account. New York: Praeger, 1988. 242. Author was imprisoned by both the Nazis and the Soviet Union. The Soviets tortured and then imprisoned him for ten years.

269. Tangley, Laura. "Scientists Campaign for Human Rights." Bioscience 34 (October 1984) 544-5. Discusses how scientists have been harassed by repressive governments.

270. Taussig, Michael. The Nervous System. New York; London: Routledge, 1992. 207. From the victim's perspective, the world and history are in a state of siege.

271. Tawil, Raymonda. My Home, My Prison. London: Zed Books, 1983. 265. A Palestinian activist details her house arrest in 1976 with no legal appeal or redress and her abduction in 1978 and solitary confinement for six weeks.

272. Taylor, Robin, exec. producer. Hooded Men. Videocassette. Narrator Eric Malling. Canadian Broadcasting Corporation, 1985. 55 minutes. This study conducted by the Canadian Broadcasting Corporation on the use of torture against political prisoners in 65 countries focuses particularly on N. Ireland, Argentina, and Nicaragua and includes interviews with the torturers and with victims and their families. Also investigates research projects into the use of white noise and other psychological and physical methods of torture.

273. Theiner, George, ed. They Shoot Writers Don't They? London: Faber and Faber, 1984. 199. Thirty articles from Index on Censorship by writers who have been victims of censorship and persecution by repressive regimes--Ilhan Endorst, Turkish publisher killed while under military escort; Rodolfo Walsh, Argentinian journalist "disappeared" from his home and never seen since; Prof. George Mangakis sentenced to fourteen years' imprisonment by the Greek colonels, et al.

274. Thiers, Naomi. "Torturers With a Human Face." Sojourners 21.7 (August-September 1992) 43-44. Review of "exhaustively researched" Children of Cain, the book by Tina Rosenberg which tells about both the victims and the violators in six Latin America countries.

275. Thoughts on Human Dignity and Freedom. New York: Amnesty International, 1991. 80. Fifty all-color photographs, poems and prose by a broad spectrum of distinguished thinkers, former political prisoners, and writers censored in their own countries.

276. "Torture as Policy: The Network of Evil." Time 108 (August 16, 1976) 31-34. In 1975 alone at least 40 countries practiced torture, which "has become a common instrument of state policy practiced against almost anyone ruling cliques see as a threat to their power."

277. Torture in the Eighties. Videocassette. Amnesty International USA, 1985. 14 min. VHS format. "Overview of torture by governments."

278. Totten, Samuel, and Milton Kleg. Human Rights. Hillside, NJ/ Aldershot Hants, UK: Enslow, 1989. 255. Chapters on the history of discrimination and racism, genocide, political prisoners, torture, hunger, and efforts to protect the victims, with lists of genocidal events in the 20th century and human rights organizations. The chapter on political prisoners begins with these words: "Over one million political prisoners are being held by one hundred or more nations today. They can be found in labor camps, jails, torture chambers, and mental hospitals....These Prisoners have not harmed anyone." The chapter on torture begins: "The use of torture is so widespread that it has been called 'an epidemic in the world.'"

279. Totten, Samuel, comp. First-Person Accounts of Genocidal Acts Committed in the Twentieth Century: An Annotated Bibliography. Westport, CT: Greenwood, 1991. 351. The twentieth century is the cenutry of genocide. Beginning with the German massacres of the Hereros in old South-West Africa in 1904, "each decade since then has witnessed its own horrific genocidal periods," all of which have involved political prisoners.

280. Totten, Samuel. "Genocide of Various Indigenous Peoples." First Person Accounts of Genocidal Acts Committed in the Twentieth Century: An Annotated Bibliography. Westport, CT: Greenwood, 1991. 311-319. Thirty-two entries mainly on Brazil and Guatemala, a sample of the book.

281. Turk, Austin T. Political Criminality: The Defiance and Defense of Authority. Sage Library of Social Research 136. Beverly Hills: Sage Publications, 1982. 232. An effort to define political crimes "produced by conflict between people who claim to be authorities and people who resist or may resist being their subjects." Bibliography pp. 211-223.

282. Turki, Fawaz. Soul in Exile: Lives of a Palestinian Revolutionary. New York: Monthly Review, 1988. 204. Turki's memoirs of his revolutionary life and nomadic existence as a "disinherited Palestinian," from war, prison, wandering as a refugee, to participating in the Palestine National Council.

283. United Nations. Yearbook on Human Rights. New York, 1946-. Covers national developments together with UN activities.

284. United States Congress. Senate Committee on Foreign Relations. Practice of Torture by Foreign Governments and U.S. Efforts to Oppose Its Use. Washington, D.C.: G.P.O., 1984. 192. About the use of in Iran, in psychiatric hospitials, etc., citing Amnesty International's "Torture in the Eighties" report.

285. United States. Department of State. Amnesty to Prisoners since the Armistice. Washington: GPO, 1920. 30. On amnesty of military and political prisoners in Great Britain, France, Italy, and Belgium.

286. The Univeral Declaration of Human Rights. New York: Amnesty International, 1988. 123. Over twenty original watercolors by Jean-Michel Folon illustrating the articles of the Universal Declaration of Human Rights, with text in the six official languages of the United Nations.

287. The Universal Declaration of Human Rights. Videocassette. S.l.: Human Rights Foundation, 1988. 21 min. Animated version.

288. USLA Reporter. New York: U.S. Committee for Justice to Latin American Political Prisoners Reporter, 1968-.

289. Valdes, Mia. "Double Standard For Human Rights." Progressive 56 (August 1992) 20-21. The much more brutal Guatemalan regime was criticized less severely than the less offending Cuba by the U.N. Human Rights Commission.

290. Vernau, Judi, and Alison Bennett. An Index to "Index on Censorship" No. 1 (1972) to No. 100 (1988). New York: Hans Zell; Writers and Scholars International, 1989. 420. Indexes articles as well as the thousands of names of political prisoners which have appeared in Index on Censorship and the status of those prisoners.

291. Voices for Freedom. London: Amnesty International, 1986. 208. A collection of accounts of political prisoners "held without trial, of torture victims, of people threatened with execution and 'disappearance,'" and of the "countless men and women...who have raised their voices in defence" over a span of 25 years.

292. Walliman, Isidor, and Michael Dobkowski, eds. Genocide and the Modern Age: Etiology and Case Studies of Mass Death. Contributions to the Study of World History No. 3. Westport, CT: Greenwood, 1987. 332. A collection of essays on genocide from various theoretical perspectives and a series of case studies.

293. Weisburd, Abe. "Prisoners." Guardian 30.24 (March 22, 1978) 11. A regular section of the Guardian that focuses on individual prisoners and their stories.

294. Weiss, Renata. Writing in Defiance: Concentration Camp Diaries in Dutch, French, and German, 1940-1945. Diss. New York University, 1971. 305. DAI 32.7. 4030. Fourteen diaries written in concentration camps in Holland and Germany.

295. Weschler, Lawrence. A Miracle, A Universe: Settling Accounts with Torturers. New York: Pantheon, 1990. 293. Examines such issues as what to do with former torturers when democratic government succeeds tyranny, given the complex conditions of the continuing power of the repressive government and whether and how to determine the truth about the victims.

296. West, Lewis J. Unclassified Bibliography: Prisoners of War, Civilian Internees, and Political Prisoners. N.p.: n.p., 1960. 201-393. Mainly prisoners of war.

297. Wheaton, Philip. "Plan Mercurio; Round Up for Political Exiles: Uruguay and Argentina Cooperate in Leftist Extermination Plan." CounterSpy 3.2 (Dec. 1976) 28-33. On the Uruguayan-Argentine-CIA joint sponsored "Plan Mercurio," designed to eliminate all Uruguayan leftists in both countries.

298. When Governments Kill. Videocassette. The Kamber Group for Amnesty International USA, 1989. 24 min. Designed specifically for college students, this video examines the death penalty both internationally and in the U.S.

299. "When Racism Wears a Badge." Amnesty Action (Spring 1993) 5. Racism is "currently on the rise all across the continent" and is reflected in police behavior. (Amnesty Action provides current information regarding human rights abuses.)

300. When the State Kills. New York: Amnesty International, 1989. 280. An extensive study of the death penalty worldwide (see The Death Penalty Briefing, 1989).

301. While There is a Soul in Prison...: The 1979 Peace Calendar and Appointment Book. New York: War Resisters League, 1978. 100. Many of the League's members have served prison terms for conscientious objection to war or to discrimination.

Included are descriptions of non-violent actions inside prisons, testimonies of prisoners, reform movements working to abolish prisons, etc.

302. Whitaker, M. "The Prisoners of Conscience." Newsweek 101 (February 14) 40-4+. Global statistics and examples: USSR, Chile, Iran, South Africa, Philippines, and other countries.

303. Wiseberg, Laurie S. and Harry M. Scoble, comps. North American Human Rights Directory 1980. 1st ed. Garrett Park, MD: Garrett Park P, 1980. 181. Directory of groups in the United States and Canada active in international human rights.

304. Wiseberg, Laurie, and Harry Scoble. Human Rights Directory: Latin America, Africa, Asia. Washington, D.C.; Human Rights Internet, 1981. 243. An annotated directory of human rights organizations in Latin America and the Caribbean, Africa, the Middle East, Asia and the Pacific.

305. Wiseberg, Laurie, and Harry Scoble. Human Rights Directory: Western Europe. Washington, D.C.: Human Rights Internet, 1982. 335. Describes 1,200 plus organizations in Western Europe actively concerned with human rights an both domestic and international levels.

306. Women in the Front Line: Human Rights Violations Against Women, an Amnesty International Report. New York: Amnesty International, 1991. 56. On the particular vulnerabilities of women, gives examples and cites countries, concludes with twelve suggestions to protect women better.

307. "Women Political Prisoners." New Women's Times 10.3 (March 1984) 4. Summarizes an AI pamphlet on eight cases of torture of women.

308. The Women's Rights Project. New York: Human Rights Watch, 1990-. Established to monitor discrimination and violence against women. Issued irregularly.

309. Women: Victims and Fighters. New York: Amnesty International, 1987. 12. Discusses the wide range of abuses against women, naming names.

310. The Writer and Human Rights. Ed. Toronto Arts Group for Human Rights. Garden City, NY: Anchor, 1983. 294.
Conference papers dedicated to writers who have been silenced by censorship, exile, torture, imprisonment, disappearance. Divided into 3 parts: contexts which lead writers to political action, kinds of action open to writers, ways governments respond oppressively.

311. Yancy, Phillip. "Lessons from the Camps; Isolating the Human Spirit: Concentration Camps, Part II." Christianity Today 23 (May 4, 1979) 25-9; 26 (May 25, 1979) 26-30. Focuses on the camps under Stalin and Hitler and continued institutionalized cruelty afterward.

312. Yearbook on Human Rights. New York: United Nations, 1946-. Annual 1946-72, biennial 1973-74--1977-78, annual again 1979 to present. The first volume contains "all declarations and bills on human rights now in force in the various countries," including each state of the U.S.

313. Yearbook on Human Rights for 1988. New York: United Nations, 1992. 150. This volume contains three parts: Part I "international developments in the field of human rights," Part II "activities of the United Nations supervisory bodies," and Part III "national developments." From the beginning in 1946, the Yearbook has focused on rights.

314. You Have Struck a Rock: Women and Political Repression in Southern Africa. London: International Defence & Aid Fund, 1980. 24. About detention without trial, banning, exile, and torture of women in South Africa, Namibia, and Zimbabwe.

315. Zivs, Samuil. The Anatomy of Lies. Tr. Nadezhda Burova. Moscow: Progress, 1982. 159. Alleges bias by AI in assigning "prisoners of conscience." E.g., Balys Gajauskas committed murders in the name of the Lithuanian Resistance, named a poc by AI. Helena Castro, Uruguayan student horribly tortured and imprisoned for many years denied poc by AI because she was accused of "Marxist subversion." AI has named no poc in N. Ireland despite much evidence of British repression and torture.

316. Zoff, Otto. They Shall Inherit the Earth. Trans. Anne Garrison. New York: John Day, 1943. 258. A plea to protect children from "the nightmare of these years." Chapters 12 and 13 tell about Jewish youth as refugees and prisoners.

AFGHANISTAN

317. Afghanistan: Reports of Torture, Ill-Treatment and Extrajudicial Executions of Prisoners, Late April-Early May 1992. New York: Amnesty International, 1992. A plea from AI to the new government to prevent abuse.

318. Afghanistan: Torture of Political Prisoners. London: Amnesty International, 1986. 51. Torture in Afghanistan "is widespread and systematic," especially for those held by the State Information Services (KHAD). Prison conditions are degrading and trials unfair.

319. Afghanistan: Unlawful Killings and Torture. London; New York: Amnesty International, 1988. 9. Gross human rights abuses during 1987-88--deliberate killings by Soviet and Afghan Government forces of refugees and "the continuing practice of torture."

320. Amnesty International Report 1980. London: Amnesty International, 1980. 176-183. Possibly 12,000 political prisoners were being confined in Kabul's prison alone, most or many without trial. There have been summary executions and disappearances after arrest. Torture was frequently used. At least 12,000 prisoners, mainly political, died in Kabul jails since April 1978. This gross pattern of violations has been condemned by the new President Babrak Karmal, who announced a general amnesty, but problems remain.

321. Amnesty International Report 1990. New York: Amnesty International USA, 1990. 27-28. Thousands of political prisoners were believed to be imprisoned by the government in 1989, and ill-treatment of prisoners continued to be reported, while the Muhjahideen reportedly carried out extrajudicial executions of prisoners and civilians.

322. "A 'CIA Confession' in Kabul." Newsweek 95 (April 14, 1980) 48. Robert Lee was coerced into confessing to be a CIA agent.

323. Martin, Frank A. Under the Absolute Amir. New York: Harper, 1907. 329. One chapter on tortures and executions under Amir Abdur Rahman.

ALBANIA

324. Albania. London: Amnesty International, 1984. 9. On the laws, unfair trials, ill-treatment of prisoners, conditions in labor camps, and death penalty (12 political, 34 total). Six case studies.

325. Albania: Political Imprisonment and the Law. London: Amnesty International, 1984. 58. Focuses on prisoners of conscience held in labor camps, unfair trials, torture and the death penalty.

326. Amnesty International Report 1980. London: Amnesty International, 1980. 253-256. The Constitution restricts expression, and in 1967 persecution of religions began. Trying to leave the country is punishable. Arbitrary arrest and banning are supported by statutes. Some torture has been substantiated. Thirty-four crimes (of which twenty-three are political and military) are punishable by death.

327. Amnesty International Report 1990. New York: Amnesty International USA, 1990. 28-29. Strict censorship limits knowledge of prisoners, but some prisoners of conscience (non-violent) are in prison or labor camps, and punishment is harsh.

328. Human Rights in the People's Republic of Albania. Minneapolis, MN: Minnesota Lawyers International Human Rights Committe, 1990. 186. A bleak account of systematic infringement of basic human rights--restrictions on religion (prohibited) and travel (attempted emigration treasonable), a system of prisons and labor camps to punish beliefs, torture, etc.

329. Korchari, Abas. Escape From Hell. New York: Vantage, 1971. 157. Account of thirteen years in prison at hard labor (1944-1953) for his opposition to the communist regime.

330. Stajka, Nika. The Last Days of Freedom. Tr. Jose Roig. New York: Vantage, 1980. 371. Arrested in 1949 as an enemy of the people and confined in forced labor camps until 1954.

ALGERIA

331. Algeria, The Imprisonment of Prisoners of Conscience in Algeria. New York: Amnesty International, 1986. 5. Appraises the arrest in 1985 of members of the Sons of Martyrs and Algerian League of Human Rights on false charges of conspiracy against the state.

332. Amnesty International Report 1980. London: Amnesty International, 1980. 321-323. In the "cleaning-up" campaign of 1979, over 1,000 people were arrested, including some opponents of the government. Moslem and Berber activism has resulted in some arrests. Former President Ahmed Ben Bella was transferred from prison to house arrest.

333. Amnesty International Report 1990. New York: Amnesty International USA, 1990. 30-31. Great improvements recently (new constitution, international human rights treaties), but some prisoners await retrials.

334. "Gilded Cage." Time 111 (February 20, 1978) 42. Former leader Ben Bella is kept under house arrest after a coup by his former army chief, Boumedienne.

ANGOLA

335. Amnesty International Report 1980. London: Amnesty International, 1980. 30-31. Although many long-term political detainees were freed in 1979, some remained and organized a hunger strike.

336. Amnesty International Report 1990. New York: Amnesty International USA, 1990. 31-33. The civil war continues to generate charges of political imprisoning and killing. Several hundred prisoners were freed, and some death sentences commuted, but harsh treatment and torture were reported.

337. People's Republic of Angola : Background Briefing on Amnesty International's Concerns. New York: Amnesty International, 1982. 40. Complains of long-term detention without trial, torture, disappearances, and death penalty. Ten individual cases are profiled.

338. Political Imprisonment in the People's Republic of Angola. New York: Amnesty International USA, 1984. 29. A history of conflicts since 1975--civil war, coup attempts, arbitrary detention, unfair trials, etc.

339. Reiss, Spencer. "SWAPO's Witch Hunt." Newsweek 144 (September 4, 1989) 33. On detainees accused by SWAPO of spying for South Africa.

ARGENTINA

340. Adler, Jerry. "Timerman's Second Ordeal." Newsweek 97 (June 22, 1981) 85. Attacks on Jacobo Timerman by U.S. Conservatives who are trying to establish a distinction between "authoritarian" (right wing dictatorships friendly to the U.S. like Argentina) and "totalitarian" (left wing regimes hostile to the U.S.).

341. Agosin, Marjorie. Circles of Madness: The Mothers of the Plaza de Mayo. Trans. Celeste Kostopulos-Cooperman. Fredonia, NY: White Pine, 1992. 98. Poetry by Agosin intermingled with photographs of the Mothers of the Plaza de Mayo carrying pictures of their children, the thousands of disappeared of Argentina during the military dictatorship of 1976-1983.

342. Amnesty International Report 1980. London: Amnesty International, 1980. 103-111. The rights to life, liberty and the security of person, and to a fair trial and due process of law continued to be systematically violated in this sixth year of a state of siege. Of the estimated 1,900 prisoners, more than 1,000 are held in preventive detention without charge, some for more than five years. Many prisoners have suffered cruel, inhuman and degrading treatment. More than 3,600 people have disappeared after arrest or kidnapping.

343. Amnesty International Report 1990. New York: Amnesty International USA, 1990. 33-35. Members of a leftist group were reportedly tortured and some disappeared after attacking a military barracks and then surrendering in 1989. Following a declaration of state of siege because of general unrest and riots, some members of opposition political parties were arrested. President Menem pardoned 39 senior military officers scheduled for trial for crimes perpetrated between 1976 and 1983 during the dirty war against alleged subversives.

344. Andersen, Martin E. Dossier Secreto: Argentina's Desaparecidos and the Myth of the "Dirty War." Boulder, CO: Westview, 1993. 412. The brutal repression by the generals who took over the country in a coup in 1976 was justified as a fight to preserve "Western Christian Civilization" against a vast army of Marxist guerrillas. This was false, a pretext for seizing power and terrorizing the civilian population. By 1983, thousands had been murdered, tortured, or disappeared. U.S. policy response alternated between condemning and condoning the power-hungry military and its atrocities.

345. Argentina 1976. London: Argentina Support Movement, 1976. 23. Mainly covers political and economic background of the repression.

346. "Argentina One Year Later--'3-10 Disappeared Each Day.'" Matchbox (Spring 1979) 1-2. One year after Argentina became the focus of world attention during the World Cup Futbol Championship (held there in June) no significant improvment in the human rights situation could be noted--over 1,500 remained missing, 4,000 detained for political reasons.

347. Argentina Today: A Dossier on Repression and the Violation of Human Rights. 2d ed. Berkeley, CA: Argentine Information Service Center, 1977. 34. Surveys the brutal terror against all kinds of citizens--trade unionists, church members, Jews, journalists, writers educators, etc.

348. "Argentina: Two Years After the Coup, A Total Disregard for Human Rights." Matchbox (Spring 1978) 9-12. Two years after the march 1976 military coup, over 15,000 people had disappeared, and 8 to 10,000 people are detained in official prisons. "This does not include the secret detention camps where torture, terrible conditions, and eventual execution are rampant."

349. "Argentina: The War Goes On." NACLA 11.1 (Jan. 1977) 3-16. Surveys the severe repression in all aspects of life--censorship, prisoners, massacres, kidnappings, etc.

350. Argentine National Commission on the Disappeared. Nunca Más: The Report of the Argentine National Commission on the Disappeared. New York: Farrar Straus Giroux; London: Index on Cesorship, 1986. 463. Details the licensed sadism of Argentine military rulers from 1976 to 1979: 12,000 plus citizens abducted, tortured and then killed.

351. "Argentine Prisoners Describe Life." Militant 40.49 (Dec. 24, 1976) 19. Testimony from two Brazilians held in an Argentine prison who experienced torture and other brutal conditions. It is estimated that about 20,000 political prisoners are still being held.

352. Blake, Patricia. "Now, the Timerman Affair." Time 117 (June 22, 1981) 20-1. Describes conservative attacks on Jacobo Timerman, imprisoned and tortured by the Argentine junta 1977-1979, because of his criticism of the Reagan administration and of both Argentine and U.S. Jews.

353. Burkhalter, Holly. "Juan Méndez: A Human Rights Pioneer." Human Rights Watch 10.1 (Winter 1992) 8. Now Director of Americas Watch, Mendez was arrested, tortured, and expelled from Argentina in 1974-75.

354. The Colours of Hope. New York: David Grubin Productions, 1985. Videocassette, 20 min. Narr. Meryl Streep. Tells story of arrest of an Argentine couple in 1975 because of the husband's union work. After her release, the wife came to the U.S. to work with AI for his release.

355. Cox, Robert. "Calling Terrorism by Name in Argentina." Matchbox (May 1982) 2-3, 13. Based on a speech Cox on state sponsored terrorism in Argentina during the 1970's.

356. Crawford, Kathryn Lee. "Due Obedience and the Rights of Victims: Argentina's Transition to Democracy." Human Rights Quarterly 12 (1990) 17-52. Analyzes the Supreme Court's ruling that security force members who had tortured and killed could not be prosecuted if they were acting under orders, and other issues regarding justice for the victims.

357. De Freitas, Nick. "Olga Talamante in Argentine Prison: Spirits High Despite Continued Torture." Workers World 17.26 (June 27, 1975) 7. Talamante, a U.S. citizen, was arrested without charge, systematically tortured, and forced to sign a confession at gunpoint.

358. The "Disappeared" of Argentina: List of Cases Reported to Amnesty International, March 1976 - February 1979. London: Amnesty International, International Secretariat, 1979. 99.

359. Dougherty, M. "Unearthing a Grim Past." Life 7 (May 1984) 34-42. Account of mass murder by Argentina's rulers. Possibly 30,000 disappeared. The military gave itself complete amnesty for their crimes.

360. Dreifus, Caludia. "'Torture is always with you': An Interview with Jacobo Timerman." Progressive 45 (Dec. 1981) 47-50. The former editor of La Opinion was tortured by the Argentine Army as punishment for publishing a series on the thousands who had been kidnapped and murdered by the military regime.

361. "Excerpts from After the Night." Connexions no. 23 (Spring 1987) 12-14. Interview with Graciela Fernández Meijide, Secretary of the Executive Commission of the Permanent Assembly for Human Rights founded in 1976 to help families of the imprisoned and disappeared. Her son, a high school student, was abducted and disappeared.

362. Fisher, Jo. Mothers of the Disappeared. Boston: South end, 1989. 168. A history of and extensive interviews with many Mothers of the Plaza de Mayo, whose children were among the 30,000 "disappeared" during the brutal military regime of 1976-1984 and whose political challenge helped effect change in Argentina.

363. "Focus on Argentina." Matchbox (May 1981) 4,8. Article based on a letter written by Amnesty International to new President-designate Roberto Viola regarding concerns about human rights violations in his country: disappearances, secret detention centers, torture, etc.

364. "Four More Argentine Trotskyists 'disappear.'" Militant 41.40 (Oct.28, 1977) 24. Four member of the political group Politica Obrera disappeared at the hands of the Videla dictatorship: Fernando Sanchez, Gustavo Grassi, Guido Puletti, and Juan José Cuello.

365. Frasca, Tim. "Argentina Torture Victim Out, Unbowed." Guardian 36.11 (Dec. 14, 1983) 16. Interview of Domiro Suarez, who spent nine years in detention, now released.

366. Girdner, William. "Torture on Trial." Nation 238 (April 21, 1984) 469. Jose Siderman is suing his government in a U.S. court for torturing him.

367. Gonzalez, Oscar Alfredo. Testimony on Secret Detention Camps in Argentina. London: Amnesty International, 1980. 63. Covers a period of 15 months in the lives of two prisoners in Buenos Aires, 1977-1979. Also gives information on 330 out of an estimated 800 prisoners who for the most part were killed. Details also on the repressive forces (all armed services had one) and the concentration camps.

368. Graham-Yooll, Andrew. A Matter of Fear: Portrait of an Argentinian Exile. Brooklyn: Lawrence Hill, 1982. 128. (Previously pub. as Portrait of an Exile). On psychological aspects of the terror.

369. Graham-Yooll, Andrew. "Publish and Be Terrified, May 1976." Cyrano's Journal 1.1 (Fall 1982) 42-43. On the abduction and disappearance of the novelist Haroldo Conti.

370. Graziano, Frank. Divine Violence: Spectacle, Psychosexualtiy, and Radical Christianity in the Argentine "Dirty War." Boulder, CO: Westview, 1992. 328. An explanation of the political repression and of state terror in Argentina and Western culture. Examines the texts that constituted the junta's discourse (including not only political and legal statements and writings but narratives, rituals, and torture methods), and finds a primitive, medieval Christian apocalyptic vision with its corresponding eschatalogical mythology of Antichrist, redemption, punishment, and sacrifice.

371. Guest, Iain. Behind the Disappearances: Argentine's Dirty War Against Human Rights and the United Nations. Philadelphia: U of Pennsylvania P, 1990. 622. An account of Argentina's maneuvers at the United Nations during the time of that military regime's brutal and systematic abductions of its citizens to concentration camps for torture and murder. Examines the UN's system of curbing human rights violations, with Argentina 1976-1983 as the test case. There is also a great deal of information on repression in other Latin American countries.

372. "Habeas Corpses." Time 113 (April 23, 1979) 57. On the brutal repression by the military regime.

372a. Historia Oficial. Dir. Luiz Puenzo. This film portrays the trauma involved in trying to locate children born in secret detention.

373. Hoeffel, Paul, and Jan Montalvo. "Missing or Dead in Argentina." New York Times Magazine (Oct. 21, 1979) 44-47. AI estimates that as many as 15,000 people have disappeared.

374. Holden, Constance. "Forensic Scientists go to Argentina's Aid." Science 225 (July 27, 1984) 397. On identifying bodies of those who disappeared under the regime.

375. "Human Rights Are Violated by Junta." City Star 4.2 (June 15, 1976) 14. On the mass arrests, and deportations.

376. Human Rights in Argentina, March 1983 Update (Incorporating a report from CELS in Buenos Aires). New York: Americas Watch Committee, 1983. 25. Testimony of Aryeh Neier of Americas Watch before the House Western Hemisphere Subcommittee on Certification of Argentina, March 16, 1983, with supporting documents, arguing against certification. "Criticizes State Dept. distortions of facts to facilitate certification."

377. Human Rights in Argentina : September 1983 Update : A Report From CELS in Buenos Aires. New York: Americas Watch Committee, 1983. 16.

378. "Imprisoned Music." America 142 (February 16, 1980) 118-121. On Argentina's efforts to silence the music and voice of one of its greatest pianists, Miguel Angel Estrella, now in prison in Uruguay at Argentina's request.

379. "In Search of the Disappeared." Time 114 (September 24, 1979) 42. Efforts to locate the thousands of desaparecidos, people who vanished during the government's reign of terror.

380. Keene, Beverly. "Adolfo Perez Esquivel." NACLA: Report on the Americas 20.5 (September 1986) 61-65. Interview of the 1980 Nobel Peace Prize recipient, who was imprisoned for fourteen months from April 1970, and tortured.

381. Knowles, Christopher. "Argentines Seek 'Missing' Prisoners." Guardian 30.3 (Oct. 26, 1979) 16. Women demanding the whereabouts of relatives have been arrested.

382. Magalis, Elaine. "Murder in Argentina." Christian Century 94 (November 9, 1977) 1030-3. On the disappearance and murder of Elizabeth Käsemann by police and the brutal treatment of her friend Diana Houstoun.

383. McCaughan, Ed. "Young Chicana Held: Political Inmates in Argentina." Guardian 27.35 (June 11, 1975) 16. Focuses on Olga Talamante.

384. "The Missing Children of Argentina." Matchbox (Feb. 1982) 8-9. Focuses on sixty-seven missing children--"some 'disappeared' with their parents after raids by security forces, others born in captivity to women pregnant at the time of their abduction."

385. "More Argentine Murders." Christian Century 100 (June 8-15, 1983) 578. AI protests the killing of two former political prisoners. Many nations demand investigation of their deaths and the disappearance of some 6,000 people during the 1970's.

386. Naipaul V.S. "Argentine Terror: A Memoir." New York Review of Books 26 (October 11, 1979) 13-16. "The society of cruelty ever renews itself... Anyone can be picked up. Torture is routine."

387. Neier, Aryeh. "The Crime of Silence Revisited." Nation 232 (June 13, 1981) 713. Discussion Nation 232 (August 8-15, 1981) 112-114. On the anti-Semitism of human rights abuses in Argentina, focusing on Timerman's Prisoner Without a Name.

388. Norman, Colin. "U.S. Scientists Protest Argentina Arrests." Science 211 (March 20, 1981) 1327. On arrest of José Westerkamp and other civil rights advocates.

389. The Ordeal of Jacobo Timerman. New York: WNET, 1981. Videocassette, 58 min. Bill Moyers' talks with one of Argentina's formerly leading journalists, who was imprisoned, tortured, and exiled by the right wing military government.

390. Partnoy, Alicia. "Another Voice From Argentina's Clandestine Prisons." National Reporter 10.3 (Spring 1987) 36-37. An excerpt from her book The Little School on prison life.

391. Partnoy, Alicia. The Little School : Tales of Disappearance & Survival in Argentina. Pittsburgh, PA: Cleis Press, 1986. 136. About the many who were killed, tortured, imprisoned, and banished by the Argentine dictatorship. The author spent seven years in prison and banishment. The Little School was the army's name for its parapolice detention and torture center.

392. Pérez, José. "Blanco, Others Still in Danger in Argentina." Militant 42.23 (June 16, 1978) 8. Thirteen Peruvians deported to Argentina have disappeared.

393. Pérez, José. "Worldwide Protest Win Hugo Blanco's Release." Militant 42.24 (June 23, 1978) 3. Due to international protests, Hugo Blanco and twelve other prisoners who had been deported from Peru are released by the Argentine government.

394. Pingel, Roy. "Alfonsin Keeps Leftist Behind Bars." Guardian 39.41 (July 29, 1987) 12. Eight prisoners, who are among the longest-held in South America, suffered illegal arrest, torture, and unfair trials; and other details of official atrocities.

395. Psychological Effects of Political Repression. Ed. Diana R. Kordon, et al. Buenos Aires: Sudamericana\Planeta, 1988. 197. The impact of imprisonment, disappeared relatives, terrorism, with attention to the Mothers of Plaza de Mayo. Sponsored by the Rehabilitation Centre for Torture Victims, Copenhagen.

396. "The Reappearance of a 'Disappeared.'" Connexions no. 23 (Spring 1987) 9-10. Interview with Alicia Portnoy, whose The Little School tells of her kidnapping, torture, and harsh prison life.

397. Reed, David. "Argentina's Apalling Reign of Terror." Reader's Digest 116 (June 1980) 100-104. The military regime has arrested thousands of people they consider "'subversive.'"

398. Reimers, Isolde. The Decline of a Social Movement: The Mothers of Plaza de Mayo. Gainsville, FL, U of Florida M.A. Thesis, 1989. 155.

399. Report of an Amnesty International Mission to Argentina, 6-15 November 1976. London: Amnesty International, 1977. 92. Surveys state violence, disappearances, and torture.

400. Repression in Argentina: The Violence of Those at the Top. Toronto: Canadian Committee for Justice to Latin American Political Prisoners, 1972. 45. Collection of brief essays published in the Buenos Aires newspaper Nuevo Hombre in 1972, which resulted in the bombing and temporary closing of the newspaper.

401. Russell, George and William McWhirter. "Living with Ghosts." Time 118 (July 20, 1981) 38-40. Describes the efforts of the Mothers of Plaza de Mayo to discover the wherabouts of their kin, the desaparecidos.

402. Sölle, Dorothee. "Argentina: Non-news about Nonpersons." Christian Century 96 (December 26, 1979) 1289-93. Describes the manifold methods of repression by the military regime and how people are fighting back.

403. Soto, David. "Big Names on 'Dirty Warrior' List." Guardian 37.9 (Nov. 28, 1984) 17. A list of over 1,000 persons guilty of human rights violations has been published and other information necessary to bringing the torturers and murderers to justice.

404. Steinberg, Jon. "More Than a World Cup." Sevendays 2.11 (July 1978) 16. The junta hosted the World Cup in 1978 to boost their image, while torturing thousands of prisoners.

405. Strejilevich, Nora. "'El Testimonio': Two Women Remember Argentina's Dirty War." National Reporter 10.3 (Spring 1987) 34. She describes the torture she suffered as the police tried to force her to confess to a crime she didn't commit.

406. "Support Grows for California Teacher." Black Panther 13.21 (July 14, 1975) 19. Olga Talamente is detained as part of Isabel Peron's martial law, accused of possessing subversive literature.

407. Talamante, Olga. "... from Olga's Prison Letters." El Gallo 8.1 (January 1976) 14. A U.S. citizen in Argentina working with a community center was imprisoned for subversive activities.

408. "Terror--Argentina Style." Matchbox (Winter 1977) 1-2. On the atrocities committed by the death squads of the Triple A--the Argentine Anti-communist Alliance: 13,000 killed in less than a year, abductions, murder, victimizations of refugees and women, etc.

409. Testimony on Secret Detention Camps in Argentina. London: Amnesty International, 1979. 31.

410. Thornton, Lawrence. Imagining Argentina. New York: Doubleday, 1987. 214. About the people who disappeared during the terrible repression.

411. Timerman, Hector. "Publishing in Argentina." Newsweek 94 (August 6, 1979) 17. Jacobo Timerman's son tells about the imprisonment and torture of his father.

412. Timerman, Jacobo. Prisoner Without a Name, Cell Without a Number. New York: Vintage Books, 1988. 164. An account of the author's brutal experiences, persecuted for his journalistic dissent and for being a Jew.

413. Timerman, Jacobo. "Reflections: No Name, No Number." Trans. Toby Talbot. New Yorker 57 (April 20, 1981) 45-130. Timerman's account of his imprisonment and torture, accompanined by family and national history.

414. Timerman, Jacobo. "Timerman--A Fight to Conquer Brutality." Matchbox (Nov. 1981) 8. Testimony of Jacobo Timerman, "a former political prisoner persecuted for his ideas, dissent, and Jewish religion.

415. "'Torture has permanent effects:'Danish Medical Team Concludes Study." Matchbox (Nov. 1980) 1. Former victims suffer long term effects similar to concentration camp survivors, such as nightmares, emotional withdrawl, and other psychiatric disturbances.

416. Tweedale, Douglas. "Argentina's New Hope." Macleans 97 (October 1, 1984) 8. Interview with exiled Argentine author Jacob Timerman "about the prospects for democracy in Argentina." Timerman recently located prisons known for torturing their prisoners.

417. Wade, Nicholas. "Physics in Argentina." Science 196 (June 17, 1977) 1302. Maximo Pedro Victoria, victim of torture in prison without being accused of a crime or being told why he was arrested.

418. Walsh, Rodolpho. A Year of Dictatorship in Argentina, March 1976- March 1977: An Open Letter to the Military Junta from Rodolpho Walsh. London: Committee to Save Rodolpho Walsh, 1977. 13. The day after he wrote this letter he was kidnapped and disapppeared.

419. Ward, Richard. "Political Prisoner Report." Guardian 30.9 (Dec. 7, 1977) 12. Findings of a survey by recently released prisoners who have left the country regarding who is arrested and for what reasons.

420. White, Judy. "Right Wing Blood Bath in Argentina." Militant 40.37 (Oct. 1, 1976) 25. Anything from disappearances to being held indefinitely without trial (20,000 poolitical prisoners), to being killed in confrontations with jail-security guards.

421. White, Judy. "United Actions for Argentine Political Prisoners." Militant 39.15 (April 25, 1975) 22. Report on the people killed and hundreds arrested during a national assault on trade unions, political organizations, and universities.

422. Why are These People In Argentine Jails? Where are the Disappeared? New York: Anti-Defamation League of B'nai Brith Argentine Prisoner Project, 1981. 15.

423. Wilde, Margaret. "Letter From an Argentine Prison." Christian Century 94 (October 12, 1977) 901-2. Describes conditions in prisons for political prisoners.

424. Willey, Fay. "The Fallen Angel." Newsweek 99 (May 31, 1982) 27. During the Falklands war, the British captured Alfredo Astiz, notorious torturer for the military regime.

425. Winchester, Simon. Prison Diary, Argentina. London: Chatto & Windus, 1983. 219. Three British journalists were imprisoned during the Falklands War for spying.

ARMENIANS (*see* TURKEY [ARMENIAN PERSECUTION])

AUSTRALIA

426. Amnesty International Report 1990. New York: Amnesty International USA, 1990. 35-6. At least nine Aboriginals died in custody in 1989 raising fears ill-treatment may have been the cause.

427. Clarke, Joan. Dr. Max Herz, Surgeon Extraordinary: The Price of Civil and Medical Bigotry in Australia. Sydney: Alternative Pub. Co-operative, 1976. 188. Tells the story of the mistreatment of aliens during World War I through the life of Dr. Max Herz, the result of crude forms of patriotism, xenophobia, and ignorance.

AUSTRIA

428. Amnesty International Report 1990. New York: Amnesty International USA, 1990. 36-7. Numerous reports of police ill-treatment of prisoners continued in 1989, sometimes amounting to torture. Foreigners were particularly mistreated.

BAHRAIN

429. Amnesty International Report 1980. London: Amnesty International, 1980. 323-24. The National Assembly was dissolved in 1975 when it opposed the government's law allowing three years of detention without trial, contrary to the constitution, and the ruling al-Khalifa family claimed discovery of a communist-inspired plot to assassinate officials of the Arabian Gulf states. Subsequent laws have further made much political activity and speech illegal, and Amnesty International now cites fourteen prisoners of conscience, but many more are detained. Trials are unfair and prisons harsh including torture.

430. Amnesty International Report 1990. New York: Amnesty International USA, 1990. 38-9. Dozens of people were detained in 1989, without charge or trial, while over 100 were serving prison terms after unfair political trials, some tortured. Most detainees were from the Shi'a community.

431. Bahrain: Violations of Human Rights. New York: Amnesty International, 1991. 15. Documents the arbitrary arrests, unfair trials, torture, and incommunicado detention of Bahrainian political prisoners.

BANGLADESH

432. Amnesty International Report 1980. London: Amnesty International, 1980. 183-86. Martial law ended in November 1979, but many political prisoners remain held, some of whom are long-term. Trials by military courts lacked standard safeguards of rights. Prisoners have been killed in prisons.

433. Amnesty International Report 1990. New York: Amnesty International USA, 1990. 39-41. Many Hindoos held without trial were released in 1989, but others arrested; reports of torture continued. Members of opposition parties, strikers, and others were arrested.

434. Bangladesh: Unlawful Killings and Torture in the Chittagong Hill Tracts. New York: Amnesty International, 1986. Describes incidents, from February to May 1986, in which tribal villagers were unlawfully killed and tortured in the context of armed opposition to the government.

435. Bleeding Bangla Desh--Crime Against Humanity. New Delhi: Sugar, 1971. 134. A history of the genocide and the events ledaing up to it.

436. Chadudhuri, Kalyan. Genocide in Bangladesh. Bombay: Orient Longman, 1972. 228. Examines the genocide that followed the army crackdown, how the people reacted to the atrocities, and details the plight faced by the refugees.

437. Hasanat Abul. The Ugliest Genocide in History. Dacca: Muktadhara, 1974. 379. Testimonies by survivors and other witnesses.

438. How Pakistan Violated Human Rights in Bangladesh: Some Testimonies. New Delhi: Indian Council of World Affairs, 1972. 62. Compiles 26 first-hand accounts about the atrocities committed by Pakistani troops.

439. Malik, Amita. The Year of the Vulture. New Delhi: Orient Longman, 1972. 159. A history of the genocide with many personal narratives by survivors.

440. Mey, Wolfgang, ed. Genocide in the Chittagong Hill Tracts, Bangladesh. Copenhagen: International Work Group for Indigenous Affairs, 1984. 190. "The Bangladesh army and air force are concluding a campaign of unparalled violence against the tribal minorities. They have been subjected to large scale evictions, torture, rape, and massacres--10,000 tribal people were killed in 1981 alone."

441. Mohan, Jag. The Black Book of Genocide in Bangla Desh: A Documentary Book. New Delhi: Geeta, 1971. 124. Gathers first-hand testimony from survivors, journalists, and other witnesses in documenting the horrors of the East Pakistan genocide.

442. Quaderi, Fazlul Quader, ed. Bangladesh Genocide and World Press. Dacca: ABCO, 1972. 455. Compiles over a hundred newspaper and journal articles from around the world to document how world opinion reacted to the killings.

443. Report of an Amnesty International Mission to Bangladesh(4-12 April 1977). London: Amnesty International, 1978. 22. Covers legal position of prisoners (laws, trial, release), the judiciary, and detention conditions. Expresses concern over martial law courts, which have imprisoned between 10,000 and 15,000 political prisoners as of 1977.

BENIN

444. Amnesty International Report 1980. London: Amnesty International, 1980. 31-32. Detention without trial, unfair trials, and the death penalty remain problems. Many students and some teachers held without charge or trial are AI prisoners of conscience; three former presidents have lived under house arrest since 1972.

445. Amnesty International Report 1990. New York: Amnesty International USA, 1990. 42-44. An amnesty released over 100 prisoners, but others were arrested for demonstrating against the Kérékou government or for membership in opposition parties, especially the Parti communiste. Two Security Court trials took pace for people accused of attempting to overthrow the state. Torture reported with some deaths resulting.

446. Benin--Political Imprisonment and Torture. New York: Amnesty International, 1988. 11. More than 200 prisoners were being held without charge or trial, many were tortured, and at least one died as the result. All were imprisoned for exercising their right to freedom of expression and association.

BHUTAN

447. Amnesty International Report 1990. New York: Amnesty International USA, 1990. 45. A campaigner for minority rights was arrested for anti-national activities, an offence punishable with death.

BOLIVA

448. Amnesty International Report 1980. London: Amnesty International, 1980. 112-113. Political instability was accompanied by some arbitrary arrests, torture, and killings.

449. Amnesty International Report 1990. New York: Amnesty International USA, 1990. 45-7. About 200 arrested in state of siege, most of them members of striking teachers' unions. Other detainees were tortured and ill-treated. The trial of former officials accused of torturing and killing has been delayed.

450. "Debray's Release." Newsweek 77 (January 4, 1971) 29-30. Writer Regis Debray, imprisoned for helping Che Guevara, is freed.

451. "Free Political Prisoners in Bolivia." Militant 44.33 (Sept. 12, 1980) 6. Report on the over 2000 people--trade unionists, journalists, teachers, religious figures, and political leaders--detained, tortured, and sometimes murdered since the July 17, 1980, military coup.

452. Henric, Laura. "Timetable of Nightmare." Guardian 32.45 (Aug. 27, 1980) 20. The current regime is trying to put down resistance by bombing mining towns and police attacks that kill or wound hundreds of people.

453/54. Valda, Roberto. Repression in Bolivia. Commonweal 97 (December 22, 1972) 268-9. The Bolivian military government of Hugo Banzer is persecuting suspected Communists and revolutionaries with a messianic zeal.

BRAZIL

455. Amnesty International Report 1980. London: Amnesty International, 1980. 113-115. Political arrests, disappearances, torture, and killings characterized Brazil in recent years, but 1979 marked an improvement by the release of most political prisoners and return of exiles by President Figueiredo and by the decrease of political arrests. But labor union leaders are increasingly threatened and arrested.

456. Amnesty International Report 1990. New York: Amnesty International USA, 1990. 47-50. Peasants, trade unionists, and campaigners for agrarian reform were detained or threatened, tortured, or killed in growing numbers--e.g., Verino Sossai, President of the Rural Workers' Trade Union of Montanha.

457. Barbosa, Roberto. "An American in Brazil: a Question of Survival." Christian Century 90 (December 12, 1973) 1222. On the arrest and disappearance of Paulo Wright, leader of Brazil's World Student Christian Federation and former member of Santa Catarina's state legislature.

458. Betto, Frei (Carlos Alberto Libanio Christo). Against Principalities and Power: Letters from a Brazilian Jail. Maryknoll, N.Y.: Orbis, 1977. 241. Member of Dominican order and director of Student Catholic Action, Betto was arrested for subversive acts, spent twenty-two months in prison awaiting trial and was sentenced to four years in prison in 1971.

459. Brazil: Authorized Violence in Rural Areas. New York: Amnesty International, 1988. 79. Hundreds of people denied protection of the law and killed by gunmen hired by landowners in northern Brazil. Hundreds more rounded up and jailed for short periods. AI is concerned by evidence that landowners' campaign is not only sanctioned but frequently assisted by the authorities.

460. "Brazil: Journalist Dies, Allegations of Torture Grow." Matchbox (Winter 1976) 2. The death by torture of journalist Vladimir Herzog sparked a massive public outcry and a document detailing political assassination in the torture chambers, 233 alleged torturers, and a list of 55 deaths under torture.

461. "Brazil: 111 Prisoners Killed by Military Police." Amnesty Action (Spring 1993). 2.

462. "A Daughter's Lament." Newsweek 77 (February 15, 1971) 42. On the arrest of Rubens Beyrodt Paiva, his wife, and daughter; Rubens has disappeared.

463. Deaths in Custody in Brazil. London: Amnesty International, 1974. 14. "A list...of 210 people that have reportedly died in mysterious circumstances."

464. Landau, Saul. "Truth Lies on Cutting Room Floor." Cine-tracts 5 (Fall 1978) 24. On the difficulty of getting his film of torture of Brazilian political prisoners distributed and shown in the United States.

465. Matthews, Adam. "Surveillance--and Worse--in Brazil, 1975." Christian Century 92 (December 31, 1975) 1205-8. Brutal repression continues in Brazil.

466. Moreira Alves, Marcio. A Grain of Mustard Seed: The Awakening of the Brazilian Revolution. Garden City, NY: Doubleday Anchor, 1973. 194. The author was forced into exile for his protests against the atrocities of the dictatorship. This book describes the rise of the repression, including a chapter on torture. Author also of Torturas e Tortuados on the methods of torture employed by the Branco regime.

467. Morris, Fred B. "Sustained by Faith Under Brazilian Torture." Christian Century 92 (January 22, 1975) 56-60. The author recounts his torture in a military prison in Recife.

468. "'Nunca Mais.'" Commonweal 113 (October 10, 1986) 517. On two new books on police torture and murder: Brasil: Nunca Mais (Torture in Brazil) and I, Rigoberta Menchú.

469. "Panel Hears Test Case: Brazilian Doctor Charged with Altering Torture Records." Matchbox (November 1980) 1, 12. One certificate falsely states suicide as a cause of death; a second that a prisoner had not been tortured despite bruises, burns, and other evidence.

470. "Price Goes Up." Newsweek 77 (January 25, 1971) 44. The government released political prisoners in exchange for the Swiss Ambassador, kidnapped by members of a revolutionary group.

471. Report on Allegations of Torture in Brazil. New York: Amnesty International USA, 1974. 27. Not Inspected.

472. The Repressive State: The Brazilian "National Security Doctrine" and Latin America. Toronto: Brazilian Studies, 1978. 97. Contains three essays on national security, political prisoners, and judicial structures. "For the past 10 years, Brazil has experienced the most complete of dictatorships, one in which torture has become a system of government," a system that has had a great influence in other Latin American countries.

473. Ring, Harry. "Moreno and Strasberg Win Freedom in Brazil." Militant 42.36 (September 29, 1978) 11. Two leading members of the Argentinian Socialist Workers Party, Nahuel Moreno and Rita Strasberg, are released from a Brazilian prison because of international protest.

474. Stahel, T.H. "A Canticle for Joao Bosco." America 155 (October 11, 1986) 179. On the murder by police of Father Burnier, because he protested the torture of two women.

475. "This is Theater." Newsweek 78 (August 16, 1971) 40. The Living Theater troupe from New York is in jail for subversion.

476. "To the President of Brazil." Christian Century 88 (December 15, 1971) 1462-3. Letter from U.S. church leaders condemning the repression (including torture) by Brazil's military dictatorship, on the eve of General Emilio Garrastazú MÉdici's visit to the U.S.

477. Torture in Brazil: Testimony Given to the Rome Session of the Russell Tribunal. Nottingham: Bertrand Russell Peace Foundation, 1976. 20. A small part of the testimony given to the Second Russell Tribunal on repression in Brazil and Latin America.

478. Wall, James M. "A Returned Key and Torture in Brazil." Christian Century 91 (October 23, 1974) 979. Arrest and torture of Fred Morris in Recife.

479. Ward, Richard. "Brazil: Torture and Repression." Guardian 30.6 (Nov. 16, 1977) 12. A letter from eleven political prisoners describes torture in Brazilian prisons.

480. Weschler, Lawrence. "A Miracle, a Universe." New Yorker 63 (May 25, 1987) 69-86 and (June 1, 1987) 72-80+. On Torture in Brazil (Brazil: Nunca Mais) compiled by Jaime Wright and Cardinal Arms about the pervasive use of torture by Brazilian military governments, 1964-1979, based on military archives they secretly photocopied. One million pages of documentation.

481. Willey, Fay. "The Herzog Case." Newsweek 86 (November 17, 1975) 62,64. On the death of journalist Vladimir Herzog in a prison cell, alleged by the police to be suicide.

BRUNEI DARUSSALAM

482. Amnesty International Report 1990. New York: Amnesty International USA, 1990. 50-1. Seven prisoners of conscience, four held for 27 years, remained confined without charge or trial.

BULGARIA

483. Amnesty International Report 1980. London: Amnesty International, 1980. 256-260. The penal code upholds punishment of anti-state expression, ethnic and religious minorities are mistreated, trying to emigrate is illegal, prisons are harsh, and torture occurs. Several people have been imprisoned for espionage after unfair trials. Pomaks, ethnic Bulgarians of the Moslem faith, have particularly been persecuted.

484. Amnesty International Report 1990. New York: Amnesty International USA, 1990. 51-3. A new government brought improvements in 1989: amnesty in November for many prisoners and relaxation of anti-Turk laws. But during the year many Turks and several human rights leaders were held without charge or trial, and some Turks were treated brutally and even killed.

485. Bulgaria: Imprisonment of Ethnic Turks. New York: Amnesty International, 1986. An account of human rights abuse of the ethnic Turk minority. Describes imprisonment, compulsory resettlement and killing of Turks since 1984 for peacefully opposing assimilation; how thousands of Turks have under threat assumed Bulgarian names; and attempts to suppress Turkish language and culture.

486. "Prisoner Watch: Bulgaria." Human Rights Watch (December 1987) 9. A call for letters to end continued internal exile of Grigor Simov Bozhilov, human rights advocate.

BURKINO FASO

487. Amnesty International Report 1990. New York: Amnesty International USA, 1990. 53-4. Twenty prisoners detained without charge since 1987 were freed, but four accused of plotting the overthrow of the government were executed without trial.

BURMA (*see* MYANMAR)

BURUNDI

488. Amnesty International Report 1980. London: Amnesty International, 1980. 33. Several dissidents have been arrested.

489. Amnesty International Report 1990. New York: Amnesty International USA, 1990. 54-6. Several prisoners released but others continued in custody without charge. Some Jehovah's Witnesses were detained.

490. Kay, Reginalda. Burundi Since the Genocide: The Minority Rights Group Report no. 20. Cambridge, MA: Cultural Survival, 1987. 12. In 1972 the ruling Tutsi-Hima faction slaughtered an estimated 150,000 Hutus, with continued repercussions against human rights.

491. Totten, Samuel. "Burundi Genocide of the Hutus." First Person Accounts of Genocidal Acts Committed in the Twentieth Century: An Annotated Bibilography. Westport, CT: Greenwood, 1991. 282-84. Fourteen entries, including films/video and use of first-person accounts, on Tutsi massacres in 1972.

CAMBODIA (*see* KAMPUCHEA)

CAMEROON

492. Amnesty International Report 1980. London: Amnesty International, 1980. 34-35. AI is concerned about political imprisonment, detention without trial, torture, and poor prison conditions. Some students, teachers, and white-collar workers have been held without trial since 1976; some dissidents have been in prison since 1960; perhaps a total of 200.

493. Amnesty International Report 1990. New York: Amnesty International USA, 1990. 57-59. Over 100 political prisoners were held in 1989 for religious belief, a 1984 coup, and other reasons. Two prisoners died allegedly from torture and neglect. Prison conditions are harsh.

494. Mukong, Albert W. Prisoner Without a Crime. Cameroon: Alfresco, 1985. 106. Imprisoned six "gruesome" years for opposing President Ahidjo.

CANADA

495. Free Quebec Political Prisoners: The Issues and Background. Toronto: Vanguard, 1970. 31. Tells about the thirteen people charged with seditious conspiracy to overthrow the governments of Canada and Quebec by force as members of the outlawed Front de Libération du Quebec.

496. Jones, Ted. Both Sides of the Wire : the Frederiction Internment Camp. Vol. I. Fredericton, N.B.: New Ireland, 1988. 325. Twenty-six Canadian internment camps were in operation by the end of WWII to house 40,000 German prisoners of war and civilian internees.

497. Kravchuk, Petro. Interned without Cause. Toronto: Kobzar, 1985. 124.

498. "Politics and Sentencing." This Magazine 19.1 (April 1985) 34-38. Protests the "extremely harsh" sentences given to five anti-war and anti-pollution bombers.

499. Repka, William. Dangerous Patriots: Canada's Unknown Prisoners of War. Vancouver, BC: New Star, 1982. 249. About the internment of left-wing citizens without trial from 1940 to 1942. Specifically, accounts by sixteen of the some 250 people interned and by three wives.

500. Repka, William. Howard Lowrie, M.D., Physician, Humanitarian. Toronto: Progress, 1977. 104. Account of Dr. Lowrie and some one hundred others imprisoned at the beginning of World War II without charge or trial but in fact for opposing imperialist wars. Chapter six describes his arrest, chapter seven the Petawauwa Internment Camp.

501. Socknat, Thomas P. Witness against War: Pacifism in Canada, 1900-1945. Toronto: U of Toronto P, 1987. 370. Chapter 8 deals with "Alternative Pacifist Service."

502. "Trial Begins For Vancouver 5." Fifth Estate 18.3 (Fall 1983) 3. Defendants are accused of destroying a generator and attacking a cruise missile plant.

503. "Vancouver 5 Latest Update." Overthrow 5.2 (July 1983) 25. Commentary on the massive show of force used in the arrest of two female and three male environmental and political activists, the press coverage that capitalizes on their arrest by fixating on sensationalism and violence, and legal advice for anyone who finds themselves in a similar situation.

CENTRAL AFRICAN REPUBLIC

504. Amnesty International Report 1980. London: Amnesty International, 1980. 35-38. Despite the overthrow of the brutal dictator Emperor Bokassa, detention of political opponents without trial continues by the new government.

505. Amnesty International Report 1990. New York: Amnesty International USA, 1990. 59-61. Several long-term detainees are held without trial.

CHAD

506. Amnesty International Report 1980. London: Amnesty International, 1980. 38-9. Civil War presents adequate investigation, but reports of serious human rights violations have been received, including disappearances and summary executions.

507. Amnesty International Report 1990. New York: Amnesty International USA, 1990. 61-2. While over a hundred were release, several hundred political prisoners were held in 1989 in secret detention centers under harsh conditions including torture. The fate of some long-term prisoners is still unknown.

508. Detentions and Arbitrary Killings in the Republic of Chad, 1982\1983. London: Amnesty International, 1983. 7.

509. "End of an Ordeal." Time 109 (February 14, 1977) 38. French archaeologist Françoise Claustre and her husband are freed from rebel tribesmen, rescued by Muammar Gaddafi.

510. Whitman, Kate. Chad: The Minority Rights Group Report no. 60. Cambridge, MA.: Cultural Survival, 1988. 16. Since 1960 a series of regimes have imposed various degrees of arbitrary rule. Thousands have died; hundreds of thousands have fled as refugees.

CHILE

511. Adams, Virginia. "Testimony as Therapy." Psychology Today 17 (June 1983) 84-5. Summarizes a report in the American Journal of Orthopsychiatry on the therapeutic value for victims of torture and their families of recounting their experiences.

512. "Adopting a Political Prisoner." Peace News 20.45 (June 3, 1977) 6. Overview of the brutal repression in Chile under Pinochet, promoting a campaign for groups to adopt individual prisoners.

513. Agosin, Marjorie. "Notes on the Poetics of the Acevedo Movement Against Torture." Trans. Miriam Ben-Ur. Human Rights Quarterly 10 (1988) 339-343. Sebastian Acevedo immolated himself in 1983 because his two children were tortured by Pinochet's secret police. The movement under his name employs "a unique poetics of actions and symbols of non-violence."

514. Agosin, Marjorie. Scraps of Life: Chilean Arpilleras. Toronto: Williams-Wallace; Trenton, NJ: Red Sea, 1987. 154. The mothers, sisters, and wives of the disappeared under Pinochet's dictatorship. Together they make wall hangings of beatings, bodies, empty chairs, etc, as instruments for their search for their missing loved ones.

515. Allende, Isabel. The House of Spirits. Trans. Magda Bogin. New York: Knopf, 1984. 380. A novel with Pinochet's coup and consequent horrors as background.

516. Allende, Isabel. Of Love and Shadows. Trans. Margaret Peden. New York: Knopf, 1987. 274. The heroine of this novel, Irene Beltrán. gradually becomes aware of death squads and the desaparecidos until she too becomes a victim.

517. Amnesty International Report 1980. London: Amnesty International, 1980. 116-122. A marked deterioration in human rights during May 1979 to April 1980, because of an increase in political imprisonment, arbitrary detention, unfair trials, torture, and killings. As many as 2000 people were arrested for political reasons during this period and perhaps most of them were taken to secret places and tortured.

518. Amnesty International Report 1990. New York: Amnesty International USA, 1990. 62-5. Further significant advances toward elected government occurred in 1989, but numerous violations of human rights continued: over 100 of the 700 disappearance cases before the courts were arbitrarily closed; security forces personnel accused of killings were treated leniently by military courts while human rights workers were treated severely; about 450 political prisoners remain in prison; trials were delayed and unfair; torture was reported.

519. Bernstein, Dennis and Connie Blitt. "Chile, Then and Now." Progressive 48 (April 1984) 14. Report on the abduction of American Suzanne Kolb and the disappearence of her Chilean companion Nano.

520. Bravo, Gabriela. Three Chilean Women: Gabriela Bravo, Ana Gonzalez, Ulda Ortiz. New York: National Chilean Center, 1978. 9. Three speeches given in Pittsburgh by the wives or mothers whose husbands and children have disappeared at the hands of the secret police.

521. Butler, Judy. "New United Nations Report Condemns Junta: Chile's Denial of Human Rights." Guardian 29.7 (November 24, 1976) 19. Outlines the 229-page report by the UN detailing the huge violations of human rights in Chile--arrests, exiles, and "disappearances."

522. Came, Barry. "The Defiant Relegado." Newsweek 101 (February 14, 1983) 49. Carlos López Vila, formerly imprisoned and tortured by Pinochet's police, now lives in exile in "Chile's Siberia."

523. Carrasco, B. "Pinochet's Political Prisoners Push for Presidential Pardon." Guardian 43.31 (June 12, 1991) 16. Over 160 prisoners still languish behind bars over a year after a new president was elected. Some of the prisoners began a hunger strike.

524. Carrasco, Rolando. Chile's Prisoners of War. Moscow: Novosti Press Agency, 1977. 312. Account of his two years of bestial brutality by the Pinochet regime backed by the United States.

525. Cassidy, Sheila. Audacity to Believe. Cleveland, Ohio: Collins-World, 1977. 335. In 1975 British physician Cassidy, in Chile to study surgery, was arrested, tortured, and imprisoned in Santiago in 1975 for treating a wounded fugitive.

526. Cassidy, Sheila. "Prayer Under Duress." National Review 29 (July 22, 1977) 826-8. Dr. Cassidy comments on her experiences.

527. Cassidy, Sheila. "Tortured in Chile." Index on Censorship 5.2 (Summer 1976) 67-73. Her testimony in 1976 in Geneva before the United Nations Ad Hoc Working Group of the Commission on Human Rights about being tortured in a Chilean prison.

528. Chile. London: Amnesty International, 1988. 19. Covers disappearences, torture, mass murder, secret graves, clandestine military and police operations, failure of court investigations.

529. Chile : Amnesty International, Briefing. London: Amnesty International, 1986. 22. Serious and systematic violations of human rights developed in Chile following the coup in 1973, and the degree of repression has escalated sharply since 1983, including abduction, torture, and murder.

530. Chile: An Amnesty International Report. London: Amnesty International, 1974. 80. Surveys summary executions, disappearances, torture, refugees, and some individual prisoners under the military junta.

531. Chile: Evidence of Torture: An Amnesty International Report. London: Amnesty International, 1983. 72. The system is examined from arrest to death. Case histories pp. 29-63.

532. "Chile: Institutionalized Brutality Against Women." Granma 10.11 (March 16, 1975) 11. Chilean women are being tortured and murdered by military junta forces.

533. Chile: The New Victims. Videocassette. Amnesty International USA, 1987. 20 min. "This video describes the situation in Chile since 1983 when clandestine death squads with links to the military have carried out a terror campaign involving killings, death threats, 'disappearances,' and torture."

534. "Chile Terror Continues, Secret Trial of 13 Ends." Guardian 27.32 (May 21, 1975) 12. Chilean dictator General Pinochet has continued to severely violate human rights including the trial of 13 members of the Chilean Movement of the Revolutionary Left (MIR) whose sentences "could range from 18 to 35 years."

535. Chile Yes, Pinochet No. Helsinki: Information Center of the World Peace Council, 1978. 35. Contains U.N. resolutions condemning Pinochet's repression.

536. The Chilean Junta: Vandals in the University. New York: National Chile Center, 1978. 14. Describes the systematic assault on the country's universities since the military coup in 1973--firings, mass detentions, torture, killings of students, faculty, and related cultural personnel and figures--and calls for international protests.

537. "Chilean Political Prisoner Campaign." Lucha 11.3 (May/June 1987) 27-28. On the fourteen prisoners facing possible execution after incommunicado detention and torture.

538. Chile's Secret Prisoners. London: Chile Committee for Human Rights, 1977. 40.

539. "Church Against State." Time 107 (January 12, 1976) 22. Dr. Sheila Cassidy has been released from prison after being tortured for having treated a political fugitive being harbored by two priests, who were also arrested.

540. Clarke, Gerald. "Missing: Fact or Fabrication?" Time 119 (March 8, 1982) 96. Discusses Costa-Gavras' film of the disappearance and murder of Charles Horman following the overthrow of President Allende with apparent U.S. complicity.

541. "Copper and Human Rights." Nation 219 (December 28, 1974) 676-7. On torture of U.S. citizen, Dr. Amy Conger, and other atrocities and outrages committed by the Pinochet government.

542. Corillon, Carol. Scientists and Human Rights in Chile: Report of a Delegation. Washington, DC: National Academy Press, 1985. 59. A report by four members of the National Academy of Sciences who investigated the severe repression in Chile in 1985: firings, internal banishment, exile, torture, disappearances, and collaboration of medical professionals in torture. Individual cases and lists of victims given.

543. Corvalán, Luis. Words from Prison. Helsinki: World Peace Council, 1975. 21. The author has been imprisoned since 1973.

544. Demand Freedom for Disappeared Prisoners in Chile!. Helsinki: World Peace Council, 1977. 23. On the "shocking" police state of Chile, individual cases, appeal for world protest.

545. "Desaparecidos: Disappeared in Chile." Matchbox (Spring 1977) 7-10. From 1973 to 1977, over 1,500 people have fallen victim to the Chilean security forces intimidation tactics--official abduction and secret detention, i.e. 'disappearance.' Many bodies turn up later in rivers, beaches, and ravines, with signs of mutilation.

546. Diaz, Gladys. "Roles and Contradictions of Chilean Women in the Resistance and in Exile: Collective Reflections of a Group of Militant Prisoners." Presented at the Plenary Session of the International Conference on Exile and Solidarity in Latin America during the 1970's. New York: Women's International Resource Exchange (WIRE), 1979. Testimony of female members of the Chilean Resistance who had been imprisoned, tortured, and exiled.

547. Diaz, Gladys and Carmen Castillo. Women in the Chilean Resistance. Berkeley: Non-Intervention in Chile, 1978. 28. Two members of the MIR (Movement of the Revolutionary Left), speak of their experiences as political prisoners and active members of the resistance.

548. Disappeared Prisoners in Chile: Dossier on Political Prisoners Held in Secret Detention Camps in Chile, March 1977. London: Amnesty International, 1977. 4 pamphlets. A selection of case histories, lists and photos of disappeared prisoners by occupation.

549. Dorfman, Ariel. Death and the Maiden. New York: Penguin Plays, 1992. 64. A play about a woman who confronts the man she believes was her torturer.

550. Ege, Konrad. "West German Cultist Concentration Camp in Chile." Counter-Spy 3.3 (Dec. 1978) 43-54. Report on the Colonia Dignidad torture camp, its origins in a Federal Republic of Germany Christian community, "Private Sociale Mission," accused of severe physical and psychological manipulation, sexual abuse, and torture, and which moved to Chile in 1961, becoming a training center for the national secret police.

551. First Session of the International Commission of Enquiry into the Crimes of the Military Junta in Chile: Dipoli, Finland, March 21-24, 1974. Helsinki: International Commission of Enquiry into the Crimes of the Military Junta in Chile, 1974. 47. Statements, appeals, and other documents, including a summary of the destruction of culture in Chile.

552. Garrett-Schesch, Adam. A Prisoner in Chile. New York: Encyclopedia Americana: CBS News Audio Resource Library, 1973. 1 cassette. The author and his wife, Patricia, graduate students doing research for their dissertations, were imprisoned and mistreated during the Chilean military coup.

553. "Global Gall." Nation 222 (June 26, 1976) 770.
On U.S. hypocrisy regarding human rights violations.

554. Greenberg, Peter. "Art, Lies, and Reality." Rolling Stone (May 13, 1982) 15,17-18,72. Interview with Constantin Costa-Gavras, director of the film Missing about the military coup that overthrew President Allende and resulted in the thousands of arrests, torture, and murder.

555. Hauser, Thomas. Missing : the Execution of Charles Horman. New York: Simon & Schuster, 1988. 258. (Orig. The Execution of Charles Horman [1978]). Examines the charge that Mr. Horman was murdered by the Chilean military with foreknowledge of U.S. Embassy officials in Santiago because he had evidence of U.S. involvement in the coup and assassination of President Allende.

556. Human Rights Concerns in Chile. New York: America's Watch Committee, 1987. 53. Covers the human rights situation in Chile from 1984 through 1987: people charged with terrorism for peaceful activity; an increase in deaths, torture and arrests; increased paramilitary squad activities, including members of the secret police, who operate at all hours and carry out assassinations and abductions; the judicial system offering no redress for victims.

557. Hurtado, María Elena. "The Caravan of Death." Index On Censorship. 19.5 (May 1990) 13-14. "As Chile prepared to return to democracy on 11 March the country was shocked by the account of the 'caravan of death' which in October 1973 travelled through Chile assassinating political prisoners."

558. International Commission of Enquiry into the Crimes of the Military Junta in Chile. Arbitrary Arrests and Detentions in Chile. Helsinki, Finland: Permanent Secretariat, 4th Session, 1976. The Commission concluded that since the military coup in 1973, the government had paid no respect to human rights but had systematically tortured and murdered its opponents and critics, arbitrarily arrested them, brutally treated them during detentions, and caused many to disappear. The first session in 1974 published statements, appeals, and other documents, including a summary of the destruction of culture in Chile.

559. Kennedy, Kit. "Women Political Prisoners Tortured." Majority Report 4.21 (February 22, 1975) 4. Describes several prisoners and a rally in New York to support them.

560. Kopkind, Andrew. "'Missing': Cultural Battlefield." Nation 234 (April 17, 1982) 466-9. Discussion (May 15, 1982) 592-3. Analyzes Flora Lewis's review of the Costa-Gavras film about the disappearance and execution of Charles Horman by Pinochet's police.

561. "List of Tortures Inflicted on Political Prisoners by Fascist Chilean Junta Revealed in Mexico." Granma 10.9 (March 2, 1975) 10. 27 techniques were described by the international commission investigating the crimes of the junta.

562. Meeting of the Juridical Sub-Commission of the International Commission of Enquiry into the Crimes of the Military Junta in Chile: Documents: Berlin, German Democratic Republic, 6 February 1977. Helsinki, Finland: International Commission of Enquiry into the Crimes of the Military Junta, Secretariat, 1977. 41. Testimonies of surviving victims of disappearance and torture; analysis of Chile's violations of international codes and conventions.

563. "Mercy Flight." Time 107 (May 17, 1976) 44. U.S. pressure to force release of political prisoners.

564. Miller, Judith. "Chile: A Survivor." Progressive 39 (January 1975) 6-7. Report on the release of Allende's ambassador to Washington, Orlando Letelier, and on the brutalities inflicted on inmates on Dawson Island, the Chilean junta's "special preserve" for political prisoners.

565. Newman, Frank C. Report of Mission to Santiago, Chile, 1st-8th November. Ed. Frank C. Newman, Bruce W. Summer, Roger Plant. New York: Amnesty International, 1974. 28.

566. 1986 Annual Report on the Human Rights Situation in Chile. Toronto: Inter-Church Committee on Human Rights in Latin America, 1987. 30. A "state of emergency"' was imposed legalizing detention without charge. Death squad activity increased--abductions, torture, execution, including the cases of Rodrigo Rojas de Negri and Carmen Gloria Quintana, who were burned alive, causing Rodrigo's death.

567. Núñoz Alarcón, Juan Rene. "Confession of a DINA Agent." CounterSpy 3.3 (Dec. 1978) 54-59. Nunoz describes how he was trained to "persecute people, to interrogate, to torture and to assassinate" for the DINA and six other Chilean secret police organizations.

568. "Objects of Barter." Time 108 (December 27, 1976) 23-4. Chile and the Soviet Union exchange political prisoners.

569. "The Open Secret: Torture and the Medical Profession in Chile. Washington D.C.: American Association for the Advancement of Science, Committe on Scientific Freedom and the Medical Profession in Chile, 1987. 82. On the participation by physicians in government-sponsored torture as well as the efforts being made by physicians in Chile to call attention to the torture and bring it to a halt.

570. Padilla, Amado and Lillian Comas-Diaz. "A State of Fear." Psychology Today 20 (Nov. 1986) 60-65. A report on the brutal repression. The authors traveled to Chile under the sponsorship of the American Psychological and Psychiatric Associations.

571. Peck, Winslow. "Death on Embassy Row: CIA Covers Up Murder Web of Chilean Gestapo With False Stories and Terrorist Operations." <u>CounterSpy</u> 3.2 (Dec. 1976) 8-15, 64-71. Focuses on the collaboration of the CIA and Pinochet's secret police, DINA, in the assassination of former Chilean Ambassador Orlando Letelier in Washington D.C. as well as documenting CIA involvment in the development of Pinochet's terror/torture state.

572. "Political Prisoners Disappear in Chile." <u>Militant</u> 40.21 (May 28, 1976) 22. Conditions in Chilean prisons worsen; reports of torture and inhumane living conditions are confirmed by family visitors.

573. "Political Prisoners in Chile Face Death Sentence." <u>Lucha</u> 11.4 (July/Aug. 1987) 20-21. Lists the fourteen condemned and summarizes the repression.

574. Rassi, Reynold. "'The Morale of the Political Prisoners in Chile is Very High and Firm.'" <u>Granma</u> 10.4 (January 26, 1975) 9. The journalist Manuel Cabieses was freed after 16 months in prison and torture.

575. <u>Refugee and Humanitarian Problems in Chile</u>. Washington: GPO, 1973. Testimony and documents of the repression.

576. <u>Report of the National Commission on Truth and Reconciliation</u>. Santiago: Secretariat of Communication and Culture, Government General Secretariat Ministry, 1991. 1350. Examines President Aylwin's Rettig Commission.

577. Ritterman, Michele. <u>Hope Under Siege : Terror and Family Support in Chile</u>. Norwood, NJ: Ablex, 1991. 264. Account of a trip to Chile by a member of a human rights commission studying the effects of terror and torture on the prisoners and their families, and the strength some prisoners and their families gain through their love for each other. The main subject is Daniel Rodriguez and his family.

578. Rothenbuecher, Bea. "A Chilling True-Life Thriller." <u>Christian Century</u> 99.8 (March 10, 1982) 260-1. Reviews the film <u>Missing</u> by Constantin Costa-Gavras, which recounts the disappearance of U.S. citizen Charles Horman at the time of the military overthrow of Allende.

579. Savren, Shelly. "Prisoners of Chilean Junta 'Disappear'." <u>Longest Revolution</u> 4.1 (October 1979) 1,11. Summarizes the disappearances and the struggles by families to trace their loved ones, with one case study.

580. Schirmer, Jennifer. "Chile: The Loss of Children." <u>Cultural Survial Quarterly</u> 10.4 (1986) 40-42. A look at "children and youths scarred by torture, detention, disappearance, execution, or exile of a close relative during the many states of emergency in Chile since 1973."

581. Serrano, Bruno. "Flowers From Sorrows." <u>Index On Censorship</u> 18.9 (Oct. 1989) 31-34. "The story of a poetry workshop with political prisoners in Chile is told by the writer who suggested the idea, carried it out, and published <u>Poesia prisionera</u>.

582. Silva, Raul, Birgitta Leander, and Sun Axelsson, comps. <u>Evidence on the Terror in Chile</u>. London: Merlin, 1974. 139. Testimonies by victims of Pinochet's torture regime, with Silva's narrative and analysis of the overthrow of Allende.

583. Smith, Michal. "Chilean Judge Under Siege." <u>Progressive</u> 52 (March 1988) 16. Judge René García Villegas is the first judge to investigate in earnest charges of torture against the secret police. The death threats he has received have necessitated 24 hour police protection.

584. Sölle, Dorothee. "To Love Means Not to Hide." Christian Century 95 (September 13, 1978) 824-28. Tells about hunger strikers in Chile attempting to gain information on the whereabouts of the more than 2,500 disappeared.

585. Styron, Rose. "Torture in Chile." New Republic 174 (March 20, 1976) 15-17. Statistics and a few case studies of the repressive ally of the U.S.

586. Valdes, Hernan. Diary of a Chilean Concentration Camp. Trans. Jo Labanyi. London: Gollancz, 1975. 160. A retrospective account of life in the Tejos Verdes military concentration camp intended to make real the "genocide, physical torture, mass psychological terror and subsepuent economic exploitation" under the military dictatorship since 1973. The purpose of the coup and of the repression was to eradicate socialism.

587. Vera, Marta (pseud.). Political Prisoners, Chilean Women No. 2: Political Prisoners in the Women's Section of Tres Alamos Concentration Camp. London: Women's Campaign for Chile and Chile Committee for Human Rights, 1976. A pamphlet containing the testimony of women imprisoned together for fifteen months.

588. Wade, Nicholas. "Chilean Doctors and the AAAS Mission." Science 213 (July 24, 1981) 421. Three physicians accused of illegal political activities have been transferred from a military to a civilian court.

589. Ward, Richard. "Political Murders Exposed." Guardian 29.7 (November 24, 1976) 12. Exposes the Pinochet regime's new policy of killing political prisoners; many new reports of prisoners "disappearing."

590. What the DINA and Pinochet Deny: The Truth about the Missing Prisoners in Chile, Their Faces, Their Lives, Their testimonies. [S.l.]: International Trade Union Committee for Solidarity with the Workers and People of Chile, 1977. 59. Over 2,500 political prisoners have disappeared since September 11, 1973. This book contains profiles and photos of a few of them and names and photos of more.

591/92. Willenson, K. and P.R. Webb. "Doctor's Ordeal." Newsweek 87 (January 12, 1976) 41. British doctor Sheila Cassidy was tortured by the police after treating a wounded guerrilla.

593. Yancey, Philip. "Holy Subversion." Christianity Today 32 (February 5, 1988) 14-20. How the Christian faith helps political prisoners survive the suffering. Focuses on Chile and Peru.

594. Zalaquet Daher, Jose. "Congressional Testimony: Human Rights in Chile Today." Matchbox (Fall 1976) 12-13. Excerpts from Zalaquet's testimony before the Subcommittee on International Organizations of the Committee on International Relations of the House of Representatives on May 5, 1976 regarding politically motivated arrests and brutal torture with no access to trial or other legal recourse. (See accompanying article on Fernando Flores.)

CHINA, NATIONALIST

595. Colman, Louis. "Cry From China." Nation 137 (August 23, 1933) 216. Alerts readers to hardships suffered by Kuomintnang repression.

596. Ming, Shih. "In a Chinese Prison: a Girl Revolutionist Tells Her Experiences as a Captive." Asia 37 (Fall 1937) 99-100. Imprisoned and tortured for being a communist, she demands release of student political prisoners.

597. Pingying, Hsieh. Girl Rebel: The Autobiography of Hsieh Pingying. With extracts from her New War Diaries. Tr. Adet Lin and Anor Lin. New York: John Day, 1940. 270. Imprisoned in 1927 for her Communist affiliation.

CHINA, PEOPLE'S REPUBLIC OF

598. "40 Million Political Prisoners in China." Fifth Estate 12.11 (October 28, 1977) 5. Focuses on the arrest of a group of dissidents called Li-I-Chi, guilty of publishing a poster critical of the government.

599. "Abuses in Tibet." Human Rights Watch (December 1987) 4. Describes the mistreatment of Tibetan prisoners, including Paldengyatso, imprisoned in 1983 apparently for criticizing the Chinese regime.

600. Achiron, Marilyn. "The Threat of the Gulag." Newsweek 109 (January 19, 1987) 33. Thousands of prisoners have been sent to labor camps in the province of Qinghai, China's Siberia.

601. Ackerly, John. The Suppression of a People : Accounts of Torture and Imprisonment in Tibet. Somerville, MA: Physicians for Human Rights, 1989. 62. Eyewitness evidence of brutal measures used by Chinese occupation forces in 1987-1988 to quell peaceful protest demonstrations, and later evidence of torture during and following arrest and harsh prison conditions.

602. Amnesty International Report 1980. London: Amnesty International, 1980. 188-94. Severe restrictions on civil liberties continue: long prison terms for "counter-revolution propaganda," unfair trials, etc. Possibly almost 3,000,000 have been "rehabilitated" and released from prison.

603. Amnesty International Report 1990. New York: Amnesty International, 1990. 65-9. A dark year for China: at least 1,000 people were killed and thousands more injured in 1989 when troops fired on demonstrators and bystanders to suppress dissent. Thousands were arrested (8,000 to 10,000 in Beijing alone), many held incommunicado and then subjected to summary and unfair trials, some sentenced to death. In Lhasa, Tibet, martial law resulted in over 1,000 arrests, some reportedly tortured, sentenced after unfair trials, or summarily executed. Long-term political prisoners continued to be held. Torture and ill-treatment of suspects remained common, and at least 273 people were executed.

604. Anderson, Harry. "'A Wave of Mass Executions.'" Time 104 (October 8, 1984) 38. Summarizes Amnesty International's report on extensive government abuse of dissidents.

605. Aredon, John. "Tibet Today: Current Conditions and Prospects." Cultural Survival Quarterly 12.1 (1988) 52-60. On the escalation of Tibet's destruction. Describes several political prisoners and life in prison for political prisoners.

606. Asia Watch Committee. Tibet: 81 Political Prisoners Held in Drachi Prison. New York: Asia Watch, 1991. 15. An official list copied from a governmental document naming 81 political prisoners; e.g., Lhakpa Tsering, a 14 year old sentenced for two years for attempting "to illegally establish a counterrevolutionary organization." Forty-seven of the eighty-one listed are nuns or monks.

607. Bao, Rou-Wang, and Rudolph Chelminski. Prisoner of Mao. London: Deutsch, 1975. 319. Bao, a French citizen (Jean Pasqualini) born in China spent seven years in prisons and labor camps from 1957 to 1964.

608. Bauman, Michael. "Free Chinese Trotskyists." Militant 40.39 (October 15, 1976) 20. Call to release Trotskyists, jailed for their political views.

609. Black, George and Robin Munro. Black Hands of Beijing: Lives of Defiance in China's Democracy Movement. New York: Wiley, 1993. 390. Narrates the lives of several key dissidents who played roles in China's democracy movement in the 70s and 80s as well as portraying life in the Chinese gulag.

610. Borderwich, Fergus M. "Into the Bamboo Gulag." Reader's Digest 136 (June 1990) 53-59. Profiles a few of the prisoners estimated to be hundreds of thousands to 20 million in prison or slave labor, "the most far-reaching system of political prisoners in the world."

611. Bowker, Michael. "The Spy and the Professor." Reader's Digest 139 (December 1991) 52-57. Narrative of the romance between a U.S. exchange professor and the Army female sargent assigned to spy on him, her imprisonment, and eventual escape to the U.S. and marriage.

612. Byron, John, and Robert Pack. The Claws of the Dragon: Kang Sheng--The Evil Genius Behind Mao and His Legacy of Terror in People's China. New York: Simon and Schuster, 1992. 560. Kang Sheng, founder of China's secret service and known as "The King of Hell," oversaw the murders of possibly a million people.

613. "Catholics in China." Time 66 (October 3, 1955) 38. Recently released prisoners tell of new drive against the Catholics in China.

614. Chen, Theodore. Thought Reform of the Chinese Intellectuals. New York: Oxford, 1961; Hong Kong: Hong Kong UP, 1960. 247. On the revolutionary universities where the educated people were sent for six months "to be remade and to have their thinking reconstructed."

615. Cheng, Nien. Life and Death in Shanghai. London: Grafton, 1986. 496; New York: Viking Penguin, 1988. 560. The wife of the former manager of Shell Petroleum's Shanghai office and herself an official in the company after his death was imprisoned for over six years at the beginning of the Cultural Revolution in 1966. (A circumstantial account that reads like a novel.)

616. Cheng, Nien. "Life and Death in Shanghai." Time 129 (June 8, 1987) 42-56. On a wealthy victim of Mao's Cultural Revolution, imprisoned 6 and a half years.

617. "China and Human Rights." Christian Century 101 (October 17, 1984) 951. Amnesty International protests imprisonment of Tibetan Buddhists and Catholic clergy.

618. China: Continued Patterns of Human Rights Violations. New York: Amnesty International, 1992. 20. Surveys human rights violations during the past three years: large-scale arbitrary arrests, long-term arbitrary detention, unfair trials, summary executions, torture, and killings of unarmed demonstrators.

619. "China Frees an Enigma." Time 101 (January 29, 1973) 42. Australian journalist Francis James was released after being imprisoned since 1969 accused of spying for the Soviet Union.

620. China: Prisoners of Conscience in the People's Republic of China. New York: Amnesty International, 1987. 37. Covers many topics: the many religious leaders who have been imprisoned since the 1950s, Catholics, Protestants, Tibetans, students, etc.

621. China : Punishment Without Crime: Administrative Detention. New York: Amnesty International, 1991. 62. Examines administrative detention under which hundreds of thousands of people are incarcerated each year in China, people held without charge or trial.

622. "China: Tiananmen Square Student Leader Tortured in Prison." Amnesty Action (Spring 1993) 2. Liu Gang, a student leader during the 1989 pro-democracy protests sentenced to six years in prison, may be in danger of his life. (Amnesty Action is full of current information on prisoners and abusive governments.).

623. China : Torture and Ill-Treatment of Prisoners. New York: Amnesty International, 1987. 46. "Torture and ill-treatment of prisoners is a persistent and widespread problem in China."

624. China: Trials and Punishments Since 1989. New York: Amnesty International, 1991. 55. The measures taken against political prisoners in China since 1989 fall far short of internationally agreed upon standards of fairness. Hundreds tried secretly, harsh sentencing, arbitrary arrest and detention without trial.

625. China: Violations of Human Rights. New York: Amnesty International, 1991. 17. Outlines the main violations reported during the past two years: mass arrests, long-term detention, unfair trials, summary executions, torture, killings.

626. "China Without Missionaries." America 94 (October 1, 1955) 8-9. Almost the last Catholic missionary has been released from prison and expelled from the country.

627. Coillie, Dries van. I Was Brainwashed in Peking. Hertogenbosch: Nederlandse Boekdruk, 1969. 320. This missionary was imprisoned three years 1951-1953 for organizing the Legion of Mary, a Catholic apostolic organization, in North China. This is his account of his struggle with his captors' efforts to persuade him to abandon his faith for theirs. Earlier Father Collie had suffered thirty months in a Japanese concentratioon camp.

628. "Communist Leniency." Time 67 (January 2, 1956) 34. Wilda and Homer Bradshaw, medical missionaries imprisoned since 1951, are released.

629. "Conspicuous Omission." New Republic 179 (December 23, 1978) 7-8. President Carter's list of the chief offenders of human rights omitted China.

630. "Continued Detention of U.S. Civilians by Communist China." United States Department of State Bulletin 33 (December 26, 1955) 1049-50. Despite a signed agreement of repatriation, China still holds U.S. citizens in prisons.

631. Continuing Religious Repression in China. New York: Human Rights Watch, 1993. 60. The escalation of repression of religious freedom in China in 1992 and 1993.

632. "Defying Death." Time 121 (February 7, 1983) 38. The death sentence of Mao's widow, Juang Qing, is commuted to life.

633. "Democracy Wall Prisoners Xu Wenli, Wei Jingsheng & Other Jailed Pioneers of the Chinese Pro-Democracy Movement." Human Rights Watch (March 1993) 51. They have been detained for thirteen years or more for alleged counterrevolutionary activities.

634. "Discussions Concerning Americans Detained in Communist China." United States Department of State Bulletin 30 (June 21, 1954) 949-50. China has acknowledged that "20 or 30" U.S. citizens are in prison in China and alleges that Chinese students have been mistreated in the U.S., a charge denied by the U.S.

635. Donnet, Pierre-Antoine. Tibet: Survival in Question. London: Zed, 1994. 256. On the devestating impact of Chinese occupation and colonization in Tibet including a destablized economy, assaults on Tibetan society and environment, and violations of human rights.

636. Donohue, J.W. "Citizens of the Celestial Kingdom." America 152 (February 23, 1985) 141-4. On the memoir of Jesuit priest Francis Xavier Chu Shu-Teh, who died in prison in 1983 after being incarcerated almost continuously since 1953.

637. Dorfman, Ron. "Wei Jingsheng, the Forgotten Man." Progressive 50 (October 1986) 30. Jingsheng was imprisoned for his essays promoting democratic reform; notes the lack of attention paid to human-rights questions in China by U.S. activists.

638. Economic Reform, Political Repression: Arrests of Dissidents in China Since Mid-1992. New York: Human Rights Watch, 1993. 28. Deng Xiaoping toured southern China speaking of the new economic reform and its blessings while political dissenters were arrested and detained all over the country in 1992.

639. Elliot, L. "Li Shuang and Emmanuel: A Love Story." Reader's Digest 129 (August 1986) 169-172. Persecution of Li Shuang for her relationship with Frenchman Emmanuel Bellefroid.

640. "End of the Ordeal." Time 94 (October 24, 1969) 59+. Anthony Grey, released from house arrest after twenty-six months, tells of his ordeal.

641. Evading Scrutiny: Violations of Human Rights After the Closing of Tibet: Supplement to the Asia Watch Report on Human Rights in Tibet. Washington, D.C.: Asia Watch, 1988. 55. Further evidence of severe abuses.

642. "Failure of Chinese Communists to Release Imprisoned Americans." U.S. Department of State Bulletin 36 (February 18, 1957) 261-63. Ten U.S. citizens are still imprisoned in China.

643. "First China Dissident." National Review 31 (May 25, 1979) 665. On the arrest of Wei Jeng-sheng for exposing wretched prison conditions, charging him with "counterrevolution," punishable by death.

644. "Flies and Freedom." Newsweek 44 (September 27, 1954) 67. Applegate and Dixon released.

645. "Forgotten Captives." Newsweek 42 (October 5, 1953) 56. On journalists Richard Applegate and Don Dixon in prison and little international protest.

646. Gordon, Eric. Freedom is a Word. London: Hodder and Stoughton, 1971. 351. This British journalist and his family were arrested as they were leaving the country with his notes on the cultural revolution. They were released two years later (1969) after he wrote a confession of his "crimes."

647. Greene, Robert, Fr. Calvary in China. New York: Putnam; Maryknoll, NY: Maryknoll, 1953. 244. Imprisoned in 1949, trials culminating in a sentence to death by beheading, sentence commuted to expulsion from the country in 1952.

648. Grey, Anthony. Hostage in Peking. London: Joseph, 1970. 343. (pbk: London: Weidenfeld, 1988). An account of his 26 months in prison.

649. Harbert, Mary Ann. Captivity: An Extraordinary Account of Imprisonment and Survival in the People's Republic of China. New York: Delacorte, 1973. 316. (Captivity: 44 Months in Red China. London: Joseph, 1974. 272.). Describes her lost years in prison 1968-1971, after being arrested while sailing off the coast of China with a friend and accused of spying.

650. "Higher Ransom for Americans." U.S. News and World Report 37 (December 24, 1954) 49-50. In China and in Eastern Europe release of imprisoned U.S. citizens has a price-- e.g., unfreezing Chinese assets in the U.S.

651. Hostage in Peking: An Interview with Anthony Grey. Culver City, CA: Social Studies School Service, 1971. Tape reel, 28 min. Interview with journalist and author of Hostage in Peking concerning his solitary confinement (ordered by Mao Tse-Tung and enacted by the Red Guard) for 26 months beginning August 18, 1967.

652. Human Rights in Tibet. Washington, New York: Asia Watch, 1988. 74. On general discrimination against Tibetans, deplorable conditions of arrest and imprisonment, and individual cases.

653. I Saw Him in the Ricefield. Maryknoll, NY: Maryknoll World Productions, 1982. 19 min. film. Story of Bishop James E. Walsh, one of the first Catholic U.S. missionaries to arrive in China and the last to leave after his release from prison in 1970.

654. If the Grain of Wheat Dies--: Fr. Francis Xavier Chu Shu-Teh, S.J. s.l.: s.n., 1984. 108. First arrested in 1953, sentenced to twenty years imprisonment in 1960 and again to twelve years in 1983, Shuh-Teh died in prison.

655. "In a Peking Prison." Newsweek 45 (January 17, 1955) 81-2. On three Fulbright scholars in prison.

656. Jones, Sidney R. "Anthems of Defeat: Asia Watch Details Detention and Torture of Pro-Democracy Activists in Hunan." Human Rights Watch 10 (Summer 1992) 9. Summarizes Anthems of Defeat: Crackdown in Hunan Province 1989-92, the story of the imprisonment of one of the founders of the Hunan Students Autonomous Federation, Tang Boqiao, and the great number of prisoners, the harsh prison conditions, and the threat of re-imprisonment following release.

657. Jones, Sidney R. "Dramatic New Report Unveils the Extent of the Crackdown in China and Sparks Strong Response." Human Rights Watch 10 (Fall 1992) 2. Reports the repression in Hunan province. About 600 pro-democracy advocates were in the 142 detention prisons at the end of 1990.

658. Jiang, Yang. Six Chapters From My Life "Downunder." Seattle; Hong Kong: U of Washington P; Chinese UP, 1984. 111. During Mao's Cultural Revolution, the author (pen name of Yang Jikang) was transferred from the university position he occupied to a cadre school in 1969.

659. Korchari, Abas. Escape from Hell. New York: Vantage, 1971. 157. The author (Chinese name Jen Shan-hsueh), a university teacher, recounts the communist repression during its early years, including his own imprisonment.

660. Kristof, Nicholas D. "Escape From Tiananmen Square." New York Times Magazine (May 5, 1991) 28-31+. Liu Xiang was arrested in connection with Tiananmen Square but managed to escape to New York.

661. Lai, Ying. The Thiry-Sixth Way: A Personal Account of Imprisonment and Escape from Red China. Tr., adapted, and ed. Eduard Behrand Sydney Liu. Garden City, NY: Doubleday, 1969. Sentenced to prison as a Catholic counterrevolutionary from 1958-1963, leaving China in 1966.

662. "Leniency for Madame Mao." Newsweek 101 (February 7, 1983) 29. Jiang Qing's death sentence commuted to life in prison.

663. Li, Fu-jen, and Peng Shu-tse. Revolutionaries in Mao's Prisons: The Case of the Chinese Trotskyites. New York: Pathfinder, 1974. 23. On the imprisonment of the socialist democrats by the regime of Stalinist Mao Tse-tung masquerading as a people's democracy.

664. Lifton, Robert. "Thought Reform of Chinese Intellectuals, a Psychiatric Evaluation." Journal of Asian Studies 16.1 (1956) 75-88. Also see "Thought Reform of Western Civilians in Chinese Communist Prisons." Psychiatry 19 (1956) 173-195. Based upon interviews of twenty-five Westerners and fifteen Chinese who had been compelled to attend a "revolutionary college" course organized to produce symbolic death and rebirth in the students.

665. Lok, Po. "Pair of State-Crossed Lovers." Maclean's 94 (November 23, 1981) 44. Li Shuang is arrested for "'debauchery' and for living illegally in a foreigner's quarters." She is engaged to marry French diplomat Emmanuel Bellefroid.

666. "Marathon in Geneva." Newsweek 47 (June 25, 1956) 49. Negotiations over release of prisoners.

667. Memorandum Submitted To the Government of the Republic of China. London: The Secretariat, 1978. 7. Criticizes the number of prisoners, especially those who are long-term, and prison conditions.

668. O'Hare, J.A. "Of Many Things." America 148 (May 14, 1983) inside cover. Four elderly Jesuit priests sentenced to long terms in prison. All four had earlier served even longer prison terms.

669. "Out of Darkness." Newsweek 46 (September 26, 1955) 48. Laurence Buol and others released.

670. "Over 30 Chinese Dissidents Arrested Since Late May." Arkansas Democrat-Gazette (July 13, 1992) 7A. Crackdowns against young intellectual reformers at universities.

671. "Over the Bridge." Time 64 (September 27, 1954) 74+. Three U.S. citizens, imprisoned 18 months for intruding into China's territorial waters, are released.

672. "Peking Frees 110,000 Political Prisoners." Militant 42.25 (June 30, 1978) 21. It is speculated that the prisoners have technical skills needed by the government. Most of the prisoners were victims of the crackdown that followed the Hundred Flowers campaign.

673. Peng, Yinhan and Charles Corwin. Return of a Chinese Patriot. S.l.: TEC China Studies Program, 1989. 208. A leading scholar of Japanese language, Taiwan-born and Japanese-educated Peng was imprisoned for 20 years because of a virulent outbreak of xenophobia, bigotry, fanaticism, and fear that resulted in Mao's catastrophic Great Leap Forward. Peng's narrative is intercalated with Corwin's explanatory commentaries and notes.

674. People's Republic of China: Preliminary Findings on Killings of Unarmed Civilians, Arbitrary Arrests, and Summary Executions Since June 3, 1989. New York: Amnesty International, 1989. 48. Between June 3 and 9 at least one thousand civilians were killed and several thousand wounded in Beijing and many thousands more in other cities, for pro-democracy demonstrations. Incommunicado detention and unfair trials of many thousands more ensued. Selected prisoner profiles and details of the killings.

675. People's Republic of China: Tibet Autonomous Region: Compilation Document. New York: Amnesty International U.S.A., 1990. Various pagings. Contains three reports: "China: Detention without Trial, Ill-treatment of detainees and Police Shooting of Civilians in Tibet" (Feb. 1988), "People's Republic of China: Torture and Ill-treatment in Detention of Tibetans" (Feb. 1989), and "People's Republic of China (Tibet Autonomous Region): One Year Under Martial Law, an Update on the Human Rights Situation" (March 1990).

676. The People's Republic of China: Torture and Ill-Treatment of Prisoners. New York: Amnesty International, 1987. Describes where, when, and why prisoners have been tortured and ill-treated in China in recent years.

677. Political Imprisonment in the People's Republic of China. London: Amnesty International, 1978. 171. Examines the legal system, penal policies, prison conditions, prison locations, and releases. Four individual cases are highlighted. Index.

678. Political Prisoners in Tibet. New York: Asia Watch (Human Rights Watch), 1992. 71. Contains three new lists of prisoners in the Tibet Autonomous Region, compiled between August and November 1991, confirming 360 cases known by name. Emphasizes the incompleteness of the report, some areas and prisons unreported.

679. "Present From Chou; Release of Richard Fecteau and Mary Ann Harbert." Newsweek 78 (December 27, 1971) 25-6. Mary Ann Harbert, picked up from a private yacht, and a CIA agent, Richard Fecteau, are released.

680. "Prison Release--and After." Time 66 (September 19, 1955) 22. China will release 41 in return for free inquiry into status of Chinese in the U.S. who wish to return home.

681. Qing, Liu. "Voice from Peking's Gulag." Time 118 (September 21, 1981) 35. A dissenter jailed without trial describes his ordeal.

682. "Red China's Policy: Hold Americans for Ransom." U.S. News and World Report 37 (December 3, 1954) 26-8. Some U.S. citizens are "unwilling prisoners or hostages," and four have died.

683. "Red China's Revenge." Time 91 (March 22, 1968) 67. Reuters' man in Peking, Anthony Grey, is under house arrest in retaliation for Britain's arresting a Chinese newsman in Hong Kong.

684. Religious Prisoners of Conscience, the People's Republic of China. New York: Amnesty International, 1987. 21. Many religious leaders have been imprisoned since the 1950s for exercising their right to freedom of religion.

685. Rickett, Allyn, and Adele Rickett. Prisoners of Liberation: Four Years in a Chinese Communist Prison. New York: Cameron Associates, 1957; rpt., Garden City, NY: Anchor\Doubleday, 1973. 344. These Fulbright students were imprisoned as spies after the outbreak of hostilities between China and the U.S. during the Korean War, and not released until 1955.

686. Rittenberg, Sidney, and Amanda Bennett. The Man Who Stayed Behind. New York: Simon and Schuster, 1993. Rittenberg, a U.S. citizen of who joined the Communists, was imprisoned in 1949 for espionage, released with apologies in 1955, and imprisoned again in 1968 for nearly ten more years.

687. Rogal, K. "'Killing the Chicken to Scare the Monkeys.'" Newsweek 101 (May 30, 1983) 76. Luo Chengxun sentenced to ten years in prison for spying for the U.S.

688. Schein, Edgar, et al. Coercive Persuasion: A Socio-psychological Analysis of the "Brainwashing" of American Civilian Prisoners by the Chinese Communists. New York: Norton, 1961. 320. Analyses the intensive indoctrination program employed to produce collaboration by a small number of U.S. civilians imprisoned between 1950 and 1956.

689. "Seventy Americans for Sixty Chinese?" U.S. News and World Report 36 (June 11, 1954) 50. The thirty-two U.S. citizens that are in Chinese jails may be swapped for Chinese in the U.S. denied exit visas.

690. "Sitting down with the Reds." Time 63 (June 28, 1954) 31-32. Negotiations over the possibly 83 U.S. citizens imprisoned or detained and the Chinese students allegedly detained in the U.S.

691. Summary of "Political Imprisonment in the People's Republic of China." London: Amnesty International, 1978. 27. Describes "the major aspects of political imprisonment"-- laws, judicial process, and political conditions. Denounces mass arrests, detention without trial, and other violations.

692. Tibet: Compilation Document: 1988-1992. New York: Amnesty International, 1991. 65. These documents focus on the death of a 20 year old prisoner of conscience while in custody; the execution of two prisoners after an alleged escape attempt; new information about solitary confinement; the beating of prisoners, etc.

693. Tibet (People's Republic of China): Repression in Tibet 1987-1992. New York: Amnesty International, 1992. 60. Human rights violations against members of the Tibetan minority in the PRC includes arbitrary arrests, torture and ill-treatment of detainees, long term detention of Prisoners of Conscience, and killings of unarmed demonstrators.

694. Tz'ong, Mi. "Trial of a Counterrevolutionary." Dissent 25.3 (Summer 1978) 261-269. The story leading up to the trial of Teng K'ing-hsan, who was convicted for speaking out against Chairman Mao; he was sentenced to be executed, a punishment later reduced to 15 years imprisonment.

695. "U.S., Red China Announce Measures for Return of Civilians." U.S. Department of State Bulletin 33 (September 19, 1955) 456-7. Mutual agreement to allow all citizens of the other country to return home. U.S. citizens in Chinese prisons are listed.

696. Vaughn, Ellen Santilli. "The Resolve to Resist." Christianity Today 32 (May 13, 1988) 16-21. Nien Cheng tells of her experiences in prison and how her faith in God helped her survive.

697. "War Criminals Released But Trotskyists are still in Mao's Jails." Militant 39.14 (April 18, 1975) 22. Questions the humanity of the decision to release "the blood-stained lieutenants of Chiang Kai-shek and Japanese imperialism" while the 200+ Trotskyists imprisoned twenty-two years before, many of whom were imprisoned under the previous regime, remain in prison without indictment or trial.

698. Watt, George. China "Spy." London: Johnson, 1972. 208; Glendale, CA: Diane, 1973. 157. The author, an engineer working for a British company in China, was convicted of espionage and sentenced in 1968 to three years in prison on no evidence whatever and incommunicado during detention and trial.

699. "What It's Like to be a Captive of Red Chinese." U.S. News World Report 39 (November 11, 1955) 58-63. An account by Rev. Harold Rigney, formerly rector of Peiking's Catholic University, imprisoned fifty months.

700. Willey, Fay. "China: Torture in 'Virtue Forest.'" Newsweek 93 (May 21, 1979) 44. Inhumane treatment continues in the former Maoist prison.

701. "The Witness of Bishop Gong." America 153 (July 27, 1985) 22-3. Bishop Ignatius Gong Pinmei freed at age 84 after being in prison since 1955.

702. Wu, Hongda Harry. Laogai, the Chinese Gulag. Trans. Ted Slingerland. Boulder: Westview, 1991. 247. China has no human rights records because both the words and investigation of the facts are forbidden: perhaps as many as 500,000 persons were punished in some way during the 1957 anti-rightist cultural revolution. The Beijing massacre of 1989 is only the tip of the iceberg. At least 990 labor reform camps exist in China; the populations of three of these camps are known to range between 50,000 to 80,000, of which about 10 percent are counter-revolutionary prisoners, the synonym for political prisoners in Chinese.

703. Wu, Hongda Harry and Carolyn Wakeman. Bitter Winds: A Memoir of My Years in China's Gulag. New York: Wiley, 1993. Wu tells the story of his triumph over degradations in Chinese labor camps and of his infiltrations of the camps years later, at grave risk of imprisonment, to show the world the horrors that still exist today.

704. WuDunn, Sheryl. "The Prisoners of Tiananmen Square." New York Times Magazine (April 8, 1990) 28-30+. A look at the Qinchens prison, where at least 200 political prisoners are held; it is suspected that those associated with Tiananmen square are also there.

705. Wu-ming-shih, pseud. The Scourge of the Sea : A True Account of My Experience in the Hsia-sa Village Concentration Camp. Taipei, Taiwan, R.O.C.: Compilation Dept., Kuang Lu Pub. Service, 1985. 118. Considered to be among the most important writers of fiction in China today, Pu Nai-fu, alias Pu Ning, was one of thousands arrested in Mao Tse-tung's Cultural Revolution that began in 1958.

706. Xu Wenli. "My Self-Defence." Index On Censorship 15.5 (May 1986) 18-25. Extracts from a 262-page manuscript, My Self-Defence, by Xu Wenli, former editor of the April Fifth Forum, who was sentenced in 1981 to 15 years imprisonment for counterrevolutionary activities.

707. "Yang Wei." Index On Censorship 17.6 (June 1988) 8. Wei, a Shanghai student, was sentenced to 2 years imprisonment in December 1987 for "counterrevolutionary propaganda and agitation."

708. Ying, Lai. The Thirty-sixth Way: A Personal Account of Imprisonment and Escape form Red China. Trans. and Ed. Edward Behr and Sydney Liu. London: Constable, 1969; 1970; Garden City, NY: Doubleday, 204. Before her escape to Macao in 1966, the author spent five years in jail and labor camps in and around Canton beginning in 1958.

CHINA, REPUBLIC OF (*see* TAIWAN)

COLOMBIA

709. Amnesty International Report 1980. London: Amnesty International, 1980. 122-125. Continued abuse of rights by state of siege laws (in force since 1949), military tribunals and unfair trials, arbitrary arrest and detention, and torture. Prisoners were systematically tortured in at least 33 military institutions.

710. Amnesty International Report 1990. New York: Amnesty International USA, 1990. 69-72. Many hundreds were killed extrajudicially; scores of people disappeared after detention; para-military organizations continued their degradations; torture and ill-treatment were reported; military courts failed to prosecute human rights violators; civilian judicial officials were killed by armed forces and paramilitary, which have close ties.

711. Colombia. New York: Amnesty International USA, 1988. 3. The Colombian armed forces have adopted a policy of terror, designed to intimidate and eliminate opponents without recourse to law, including disappearances and murder. Whole sectors of society are at risk of being considered "subversive," and in Colombia that is tantamount to a death sentence.

712. Colombia. New York: Amnesty International, 1988. 16. Describes the armed forces "policy of terror" to "intimidate and eliminate opponents without recourse to law." Over one thousand political killings occurred in 1987.

713. Colombia: Briefing. New York: Amnesty International, 1988. 18. Focuses on political killings, disappearances, torture and the activities of the clandestine death squads in Colombia.

714. "Colombian Regime Steps Up Repression." Militant 43.11 (March 23, 1979) 8. Arrests of socialists continue daily.

715. Frankel, David. "Colombia: Trotskyist Leader in Danger." Militant 43.15 (April 20, 1979) 10. Libardo González, leader of the Revolutionary Socialist Party, is being held incommunicado, and Gloria Stella Gallego of the Socialist Workers Party also.

716. "Free Gonzalez and Gallego." Militant 43.16 (April 27, 1979) 2. On the government's campaign to repress the labor movement.

COMOROS

717. Amnesty International Report 1980. London: Amnesty International, 1980. 39-40. Forty-three leaders of the government have been held without trial since President Abdallah came to power in 1978, and some students protesters have been jailed more recently.

718. Amnesty International Report 1990. New York: Amnesty International, 1990. 72-3. After the Head of State was assassinated and the foreign mercenaries who supported him left the country, over 70 political prisoners were released in December 1989, some long-term, but some 25 prisoners were unaccounted for.

CONGO

719. Amnesty International Report 1980. London: Amnesty International, 1980. 40-41. In 1979 amnesty was granted to prisoners held since 1977 and 1978 for alleged conspiracy. But the former President is being held without trial.

720. Amnesty International Report 1990. New York: Amnesty International, 1990. 73-4. Some opponents of the government were released in 1989, but others held without trial continued confined.

721. Reed, David. 111 Days in Stanleyville. New York: Harper and Row, 1965. 279. The story of the Simba rebellion in 1964 in which U.S. citizens were confined and some murdered.

COSTA RICA

722. Weissburg, Arnold. "Campaign Set to Free Costa Rican Prisoners." Militant 41.48 (December 23, 1977). Eight people were arrested for demonstrating for better housing.

CÔTE D'IVOIRE (IVORY COAST)

723. Amnesty International Report 1980. London: Amnesty International, 1980. 52. A dozen protesting students were conscripted and treated harshly.

724. Amnesty International Report 1990. New York: Amnesty International, 1990. 75. Five opponents of the government were detained and some expelled from the country. Another opponent was sentenced to 20 years in prison on criminal charges in an unfair trial.

CROATIA

725. Dedijer, Vladimir. The Yugoslav Auschwitz and the Vatican. Buffalo, NY: Prometheus, 1992. 375. An account of the concentration camp in Jasenovic during WWII and its support by the Catholic Church.

CUBA

726. Amnesty International 1980. London: Amnesty International, 1980. 126-29. Some 3,600 prisoners of all kinds were released in 1979, including many political prisoners, but harassment, harsh prison conditions, and summary trials continue, and perhaps 250 long-term political prisoners are still held.

727. Amnesty International 1990. New York: Amnesty International, 1990. 75-8. At least 60 critics of the government were arrested in 1989 and at least 33 of them remain in custody after unfair trials. Some had been detained at length without charge or legal advice. Release of long-term prisoners continued.

728. Brecher, John, et al. "Gift Horse from Fidel Castro." Newsweek 96 (October 27, 1980) 74,77. Diverse U.S. prisoners released.

729. Brown, Charles J. The Politics of Psychiatry in Revolutionary Cuba. Washington, D.C.: Freedom House of Human Rights, 1991. 217. On psychiatric abuse, containing case histories. Biblio. and Index.

730. Camejo, Mary Jane. "Cuba's Civil Society Besieged: Dissent Persists Despite Prohibitions." Human Rights Watch 10.1 (Winter 1992) 4. On the arrest of Maria Elena Cruz and other advocates of democracy.

731. "Castro and his 3,000 prisoners." U.S. News and World Report 85 (December 4, 1978) 12. Castro to allow 3,000 political prisoners to leave Cuba.

732. Cisneros, Evangelina. The Story of Evangelina Cisneros (Evangelina Betancourt Cosio y Cisneros). New York: Continental, 1985. 257. Memoir of her imprisonment and rescue.

733. Conaway, Janelle. "A Pastor Describes Brutal Conditions in Cuban Prisons." Christianity Today 28 (August 10, 1984) 61-62. Nobel Alexander was held 22 years "for preaching the gospel," released when Rev. Jessie Jackson visited.

734. Copa, Victorio M. "Cuba: Fidel Castro Statements." Direct From Cuba 98 (December 1, 1978) 1. Castro's program to release 3,000 "counterrevolutionary" political prisoners depends on the readiness of the U.S. government to issue entry permits.

735. Copa, Victorio M. "Cuba: Situation of Prisoners." Direct From Cuba 2.20 (October 30, 1979) 4-5. Despite U.S. encouragement and aid in conducting counterrevolutionary action against Cuba, political prisoners' efforts to enter the U.S. are hampered by dilatory procedures for issuing visas.

736. Cuba : Political Imprisonment : An Update. New York: Amnesty International, 1988. 7. Updates earlier reports regarding the number of prisoners, long-term prisoners, plantados, and individual cases.

737. Cuba: Recent Developments Affecting the Situation of Political Prisoners and the Use of the Death Penalty. New York: Amnesty International, 1988. 37(unpaged). A report of AI's Secretary General's visit to Cuba in March 1988. Surveys AI's concerns regarding detention and trial procedures, ill treatment of prisoners, and the death penalty. Recent legislation has led to improved guarantees for political prisoners--reduced death sentences and executions, and the release of 15,000 prisoners, down to less than 500.

738. Cuban Political Prisoners: Hearing before the Subcommittee on Human Rights and International Organizations of the Committee on Foreign Affairs, House of Representatives, Ninety-ninth Congress, second session, September 24, 1986. Washington: GPO, 1987. 107. Testimony from a former prisoner, representatives of the State Dept., Americas Watch, and AI.

739. "Deliverance." Time 120 (November 1, 1982) 57. Release of Cuban poet A. Valladares through French intervention.

740. Farber, Samuel. "Socialist Dissident in a Cuban Prison." Changes Socialist Journal 7.3 (March 1985) 8. Ariel Hidalgo, a Cuban revolutionary writer, Marxist, and vocal activist who "concluded that what existed in Cuba was a far cry from what Marx and Engels had in mind" was arrested and sentenced to eight years in 1980 for his beliefs.

741. Feldman, F. "Why Capitalist Press Parade Matos." Militant 43.43 (November 9, 1979) 6. Huber Matos, counterrevolutionist, is released from jail.

742. Fite, Clifton E. In Castro's Clutches. Chicago. Moody, 1969. 158. The story of the imprisonment on charges of espionage of two Southern Baptist missionaries--David Fite and Dr. Herbert Caudill.

743. "Free Cuban Human Rights Activists!" Against the Current 23 (November 1989) 5. The president of the Cuban Commission of Human Rights and two others are being tried on the charge of "disseminating false news." Also, the leader of a group of Green-Pacifist activists was arrested.

744. Fuller, Elaine. "Human Rights in Cuba." CubaTimes 4.4 (May 1984) 1. A comparative assessment of the U.S. State Department's Country Reports on Cuba, 1979 and 1983: it is a political "tool" used to attack political enemies.

745. Genet, Harry. "Bible Smuggling Comes Home to Roost." Christianity Today 23 (September 7, 1979) 75. When their plane crashed just outside of Montego Bay, Tom White, Michael Wurmbrand, and Melvin Bailey (the pilot) were arrested by Cuban officials and charged with "illegal entry and dissemination of anti-state propaganda."

746. Greenfield, Charles. "Inside Cuba's Jails." Maclean's 96 (November 7, 1983) 12-13. Interview with Armando Valladares, a Cuban poet who spent 22 years in jail on charges of counter-revolutionary activity."

747. A Haggard Poet Scales the Rainbow." Newsweek 100 (November 1, 1982) 55. Armando Valladares released.

748. Hammarberg, Thomas, and Roger Plant, eds. Memorandum Submitted to the Government of the Republic of Cuba. London: Amnesty International, 1978. 7. Especially concerned over the many extremely long-term prisoners and the harsh treatment of some prisoners and released prisoners.

749. Hildalgo, Ariel. "The Sin of Thinking." Index On Censorship 18.3 (March 1989) 18-19. Ariel Hidalgo, a Cuban academic and writer, was arrested in 1981, charged under article 108-1 of the Cuban Penal Code ("Enemy Propaganda"), and sentenced to eight years imprisonment.

750. In A Place Without a Soul : The Testimony of Former Cuban Political Prisoners. Washington, D.C.: U.S. Information Agency, 1989. 56. Twenty three testimonies.

751. Inside Cuba with Richard Whitcomb. Videocassette, 81 min. Nar. Richard Whitcomb. WCKT-TV News Special, Miami (3 Jan. 1978-13 Feb. 1978). Social, economic, and political report.

752. Inter-American Commission on Human Rights. Report on the Situation of Political Prisoners and their Relatives in Cuba. Washington D.C.: Pan American Union, 1963. Focus on mistreatment in prison, with one chapter on women.

753. Inter-American Commission on Human Rights. Second Report on the Situation of Political Prisoners and Their Relatives in Cuba. Washington, DC: General Secretariat of the Organization of American States, 1970. 45. On the gap between legal rights and actual treatment of prisoners and their relatives.

754. Inter-American Commission on Human Rights. Fifth Report on the Situation of Human Rights in Cuba. Washington D.C.: General Secretariat of the Organization of American States, 1976. 94. Summarizes the many violations of human rights--unfair trials, torture, etc. Over 300 political prisoners are named.

755. Inter-American Commission on Human Rights. Sixth Report on the Situation of Political Prisoners in Cuba. Washington D.C.: General Secretariat, Organization of American States, 1979. 39. On prison conditions, individual cases, etc.

756. Joe, Barbara. "Breaking the Silence." Commonweal 112 (February 22, 1985) 114-15. Testimony of 26 prisoners released through efforts of Jesse Jackson.

757. Levi, Jeffrey. "Political Prisoners in Cuba." Dissent 25.3 (Summer 1978) 283-85. Story of Pierre Golendorf's experiences in Cuba--falsely arrested in 1969 for being a CIA agent, and then held for 38 months, six of which were solitary confinement leading up to the trial.

758. Lippert, Ronald P. Ten Years/Ten Days: A True Story of Life and Death in Cuban Prisons, Counter Revolution, and Nicaragua. New York: Vantage, 1988. 200. A Canadian caught working for the anti-Castro underground (flying in arms and explosives) spent ten years in prison.

759. Lunt, Lawrence K. Leave Me My Spirit. Tempe, AZ: Affiliated Writers of America, 1990. 277. Lunt, an American in Cuba arrested as a CIA agent and imprisoned from 1965 to 1979, exposes the brutality of Castro's labor camps.

760. Medina, Reinaldo. The Gospel Behind Bars. Miami, FL: J. Flores, 1991. 290. The author, a Baptist minister, spent 13 years in Castro's prisons beginning in 1965, accused of plotting the overthrow of the government.

761. Mencia, Mario. Time was on Our Side. La Habana: Editora Politica, 1982. 281. On the struggle Fidel Castro waged while in prison following his capture after the attack on Batista's Moncada Garrison. How Fidel "in solitary, conceived, prepared and organized the elements that enabled him to go on to create the 26th of July movement."

762. Montane, Oropesa Jesus. "There is Honor in Being in Prison." Granma 10.21 (May 25, 1975) 5. On revolutionary activities by Fidel Castro and his comrades while in prison.

763. Neier, Aryeh. "Cuba: The Human Rights Show." New York Review of Books 36 (June 15, 1969) 33-5. On Castro's suppression of human rights dissidents.

764. Nelson, A. "Politics of Political Prisoners." Nation 227 (December 9, 1978) 629-30. On the slow process the U.S. has improvised for admitting political prisoners Castro has offered to free.

765. Of Human Rights. Washington D.C.: Of Human Rights Inc., 1977. Semiannual. The first two volumes of this magazine supports Cuban political prisoners.

766. Peerman, Dean. "Twenty-two Years in Castro's Prisons." Christian Century 104 (November 18, 1987) 1029-33. Review of Against All Hope by Armando Valladores.

767. "Perfecting" the System of Control: Human Rights Violations in Castro's 34th Year. New York: Human Rights Watch, 1993. 26. Amidst all of the economic and political problems in Cuba, the government feels even more compelled to retain power by violence.

768. Pierce, K.M. "A Mixed Bag from Fidel's Jails." Time 124 (July 9, 1984) 11. Jesse Jackson brought back 48 prisoners from Havana, 26 of them political--calling themselves plantados, planted firmly in opposition to Castro.

769. Platt, T. "Cuba and the Politics of Human Rights." Social Justice 15.2 (Summer 1988) 38-54. The article focuses on human rights abuses in Cuba, the number of political prisoners, and U.S. government reactions.

770. Political Imprisonment in Cuba. New York: Amnesty International, 1986. 23. On prison conditions. Individual prisoners described.

771. Political Imprisonment in Cuba : A Special Report From Amnesty International. Washington, D.C.: Cuban-American National Foundation, 1987. 36. Examines prison conditions of the main prisons, assesses the kinds of prisoners of conscience, describes several prisoners, trial procedures, and other information.

772. The Political Prisoners in Cuba : 1981 report. Washington, D.C.: Of Human Rights, 1982. Describes several prisons and gives details on 294 prisoners.

773. Prepared Statement of Amnesty International USA on the Human Rights Situation in Cuba. New York: Amnesty International, 1984. 7. Report to Congressional Committees.

774. Reed, David. "Man Who Defied Castro." Reader's Digest 116 (April 1980) 117-122. Unbroken by 20 years in prisons, "Huber Matos remains a symbol of principled resistance against dictatorship."

775. Ring, Harry. "Political Prisoner 'Report' on Cuba Is Anticommunist Fraud." Militant 47.39 (October 1983) 14-15. Analyzes an Americas Watch report.

776. Rodriguez Quesada, Carlos. David Salvador, Castro's Prisoner. New York: Labor Committee to Release Imprisoned Trade Unionists and Democratic Socialists, 1961. 23. On the imprisonment without trial of the elected leader of Cuba's trade unions.

777. Shamma, Geraldine. Cuban-American Spy for Freedom : the Story of Geraldine Shamma. As told to Virginia Lee Turney. New York: Vantage, 1982. 105. Imprisoned for counterrevolutionary work aided by U.S. intelligence forces against Castro.

778. Shorris, Earl. "Imaginary Persons, Imaginary Prisons." Nation 243 (December 20, 1986.) 708-14. On the prison memoirs of Armando Valladares Perez.

779. Spring, Beth. "Christianity Today Talks to Armanda Valladares." Christianity Today 30 (November 21, 1986) 41. Valladares tells her that "there are thousands of political prisoners in Cuba who are subject to inhumane torture."

780. Trantmann, E. "Cuban Poet Freed After 22 Years." Matchbox (February 1983) 1. Armando F. Valladares Pérez was released from prison in 1982. He had been adopted as a prisoner of conscience by Amnesty International.

781. Valdés, Mia. "Double Standard for Human Rights." Progressive 56 (August 1992) 20-21. The much more brutal Guatemalan regime was criticized less severely than the less offending Cuba by the U.N. Human Rights Commission.

782. Valladares, Armando. Against All Hope: The Prison Memoirs of Armando Valladares. Trans. Andrew Hurley. New York: Knopf, 1987. 380; Sevenoaks: Coronet, 1987. 544. Account of his 22 years in Castro's prisons until his release in 1982.

783. Valladares, Armando. Against All Hope. Audiocassette. Read by Christopher Hurt. Ashland, Oregon: Classics on Tape, 1989. 12 audiocassettes. (See Valladares' Against All Hope: The Prison Memoirs of Armando Valladares.)

784. Valladares, Armando. "Inside Castro's Prisons." Time 122 (August 15, 1983) 20-2. Account of his 22 years of imprisonment for criticizing Castro's pro-Soviet policies.

785. Valls, Jorge. Twenty Years and Forty Days: Life in a Cuban Prison. New York: Americas Watch, 1986. 125. Imprisoned both by Batista and Castro, the latter for 20 years. He describes all aspects of prison life.

786. Wallance, Gregory. The Treatment of Political Prisoners in Cuba and the American Response. New York: Americas Watch Committee, 1983. 51. Criticizes the repression in Cuba--at least 250 long-term prisoners, over 1000 former prisoners languishing as pariahs.

787. "Why Castro Plays Good Neighbor." U.S. News and World Report 89 (October 27, 1980) 14. Castro frees 33 U.S. citizens jailed in Cuba.

788. Will, G.F. "Not Your Basic Beach Book." Newsweek 108 (July 7, 1986) 68. On Armando Valladores's Against All Hope, a memoir of twenty-two years in prison.

CYPRUS

789. Amnesty International 1980. London: Amnesty International, 1980. 260. People are still missing since the hostilities of 1974.

790. Amnesty International 1990. New York: Amnesty International, 1990. 78-9. Two conscience objectors to military service were imprisoned, no alternative service allowed.

791. Penintaex, George. "A Question of Conscience." Cyprus View 6 (July 1992) 12-13. A new law ends imprisonment of religious and conscientious objectors to military service.

CZECHOSLOVAKIA

792. "Act of Artistic Unfreedom." Time 133 (March 6, 1989) 45. Václav Havel and eight other dissidents are arrested while laying flowers in memory of Jan Palach.

793. Amnesty International Report 1980. London: Amnesty International, 1980. 260-64. Mistreatment of political dissenters is widespread: abuse by police, arbitrary detention, unfair trials, and harsh prison conditions. The Committee for the Defence of the Unjustly Persecuted and others were imprisoned for subversion. Roman Catholic priests and laity have been widely harassed.

794. Amnesty International Report 1990. New York: Amnesty International, 1990. 79-81. All known prisoners of conscience were released and charges against others dropped in 1989. One conscientious objector against military service was imprisoned. Many reports of ill-treatment by police during arrest and detention.

795. Bugajski, Janusz. Czechoslovakia: Charter 77's Decade of Dissent. The Washington Papers No.125. New York: Prager; London: Center For Strategic and International Studies, 1987. 118. On the history of the Charter 77 campaign, surviving official attempts to imprison all vocal opposition, intimidation, harassment and other persecutions.

796. Chelmiwski, Rudolph. "In the Hands of God." Reader's Digest 133 (September 1988) 154-158. The author was imprisoned in a psychiatric hospital for campaigning for religous freedom.

797. Czechoslovakia: Amnesty International Briefing. 2nd edition. London: Amnesty International, 1981. 17. (1st ed. 1977, 16). Focuses on imprisonment for exercising human rights, unfair trials, harsh prison conditions, and death penalty.

798. "A Debased Judiciary." East European Reporter 3.3 (Fall 1988) 14. About the persecution of Pavel Wonka, who died in prison.

799. "Freedom for Czech Political Prisoners: Two Documents." Critique 7 (Winter 1976) 106. A letter from fifteen former Czech political prisoners to the grieving relatives of dissidents still imprisoned, testifying to the inhuman conditions of Czech prisons.

800. Glusman, J.A. "Jazz Leaders Face Trial in Czechoslovakia." Rolling Stone (April 9, 1987) 16. On the persecution of seven members of the Jazz Section of the Czech Musicians' Union by arrest on a trumped up charge of "unauthorized business activities."

801. Havel, Václav. Disturbing the Peace : A Conversation with Karel Hvízdala. New York: Knopf, 1991. 256. Chapter 4, "Public Enemy," discusses his prison experiences.

802. Havel, Václav. Letters to Olga: June 1979-September 1982. Trans. Paul Wilson. New York: Holt, 1989. 397. Originally a samizdat (self-published) version of 125 letters written in prison.

803. Havel, Václav. "A Statement to the Court." New York Review of Books 36 (April 27, 1989) 41. Response to his sentence to prison on charges of incitement and obstruction.

804. Havel, Václav and Antoine Spire. "An Interview with Vaclav Havel: My Prison...My Country." Matchbox (June 1983) 7.

805. Hochman, Jiri. "Letters From a Czech Prison: The 'Prague Spring' Remembered: Despair--and Hope--Behind the Iron Gates of Ruzyn." Trans. Marion Sling. Progressive 42 (September 1978) 16-20. Excerpts from letters Hochman smuggled out of prison to his wife in which he discusses political "crimes," life in a political prison, and resistance to their captors.

806. "Human Rights and All That Jazz." Newsweek 109 (March 23, 1987) 36. Members of the outlawed Jazz Section sent to prison.

807. "International Solidarity with Prisoners." East European Reporter 3.4 (Spring 1989) 72-73. Prints samples of appeals for support of Czech prisoners.

808. "Jazz Section Latest." End Journal 26 (February 1987) 4. Report on the intense harrassment and arrests of the eight members of the Prague Jazz Section of the Czech Union of Musicians.

809. Kavan, J. "The Official Finding of the Trial of Machacek and Lastuvka." Critique 10 (Winter 1978) 140-164. Vladimir Lastuvka and Ales Machacek were found guilty of the "crimes" of distributing literature, including The Dialectic of Power and The Gulag Archipelago.

810. Kyncl, Karel. "Ivan Jirous." Index On Censorship 18.1 (Jan. 1989) 28. In October Jirous was again arrested. During the past twenty years he has spent a total of eight years in Chekoslovak prisons--almost a fifth of his whole life.

811. Laber, Jeri. "Fighting Back in Prague." New York Review of Books 36 (April 27, 1989) 39-41. The "chill of persecution is worse" since the VONS trials of 1979.

812. Langer, Jo. Convictions: Memories of a Life Shared with a Good Communist. London: Deutsch, 1979. 206. Tells the story of her communist husband's arrest, trial, forced confession, and lengthy imprisonment, until he was rehabilitated, but soon died.

813. Levy, Alan. "The Class of '72, Prague-Style." Saturday Review (September 23, 1972) 7-8+. An account of the summer 1972 purge trials of 46 Dubcek adherents charged with pamphleteering.

814. Levy, Alan. Good Men Still Live! ("I am the Other Karel Capek.") The Odyssey of a Professional Prisoner. Chicago: O'Hara, 1974. 315. Levy was first jailed in 1949 for "crimes against the state"; he spent eleven years in prison camps and slave labor in uranium mines. Released in 1960, he escaped from the country in 1969.

815. Levy, Alan. Rowboat to Prague. New York: Crossman, 1972. 531. On the 1968 Soviet invasion and subsequent repression.

816. Loebl, Eugen. My Mind On Trial. New York: Harcourt Brace Jovanovich, 1978. 235. This former Czech official tells of his fraudulent trial for treason and eleven years in prison including five years of solitary confinement.

817. McGlynn, B. "Czechoslovakia Takes Aim At Dissident." In These Times 11.22 (Apr. 29, 1987) 5. Surveys the activities of Czech dissident Petr Pospichal.

818. Medical Mission to Czechoslovakia. New York; Sommerville, MA: Helsinki Watch; Physicians for Human Rights, 1988. 36. On the serious illnesses of several prisoners, visited by U.S. representatives of Physicians for Human Rights.

819. Mucha, Jiri. Living and Partly Living. Tr. Ewald Osers. London: Hogarth P., 1967. 224; New York: McGraw-Hill, 1968. 223. Confined first to solitary for a year and then sentenced to six years labor in a mine, 1951-54.

820. "The Other Face." Time 100 (August 14, 1972) 35. Trials of supporters of Alexander Dubcek's government continue.

821. Pagác, Stefan. State Secret no. 1: Warning for the Free World. New York: Edition "Brotherhood", 1982. 151. The author was imprisoned by the Nazis in 1944 and by the Czech communist government in 1954. Released in 1968, he emigrated to the U.S. in 1969. This book derives form his incarceration in the Ruzyne Prison 1959-

1962 with Bohumil Lausman, former Prime Minister and Chairman of the Social Democratic Party, whose story it is, his abduction, imprisonment, trial and death.

822. "Repression Still the Answer." East European Reporter 3.3 (Fall 1988) 11. Describes the imprisonment and death of Pavel Wonka.

823. Roth, Kenneth. "Prague and the Perils of Jazz." Commonweal 114 (June 5, 1987) 351-4. Persecution of the Jazz Section of the Union of Musicians.

824. Ryan, William. "Czech Dissidents Convicted." Guardian 32.5 (November 7, 1979) 12. Six prominent opponents of the government were convicted of subversion and given prison sentences of up to five years.

825. Ryan, William. "Czechoslovakia: Critics Sentenced." Guardian 30.4 (November 2, 1977) 13. Two critics of the government were sentenced to prison terms and two more received suspended sentences.

826. Ryan, William. "Czechoslovakia: Opponents Arrested." Guardian 31.39 (july 4, 1979) 10. Ten members of the human rights group Charter '77 and the Committee to Defend the Unjustly Prosecuted were arrested on charges of subversion.

827. Shapiro, L. "The Devil in Eastern Europe." Newsweek 113 (April 24, 1989) 77-8. About Vaclav Havel's play about crushing political dissent.

828. Siklová, Jirina. "Save These Books." Index on Censorship 12.2 (April 1983) 37-39. Imprisoned for helping banned Czech writers send their books out of the country; her trial was never held.

829. Silhanova, L. "'Once Abused, the Law Ceases.'" East European Reporter 3.3 (Fall 1988) 15. An interview of Pavel Wonka before he died in prison.

830. Skorecky, Josef. "Jamming the Jazz Section." The New York Review of Books 35 (June 30 1988) 40-2. On the trial of the Jazz Section of the Czech Musicians Union.

831. Sproul, B.C. "Before the Law." New York Review of Books 30 (December 8, 1983) 52. On the prison experiences of dissident Rudolf Battek.

832. "The Struggle in Czechoslovakia." Militant 43.38 (July 20, 1979) 20. Interview with dissident socialist Peter Uhl, one of ten human rights activists held and faced with one to ten years for "subversion" and "activities inimical to the interest of the state."

833. Tal, David. "Improvising in a Rigid Structure When Party Music Isn't Danceable." In These Times 11.26 (May 27, 1987) 21. On the arrest of seven leaders of the Jazz Section, a jazz lovers' organization, and the imprisonment of Karel Srp and Vladimir Kouril. State officials hate rock music and avant garde music in general.

834. Uhl, P. "Srp's Back!" East European Reporter 3.2 (march 1988) 11-12. Interview of Karel Srp, head of the Czech Jazz Section, following his release from prison.

835. Uhlir, Frank. The Call of The Cross : The Story of a Cabinet Minister in the Government of Pre-Communist Czechoslovakia Who Became an Anglican Priest in Canada. Gatineu, Quebec: Temple Pastures Mission, 1985. 159. Chaps. 4 and 5 describe the author's imprisonment following the communist coup. He escaped through the aid of resistance fighters.

836. "Wave of Arrests." Time 99 (March 6, 1972) 32. On the first large-scale mass arrests since Dubcek's downfall.

837. Weschler, Lawrence. "From Kafka to Dreyfus." The New Yorker (Nov. 2, 1992) 62-63. On the unfair trials of Jan Kavan and the "witch-hunting hysteria" sweeping the country. Also see the author's "The Velvet Purge: The Trials of Jan Kavan" (Oct. 19, 1992).

838. Wyatt, Jiai. "Show Trials Return to Prague." Nation 233 (July 25-Aug. 1, 1981) 74-6. The arrest of twenty-six activists will be the biggest political trial in Eastern Europe since the 1950's and the most determined assault on dissent in Czechoslovakia since 1968.

839. Zimmermann, Matilde. "Trial of Czech Dissidents Stirs Protests." Militant 41.42 (November 11, 1977) 24. Four Czech dissidents, Jiri Lederer, Václav Havel, Frantisek Parlicek, and Ota Ornest, were sentenced to prison for heir actions against the Czech governmaent. All but Ornest signed the Charter 77, a civil liberties manifesto.

DJIBOUTI

840. Amnesty International Report 1980. London: Amnesty International, 1980. 41-43. Critics of the government and suspects in rebel attacks have been detained and systematically tortured with some deaths resulting.

841. Amnesty International Report 1990. New York: Amnesty International, 1990. 81-2. Government critics were detained, some for several months; one died in custody, possibly by torture. Prison conditions are harsh.

DOMINICAN REPUBLIC

842. Amnesty International Report 1980. London: Amnesty International, 1980. 129-130. Since President Guzmán took office in 1978, human rights have improved, but short-term political detentions still occur, and brutality towards Haitian refugees and immigrant workers is a major problem.

843. Amnesty International Report 1990. New York: Amnesty International, 1990. 82. Arrests of demonstrators and trade unionists were reported. Two disappeared detainees (1974 and 1982) still not accounted for.

844. Dayer, Augusta. "The Disappeared Ones." Maclean's 99 (February 10, 1986) 42. As many as 65 people over the course of 1985-86 have been arrested and beaten simply because "they had fallen into police disfavor."

845. "Demand Freedom for 3 PSP Members in Dominican Prisons." Militant 39.26 (July 25, 1975) 25. A statement from the Liga Juvented Comunista asks for the release of three political prisoners being held in the Dominican Republic for supporting the Puerto Rico independent movement.

846. Destrot is Innocent. Roseau, Dominica: Committee in Defense of Desmond Trotter and Political Prisoners in Dominica, 1976. 14. An appeal for the release of Trotter.

847. "Prisoners Charge Dominican Government with Torture." Militant 39.27 (July 18, 1975) 5. Three political prisoners, jailed for supporting the Puerto Rican independence movement, confessed to crimes after being tortured.

848. Weissberg, Arnold. "Support Jailed Dominicans." Militant 41.11 (March 25, 1977) 25. Four political prisoners are starving to death, psychologically and physically tortured.

849. White, Judy. "Dominican Government Frees Claudio Tavárez." Militant 41.38 (October 14, 1977) 25. The article details how Dominican teacher Tavárez was released from prison after he was exonerated of "violating three Dominican anticommunist statutes."

ECUADOR

850. Amnesty International Report 1980. London: Amnesty International, 1980. 130. A general amnesty marked the return to civilian rule in 1979, though not all political prisoners were released, and in 1980 some 100 protestors against prices were jailed for a few days.

851. Amnesty International Report 1990. New York: Amnesty International, 1990. 83-4. Torture and ill-treatment of prisoners continue. Some deaths during custody probably from torture. Past disappearances still not explained, but one murdered by naval and police officers.

852. Dongen, Toine van. "The Restrepo Case: Murky Waters." Human Rights Quarterly 14 (1992) 289-302. An account of torture, murder, and secret disposal of the bodies of two teenagers by members of the National Police.

853. Murphy, Fred. "Massacre of Sugar Workers in Ecuador." Militant 41.42 (November 11, 1977) 21. Police killed 120 strikers and wounded many more.

EGYPT

854. Aikman, David. "A Dangerous Confession." Christianity Today 35 (April 8, 1991) 57. Christians in Egypt often face harsh treatment ranging from rejection by their families to electric shock in prisons.

855. Amnesty International Report 1980. London: Amnesty International, 1980. 326-28. Arbitrary detention without trial, especially of left-wing opponents of the government, is common under a state of emergency in force for many years. AI supports over 100 adoptees, but many more political prisoners exist, not only communists but members of religious groups.

856. Amnesty International Report 1990. New York: Amnesty International, 1990. 84-6. More than 8,000 political prisoners (mainly Islamic opposition) were detained for periods of one to three months without charge or trial, some repeatedly. The 1981 state of emergency remained in force.

857. Booth, Marilyn. "Sheikh Imam the Singer: An Interview." Index On Censorship 14.3 (June 1985) 18-21. Egypt's most famous dissident political singer and his songwriter, Najm, were imprisoned for three years (1969--1971) in solitary confinement by President Sadat, re-arrested and released periodically from 1972 to 1978. Imam discusses oppositional political poetry in Egypt and the Arab world.

858. Brecher, J. and R. Wilkinson. "Russians are Going." Newsweek 98 (September 28, 1981) 52+. After jailing over a thousand dissidents, President Sadat has expelled the Soviet Ambassador, accusing him of fomenting the trouble.

859. "Cracking Down." Time 118 (September 14, 1981) 48. Sadat jailed at least 1,100 of his most volatile critics in an alleged response to Muslim and Coptic violence.

860. Egypt : Arbitrary Detention and Torture Under Emergency Powers. New York: Amnesty International, 1989. 40. State of emergency legislation almost continuous since 1967 has been used widely to detain without trial critics of the government, and torture and ill-treatment of these detainees have been widely reported.

861. Egypt : Recent Human Rights Violations Under the State of Emergency; Summary. New York: Amnesty International USA, 1990. 40. Illegal judicial procedures, torture, etc.

862. Egypt: Security Police Detentions Undermine the Rule of Law. New York: Amnesty International, 1992. 16. Since the imposition of the state of emergency in 1981 thousands of people have been arbitrarily arrested and detained without charge or trial.

863. Egypt: Ten Years of Torture. New York: Amnesty International, 1991. 17. Even though Egypt attended the United Nations convention against torture in 1986, many of its basic measures have not been implemented. Includes interviews and forensic reports.

864. Egypt, Update to 1983 Report. London: Amnesty International, 1984. 15. Criticizes detention and trial of non-violent opponents of the government.

865. Egypt, Violations of Human Rights. London: Amnesty International Publications 1983. 38. Contains six case histories of prisoners of conscience, summarizes the trial of 176 persons jailed in connection with the Food Riots in 1977, shows how judicial independence has been undermined by executive veto. Torture and ill-treatment are also exposed.

866. "Freeing a Pope." Time 125.2 (January 14, 1985) 65. Pope Shenouda III is freed from a three-year house arrest. He leads the Copts, the largest Christian group in any Arab nation.

867. Golan, Aviezer. Operation Susannah. Trans. Peretz Kidron. New York: Harper & Row, 1978. 383. The story of four Israelis imprisoned for fourteen years for their underground operations in Egypt.

868. Neier, Aryeh. "Watching Rights." Nation. 256.20 (May 24, 1993) 691. Torture has "long been practiced in Egypt" and its frequency "seems to be increasing."

869. Ragal, Kim and Julian Nurdy. "The Crackdown in Cairo." Newsweek 98 (September 21, 1981) 62. As ordered by President Anwar Sadat, 1,536 religious activists, journalists, lawyers, and professors have been arrested.

870. Reese, Michael and Glass, Charles. "Mubarek Cracks Down." Newsweek 98 (October 26, 1981) 26. Widespread arrests of Islamic fundamentalists.

871. Saadawi, Nawal el. "In the Women's Prison." Index On Censorship 14.4 (August 1985) 36-43. Extracts from her book In the Women's Prison recounting her arrest and imprisonment. Dr. Saadawi was among the 1,563 people detained without charge by President Sadat in 1982.

872. Saadawi, Nawal el. Memoirs From the Women's Prison. London: Women's Press, 1986. 197. After a distinguished career as a doctor, sociologist, novelist, and feminist, she was dismissed from her post as Director of Health Education and later imprisoned in 1981 for alleged "crimes against the State." Her book describes her arrest and prison experiences.

873. Smith, W. E., and others. "Democracy with a Bite." Time 118 (September 21, 1981) 26-7. Alleging a conspiracy against his government, Sadat is cracking down on dissidents; including Omar Telmissani, head of the Moslem Brotherhood, and Dr. Hilmy Gazzar, leader of militant student groups.

874. Soames, Emma. "The 'Electric Shock' Treatment." Maclean's 94 (September 21, 1981) 29+. Anwar Sadat declares that even though 1600 religous and political leaders were arrested, "'Democracy is flourishing...the electric shock was necessary to counter dissident activities by haters and traitors.'"

875. Soames, Emma. "The Islamic Thunderer." Maclean's 95 (January 4, 1982) 22. Sheik Abdel Hamid Kishk has been arrested on numerous occasions for speaking out against the Egyptian government in his sermons.

876. Torture in Egypt in 1989. New York: Lawyers Committee for Human Rights, 1990. Various pagings. The first in a series of reports circulated by the Lawyers Committee for Human Rights. The EOHR is the Egyptian branch of the Arab Organization for Human Rights, founded in 1983. Its report charges Egyptian security forces of torturing "as a matter of policy," by 1989 "a matter of routine" not only in prisons or the headquarters of the State Security Intelligence, but in a large number of police stations and provincial security offices.

EL SALVADOR

877. 1986 Annual Report on the Human Rights Situation in El Salvador. Toronto: Inter-Church Committee on Human Rights in Latin America, 1987. 20. Examines the economic and military situation, disappearances, killings, torture, displacement of citizens, etc.

878. Alegrín, Claribel. They Won't Take Me Alive: Salvadorean Women in Struggle for National Liberation. Trans. Amanda Hopkinson. London: Women's Press, 1987. 145. Story of Salvadoran guerilla commander Eugenia (a pseudonym) in all aspects of her life, as political leader, soldier, revolutionary, proletarian, mother and wife fighting for basic human rights against El Salvador's brutal military regime.

879. Amnesty International Report 1980. London: Amnesty International, 1980. 131-138. A major human rights violator--torture and murder of prisoners, the disappearance of activists, systematic violence against individuals and institutions that defend human rights. A Following a coup in 1979 the new "security forces acted with the same brutality as those under [General] Romero," in fact conditions "worsened." (Despite the high level of violence, President Carter promised military assistance.)

880. Amnesty International Report 1990. New York: Amnesty International, 1990. 86-9. Union leaders and academics continued to disappear or openly murdered by the military death squads. Most arrests of government opponents also persisted, including students, church workers, and trade unionists. "Torture and ill-treatment were routinely used to extract 'confessions.'" Human rights offices were bombed and rights workers arrested.

881. Bader, E. "Political Prisoner's Trials." New Directions for Women 19.3 (May 1990) 1. Jennifer Casolo, imprisoned for alleged arms possession, tells of torture in prison.

882. Bilski, Andrew. "Under Suspicion." Maclean's 102 (December 4, 1989) 52. Karen Ridd was arrested and tortured mentally and physically by the Treasury police, accused of aiding leftest rebels, but was released.

883. Camarda, Renato. Forced to Move: Salvadorean Refugees in Honduras. San Francisco: Solidarity, 1985. 98. Refugees are a kind of political prisoner in the sense of being forced by persecution to flee outside their country of nationality. In 1980 the government of El Salvador "began a campaign of indiscriminate extermination [including kidnapping and torture] of the population, forcing many to leave."

884. Carter, Brenda, et al. A Dream Compels Us: Voices of Salvadoran Women. Ed. New American Press Collective. Boston: South End, 1989. 248. Essays depict women's participation in the revolutionary period 1980- 1988 in El Salvador and the brutal repression they in turn received: disappearances, imprisonment, rape, mutilation, exile, etc.

885. The Civilian Toll 1986-87: Ninth Supplement to the Report on Human Rights in El Salvador. New York: America's Watch Committee, 1987. 325. Interviews civilian victims regarding the serious, systematic abuses by the armed forces, and some by the guerrillas.

886. "Co-Madres." Connexions 17 (Summer 1985) 56-57. Interview of an El Salvadoran woman and member of Co-Madres, a protest group pursuing many activities for peace and against the state tyranny--sit-ins, visiting political prisoners, etc.

887. Condoning the Killing: Ten Years of Massacres in El Salvador. Ed. Ecumenical Program on Central America and the Caribbean (EPICA). Washington, DC: EPICA, 1990. 75. An account of 32 massacres of civilians by the U.S.-backed military. Over 72,000 political killings and eleven years of U.S. aid.

888. De La Locura a la Esperanza (From Madness to Hope). New York: Report of the El Salvador Truth Commission, 1993. n.p. The terrible details of the 12-year war against the people of El Salvador by the government maintained by the U.S.

889. A Decade of Abuse: Human Rights in El Salvador January, 1990. San Anselmo, CA: Marin Interfaith Task Force on Central America, 1990. 18. Describes the pattern of human rights abuses in El Salvador during the 1980's: mass killings, torture, imprisonment, exile. Includes testimonies of five torture victims and a member of a death squad, and many photographs.

890. Diaz, Nidia. I Was Never Alone: A Prison Diary from El Salvador. New York: Ocean\Talman, 1992. 210. A guerrilla commander's 190 day ordeal shows how one individual survived isolation and brutality.

891. El Salvador. New York: Amnesty International, 1978. 11. Torture, etc.

892. El Salvador: Amnesty International's Continuing Concerns. New York: Amnesty International, 1991. 19. Information gathered during the second half of 1990 indicates that the government is still failing to fulfill its commitments to respect human rights.

893. El Salvador: Death Squads--a Government Strategy. New York: Amnesty International, 1988. 49. Amnesty International concerned over the escalation of torture, disappearances and extrajudicial executions carried out by uniformed and plainclothes death squads (clandestine paramilitary groups of the official security apparatus).

894. El Salvador : Killings, Torture, and "Disappearances." New York: Amnesty International, 1990. 29. Documents increase in killings and discusses extra-judicial executions, disappearances, torture, arbitrary detention, and the lack of effective investigations into human rights violations.

895. El Salvador : Pt. 1 Recent Allegations of Torture of Political Detainees, October 1985 : Pt. 2 Amnesty International's Current Concerns in El Salvador, June 1985. New York: Amnesty International, 1985. Various pagings. Surveys the torture system accompanied by testimonies, followed by a general survey of the atrocities committed against the populace by government forces.

896. El Salvador's Decade of Terror: Human Rights Since the Assassinatoin of Archbishop Romero. New Haven: Yale UP/Americas Watch, 1991. 207. On the continuing persecution of the population by the ruling oligarchy and its army with U.S. support.

897. Hassett, John, and Hugh Lacey, eds. Towards a Society That Serves Its People: The Intellectual Contribution of El Salvador's Murdered Jesuits. Washington D.C.: Georgetown UP, 1993. 406. The writings of three of the six Jesuits slain by the army in 1989.

898. "Home for the Holidays--From El Salvador." Newsweek 114 (December 25, 1989) 52. U.S. citizen Jennifer Casolo released.

899. Kernaghan, Charles. "Duarte's War on Labor." Guardian 40.2 (Oct. 7, 1987) 10-11. Assaults, imprisonment, and torture of trade union leaders.

900. "Murder of CDHES General Coordinator Ernesto Anaya Sanabria." Human Rights Internet Reporter 12.1 (Fall 1987) 45-46. Anaya, father of five children, is the seventh Human Rights Commission official to be slain in the past seven years.

901. Neier, Aryeh. "Watching Rights." Nation 256.14 (April 12, 1993) 475. The U.N. Truth Commission has authoritatively resolved what was well known, that the government and military were the source of the systematic mass killings, tortures, and disappearances, and the equally systematic coverups, all aided and abetted by the U.S. government ($6 billion in military aid).

902. Nemeth, Mary. "Fear in the Midst of War." Maclean's 102 (December 4, 1989) 48. Six priests have been killed and at least 40 other church workers have been detained by government security forces.

903. Popkin, Margaret. Waiting for Justice : Treatment of Political Prisoners Under El Salvador's Decree 50. Washington D.C.: International Human Rights Law Group, 1987. 108. Rights abuses by the army and security forces continue under Decree 50, which was claimed to reform earlier laws, during 1984-1986.

904. Reissner, Will. "El Salvador Junta Arrests Union Leaders." Militant 44.33 (September 12, 1980) 6. U.S. financed Salvadoran troops break a strike of 1,500 electrical power workers and jail union leaders.

905. Rivard, Robert. "A Day Inside La Esperanza." Newsweek 103 (February 13, 1984) 34. A rare interview of political prisoners reveals secret arrests, arbitrary detention, and physical abuse.

906. Torture in El Salvador : From La Esperanza (Mariona) Prison, San Salvador, El Salvador, C.A. Ed. Human Rights Commission of El Salvador (CDHES). San Salvador: The Commission, 1986. 161. Details of the atrocious repression: chaps. on the 40 types of torture, testimony by individual victims, etc., and a passionate indictment of the Reagan Administration's support of the torture/murder military system.

907. "We Organized!" Connexions 14 (Fall 1984) 21. An interview of six political prisoners in Iolonga Prison by a delegation of women from the U.S.

EQUATORIAL GUINEA

908. Amnesty International Report 1980. London: Amnesty International, 1980. 43-44. Brutal dictator Nguema was overthrown in 1979, and political prisoners were ordered released by the new government, but some people are still in jail and some beaten for political reasons.

909. Amnesty International Report 1990. New York: Amnesty International, 1990. 89-90. About a dozen prisoners, victims of unfair trial in 1983, 1986, and 1988, continue confined. Evidence of torture in 1988 has appeared.

910. Equatorial Guinea: Arrests of Pro-Democracy Activists--A Changing Pattern of Human Rights Violations. New York: Amnesty International, 1991. 7. A new pattern of political arrests have emerged over the last year in response to increasing internal pressure for reform.

ETHIOPIA

911. Abeba Tesfagiorgis. A Painful Season & a Stubborn Hope: the Odyssey of an Eritrean Woman in Prison. Trenton, N.J.: Red Sea, 1992. 210. Memoir of suffering and survival.

912. Amnesty International Report 1980. London: Amnesty International, 1980. 45-48. Large-scale political imprisonment, torture, and killings; long-term detention without trial; and harsh prison conditions.

913. Amnesty International Report 1990. New York: Amnesty International, 1990. 90-3. Detention without trial, incommunicado detention, torture and ill-treatment, and extra-judicial executions were among the human rights violations that continued. Several hundred remained in prison without charge or trial.

914. Ethiopia: End of an Era of Brutal Repression--A New Chance for Human Rights. New York: Amnesty International, 1991. 41. The sudden flight into exile of President Mengistu Haile-Mariam on 21 May 1991 and the defeat of the government's armed forces by opposition groups mark the end of nearly two decades of human rights violations. Amnesty International appeals for a new commitment to human rights.

915. Ethiopia: Political Imprisonment and Torture. New York; London: Amnesty International, 1986. 18. On the several thousand imprisoned opponents of the government, some held since 1974, when Emperor Selassie was overthrown.

916. Ethiopia: Political Imprisonment in Ethiopia. New York: Amnesty International, 1989. 13. "Serious abuses of human rights continue": torture, extrajudicial executions, and disappearances. This report deals with long-term detention either without trial, or after unfair trial, or after secret sentencing.

917. "Ethiopia: Torture and Political Killings." Matchbox (Autumn 1978) 9, 16, 21. A report on human rights violations since the military coup in 1974--large scale political imprisonment, harsh prison conditions, torture, and politically motivated killings.

918. Human Rights Violations in Ethiopia: Report. Stockholm: Swedish Action Group for the Political Prisoners in Ethiopia, 1977. 26. Gives data and expresses concern for the torture and other outrages.

919. "A Pilgrimage of Thanks From Ethiopia to Maine." Amnesty Action (Winter 1993) 9. Mulugetta Mosissa, 11 years in prison, visits the Amnesty group who worked for his release.

920. Waal, Alex de. Evil Days: Thirty Years of War and Famine in Ethiopia. New York: Human Rights Watch, 1991. 386. Sets forth a broad range of abuses under Mengistu Haile Mariam's brutal regime (1974-1991) and advocates prosecution of the perpetrators.

921. Ward, Richard. "Ethiopia: Leftist Executed." Guardian 30.5 (November 9, 1977) 12. Eight men convicted of counterrevolutionary activities were executed by Ethiopia's military regime.

922. Willenson, Kim, et al. "Hardship Post." Newsweek 86 (September 29, 1975) 57. Rebels have captured several U.S. citizens.

FIJI

923. Amnesty International Report 1990. New York: Amnesty International, 1990. 93-4. A few critics of the government were briefly detained, and others arrested in 1988 were convicted but none imprisoned. Detainees reported experiences of torture and ill-treatment.

924. Tinker, Hugh, et al. Fiji: Minority Rights Group Report no. 75. Cambridge, Mass.: Cultural Survival, 1987. 15. The 1970 racist constitution allowed special privileges to Fijians over Indian descendants, until a coup in 1987.

FINLAND

925. Amnesty International Report 1990. New York: Amnesty International, 1990. 94. Although alternative civilian service is allowed to conscientious objectors, the term is twice the length of military service; several conscientious objectors have chosen prison.

FRANCE

926. Alleg, Henri. The Question. Introduction by Jean-Paul Sarte. New York: Braziller, 1958. 123. A protest against political prisoners to make them betray others, and an account of the author's detention and torture for a month by French paratroops. Despite being banned and confiscated in France, the book sold well throughout the world. Alleg was editor of the Alger Républican, which was banned.

927. Amnesty International Report 1980. London: Amnesty International, 1980. 265-68. Conscientious objectors are imprisoned when their conscientious objector status is rejected, and all applications have been refused since August 1979. An appeal court overturned these sentences, but their re-arrest is probable at next call-up time. Summary courts are employed to punish demonstrators (e.g., against construction of a nuclear power station).

928. Amnesty International Report 1990. New York: Amnesty International, 1990. 95-6. Hundreds of conscientious objectors to military service, most of them Jehovah's Witnesses, were in prison.

929. de Beauvoir, Simone, and Gisele Halimi. Djamila Boupacha: The Story of the Torture of a Young Algerian Girl which Shocked Liberal French Opinion. Trans. Peter Green. London: Andre Deutsch and Weidenfeld and Nicolson, 1962. 250. On the imprisonment and torture of Boupacha, of the Algerian F.L.N., by French military.

930. Ingram, Norman. The Politics of Dissent: Pacifism in France 1919-1939. Oxford, Eng.: Clarendon, 1991. 366. Bits of information about the incarceration of conscientious objectors (e.g., pp. 163-64).

931. Maran, Rita. Torture: the Role of Ideology in the French-Algerian War. New York: Praeger, 1989. 214. On "the role of ideology in legitimating the use of torture by successive French governments in their attempt to suppress the Algerian 'war of liberation'" (1954-1962). France's claim of a civilizing mission in Algeria was belied by its persistent use of torture during the war.

932. Reflections from Captivity: Phan Boi Chau's "Prison Notes," Ho Chi Minh's "Prison Diary.'" Trans. Christopher Jenkins, et al. Ed. David Marr. Athens, OH: Ohio UP, 1978. 113. A French court sentenced Phan to death in absentia in 1913, then imprisoned by a warlord opposing the Kuomintang 1914-1917, then kidnapped by the French secret police, put on trial for his life in 1925, and sentenced to house arrest for the remaining fifteen years of his life in Hue. Ho's diary in the form of poems were written while he was incarcerated by the Kuomintang 1942-43.

933. "Total Resister Free." Peace News 21.9 (December 7, 1979) 5. On the military trial of Jean Fabre, a conscientious objector to conscription.

934. Webster, Paul. Pétain's Crime: The Full Story of French Collaboration in the Holocaust. London: Macmillan, 1990. 225. Examines the twenty camps in France, run under French administration and guarded by French police, responsible for the deaths of 76,000 French, foreign, and stateless Jews; a system "begun without pressure from the Germans." Webster also studies the forty years deliberate attempt to hide the truth.

GABON

935. Amnesty International Report 1980. London: Amnesty International, 1980. 48. An amnesty in 1980 freed several prisoners, but several others remain without trial.

936. Amnesty International Report 1990. New York: Amnesty International, 1990. 96-7. Several people arrested in connection with an alleged plot against the government were still detained without charge, and two died in custody as the possible result of mistreatment.

GAMBIA

937. Sallah, Halifa. An Emergency Situation! : How Many More Will Have to Die? : A Focus on the Situation at Mile II Prison. Banjul, Gambia: Fund to Ease Human Suffering, 1987. 8. Prison conditions are killing inmates.

GERMANY

938. Fischer, Louis. "Class Justice in Germany." Nation 120 (June 3, 1925) 624-5. Double justice, the right treated much less severely than the left for similar crimes.

939. Luxemburg, Rosa. The Letters of Rosa Luxemburg. Ed. Stephen E. Bronner. Boulder, CO: Westview, 1978. 259. Letters written during 1916-1918 by Red Rosa, a leader in the German Social Democratic Party.

940. Luxemburg, Rosa. "Letters from Prison." Trans. Eleanor Clark. Partisan Review 5.1 (June 1938) 3-23. "Letters from Prison." Trans. Ralph Mannheim. Partisan Review 10.4 (July-August 1943) 362-71. Written during her imprisonment 1917-1918.

941. Salomon, Ernst von. The Captive: The Story of an Unknown Political Prisoner. Trans. James Kirkup. London: Weidenfeld and Nicolson, 1960. 184. The story of "A.D.," as told to Salomon, of twenty-seven years in the prisons of the Weimar Republic, the Nazis, and the U.S. occupation forces.

942. Toller, Ernst, and R.E. Ellis. Look Through the Bars; Letters from Prison, Poems, and a New Version of "The Swallow Book." New York: Farrar & Rinehart, 1937. 305. The author was imprisoned briefly in 1918 for opposing the war, released, and then imprisoned again in 1919, this time for five years, for defending the Bavarian Free State, of which he was a member of the government at age 24. The contents of this book were written during this period.

GERMANY, GERMAN DEMOCRATIC REPUBLIC (EAST GERMANY)

943. Amnesty International Concerns with Respect to Political Trials in the German Democratic Republic (GDR). New York, 1984. 18. On the unfair trial procedures: exclusion of the public, restricted access to lawyers, etc.

944. Amnesty International Report 1980. London: Amnesty International, 1980. 269-72. Many laws deprive citizens of their human rights--e.g. expression and association, emigration. Even those who attempt to leave legally are subject to arrest and imprisonment.

945. Amnesty International Report 1990. New York: Amnesty International, 1990. 97-9. During 1989 thousands of political prisoners were detained under laws restricting freedom of expression, association, assembly, and movement: many were convicted in secret and unfair trials; and many ill-treated by security forces. But at the end of the year amnesties freed most of the prisoners, reflecting new laws guaranteeing liberties.

946. Battle, Hellen. Every Wall Shall Fall. Old Tappan, NJ: Fleming H. Revell, 1972. 319. An account of the author's imprisonment for trying to help an East German leave the country.

947. The Case of Rudolf Bahro: A Socialist in an East German Prison. Nottingham, Eng: Bertrand Russell Peace Foundation, 1979. 22. Urges his release.

948. "Efforts to Leave East Germany Constitute Most Common Offense." Matchbox (Feb. 1981) 1,5. Crossing, preparing to cross the border, or even applying for permission to leave the country carries heavy prison punishment.

949. "Freedom Sought for Medical Physicist in East Germany." Intellect 103 (December 1974) 144. The story of Jurgen Richter's imprisonment and the international efforts to gain his release.

950. "Friend in Dresden." Time 72 (July 14, 1958) 68. An interview of the nine U.S. soldiers held incommunicado since their helicopter was forced down last month. The GDR was using them to pressure the U.S. into recognizing its government.

951. German Democratic Republic (GDR). London: Amnesty International Publications, 1977. 12. Expresses concern over laws in violation of the U.N. Declaration of Human Rights, prolonged pre-trial detention and imprisonment of critics of the government, and the death penalty for political offenses.

952. Johnson, William O. "Thrown Free." Sports Illustrated 74 (January 21, 1991) 50-69. GDR record discuss-thrower Wolfgang Schmidt was sentenced to hard labor for plotting to leave the country.

953. Juretzko, Werner. Years without Hope. Chicago: Krause, 1970. 127. Story of a West German spy sentenced to 13 years (reduced to 8).

954. Kavan, Jan. "Hidden Opposition of the GDR." East European Reporter 3.3 (Fall 1988) 65. Interview of Werner Fischer, who was arrested for treason and then expelled from the country.

955. Lewis, Peter. "Freedom with a Price Tag." Macleans 96 (Jan. 24, 1983) 7. Rainer Barzel talks about the practice of exchanging West German money for East German prisoners.

956. "Open Letter Demands: Free Rudolf Bahro!" Militant 42.28 (July 21, 1978) 24. Bahro is in prison accused of espionage, but he is guilty only of publishing his ideas.

957. Prison Conditions in East Germany: Conditions for Political Prisoners. London: Amnesty International, 1966. 56. Surveys the judicial system, the prisoners, and the prisons. Despite several thousand releases since 1964, many more remain incarcerated and more are continually being sentenced.

958. Prittie, Terence. "Woe to Him Who Thinks." New Republic 144 (June 5, 1961) 8-9. Statistics and a few individual cases.

959. Reed, David. "East Germany: People for Sale." Reader's Digest 109 (Oct. 1976) 150-4. Lawyer Wolfgang Vogel has convoyed more than 10,000 prisoners from East German jails to West Germany.

960. Rothenbacher, Wulf, and Wilfried Vemmer, eds. Political Imprisonment in the GDR : A Survey of Former Political Prisoners From the GDR About Their Imprisonment in the GDR, 1986. Franfurt\Main, West Germany: International Society for Human Rights, German Section, Committee on The Civil Rights Movement and Political Prisoners in the GDR, 1987. 64. Based upon testimony from former prisoners. Arrest, detention, courts, prison conditions, and individual cases are presented.

961. Stamets, Bill. "Sybille Schonemann: Back in Court." In These Times 16.24 (May 13-19, 1992) 4-5. Schonemann, imprisoned a year in 1984 and then exiled, returned to make a film about her persecutors, Locked Up in Time.

962. "Thousands Attend Meeting for Bahro." Militant 42.48 (Dec. 22, 1978) 22. An estimated 3,500 people attended the International Congress in West Berlin to demand Rudolf Bahro's freedom.

963. "Ulbricht's Prisoners." Time 96 (November 9, 1970) 27. Western and U.S. students have been imprisoned for such crimes as putting up posters or "slandering" the state.

964. Wallach, Erica. Light at Midnight. Garden City, NY: Doubleday, 1967. 397. Describes her five years in East German and Soviet prisons beginning in 1950, charged with spying (she had entered East Berlin to find her foster parents).

965. Young, Jacob. "Political Prisoners for Sale." Newsweek 102 (August 29, 1983) 32. Every year, West Germany spend on an average of $5 million to buy the freedom of some 1,000 East German political prisoners.

GERMANY, FEDERAL REPUBLIC OF (WEST GERMANY)

966. "13,175 Miles Around the Yard." Time 106 (July 28, 1975) 31. Describes Albert Speer's Spandau Diaries. Speer spent twenty years in prison as a Nazi war criminal--forcing millions of non-Germans to work as slave laborers.

967. Amnesty International Report 1980. London: Amnesty International, 1980. 272-76. Some people have been prosecuted for defaming the state, some defense lawyers of political prisoners have been harassed, and prison conditions have been harsh for members of revolutionary groups (e.g. Red Army Faction).

968. Amnesty International Report 1990. New York: Amnesty International, 1990. 99-101. Prisoners detained under anti-terrorist legislation continue confined in isolation.

969. Amnesty International's Work on Prison Conditions of Persons Suspected or Convicted of Politically Motivated Crimes in the Federal Republic of Germany: Isolation and Solitary Confinement. London: Amnesty International, 1980. 35. Expresses opposition to solitary and small group isolation "in which a considerable number of prisoners have been and still are held while in high security detention." AI seeks international standards for isolation.

970. Baumann, Michael. "Germany: Tanks in Streets, 'Suicides' in Prison--Government Uses Terrorism as Pretext for Repression." Militant 41.41 (Nov. 4, 1977) 9. Three leading members of the Red Army Faction did not commit suicide in prison as the government claimed.

971. Bend, Jill. "Crackdown on West German Feminists." Spare Rib no. 189 (April 1988) 24-5. Many homes were searched and 23 women were detained in a sweeping search for "terrorist" opponents of genetic engineering and immigration policy.

972. Ege, Konrad. "Mossad in West Germany." CounterSpy 4.3 (Summer 1980) 5-6. The Bundesnachrichtendienst secretly allows MOSSAD to interrogate Palestinians in jails, and the use of torture and mind-altering drugs has been reported.

973. Franklin, A. "Terrorism: the State Marches On." Fifth Estate 12.12 (Dec. 1977) 1,8. Deaths in jail and torture are compared to S. Africa.

974. Holmes, Judith. "Prisoners' Hunger Strike Protests Isolation Techniques." Guardian 37.19 (Feb. 13, 1985) 15. Thirty-nine prisoners from the Red Army Faction and other groups protest against severe isolation regulations.

975. Jungwirth, Barbara. "Charge Isolation in Prison is Torture." Guardian 38.29 (April 23, 1986) 14. On the extreme isolation of Red Army Faction members of supporters--23 hours a day in sound proof cells.

976. Ryan, William. "War Protesters Tried." Guardian 30.30 (May 3, 1978) 13. Examines a trial "on charges stemming from a mass anti-Vietnam war protest" and discusses the increase of repression.

977. "West German Revolutionary Raped, Hanged in Cell: New Evidence in Meinhof Case Points to Murder, Not Suicide." CounterSpy 3.2 (Dec. 1976) 24-25, 35. Evidence indicates Ulrike Meinhof did not hang herself but was throttled.

978. Wood, S. "Ulrike Meinhoff Dies in Prison." Workers World 18.23 (June 4, 1976) 15-6. She was possibly murdered or tortured to death.

GERMANY, NAZI

Studies of the Jewish genocide fill several bibliographies. I have selected books and articles which focus on imprisonment.

979. Adelson, Alan and Robert Lapides. Lodz Ghetto: Inside a Community Under Siege. New York: Viking, 1989. 526. Compilation of first-person accounts of life in the Lodz Ghetto gathered from survivors and from diaries and memoirs of those who perished.

980. Ainsztein, Reuben. Jewish Resistance in Nazi-Occupied Eastern Europe with a Historical Survey of the Jew as Fighter and Soldier in the Diaspora. New York: Barnes & Noble, 1974. 970. Parts six and seven (seven chapters) on ghetto revolts, eight on revolts in the death camps.

981. Améry, Jean. At the Mind's Limits: Contemplations by a Survivor on Aushwitz & Its Realities. Trans. Sidney Rosenfeld and Stella P. Rosenfeld. Bloomington, IN: Indiana UP, 1980, 111; New York: Schocken, 1986. 128. (First ed. 1966). On the victims of the Third Reich, e.g., torture, the Jewish victim, the intellectual in the concentration camp, not a documentary but a phenomenological description of the existence of the victim.

982. Améry, Jean. Radical Humanism: Selected Essays. Trans. and ed. Sidney Rosenfeld and Stella P. Rosenfeld. Bloomington, IN: Indiana UP, 1984. 144. One essay on being a Jew and imprisoned, another on the Warsaw ghetto.

983. Apenszlak, Jacob, ed. The Black Book of Polish Jewry. New York: American Federation of Polish Jews; Roy, 1943. 343. Compiled during the war from scattered reports, this is one of the first accounts of the holocaust.

984. Arad, Yitzhak. Belzec, Sobibor, Treblinka: The Operation Reinhard Death Camps. Bloomington: Indiana UP, 1987. 437. On the development and construction of these extermination camps, extermination techniques, portraits of the perpetrators, prisoners' daily life, diseases, suicides, resistance, and escapes.

985. Arad, Yitzhak, ed. The Pictoral History of the Holocaust. New York: Macmillan, 1990. 396. Ghettos, mass killings, deportations to death camps, death camps, armed resistance, etc.

986. "Autumn Roundup." Time 36 (November 4, 1940) 28+. Random accounts of Gestapo arrests.

987. Avni, Haim. Spain, the Jews, and Franco. Tr. Emanuel Shimoni. Philadelphia: Jewish Pub. Soc., 1982. 268. How Spanish diplomats saved thousands of Jews in Nazi-occupied countries.

988. Barnouw, David and Jerrold van der Stroom, eds. The Diary of Anne Frank. The Critical Edition. New York: Doubleday, 1989. 719. Published in response to so-called "revisionists" who question whether the Holocaust ever occured and question the authenticity of first-person accounts of the Holocaust, this book establishes the history of the Frank family, includes a 270 page study of the handwriting in the diary, and reproduces three versions of Anne Frank's diary: the original; the revisions made by Anne; and the diary as editied by her father Otto Frank.

989. Bauer, Yehuda. American Jewry and the Holocaust: The American Jewish Joint Distribution Committee, 1939-1945. Detroit: Wayne State UP: 1981. 522. JDC rescue operations throughout Europe.

990. Bauer, Yehuda. A History of the Holocaust. New York: Franklin Watts, 1982. 398. A chronological, comprehensive account of 1933-1945: Chap. 6 "German Jewry," Chap. 7 "Poland," Chap. 8 "Ghettoes," Chap. 9 "The Final Solution," etc.

991. Berkowitz, Sarah. Where Are My Brothers? New York: Helios Books, 1965. 127. A memoir of Bergen-Belsen.

992. Bernadac, Christian. Devil's Doctors: Medical Experiments on Human Subjects in the Concentration Camps. Paris: France-Empire, 1967. 254. A compilation of testimony by former Nazi doctors and survivors taken from the archives of the Nuremberg Trials, journals, and personal interviews.

993. Bethge, Eberhard. Dietrich Bonhoeffer: Man of Vision, Man of Courage. Trans. Eric Mosbacher, et al. Ed. Edwin Robertson. New York: Harper & Row, 1970. 867. The final two chapters trace his arrest, imprisonment, trial, death sentence, and execution from 1943 to April 1945.

994. Bettelheim, Bruno. The Informed Heart: Autonomy in a Mass Age. Glenco, Ill.: Free Press, 1960. 309; New York: Avon, 1971. 304. Discusses the victims' psychological responses to their fate.

995. Bezwinska, Jadwiga, and Danuta Czech, eds. Amidst a Nightmare of Crime: Manuscripts of Members of the Sonderkommando. Trans. Krystyna Michalck. Auschwitz: State Museum of Oswiecim, 1973; New York: H. Fertig, 1992. 207. An anthology taken from the diaries of the Sonderkommando, or crematoria workers, most of whom were themselves gassed after about three months of their work.

996. Birenbaum, Halina. Hope Is the Last to Die. Trans. David Welsh. New York: Twayne, 1971. 246. A personal documentation of the Nazi terror by a Polish survivor of Auschwitz, Majdanek, and other camps.

997. Blady Szwajger, Adina. I Remember Nothing More: A Memoir of the Warsaw Children's Hospital and the Jewish Resistance. New York: Pantheon, 1991; London: Collins Harvill, 1990. 184. By a nurse in the children's hospital in the Warsaw ghetto.

998. Boas, Jacob. Boulevard des Misères: The Story of Transit Camp Westerbork. Hamden, CT: Archon, 1985. 169. Approximately 104,000 of Holland's 140,000 Jews passed through Websterbork on their way to extermination camps.

999. Boehm, Erich H., ed. We Survived: The Stories of Fourteen of the Hidden and the Hunted of Nazi Germany. New Haven: Yale UP, 1949. 308. [Republished in 1985 under the title We Survived: Fourteen Histories of the Hidden and Hunted of Nazi Germany. Santa Barbara, CA: ABC-Clio. 316.] The first-person accounts include Jewish survivors, underground oppositionists, communists, clergymen, several who were involved with the failed attempt to assassinate Hitler, etc.

1000. Bonhoeffer, Emmi. Auschwitz Trials: Letters From an Eyewitness. Trans. Ursula Stechow. Richmond, VA: John Knox Press, 1967. 61. About the survivors of Auschwitz atrocities who came to Frankfurt to testify against the officials of the camp.

1001. Bor, Josef. Terezin Requiem. Trans. Edith Pargeter. New York: Knopf, 1963. 112; Avon, 1978. 119. A memoir based on a famous incident at Theresienstadt in which inmates sang Verdi's "Requiem" shortly before being transported to their deaths.

1002. Bosanquet, Mary. The Life and Death of Dietrich Bonhoeffer. New York: Harper & Row, 1968. 287. The final two chapters relate his imprisonment, trial, and execution.

1003. Bower, Tom. Klaus Barbie: The Butcher of Lyons. New York: Pantheon, 1984. 255. The first biography of the notorious Gestapo head in Lyons who, after the war, was used by the Americans as a paid informer.

1004. Braham, Randolph L., ed. The Destruction of Hungarian Jewry. 2 vols. New York: World Federation of Hungarian Jews, 1963. 969. A documentary account of what befell Hungarian Jews, containing a comrehensive list of documents with synopses in English.

1005. Braham, Randolph L., comp. The Hungarian Jewish Catastrophe: A Selected and Annotated Bibliography. 2nd ed. East European Monographs 162. New York: Columbia UP, 1984. 501. Most of the 564,507 Hungarian jews were killed during the last year of the war after the Nazis occupied Hungary on March 19, 1944. Some 3000 references in a variety of languages, mainly Hungarian.

1006. Braham, Randolph L., ed. The Politics of Genocide: The Holocaust in Hungary. 2 vols. New York: Columbia UP, 1980. 1269. An account of every phase of the holocaust in Hungary.

1007. Breitowicz, Jacob. Through Hell to Life. New York: Shengold, 1983. 138. How a couple and their child survived the Holocaust.

1008. Browning, Christopher R. The Final Solution and the German Foreign Office: A Study of Referate DIII of Abteilung Deutschland 1940-43. New York: Holmes &

Meier, 1978. 276. On the Foreign Office's participation in the mass murder of the Jews through the mass deportations.

1009. Buber-Neumann, Margarete. Milena: The Story of a Remarkable Friendship. Trans. Ralph Manheim. New York: Schocken, 1977; Seaver, 1988. 213. Loved by Franz Kafka, Milena Jesenská opposed Hitler and was sent to Ravensbrück concentration camp, where she met Buber-Neumann and died in 1944.

1010. Buber-Neumann, Margarete. Under Two Dictators. New York: Dodd, Mead; London: V. Gollancz, 1949. 331. A memoir of life in both Nazi and Soviet concentration camps.

1011. Burney, Christopher. The Dungeon Democracy. London; Toronto: William Heinemann, 1945. 100. An account of his fifteen months in the "savage" Buchenwald prison.

1012. Burney, Christopher. Solitary Confinment. London: Macmillan; New York: St. Martin's, 1961. 172. He spent eighteen months in solitary as a prisoner of the Nazis.

1013. Cargas, Harry James. ed. The Holocaust: An Annotated Bibliography. Haverford, Pa.: Catholic Library Association, 1977. 86. Divided into twelve categories, "History", "Hitler and Associates", "Children's Literature", etc., and concentrated on works published exclusively in the U.S.

1014. Cargas, Harry James, ed. Voices From the Holocaust. Lexington: U of Kentucky P, 1992. 184. Interviews of people involved in the holocaust from many perspectives, including an essay on the psychological impact of the holocaust on survivors.

1015. Cargas, Harry James, ed. When God and Man Failed: Non-Jewish Views of the Holocaust. New York: Macmillan, 1981. 238. A collection of essays by Christian students of the Holocaust, some of few Christians who raised a voice of protest while the Nazi atrocities were being perpetrated.

1016. Chary, Frederick B. The Bulgarian Jews and the Final Solution 1940-1944. Pittsburgh, PA: U of Pittsburgh Press, 1972. 246. Focuses on the deportation of the Jews from Greek and Yugoslav territories occupied by Bulgaria, while Bulgarian Jews were mostly saved.

1017. Cohen, Elie A. The Abyss. New York: Norton, 1973. 111. Because he was a doctor, this (Dutch) Jewish man had skills which allowed him to survive at Auschwitz, although his young family did not.

1018. Cohen, Elie A. Human Behavior in the Concentration Camp. New York: Norton, 1953. 295; Columbia UP, 1989. 336. A psychological perspective by a survivor of Auschwitz and Mauthausen.

1019. Crome, Len. Unbroken : Resistance and Survival in the Concentration Camps. New York: Schocken, 1988. 174. Tells the story of a group of mostly communist young people who resisted the Nazis before and after their seizure of power in 1933, including resistance in concentration camps.

1020. Dafni, Reuven and Yehudit Kleiman, eds. Final Letters From Victims of the Holocaust. New York: Paragon House, 1991. 128. The editors provide personal and historical explanations of the letters.

1021. Dawidowicz, Lucy S. The Holocaust and the Historians. Cambridge, MA: Harvard UP, 1981. 187. Tries to explain "why so many historians in so many countries have failed to deal even adequately with the Holocaust."

1022. Dawidowicz, Lucy S. The War Against the Jews 1933-1945. New York: Holt, Rinehart and Winston, 1975. 460. Organized in 2 parts: "The Final Solution" and "The Holocaust," covering such topics as anti-Semitism, the SS, and building the death camps, to Jews in Germany and the Jewish Councils (Judenräte). Also country by country appendices.

1023. Delbo, Charlotte. None of Us Will Return. Trans. John Githens. New York: Grove Press, 1968; Boston: Beacon, 1978. 128. Delbo, a member of the French Resistance who was caught and brought to Auschwitz in 1942, remembers camp life.

1024. Des Pres, Terrence. The Survivor. New York: Oxford UP, 1976. 218; Pocket Books, 1978. 257. "An Anatomy of Life in the Death Camps" is the subtitle of this book, which focuses on the psychology of survival in German and Russian concentration camps.

1025. D'Harcourt, Pierre. The Real Enemy. New York: Scribner's, 1967. 186. A Christian imprisoned in concentration camps.

1026. Directory of Holocaust Institutions. Washington, D.C.: U.S. Holocaust Memorial Council, 1988. 56. Lists 99 organizations and institutions in the U.S. and Canada that provide services, assemble resources, and conduct programs related to the Holocaust.

1027. Dobroszycki, Lucjan, ed. The Chronicle of the Lodz Ghetto, 1941-1944. Trans. Richard Lourie, et al. New Haven, CT: Yale UP, 1984. 551. This secret chronicle of the Jewish community's life under Nazi terror in the Lodz Ghetto was written and compiled by a group of Jewish scholars, historians, journalists, and scientists, all of whom but one perished in the final liquidation of the Ghetto in August 1944.

1028. Donat, Alexander, ed. The Death Camp at Treblinka. New York: Holocaust Library, 1980. 320. Treblinka became the graveyard for Warsaw Jews as well as for Jews from other European countries. More than one million men, women, and children died there. On August 2, 1943, the thousand prisoners left alive rebelled, setting fire to the death factory. Two hundred broke through, although only fifty survived to tell the story. This book consists mainly of the testimony of survivors.

1029. Donat, Alexander. The Holocaust Kingdom: A Memoir. New York: Holt, Rinehart & Winston, 1965; Holocaust Library, 1978. 361. A detailed memoir of surviving death and labor camps.

1030. Dorian, Emil S. The Quality of Witness: A Romanian Diary, 1937-1944. Ed. Marguerite Dorian. Trans. Mara Soleanu Vamos. Philadelphia: Jewish Publication Society, 1982. 350. The day to day diary by a Romanian writer and physician of the Holocaust in Romania.

1031. Dribben, Judith Strick. A Girl Called Judith Strick. New York: Cowles, 1970. 340. The autobiographical account of a woman who survived the underground, the Gestapo, prison, and Auschwitz.

1032. Dufournier, Denise. Ravensbrück: The Woman's Camp of Death. London: Allen & Unwin, 1948. 150. Dufournier, a French member of the underground, survived Ravensbrück.

1033. Dwork, Debórah. Children With a Star: Jewish Youth in Nazi Europe. New Haven, CT: Yale UP, 1991. 354. One-and-a-half million Jewish children were killed. This book is about their persecution and murder. ("Jewish youth" is defined as "those children whom the Nazis and their allies considered to be Jews.")

1034. Dying We Live : Letters Written by Prisoners in Germany on the Eve of Execution. Ed. Helmut Gollwitzer, et al. Trans. Reinhard Kuhn. London: Collins; Fount, 1983. 224. Orig. pub. Harvill P, 1956. Fifty-three German opponents of the Nazis write farewell.

1035. Edelheit, Abraham, and Hershel Edelheit, comps. Bibliography on Holocaust Literature. Boulder, CO: Westview, 1986. 842. Includes scholarly studies and popular works from the 1930s to the 1990s, a new section on Soviet antisemitism and expanded coverage of neo-Nazism/neo-Fascism, extensive cross-references, a glossary, and author/title and subject indexes.

1036. Edelheit, Abraham, and Hershel Edelheit, comps. Bibliography on Holocaust Literature: Supplement, Volume Two. Boulder, CO: Westview, 1992. 564. This second supplement contains 4,000 new entries. Includes both scholarly and popular works dating as far back as the 1930s and as recent as 1992. Extensive cross-references, a glossary, and author/title and subject indexes.

1037. Edelheit, Abraham, and Hershel Edelheit. History of the Holocaust: A Handbook and Dictionary. Boulder, CO: Westview, 1993. History and assessment in the first part, dictionary of terms in the second, along with graphs, charts, tables, maps, photographs.

1038. Edelstein, Dov. Worlds Torn Asunder. New York: Ktav, 1984. 176. The author, a pious Hasidic youth from the town of Szatmár in Hungary, was sent to Auschwitz at the age of seventeen.

1039. Ehrenburg, Ilya and Vasily Grossman, eds. The Black Book. Trans. John Glad and James S. Levine. New York: Holocaust Library, 1981. 595. Prepared in 1946, and removed from the press at Stalin's orders, this is an anthology of documents on the Holocaust in Russia.

1040. Eisenberg, Azriel, ed. The Lost Generation: Children in the Holocaust. New York: Pilgrim, 1982. 380. Compiles over one hundred eyewitness accounts of horrors perpetrated against Jewish children under the Nazi regime.

1041. Eisenburg, Azriel, ed. Witness to the Holocaust. New York: Pilgrim, 1981. 649. Compiled excerpts from journals, diaries, letters, and books that concern the Holocaust.

1042. Eisner, Jack. The Surivor. Ed. Irving A. Leitner. New York: William Morrow, 1980; Bantam, 1982. 320. Memoir of resistance and survival by the founder of the Warsaw Ghetto Resistance Organization.

1043. Eitinger, Leo, et al. The Psychological and Medical Effects of Concentration Camps and Related Persecutions on Survivors of the Holocaust: A Research Bibliography. Vancouver: U of British Columbia P, 1985. 168. Topics include: I. Direct observations of and direct reactions to the concentration camp during imprisonment and immediately after liberation; II. Compensation-rehabilitation; III. Physical and Psychological results; IV. Children as Survivors; and V. Second Generation.

1044. Elkins, Stanley. Slavery. New York: Universal Library, 1963. 247. Discusses slavery in Nazi concentration camps and its relationship to other kinds of slavery, pp.103-115.

1045. Facing History and Ourselves: Elements of Time--Holocaust Testimonies. Brookline, MA: Facing History and Ourselves, 1989. 402. Designed specifically to teach about and prepare teachers to teach about the Holocaust, this volume is a companion to the Facing History videotape collection of Holocaust testimonies and includes transcriptions of the videos, descriptions of the speakers, and guidelines for classroom use. It also includes essays about various aspects of Holocaust testimony.

1046. Falstein, Louis, ed. The Martyrdom of Jewish Physicians in Poland. New York: Exposition, 1964. 500. An important anthology of first-person accounts of the persecution of Jewish doctors in ghettos and death camps.

1047. Feig, Konnilyn. Hitler's Death Camps: The Sanity of Madness. New York: Holmes & Meier, 1981. 547. An interdisciplinary account of each of the major concentration and death camps.

1048. Fein, Helen. Accounting for Genocide: National Responses and Jewish Victimization During the Holocaust. New York: Free, 1979. 468. Attempts to understand the will of Germany to annihilate the Jews; the lack of response outside Germany to the ongoing extermination; and the responses of Jews.

1049. Fenelon, Fania. Playing For Time. New York: Atheneum, 1977; Berkeley Press, 1977. 262. This is a personal narrative told by a member of the female orchestra of the Auschwitz concentration camp. (Arthur Miller wrote a play from Fenelon's memoir by the same title, which was made into a film for tv.)

1050. Ferencz, Benjamin. Less Than Slaves. Cambridge, Mass.: Harvard UP, 1980. 249. Tells the story of Jewish labor conscripted by the major German industrial concerns during WWII. It also recounts the usually futile attempts of the former slave laborers to collect reparations after the Holocaust.

1051. Filipek, Jan. The Shadow of the Gallows : A True Story. Palm Springs, CA: Palm Springs Pub., 1985. 316. A Czech's account of four years in Nazi prisons during WWII.

1052. Friedman, Ina R. The Other Victims: First-Person Accounts of Non-Jews Persecuted by Nazis. Boston: Houghton Mifflin, 1990. 176. This book was developed for a young audience (4th-9th grade) and includes accounts of Nazi persecution of gypsies, homosexuals, Jehovah's Witnesses, Blacks, and accounts of sterilization, censorship, forced labor, etc.

1053. Friedman, Philip. Roads to Extinction: Essays on the Holocaust. New York: Jewish Pub. Soc., 1980. 610. Twenty-four essays on the yellow star, segregation system, etc.

1054. Friedman, Saul, ed. Holocaust Literature: A Handbook of Critical, Historical, and Literary Writings. Westport CT: Greenwood, 1993. 677. Covers biographies of Hitler, concentration camps, belles letters, etc.

1055. Friedman, Saul, ed. The Terezin Diary of Gonda Redlich. Trans. Laurence Kutler. Lexington: U of Kentucky P, 1992. 200. Terezin was a way station to Auschwitz. Redlich kept his diary from 1941 to 1944, when he was also sent to Auschwitz, and when he hid the diary, not discovered until 1967.

1056. Fromer, Rebecca. The Holocaust Odyssey of Daniel Bennahmias, Sonderkommando. Tuskegee: Alabama UP, 1993. 152. An account of the boy's transport from Greece to Auschwitz/Birkenau, the exxtermination of his parents upon arrival, his assignment to the job of preparing gas chamber victims for cremation, an abortive prison rebellion, a final march from Auschwitz to Ebensee, and rescue by U.S. soldiers.

1057. Geve, Thomas. Guns and Barbed Wire: A Child Survives the Holocaust. Chicago: Academy Chicago, 1987. 220. Revised edition of Geve's Youth in Chains (see below).

1058. Geve, Thomas. Youth in Chains. Jerusalem: Rubin Maas, 1981. 262. A memoir of the author's youth in concentration camps.

1059. Gilbert, Martin. The Holocaust: A History of the Jews of Europe During the Second World War. New York: Holt, Rinehart, and Winston, 1985. 959. "This book is an attempt to draw on the nearest of the witnesses, closest to the destruction, and through their testimony to tell something of the suffering of those who perished.

1060. Gill, Anton. The Journey Back from Hell--An Oral History: Conversations with Concentration Camp Survivors. New York: Morrow, 1988. 494. 120 interviews dealing with the suffering and the later adjustments.

1061. Glatstein, Jacob, et al., eds. Anthology of Holocaust Literature. New York: Atheneum, 1977. 412. Selections from books in hopes that it will be a precursor to a definitive anthology derived from many languages (especially Yiddish and Hebrew) and places, by victims, witnesses, and fighters of Nazi perfidy.

1062. Gray, Martin. For Those I Loved. Trans. Anthony White. Boston: Little, Brown, 1971. 351. A memoir of the death camps, escape, and the post-Holocaust years.

1063. Gross, Leonard. The Last Jews in Berlin. New York: Simon and Schuster, 1982; Bantam, 1983. 349. An account of the few thousand Jews who hid in the capitol of the Third Reich during the Holocaust.

1064. Guernsey, Isabel Russell. Free Trip to Berlin. Toronto: Macmillan, 1943. 230. This Canadian citizen was captured at sea by the Germans and interned for a year.

1065. Guide to Yale University Library Holocaust Video Testimonies. New York: Garland; Fortunoff Video Archive, 1990. 116. Summarizes each of the 1500 testimonies and provides several indexes.

1066. Gutman, Israel, et al. eds. The Encyclopedia of the Holocaust. 4 vols. New York: Macmillan, 1990. 1903. Covers 900 entries. Vol. 4 includes a glossary, chronology of events, and an index of 100pp.

1067. Haas, Albert. The Doctor and the Damned. New York: St. Martin's, 1984. 333. The memoir of a French-Hungarian doctor who served in the French underground, was caught by the Nazis, and was deported to Auschwitz, where he was forced to practice medicine.

1068. Handler, Andrew, ed. The Holocaust in Hungary: An Anthology of Jewish Response. Tuscaloosa, AL: U of Alabama P, 1982. 162. Responses of "those who detected the danger signals...and those who bore the burdens of survival."

1069. Hart, Kitty. Return to Auschwitz: The Remarkable Story of a Girl who Survived the Holocaust. New York: Atheneum, 1982. 178. The basis for a TV documentary, this memoir describes life in the Lublin Ghetto, slave labor, and eighteen months in the most dreaded of all concentration camps.

1070. Heimler, Eugene. Concentration Camp (orig. title, Night of Mist). New York: Pyramid Books, 1961; Vanguard, 1969; Westport, Conn.: Greenwood, 1978. 190. Semi-fictional account of a young Hungarian's imprisonment in Auschwitz and Buchenwald.

1071. Hellman, Peter (text). The Auschwitz Album. New York: Random House, 1981. 167. An album of 180 photographs of one group of Hungarian Jews arriving at Auschwitz in 1944.

1072. Hilberg, Raul, ed. Documents of Destruction: German and Jewry 1933-1945. Chicago: Quadrangle, 1971. 242. Anthology of papers written by German perpetrators or Jewish victims during the Holocaust.

1073. Hilberg, Raul, et al., eds. The Warsaw Diary of Adam Czerniakow. Trans. Stanislaw Staron, et al. New York: Stein and Day, 1979. 420. Czerniakow, chairman of the Warsaw Ghetto Judenrat, committed suicide after being ordered to round up children for the death camp.

1074. Hoess, Rudolf. Death Dealer: The Memoirs of the SS Kommandant at Auschwitz. Trans. Andrew Pollinger; ed. Steven Paskuly. Buffalo, NY: Prometheus, 1993. 390. (Kommandant in Auschwitz: The Autobiography of Rudolf Hoess. Trans. Constantine FitzGibbon. Cleveland and New York: World, 1960; New York: Popular Library, 1961. 285.) Perhaps the greatest mass-murderer in history tells how the final solution of the Jews (and Gypsies, homosexuals, free thinkers, political dissidents, and the disabled) was carried out.

1075. Horowitz, Gordon. In the Shadow of Death: Living Outside the Gates of Mauthausen. New York: Free P, 1990. 236. Records recollections of those who lived near Austria's death camp.

1076. Huberband, Simon. Kiddush Hashem: Jewish Religious and Cultural Life in Poland During the Holocaust. Trans. David E. Fishman, et al. New York: Ktav, 1987. 474. The material in this text was compiled by Huberband and others in the Warsaw Ghetto and is divided into four sections: I, autobiographical materials; II, daily life and death in the Warsaw Ghetto; III, Jewish religious life in Nazi-occupied Europe; and IV, the destruction of East European Jewry.

1077. Hunt, Antonia. Little Resistance: A Teenage English Girl's Adventures in Occupied France. London: Secker & Warburg, 1982. 149. Experiences of an English teenager in German occupied France, in an internment camp and Gestapo headquarters in Paris suspected of Resistance activities.

1078. International Auschwitz Committee. Nazi Medicine: Doctors, Victims and Medicine in Auschwitz. New York; Fertig, 1986. Compilation of articles, essays and testimonies from the special issues of the scientific journal Przeglad Lekarski (Medical Review) that dealt specifically with the medical atrocities of the Nazi period.

1079. Jackson, Livia E. Bitton. Elli: Coming of Age in the Holocaust. New York: Times Books, 1980; Harper & Row, 1983. 248. An account of an adolescent's incarceration in Auschwitz and the first months of liberation.

1080. Joseph, Sharon, ed. The Holocaust: An Annotated Bibliography. Montreal, Quebec: National Holocaust Remembrance Committee, Canadian Jewish Congress, 1980. 35. Section one cover historical material (ghettos and camps, war crimes and trials, etc), section two is divided into various themes: art, braille, teacher's guides, etc.

1081. Kantor, Alfred. The Book of Alfred Kantor. New York: McGraw-Hill, 1971. 42. Drawings and commentaries by an inmate of three concentration camps (Terezin, Auschwitz, Schwarzheide).

1082. Kaplan, Chaim A. Scroll of Agony: The Warsaw Diary of Chaim A. Kaplan. Trans. Abraham I. Katsh. Seamen, OH: Collier, 1981. 350. Kaplan's diaries, discovered about twenty years after the liquidation of the Warsaw Ghetto and the author's death at Treblinka, record the bloody period from the Occupation in 1939 to the deportations in 1942.

1083. Karski, Jan. Story of a Secret State. Boston: Houghton Mifflin, 1944. 389. Karski, a member of the Polish Underground, witnessed the mass killings at Belzec, and in 1942 presented the first eyewitness accounts of the Holocaust to Churchill and Roosevelt.

1084. Katz, Esther and Joan Ringelheim, eds. Women Surviving the Holocaust. New York: Institute for Research in History, 1983. 196. Includes interviews and personal accounts pertaining specifically to the experiences of Jewish women in the ghettos and concentration camps.

1085. Katz, Joseph. One Who Came Back: The Diary of a Jewish Survivor. New York: Bergen-Belsen Memorial Press; Herzl Press, 1973. 277. Katz was fifteen when Hitler came to power; by the war's end, he had lived through ghettos, concentration and death camps, and a death march.

1086. Katz, Robert. Black Sabbath: A Journey Through a Crime Against Humanity. New York: Macmillan, 1969. 398. The deportation of Jews from Rome in October, 1943.

1087. Katz, Robert. Death in Rome. New York: Macmillan, 1967. 334. The history of the razzia (roundup for deportation) of Rome's Jews in March 1944.

1088. Kehr, Helen, and Helen Langmaid, eds. The Nazi Era 1919-1945: A Select Bibliography of Published Works From the Early Roots to 1980. London: Mansell, 1982. 621. Divided into nine sections, including V, The Criminal State--B. Persecution and Resistance; and VIII, War Crimes--C. The Holocaust--Individual Accounts.

1089. Kehr, Helen, ed. Persecution and Resistance Under the Nazis. Catalogue Series No. 7. London: Institute of Contemporary History and Wiener Library, 1978. 500. Bibliography of information on Nazi German oppression divided into seven sections: I, Reference Books; II, Persecution in Nazi Germany; III, German Resistance; IV, Persecution and Resistance in Nazi-Occupied Territories; V, Persecution and Resistance of the Jews; VI, War Crimes and Crimes Against Humanity; VII, Aid to the Persecuted.

1090. Kenrick, Donald and Grattan Puxon. The Destiny of Europe's Gypsies. New York: Basic, 1972. 256. Presents a history of Gypsy persecution in Europe and details the Nazis' attempt to exterminate them during the Holocaust.

1091. Kermish, Joseph, ed. To Live With Honor and Die With Honor! Selected Documents from thek Warsaw Ghetto Underground Archives "O.S. [ONEG SHABBAT]." Jerusalem: Yad Vashem, 1986. 790. Presents a wide range of all types of documents discovered in the secret Archives: daily life, forced labor, the "Judenrat," the fate of children, extermination, etc.

1092. Kessel, Sim. Hanged at Auschwitz. Trans. Melville and Delight Wallace. New York: Stein & Day, 1972. 192. Memoir of a man's narrow escapes from death.

1093. Kielar, Wieslaw. Anus Mundi: 1,500 Days in Auschwitz/ Birkenau. Trans. Susanne Flatauer. New York: Times Books/Harper & Row, 1980. 312. The vivid account of a non-Jewish political prisoner, now a Polish film director, of the most terrible death camp.

1094. Klarsfeld, Serge. The Children of Izieu: A Human Tragedy. New York: Holocaust Library, 1985. 134. Contains the letters of Jewish orphans, as young as four years, who were arrested by the Gestapo on April 6, 1944 and deported to Auschwitz where they were immediatly murdered.

1095. Klarsfeld, Serge. Memorial to the Jews Deported from France, 1942-1944. New York: Beate Klarsfeld Foundation, 1983. 633. A list of names of the over 75,000

French Jews deported in the eighty-seven convoys between March 1942 and August 1944, with notes and documents.

1096. Klein, Gerda. All But My Life. New York: Hill & Wang, 1957. 246. An autobiographical account of a woman who became a slave laborer.

1097. Koestler, Arthur. Scum of the Earth. New York: Macmillan, 1968. 287. About the concentration camps and those who worked in them.

1098. Kogen, Eugen. The Theory and Practice of Hell: The German Concentration Camps and the System Behind Them. Trans. Heinz Norden. New York: Berkley-Medium, 1958; Octagon, 1973. 307. An account of the SS and concentration camp system.

1099. Kohner, Hanna, and Walter Kohner. Hanna and Walter: A Love Story. New York: Random House, 1984. 207. About a couple who fell in love, were in separate concentration camps during the Holocaust, and survived to find one another in an accidental reunion.

1100. Korman, Gerd, ed. Hunter and Hunted: Human History of the Holocaust. New York: Viking, 1973. 320. A collection of essays and fragments of personal narratives assembled to provide a chronological frame of reference for the Holocaust, from events preceding WWII to the liberation of concentration camp survivors.

1101. Kraus, Ota, and Erick Kulka, eds. The Death Factory: Documents on Auschwitz. Oxford and London: Oxford UP, 1966; New York: Pergamon, 1966. 284. An anthology.

1102. Krausnick, Helmut, et al. Anatomy of the SS State. Tr. Richard Barry, et al. New York: Walker, 1968. 614. Chapters on the persecution of the Jews, the SS, the concentration camps, and mass murder.

1103. Kren, George M. and Leon Rappoport. The Holocaust and the Crisis of Human Behavior. New York: Holmes & Meier, 1980. 176. Argues that the Holocaust should be understood as something new and totally unique in human history. Chapters II and III focus on Germany and the SS; Chapters IV and V focus on the victims and their resistance.

1104. Laks, Szymon. Music of Another World. Trans. Chester A. Kisiel. Evanston, IL: Northwestern UP, 1989. 130. (Revised from the original version published in French, 1948). About the orchestra in Auschwitz II-Birkenau, the German persecutors' hunger for music, the prisoners' hunger for food, and the role of music in the extermination camps.

1105. Langer, Lawrence L. Holocaust Testimonies: The Ruins of Memory. New Haven, CT: Yale UP, 1991. 216. These narratives "raise few expectations of renewal or hopes of reconciliation," but tell of "disruption, absence, and irreversible loss."

1106. Langhoff, Wolfgang. Rubber Truncheon: Being on Account of Thirteen Months Spent in a Concentration Camp. Tr. Lilo Linke. New York: Dutton, 1935. 280. The author, an actor, was arrested in 1933 for his political views and social activities.

1107. Laska, Vera, comp. Nazism, Resistance & Holocaust in World War II: A Bibliography. Metuchen, NJ: Scarecrow, 1985. 183. A mostly non-annotated bibliography of books divided into thirteen categories: Jews and Anti-Semitism; Nazism; Resistance; Resistance-Women; Jewish Resistance; Holocaust; Holocaust-Women; Women in Hiding; War Crimes; Art and Photographs; Philosophy and Interpretation; and Literature.

1108. Laska, Vera, ed. Women in the Resistance and the Holocaust: The Voices of Eyewitnesses. Westport CT: Greenwood, 1983. 330. The three sections, "Women in the Resistance," "Women in Concentration Camps," and "Women in Hiding," include over 25 personal narratives.

1109. Last Letters of Resistance : Farewells from the Bonhoeffer Family. Philadelphia: Fortress, 1986. 117. Testimonies from the period before they were killed in connection with the plot of July 20, 1944 to assassinate Hitler.

1110. Leber, Annedore. Conscience in Revolt. Trans. Rosemary O'Neill. Widerstand Series: Dissent & Resistance in the Third Reich. Boulder, CO: Westview, 1994. 270. (Originally published in 1954). Brief biographies of sixty-four members of the German Resistance against the Nazis.

1111. Leitner, Isabella. Fragments of Isabella: A Memoir of Auschwitz. Ed. Irving A. Leitner. New York: Crowell, 1978; Dell, 1980. 112. A series of vignettes about Auschwitz, the memoirs of a survivor.

1112. Leitner, Isabella, and Irving Leitner. Saving the Fragments: From Auschwitz to New York. New York. New American Library, 1985. 145. Biographies of holocaust survivors in the United States.

1113. Lengyel, Olga. Five Chimneys. Chicago: Ziff-Davis, 1947. 213. A memoir of Auschwitz.

1114. Lenz, John M. Christ in Dachau or Christ Victorious: Experiences in a Concentration Camp. Trans. Barbara Waldstein. Vienna: n.p., 1960. 328. A priest's personal account of his arrests and imprisonments, mainly in Dachau, where 2,720 clerics (mainly Catholics) were incarcerated, 1,034 of whom died.

1115. Letters From the Doomed : Concentration Camp Correspondence 1940-45. Ed. and trans. Richard S. Geehr. Lanham, MD: UP of America, 1992. 71. Misc. letters written from 1940 to 1944 from Dachau and other Nazi concentration camps.

1116. Letulle, Claude J. Nightmare Memoir: Four Years as a Prisoner of the Nazis. Baton Rouge: Louisiana State UP, 1987. 132. This French prisoner of war assigned to a job at a Nazi experimental hospital describes victims tortured as guinea pigs in the cause of "racial science."

1117. Levi, Primo. The Drowned and the Saved. Trans. Raymond Rosenthal. New York: Summit, 1986. 203. A study of the extermination camps, "the central event, the scourge, of this century"--collaborators, resisters, the SS, guilt felt by survivors, etc.

1118. Levi, Primo. Survival in Auschwitz: The Nazi Assault on Humanity (orig. title, If This Be A Man). Trans. Stuart Woolf. New York: Orion, 1959; Collier, 1973. 157. Account of one man's strategy for survival.

1119. Levy, Claude and Paul Tillard. Betrayal at the Vel d'Hiv. New York: Hill and Wang, 1969. 284. On the roundup and deportation of Parisian Jews in July 1942.

1120. Lévy-Hass, Hanna. Inside Belsen. Trans. Ronald Taylor. Sussex, Eng: Harvester; Totowa, NJ: Barnes & Noble, 1982. 134. (First published in Berlin, 1979). The author kept her diary during 1944-1945 when Belgen-Belsen became a dumping ground for the camps being closed (28,000 arrived during one week in 1945) and organization collapsed, food disappeared, disease killed thousands daily, and jungle law prevailed.

1121. Lewinska, Pelagia. Twenty Months at Auschwitz. Trans. Albert Teichner. New York: Lyle Stuart, 1968. 155. A memoir of Auschwitz.

1122. Lifton, Robert Jay. The Nazi Doctors: Medical Killing and the Psychology of Genocide. New York: Basic, 1986. 561. Focuses on the tasks of the physician during the Holocaust: selecting victims, supervising the gassings, falsifying death certificates, medical experimentation on human subjects, etc.

1123. Lorant, Stefan. I was Hitler's Prisoner: A Diary. New York: Putnam, 1935. 318. The author, editor of a large newspaper in Munich, was imprisoned 6 months in 1933 without charge or trial, and his wife was imprisoned briefly for protesting.

1124. Luel, Steven A. and Paul Marcus, eds. Psychoanalytic Reflections on the Holocaust: Selected Essays. New York: Holocaust Awareness Institute, Center for Judaic Studies, University of Denver; Ktav, 1984. 239. Anthology of essays approaching the "physical horror" of the Holocaust from various psychodynamic perspectives: I, Ideological and Cultural Perspectives; II. Differing Views of Survivorship; III, A Generation After.

1125. Machlejd, Wanda. Experimental Operations on Prisoners of Ravensbrück Concentration Camp. Warsaw: Zachodnia Agencja, 1960. 58. An account of the terrifying experimental operations the Nazis performed on the women of Ravenbrück.

1126. Marrus, Michael R. The Holocaust in History. Hanover, NH: UP of New England, 1987. 267. Several chapters on the mass murders of the Final Solution.

1127. Marrus, Michael R., ed. The Nazi Holocaust: Historical Articles on the Destruction of European Jews. 9 vols. Westport, CT: Meckler, 1989. Vol. 3: The "Final Solution": The Implementation of Mass Murder; Vol. 4, The "Final Solution" Outside Germany. Vol. 6: The Victims of the Holocaust, 1259, includes articles on the extermination camps--Operation Reinhard, the gas chambers, Belzec, Auschwitz, Sajmiste, etc.

1127a. Marrus, Michael R. and Robert O. Paxton. Vichy France and the Jews. New York: Basic Books, 1981. 432. On Vichy anti-Semitism and the process of rounding up, deporting, and exterminating Jews.

1128. Maurel, Micheline. An Ordinary Camp. Trans. Margaret S. Summers. New York: Simon & Schuster, 1958. 141. An account of daily life in Neubrandburg concentration camp.

1129. Mayer, Arno J. Why Did the Heavens Not Darken? The "Final Solution" In History. New York: Pantheon, 1988. 492. A survey of the Holocaust from begining to end: two chapters on Operation Barbarossa (the savage, total war against "Judeobolshevism"), one chapter on Auschwitz, a chapter on other extermination sites.

1130. Mechanicus, Phillip. Waiting for Death: A Diary. Trans. Irene R. Gibbons. London: Calder & Boyars, 1968. 267. (Year of Fear: A Jewish Prisoner Waits for Auschwitz. New York: Hawthorn, 1968. 267.) The diary of a year in Westerbork 1943-44, the Dutch transit camp, written by a Dutch-Jewish journalist who perished in Auschwitz.

1131. Mendelsohn, John and Donald S. Detwiler, eds. The Holocaust: Selected Documents in Eighteen Volumes. New York: Garland, 1982. Volumes 8-13, "The Killing of the Jews"; volumes 14-16, "Rescue Attempts"; volumes 17-18, "Punishment" (i.e. of the perpetrators). Volume 8 on deportations; volume 9 on medical experiments in concentration camps; volume 10 on murder commandos; volume 11 on Wannsee and Auschwitz; volume 12 on the extermination camps; volume 13 on the judicial system.

1132. Merson, Allen. Communist Resistance in Nazi Germany. London: Laurence & Wishart; Atlantic Highlands, NJ: Humanities, 1985. 372. Chapter Seven, "A Losing

Battle," surveys the mass arrests and imprisonments 1933-1936; later chapters have scattered details.

1133. Michaelis, Meir. Mussolini and the Jews: German-Italian Relations and the Jewish Question in Italy, 1922-1945. New York: Oxford UP, 1978. 472. An account of Mussolini's relatively "tolerant" attitude toward the Jews until 1937, and the attempts made by many Italian officials to sabotage the final solution thereafter.

1134. Micheels, Louis J. Doctor #117641: A Holocaust Memoir. New Haven, CT: Yale UP, 1989. 199. The author tells how he and his fiancée survived Auschwitz.

1135. Michel, Jean, and Louis Nuoera. Dora. Trans. Jennifer Kidd. New York: Holt, Rinehart & Winston, 1980. 308. Dora was a German slave labor camp.

1136. Mikhel'son, Frida. I Survived Rumbuli. Ed. and Trans. Wolf Goodman. New York: Schocken, 1979. 232. A memoir by one of the two survivors of the Riga Ghetto.

1137. Miller, Arthur. Playing For Time. Chicago: Dramatic Publishing, 1985. 91. Full length stage play based upon Fania Fenelon's Playing For Time (see above).

1138. Mirchuk, Petro. In the German Mills of Death, 1941-1945. 2nd ed. Washington, D.C.; Rochester, NY: The Survivors of the Holocaust; Ukrainian American Freedom Foundation, 1985. 225. Circumstantial account of one Ukrainian's perilous experiences in Nazi prisons and concentration camps.

1139. Mishell, William M. Kaddish for Kovno: Life and Death in a Lithuanian Ghetto, 1941-1945. Chicago: Chicago Review, 1988. 384. Mishell's recording of the horrors of the Kovno Ghetto under the Nazis and their Lithuanian, Latvian, and Ukrainian collaborators, including descriptions of many mass executions of Jews.

1140. Mitscherlich, Alexander, and Fred Mielke. Doctors of Infamy. Trans. Heinz Norden. New York: H. Schumann, 1949. 172. Nazi medical crimes.

1141. Mommsen, Hans. From Weimar to Auschwitz. Princeton, NJ: Princeton UP, 1991. 367. Essays on German resistance to Hitler and on the final solution.

1142. Morais, Fernando. Olga: The "Gift" to Hitler. London: Halban, 1990. 245. Olga Benario, German Jew and Communist activist married to the leader of the Brazilian Communist Party, was arrested and deported to Nazi Germany.

1143. Mortality Among Netherlands Concentration Camp Survivors. The Hague: Netherlands Central Bureau of Statistics, 1977. 69. Comparison of mortality rates of Dutch concentration camp survivors to rates of entire Dutch population shows a considerably lower rate among survivors.

1144. Muffs, Judith Herschlag, ed. The Holocaust in Books and Films: A Selected, Annotated List. New York: Anti-Defamation League of B'nai B'rith, 1982. 67. Covers many topics including "Camps, Ghettos, In Hiding" and "Resistance and Rescue."

1145. Muller, Filip. Eyewitness Auschwitz: Three Years in the Gas Chambers at Auschwitz. Ed. and Trans. Susanne Flatauer. New York: Stein & Day, 1979. 180. Muller survived working in the gassing installations and crematoria from May 1942 and was still alive when the gassings ceased in November 1944.

1146. Nahon, Marco. Birkenau, The Camp of Death. Ed. Steven Bowman. Trans. Jacqueline Bowers. Tusçaloosa: U of Alabama P, 1989. 144. The experiences of a Greek Jewish medical doctor in concentration camps.

1147. Naumann, Bernd. Auschwitz. New York: Praeger, 1966. 433. Contains much testimony and documentation on Auschwitz, in part based on the Frankfurt trials of those accused of war crimes.

1148. Niewyk, Donald, ed. The Holocaust: Problems and Perspectives on Interpretation. Problems in European Civilization Series. Lexington, MS: D.C. Heath, 1992. 267. Chapter two, "The Holocaust Experience," contains essays mainly on the victims' will and ability to survive.

1149. Nomberg-Przytyk, Sara. Auschwitz: True Tales from a Grotesque Land. Eds. Eli Pfefferkorn and David H. Hirsch. Trans. Roslyn Hirsch. Chapel Hill: U of North Carolina P, 1985. 185. (Originally in Polish, 1966). Narrates her experiences in the camp and the victims there--e.g., a young couple in love who escape but are captured, tortured, and executed.

1150. Nyiszli, Miklós. Auschwitz: A Doctor's Eyewitness Account. Trans. Tibére Kremer, et al. New York: Frederick Fell, 1960; Crest, 1973; Fawcett, 1977. 222. An account of the infamous medical experiments, including those of Josef Mengele.

1151. Oberski, Jona. Childhood. Trans. Ralph Manheim. Garden City, NY: Doubleday, 1983; Plume Books/New American Library, 1984. 119. Partially fictional memoir covering life under Nazi occupation, in a transit, a concentration camp, and, finally, the first days after liberation.

1152. Pawelczynska, Anna. Values and Violence in Auschwitz: A Sociological Analysis. Berkeley: U of California P, 1979. 170. The author was a resistance fighter arrested by the Gestapo in 1942 and sent to Auschwitz. This book focuses on "individual resistance to coercion."

1153. Phillips, Raymond, ed. Trial of Jesef Kramer and Forty-Two Others (The Belsen Trial). London: William Hodge, 1949. 749. Contains the evidence presented against the Nazis who ran Bergen-Belsen, the testimony of survivors and liberators which details the horrors of the death camp.

1154. Phillips, Walter. The Tragedy of Nazi Germany. London: Routledge & K. Paul, 1969. 241. Chapter 4 on concentration camps and the extermination policy.

1155. Pies, Otto. The Victory of Father Karl. Trans. Salvator Attanasio. New York: Farrar, Strauss and Cudahy, 1957. 210. Biography of Karl Leisner, a German priest, including his arrest at the age of 24 from a tubercular ward, his interrogation by the Gestapo, and his life in Dachau concentration camp.

1156. Playing For Time. Dir. Daniel Mann. Prod. Linda Yellen. With Vanessa Redgrave. Syzygy Productions Ltd., 1984. 148 min. Based on Fania Fenelon's Playing For Time (see above).

1157. Poller, Walter. Medical Block, Buchenwald: The Personal Testimony of Inmate 966, Block 39. London: Corgi, 1965. 254. Details the various medical experiments on human beings committed in Buchenwald.

1158. Pressac, Claude. The Crematoria of Auschwitz: The Machinery of Mass Murder. Paris: National Center for Scientific Research, 1993. 100. Describes how German companies competed for contracts to build the gas chambers and how engineers, contractors, and workers struggled to keep them operating and more efficient. The first oven at Dachau in 1939 burned two corpses an hour; by the end of the war more than 4,300 were burned at Auschwitz daily.

1159. Presser, Jacob. The Destruction of the Dutch Jews. Trans. Arnold Pomerans. New York: Dutton, 1965. 556. An account, part-history, part-memoir, of the life and death of Dutch Jews under Nazi occupation.

1160. Ramati, Alexander. And the Violins Stopped Playing: A Story of the Gypsy Holocaust. New York: Franklin Watts, 1986. 237. Roman Mirga, a Gypsy survivor of Birkenau, tells of that death camp, the early years of Nazi persecution of the Gypsies, and execution of the Gypsies on the road to Lukov.

1161. Rawicz, Piotr. Blood From the Sky. Trans. Peter Wiles. New York: Harcourt, Brace & World, 1964. 316. Records the steps to extinction and the frantic activities of the doomed.

1162. Rector, Frank. The Nazi Extermination of Homosexuals. New York: Stein and Day, 1981. 189. Details the policy of extermination, treatment in camps, and includes personal testimony.

1163. Return to Auschwitz, A. Videocassette. Dir. Peter Morley. Prod. Peter Morley and Kevin Sim. Chicago: Films Incorporated, 1979. 90 min. Thirty-four years after her liberation, Kitty Felix Hart (see above) visits the grounds of Auschwitz where she was an inmate.

1164. Rigby, Françoise (née Labouverie). In Defiance. London: Eleck, 1960. 224. The memoirs of a Belgian Resistance member during WWII, imprisoned in 1944 but released the same year when Brussels was liberated.

1165. Ringelblum, Emmanuel. Notes from the Warsaw Ghetto: The Journal of Emmanuel Ringelblum. New York: Shocken, 1975. 369. Details the day to day struggle of the Jews in all aspects of life as well as the personal views and torments of Ringelblum, the important archivist and historian who founded the Underground Archives in the Warsaw Ghetto and later died in Auschwitz.

1166. Ringelheim, Joan and Esther Katz. A Catalogue of Audio and Video Collections of Holocaust Testimony. New York: Institute for Research in History, 1986. 238. Lists and details the contents of 41 audio and video collections of Holocaust testimony in the U.S. and Canada.

1167. Robinson, Jacob and Mrs. Philip Friedman. The Holocaust and After: Sources and Literature in English. Jerusalem: Yad Vashem and YIVO Institute for Jewish Research, 1973. 353. Bibliography covers books, periodicals, films and television, gives summaries and reviews in English of books and articles in other languages, and is divided into seven sections: General; Background; Persecution and Extermination; The Jews in and Outside the Nazi Terror; etc.

1168. Robinson, Jacob and Henry Sachs, eds. The Holocaust: The Nuremberg Evidence--Part One: Documents. Jerusalem: Yad Vashem and YIVO Institute for Jewish Research, 1976. 370. Bibliography contains many listings and annotations of first-person accounts by survivors of the Holocaust on many topics: camps, mass extermination, children and infants, sterilization and other medical procedures and experiments, etc.

1169. Rosenberg, Alan and Gerald E. Myers, eds. Echoes From the Holocaust: Philosophical Reflections on a Dark Time. Philadelphia: Temple UP, 1988. 453. Anthology of presentations from a conference of philosophers May 1985, concerning choice in the death camps and other philosophical issues.

1170. Rothchild, Sylvia, ed. Voices from the Holocaust. New York: New American Library, 1981. 456. A compilation of Holocaust testimonies from survivors of all walks of life who are now living in the U.S.

1171. Rousset, David. The Other Kingdom. Trans. Ramon Guthrie. New York: Reynal & Hitchcock, 1947. 173. Memoir of the concentration camp universe.

1172. Rudolf, Anthony, ed. I'm Not Even a Grown-Up: The Diary of Jerzy Feliks Urman. Trans. Anthony Rudolf and Joanna Voit. London: Menard/Kings, 1991. 54. A Jewish child's diary of his family's efforts to hide from the Nazis in West Ukraine. At the age of eleven he committed suicide to avoid arrest, after hiding eight months in one room with his parents and two relatives.

1173. Sable, Martin. Holocaust Studies: A Directory and Bibliography of Bibliographies. Greenwood, FL: Penkevill, 1987. 115. Includes listings of bibliographies published in numerous different languages, multi-lingual bibliographies, organizations, archives, libraries and publishers, information and research centers, etc.

1174. Sanbar, Moshe. My Long Year in the Hungarian Labor Service and in the Nazi Camps. Trans. S.C. Hyman. Jerusalem: Yad Vashem, 1968. 114. On an aspect of the Holocaust in Hungary.

1175. Schlabrendorff, Fabian von. The Secret War Against Hitler. Trans. Hilda Simon. Widerstand Series: Dissent & Resistance in the Third Reich. New York: Pitman, 1965; Boulder, CO: Westview, 1994. 438. Schlabrendorff's memoir of his days in the German Resistance against the Nazis.

1176. Schoenfeld, Joachim. Holocaust Memoirs. New York: Ktav, 1984. 328. What it was like in the Lwów Ghetto and the nearby Janowska concentration camp.

1177. Scholl, Inge. Students Against Tyranny: The Resistance of the White Rose, Munich, 1942-1943. Trans. Aurthur R. Schultz. Middletown, CT: Wesleyan UP, 1970. 160. Reissued in paper as The White Rose, Munich 1942-43 (1983). On the students and professors executed or imprisoned for opposing Hitler in Munich and Hamburg.

1178. Schreurs, Joannes J. M. H. A Will to Resist. San Mateo, CA: Western Book Journal, 1988. 122. The author, an underground fighter in the Netherlands, was caught trying to escape into Spain, tortured, escaped, and captured again.

1179. Schwarberg, Guenther. Murders at Bullenhauser Dam: The S.S. Doctor and the Children. Trans. Erna Rosenfeld, et al. Bloomington: Indiana UP, 1984. 178. On the torture and murder in April 1945 of twenty Jewish children, ages five to twelve, by SS doctor Kurt Heissmeyer.

1180. Schwartz, Leo, ed. The Root and the Bough: The Epic of an Enduring People. New York: Rinehart, 1949. 362. 32 personal narratives by survivors of the Holocaust.

1181. Selzer, Michael. Deliverance Day: The Last Hours of Dachau. New York: Lippincott, 1978. 253. An account of the last days of the concentration camp, as seen from the perspectives of the Germans, the Jewish and other prisoners, and the liberating American army.

1182. Sereny, Gitta. Into That Darkness: From Mercy Killing to Mass Murder. New York: McGraw-Hill, 1974. 379. Based upon interviews with the Kommandant of Sobibor and Treblinka extermination camps, augmented by other interviews and research.

1183. Sevillias, Errikos. Athens-Auschwitz. Trans. Nikos Stavroulakis. Athens, Greece: Lycabettus, 1983. 109. A memoir of life in Athens during the Holocaust and of deportation to Auschwitz.

1184. Shapell, Nathan. Witness to Truth. New York: McKay, 1974. 386. Memoir of Auschwitz.

1185. Shelly, Lore, ed. Secretaries of Death: Accounts by Former Prisoners Who Worked in the Gestapo of Auschwitz. New York: Shengold, 1986. 378. Gives the accounts of 27 Jewish women and four non-Jewish men who were forced to work for the Gestapo in Auschwitz keeping records of the living and the dead, and recording interrogation/torture sessions.

1186. Sherwin, Byron L. and Susan G. Ament, eds. Encountering the Holocaust: An Interdisciplinary Survey. Chicago: Impact, 1979. 502. Designed as a text-manual and model curriculum for U.S. colleges and universities. Has chapters on law, psychology, diaries and memoirs, imaginative literature, etc.

1187. Shub, Boris, ed. Hitler's Ten-Year War on the Jews. New York: Institute of Jewish Affairs of the American Jewish Congress, 1943. 311. Country by country survey.

1188. Simon Wiesenthal Center Annual (1984-). "The first serial publication in the United States focusing on the scholarly study of the Holocaust." Vol. 1 contains articles on the postwar German judiciary and Nazi crimes, women in the Holocaust, Auschwitz, rescue attempts, etc.

1189. Smith, Marcus J. The Harrowing Hell: Dachau. Albequerque: U of New Mexico P, 1972. 291. A scholarly look at the structure of Dachau and at its many kinds of torture.

1190. Smolen, Kazimierz, ed. From the History of KL-Auschwitz. Trans. Krystyna Michalik. New York: Howard Fertig, 1982. 225. (Originally published in Polish, 1967). Essays on the organization of Auschwitz-Birkenau, the system of punishment, medical experiments, starvation, escapes, most important events in its history, and individual cases. "KL" stands for Concentration Camp.

1191. Sosnowski, Kiryl. The Tragedy of Children Under Nazi Rule. New York: Howard Fertig, 1983. 381. Part II deals with children of other nations--expulsion, kidnapping, direct extermination of 1,200,000 Jewish children, 60,000 mentally or physically handicapped children in Germany alone, forced labor, etc.

1192. Stiffel, Frank. The Tale of the Ring: A Kaddish. Wainscott, NY: Pushcart, 1984. 358. Stiffel kept diaries throughout his incarceration at Auschwitz, where he was made a hospital orderly and was able to learn about the systematic murders and the gruesome medical experimentation being conducted by Mengele and Koenig.

1193. Strauss, Walter, ed. Signs of Life: Jews from Württemberg, Reports for the Period After 1933 in Letters and Descriptions. New York: Ktav, 1982. 389. Nearly 500 first-person accounts describing their suffering under Nazi rule.

1194. Szajkowski, Zosa. Jews and the French Foreign Legion. New York: Ktav, 1975. 280. On the deportation and internment as forced laborers in North African concentration camps of Jewish refugees who had voluntarily served in the French armed forces against the Germans until the fall of France in 1940.

1195. Szmaglewska, Seweryna. Smoke Over Birkenau. Trans. Jadwiga Rynas. New York: Holt, Rinehart & Winston, 1947. 386. Memoir about Birkenau.

1196. Szonyi, David M. ed. The Holocaust : An Annotated Bibliography and Resource Guide. New York: KTAV for the National Jewish Resource Center, 1985. 396. Thirteen general topics are covered, such as Memoirs, Other Nonfiction of the Holocaust (the largest section), Literature of the Holocaust, and Bibliographies on the Holocaust for Young People.

1197. ten Boom, Corrie. A Prisoner--and Yet!. Toronto: Evangelical, 1947. 170. She was imprisoned in 1944 with her sister and father for harboring Jews in their home in Haarlem, Holland (her father and sister died in prison).

1198. Tillion, Germaine. Ravensbrück. Garden City, NY: Doubleday, 1975. 256. A survivor of Ravensbrück, the largest women's concentration camp, details the drudgery of daily life, of forced labor, and of death in the camp.

1199. Totten, Samuel, comp. "Fate of the Gypsies During the Holocaust Years." First-Person Accounts of Genocidal Acts Committed in the Twentieth Century: An Annotated Bibliography. Westport, CT: Greenwood, 1991. 261-273. 61 entries.

1200. Totten, Samuel, comp. "Holocaust (1939-1945)." First-Person Accounts of Genocidal Acts Committed in the Twentieth Century: An Annotated Bibliography. Westport, CT: Greenwood, 1991. 91-260. 700 entries, the largest section of the book, covering, besides first-person accounts, bibliographies, archival guides, filmographies, newsletters and journals, organizations, repositories, oral history projects, essays on first-person accounts, use of first-person accounts in reports, studies and research, and films/videotapes.

1201. Trial of the Major War Criminals Before the International Military Tribunal, Nuremberg, 14 November 1945-October 1946. 42 vols. Nuremberg: International Military Tribunal, 1947-1949. Official Blue Series transcripts of the International Military Tribunal's trial of the major Axis war criminals containing pretrial documents, judgements and sentencing, as well as tens of thousands of incriminating documents and testimony of those who suffered the atrocities committed by the Nazi regime.

1202. Trial of War Criminals Before the Nuremberg Military Tribunals Under Control Council Law No. 10. 15 vols. Washington, D.C.: U.S. Government Printing Office, 1949-1953. Official Green Series transcripts of the Nuremberg Trials--330,000+ pages of incriminating documentary evidence and judgements pertaining to the Holocaust.

1203. Von Hassell, Fey. Hostage of the Third Reich : The Story of My Imprisonment and Rescue From the SS. Ed. David Watt. New York: Scribner, 1989. About a fourth of the book is about her arrest as a hostage, because she was the daughter of one of the plotters to kill Hitler in 1944 (he was executed).

1204. Vrba, Rudolph, and Alan Bestic. I Cannot Forgive. New York: Grove, 1964. 281. Exposes the savagery of the SS prison system. Vrba endured Maidenek and Auschwitz, escaped from Auschwitz in 1944, and joined a Czech partisan unit.

1205. Weinstock, Earl, and Herbert Wilner. The Seven Years. New York: Dutton, 1959. 254. Remininscences of a childhood and youth in a concentration camp.

1206. Wells, Leon W. The Janowska Road. London: Cape, 1966. 307. (Retitled The Death Brigade. New York: Macmillan, 1963; Holocaust Library, 1978.) Imprisoned by the Nazis at the age of sixteen, he twice escaped Janowska Prison, where he endured great hardship. His parents, two brothers, and four sisters disappeared.

1207. Wiechert, Ernst. The Forests of the Dead. Trans. Ursula Stechow. New York: Greenberg, 1947. 135. Autobiographical account of the concentration camp experience by a non-Jewish German writer.

1208. Wiesel, Elie. Night. Trans. Stella Rodway. New York: Hill & Wang, 1960; Avon, 1972. 116. Recounts the author's years in concentration camps and the loss of his family, together with the moral dilemma regarding religious faith and conviction.

1209. Wytwycky, Bohdan. The Other Holocaust: Many Circles of Hell--A Brief Account of 9-10 Million Persons Who Died With the 6 Million Jews Under Nazi Racism. Washington, D.C.: The Novak Report on the New Ethnicity, 1980. 95. Focuses on the Gypsies, Poles, Ukrainians, Belorussians, prisoners of war, and slave laborers.

1210. Yahil, Leni. The Holocaust: The Fate of European Jewry, 1932-1945. Trans. Ina Friedman and Haya Galai. New York; Oxford: Oxford UP, 1990. 808. On the mass murder of Europe's Jews and their struggle for life, divided into three historical periods: 1932-1939, 1939-1941, 1941-1945. Bibliography of sources pp.753-784 divided into 7 sections.

1211. Young, Richard John. Hitler, His Generals and the Commissar Order. Washington D.C.: Georgetown U, 1978. 92. The Order that separated Soviet political officers from other prisoners for summary execution.

1212. Zahn, Gordon C. In Solitary Witness: The Life and Death of Franz Jägerstäetter. New York: Holt, Rinehart & Winston, 1964. 277. For refusing induction in the army in WW II Jägerstätter was imprisoned and then beheaded in 1943 after a military trial.

1213. Zeller, Eberhard. The Flame of Freedom: The German Struggle Against Hitler. Trans. R.P. Heller and D.R. Masters. Widerstand Series: Dissent & Resistance in the Third Reich. Boulder, CO: Westview, 1994. 471. (Originally published in 1963). Historical account of the German Resistance, including the attempted assassination of Hitler on 20 July, 1994.

1214. Zubatsky, David S., ed. Jewish Autobiography and Biographies: An International Biography of Books and Dissertations in English. New York; London: Garland, 1989. 370. Includes citations of autobiographies and memoirs by 138 survivors of the Holocaust and thirteen works by Holocaust victims.

GHANA

1215. Adjei, Mike. "Government Rings." Index on Censorship 17.6 (June 1988) 23-26. Adjei was arrested for writing an article on Flt.Lt. Jerry Rawlings, the head of the military government.

1216. Amnesty International Report 1980. London: Amnesty International, 1980. 49-50. A coup in 1979 led by Lt. Jerry Rawlings resulted in quick executions of three former heads of state and other officials without fair trials, and numerous people were beaten, flogged, and detained in army camps, and sentenced to long terms without fair trials. Civilian government has been restored, but the house-cleaning trials continue. Several hundred prisoners arrested before the coup were amnestied by the new government.

1217. Amnesty International Report 1990. New York: Amnesty International, 1990. 101-2. At least 50 prisoners detained after alleged coup attempts in 1982 and 1985 are still held without charge or trial. Two leading officials of the Bar Association were held without charge for two and three weeks respectively.

1218. Amnesty International. Amnesty International's Concerns in the Republic of Ghana : An Amnesty International Background Paper. New York: Amnesty International, 1983. 17. On detention without charge, unfair trials, torture, and arbitrary killings. Many detainees identified by name.

1219. Appiah, Joe. The Man, J.B. Danquah. Accra: Academy of Arts and Sciences, 1974. 51. About the "co-architect of independence" of Ghana, who was imprisoned in 1961 for opposing Nkrumah's detention law and other dissent.

1220. DeCormis, Anna. "Ghana: Amnesty International Decries Journalists' Arrest." Guardian 40.18 (Feb. 3, 1988) 12. Seven journalists have been jailed without charge by the Rawlings regime for six months.

1221. DeCormis, Anna. "Ghana: One Year Later, Opposition leaders Still in Jail." Guardian 40.37 (June 15, 1988) 13. Kwame Karikari, university professor and journalist, and others are imprisoned without charge or trial.

1222. DeCormis, Anna. "Ghana: Rawlings Frees Journalist." Guardian 41.16 (Jan. 18, 1989) 16. Journalist Kwame Karikari has been released, detained without charge since 1987.

1223. Dr. J.B. Danquah: Detention and Death in Nsawam Prison: Extracts form Evidence of Witnesses at the Commission of Enquiry into Ghana Prisons. Accra-Tema: Ministry of Information, 1967. 212. Contains a summary of his detention and death, testimonies of 22 witnesses, and (the bulk of the book), various petitions by Danquah.

1224. Ghana. Commission of Enquiry into Ghana Prisons. Mr. E. Obetsebi-Lamptey: Detention and Death in Nsawam Prison: Extracts From Evidence of Witnesses at the Commission of Enquiry into Ghana Prisons. Accra-Tema, Ghana: Ministry of Information, 1967. 51.

1225. Kesse-Adu, Kwame. The Politics of Political Prisoners. Tema: Ghana Pub. Corp., 1971. 225. A survey of the repressive regime of Nkrumah. Includes the petitions written by Dr. J.B. Danquah while in prison.

1226. Safo-Adu, Kwame. Quo Vadis, Africa?: Letters From Ghana Prison, 1972. New York: Vantage, 1985. 63. Imprisoned for 18 months by the military junta which overthrew the democratically elected government, of which the author was Agriculture Minister. The six letters were written in 1972.

1227. Thompson, D. Odotei. I Was Nkrumah's Prisoner. Accra: D.O. Thompson, 1971. 48. An account of his experiences as a prisoner of Kwame Nkrumah's regime in Ussher Fort Prison for over three years.

GREECE

1228. Amnesty International Report 1980. London: Amnesty International, 1980. 276-77. Greece legally recognized conscientious objection to military service in 1977 and offered alternative service, but Jehovah's Witnesses refuse any service and are imprisoned.

1229. Amnesty International Report 1990. New York: Amnesty International, 1990. 102-3. Some 400 conscientious objectors to military service are in prison under four to five year sentences, most of them Jehovah's Witnesses. Some alleged ill-treatment by police.

1230. Becket, James. Barbarism in Greece: A Young Lawyer's Inquiry into the Use of Torture in Contemporary Greece, with Case Histories and Documents. New York: Tower, 1970. 245. New York: Walker, 1970. 147. Ten case histories of representative victims (an actress, a priest, documents from Amnesty International, the Red Cross), torture methods and places, names of torturers, and a list of victims.

1231. Boetsch, Jacques. "The Monday of Mikis Theodorakis." Saturday Review 53 (May 9, 1970) 14-15, 71. An account of Jean-Jacques Servan-Schreiber's successful mission to Athens to free Theodorakis.

1232. "Conspiracy of Conscience." Time 98 (October 11, 1971) 53. Lady Amalia Fleming was sentenced to prison for aiding the aborted plot to free Alexandros Panaghoulis, who had attempted to assassinate the dictator George Papadopoulos.

1233. "Escape by Red Carpet." Time 99 (May 1, 1972) 27. Professor George-Alexander Mangakis, authority on penal law, is released form prison. He had been sentenced to an eighteen-year term for attempting to topple the military regime.

1234. Fleming, Amalia. A Piece of Truth. London: Jonathan Cape, 1972; Boston: Houghton Mifflin, 1972. 257. Lady Fleming was prosecuted in 1971 for her opposition to the repression of the military dictators of Greece, and then exiled to England. This is her story.

1235. "Flight to Freedom." Newsweek 75 (April 27, 1970) 56+. Mikis Theodorakis is freed.

1236. Free Speech on Trial: Government Stifles Dissent on Macedonia. New York: Human Rights Watch, July 1993. 7. Increased repression including tampering with prosecutions out of fear of the former Yugoslav Republic of Macedonia.

1237. "Furor over Prisoners." Time 91 (April 19, 1968) 38. Charges of brutality and torture of political prisoners under the regime of Colonel George Papadopoulos.

1238. Gage, Nicholas. "The Prisoner of Amorgos." New York Times Magazine (Sept. 21, 1969) 23-5+. Discussion (Oct. 12, 1969) 16, (October 26, 1969) 16. About army officers arrested and exiled to villages following the 1967 coup.

1239. Goldbloom, Maurice. "How the Military Rules 8 Million Greeks." New York Times Magazine (Sept. 24, 1967) 26-7. Report on the thousands of arrest following the military takeover and the incarceration of prisoners in a concentration camp on Yiaros Island.

1240. Goldbloom, Maurice. "The Two Greeces." Commonweal 93 (February 5, 1971) 441-4. The Greek military government and the U.S. government claim Greece is working toward democracy, but the truth is the opposite.

1241. Greece: Torture and Ill-Treatment. New York: Amnesty International, 1992. 55. The systematic torture of political prisoners ended with the fall of the military government in 1974, yet detainees are still at risk in police stations and prisons in Greece.

1242. Greek Women in Resistance: Journals, Oral Histories. Ed. Eleni Fourtouni. New Haven: Thelphini, 1980. 163. Covers the period 1940-1950--the resistance against the Germans during WWII and the civil war 1945-1950. These accounts include prison and trial experiences. Also see Concentration Camps for Women (in Greek) edited by Victoria Theodorou (1976).

1243. Hellinas, Enas (pseud.). Greece Today: One More Dark Page in Mankind's History. New York: Exposition, 1971. 30. Six poems on the military regime 1967-.

1244. Horn, E.M. Greek Tragedy in Seven Acts. London: Union of Democratic Control, 1957. 19. A short story about the lives of families and friends of political prisoners.

1245. Kobbe, Jeffrey. "The Greek Colonels' Revenge." Nation 210 (June 29, 1970) 789. On the extreme abuse Alexandros Panaghoulis is suffering in prison, after attempting tyrannicide.

1246. Koroveses, Perikles (Pericles Korovessis). The Method: A Personal Account of the Tortures in Greece. Tr. Les Nightingale and Catherine Patrakis. London: Allison & Busby, 1970. 87. The author was arrested in 1967 for suspected Communist membership (completely baseless) and tortured by beating, electric shock, and numerous other physical and psychological terrors. Torture occurs throughout Greece.

1247. Lake, Christopher. Political Prisoners in Greece. London: Peace News, 1963. 16.

1248. "The Long View." Newsweek 71 (January 8, 1968) 37. Some 300 prisoners were released, but 2,600 remain held without charges or trials.

1249. Mangakis, G. "Letter in a Bottle from a Greek Prison." Atlantic Monthly 228 (October 1971) 53-9. The author, Chair of Penal Law at Athens University, was arrested in July, 1969, tortured, and sentenced to eighteen years' imprisonment for plotting to overthrow the regime. His wife was also imprisoned for telling newsmen her husband was being tortured.

1250. Minis, Anastassios. "Interrogation in Athens: Diary of the Man in the Green Circle." New York Times Magazine (Aug. 5, 1973) 8-9. Reply L. Eisenberg (Sept. 9, 1973) 22. Account of the severe 111-day interrogation of Minis, WWII hero arrested for planting bombs in Athens in protest against the dictatorship.

1251. Mylonas, George. Escape from Amorgos. New York: Scribner, 1974. 228. The story of his arrest, imprisonment, exile, and escape from the Greek dictatorship.

1252. News of Greece. Newspaper about the dictatorship published by the U.S. Committee for Democracy in Greece, 1968-.

1253. "One Man's Odyssey." Newsweek 74 (October 20, 1969) 54. George Mylonas is rescued from exile on the island of Amorgos.

1254. "Pronouncements on Prisoners." Time 90 (September 15, 1967) 39. Tells about two: composer Mikis Theodorakis and Andreas Papandreou, son of former Premier George Papandreou.

1255. Siegrist, Roland. The Protection of Political Detainees : The International Committee of the Red Cross in Greece, 1967-1971. Montreux: Editions Corbaz, 1985. 171. After the coup d'etat by the military in April 21, 1967, the entire political leadership and public figures and over 5,000 communists were arrested and many of them deported. Persecution became widespread. The ICRC intervened during those years to assist the prisoners.

1256. "The Silenced Lady." Newsweek 78 (September 13, 1971) 36+. The four who tried to free Alexandros Panagoulis, who attempted to kill the dictator of Greece, were caught and are in prison.

1257. Sotiris, Angelos. "There's the Greece of Greeks and There's the Tourist's Greece." New York Times Magazine (July 25, 1971) 12-14. Describes the repression under the junta and the methods used to hide it.

1258. Styron, R. "Greek Tragedy." Inquiry 4.2 (Dec. 29, 1980) 24. Review of Orianna Fallaci's A Man, about Alexander Panagoulis, hero of the Greek Resistance imprisoned by the junta for five years and tortured.

1259. Theodorakis, Mikis. Journal of Resistance. New York: Coward, McCann, and Geoghegan; London: Hart-Davis MacGibbon, 1973. 333. Journal of his resistance to the tyranny of the Greek colonels--from his move underground to his capture, imprisonment, and exile. Theodorakis is a notable poet and composed the music for Z and Zorba the Greek.

1260. Thoedorakis, Mikis. "Theodorakis." New Yorker 46 (Aug. 15, 1970) 22-3. An interview of Theordorakis, Greece's most celebrated composer, former member of the abolished Parliament, and former prisoner.

1261. "Torture." Newsweek 74 (December 15, 1969) 52. The Council of Europe's Human Rights Commission has compiled a 1,200 page report on torture by the Greek dictatorship.

1262. "The Unmentionable Issue." Time 94 (December 12, 1969) 39-40. On the mounting evidence of torture in the prisons of the government of Premier George Papadopoulos and his fellow colonels.

1263. Vlachos, Helen. House Arrest. London: Deutsch, 1970. 158; Boston: Gambit, 1970. 183. An account of her house arrest by the Colonels' regime in 1967 for two months until her escape. She and her husband published a prominent newspaper in Athens, the Kathimerini, which was closed after the coup.

GRENADA

1264. Amnesty International Report 1980. London: Amnesty International, 1980. 138. Following the overthrow of the government of Eric Gairy by Maurice Bishop, former officials and others were detained without trial, but releases reduced the number to 56 in 1980.

1265. Amnesty International Report 1990. New York: Amnesty International, 1990. 103-4. Appeals continue of death sentence by former members of the government convicted of murdering Prime Minister Maurice Bishop.

1266. Coard, Phyllis. U.S. War on One Woman : My Conditions of Imprisonment in Grenada (Oct. 1983-August 1986). London: Karia, 1988. 94. Written in prison where she is under sentence of death. She was a supporter of Maurice Bishop, whose government and New Jewel Movement was overthrown by an invasion by U.S. troops.

1267. The Frame-Up of Cecil Prime: Five Years of Crimes Against a Grenadian Patriot. New York: Friends for Jamaica, 1989. 42.

1268. Grenada Update. Kingston, Jamaica: Jamaica Committee for the Defence of Human Rights in Grenada, 1984. 45. On the continuing violations of human rights in Grenada since the U.S. led military invasion on October 25, 1983.

1269. "In Grenada, Victors' Justice." Progressive 53 (March 1989) 15-16. Report on the condition of the Grenada 17, including ten political leaders of the 1983 coup convicted on a doctrine of having "common purpose" with those who killed Prime Minister Maurice Bishop, notes the appellants severe beatings, lack of medical care, and evidence of malnutrition.

1270. Kittson, Doris. "Bishop Trial Defendants to be Hanged." Guardian 39.12 (Dec. 17, 1986) 13. Fourteen of 24 accused of murdering former Prime Minister Bishop and others were sentenced to death. They pled innocent.

1271. The Side You Haven't Heard: Maurice Bishop Murder Trial. Testimony By the Defendants and Analysis by Njm and Other Grenadians. Part II. New York: Friends for Jamaica, 1987. 250. Documents from Lt. Col. Layne, Phyllis Coard, and others, Oct. 19th. Part I gives Bernard Coard's testimony.

GUATEMALA

1272. 1986 Annual Report on the Human Rights Situation in Guatemala. Toronto: Inter-Church Committee on Human Rights in Latin America, 1987. 20. Collective human rights abuses in the course of the military government's army operations continue and no investigation regarding the thousands of disappeared has taken place.

1273. Amnesty International Report 1980. London: Amnesty International, 1980. 139-145. A major terror government: torture and murder of prisoners, disappearances and killings by troops and paramilitary groups. Death squad killings between January and June 1979 were 1,222, by November 3,252, most apparently after being tortured. The government of Lucas Garcia denied responsibility and accused Amnesty International of being pro-communist.

1274. Amnesty International Report 1990. New York: Amnesty International, 1990. 105-7. Security forces and death squads implicated in hundreds of extrajudicial executions and disappearances. Numerous reports of torture by survivors of kidnapping and detention. Scores of political opponents were harassed and assaulted by military forces. President Cerezo granted immunity from prosecution to human rights violators in previous administrations.

1275. Black, George, et al. Garrison Guatemala. New York: Monthly Review, 1984. 198. The Guatemalan terror regime rules through its secret police and through brute military force--many witnesses tell of detention without charge, disappearances, torture and mass killings.

1276. Bowen, Gordon. "Four Candles in the Wind." Commonweal 114 (December 18, 1987) 726-7. Three Catholic catechists disappeared after being kidnapped by uniformed soldiers, joining the more than 35,000 Guatemalan disappeared in recent years.

1277. Carmack, Robert M. Harvest of Violence: The Maya Indians and the Guatemalan Crisis. Norman: U of Oklahoma P, 1988. 334. A collection of essays by anthropologists examining the fate of the Mayan Indians at the hands of the Guatemalan government and its sanctioned genocide against all native populations.

1278. Clandestine Detention in Guatemala. New York: Human Rights Watch, 1993. 18. Contains testimonies of major human rights abuses by the military to gain information concerning the Guatemalan Revolutionary Unity guerillas.

1279. Fried, Jonathan. "Rights Report Describes a 'Nation of Prisoners'." Guardian 36.21 (Feb. 29, 1984) 14. With U.S. military aid, Guatemala continues its gross abuse of human rights.

1280. Gold, Donna L. "A Guatemalan Woman's Grief." Progressive 48 (December 1984) 14. Story of Irma Leticia Chavez, whose efforts to avert politically motivated firings at a hospital resulted in an attack by a soldier with a shotgun ("she lost an arm and parts of her stomach, liver, and thigh"), two and a half years in a hospital, and the abduction and disappearance of her youngest son.

1281. Guatemala. Amnesty International briefing 8. London: Amnesty International, 1976. 16. A general survey of history, legal and illegal, and indicts the frequent extrajudicial executions of political dissidents, torture, and abduction.

1282. Guatemala: Amnesty International's Current Human Rights Concerns. New York: Amnesty International, 1991. 14. Torture, disappearances, and death squad killings continue.

1283. Guatemala: Children in Fear: Street Children and Street Educators Continue to be Targeted. New York: Amnesty International, 1992. 39. Contains details of continuing human rights violations directed against street children by security forces. Sources estimating over 1500 civilians killed and the number of arrests exceeding 300. Thousands of people have been forced into hiding; tens of thousand have fled in search of asylum.

1284. Guatemala: A Government Program of Political Murder. New York: Amnesty International, 1981. "People who oppose or are imagined to oppose the Guatemalan Government are systematically seized without warrant, tortured and murdered--all part of a deliberate and long standing program of the goverment." Portion reptd. New York Review of Books 28 (March 19, 1981) 38-40.

1285. Guatemala: Human Rights Violations Under the Civilian Government. New York: Amnesty International, 1989. 75. Despite promises by President Cerezo's government that human rights abuses in Guatemala would end during his administration, Amnesty International documents a renewed wave of killings and disappearances.

1286. Guatemala: A Nation of Prisoners. New York: Americas Watch, 1984. 260. Details the plight of the Guatemalan people under the ever increasing brutality of the government and a growing number of detentions, torture, disapppearances, and executions.

1287. Holdenried, F.X. "Terror in Guatemala." America 147 (July 17, 1982) 31-4. On the disappearance of Jesuit priest Carlos Perez Alonso.

1288. Human Rights in Guatemala: No Neutrals Allowed. New York: Americas Watch, 1982. 133. The Guatemalan government's paranoid counterinsurgency campaign does not allow for human rights in its destruction of life and culture and creation of a terror state. This report notes the indifferent attitude of the U.S. Government toward refugee accounts of massacres.

1289. "In Guatemala: 'Death or Exile'." Matchbox (November 1979) 3. In the first five months of General Lucas Garcia's government there were reports of 500 victims of violence, 200 of whom were tortured; murders almost every day. Secret cemetaries and mass graves have been discovered: an estimate of those murdered by death squads from 1966-1979 numbers over 20,000.

1290. Jonas, Susanne, et al., eds. Guatemala, Tyranny on Trial: Testimony of the Permanent People's Tribunal. San Francisco: Synthesis, 1984. 301. Transcripts of the People's Tribunal in Madrid concerning the atrocious violations of human rights by the Guatemalan government, including a waged genocide against the indigenous populations.

1291. Lindorff, Dave. "State Terror in Guatemala." In These Times 5.17 (March 18, 1981) 4. On the disappearance of feminist Alaide Foppa.

1292. Manuel, Anne. "Guatemala: Deadly Repression Continues." Human Rights Watch 10.1 (Winter 1992) 13. The country is "one of the hemisphere's most horrendous human rights situations." Focuses on attacks on human rights workers.

1293. Manz, Beatriz. Refugees of a Hidden War: The Aftermath of Counterinsurgency in Guatemala. SUNY Series in Anthropological Studies of Contemporary Issues. Albany, NY: State U of New York P, 1988. 286. Focuses on the aftermath of the 1981-83 Guatemalan military counter-insurgency campaign: climate of fear, severely restricted freedoms, mass killings, and a mass exodus of refugees (20,000 to Mexico alone).

1294. Maximizing Deniability: The Justice System and Human Rights in Guatemala. Washington D.C.: International Human Rights Law Group, 1989. 104. Discusses the large number of killed and disappeared since the inauguration of President Cerezo in 1986, and the failure of the criminal justice system to defend basic human rights.

1295. Menchú, Rigoberta. I, Rigoberta Menchú: An Indian Woman in Guatemala. Trans. Ann Wright. London: Verso, 1984. 251. A Quiché Indian, she survived the genocide that destroyed her family and community and now confronts the systematic extermination of her people by learning the Spanish language of the oppressors. One chapter gives an account of an attack by the army; another the murder of a young woman ordered by the son of a wealthy landowner; another the torture and murder of her brother; etc.

1296. "Ortiz v. Gramajo." Docket: Fall 1992. New York: Center for Constituional Rights, 1992. 13-14. Sister Dianna Ortiz, a U.S. nun who was teaching in Guatemala, filed suit in the District Court of Massachusetts against Guatemalan ex-Defense Minister Hector Gramajo, who was responsible for Ortiz being "stripped, raped, burned with a lit cigarette, and held in a pit filled with dead bodies and live rats while being interrogated." (See also "Xuncax v. Gramajo.")

1297. Pall, Ellen. "When Love Overcomes Fear in Guatemala: Talking with Manuel Mejía Tol." Human Rights Watch 10.1 (Winter 1992) 7. On the rural human rights group, CERJ, and its director. Eleven members have been killed and eight have disappeared.

1298. Scientists and Human Rights in Guatemala: Report of a Delegation. Washington, D.C.: National Academy, 1992. 68. Focuses on extreme violence against more than 50 scientists by murder, abduction, and disappearances. The victims are named and the atrocities described. Report sponsored by the U.S. National Academy of Sciences and the Institute of Medicine.

1299. Special Courts. Managua, Nicaragua: Guatemalan Church in Exile, 1983. 19. Testimony of the persecution.

1300. Sywulka, S.R. "Priest Who Came in from the Cold." Christianity Today 25 (Nov. 20, 1981) 56+. Luis Eduardo Pellecer Faena was apparently brainwashed into making statements for his country's military regime.

1301. Testimonies From Peasants of El Peten : Stories of Guatemalan Peasants Who Survived the Attacks of the Guatemalan Army on Their Villages and Cooperatives. Detroit: Latin American task Force, 1981. 11.

1302. Woolfe, Henry. "Brainwashing in Guatemala?" America 146 (January 2-9, 1982) 9,12. The case of Fr. Luis Eduardo Pellecer, who is confessing to crimes and attacking his church over TV, after having been secretly abducted and imprisoned, and other examples of the worst violence and repression in Guatemala's history.

1303. "Xuncax v. Gramajo." Docket: Fall 1992. New York: Center for Constitutional Rights, 1992. 12-13. Report on the CCR suit on behalf of nine plantiffs (who represent tens of thousands of indigenous Guatemalans) against ex-Defense Minister Hector Gramajo, who "designed, ordered, implemented and directed a program of massacres, murders, disappearances, widespread torture, and arbitrary arrest" known as "the Guatemala Solution."

GUINEA

1304. Alata, Jean-Paul. "In an African Prison: A Memoir." Dissent 24.4 (Fall 1977) 418-424. Excerpts from Alata's book that describe a torture scene, collective madness in Conakry, and a telephone conversation between...Alata and Presedent Sékou Touré.

1305. Amnesty International Report 1980. London: Amnesty International, 1980. 51-2. Most of the prisoners arrested by President Sékou Touré in 1971 and 1976 have been freed or died or were killed in prison: five hundred known by name have not reappeared; perhaps as many as 4,000 did not survive. New arrests occurred in 1979.

1306. Amnesty International Report 1990. New York: Amnesty International, 1990. 107-8. At least six suspected dissidents were detained and tortured. Some prisoners convicted in unfair trials in 1986 apparently are still in custody.

1307. Guinea. London: Amnesty International, 1978. 12. Prolonged detention without trial, secret courts, starvation, torture, and executions continue among the 2000 to 4000 (perhaps more) political prisoners.

1308. "Guinea (Conakry)--A Small but Terrible Country." Matchbox (Summer 1978) 11,22. Political detainees run as high as 2,000-4,000--one out of every 1,500 people--and face brutal torture, harsh prison conditions, and forced starvation as a form of death penalty.

1309. Human Rights Violations in the Popular and Revolutionary Republic of Guinea: An Account of 'Disappearances', Extrajudicial Executions, Torture, and Incommunicado Detentions. New York: Amnesty International, 1982. 25. Includes a list of 78 disappeared prisoners. Some 4,000 people were arrested for political reasons between 1969 and 1976.

GUINEA-BISSAU

1310. Amnesty International Report 1990. New York: Amnesty International, 1990. 108-9. Some long-term (1986-) prisoners convicted after unfair trials remain in prison.

1311. Urdang, Stephanie. Fighting Two Colonialisms: Women in Guinea-Bissau. New York: Monthly Review Press, 1979. 320. Focuses on the need for women of Guinea-Bissau to "fight against two colonialisms--the one of the Portuguese and the other of men."

GUYANA

1312. Amnesty International Report 1980. London: Amnesty International, 1980. 145-46. One of the members of the opposition party is being tried for arson, another was killed while allegedly stealing, both charges dubious.

1313. Amnesty International Report 1990. New York: Amnesty International, 1990. 109-110. Over 200 strikers were arrested for short periods during peaceful demonstrations against economic conditions. Three men have been charged with treason and allegedly tortured for confession.

HAITI

1314. Amnesty International Report 1980. London: Amnesty International, 1980. 146-48. Human rights have again deteriorated by an increase of arbitrary detentions, illegal deportations, police harassment, and torture and deaths in prison, and the rights of assembly, expression, thought, and information were severely repressed during the year.

1315. Amnesty International Report 1990. New York: Amnesty International, 1990. 110-112. Many have been detained without warrant or charge for peaceful protests or criticizing the government. Many of these reported torture or ill-treatment in harsh prisons. Members of grassroots organizations and sympathetic journalists were also arrested. Torture and ill-treatment were widespread.

1316. Bouillard, Thomas. "'Culture of Terror' Reigns in Haiti." Arkansas Democrat-Gazzette (May 22, 1993) 6A. More than 3,000 political murders have occured since the military putsch which deposed President Jean-Bertrand Aristide, and torture is suspected to be widespread. Some 7,000 police and soldiers are backed up by 16,000 civilian "thugs" and the 568 Chefs de la Section each of whom have up to 200 employees.

1317. Haiti: Amnesty International Briefing. New York: Amnesty International, 1985. 14. Systematic repression including incommunicado detention sometimes for long periods, torture, and disappearance continue under the government's armed militia, the tontons macoutes.

1318. Haiti: Deaths in Detention, Torture and Inhumane Prison Conditions. New York: Amnesty International, 1987. 44. Amnesty International is now seriously concerned for the safety of anyone who is arrested in Haiti.

1319. Haiti: Killing the Dream. Film. San Francisco: Speak Out!, 1992. The story of terror and repression and the moral failure of U.S. foreign policy.

1320. "Paul v. Avril." Docket: Fall 1992. New York: Center for Constitutional Rights, 1992. 11-12. Report on the CCR suit against former military dictator Prosper Avril on behalf of six prominent Haitian political activists who suffered brutal torture under Avril's regime.

1321. Rawls, Wendell, Jr. "Baby Doc's Haitian Terror." New York Times Magazine (May 14, 1978) 14-16+. Lucien Rigaud's account of his fall from "a high-level envoy of Jean-Claude (Baby Doc) Duvalier to a prisoner in the Haitian dictator's jails, where beatings still occur regularly, deaths daily, and the regime's opponents languish for years in squalid cages."

1322. Silencing a People: The Destruction of Civil Society in Haiti. New York: Human Rights Watch (with National Coalition for Haitian Refugees), 1992. 152. The military has supressed the civil society as a way to undermine Aristide if he returns.

1323. "U.S. Acting as 'Gate Keeper' for Repression Says Healey." Amnesty Action (Summer/Fall 1992) 8. The U.S. government has built a Caribbean Curtain to keep Haitians in Haiti.

HONDURAS

1324. Amnesty International Report 1980. London: Amnesty International, 1980. 149-50. Several trade unionists were jailed in poor conditions in the course of disputes with employers. Several leaders of a peasant party and two priests were murdered.

1325. Amnesty International Report 1990. New York: Amnesty International, 1990. 112-114. Frequent reports of torture during incommunicado detention and reports of disappearances, murder, and death threats.

1326. Honduras: "Disappearances" in Honduras: A Wall of Silence and Indifference. New York: Amnesty International, 1992. 41. AI calls on the government of President Leonardo Callejas to establish a commission of inquiry into the disappearances prior to the current administration.

1327. Honduras: Human Rights Violations. New York: Amnesty International, 1988. A research paper on unacknowledged detentions, torture, disappearances and extrajudicial executions.

1328. Honduras: Persistence of Human Rights Violations. New York: Amnesty International, 1991. 35. Though human rights violations have diminished since the early 1980's, serious human rights violations persist.

1329. Human Rights in Honduras: Central America's "Sideshow". New York: Americas Watch Committee, 1987. 150. Focuses on human rights abuses by the Honduran military, especially the Fuerzas de Seguridad (security forces) and its intelligence branch, the Direccion Nacional de Investigacion (DNI), who are responsible for routine torture and murder of detainees for political reasons. The report evidences close ties between the CIA and the death squads.

1330. Medea, Benjamin, ed. Don't Be Afraid, Gringo: A Honduran Woman Speaks From the Heart. San Francisco: Institute for Food and Development Policy, 1987. 173. Biography of Elvia Alavorado, founder of the Honduran Federation of Peasant Women and an Organizer with the National Congress of Rural Workers, who has been harrassed, arrested and tortured for her work.

HONG KONG

1331. Amnesty International Report 1990. New York: Amnesty International, 1990. 114-115. A few demonstrators were arrested and reportedly beaten, but all except one were acquitted. Vietnamese asylum-seekers were reportedly mistreated.

HUNGARY

1332. Amiel, Barbara. "Enduring Vein of Courage." Macleans 94 (June 29, 1981) 40. George Gabori, a Hungarian Jewish activist, has released his memoirs detailing his experiences in death camps and with the communist secret police.

1333. Amnesty International Report 1980. London: Amnesty International, 1980. 277-78. Critics of the government are being imprisoned, and freedom of movement (emigration) is restricted and punishable by prison.

1334. Amnesty International Report 1990. New York: Amnesty International, 1990. 116. Some 70 conscientious objectors were released as alternatives to military service were introduced.

1335. Bone, Edith. Seven Years Solitary. London: Hamish Hamilton, 1957. 212. She spent 1949-1956 in prison, several of those years in solitary, accused of being an British spy. She taught herself Greek, wrote a diary, and studied mathematics, privileges won through a language strike--refusing to speak Hungarian.

1336. Dupré, Peter. Caught in the Act : A True Story. Tunbridge Wells : Costello, 1988. 250. The author was imprisoned for trying to help an East German family escape to the West.

1337. Fehervary, Istvan. The Long Road to Revolution : The Hungarian Gulag, 1945-1956. Ed. Krisztina Fehervary. Santa Fe, NM: Pro Libertate, 1989. 228. A history of the prison world that Hungary became under the Stalinist Rakosi regime. The author spent eight years in prison (1949-1956), until released during the revolution of 1956, when he escaped to Vienna.

1338. Ignotus, Paul. Political Prisoner. New York: Macmillan, 1960. 201. Press Secretary at the Hungarian Legation in London during WWII, he was arrested in Budapest in 1949 and imprisoned (and his wife) for seven years.

1339. Kiszely, Karoly. "My Time Inside for Saying No to Arms." End: Journal of European Nuclear Disarmament 16.17 (Summer 1985) 10. The author was the first Catholic to refuse to bear arms, for which he served 33 months 1976-1977.

1340. Kiszely, Karoly. "Pacifism Under Fire." Across Frontiers. 2.3 (Spring 1986) 27. Reprint of Kiszely's letter to the Budapest Cultural Forum on behalf of imprisoned conscientious objectors.

1341. Krokavay, Zsolt. "Politics and Punk." Index On Censorship 14.2 (April 1985) 17-21. Examines the sentencing of members of the Coitus Punk Group to two years in jail.

1342. Lemmé, Janet E. Conviction. New York: Norton, 1970. 282. A U.S. citizen imprisoned (in 1966 for six months in the Marko Prison in Budapest) for attempting to help relatives escape from East Germany through Hungary.

1343. Paloczi-Horvath, George. The Undefeated. Boston: Little Brown, 1959. 305. Head of the Hungarian Broadcasting and News Agency, he was imprisoned in 1949 for five years. The book tells of his life in prison and of how purge trials are prepared.

1344. Szász, Béla. Volunteers for the Gallows; Anatomy of a Show Trial. Tr. Kathleen Szász. New York: Norton, 1972. 244. A picture of the Stalinist purges and show trials which culminated in the execution of Lászlő Rajk, former Minister of the Interior. The author was tortured to extract evidence against Rajk, but he refused, and was sentenced to ten years hard labor, serving five years, 1949-1954.

INDIA

1345. Advani, Lal K. A Prisoner's Scrap-book. New Delhi: Arnold-Heinemann, 1978. 327. The author describes his imprisonment in various jails 1975-76 during the repression of under Indira Gandhi.

1346. Amnesty International Report 1980. London: Amnesty International, 1980. 194-98. Preventive detention, "serious" police brutality, and long-term detention without trial are some of the problems. Some cases of torture were documented.

1347. Amnesty International Report 1990. New York: Amnesty International, 1990. 116-119. Thousands of prisoners are held without charge or trial under "anti-terrorist" or preventive detention laws; many for peaceful political activities. "Torture and ill-treatment were widespread," with possibly over 50 people tortured to death. Several disappeared after arrest and "several hundred may have been extrajudicially executed."

1348. Balan, C.A. In the Shadow of the Gallows. Trans. Saraswathy Menon. Madras: Sangam Books, 1979. 98. Served twelve years and eight months, 1950-1963, originally sentenced to death for a murder (of which he was innocent) only because he was a communist.

1349. Dasagupta, Sudhamsu. How We Became Communist in Jails: The Story of the Past. Calcutta: Nishan Prakashani, 1985. 140. How a group of revolutionary terrorists turned to communism during incarceration in Andaman Prison.

1350. Davidon, Karen. "India Holds Over 60,000 Political Prisoners." Guardian 27.42 (August 13, 1975) 10. Indira Gandhi's state of emergency detains over 60,000 people. This article details how Gandhi used the Indian Parliament to escape conviction.

1351. Fernandes, George. "A Prisoner in Mrs. Gandhi's India." Dissent 24.1 (Winter 1977) 11-12. A letter from George Fernandes, Chairman of the Socialist party of India, to a friend that describes his false arrest for "planned sabotage" and the horrible conditions in the prisons.

1352. "Gandhi in the Slammer." Time 113 (January 1, 1979) 68. Indira Gandhi sent to jail for contempt by Parliament.

1353. Ghose, Aurobindo. Tales of Prison Life. Calcutta: Sri Aurobindo Pathamandir, 1974. 124. Trans. of Karakahini (1908). The story of his solitary incarceration for one year, accused of terrorism.

1354. Ghosh, Ajoy. Bhagat Singh and His Comrades. New Delhi: Communist Party of India, 1979. 51. Ghosh was General Secretary of the Communist Party of India 1951-62 and was imprisoned several times. Singh was executed in 1931 for bombings.

1355. Gossman, Patricia. "India Tries to Squash Protests Against Massive Narmada Dam Project." Human Rights Watch 10 (Fall 1992) 1, 9. Protestors against the Narmada Dam in western India have been treated with police violence, arbitrary arrest, illegal detention, and beatings.

1356. Gossman, Patricia. "Widespread Rape in Kashmir Escapes the Spotlight." Human Rights Watch 11.2 (Spring 1993) 3. Not only rape but summary executions, systematic torture, and civilian massacres by government troops are familiar, and assassinations, kidnappings, and bombings by insurgent groups.

1357. Hardwari, Lal. 555 Days in Jail: Recollections of a MISA Detenu. Chandigarh: Printing Promoters, 1977. 128. Account of nineteen months in different jails as part of India's arrest of opposition leaders in the 1975 "emergency."

1358. Harsch, Ernest. "India/The View from Gandhi's Jail." Militant 40.25 (June 25, 1976) 19. Repression in the forms of jailing, censorship and overall human rights violations are becoming large scale in Indiri Gandhi's regime.

1359. Harsch, Ernest. "Thousands Jailed as Gandhi Cracks Down on Opponents." Militant 39.34 (Sept. 19, 1975) 19,22. Since Indira Gandhi's "coup" of June 26, 50,000 to 80,000 detainees were added to the tens of thousands of political prisoners already in jail.

1360. The Human Rights Crisis in Kashmir, A Pattern of Impunity. New York: Human Rights Watch (with Physicians for Human Rights), 1993. 224. The Indian "catch and kill" policy has increased the number of human rights violations.

1361. India: Human Rights Violations in Punjab: Use and Abuse of the Law. New York: Amnesty International, 1991. 62. Since the beginning of the Sikh independence movement in 1983, a well-documented pattern of human rights abuse by both government and opposition forces has emerged.

1362. "India--One Year Later." Matchbox (Summer 1976) 1-2. On Indira Gandhi's declaration of "internal emergency" on top of a "state of emergency" already in place, leading to thousands of arrests of political opponents, critics, and other innocent people, adding to the 75,000-175,000 political prisoners already detained.

1363. India: Torture, Rape and Deaths in Custody. New York: Amnesty International, 1992. 195. Torture of men, women, and children, is routine in every one of India's 25 states. Includes the cases of over 400 deaths since 1985 and calls on the government to acknowledge the violations and take steps to stop them.

1364. "India: Torture in the Cradle of Non-Violence." Amnesty Action (Summer/Fall 1992) 5. "Torture and rape occur routinely and systematically and are reserved for the poorest citizens."

1365. "India's Political Prisoners." International Bulletin 2.4 (Feb. 1975) 3. Indira Gandhi's government holds "15,000 to 40,000 political prisoners," many without trial, and some tortured. Many of the prisoners are Naxalites (Marxist-Leninist Communist).

1366. International Work Group For Indigenous Affairs (INGIA). The Naga Nation and its Struggle Against Genocide. Cambridge, Mass.: Cultural Survival, 1986. 230. Oppression is the rule in Nagaland under Indian rule.

1367. Jela Kavitaem/Poems from Prison. Nai Dilli: Hiravala Prakasana, 1978. 31. English and Hindi on opposite pages. Poems written originally in English by the communist prisoners in West Bengal and Bihar during the emergency in India, 1975-1977.

1368. Kistemaker, Peter. "Radical Writers' Group Hounded in India." Guardian 35.17 (Jan. 26, 1983) 15. For twelve years an association of some 500 writers has been the target of government censorship, arbitrary jailings, and a protracted conspiracy trial.

1369. Kumara, Santa. A Chief Minister's Prison Diary. New Delhi: Vikas, 1979. 90. The author's memoir of his five arrests, particularly his fifth in 1975 following Indira Gandhi's State of Emergency.

1370. Lewis, Primila. Reason Wounded: An Experience of India's Emergency. New Delhi: Vikas, 1978. 207. Imprisoned in 1975 during the Emergency declared by Mrs. Gandhi's government, for supporting a union for poor agricultural workers.

1371. Malkani, K.R. The Midnight Knock. New Delhi: Vikas, 1978. 98. A memoir of his prison experiences during Indira Gandhi's state of emergency.

1372. Mehta, Ved. "Department of Amplification." New Yorker 52 (Oct. 4, 1976) 105-110. Describes the repression under Indira Gandhi's national emergency decree, resulting in 30,000 to 250,000 political prisoners who have been subjected to brutal treatment.

1373. Namo, Dalle. The Prisoner From Nagaland. Tuli, Nagaland: D. Namo, 1987. 135. An account of the Naga independence movement and the author's role in it, including imprisonment in 1957, where he wrote this book which was kept hidden until 1987.

1374. Narayan, Jayaprakash. "India, My India!" New York Times Magazine (March 27, 1977) 35-7+. "In a diary written during four months as Indira Gandhi's most famous political prisoner, Narayan, spiritual leader of the oppositon, reflects on the decline and fall of his nation's democracy."

1375. Narayan, Jayaprakash. Prison Diary, 1975. 2nd ed. Pune: Abhay Prakashan, 1977. 127. Also published Bombay: Popular Prakashan, 1977; Seattle: U of Washington P, 1978. First edition was printed under censorship conditions; this second edition is complete. Narayan was imprisoned following "Mrs. Indira Gandhi's midnight coup" when political opponents were arrested.

1376. Nargolkar, Vasant. A Non-Entity Fasts for Freedom. Bombay: Vijnanashram, 1978. 121. The author fasted twice--for twenty-five and for twenty-seven days--to persuade Indira Gandhi to end her "misrule" and to restore democracy.

1377. Nayar, Kuldip. In Jail. New Delhi: Vikas, 1978. 152. Based on his diary kept for two months in 1975 after he was detained under Indira Gandhi's repressive Maintainance of Internal Security Act (MISA). The journalist/author was a critic of Gandhi.

1378. No End in Sight: Human Rights Violations in Assam. New York: Human Rights Watch, 1993. 22. Reports on a large-scale search-and-arrest policy carried out by the Indian army.

1379. Rape in Kashmir: A Crime of War. New York: Human Rights Watch (with Physicians for Human Rights), 1993. 19. Details the conflict between Indian security forces and Muslim insurgents and the security forces use of rape against women thought to be militant sympathizers.

1380. The Real Face of India's "Democracy" : Documentary Evidence of Political Repression in Post-Independence India. Vancouver: Indian People's Association in North America, 1979. 72. The people of India "have very few democratic rights." The report gives evidence of "the extreme brutality of the Indian state."

1381. Reddy, Snehalata. A Prison Diary. Karnataka State, Mysore, India: Human Rights Committee, 1977. 22. This leading Indian actress was jailed without charges in 1976 presumably for friendships with socialist leaders. Released for medical reasons, she died five days later.

1382. Report of an Amnesty International Mission to India, 31 December 1977-18 January 1978. London: Amnesty International, 1979. 84. Gives a background of the Emergency under Indira Gandhi and the infamous Maintenance of Internal Security Act (MISA) under which widespread human rights volations occurred, including torture and deaths. Some 17,754 prisoners were held in preventive detention by the end of the Emergency, and perhaps 1000 left-wing "Naxalites" remain imprisoned.

1383. Sarin, Garish. "Indian Communists Acquitted." Guardian 31.37 (June 20, 1979) 15. Kanu Sanyal and Souren Bose, leaders of the Communist Party of India-Marxist-Leninist, spent nine years in jail without trial and were tortured repeatedly.

1384. Singh, Gulab. Thorns and Thistles: (Autobiography of a Revolutionary). Bombay: National Information & Publications, 1948. 274. Pub. 1964 under title: Under the Shadows of Gallows. Sentenced to death for revolutionary activities.

1385. Strasser, Steven. "Back Like Thunder?" Newsweek 93 (January 1, 1979) 32. Indira Gandhi jailed.

1386. "Symbol in Chains." Time 108 (October 18, 1976) 51. George Fernandez, chairman of the Socialist Party of India and former president of the India Railwaymen's Federation and 21 co-defendants face prosecution for conspiracy against Prime Minister Indira Gandhi's Government.

1387. Torture of Political Prisoners in India. New Delhi: Printox, 1977. 48. Case studies of the repression since 1975 in which "torture and inhumane treatment of demonstrators was order of the day."

1388. Tyler, Mary. My Years in an Indian Prison. Bombay: B.I., 1978. 191. London: Gollancz, 1977. 191. She was imprisoned for five years accused of supporting peasant rebellion, the Naxalite movement. She was allowed to return to England in 1975, but her husband remained in prison.

1389. "Under Gandhi's State of Emergency." Militant 40.3 (Jan. 23, 1976) 19. Interview with an Indian Trotskyist who states "the people have been deprived of all their basic rights."

1390. Ward, Richard. "Thousands Arrested." Guardian 28.34 (June 2, 1976) 12. Sweeping arrests in India by the Indira Gandhi government are part of a "drive to halt the flow of 'objectionable' antigovernment literature in India."

1391. Yunus, Mohammad. Letters from Prison. New Delhi: Vikas, 1986. 205. "Stray reflections" about his incarceration from 1942-1945 for participating in the Quit India Movement, earlier published in Hindi and Urdu editions. Mr. Yunus was a leader in the Congress Party and close friend to Nehru, Indira Gandhi, and Rajiv Gandhi.

INDONESIA

1392. Administration of Justice in Indonesia: An Account of the Treatment of Netherlands Prisoners and Defence Counsel in Indonesia 1953-1955. 's-Gravenhage: Netherlands Ministry of Foreign Affairs, 1955. 40. 23 Dutchmen await trial for over a year accused of plotting against the new Indonesia. Many have been tortured.

1393. Amnesty International Report 1980. London: Amnesty International, 1980. 198-204. The government continues to release political prisoners arrested in 1965 who were never brought to trial, but harassment continues after release. Severe violations of human rights in East Timor are widespread, including imprisonment without trial and summary executions. Many students and Moslems who opposed President Suharto's re-election or who advocate secession are in jail.

1394. Amnesty International Report 1990. New York: Amnesty International, 1990. 119-122. Several thousand people were temporarily detained, and several hundred are confined, the majority in East Timor, some long term. Trial fairness is often suspect. The government admitted killing some 5,000 "petty criminals" between 1983 and 1986. Torture and ill-treatment were frequently reported, some died as the consequence, and some were extrajudicially executed.

1395. Carroll, Raymond. "Indonesia: Devil's Island." Newsweek 91 (January 2, 1978) 29. Tens of thousands of Indonesians were imprisoned without trial in 1965 in an effort to destroy communist membership. About 10,000 have just been released; perhaps as many as 100,000 remain. Reports of torture and murder are increasing.

1396. Dunn, James. Timor: A People Betrayed. Queensland, Australia: Jacaranda, 1983. 402. Details the perilous situation in Timor in the wake of the Indonesian invasion: massacres, torture, disappearances, etc. An estimated one-third of the population in Timor have died in military assaults, massacres, and by disease and starvation.

1397. Frency, Denis. "US-Australian Role in East Timor Genocide." CounterSpy 4.2 (Spring 1980) 10-21. Suharto's military regime in Indonesia launched a full scale invasion of East Timor in 1975 backed by the U.S. By 1980 some 100,000 of an estimated population of 689,000 (in 1974) had been killed.

1398. Gellen, Karen. "Another Vietnam." Guardian 30.6 (November 16, 1977) 13. Details the "search and destroy" policy of the Indonesian military in East Timor and the plight of political prisoners.

1399. Indonesia: An Amnesty International Report. London: Amnesty International, 1977. 146. "With regard to numbers, time-scale, methods used by the government, and the history of mass killings and massive arrests, political imprisonment in Indonesia is without parallel today." As many as 100,000 prisoners have been held captive without trial, the majority over 11 years. This report includes a history of the repression and describes the prison system, trials, individual cases, and women.

1400. "Indonesia: Anguished Archipelago." Christian Century 95 (February 22, 1978) 179-80. The military government has announced their intention to release 10,000 political prisoners ("Tapols") though it has not given names as promised and past promises about releases have not been fulfilled. Furthermore, 10,000 are "but a fraction" of the number held, according to Amnesty International.

1401. "Indonesia: An Asian Gulag." Matchbox (Fall 1976) 7-10. Up to 100,000 Indonesians have been detained indefinitely under brutal cicumstances without charge or trial in archipelago gulags.

1402. Indonesia : Continuing Human Rights Violations in Irian Jaya. New York: Amnesty International, 1991. 38. Advocates of independence have been imprisoned, tortured, and extrajudicially executed. In April 1991 there are about 130 political prisoners, some for life.

1403. Indonesia\East Timor: Violations of Human Rights: Extrajudicial Executions, "Disappearances," Tortures and Political Imprisonment, 1975-1984. New York: Amnesty International, 1985. East Timor was invaded by Indonesian forces in 1975.

1404. Indonesia: Muslims on Trial. London: TAPOL, British Campaign for the Defense of Political Prisoners and Human Rights in Indonesia, 1987. 114. On the massacre of several hundred Muslims in the port slum of Tanjung Priok in Jakarta in 1984 under the Suharto regime, and the trials of Muslim activists which followed in which defedants were convicted of subversion or related offenses and handed exemplary punishment.

1405. Indonesia: Muslim Prisoners of Conscience. New York: Amnesty International, National Office, 1986. 45. Of the over 100 persons sentenced to heavy terms for participation in a disturbance at Tanjung Priok, at least half had been peacefully expressing their views.

1406. Indonesia Special. Amsterdam: Amnesty International, Dutch Section, 1973. 31. On the situation of more than 55,000 untried political prisoners in Indonesia and the plight of their children, wives and families; many of these prisoners are long-term and in bad conditions.

1407. Jendrzejczyk, Mike. "Killing of Demonstrators Sparks Cutoff of Military Training Aid to East Timor." Human Rights Watch 10 (Fall 1992) 7. The massacre of at least 75 civilians in Dili resulted in the ending of U.S. training of military officers.

1408. King, Dwight. "Human Rights Practices and Indonesian Middle Class." Bulletin of Concerned Asian Scholars 19.1 (January 1987) 4-13. Respect for human rights "has deteriorated during the 1980's," and middle-class groups are growing critical of the abuses.

1409. Military Repression Against the Batak Church. New York: Human Rights Watch, 1993. 9. Military choice of archbishop set off protests followed by arbitrary detention, house searches without warrants, and press censorship.

1410. Miller, John M. "Free Xanana!" Nonviolent Activist (July-August 1993) 20. East Timor's resistance leader was sentenced to life in prison for opposing Indonesia's forced annexation of his country, which is not recognized by the UN.

1411. Nusa, Pandu. "The Path of Suffering." Bulletin of Concerned Asian Scholars 19.1 (January 1987) 15-23. An account of the author's prison experiences following his arrest after the 1965 attempted coup, when the Indonesian Communist Party (PKI) was destroyed, appalling massacres occurred, perhaps one-and-a-half million people were imprisoned, and thousands died from malnutrition and brutal treatment.

1412. Oakely, R.B. "Human Rights in Indonesia; Statement, October 18, 1977." United States Department of State Bulletin 77 (December 12, 1977) 848-52. On the approximately 28,000-30,000 in detention without judicial process since 1965. The subjugation of East Timor by Indonesia is also discussed.

1413. Otto, J. "1 Million Indonesians Killed Since CIA-led Coup of 1965." Workers World 18.14 (April 2, 1976) 7,11. History of the U.S. backed coup of 1965 and the resulting "bloodbath of horrendous proportions." 1 million executed and over one hundred thousand suffering in political prisons.

1414. Payer, Cheryl. "Letter from Indonesia." Pacific Research 8.2 (January 1977) 7-11. A wide-ranging article, including an interview of two former prisoners and the repression of East Timor.

1415. Prison Conditions in Indonesia : an Asia Watch Report. New York: Human Rights Watch, 1990. 76. "The rule of law is only fitfully respected in Indonesia," where the police are part of the armed forces, and the Ministry of Justice "has no control over what happens in police lock-ups."

1416. Remembering History in East Timor: The Trial of Xanana Gusamao. New York: Human Rights Watch, 1993. 44. Summarizes the findings of the Asian Watch visit to Jakarta and Dili in March 1993 and focuses on one trial of a guerilla fighter.

1417. Retboll, Torben, ed. East Timor: The Struggle Continues. Copenhagen: International Work Group for Indigenous Affairs, 1984. 219. A history of the genocide in East Timor from the Indonesian invasion in 1975 through 1984.

1418. Students Jailed for Puns. New York: Human Rights Watch, 1993. 4. Two Indonesian college students were charged with blasphemy and sentenced to two-and-a-half years because of puns on phrases from the Quran.

1419. Taylor, John. Indonesia's Forgotten War: The Hidden History of East Timor. UK: Zed Books and Pluto Press, 1991. 224. Possibly as many as one-third of East Timor's 600,000 people have been killed since the Indonesian invasion of 1975, and human rights have been systematically repressed.

1420. Totten, Samuel. "Indonesian Genocide in East Timor." First-Person Accounts of Genocidal Acts Committed in the Twentieth Century: An Annotated Bibliography. Westport, CT: Greenwood, 1991. 285-86. Five entries on the Indonesian invasion, massacres, torture, disappearances, starvation of the Timorese.

1421. "'Transmigration' Does Not Mean Freedom." Southeast Asia Chronicle 63 (July 1978) 5-17. Questions Indonesian government's claim of having released 90 percent of its political prisoners.

IRAN

1422. "AI Confirms Reports of Torture, Execution." Matchbox (Feb. 1983) 7. Confirmed testimony includes: mothers tortured before their children; brutal whippings, electric shock torture, 30-60 executions each day, etc.

1423. Aikenhead, Sherri. "A Champagne Homecoming." Macleans 100 (Feb. 23, 1987) 13. Phillip Engs, a Canadian engineer working in Iran, was arrested and held 69 days while being interrogated about espionage.

1424. Amnesty International Documentation on Iran. New York: Amnesty International, U.S. Section, 1982. 11. Exposes the executions, cruel, inhuman and degrading treatment of prisoners, unfair trials, and other abuses in Iran since the 1979 revolution.

1425. Amnesty International Report 1980. London: Amnesty International, 1980. 329-31. Hostages in the U.S. Embassy in Teheran are still held (since November 1979). Many people associated with previous government (the Shah) have been imprisoned or await trial, trials are unfair under the Revolutionary Tribunals, executions are numerous (an estimated 800 to 1000 since the revolution of February 1979).

1426. Amnesty International Report 1990. New York: Amnesty International, 1990. 122-125. Hundreds of long-term prisoners remain in prison in 1989, and new arrests are occurring followed by unfair trials before Islamic Revolutionary Courts. At least 2,000 prisoners were killed in 1988 following the cease-fire in the war with Iraq.

1427. Amensty International Report on Iran. Videocassette. Amnesty International USA, 1987. 15 min. "A documentary on human rights abuses occuring in Iran today, with commentary on the domestic and international legal standards contravened by these abuses."

1428. "Appeal for Iranian Women Prisoners." Militant 44.7 (February 29, 1980) 7. Mahsa Hashemi and Fatima Fallahi, members of the Iranian Workers Party (HKE) and supporters of women's equality, remained imprisoned despite the release of all twelve other male HKE members.

1429. Baraheni, Reza. The Crowned Cannibals: Writings on Repression in Iran. New York: Vintage, 1977. 279. The author was imprisoned and tortured for his writings protesting the Shah's repression. This book includes essays on the terror, the repression of writers, his prison memoirs, memoirs of other prisoners, and poems. He is a novelist, a poet, a translator of Shakespeare, Camus, and other writers, and a founder of modern literary criticism in Iran.

1430. Baraheni, Reza. God's Shadow Prison Poems. Bloomington: Indiana UP, 1976. Poems about author's confinement and torture in Iran's notorious Committee Prison in 1973.

1431. Baraheni, Reza. "The Savak Documents." Nation 230 (February 23, 1980) 193, 198-202. Documents of torture and murder of fifty political prisoners by Savak, the Shah's secret police.

1432. Baraheni, Reza. "'There is only one Terrorist in Iran--The Shah Himself.'" The Militant 39.47 (Dec. 19, 1975) 21,22. Former prisoner under the Shah and now in exile, the author denounces the "Shah's torture machine."

1433. Bennett, Ralph K. "Iran's Government by Extermination." Reader's Digest 120 (March 1982) 23-26. Since 1979 when Khomeini came to power, Islamic Guards have executed at least 4,000 prisoners, many of them political.

1434. Brecher, John. "The Hostages Left Behind." Newsweek 97 (February 2, 1981) 34. Seven British and U.S. citizens are in prison on no charges or charged with espionage.

1435. Clifton, Tony. "Death Inside Khomeini's Jails." Newsweek 103 (June 18, 1984) 57. On the persecution, including execution, of Iran's Bahais, considered heretical by Iran's Islamic leaders.

1436. Dihqani, Ashraf. Torture and Resistance in Iran: Memoirs of the Woman Guerilla Ashraf Dehghani. New Delhi: Iran Committee, 1978. 132. On her resistance, arrest, torture, and escape.

1437. Dowden, Richard. "In the Terror of Tehran." New York Review of Books 31 (February 2, 1984) 8-12. Summary of Iranian Islamic Republic's torture and killing. Possibly as many as 6,000 Mujahadeen opponents were executed between 1979 and 1983.

1438. Evidence of Torture in Iran. New York: Amnesty International USA, 1984. 9. Testimonies given by former Iranian prisoners of torture dating from August 1981 to early 1984 typical of many others collected by Amnesty International, revealing a pattern of torture of political detainees. All of this despite Iran's official support for the UN Declaration on Torture.

1439. Ferdowsi, Faran. "In Iran, a 'campaign of terror' against Baha'is." Matchbox (October 1983) 11. Ferdowsi was "forced to flee with his family last year or face execution for his beliefs." His testimony relates the brutal persecution of Baha'is in Iran: assassinations, executions, lynchings, stonings, "disappearances," detention under severe conditions, torture, etc.

1440. "Frame Ups Can't Silence Us." Militant 43.31 (Aug. 10, 1979) 10. A letter from fourteen members of the Iranian-Socialist Workers Party arrested without formal charges.

1441. Frankel, David. "Stop Execution of Socialists in Iran." Militant 43.34 (Sept. 7, 1979) 1. Twelve members of the Iranian Socialist Workers Party (HKS) were sentenced to death and two to life imprisonment in a secret trial solely for their beliefs.

1442. Gellen, K. "Surviving Torture." Guardian 29.20 (February 23, 1977) 13. Ashraf Dehghani, a member of the Organization of Iranian Fedai Guerillas, wrote a diary of her prison experiences and outlined nine points on revolutionary resistance to torture.

1443. Goering, Curt. "The Baha'is of Iran: Persecution is Government Policy." Matchbox (November 1981) 1,5. Baha'is constitute the largest religious minority in Iran yet are not recognized by the Constitution of the Islamic Republic as are other religious minorities, are subject to severe persecution--killings, imprisonment and torture, destruction of schools, shops, and homes, etc--, and have no legal protection.

1444. Hontz, Craig. "OCAW Vice-President Protests Arrests in Iran." Militant 43.30 (Aug. 3, 1979) 6. Three leaders of the Iranian oil workers council were imprisoned, and fifteen imprisoned members of the Iranian Socialists Workers Party remained in danger of execution.

1445. Hontz, Craig. "Urgent Protests Needed for Iranian Trotskyists." Militant 43.29 (July 27, 1979) 7. Fifteen members of the Iranian Socialist Workers Party were detained without charges in Ahwaz along with oil worker militants and hundreds of others, all of whom face probable execution.

1446. Human Rights in Iran : Testimony on Behalf of Amnesty International by Brian Wrobel Before the Subcommittee on International Organizations of the Committee on International Relations, House of Representatives, United States Congress. London: Amnesty International, 1978. 63. On the unfair trial of 11 defendants accused of "anti-state" activities.

1447. "Inside a Khomeini Prison." Time 118 (October 12, 1981) 55. A relative of a hiding dissident recounts his tortures in prison.

1448. Iran. London: Amnesty International, 1976. 12. Discusses arbitrary arrests of political opponents, long incommunicado detention, unfair trials, torures, and extra-legal executions.

1449. Iran : Imprisonment, Torture and Execution of Political Opponents. New York: Amnesty International, 1992. 10. Serious violations of human rights continue in Iran despite the release of many political prisoners.

1450. Iran : Photographs and Documents on the Continuing Grave Violation of Human Rights : A Report on 64 Forms of Torture Practised by the Khomeini Regime. Baghdad: International Relations of the People's Mojahedin Organization of Iran, 1986. 31.

1451. Iran Violations of Human Rights : Documents sent by Amnesty International to the Government of the Islamic Republic of Iran. London: Amnesty International, 1987. 99. Describes patterns of human rights violations, examines the Penal Code, and presents testimonies of former prisoners.

1452. Iran, Violations of Human Rights : 1987-1990. New York: Amnesty International USA, 1990. 64. Serious human rights violations continue: extrajudicial executions, unfair trials, long-term prisoners, torture, thousands executed between 1987 and 1990, including more than 2,000 political prisoners.

1453. Iran: Violations of Human Rights. New York: Amnesty International, 1987. A major report documenting a pattern of political arrest and detention, unfair trials, torture, amputations and executions. Includes memoranda sent by Amnesty International to the government and testimonies of victims.

1454. The Iranian Bulletins: The News Bulletins of the Committee for the Defence of Political Prisoners in Iran. London; New York: Index on Censorship, 1979. 119. Details on people arrested, imprisoned, their families, police brutality, hunger strikes, the disappeared, prison conditions, etc., April 1978-Jan. 1979.

1455. Jaquith, Cindy. "Campaign Grows to Free 9 Trotskyists in Iran." Militant 43.24 (June 22, 1979) 6. On the Socialist Workers Party's efforts to free nine of their members imprisoned by the Khomeini/Bazargan government for demonstrating for Arab rights, despite their record for opposition to the Shah.

1456. Kaplan, Carl, and Fred Halliday. "The Savak-CIA Connection." Nation 250 (March 1, 1980) 229-30. The CIA trained the future torturers in interrogation methods, knew about the torture, and kept it secret from the public "for more than a quarter of a century."

1457. "Khomeini's Revenge: the Firing Squad." U.S News and World Report 93 (September 27, 1982) 12. The execution of Sadegh Ghotbzadeh, former Foreign Minister, among the estimated 4,500 to 15,000 executions for opposing Khomeini's regime.

1458. Lynn, J. "World Labor Cry Makes Impact in Iran." Militant 43.36 (Sept. 21, 1979) 11. Twelve imprisoned members of the Iranian Socialist Workers Party were condemned to death in a secret trial August 26, 1979 on false charges.

1459. Moghadam, Val. "Political executions Follow End of War." Guardian 41.3 (Oct. 12, 1988) 12. Hundreds of Communist prisoners have been executed and possibly 2,000 more are to be killed.

1460. "More Martyrs, More Blood." Time 118 (September 21, 1981) 31. Khomeini's political executions.

1461. Moreau, Ron. "Serving Time in Hell." Newsweek 101 (February 14, 1983) 44. Torture of female opponents of Ayatollah Khomeini.

1462. Murphy, Fred. "Iran: Baraheni Released From Prison." Militant 46.2 (January 1982) 3. Dr. Reza Baraheni, a prominant Iranian poet and writer, was released from prison due to a massive international telegram campaign.

1463. Najafi, Parvin. "Massive Protests Rock Shah's Regime." Militant 42.19 (May 19, 1978) 24. Protests in the form of nationwide bazaar strike, a hunger strike in a political prison, and demonstrations in approximately fifty-five towns and cities are a response "to honor those killed by the Shah's army during the huge antigovernment demonstrations in Tabriz."

1464. Najafi, Parvin. "Political Prisoners Indict Butcher of Tehran." Militant 42.43 (Nov. 17, 1978) 7. A few hundred released political prisoners (tens of thousands remain) testify in mass meetings of the Shah's torture regime.

1465. Namvar, Majid. "'Hot Table' Exposed: New Reports from Iran Document Shah's Torture of Political Prisoners." Militant 39.5 (February 14, 1975) 4. Prisoners held incommunicado for months of severe torture, including use of the "hot table," an iron frame covered with a wire mesh which prisoners would be strapped to while it was heated until it became red hot.

1466. Naraghi, Ehsan. From Palace to Prison: Inside the Iranian Revolution. Trans. Nilou Mobasser. Chicago: Ivan Dee, 1993. 352. In the second half of the book the author recalls his 33-month experience in prison. Naraghi founded Teheran University's Institute of Social Studies in the early 1960s.

1467. Omidi, Behzad. "Iran Solidarity: U.N. Picket targets Execution of Prisoners." Guardian 41.13 (Dec. 21, 1988) 4. An estimated 5,000 prisoners have been executed during the past two months.

1468. "Persia Today: No Magic Carpet Ride." Matchbox (Fall 1976) 1. On the Shah's National Intelligence and Security Organization, SAVAK's pervasive activities--detention without trial, torture, etc.

1469. "Plot Uncovered." Time 119 (May 3, 1982) 38. Former Foreign Minister Ghotbzadeh and 45 others were arrested for plotting overthrow of Khomeini.

1470. Rejali, Darius. Torture and Modernity: Self, Society, and State in Modern Iran. Boulder, CO: Westview, 1993. 225. Focuses on Iran but also investigates the global politics and psychology of modern torture.

1471. Russell, G. "Revolution Devouring Its Own." Time 120 (September 27, 1982) 35. Former Foreign Minister Sadegh Ghotbzadeh was executed, accused of attempting to overthrow the Ayatollah Khomeini.

1472. Scanlon, Kevin, and Carole Jerome. "An Execution in Tehran." Maclean's 100 (Oct. 12, 1987) 32. Mehdi Hashemi, who made public the Iran/U.S. arms negotiations, was executed by firing squad.

1473. Seidman, Peter. "Protests in Iran Defy Shah, Demand Rights." Militant 41.46 (Dec. 9, 1977) 8. Several writers were among those arrested during the protests: Mahmoud Etemadzadeh (Beh-Azin), Dr. Homa Nateg, and Nemat Mirzazadeh. The latter two were connected with the Iranian Writers Association.

1474. "The Sergeant's Saga." Time 113 (March 5, 1979) 39. Story of Marine captured at takeover of the U.S. Embassy in Teheran.

1475. "Shah to Kill 10 Political Prisoners." Guardian 28.14 (January 14, 1976) 12. The Shah of Iran continues his policy of repression against those disagreeing with his regime, and the U.S. helps train the military for such actions.

1476. Shirvani, Ali. "Iran/Khomeini's 4-Month Death Toll: 12,000." Guardian 41.16 (Jan. 18, 1989) 15. Marxists, communists, leftists, and Kurds are suffering mass executions.

1477. Strasser, Steven, et al. "Grim Tales of Brutality." Newsweek 97 (February 2, 1981) 33-36. After fourteen months of captivity the U.S. Embassy hostages are released.

1478. Taylor, Deb. "Women Tortured in Iran. Big Mama Rag 5.8 (Oct. 1977) 6. Some 4000 women are in the Shah's jails.

1479. Thought Control in Iran: Limits on Freedom of Expression. New York: Human Rights Watch, June 1993. 80. Examines the thoroughness of Iran's censorship policy from film and radio to the fatwa against Salmon Rushdie.

1480. Totten, Samuel. "The Threatened Genocide of the Bahá'ís." First-Person Accounts of Genocidal Acts Committed in the Twentieth Century: An Annotated Bibliography. Westport, CT: Greenwood, 1991. P. 310. Two entries on the brutality faced by the Bahá'í.

1481. U.S. House of Representatives Committee on Foreign Affairs, May 2, 1984. Religious Persecution of the Bahá'ís in Iran. Washington, DC: Government Printing Office, 1984. 107. The Bahá'ís are the largest religious minority in Iran and face daily persecution at the hands of the government: confiscation of all properties, torture, exile, execution, etc.

1482. Wang, Diane. "Happy New Year." Militant 42.13 (April 7, 1978) 27. The case of Vida Hadjebi Tabrizi, held in prison by the Shah; included is a poem written by Kay Boyle.

1483. Ward, Richard. "Political Prisoners Strike." Guardian 30.26 (April 15, 1978) 12. Discusses a hunger strike by political prisoners at Qasr.

1484. "What Is to Happen to Me Tonight?" Time 117 (February 16, 1981) 24-5. Time reporter Raji Samghabadi was subjected to a mock execution.

IRAQ

1485. al-Khalil, Samir. Republic of Fear: The Politics of Modern Iraq. Berkeley: U of California P, 1989. 310. Chapter 1, "Institutions of Violence," chapter 2, "A World of Fear."

1486. Amnesty International Report 1980. London: Amnesty International, 1980. 331-337. Saddam Husain (Hussein) assumed power in July 1979, alleged a conspiracy and began executions of Ba'ath Party members and of armed forces. Widespread arrests of Shi'is occurred (some 10,000 people), and arbitrary detention and torture of members and supporters of the once legal Iraqi Communist Party became "routine." Kurds have also been arrested and some executed. Trials summary and secret, confessions extracted by torture, mass arrests, numerous executions--Iraq is a major repression regime.

1487. Amnesty International Report 1990. New York: Amnesty International, 1990. 125-128. Thousands of prisoners continued to be held without charge or trial, or after unfair trials, and torture "remained widespread." Thousands of prisoners have disappeared.

1488. "Farzad Bazoft." Index On Censorship 19.1 (Jan. 1990) 34. "A British-based journalist, Farzad Bazoft has been imprisoned in Baghdad since 15 September 1989 following an Iraqi government-orchestrated media operation that backfired."

1489. Genocide in Iraq: The Anfal Campaign Against the Kurds. New York: Human Rights Watch, 1993. 400. Details the history of Kurdish torment and forced exile at the hands of the Iraqi government (uses previously unpublished Iraqi government documents).

1490. Iraq: Evidence of Torture. London: Amnesty International, 1981. 44. Medical reports of victims, fifteen case histories, human rights documents, etc.

1491. Iraq: Human Rights Since the Uprising: A Summary of Amnesty International's Concerns: The Need for Further United Nations Action to Protect Human Rights in Iraq. New York: Amnesty International, 1991. 24. This report voices concerns for people who were involved in the uprising in Iraq after the withdrawal of Iraqi troops from Kuwait. Widespread arrests, torture and mass extrajudicial killings of many innocent victims, including women and children.

1492. Iraq-occupied Kuwait, the Health Care Situation: a Report by Physicians for Human Rights/Denmark and Physicians for Human Rights/USA. Sommerville, Mass.: Physicians for Human Rights, 1991. 35. Two pages on torture.

1493. Janabi, Nabil. "Memoir of Terror." Index On Censorship 18.1 (Jan. 1989) Backcover. "Nabil Janabi, a poet, was arrested in Iraq in March 1976...he describes the reasons for his arrest and the torture that followed when he was under interrogation."

1494. Makiya, Kanan. "Rape in the Service of the State." Nation 256.18 (1993) 627-630. On the widespread use of rape as a method of repression. Adapted from author's Cruelty and Silence.

1495. Saddam's Iraq: Revolution or Reaction? London: 2nd ed; Committee Against Repression and for Democratic Rights in Iraq, 1986. 254. Describes the administration and policies of the Ba'th regime ("Husain rules by right of execution and assassination"), the brutal suppression of Kurdish and other minorities, opposition political groups, womens organizations through mass deportation, torture, detention without trial, mass executions, etc. Includes an interview with an Iraqi mother whose two sons were abducted and imprisoned without charges and tortured to death: amputation of legs, arms, eyes, nose; burning, and flaying; and a speech by Dr. Su'ad Khairi of the Iraqi Women's League, a political opponent of the Ba'thists and victim of torture (108-119).

1496. Torture in Iraq, 1982-1984. New York: Amnesty International USA, 1985. 24. Mainly composed of case histories.

1497. "Torture in Iraq: An AI Report." Matchbox (May 1981) 1-2. Evidence of brutal torture inflicted by security forces based on medical evidence and interviews with 15 exiles.

1498. Whitley, Andrew. "Iraqi Kurdistan: Bones Tell the Tale of Abuses." Human Rights Watch 10.2 (Spring 1992) 3. Possibly 100,000 Kurds disappeared under the Iraqi repression during the late 1980s.

IRELAND

1499. Amnesty International Report 1980. London: Amnesty International, 1980. 279. A Special Criminal Court for political crimes exists without full safeguards for fair trials, and one prisoner was convicted on the basis of his confession, which he alleges was forced during prolonged incommunicado detention, but Amnesty International has no prisoners of conscience in Ireland.

1500. Amnesty International Report 1990. New York: Amnesty International, 1990. 128-129. Two former prisoners pursued civil actions against the government for allegedly torturing them for confessions.

ISRAEL

1501. Ala Turabina Al-watani Nuhaqqiqu Hurriyatana = Leheyot Am Hafshi Bemoladtenu = We Will be Free in our Homeland. Chicago: Palestine Human Rights Campaign, 1986. 141.

1502. Amnesty International Report 1980. London: Amnesty International, 1980. 337-42. Israel's abuses in the Occupied Territories include imprisonment for political belief, restrictions without due process, detention without trial, and mistreatment in prisons.

1503. Cohen, Stanley. The Interrogation of Palestinians During the Intifada: Ill-treatment, "Moderate Physical Pressure" or Torture? Jerusalem: B'tselem, Israeli Information Center for Human Rights in the Occupied Territories, 1991. 151. Torture used to quell the uprising.

1504. Corrigan, Edward. "A Year of the Palestinian Uprising." Against The Current 3.5 (Nov. 1988) 4. A survey of Israel's repression of the intifada's first year: over twenty journalists detained, deportation, house demolitions, killings.

1505. Cossali, Paul, and Clive Robson. Stateless in Gaza. London: Zed, 1986. 159. Collection of interviews with the Palestinians of Gaza, many of whom have been in prison under the Israeli occupation army.

1506. Cox, Sophie. "Land Before Honour." Spare Rib 1.39 (February 1984) 26-29. On abuse of female prisoners.

1507. Darwish, Adel. "Palestinian Journalist Sam'an Khoury." Index on Censorship 19.4 (April 1990) 30. Agence France Presse reporter Khoury has been detained a year charged with writing inciting leaflets.

1508. Dawli, T. "Prisoners' Hunger Strike Victorious." Guardian 37.05 (Oct. 31, 1984) 14. Palestinians in the Jnaid Prison near Nablus in the West Bank won demands for better conditions.

1509. "Defending Israel's Palestine Prisoners." Militant 41.35 (September 23, 1977) 20. Interview with Lea Tsemel, member of Israel League for Human Rights, discussing poor prison conditions.

1510. Deming, Angus. "A Costly Prisoner Exchange." Newsweek 105 (June 3, 1985) 40. Israel exchanges over 1000 prisoners for three Israelis held in Syria.

1511. Finkel, David. "The Case of Michael Warschawsky." Red Bass No. 12 (1987) 42-3. The police closed and took the equipment from the peace activist Alternative Information Center, arrested its staff, and its head, Warschawsky, who is now on trial under the Prevention of Terrorism Act.

1512. "Free Lebanon--Free Suha Bishara." Spare Rib 201 (May 1989) 45. For attempting to assassinate a South Lebanon Army commander, she was transferred to Israel, in violation of international law, where she was tortured.

1513. Gover, Yerach, and Ella Shohat. "In Defence of Mordechai Vanunu: Nuclear Threat in the Middle East." Social Text No. 18 (Winter 1987/88) 95-97. Vanunu, who disclosed Israel's nuclear capabilities, is considered a traitor in Israel, but a hero elsewhere. Vanunu claims his civil disobedience was in the name of peace and justice.

1514. Habib, Shafiq. "'I Didn't Feel Alone During Detention.'" Index On Censorship 19.10 (Oct. 1990) 20. "Police came to Shafiq Habib's house on 16 June, arrested him and held him for five days."

1515. Hiltermann, Joost. Israel's Deportation Policy and the Occupied West Bank and Gaza. Ramallah: al-Haq, 1986. 110. Focuses on the August 4, 1985 revival by the Israeli government of punishment by exile of Palestinians accused of infiltration or of incitement--extra-judicial punishment "in which no formal charges are brought against the deportee, no trial is held, and the person is deported on the basis of evidence to which neither he/she nor his/her lawyer can have access." List of Palestinians deported from Occupied Territories in 1985 and 1986.

1516. Hunt, Paul. Justice? The Military Court System in the Israeli Occupied Territories. Ramallah: al-Haq, 1987. 40. Describes the Israeli military court system--arrest, interrogation, charge, trial, and sentence--, evidences the injustice of this system for those detained, and notes the violations of international human rights and humanitarian laws.

1517. Isolation of Jerusalem: Restrictions in Movement Causing Severe Hardship in Occupied Territories. New York: Human Rights Watch, 1993. 9. Describes the trouble that some 1.8 million Palestinians are having while Israel continues its entry ban to these people who have no way of getting to work, the mosques, hospitals, etc.

1518. "Israel and the Occupied Territories." Amnesty International Report 1990. New York: Amnesty International, 1990. 129-132. About 25,000 Palestinians have been arrested in connection with the intifada (uprising), over 4,000 were detained without charge or trial, thousands more were tried by military court, and over 13,000 remained in prison at the end of 1989. Thousands were beaten and tortured, and at least 8 died as the result.

1519. Israel and the Occupied Territories: Amnesty International's Concerns in 1988. New York: Amnesty International, 1988. 76. A compilation of recent documents on the use of live ammunition by the Israel Defense Force, misuse of tear gas, excessive force, beatings, conscientious objection, etc.

1520. Israel and the Occupied Territories: Fear of Torture or Ill-Treatment. New York: Amnesty International, 1992. 5. AI is concerned that detainees arrested on 22 January may have been subjected to torture or ill-treatment while under interrogation and may be further at risk.

1521. Israel and the Occupied Territories: The Military Justice System in the Occupied Territories. New York: Amnesty International, 1991. 75. Protests against the prolonged incommunicado detention of Palestinians after arrest, facilitating arbitrary arrest as well as torture or ill-treatment.

1522. "Israel: Palestinian Prisoners Protest." Peace News 20.39 (March 11, 1977) 7. Report on the dismal living conditions of Palestinian prisoners in Israel and their protests through hunger strikes and threatened mass suicide.

1523. Israel\South Lebanon : The Khiam Detainees: Torture and Ill-treatment. New York: Amnesty International, 1992. 53. Detainees have routinely faced torture and ill-treatment, and although the center is staffed by the South Lebanon army militia, AI believes that Israeli authorities have responsibility for the treatment and fate of detainees.

1524. Israel and Torture. New York: Americans for Middle East Understanding, 1977. 33. Reprint of articles appearing in The Sunday Times of London, June 19-July 10, 1977 on the routine ill-treatment and often torture of Arab prisoners.

1525. Israel and Torture : A Special Investigation. London: Arab Dawn, 1977. 72. Personal narratives.

1526. "Israeli Mistreatment Kills Political Prisoners." Palestine 2.5 (September 1980) 2. Two Palestinian prisoners died as the result of forced feeding during a hunger strike in the Nafha Prison.

1527. Jaber, S. "Repression Knows No Frontiers." International Viewpoint 147 (September 19, 1988) 8. Describes the police harrassment, state-of-emergency detention in harsh prison conditions, the use of torture to extract confessions, etc., suffered by the Sons of the Country movement.

1528. Jabora, Abdeen. "Palestinians/ Freedom still a Dream for Abu Eain." Guardian 36.19 (Feb. 15, 1984) 13. Despite the release of 4,500 Palestinians in exchange for Israeli prisoners, some Palestinians remain confined.

1529. Jammal, Laila. Contributions by Palestinian Women to the National Struggle for Liberation. Washington, D.C.: Middle East Public Relations, 1985. 104. From

British colonial rule to 1985. One section on women detainees in Israeli jails, another on women prisoners in Ansarit Prison in Lebanon.

1530. Johnson, Alexandra. Israeli Tortue of Palestinian Political Prisoners in Jerusalem and the West Bank: Three State Department Reports. New York: Americans for Middle East Understanding, 1979. 11. Summaries of three reports by a U.S. consular officer on interviews of twenty-nine Palestinians which indicate that brutality is widespread and systematic.

1531. Khaled, Leila, with George Hajjar. My People Shall Live: The Autobiography of a Revolutionary. London: Hodder and Stoughton, 1973. 229. Khaled, expelled from her home in Haifa and from her homeland in 1948 at the age of four, describes her transformation from Palestinian refugee to revolutionary and humanist. She was arrested for attemting to hijack an Iraeli airplane but soon released in hostage exchange.

1532. The Khiam Detainees: Torture and Ill-Treatment. New York: Amnesty International, 1992. At Khiam, a detention center set up by the Israelis, through their creature, the South Lebanon Army, prisoners are subjected to sexual, physical, and psychological abuse.

1533. Langer, Felicia. These are my Brothers: Israel and the Occupied Territories. London: Ithaca, 1979. 145. The second of two volumes on the oppression--including torture--of Palestinians in Gaza and the West Bank, by the President of the League of Human and Civil Rights in Israel.

1534. Langer, Felicia. With My Own Eyes: Israel and the Occupied Territories 1967-1973. London: Ithaca, 1975. 166. The first of two volumes on cases of persecution, oppression, and torture by Israel against the Palestinians and Israeli citizens who supported them.

1535. A License to Kill: Israeli Undercover Operations Against Wanted & Masked Palestinians. New York: Human Rights Watch, August 1993. 200. Case studies expose the lack of accountability among Israeli undercover forces.

1536. McGeary, Johanna. "Behind Barbed Wire." Time 131 (June 13, 1988) 34-5. Thousands of Palestinians are detained without charge or trial in Ketziot Prison in the Negev Desert.

1537. "Middle East: Warschawsky in Jeopardy." International Viewpoint 147 (September 19, 1988) 10. Michel Warschawsky and other supporters of peace with the Palestinians are facing harsher sentences.

1538. O'Brien, S. "Palestinian Support: Prisoners of Conscience Backed." Guardian 36.31 (May 9, 1984) 4. A forum on Palestinian and U.S. political prisoners discussed the "Nuremberg defense" and other issues.

1539. Palestinian Political Prisoners and Repression in Israel and the Occupied Territories. Switzerland: Lebanese Association for Information on Palestine, 1975. 12. Individual cases, the prisons, and tortures surveyed.

1540. Palestinian Political Prisoners: Struggle Behind Iron Bars. Beirut, Lebanon: PLO Unified Information, Foreign Information Department, Committee for the Defense of Political Prisoners in Israeli Jails, 1979. 105. Twelve cases of "brutal and inhuman" practices in Israeli jails.

1541. Posner, Michael H. An Examination of the Detention of Human Rights Workers and Lawyers from the West Bank and Gaza and Conditions of Detention at Ketziot. New York: Lawyers Committee for Human Rights, 1988. 122. A report about the jailing without charge of four Palestinian human rights workers and two lawyers in

Ketziot prison, which violates the Fourth Geneva Convention, as do conditions in Ketziot prison. Over 18,000 Palestinians have been imprisoned in the past year.

1542. Prison Conditions in Israel and the Occupied Territories: a Middle East Watch Report. New York: Human Rights Watch, 1991. 118. The team visited most of the prisons and detention camps but not the interrogation centers where physical force occurs.

1543. Rahman, Asaad Abdel. A Prisoner of the Israelis. Ottawa: Middle East Research Centre, 1969. 99. An account of his arrest, interrogation, and imprisonment for a year.

1544. A Report on the Treatment of Security Prisoners at the West Bank Prison of al-Faara. Ramallah (West Bank, Israel): Law in the Service of Man, 1984. 9. On mistreatment of Palestinian prisoners.

1545. Report and Recommendation of an Amnesty International Mission to the Government of the State of Israel, 3-7 June 1979: Including the Government's Response and Amnesty International Comments. London: Amnesty International, 1980. 71. Focuses on ill-treatment in detention and unfair court procedures.

1546. Rubin, Robin. "MOSSAD's Long Arm." CounterSpy 4.3 (Summer 1980) 7-8. Three Palestinians and two West Germans were secretly extradited in violation of international law from Kenya to a secret military camp in Israel, and held incommunicado for four months of severe torture to extract confessions.

1547. Ryan, Sheila. "Esmail Exposes Israel's Jails." Guardian 31.6 (November 15, 1978) 7. Sami Esmail was released from an Israeli prison where he was held for "membership in an illegal organization" and was subjected to mental and physical torture.

1548. Ryan, Sheila. "Political Prisoners Tortured." City Star 3.2 (June 1975) 14. Israel employs brutal collective punishment, deportation, and torture to maintain its occupation. Over the last eight years some 27,000 Palestinians have been detained for political reasons.

1549. "Salah Tamari." Journal of Palestine Studies 8.4 (Summer 1984) 46-69. Memoir of his arrest and imprisonment in 1982 in Ansar Prison Camp, which is thoroughly described.

1550. Seidman, Peter. "Tsemel Touring U.S. on Palestinian Rights." Militant 41.38 (Oct. 14, 1977) 23. Lea Tssemel, "a prominent Israeli attorney who has defended Palestinian prisoners," toured the U.S. to speak about Palestinian human rights.

1551. Shehadeh, Raja. Occupier's Law: Israel and the West Bank. Washington, D.C.: Institute for Palestine Studies, 1985. 212. Israel's intent to drive out the Palestinians and annex the occupied territory. Chapter Six describes the conditions for Palestinians in Al-Fara'a Prison, "a detention centre for people suspected of endangering security...against whom no specific charge could be made."

1552. Silver, Eric. "A Scandal in the Ranks." Macleans 100 (May 4, 1987) 28+. Izat Napso, an army lieutenant, confessed after 19 days of torture to giving arms and information to an unknown enemy.

1553. Smith, David. Prisoners of God: The Modern-Day Conflict of Arab and Jew. London: Quartet, 1988. 239. Israeli and Palestinian conflict has resulted in killings, mass arrests, and thousands of imprisonments.

1554. Smith, W.E. "Fallout of an Ugly War." Time 125 (June 3, 1985) 28-9. Israel exchanges over a thousand prisoners for three Israelis.

1555. "Solidarity with Michael Warshawsky." Against the Current 24 (January 1990) 12. On the persecution of the director of the Alternative Information Center in Jerusalem who is a leading anti-war and anti-occupation activist.

1556. Spaniola, Thomas. "Sami Esmail Fights Israeli Gov't Frame-Up." Militant 42.9 (March 10, 1978) 23. Esmail, a U.S. graduate student, was imprisoned in Israel on false charges of being a member of the Popular Front for the Liberation of Palestine (PFLP).

1557. Stevens, Janet. "Shiite Sit-in Condemns Israeli Occupation." Guardian 35.28 (April 13, 1983) 15. The arrest of Sheikh Raghib Harb, who refused to cooperate with the occupation forces, has triggered strikes demanding his release.

1558. "Thrice Rebuked." Time 129 (June 8, 1987) 40. Azat Napso is released from prison, where he had spent seven-and-a-half years on false espionage and treason charges.

1559. "A Time Bomb for Israel." Time 113 (February 19, 1979) 37. Israeli torture of Palestinians.

1560. Torture and Intimidation in the West Bank: The Case of Al-Fara'a Prison: A Report. Geneva, Switzerland: International Commission of Jurists: Law in the Service of Man, 1984. 56. This second report covers the period 1982-1984. Al-Fara's is not a prison but a torture center where confessions are manufactured.

1561. Toscano, Louis. Triple Cross: Israel and the Atomic Bomb and the Man Who Spilled the Secret. New York: Birch Lane\Carol, 1990. 321. Mordechai Vanunu was sentenced to 18 years in prison for revealing that Israel had over 200 nuclear warheads. Vanunu hoped the exposure would increase the possibility of peace.

1562. Tzemei, L. "No Court, No Trial, No Jury." Connexions 14 (Fall 1984) 24. On the difficulties for women in prison and under occupation.

1563. Vanunu, Mordechai. "Israel's Nuclear Arsenal." Covert Action Information Bulletin No. 30 (Summer 1988) 45. The story of Vanunu's arrest and confinement by Israeli's for his confirmation of Israel's nuclear power.

1564. Vitullo, Anita. "West Bank Erupts Again." Guardian 39.29 (April 22, 1987) 1. On hunger strikes in Israeli prisons by Palestinians, the shooting of a student, the arrest of journalists, unionists, and political activists.

1565. "Voices from Prison." Ground Zero 11 (Summer 1992) 11. The story of Mordechai Vanunu, who because he told the world about Israel's nuclear weapons program was kidnapped and imprisoned by his government.

1566. Wattenmaker, Steve. "Palestinians in Israeli Jails." Militant 41.27 (July 15, 1977) 20. On the physical, psychological, and sexual torture of Palestinian prisoners.

1567. Wollin, A. "Palestinian Resister Fights Deportation." Guardian 36.26 (April 4, 1984) 13. After Abdel Aziz Ali Shaheen ("Abu Ali") served fifteen years in prisons, he was exiled to a guarded village and now faces deportation.

1568. Ya'ari, Ehud. "Israel's Prison Academies." The Atlantic 264 (October 1989) 22-30. Trans.Ina Friedman. The Palestinian uprising was partly produced by the Israeli penal system, in which tens of thousands of political prisoners welded the intifada.

ITALY

1569. Amnesty International Report 1980. London: Amnesty International, 1980. 279-82. Prolonged detention for investigation is a continuing problem. New statutes expand police powers at the expense of individual rights. Amnesty International had adopted nine conscientious objectors as prisoners of conscience.

1570. Amnesty International Report 1990. New York: Amnesty International, 1990. 132-134. Hundreds of conscientious objectors to the draft were in prisons, and political trials continued to be slow. Ill-treatment in prisons was frequently reported.

1571. Fiori, Giuseppe. Antonio Gramsci: Life of a Revolutionary. Trans. Tom Nairn. New York: Dutton, 1971. 304. In November 1926 all opposition parliamentary deputies were arrested, including the communists, of which Gramsci was one. He was to spend 10 years in fascist prisons. Chapter 23 tells of his initial imprisonment; Chapter 24 of his trial, etc.

1572. Gramsci, Antonio. Prison Notebooks. Ed. Joseph Buttigieg. Trans. Joseph Buttigieg and Antonio Callari. Vol. 1. New York: Columbia UP, 1992. 608. The author was imprisoned in 1926 for his opposition to Mussolini. He was a founder of the Italian Communist Party.

1573. Johnstone, Diana. "Bulgarian Connection/Finger Pointing in the Pontif Plot Labyrinth." In These Times 10.10 (Jan. 29, 1986) 11,22. Francesco Pazienza has been jailed in New York at the request of the Italian government, which is seeking his extradition in regard to Ali Agca's claim that he shot the Pope for the Bulgarian government.

1574. Meda, Luigi. "Prison Memories." Commonweal 44 (July 19, 1946) 332-5. Part of Meda's account of his imprisonment by the Nazis.

1575. Nitti, Francesco Fausto. Escape: The Personal Narrative of a Political Prisoner who was Rescued from Lipari, the Fascist "Devil's Island." New York: Putnam's; London: Knickerbocker, 1930. 267. An account of life on the prison island of Lipari and how three prisoners escaped.

1576. Pavese, Cesare. The Political Prisoner. Trans. W.J. Strachan. London: P. Owen, 1955. 237. Two short novels about his arrest and imprisonment in 1935 for his work as editor of the anti-Fascist journal La Cultura.

1577. Rossi, Carlo. In the Dungeons of Mussolini. New York: Italian Patronati to Aid the Political Prisoners of Italy, 1936. 31. The persecuation of anti-Fascists.

1578. "Songs of the Pentiti." Time 119 (March 22, 1982) 46. Trial of Red Brigades members who had kidnapped Brig. General James Dozier.

1579. Spriano, Paolo. Antonio Gramsci and the Party: The Prison Years. Trans. John Fraser. London: Lawrence and Wishart, 1979. 192. Gramsci, the general secretary of the Italian Communist Party, was arrested and imprisoned on November 8, 1926 as part of the purging of parliamentary opposition to Mussolini, and was not released until October 1934.

IVORY COAST (*see* CÔTE D'IVOIRE)

JAMAICA

1580. Amnesty International Report 1990. New York: Amnesty International, 1990. 134-136. No political prisoners were reported, but unfair trials and delays in appeals of capital criminal cases were common.

1581. Charles, Pearnel. Detained: 283 Days in Jamaica's Detention Camp, Struggling for Freedom, Justice and Human Rights! Kingston, Jamaica: Kingston, 1977. 207. His story of nine months of incarceration during a State of Emergency 1n 1976 in which members of the opposition party were detained.

1582. Human Rights in Jamaica: Death Penalty, Prison Conditions & Police Violence. New York: Human Rights Watch, 1993. 13. Describes the death penalty, police violence (including torture as a form of coercion), and conditions within the prisons.

JAPAN

1583. Amnesty International Report 1980. London: Amnesty International, 1980. 204. AI's only concern is the death penalty.

1584. Collar, Hugh. Captive in Shanghai. Hong Kong; New York: Oxford UP, 1990. 160. Collar was Chairman of the British Residents' Association of Shanghai when the Japanese interned all British citizens. This is an account of his years in prison as leader of the British prisoners 1941-1945.

1585. Mitchell, Richard H. Janus-Faced Justice: Political Criminals in Imperial Japan. Honolulu: U of Hawaii P, 1992. 235. Focuses on a study of the 1930s and 1940s but reaches back to 1868, and the treatment of leftists, who were the most affected by the state's obsession to stamp out communism.

1586. Roth, Andrew. "Prisoners We Forgot." Nation 161 (September 29, 1945) 305-6. U.S. is neglecting the thousands of Japanese anti-militants imprisoned by their government during the war.

JORDAN

1587. Amnesty International Report 1980. London: Amnesty International, 1980. 342-43. Martial law, since 1967, continued 1979-80, allowing arbitrary arrest, detention without trial, and military courts for political prisoners.

1588. Amnesty International Report 1990. New York: Amnesty International, 1990. 137-139. Over 1000 suspected opponents of the government were arrested in 1989, and most were detained without charge or trial for several months. About twenty prisoners were tried by the unfair Martial Law Court. Torture and ill-treatment were reported.

1589. "Befuddled Fedayeen." Time 102 (October 1, 1973) 43. King Hussein gives amnesty for all Palestinian political prisoners (about 970) except for those convicted of espionage and murder.

KAMPUCHEA (CAMBODIA)

In recent decades, the nation has been known by several names. Between 1953, when Prince Norodom Sihanouk declared the nation's independence from France, and 1970, when General Lon Nol deposed the Sihanouk regime in a military coup, until 1975, the country's official name was the Khmer Republic, referring to the nation's dominant ethnic group. In early 1976, when Khmer Rouge forces captured Phnom Penh and evacuated its people, their leaders changed the country's name to Democratic Kampuchea (DK). Then, when the Vietnamese army overran the DK regime in January 1979, it installed a new regime called the People's Republic of Kampuchea (PRK). In 1982, three major forces opposing this regime joined in a loose coalition called the Coalition Government of Democratic Kampuchea. Since both the Phnom Penh-based government and the rebel coalition, which is recognized by the United Nations, include Kampuchea in their official names, we do so as well.

1590. Abrams, Floyd and Diane Orentlicher. Kampuchea: after the Worst. New York: Lawyers Committee for Human Rights, 1990. 161. Based upon two missions in 1984-1985 by the Lawyers Committee for Human Rights to areas on both sides of the Thai-Kampuchean border. Studies human rights violations by The People's Republic of Kampuchea, The Democratic Kampuchea Guerrillas (DK, Khmer Rouge), and the Khmer People's National Liberation Front.

1591. Amnesty International Report 1980. London: Amnesty International, 1980. 204-206. Civil war continues between the government and the former government of Khmer Rouge under Pol Pot and Ieng Sary (overthrown January 1979) whose policies amounted to genocide. The new government imprisoned captured Khmer Rouge soldiers, but has claimed to have released most of them.

1592. Amnesty International Report 1990. New York: Amnesty International USA, 1990. 56-7. Civil war caused numerous charges of illegal imprisoning and mistreatment. The government jailed many people suspected of supporting opposition parties. Several hundred prisoners jailed without trial as long ago as 1979 remain imprisoned.

1593. Barron, John and Anthony Paul. Murder of a Gentle Land: The Untold Story of Communist Genocide in Cambodia. New York: Crowell, 1977. 240. The authors compiled three hundred interviews of Cambodian refugees from all levels of society and geographic locale in producing this early account of the Khmer Rouge genocide.

1594. Brecher, John. "Pol Pot's Hatchet Man." Newsweek 96 (September 8, 1980) 42. Portrait of "Brother Deuch," head of Khmer Rouge secret police and responsible for the deaths of as many as one million people.

1595. "Cambodia Witness." Matchbox (June 1983) 8-10. Report on the "photographic documentation of a government's mass murder of its citizens," the Cambodia Witness exhibit that toured the United States in 1983.

1596. Criddle, Joan D. and Mam Teeda Butt. To Destroy You Is No Loss: The Odyssey of a Cambodian Family. New York: Atlantic Monthly, 1987. 289. Teeda's personal narrative of survival amidst the Khmer Rouge genocide. The title of this book comes from the Khmer Rouge slogan and basic philosophy: "To keep you is no benefit; to destroy you is no loss."

1597. Hannum, Hurst. "International Law and Cambodian Genocide: The Sounds of Silence." Human Rights Quarterly 11 (1989) 82-138. Argues that the Khmer Rouge under Pol Pot did commit genocide and explains why an application to the International Court of Justice would be legally feasible and morally and politically desireable.

1598. Kampuchea : Campaign to Stop Torture and Political Imprisonment in the People's Republic of Kampuchea (Cambodia). New York: Amnesty International USA, 1987. 15. Widespread abuses of human rights continue.

1599. Kampuchea : Political Imprisonment and Torture. New York: Amnesty International, 1987. 84. Political prisoners are detained without charge or trial, or after unfair trials, and many have been tortured.

1600. Marston, John, ed. An Annotated Bibliography of Cambodia and Cambodian Refugees. Minneapolis, MN: Southeast Asian Refugee Studies Project, Center for Urban and Regional Affairs, 1987. 121. Contains numerous citations of materials pertaining to the Khmer Rouge genocide.

1601. May, Someth. Cambodian Witness: The Autobiography of Someth May. Boston: Faber and Faber, 1986. 287. Someth survived the starvation, slave labor, and mass executions that claimed most of his family during the Khmer Rouge genocide.

1602. Ngor, Haing and Roger Warner. Haing Ngor: A Cambodian Odyssey. New York: Macmillan, 1988. 478. Ngor gives his personal account of life and genocide under the Khmer Rouge regime and presents a history of events that led up to Khmer Rogue rule and the genocide.

1603. Shenon, Philip. "U.N. Finds Uniformed Cambodians able to Kill Civilians with Impunity." Arkansas Democrat-Gazette (July 11, 1993) 16A. Civilians live in fear of the security forces of Cambodia's Vietnamese-installed government: soldiers kill innocent people without cause, brutal torture still prevails in government prisons, and the intransigence of Cambodian military and police commanders makes prosecution nearly impossible.

1604. "Testimony of a Survivor." Matchbox (October 1983) 1-2. Excerpts from Cambodian genocide survivor Arn Chorn's address to Amnesty International USA's Annual General Meeting on his experiences: "I saw so much death, life itself lost all meaning."

1605. Totten, Samuel. "The Khmer Rouge Genocide in Cambodia." First-Person Accounts of Genocidal Acts Committed in the Twentieth Century: An Annotated Bibliography. Westport, CT: Greenwood, 1991. 287-309. Eighty-nine entries on atrocities and mass carnage committed by the Khmer Rouge 1975-1979.

1606. Yathay, Pin with John Man. Stay Alive, My Son. New York: Free Press, 1987. 240. Yathay lost all seventeen members of his family in the Khmer Rouge genocide; his testimony shows "how fine-sounding ideas of justice and equality can be perverted by fanatics to create brutal oppression and an equality of misery."

KENYA

1607. Amnesty International Report 1990. New York: Amnesty International, 1990. 139-140. Over 50 prisoners were in prison part or all of 1989. Trials were illegally delayed and unfair when performed, and prison conditions were harsh. Asylum seekers from Uganda and Somalia were returned, and some of those from Somalia were killed.

1608. "Arrest and Detention in Kenya." Index On Censorship 16.1 (January 1987) 23-29. Background to the arrests and detentions. Descriptions of over 50 prisoners and some possibly disappeared, for dissent, many accused of sedition.

1609. Awwori, Horace. "Political Prisoners Lose Fight." Africa News 22.21 (May 21, 1984) 9-10. The Supreme Court rejected petitions for freedom from politicians detained without trial since 1984.

1610. Bini, O. "Kenya Political Prisoners Released." Guardian 31.12 (December 27, 1978) 12. President Daniel Arap Moi ordered his government to release all the country's political prisoners (16 total) but stated that the act enabling "arbitrary detentions without trial" was still intact.

1611. DeCormis, Anna. "Imprisoned Activist Fights From His Jail Cell." Guardian 40.31 (May 4, 1988) 13. As a part of President Daniel Arap Moi's offensive against opposition intellectuals, Wanyiri Kihoro and others have been held incommunicado under a law which permits detention without trial. He and others had sued the government over this law.

1612. Kariuki, Josiah Mwangi. Mau Mau Detainee: The Account by a Kenya African of his Experiences in Detention Camps, 1953-1960. Nairobi: Oxford UP, 1963. 188. Rptd. with postscript 1976. About the rebellion by the Kikuyu tribe under Jomo Kenyatta against their British colonial rulers, and the sometimes brutal treatment of prisoners in the detention camps.

1613. Kenya: Torture, Political Detention, and Unfair Trials. London: Amnesty International, 1987. 58. Describes and condemns a variety of police state practices during 1986-87.

1614. Kihoro, Wanjiru. "Terror Worse Then Death." Spare Rib 175 (February 1987) 7. On the strong reaction by the government to increasing political tensions: five people arrested for raising concern over the government's family planning policies; over 100 arrested for political reasons and tortured to obtain confessions; an increasing number of detention without arrest, etc.

1615. Law as a Tool of Political Repression in Kenya. London: Committee for the Release of Political Prisoners in Kenya, 1982. 14. On the glaring cases of Kenya's kangaroo courts.

1616. Likimani, Muthoni. Passbook Number F.47927: Women and Mau Mau in Kenya. London: Macmillan, 1985. 209. On the impact of the Mau Mau revolt in Kenya in the 1950s on women's daily lives. One chapter describes interrogation and torture.

1617. "Maina Wa Kinyatti--Prisoner of Conscience." Index On Censorship 16.6 (June 1987) 22-25. A Kenyatta University senior lecturer, Maina was sentenced to 6 years imprisonment for possessing "seditious literature."

1618. "Moi Deals Himself a Better Hand." Africa News 30.4 (August 2, 1988) 1. There has been no case in recent Kenyan history in which a magistrate ruled against the government, and "For the first time people are being tortured in Kenya, tortured to death."

1619. Presley, Cora Ann. Kikuyu Women, The Mau Mau Rebellion and Social Change in Kenya. Boulder, CO: Westview, 1992. 213. On the importance of women's political involvement in Kenyan nationalism--e.g., the Mau Mau rebellion and prison conditions.

1620. "Repression Intensifies in Kenya: The Need for Solidarity." Reviews of African Political Economy 25 (September 1982) 112-117. This report on the "government's campaign of arrests, detentions and harassment of university lecturers, students, writers, lawyers, peasants, workers and members of parliament and the systematic attacks on intellectual, political and cultural life" includes a political tract that is a criminal offence to possess in Kenya.

1621. Repression Intensifies in Kenya Since the August 1st Coup Attempt. London: Committee for the Release of Political Prisoners in Kenya, 1983. 14. House arrests, detentions without trial, hundreds sentenced to death or up to 25 years, travel restrictions--the repressive situation has worsened.

1622. Thacker, Elmira. "A Rough Time for Dissidents." Africa News 18.7 (February 15, 1982) 7-9. President Moi has neutralized a number of opponents recently by legal maneuvers and trials.

1623. Thiong'o, Ngugi wa. Detained : A Writer's Prison Diary. London/Nairobi: Heinemann, 1981. 232. This notable novelist, playwright, and essayist was detained without trial in 1978 as punishment for one of his plays. The first part gives his experiences in prison, the second his letters from prison, and the third his struggle to regain employment after his release, and other harassments.

1624. Wamwere, Koigi wa. Conscience on Trial: Why I Was Detained, Notes of a Political Prisoner. Trenton: Africa World Press, 1988. 143. About detention without trial in Kenya between 1975 and December 1978 and 1982-1985, through the author's letters and poems written while in prison.

KOREA, NORTH

1625. Amnesty International Report 1980. London: Amnesty International, 1980. 206-207. Because of the government of Kim Il Sung severely restricts access to the country, little is known about human rights there.

1626. Amnesty International Report 1990. New York: Amnesty International, 1990. 141. Harsh censorship laws put critics of the government in jeopardy but also prevent investigation of the facts. Possibly thousands of opponents are in prison.

1627. Amnesty International's Concerns in the Democratic People's Republic of Korea. New York: Amnesty International, 1985. 15. On the scarcity of information about the DPRK.

1628. "Freed Missionaries Reach America." Christian Century 70 (May 27, 1953) 621. Methodist missionaries and other civilians captured at the outbreak of war in 1950 are freed.

1629. Johnson, L.B. and D. Rusk. "Crew of U.S.S Pueblo Released at Panmunjon; U.S. Position on Facts Unchanged." Department of State Bulletin 60 (January 6, 1969) 1-3. Crew captured by Democratic People's Republic of Korea and accused of illegally intruding in their territorial waters were released.

1630. Lameda, Ali. A Personal Account of the Experience of a Prisoner of Conscience in the Democratic People's Republic of Korea. London: Amnesty International, 1979. 39. The author, a Venezuelan poet, was detained one year without trial, then placed under house arrest, and finally tried and sentenced to twenty years in prison, of which he served six.

1631. "Rights Group Denounces North Korea." Arkansas Democrat-Gazette (October 15, 1993) 6A. Amnesty International reported that "thousands of people have reprotedly been tortured or summarily executed and tens of thousands of others" have been detained "over the past 30 years."

KOREA, SOUTH

1632. "Amnesty for the Opposition." Macleans 100 (July 2, 1987) 24. Amnest for 2,335 political prisoners was granted.

1633. Amnesty International Report 1980. London: Amnesty International, 1980. 207-212. The new President Choi Kyu-hah rescinded the law under which an estimated 200 political prisoners were held, and released 68, but others remain in prison under other laws. For example, seven accused of being socialists endured a long, harrowing trial that included "confessions" by torture.

1634. Amnesty International Report 1990. New York: Amnesty International, 1990. 141-144. About 800 people were imprisoned for opposition activities in 1989, and thousands more were temporarily detained for trade union and other activities. Six long-term prisoners remained confined, one after 18 years.

1635. "An Erratic Shot at Democracy." Macleans 95 (Dec 27, 1982) 19. The South Korean government works "to improve its badly stained human rights record" by improving the treatment of its political prisoners in order to look good to the U.S.

1636. Bini, O. "South Korea: Limited Amnesty Decree." Guardian 31.13 (January 3, 1979) 10. South Korea dictator Pak Jung Hi ordered the release of 107 political prisoners.

1637. Brill, Julie. Assessing Reform in South Korea: a Supplement to the Asia Watch Report. Washington D.C.: Asia Watch, 1988. 54. Some reforms have been instituted, but several hundred political prisoners remain confined, some fifty long term prisoners are held in preventive custody after their terms expired. There have been unfair trials, arbitrary arrests, and abuses in detention including torture.

1638. Butler, William Jack, ed. Political Repression in South Korea: Report of Commission to South Korea for Amnesty International. London: Amnesty International, 1974. 12. Unfair trials, preventive detention, etc.

1639. "Cauldron that is South Korea." Guardian 31.13 (January 10, 1979) 19. On the release of South Korean political prisoners and former New Democractic Party leader Dae Jung Kim.

1640. "Church Goes Against State." Newsweek 84 (August 5, 1974) 46. Dictator Park Chung Hee has again arrested poet Kim Chi Ha, this time to sentence him to life in prison; many other opponents are in prison or on trial.

1641. Easter, David. "South Korea Has World's Longest Held Prisoners." Guardian 43.20 (March 13, 1991) 16. Roh Tae Woo has arrested more people on political charges in his three years as president as the previous dictator, Chun Doo Hwan, did in his seven year rule. At the beginning of this year there were 1,332 political prisoners, 147 of them long-term.

1642. Elam, F. "Death Sentences Upheld." Guardian 33.15 (January 14, 1981) 12. Three South Koreans are sentenced to death on charges stemming from antigovernment uprisings.

1643. "Freedom's Price." Time 102 (November 5, 1973) 61. Opposition leader Dae Jung Kim was freed from house arrest.

1644. Harvey, Pharis. "Commentary on Korea." Human Rights Internet Reporter 12.1 (Fall 1987) 9-10. Despite the promise of democratic reforms of June 29, 1987, between 300 and 800 political prisoners remain detained, hundreds more arrested, no promised legal reforms have been introduced, and no efforts to dismantle the huge secret police have been made.

1645. Hill, P. "Student Revolt Brewing in South Korea." Guardian 35.17 (Jan. 26, 1983) 15. The release of 49 prisoners, including Dae Jung Kim , but in a new crackdown the government has arrested at least 50 people for participating in leftist study groups.

1646. Kim, Dae Jung. Prison Writings. Trans. Choi Sung-Il and David R. McCann. Berkeley, CA: U of California P, 1987. 333. One of South Korea's foremost prisoner dissidents expresses his views about the government, prison life, etc. Kim has been kidnapped and almost murdered, sentenced to death, kept in solitary confinement, and other punishments beginning in 1971.

1647. "Korea: Kim Keun-Tae Still in Prison." HRI Reporter 12.1 (Fall 1987) 46. Kim, imprisoned for causing "social unrest" and "for spreading groundless rumours," has been tortured with electricity, beaten, deprived of food, and currently suffers from many medical problems.

1648. "Korean Amnesty." Christian Century 100 (January 26, 1983) 64. Timothy Moon (Moon Ik Whan) and Kim Dae Jung and other dissidents have been released from confinement.

1649. Krisher, Bernard. "Seoul: an Acute Sense of Timing." Newsweek 89 (May 2, 1977) 63-4. More crackdowns on dissenters to Park Chung Hee's regime.

1650. Marginalization of Peoples: Racial Oppression in Japan, Political Repression in South Korea, Economic Slavery in Brazil. New York: Idoc/North America, 1974. 68. The section on South Korea was written by William J. Butler for A.I. It gives a history of the "struggle for democracy" from 1910 to the present, including recent torture.

1651. "A Matter of Conscience." Time 108 (September 13, 1976) 36. Eighteen distinguished dissidents sentenced to prison for writing a "Declaration for the Restoration of Democracy."

1652. Moon, Stephen. "'Joy on the Way': Life in a Korean Prison." Christian Century 95 (November 29, 1978) 1160-2. An account of his 22 months in prison for participating in protests against the Park Chung Hee government's martial law; Dr. Moon is a Presbyterian and former professor at Hankuk Theological Seminary in Seoul.

1653. Nicolaus, Martin. "South Korea Prisoners Tortured." Guardian 27.22 (March 12, 1975) 12. Describes the torture of a 26 year old student, Na Byung Sik, and the continued meetings held, despite threats of torture, to plan the release of the remaining 35 political prisoners.

1654. The Plantados of Asia: "Non-converted" Political Prisoners in South Korea. New York: Asia Watch, 1990. 9. Fifty-seven long-term prisoners in Taejon Prison outside Seoul, fifty serving life sentences, fifteen held since the 1950s, all but two charged with espionage for N. Korea.

1655. Political Imprisonment in the Republic of Korea. London: Amnesty International, 1987. 25. Mainly case histories of ill-treatment, torture, and other abuses.

1656. Report of an Amnesty International Mission to the Republic of Korea, 27 March--9 April 1975. 2nd ed. London: Amnesty International, 1977. 45. Indicts detainment without trial, torture, and other human rights violations frequently used by law enforcement agencies.

1657. Republic of Korea Violations of Human Rights: An Amnesty International Report. London: Amnesty International, 1981. 43. The laws, trial procedures, torture testimonies, case histories, and other information. Martial law declared in 1980 produced mass arrests and degradation of human rights--detention without charge, torture, etc.

1658. Schwen, Marcia. "In Prison: Flowers, a Spiderweb and Prayer: An Interview with Kim Dae Jung." Matchbox (Feb. 1983) 2. A former political prisoner describes conditions in a South Korean prison.

1659. Seiden, Matthew, ed. "South Korea: Letters from Solitary." Ms 4 (August 1975) 91-2. Letters from a young woman and former student to her mother written from prison, where she was sentenced by a military court to 9 years for demonstrating against the government.

1660. "Seoul Jails 96 Dissidents." Guardian 32.9 (December 5, 1979) 16. Police arrested 96 people at an antigovernment protest.

1661. Shelton, Sharon. "Risking Her Life: Korean Woman Exposes Rape, Torture by Pak's Police." Workers World 18.3 (January 16, 1976) 4. Kwon Mal Ja was "systematically tortured, sexually abused, threatened with death, and forced into signing a confession that she had engaged in political activities."

1662. Shorrock, Tim. "Seoul Attempts Democratic Facade." Guardian 32.8 (November 28, 1979) 16. The same day South Korea announced that it would release its 200 political prisoners, 23 people were arrested and charged with "being part of a communist guerilla network," including journalists and Amnesty International leaders.

1663. South Korea: Long-term Political Prisoners: Return to Repressive Force and Torture. New York: Amnesty International, 1990. 35. Over 200 prisoners are serving long sentences, on charges of being North Korean agents. Some have been held up to 30 years, and some are guilty only of the peaceful exercise of their opinions.

1664. South Korea: Prisoners Held For National Security Reasons. New York: Amnesty International, 1991. 45. Examines the 200 prisoners held on national security grounds and the some 60 held for their political views, and 30 whose confessions were forced.

1665. "South Korea: Still Guilty." Christianity Today 21 (Jan 21, 1977) 42-43. Eighteen South Korean leaders arrested for speaking out against the government were convicted and sentenced to eight years; the court of appeals reduced sixteen of the sentences and suspended the other two.

1666. "South Korea Jails Kim Chi Ha." Militant 41.3 (January 28, 1972) 22. Kim Chi Ha is sentenced to seven years prison for his communist writings.

1667. South Korea: Violations of Human Rights. London: Amensty International, 1986. 109. Since the early 1970s, thousands of people have been arrested in South Korea for the non-violent exercise of their right to freedom of expression and association. Many have been sentenced to death, beaten, and tortured.

1668. "South Korean Poet Faces Death Sentence." Militant 39.40 (October 31, 1975) 25. Kim Chi Ha was tortured into a confession of being a communist. He has been arrested four times since 1970, including a death sentence in 1974.

1669. Stentzel, Jim. "Korean Diary: Courage and Faith." Christian Century 91 (December 11, 1974) 1175-7. Protests by Christians against government repression.

1670. Strasser, S. and Camper, D. "South Korea; Bad Reviews." Newsweek 92 (July 31, 1978) 34. Account of imprisoning of journalists Lee Yong Hui and Paik Nak Chung for alleged sympathy with Communist China.

1671. Tan, Lek Hor. "'Guiding' the Press." Index On Censorship 16.5 (May 1987) 28-36. Censorship is severe, including arrests of journalists and publishers critical of the government. Detailed information restrictions have been established. Imprisoned individuals are described.

1672. Violations of Human Rights in South Korea. New York: Kwangju Massacre Indictment Committee, 1981. 36. Describes the deterioration of human rights after martial law declared in 1980: widespread detention without charge, unfair trials, torture, death penalty.

1673. Wenzel, D. "A Question of Courage." Christian Century 96.26 (August 15, 1979) 779-81. On Korean CIA harassment of the Korean Christian Academy and general persecution of critics of the government.

KUWAIT

1674. Amnesty International Report 1990. New York: Amnesty International, 1990. 145-146. About twenty opponents of the government were arrested and about 20 were sentenced to prison after unfair trials. Several long-term prisoners remained confined.

LAOS

1675. Amnesty International Report 1980. London: Amnesty International, 1980. 212-216. Ten to fifteen thousands continue imprisoned without charge since 1975, arrests continue on political grounds, trials lack safeguards, and prison conditions are poor.

1676. Amnesty International Report 1990. New York: Amnesty International, 1990. 146-147. Several hundred opponents of the government are confined in re-education camps, some long-term.

1677. Democratic People's Republic of Laos. New York: Amnesty International, 1985. 17. About the continued detention in remote parts of the country of large numbers of people (6000 to 7000) without charge or trial for re-education since 1975-76. The number of detainees decreased in 1982, but the number began to increase again during 1984.

1678. Political Prisoners in the People's Democratic Republic of Laos. London: Amnesty International, 1980. 22. Focuses on prisoners in re-education camps without charge or trial. Profiles 17 prisoners. Over 10,000 political prisoners are in the camps.

1679. "Thorns Appear in Lotus Island." Time 111 (February 20, 1978) 41. On Pathet Lao concentration camps called "re-education" camps, where possibly 40,000 people are incarcerated.

LEBANON

1680. Amnesty International Report 1990. New York: Amnesty International, 1990. 147-149. Hundreds of people were arbitrarily arrested for political opposition and some were killed in possibly extrajudicial executions, in a country extremely fragmented by opposing armed groups.

1681. Lebanon's Lively Press Fears Worst Crackdown Since 1976. New York: Human Rights Watch, 1993. 48. The Hrawi government in Lebanon "shut down four news organizations and filed criminal charges against four journalists for violating Lebanon's restrictive press regulation."

LESOTHO

1682. Amnesty International Report 1980. London: Amnesty International, 1980. 53-54. Conflict between the ruling party and its chief opposition party has resulted in killings, assaults, and detentions.

1683. Amnesty International Report 1990. New York: Amnesty International, 1990. 149-150. Two brief detentions without trials occurred and inquiry into some past killings continued.

1684. Lesotho: Torture, Political Killings and Abuses Against Trade Unionists. New York: Amnesty International, 1992. 15. The new constitution has failed to protect the rights of citizens, especially members of trade unions.

LIBERIA

1685. Amnesty International Report 1980. London: Amnesty International, 1980. 54-56. Possibly several hundred people were arrested in 1979 by the Tolbert government, some charged with treason for protesting price increases, but later amnestied. Three student leaders were charged with treason in 1980 for writing a letter, but later freed. About 90 political opponents were also arrested. Tolbert was killed in 1980 during a coup led by Sgt. Samuel Doe, who immediately arrested leaders of the former government with a charge of treason, and executed several without fair trial.

1686. Amnesty International Report 1990. New York: Amnesty International, 1990. 150-152. Several prisoners arrested in 1988 remained confined. Many extrajudicial killings were committed during an attempted invasion.

1687. "Doe Frees Former Official." Africa News 95.7 (October 7, 1985) 12. The opposition leader and former head of the Liberian Development Bank was sentenced to ten years for criticizing General Doe, who then released her.

1688. "Ezekiel B. Pajibo." Index On Censorship 14.3 (June 1985) 43. The acting president of the National Students Union was arrested for protesting the government's closing of the University of Liberia and dismissal of its faculty and officers. Pajibo was sentenced to death in 1982 for protesting the government's ban on political activities, but was released.

LIBYA

1689. Amnesty International Report 1980. London: Amnesty International, 1980. 344-47. An increasing number of people were detained for their political beliefs, many given life sentences, and a large number of offences, many of them political, carry the death penalty. Harsh treatment--beatings and electrical shock--is occurring at arrest and detention.

1690. Amnesty International Report 1990. New York: Amnesty International, 1990. 152-153. Over 50 political prisoners arrested in previous years were still held. At least 60 more were detained incommunicado without charge in 1989.

1691. Committee for the Defence of Human Rights and Political Prisoners in Libya. Selected Documents. London: The Committee, 1981. 71. An indictment of Muammar Ghaddafy's tyranny, citing many cases.

1692. Libya: Amnesty International's Prisoner Concerns in the Light of Recent Legal Reforms. New York: Amnesty International, 1991. 69. In 1988 Col. Gadaffi released 400 political prisoners and promised reforms, but the reforms fall "short of the international human rights standards and in many cases have not been implemented." In June of 1991 there are "at least 467 political prisoners." Lists some of the prisoners imprisoned since 1973, 1970-1986, 1989-1990.

1693. Libya, Summary of Amnesty International's Prisoner Concerns. New York: Amnesty International, 1987. 12. A wide-ranging study of the over 200 victims of arbitrary arrest, prisoners held despite expiration of sentence or acquittal, etc. 221 prisoners are listed with details.

1694. Violations of Human Rights in the Libyan Arab Jamahiriya. New York: Amnesty International, 1984. 12. On the killing or attempted killing of opponents abroad, the imprisonment of about 100 opponents some long term, and the torture and ill-treatment of detainees. A list of some of the prisoners is given.

MADAGASCAR

1695. Amnesty International Report 1980. London: Amnesty International, 1980. 57. Several people have been detained incommunicado recently, and others held in lengthy pre-trial detention.

1696. Amnesty International Report 1990. New York: Amnesty International, 1990. 153-154. Summary killings of hundreds of people in 1988 remained uninvestigated. At least 50 people were arrested protesting the re-election of President Ratsiraka. Prison conditions were extremely harsh, causing possibly ten inmates a month to die.

MALAWI

1697. "Amnesty Celebrates Release of Vera Chirwa, Mourns Death of Orton Chirwa." Amnesty Action (Spring 1993) 10. The Chirwas were Africa's longest serving known prisoners of conscience (11 years). Her husband died in prison shortly before her release.

1698. Amnesty International Report 1980. London: Amnesty International, 1980. 58-59. Detention without trial, harsh prison conditions, and mistreatment of Jehovah's Witnesses. Detention without trial existed since independence in 1964 but declined since 1977 when more than 2000 long-term prisoners were released.

1699. Amnesty International Report 1990. New York: Amnesty International, 1990. 154-155. Dozens of political opponents were detained without charge and several imprisoned in previous years were still held, some without charge and some after unfair trials. Reports of ill-treatment and torture.

1700. "Banda Frees Young Chirwa." Africa News 22.10 (March 5, 1984) 8. Orton Chirwa, his wife Vera, and their son Fumbani were abducted in 1981 and sentenced to death in 1982, but the sentences were not carried out, and Fumbani has now been released.

1701. Kelemba, Robert. "Life Censor Banda." Index on Censorship 18.10 (Nov. 1989) 32-34. The severe repression is described--horrible prisons, extreme censorship, etc. The author, a journalist, describes his imprisonment and torture.

1702. Malawi. London: Amnesty International, 1976. 10. Concern is expressed over widespread use of prolonged detention without trial to quell dissent, suppression of religious groups not conforming to government dictates, torture, death penalty without proper judicial process.

1703. "Malawi Frees 10 Political Prisoners, Grants Bail to Detained Labor Leader." Arkansas Democrat-Gazette (July 12, 1992) 18A. Release of these 10 prisoners after 12 years may indicate a slight relaxation by the dictator Kamuzu Banda, who seeks Western money.

1704. Malawi: Human Rights Violations 25 Years After Independence. London: Amnesty International, 1989. 9. Unfair trials, etc., 1964-.

1705. Malawi: Prison Conditions, Cruel Punishment and Detention Without Trial. New York: Amnesty International, 1992. 17. Political prisoners suffer cruel, inhuman or degrading treatment.

MALAYSIA

1706. Amnesty International Report 1980. London: Amnesty International, 1980. 216-17. Some 1,000 people are detained without trial in wretched conditions--critics of the government, trade unionists, and others.

1707. Amnesty International Report 1990. New York: Amnesty International, 1990. 156-157. The last of the opposition leaders arrested in 1988 were released. Several of these reported police torture and forced confessions.

1708. "Chandra Muzaffar and Other Human Rights Advocates Held in Unprecedented Sweeping Arrests Under ISA." HRI Reporter 12.1 (Fall 1987) 47-48. Muzaffar, president of the social reform movement Aliran, and over 90 others, including members of Parliament, social and political activists, and educators, have been detained under the Internal Security Act, which cannot be challenged in a court of law.

1709. Hamid, Rizu. "Woman Detained Without Trial." Spare Rib 186 (January 1988) 12. Cecilia Ng Choon Sim, a leading women's rights activist, is one of many Malaysians detained without trial in an apparent "clampdown on government critics."

1710. International Mission of Lawyers. The Report of the International Mission of Lawyers to Malaysia, 1982. Washington, D.C.: International Human Rights Law Group, 1982. 91. Discusses criminal procedures, prisoners, laws, etc.

1711. Ishak, Abdul Aziz. Special Guest: The Detention in Malaysia of an Ex-cabinet Minister. Singapore: Oxford UP, 1977. 210. The author was imprisoned one year for allegedly collaborating with Indonesia, which was at war with Malaysia.

1712. Kua, Kia Soong. 445 Days Behind the Wire: an Account of the October 1987 Detentions. Kuala Lumpur: Resource and Research Centre, Selangor Chinese Assembly Hall, 1989. 191. An account of the author's arrest, trial, and imprisonment for fifteen months under the Internal Security Act, when his only crime was advocating racial harmony. An indictment of a corrupt government and destroyed judiciary.

1713. "Malaysia Arrests Environmentalists." Not Man Apart 17.6 (November 1987) 1. Report on the arrest, without charges, of over 100 environmentalists: "most remain in solitary confinement, undergo regular interrogation and have no access to legal counsel."

1714. "Prisoner Watch: Malaysia." Human Rights Watch (December 1987) 9. A call for letters urging the release of human rights activists.

1715. Report of an Amnesty International Mission to the Federation of Malaysia, 18 November-30 November 1978. London: Amnesty International, 1979. 67. Surveys repression of dissent--detention without charge or trial, long-term detention, torture, etc. Includes thirteen cases.

1716. "Repression in Malaysia." Science For The People 20.2 (March/April 1988) 16-18. Since October 1987 over 150 people have been arrested for criticising Prime Minister Datuk Seri Mohathir Mohamed and his regime.

1717. The State of Human Rights in Malaysia: A Collection of Documents Relating to Political Detainees, Political Banishees and their Struggles, and also to the Laws and Procedures. Hong Kong: Asia Forum on Human Rights, 1979. 197. Documents from the files of AFHR on the thousands of victims during the past thirty years. Over one-thousand political detainees exist in 1979, many long-term. Brutality has been widespread, prison conditions deplorable.

MALDIVES

1718. Amnesty International Report 1990. New York: Amnesty International, 1990. 157. Over 70 people involved in an attempted coup received varied prison sentences.

MALI

1719. Amnesty International Report 1980. London: Amnesty International, 1980. 59-62. Detention without trial, political killings, torture, extremely poor prison conditions. In 1979 several opponents of the sole political party were sentenced to prison for insulting the Head of State. In 1979 and 1980 student protests led to extremely brutal police reaction.

1720. Amnesty International Report 1990. New York: Amnesty International, 1990. 157-158. Four students were held incommunicado and tortured, a reminder of the many students and teachers tortured in 1980. Others were arrested for leafletting.

MAURITANIA

1721. Amnesty International Report 1980. London: Amnesty International, 1980. 62-63. Detention without trial still a problem in 1979 and 1980, but the end of the civil war, the release of 22 prisoners, and a moratorium on "Arabization" has reduced conflict.

1722. Amnesty International Report 1990. New York: Amnesty International, 1990. 158-160. Over 200 people were detained without charge in 1989, and over 60 continued to serve sentences imposed in earlier years, mostly after unfair trials. Numerous reports of torture, some resulting in death, and possibly as many as 30 extrajudicial killings.

1723. Mauritania 1986-1989: Background to a Crisis. New York: Amnesty International, 1989. Three years of political imprisonment, torture and unfair trials.

MAURITIUS

1724. Amnesty International Report 1990. New York: Amnesty International, 1990. 160-161. Nine critics of the government were arrested in 1989.

MEXICO

1725. Amnesty International Report 1980. London: Amnesty International, 1980. 150-53. Human rights violations include arbitrary detention, incommunicado detention, torture, disappearances. The army's Brigada Blanca in Mexico City runs a torture center at its base.

1726. Amnesty International Report 1990. New York: Amnesty International, 1990. 161-164. The new government released numerous prisoners in 1989 and promised to investigate disappearances, torture, and killings. Many peasants have been threatened and killed over land disputes.

1727. Bergman, Gregory. "Target For Repression in Mexico." Christian Century 95 (March 29, 1978) 337-40. Army repression of students and faculty at Juarez University in Oaxaca.

1728. Bini, Obi. "Mexico: 'Investigation' of the Disappeared." Guardian 31.20 (February 21, 1979) 12. Civil rights, human rights, and labor groups, as well as the relatives of "disappeared" political activists refute the government's claim that guerrillas, gangs and drug dealers are responsible for the disappearance of over 350 people.

1729. Crespi, Robert. "Quiet Day in Mexico: Letter." Nation 211 (September 28, 1970) 277. On political prisoners in Mexico City jails, following the Tlatelolco "massacre."

1730. Davis, Angela. "To Mexican Political Prisoners." Transcontinental 6.66 (September 1971) 5. Supports those imprisoned in Mexico City in 1971 following demonstrations. Written from Marin County Jail, San Rafael, California.

1731. Fainlight, Ruth. "Mexico: Israel Gutierrez Hernandez." Index On Censorship 17.6 (June 1988) 3. The writer Gutierrez has been sentenced to prison accused of bank robbery based upon a forced confession.

1732. Frankel, David. "Mexico: Movement Against Repression Grows." Militant 42.38 (Oct. 13, 1978) 8. Protests and documented evidence fuel the movement against tyranny.

1733. Goldman, Robert and Daniel Jacoby. Report of the Commission of Enquiry to Mexico. New York: The International League for Human Rights, 1978. 31. Surveys arbitrary arrests, detentions, torture, and other cruel punishment, unfair trials and intimidation of relatives of some one hundred political prisoners based upon their testimony and that of relatives and lawyers. Testimony regarding 301 disappeared persons was also taken. The names of the prisoners and the disappeared are listed.

1734. Horowitz, Gus. "Torture in Mexican Jails." Militant 44.2 (January 25, 1980) 17. Berthia Alica López de Zazueta, one of hundreds of "disappeared" leftist dissidents released from secret jails, describes her four-month ordeal at the hands of the government sanctioned right-wing paramilitary group, the White Brigade, during which she was subjected to electrical shock torture, sexual abuse, and was forced to watch the electrical shock torture of her fourteen-month-old baby daughter.

1735. Marroquín, Héctor. "Héctor Marroquín: My Story." Militant 42.3 (Jan. 27, 1978) 19-22. A student leader in Monterrey falsely accused of murder fled to the U.S. for asylum.

1736. Mexico: Human Rights in Rural Areas. New York: Amnesty International, 1986. Investigation into human rights abuses in the states of Oaxaca and Chiapas. Human rights violations include: political killings, torture and ill-treatment, political imprisonment, and unfair trials.

1737. de Piedra, Rosario Ibarra. "Right Leader Details Mexico Repression." Militant 43.15 (April 20, 1979) 20. On torture of innocent prisoners.

1738. Rohde, Clifford. "Unceasing Abuses: Human Rights Crimes Go Unpunished in Mexico." Human Rights Watch 10.1 (Winter 1992) 6. On the murder of human rights activists.

1739. Roland, Jane. "New Report Documents Repression in Mexico." Militant 43.1 (Jan. 12, 1979) 9. Three human rights groups presented evidence of widespread abuses against political opponents.

1740. Rudentstein, Roger. "Piedra Blasts Mexican Government Coverup." Militant 43.7 (Feb. 23, 1979) 11. Denounces kidnappings and other secret police crimes.

1741. Russell, J.W. "Missing." Progressive 46 (July 1982) 19. Florencio Coronel's violent abduction by ten members of Mexico's Brigada Blanca highlights this report on the disappearences of over 500 political dissidents since 1970, and the existence of secret political prisons, torture, and paramilitary squads.

1742. "Tyranny and Soccer." Nation 210 (February 2, 1970) 101. On the some 150 political prisoners in Lecumberri Prison in Mexico City, mainly students and teachers.

1743. U.S. Citizens Imprisoned in Mexico; Hearings Before the Subcommittee on International Political and Military Affairs of the Committee on International Relations House of Representatives, Ninety-Fourth Congress. Part II. October 22, 1975 and January 27, 1976. Washington: G.P.O., 1976. 110. Efforts to clarify the situations of individual prisoners and to improve trial and prison conditions.

1744. "Vatican Receives Appeal from Ninety-one Mexican Political Prisoners." Christian Century 87 (February 4, 1970) 135. Students arrested in 1968 still not tried.

1745. Weissberg, Arnold. "Mexico: Free All Political Prisoners." Militant 42.34 (Sept. 15, 1978) 4. The Committee to Defend Political Prisoners, the Politically Persecuted, Exiled, and Disappeared organized a strike in a cathedral in Mexico City for four days until the Mexican President agreed to meet with them.

1746. Weissberg, Arnold. "Mexican Activist Fights for Political Asylum in U.S." Militant 41.40 (Oct. 28, 1977) 4-5. About student Héctor Marroquín falsely charged with murder, conspiracy, and subversion. (Also Feb. 17, 1978, 6).

1747. Weissberg, Arnold. "We Fight for Justice in Mexico." Militant 42.14 (April 14, 1978) 10. Interview with Rosario Ibarra de Piedra about political persecution in the country.

MOROCCO

1748. Amnesty International Report 1980. London: Amnesty International, 1980. 347-50. Problems are detention without trial, unfair trials, ill-treatment of prisoners, poor prison conditions, persecution of trade unionists, students, and Moslem activists, all exacerbated by Morocco's war against the Polisario Front for control of the Western Sahara.

1749. Amnesty International Report 1990. New York: Amnesty International, 1990. 164-166. Over 300 people were detained in 1989, and many were sentenced after unfair trials. Over 100 prisoners sentenced in previous years remained in prison. Torture was reported, and prisons were cruelly harsh. About 100 former military personnel imprisoned in the early 1970s and many people of Sahara origin arrested in the mid-1970s have apparently disappeared.

1750. Chaoui, Abdelkader. "Blindfold Justice." Index On Censorship 18.1 (Jan. 1989) 20-22. "A Moroccan author serving a 20-year sentence for allegedly "plotting against the state" describes scenes from a mass political trial in 1977.

1751. "Detainees, War Prisoners Freed." Guardian 41.34 (May 24, 1989) 16. King Hassan granted amnesty to 200 prisoners, some of them held up to 30 years, but many others remain incarcerated.

1752. Edling, Joyce. "Moroccans Sentenced for Cultural Activities." Index On Censorship 18.1 (Jan. 1989) 21. "In Morocco, a large number of intellectuals are imprisoned solely on account of their political beliefs."

1753. Elansari, Nour al-Din. "A Tale of Two Brothers." Index On Censorship 14.3 (June 1985) 14-16. The author fled into exile to avoid arrest, while his younger brother, Ibrahim, was imprisoned "solely for his poetry."

1754. Farhi, Moris. "Ali Idrissi Kaitouni: Poet in Prison." Index On Censorship 19.1 (Jan. 1990) 22. Student Idrissi was "indicted for 'insulting the King's dignity', for 'undermining the inviolability of national institutions', for 'inciting crimes against internal security of the state'", etc. He was sentenced to fifteen years imprisonment on 18 May 1982.

1755. Griffith, Aline. The Spy Wore Silk. New York: Putnam, 1991. 316. About a mission by the author with William Casey to save King Hassan II, a loyal U.S. client who enforced his regime with torture of political prisoners.

1756. Morocco. London: Amnesty International, 1977. 16. Summary analysis of incommunicado detention, unfair trials, terrible prison conditions, and death penalty.

1757. Morocco: AI's Concerns February--June 1990. New York: Amnesty International, 1991. 8. The government has taken certain actions to improve its human rights record since 1991, but over 600 political prisoners, including prisoners of conscience, are still detained after unfair trials.

1758. Morocco: Human Rights Violations in Garde a Vue Detention. New York: Amnesty International USA, 1990. 28. On the systematic ill-treatment, torture, and even deaths of detainees held incommunicado by police. A report on the same conditions and a 1988 protest by Amnesty International have gone unheeded.

1759. Morocco : A Pattern of Political Imprisonment, Disappearances, and Torture. New York: Amnesty International, 1991. 76. Widespread human rights violations have been common in Morocco since the early 1960s, including unfair trials, torture, and disappearances.

1760. Report of an Amnesty International Mission to the Kingdom of Morocco, 10-13 February, 1981. London: Amnesty International, 1982. 74. Particularly concerns violations of human rights during the period of garde a vue (incommunicado) detention. Lists of prisoners and disappeared given.

1761. Torture in Morocco. New York: Amnesty International, 1986. 15. Prisoners are routinely subjected to torture especially during incommunicado detention following arrest, and several have died.

MOZAMBIQUE

1762. Amiel, Barbara. "A Flagrant Violation of Rights." Macleans 94 (Jan. 19, 1981) 4. Author tells how she was held in inhumane Machava prison after being arrested with two other Canadian journalists on false charges of bribing and espionage. Also see Feb. 16, 1981, 44.

1763. Amnesty International Report 1980. London: Amnesty International, 1980. 63-64. Detention without trial remains and in 1979 27 people were convicted of treason and other crimes and several executed, but in 1979 and 1980 "large numbers of detainees were released."

1764. Amnesty International Report 1990. New York: Amnesty International, 1990. 166-168. Several hundred people detained without trial or sentenced after unfair trials in previous years were released, but 140 untried detainees remained confined, and 300 new arrests occurred in 1989. Ill-treatment and torture were reported. The fate of dozens of prisoners who disappeared in the 1970s remained unclarified.

1765. Reports of the Use of Torture in the People's Republic of Mozambique. New York: Amnesty International, 1985. 16. On cruel and inhuman treatment of detainees mainly by government forces but also by the armed opposition.

MYANMAR (BURMA)

1766. Amnesty International Report 1980. London: Amnesty International, 1980. 187. Although information is severely restricted, allegations of arbitrary arrest without charge and torture have been made. One man was sentenced to life in prison for possession of poetry critical of the government.

1767. Amnesty International Report 1990. New York: Amnesty International, 1990. 168-171. Possibly thousands of government opponents were detained without charge or sentenced after unfair trials in 1989. Torture and extrajudicial killings were widely reported. Killings of thousands of pro-democracy demonstrators by troops remained uninvestigated.

1768. Brady, Diane. "A Fight for Rights." Maclean's 104 (October 28, 1991) 84. Daw Aung San Suu Kyi is awarded the Nobel Peace Prize for her "nonviolent struggle for democracy and human rights" in Burma.

1769. Burma: Extrajudicial Execution and Torture of Members of Ethnic Minorities. New York: Amnesty International, 1988. Testimonies from refugees describing almost 200 cases of unlawful killing, torture, and ill-treatment. Details of 60 cases of what AI believes were extrajudicial executions by army units assigned to counter-insurgency duties.

1770. "Burma: Rape, Forced Labor and Religious Persecution in Northern Arakan." New York: Asia Watch, 1992. 28. Details about the military dictatorship's repression in one part of the country.

1771. Clements, Alan. Burma: The Next Killing Fields? Berkeley, CA: Odonian, 1992. 95. An explanation of the civil war and repression by a former Buddhist monk who lived in Rangoon. The governing State Law and Order Restoration Council (SLORC) is pursuing a policy of violent repression against all who want a democratic government. Foreward by the Dalai Lama.

1772. Clements, Alan. "Terror in the Golden Land." Utne Reader 58 (July/Aug. 1993) 79-87. Adapted from Burma: The Next Killing Fields. Also published in New Age Journal (March/April 1993). From the 1988 massacres to the present repression, Myanmar has filled prisons "with thousands of innocent men, women, and children" arrested "on the slightest suspicion of dissent against its politics."

1773. Kyi, Aung San Suu. Freedom From Fear and Other Writings. Ed. Michael Aris. New York: Viking, 1991. 338. She has been under house arrest since 1989 because of her political endeavors. She received the 1991 Nobel Peace Prize for her "non-violent struggle for democracy and human rights."

1774. Lazar, Edward. "Burma's Aung San Suu Kyi." Humanitas 4 (1991) 2-3. Suu Kyi, 1991 recipient of the Nobel Peace Prize and activist for democratic reform, has been under house arrest since July 20, 1989.

1775. McFadden, Robert D. "Burmese Rulers Releasing a Dozen Political Prisoners." New York Times (April 26, 1992) 3Y. The military junta of Myanmar released a dozen political prisoners in response to mounting international pressure over its dismal human rights record.

1776. Mirante, Edith. Burmese Looking Glass: A Human Rights Adventure and a Jungle Revolution. New York: Grove, 1993. 333. On her experience with General NeWin's dictatorship's gross and systematic abuses, of which she made a report.

1777. Myanmar (Burma) : Prisoners of Conscience : a Chronicle of Developments Since September 1988. New York: Amnesty International, 1989. 76. A history of the repression since 1988: thousands of killings, many more thousands of arrests, torture, unfair trials, detention without charge or trial, house arrest. Many prisoners are named.

1778. Myanmar: Human Rights Violations Against Muslims in the Rakhine (Arakan) State. New York: Amnesty International, 1992. 25. Reports a general pattern of repression by security forces against the Muslims in the Rakhine State--part of the gross and consistent pattern of human rights violations committed by the SLORC (State Law and Order Restoration Council) against all forms of political opposition and dissent.

1779. Myanmar: 'In the National Interest' Prisoners of Conscience, Torture, Summary Trials Under Martial Law. New York: Amnesty International, 1990. 55. A coup that overthrew the dictatorship of General Ne Win, promising democratic reforms, has resulted in continued repression. Thousands have been shot and more thousands have been detained by the military, including the main opposition party leaders. Death penalty, long terms with hard labor, widespread torture, and other abuses continue.

1780. Roberts, Kim. "Human Rights Quagmire in Burma." Humanitas No. 2 (1989) 1-3. On the brutal repression of peaceful demonstrators in 1988 and following. Thousands have been killed, more arrested and abused.

1781. Shenon, Philip. "Family of Detained Nobelist Flies to Burma for Rare Visit." New York Times (May 3, 1992) 8Y. The military junta allowed Aung San Suu Kyi, the Nobel peace prize recipient under house arrest since 1989, to see her husband and their two children for the first time in over two years.

1782. Union of Myanmar (Burma) : Arrests and Trials of Political Prisoners January-July 1991. New York: Amnesty International Publications, 1991. 55. At least 200 opposition political figures were arrested between Jan. and July 1991.

NAMIBIA (formerly South West Africa; *see also* SOUTH AFRICA)

1783. Amnesty International Report 1980. London: Amnesty International, 1980. 65-67. South Africa responded to the struggle for independence with martial law, incommunicado detention, detention without trial, bannings, and poor prison conditions.

1784. Amnesty International Report 1990. New York: Amnesty International, 1990. 171-174. Namibia's impending independence from South Africa caused the release of all political prisoners, though many remained unaccounted for and had apparently disappeared. More reports of torture in previous years were made.

1785. "Free at Last." Time 123 (March 12, 1984) 47. Herman Toivo ja Toivo, independence leader of SWAPO, released after 16 years.

1786. Human Rights Violations in SWAPO Camps in Angola and Zambia. London: International Society for Human Rights, British Section, 1988. (Unpaged). Systematic repression within SWAPO.

1787. Namibia: Amnesty International Briefing. London: Amnesty International, 1977. 16. On the widespread detention without trial, torture, and imprisonment under S. Africa's continued state of emergency.

1788. Remember Kassinga, and Other Papers on Political Prisoners and Detainees in Namibia. London: International Defence and Aid Fund, 1981. 52. Kassinga was a massacre in 1981 by South African jet bombers and paratroops of more than 600 Namibian refugees in Angola. At least 118 of the survivors are still detained.

1789. Torture: A Cancer in Our Society; A Report. London: Catholic Institute for International Relations: British Council of Churches, 1978. 67. Contains the sworn affidavits of Namibian victims. Banned prior to publication.

NEPAL

1790. Amnesty International Report 1980. London: Amnesty International, 1980. 219-21. Despite an amnesty, some detainees remain, and new arrests are occurring.

1791. Amnesty International Report 1990. New York: Amnesty International, 1990. 174-175. Hundreds of opponents of the government were held without charge in 1989, and thousands were detained briefly for participating in peaceful demonstrations, around 3,000 in September alone. Allegations of torture were "persistent." Prison conditions were extremely harsh.

1792. Nepal : A Pattern of Human Rights Violations. New York: Amnesty International, 1987. 48. In this country in which all political party activity is banned, political imprisonment is "a persistent feature."

1793. Nepal: A Summary of Human Rights Concerns. New York: Amnesty International, 1992. 39. Describes a pattern of widespread human rights violations including detention without trial, torture, "disappearance," and extrajudicial execution.

1794. "Party for a Political Prisoner." New Yorker 54 (July 31, 1978) 23-4. B. P. Koirala, former prime minister of Nepal, reformer and democrat, and prisoner of the King for eighteen years, attends a party in New York while out on parole for an operation.

NICARAGUA

1795. Amnesty International Report 1975-1976. London: Amnesty International, 1976. 105-107. "Torture, arbitrary detention and 'disappearance' appear increasingly characteristic of the human rights situation in Nicaragua" under the state of siege decreed by the Somozo regime.

1796. Amnesty International Report 1980. London: Amnesty International, 1980. 153-57. The government of Anastasio Somoza Debayle was overthrown in 1979 after 50 years of repression--thousands of arbitrary arrests, summary executions, and torture. The Constitution of the new government gives full recognition of human rights, including the abolition of the death penalty, but some 100 of Somoza's National Guard were executed in the first days of the overthrow, and 7,000 to 9,000 soldiers and officials have been detained, trials pending.

1797. Amnesty International Report 1990. New York: Amnesty International, 1990. 175-179. Several prisoners who disappeared in 1987 and 1988 are not accounted for. Over 1000 former Somozen National Guard members were released, but over 1000 contras were still held by the Sandinista government, convicted by special courts in possibly unfair trials.

1798. Human Rights in Nicaragua 1986. New York: Americas Watch Committee, 1987. 174. The U.S. backed 'contras' continue to abuse human rights: selective but systematic killing of those suspected of supporting the government, abuse of prisoners, widespread kidnapping of civilians and children, etc.

1799. Light, J. "Nicaragua/Some Joyful, Many Bitter As Guards Released." Guardian 41.26 (March 29, 1989) 13. The government pardoned nearly 1,900 former Somozan National Guard members.

1800. The Republic of Nicaragua: An Amnesty International Report Including the Findings of a Mission to Nicaragua, 10-15 May 1976. London: Amnesty International, 1977. 75. On the worsening repression since the suspension of constitutional guarantees December 28, 1974 by President Somoza Debayle.

1801. Suarez, Jacinto. "Seven Years, Four Months, 21 Days of Apprenticeship." Nicaraguan Perspectives 9 (Fall 1984) 14. His experiences in prison for attempted robbery for the Sandinista cause.

1802. Thayer, Millie. "Ortega Bids for Foreign Support." Guardian 42.16 (Feb. 14, 1990) 14. The Sandinistas released over 1000 contra prisoners and the remaining 39 ex-National Guard troops still in jail.

NIGER

1803. Amnesty International Report 1990. New York: Amnesty International, 1990. 179. All remaining 12 prisoners were released in 1989.

NIGERIA

1804. Adams, Lois. "The Prison and Post-Prison Writing (1967-1973) of Wole Soyinka." Diss. U of Wisconsin, 1981. 231. A dissertation on his prose writings. Soyinka was accused of conspiring with the rebels and was imprisoned during the Nigerian Civil War.

1805. Agetua, John. When the Man Died: Views, Reviews, and Interview on Wole Soyinka's Controversial Book. Benin City, Nigeria: Newspaper Corp., 1975. 47. About Soyinka's The Man Died, an account his arrest and detention during the civil war and an attack of the structures of repression in the country.

1806. Amnesty International Report 1980. London: Amnesty International, 1980. 67-68. Return to civilian rule ended the military tribunals which had imposed mandatory death sentences on seven crimes including treason.

1807. Amnesty International Report 1990. New York: Amnesty International, 1990. 179-181. At least 30 critics of the government were detained without charge for various lengths, some for several months in harsh prison conditions. The life sentences of 11 trade union leaders after a strike were reduced to 10 years.

1808. Babatope, Biola. Detainee's Wife. Lagos, Nigeria: Update Communications, 1989. 214. Chronicles the experiences of the wife of a political activist detained for 18 months in 1984.

1809. Cain, Joy. "American Jailed in Nigeria." Essence 15 (Nov. 1984) 62. Marie McBroom has been imprisoned without charge but apparently because she did business with the former government.

1810. Ikoku, Sam. "Coup d'État." Index On Censorship 15.1 (January 1986) 21-24. Ikoku has been imprisoned without trial often. He was imprisoned in 1983 along with other officials when the government of Shehu Shagari was overthrown. After he was released he published an account of his experiences in Nigeria's Fourth Coup d'État, which was banned and the author imprisoned again. This excerpt tells of the moment of the 1983 coup.

1811. Maja-Pearce, Adewale. "The Mark of the Beast: Nigeria in the Year 1989." Index on Censorship 18.9 (Oct. 1989) 14-20. An account of the repression of successive regimes and the bravery of a few journalists, academics, and opposition politicians. Individual cases cited.

1812. Marsh, Dave. "Afrobeat Creator 'Rots in Prison'." In These Times 9.16 (March 20, 1985) 14. After hundreds of arrests and jailings which included beatings,

Fela Anikulapo Kuti was sentenced to five years in prison on a currency charge. He was one of the most persistent critics of the autocracy.

1813. Military Injustice: Major General Zamani Lekwot and Others Face Government-Sanctioned Lynching. New York: Human Rights Watch, March 1993. 11. "Fifteen Nigerians are currently imprisoned, awaiting death by hanging for their supposed participation in ethnic-religious riots in Northern Nigeria in May 1992."

1814. Oliver, April. "Nigeria's Havel?" In These Times 17.24 (October 18, 1993) 10-11. Wole Soyinka, winner of the 1986 Nobel Prize in Literature, stands against dictatorship, which led to his imprisonment for two years in the late '60s, an experience described in The Man Died.

1815. Otu, Igbuku. Kill Them Young: The Prison Notes of Igbuku-Otu. s.l.: African Network International Communications, 1989. 135. Otu was imprisoned in 1983-84, accused of "treasonable felony" (attempting to overthrow the government).

1816. Otubushin, Christopher. The Exodus and the Return of Chief Obafemi Awolowo. Yaba: Pacific Printers, 1966. 46. On the treason trial of Awolowo and 25 fellow party members and Awolowo's sentencing in 1963 to 10 years imprisonment. He and others were released in 1966.

1817. Soyinka, Wole. The Man Died: The Prison Notes of Wole Soyinka. New York: Noonday, 1988. 317. Soyinka was jailed for dissenting against the military dictatorship and for supporting the secession of Biafra in the press. He wrote the book secretly while in prison. Soyinka received the Nobel Prize for Literature in 1986. The title means: "The man dies in all who keep silent in the face of tyranny."

1818. Threats to a New Democracy: Human Rights Concerns at Election Time. New York: Human Rights Watch, June 1993. 23. The Nigerian military government increased attacks on journalists and human rights activists just prior to the June 12 elections.

PAKISTAN

1819. Ali, Tariq. "Military Intrigue and Secret Trial Show Cracks in Zia's Dictatorship." In These Times 9.17 (March 27, 1985) 9,22. On the trial of more than 100 dissident military officers accused of conspiring to overthrow the government.

1820. Amnesty International Report 1980. London: Amnesty International, 1980. 221-224. President Zia banned elections, political parties, trade union activists, press freedom, and appeal of military court verdicts, and arrested leaders of opposition parties. Some reports of torture and deaths while in custody.

1821. Amnesty International Report 1990. New York: Amnesty International, 1990. 181-184. At least 100 were detained for political and religious activities in 1989, though most only for short periods. Torture was "widespread," sometimes resulting in death.

1822. Baluch, Akhtar. "Preface to Akhtar Baluch's Prison Diary." Race and Class 18.4 (Spring 1977) 389-395. An eighteen-year-old college student, she was imprisoned in 1970 charged with supporting Sindhi nationalist leaders.

1823. Baluch, Akhtar. "'Sister, Are You Still Here?': The Diary of a Sindhi Woman Prisoner." Race and Class 18.3 (Winter 1977) 219-45. Introduction and Notes by Mary Tyler.

1824. Buckley, William F., Jr. "In re Bhutto." National Review 31 (March 16, 1979) 381. On the approaching execution of former Prime Minister Zulfikar Ali Bhutto.

1825. "Iran and Bhutto." Nation 228 (March 3, 1979) 230. On the impending execution of Zulfikar Ali Bhutto, former Prime Minister, after an unfair trial.

1826. Pakistan: Arrests of Political Opponents in Sindh Province, August 1990 - Early 1992. New York: Amnesty International, 1992. 49. Political prisoners in this province have been held in unacknowledged detention and reportedly subjected to torture and rape. Includes reports of death in custody and extrajudicial executions.

1827. Pakistan: the Trial and Treatment of Political Prisoners Convicted by Special Military Courts. London: Amnesty International, 1985. 56. Over 130 prisoners convicted by military courts for political reasons. Many cases cited.

1828. "Re: Raza Kazim." Nation 238 (March 17, 1984) 308. On the disappearance of Raza Kazim, lawyer, while U.S. aid flows despite U.S. law forbidding aid to human rights violating countries.

1829. Totten Samuel. "Pakistani Genocide in Bangladesh." First-Person Accounts of Genocidal Acts Committed in the Twentieth Century: An Annotated Bibliography. Westport, CT: Greenwood, 1991. 277-281. 19 entries on the mass slaughter perpetrated by the West Pakistani military against the East Bengals.

1830. The Trial and Treatment of Political Prisoners Convicted by Special Military Courts in Pakistan. New York: Amnesty International USA, 1985. 56. Discusses the over 130 prisoners convicted and the 38 awaiting verdicts. The trials of all were unfair. Names and details about the prisoners are provided.

1831. "Women in Double Jeopardy of Sexual Abuse During Police Custody in Pakistan." Human Rights Watch 10 (Fall 1992) 4. Women are often denied the basic protections and are routinely subjected to physical and sexual abuse.

PANAMA

1832. Amnesty International Report 1990. New York: Amnesty International, 1990. 184-186. In 1989, prior to the U.S. invasion in Dec., hundreds of opponents of General Noriega's government had been held shortly without charge. Military officers confined after two failed coup attempts in 1988 and 1989 continued in prison, but some were reported summarily executed. Some torture was reported. After the invasion several thousand supporters were detained on U.S. army bases.

1833. "Panama: Reminder of Things to Come?" Philippine Human Rights Update 5 (January 15 - February 14, 1990) 11-15. Concerning U.S. military intervention in Panama (Dec. 20, 1989-Jan. 1990) and of the U.S. refusal to withdraw even after being urged to do so by the United Nations and the Organization of American States.

PAPUA NEW GUINEA

1834. Amnesty International Report 1990. New York: Amnesty International, 1990. 186-188. Dozens of people suspected of supporting armed opposition on the island of Bougainville were detained without charge, some tortured, and a few possibly executed extrajudicially.

1835. Papua New Guinea : Human Rights Violations on Bougainville, 1989-1990. New York, Amnesty International USA, 1990. 47. At least 19 people have died while in police or military custody, either executed or tortured to death, and at least 50 people have been tortured, beaten, threatened with death, or sexually harassed, in the context of counter-insurgency operations.

PARAGUAY

1836. Amnesty International Report 1980. London: Amnesty International, 1980. 158-161. Under General Alfredo Stroessner's 26-year state of siege, people have suffered prolonged detention without trial, denial of habeas corpus, incommunicado detention, disappearances, and torture, all of which continue.

1837. Amnesty International Report 1990. New York: Amnesty International, 1990. 188-190. Human rights improved in 1989 following the overthrow of General Stroessner, who had ruled 34 years, but short-term arrests and ill-treatment continued especially relating to land and labor conflicts.

1838. Arens, Richard, ed. Genocide in Paraguay. Philadelphia: Temple UP, 1976. 171. The Aché Indians have been hunted for sport, forced onto reservations, had their children stolen and sold, enslaved as field labor and for prostitution, and many have died due to starvation, inadequate medical care, disease, etc.

1839. Barbosa, Roberto. "New Hope of Paraguay's Prisoners." Christian Century 94 (March 30, 1977) 301-2. Dictator General Stroessner has agreed to the trials of some of the political prisoners.

1840. Benjamin, R. "Prisoners in Paraguay." Time 52 (August 30, 1948) 30. Describes the Paraguayan police state and its political prisons.

1841. Bridges, S. "A Cry of Despair in Paraguay." Christian Century 95 (November 8, 1978) 1062-3. Seventeen political prisoners refuse to eat.

1842. Deaths Under Torture and Disappearance of Political Prisoners in Paraguay. London: Amnesty International, 1977. 17. "There is increasing evidence of deaths under torture and 'disappearances' after arrest.'

1843. "Forgotten Man." Nation 218 (April 20, 1974) 485. Appeals for support of Dr. Antonio Maidana, professor of history held in jail since 1958 by dictator Alfredo Stroessner. His crime: being a communist and organizing a strike.

1844. Herman, Edward. "Paraguayan 'Horror Files.'" Lies of Our Times 4.9 (Sept. 1993) 24. Further exposure of the New York Times' failure to report adequately the "horrendous state terror" with "U.S. complicity" by U.S. client states.

1845. Lernoux, Penny. "'Land' is a Dirty Word in Paraguay." Nation 231 (October 11, 1980) 343-5. On censorship of newspapers and imprisonment and intimidation of journalists, particularly of Gonzalez Delvalle.

1846. Nadler, Eric. "Paraguay Torture in U.S. Courts." Nation 234 (May 8, 1982) 551-2. Dr. Joel Filartiga, himself a victim of torture by Stroessner's police, is suing the former police official accused of torturing his son to death.

1847. Paraguay. London: Amnesty International, 1976. 13. On General Stroessner's illegal procedures: wide-scale arrests and disappearances, long term detention without trial, harsh prison conditions, and torture.

1848. Paraguay. London: Amnesty International, 1978. 13. Surveys prisoners, prisons, conditions, torture, and released prisoners.

1849. Prison Conditions in Paraguay: Conditions for Political Prisoners. London: Amnesty International, 1966. 34. Political background, press censorship, police interrogation, and prison conditions in this government of "corrupt despotism."

1850. "Prisoner Watch: Paraguay." Human Rights Watch (December 1987) 9. A call for letters urging the release of Dr. Rafael Hermes Saguier.

1851. Steif, William. "The Dictator and the Journalists." Progressive 53.10 (October 1985) 16-18. Report on the repression of journalists, including imprisonment and brutal torture, under the Stroessner military regime.

1852. Steif, William. "Hope for Paraguay." Progressive 53.7 (July 1989) 16-17. Report on Carmen de Lara Castro, chair of Paraguay's nongovernmental Commission for Defense of Human Rights for over twenty years, and of the suffering she has endured for her cause, including the torture and imprisonment of her children.

1853. "A Verdict on Torture." Newsweek 103 (January 23, 1984) 70. A U.S. court fined a Paraguayan torturer $10 million in damages.

PERU

1854. Amnesty International Report 1980. London: Amnesty International, 1980. 161-62. Massive arrests of peaceful protesters have occurred periodically from 1975 and continue. Sometimes brutal treatment of compesinos and Indians occur. Striking teachers were jailed, fired, and killed.

1855. Amnesty International Report 1990. New York: Amnesty International, 1990. 190-194. In 1989, over 500 people, including 69 children and young people, disappeared and hundreds more were extrajudicially executed. Torture was reported throughout the country. A commission reported the disappearance of 5,877 people during the 1980s.

1856. 1986 Annual Report on the Human Rights Situation in Peru. Toronto: Inter-Church Committee on Human Rights Abuses in Latin America, 1987. 19. Imposition of a "state-of-emergency" resulted in thousands of arrests in Lima and Callao; systematic human rights violations by the military and by revolutionary groups such as the Shining Path continue: torture, disappearences, summary executions, massacres of peasants, etc.

1857. Briefing: "Caught Between Two Fires". New York: Amnesty International, 1989. 17. AI reports a dramatic increase in "disappearances," extrajudicial executions and torture, particularly in Peru's emergency zones, of which women, human rights activists, trade unionists and children are often the target.

1858. Burkhalter, Holly. "Fujimori Attacks Human Rights Groups, While the Killing Continues in Peru." Human Rights Watch 10.1 (Winter 1992) 10. President Fujimori is attacking Americas Watch and Amnesty International as tools of the Sendero Luminoso rebels.

1859. Campos, Carlos Taipe. "Peru: Fight for Survival." Akwesasne Notes 17.2 (Spring 1985) 21. A letter written by Campos from a city jail in Peru describing his prison experiences and repression in Peru.

1860. Cornell, Angela and Kenneth Roberts. "Democracy, Counterinsurgency, and Human Rights: The Case of Peru." Human Rights Quarterly 12 (1990) 529-553. Describes the "sharp upsurge" of rights violations since turning to democratic rule in 1980, as the consequence of the government's campaign against the Sendero Luminoso revolutionary movement.

1861. "Free Peruvian Political Prisoners." Militant 42.21 (June 2, 1978) 2. Hundreds of Peruvian workers are thrown in jail for protesting increases in food prices.

1862. Human Rights in Peru: One Year After Fujimori's Coup. New York: Human Rights Watch, 1993. 56. Peru's democracy has been dismantled; Fujimori's forces use violent tactics such as extrajudicial executions, "disappearances," torture and rape to maintain control.

1863. International Committee for Political Prisoners. Political Prisoners Under the Dictatorship in Peru. New York: The Committee, 1940. 11.

1864. López, L. "Behind Bars with the Senderistas." Time 131 (May 9, 1988) 57. U.S. anthropologist Cynthia McNamara imprisoned four months, accused of supporting the Sendero Luminoso rebels.

1865. Murphy, F. "Peruvian Junta Jails Opponents." Militant 43.3 (Jan. 26, 1979) 3. Hundreds of trade-union and political leaders have been jailed to prevent a general strike.

1866. Murphy, F. "Release USLA Executive Secretary." Militant 43.3 (Jan 26, 1979) 3. Mike Kelly, Executive Secretary of the U.S. Committee for Justice to Latin American Political Prisoners, has been in jail since January 10 for taking photos.

1867. Peru: Briefing. New York: Amnesty International, 1985. "Disappearances," political killings and torture in the Andean Emergency Zone. Includes a comprehensive list of people who "disappeared" between January 1983 and October 1984.

1868. Peru: "Disappearances," Torture and Summary Executions by Government Forces After the Prison Revolts of June 1986. New York: Amnesty International, 1987. 71. The massacre of political prisoners who took part in revolts in three prisons; the secret detention of survivors.

1869. Peru : Human Rights During the Government of President Alberto Fujimori. New York: Amnesty International, 1992. 35. Gross human rights violations including "disappearances," extrajudicial executions by security forces, death threats, attacks and killing human rights defenders.

1870. Peru: Human Rights in a Climate of Terror. New York: Amnesty International, 1991. 76. This report covers widespread human rights abuses over the last ten years, despite the hope raised by President Fujimori in 1990.

1871. Peru Under Fire: Human Rights Since the Return to Democracy. New Haven: Yale UP; Americas Watch, 1992. 176. "More than half of Peru's twenty million citizens live under a sustained state of emergency, effectively governed by the military and lacking basic protections against arbitrary arrest, disappearance, and extrajudicial execution by the armed and police forces or the paramilitary groups they tolerate." Over 23,000 have been murdered since 1980.

1872. "We Condemn the Massacre of Political Prisoners in Peru: We Oppose All U.S. Military Intervention There." Nation 255.11 (October 12, 1992) 393. A call for protest against the Canto Grande Prison Massacre, where over 40 political prisoners were murdered and nearly 100 wounded, and the indifferent response of the U.S. government.

PHILIPPINES

1873. Aguilar, Delia. "Filipina Poet Uncaged." Guardian (March 12, 1986) 1. Mila Aguilar, poet, teacher, and journalist was released by the new Aquino government.

She had been imprisoned, charged but not tried for leadership in a banned political organization, since 1984.

1874. Aguilar, Mila D. A Comrade is as Precious as a Rice Seedling. 2nd ed. Latham, NY: The Kitchen Table Women of Color Press, 1987. 68. Filipina revolutionary poet Aguilar writes about the Marcos dictatorship and the liberation for which she hopes. On August 6, 1984 she was charged with "subversion and conspiracy to commit rebellion" and placed in solitary confinement for writing these poems. This second edition includes poems written in prison.

1875. Amnesty International Report 1980. London: Amnesty International, 1980. 225-227. As President Marcos entered his eighth year of martial law, both opposition and army repression intensified: imprisonment without trial, extra-judicial killings, torture, disappearances. Mass arrests of peasants have occurred.

1876. Amnesty International Report 1990. New York: Amnesty International, 1990. 194-197. Over 200 people were killed in apparent extrajudicial executions, many others disappeared, and over 600 opponents remained in prison. Torture and ill-treatment were frequently reported.

1877. Balais-Serrano, Evelyn. "Effects of Detention and Disappearance on Women and Families." Philippine Human Rights Update 4 (July 15 - August 14, 1989) 16-17. Degradations in order to visit, threats, etc.

1878. Bandiola, Amy. "Press Freedom Situation Much worse After EDSA." Philippine Human Rights Update 5 (June 15 - July 14 1990) 12-15. On the increase of censorship and murder to journalists under the presidency of Aquino.

1879. "Baylosis, De Vera and Palo: Reaching Out." Philippine Human Rights Update 4 (June 15-July 14, 1989) 9+. Tells about three leaders of the Communist Party of the Philippines now in prison.

1880. Beyond the Walls of the Prison. Videocassette. N.p.: Asia Media Foundation, 1986. 60 min. Describes the difficulties of political prisoners held under the Marcos regime and of adjusting upon their return to society. Includes five interviews with former detainees and some footage of police action against protestors.

1881. Came, Barry. "A Chiller in Manila." Newsweek 91 (April 24, 1978) 59. On dictator Marcos's mass arrests of dissidents.

1882. Chan, Connie. "Mila Aquilar: The Philippines." Gay Community News 12.41 (May 4, 1985) 8. Filipina poet held without charge for almost a year has imspired international protests.

1883. Deming, Angus, et al. "Aquino's Amnesty: Empty the Jails." Newsweek 107 (March 10, 1986) 24. President Corazon Aquino has released hundreds of prisoners.

1884. "A Dialogue on a Mission to the Philippines." Matchbox (Nov 1982) 1-2, 13. On the documented violations of human rights under Marcos: torture, disappearances, illegal detentions and murder.

1885. Documentation Committee for Philippine Political Prisoners (Los Angeles). Political Prisoners in the Philippines. Los Angeles: National Coordinating Committee of the Anti-Martial Law Movement (Philippines), 1975. 40.

1886. Fight For Us (orig. Orapronobis; French Les Insoumis). Film. Dir. Lino Brocka. 1990. 92 min. On the worsening human rights violations under President Aquino (200,000 victims in 1988 alone).

1887. Forché, Carolyn. "Poems By Mila D. Aguilar." Bulletin of Concerned Asian Scholars 18.3 (July 1986) 4. Collection of Aguilar's work with an introduction by

Forché recounting Aquilar's brutal treatment in detention, and addressing the issue of severe human rights violations in the Philippines and its archipelago of 174 political prisons.

1888. Free Sison!: Free Jose Maria Sison, Philippine Political Prisoner. Mansfield Depot, CT: 1983. 15.

1889. Gaspar, Karl. How Long? Quezon City, Philippines: Claretian, 1985. 235. Letters from prison of Karl Gaspar, who "disappeared" in 1983 and spent over two years in prison.

1890. "The Hernandez Doctrine What Now?" Philippine Human Rights Update 5 (May 15 - June 14, 1990) 10-14. Discusses decrees, laws, and individual cases regarding political prisoners and trials.

1891. Human Rights in the Philippines: Report by Amnesty International: Hearing before the Subcommittee on International Organization of the Committee on International Relations, House of Representatives, Ninety-fourth Congress, Second Session. Washington D.C.: U.S. G.P.O., 1976. 29. At least 6,000 political prisoners many of them log term suffer without specific charges, trial, or right to bail, and torture is "widespread and systematic."

1892. "Interview: Sr. Helen Graham." Philippine Human Rights Update 5 (December 15-January 14, 1990) 5-7. About her work with the Task Force Detainees of the Philippines (TFDP), a human rights group.

1893. Jones, Tom. "Philippines Report: President Marcos and Martial Law." Matchbox (Winter 1977) 12-13. On the thousands of political prisoners held without charge or trial, subject to systematic and widespread torture and sexual assault.

1894. Legal Rights of Political Detainees Under Martial Law. Magallanes Village, Makati, Metro Manila: Civil Liberties Union of the Philippines, 1977. 87. Analyzes Geneva Conventions and other international laws.

1895. Legal Rights of Political Detainees Under Martial Law. Magallanes Village, Makati, Rizal: Civil Liberties Union of the Philippines, 1977. 145. General rights, rights during arrest and search, rights under detention, rights during preliminary investigation and trial.

1896. "Lest We Forget." Philippine Human Rights Update. (International Edition). A regular feature about people who have disappeared or been murdered for their work for people's rights.

1897. "Marcos' Martial Law." Time 100 (October 2, 1972) 32. Not only guerrillas but political opponents of Ferdinand Marcos are being arrested.

1898. Mindanao: The Bleeding Land. Philippines: s.n., 1981. Collection of reports of military abuses since September 21, 1972, when martial law was declared.

1899. Mydans, Seth and Richard Vokey. "The 'Militant Detainee.'" Newsweek 101 (February 14, 1983) 52. Journalist Saturnino Ocampo imprisoned already five years with case dragging on.

1900. The Pain Will Go On Until Justice Is Done: What Can We Do To Enforce Human Rights in the Philippines? N.p.: Human Rights Desk, National Council of Churches in the Philippines, 1986. 109. Describes specific cases of human rights violations under the Marcos regime and includes statistics on the number of arrested, tortured, missing, massacres, etc.

1901. Philippine Human Rights Update. Vol. 1, no. 1 (Sept. 15, 1985). Cubao, Quezon City: Documentation Desk of the Task Force Detainees of the Philippines--National Center, 1985. Packed with articles on political trials, prisoners, disappearances, murders, plus articles on law, human rights, and history.

1902. "Philippine Political Fast." America 132 (January 18, 1975) 25. On Fr. Edicio de la Torre's fast to protest illegal detention and torture of political prisoners by Marcos's government.

1903. Philippines : "Disappearances" in the Context of Counter-Insurgency. New York: Amnesty International, 1991. 41. More than 50 critics of the government disappeared during 1990, at least five of whom died while in custody some apparently from torture.

1904. Philippines : Human Rights Violations and the Labor Movement. New York: Amnesty International, 1991. 50. Includes extrajudicial executions, arbitrary arrest and "disappearance," torture and ill-treatment while in police or military custody.

1905. Philippines: The Killing Goes On. New York: Amnesty International, 1992. 119. Extrajudicial executions under the government of President Corazon Aquino since 1988.

1906. The Philippines : The Philippines Government's Response to the Report of an AI Mission to the Republic of the Philippines 11-28 November 1981 and AI's Response to the Government's Response. London: Amnesty International, 1983. 18. On human rights abuses of the utmost gravity, which the government tries to deny. AI sticks by its evidence and its principles regarding detention, torture, etc.

1907. Philippines: Unlawful Killings by Military and Paramilitary Squads. New York: Amnesty International, 1988. Documents cases in which human right of men, women and children continue to be violated by government and government-backed forces.

1908. Pintig: Poems and Letters From Philippine Prisons. Hong Kong: Resource Centre for Philippine Concerns, 1979. Also includes artwork and statements by male and female political prisoners. Journalist Clarita Roja (Mila Aguilar, pseud.) has a poem.

1909. "Political Detainees Cry Freedom!" Philippine Human Rights Update 5 (November 15 - December 14, 1989) 6-8. Describes prison conditions and statistical information of the 550 political prisoners still in detention under President Aquino.

1910. Political detainees in the Philippines. Manila: Assoc. of Major Religious Superiors in the Philippines, 1976. 127. On torture, deaths, disappearances, and cruel prison conditions. One chapter on the church and detainees. Four individual cases are presented.

1911. Political Detainees in the Philippines: Documentation Report of Signs of the Times, a Publication of the Association of Major Religious Superiors in the Philippines, Manila, March 31, 1976. Los Angeles: Anti-Martial Law Coalition, 1976. 58. An "indictment of the brutal and inhuman treatment inflicted upon the detainees by the Philippine military." Four case studies.

1912. Political Detainees in the Philippines, (book two). Los Angeles: Association of Major Religious Superiors in the Philippines (reprinted in the U.S. by Anit-Martial Law Coalition), 1977. 52. Locates the main twenty-five detention centers, cites evidence of continued torture despite official denials, praises the efforts of the Church to mitigate government brutality, and sets forth fifteen recommendations.

1913. Political Detainees of the Philippines, Book 3. s.l.: Task Force Detainees of the Philippines, 1978. 130.

1914. "Political Detention in the Country Today." Philippine Human Rights Update 4 (June 15 - July 14, 1989) 10-12+. Analyzes the categories, rights, and legalities of political prisoners.

1915. Political Prisoners of Our Time. Quezon City, Philippines: The Task Force, 1989. 62. Under martial law the Marcos government imprisoned thousands of political opponents, a practice continued by the Aquino government. Several charts classify the prisoners, the legal system is explained, prison conditions described, and many individual prisoners profiled (pp. 17-62).

1916. "Political Prisoners Score Double Standard of Justice." Philippine Human Rights Update 5 (May 15 - June 14, 1990) 15-16. Denounces the "rebellion complex" charge under which many political opponents of the government have been imprisoned.

1917. "A Prison Cell is not a Home." Philippine Human Rights Update 5 (July 15 - August 14, 1990) 15. On the arrest and torture of two women for association with a communist.

1918. Pumipiglas: Political Detention and Military Atrocities in the Philippines, 1981-1982. Quezon City: Task Force Detainees of the Philippines, Association of Major Religious Superiors in the Philippines, 1986. 169.

1919. "The Quality of Justice in Manila." America 137 (December 10, 1977) 410. Marcos's chief political rival, Senator Benigno Aquino, has been sentenced to death by firing squad.

1920. Quinn-Judge, P. "Snaring a Rebel Wunderkind." Macleans 95 (Aug 2, 1982) 25-6. The story of Horacio (Boy) Morales--a young star in the Philippine government until late 1977--who was arrested and tortured.

1921. "Renewing Our Call For the Freedom of All Political Prisoners." Philippine Human Rights Update 4 (June 15 - July 14, 1989) 1. Appeal to Aquino Government in a special issue on political prisoners.

1922. Report of an Amnesty International Mission to the Republic of the Philippines, 22 November-5 December 1975. 2nd ed. London: Amnesty International, 1977. 95. Includes interviews of prisoners, evidence of torture, and analysis of martial law.

1923. Reysio-Cruz, Amelita. Prison Diary of Amelita Reysio-Cruz: Detainee, Camp Crame, Quezon City, Philippines. Quezon City: Regal, 1986. 346. A journalist imprisoned for "insurrection, rebellion and subversion." An account of her experiences in the context of contemporary Philippine politics.

1924. Right-Wing Vigilantes and US Involvement: Report of a US-Philippine Fact-Finding Mission to the Philippines, May 20-30, 1987. Manila: Philippine Alliance of Human Rights Advocates, 1987. 75. Examines the harrassment, torture and execution of civilians by right-wing vigilantes in the Philippines in the context of US involvement with that country.

1925. "Salvaging: Philippine Style." Christian Century 96.19 (May 23, 1979) 582. Information compiled by the Roman Catholic Task Force on Detainees "constitutes an appalling indictment" of the Marcos Regime.

1926. San Juan, E., Jr. "Aquino Releases Communist Leader." Guardian 38.24 (March 19, 1986) 7. Jose Maria Sison, founder of the Communist Party of the Philippines, and Bernabe Buscayno, former commander of the New People's Army, have been released. Aquino has also restored the writ of habeas and made other reforms as promised during her campaign.

1927. San Juan, E., Jr. Crisis in the Philippines: The Making of a Revolution. South Hadley, MA: Bergin & Garvey, 1986. 264. Indicts "the unrelenting massacre of 'hamletted' village folks; the jailing, torture, and killing of civilian dissenters, workers on strike, protesting students, journalists, clergy" under the Marcos dictatorship supported by the U.S.

1928. Schnookal, Deb. "Filipino Political Prisoner Speaks Out on Growing Opposition to Marcos." Militant 48.46 (December 1984) 8-9. Interview with the journalist Satur Ocampo, "one of the longest-held political prisoners in the Philippines today" (arrested 1976).

1929. Startup, Patricia and Eileen Laird, eds. Truth Uncovered: Fact-Finding Report--Cotabato & Zamboanga Del Sur--May 1985. Quezon City: Claretian, 1985. 162. On the deaths, arrests, massacres, evacuations, burnings, looting and other activities by the military in North Cotabato and Zamboanga del Sur.

1930. "Supreme Court Ruling on Warrantless Arrests." Philippine Human Rights Update 5 (July 15 - August 14, 1990) 12-15. Arbitrary arrest justified in cases of "subversion," which the Court ruled was a continuous crime.

1931. Swomley, John Jr. "Inside Marcos's Concentration Camps." Christian Century 91 (November 13, 1974) 1066-8. Many camps hold prisoners under martial law.

1932. "Teacher Arrested." Philippine Human Rights Update 5 (November 15-December 14, 1989) 5. Tells of the arrest without warrant of Eric Torres, chairman of The Alliance of Concerned Teachers (ACT).

1933. "The Three-Year Human Rights Record of the Aquino Government." Philippine Human Rights Update 5 (November 15-December 14, 1989) 9-15. Includes ten tables illustrating arrests, killings, and human rights violations for 1987-1989. The article states that only 2.5% of the 14,207 arrests are legal.

1934. TRENDS, a TFDP Report on Political Detention, Salvaging and Disappearances, January-June 1984. Quezon City: Task Force Detainees of the Philippines, 1984. 35.

1935. Visvayas Monitor: A Tri-Mestral Publication of the Task Force Detainees of the Philippines--Visayas Region. Cebu City, Philippines: TFDP, 1984. Three issues yearly 1984-, monthly 1987-.

1936. "Waiting For Justice." Philippine Human Rights Update 4 (June 15 - July 14, 1989) 7-8. Describes the case of the Leyte 26, accused of various crimes including rebellion.

1937. Ward, Richard. "Philippines Relations Strained." Guardian 29.15 (January 19, 1977) 12. A State Department report on torture, and estimates that anywhere from 500 to 6000 prisoners are being held.

1938. "What Happened in ...?" Philippine Human Rights Update. A regular summary (e.g., "What Happened in the First Quarter of 1989") of rights abuses: arrests, salvaging victims, massacres, murders, torture victims, and missing.

1939. Whipple, Christopher, et al. "Great Escape?" Newsweek 90 (October 17, 1977) 62. Eugenio López Jr. and Sergio Osmeña III escaped from Manila's Fort Bonifacio Prison.

1940. Wofford, Carrie. "Celebrating Freedom." Gay Community News 19.14 (October 20, 1991) 3. "Filipina poet and former political prisoner Mila Aguilar makes first trip to U.S., is honored with Freedom to Write Award."

POLAND

1941. Amnesty International Report 1980. London: Amnesty International, 1980. 283-88. Human rights activists have been systematically and increasingly persecuted--preventive detention without charge, summary imprisonment, unfair trials, police brutality. On "a number of occasions" mass detentions attempted to forestall demonstrations. False charges, torture, and other methods are being used to silence critics of the government.

1942. Amnesty International Report 1990. New York: Amnesty International, 1990. 197-198. Many people were briefly detained for exercising speech and association, and reports of ill-treatment continued during the first half of 1989 prior to the election victory of Solidarity.

1943. Appendixes on the Human Rights Situation in the Polish People's Republic. New York: Committee in Support of Solidarity, 1984. (irreg. pag.) "Gross and massive violations of human rights" continued in 1983--an increase in killings and beatings, new legislation allowing for broad powers of arrest against association, assembly and expression. Includes 94 pages of documentation.

1944. Bielecki, Czeslaw. "Good Times Will Return." Index On Censorship 15.9 (October 1988) 10-14. Founder of one of Poland's largest underground publishing houses, CND, Bielecki was captured and imprisoned from 1982 to 1986. Here are excerpts from his letters to his sons.

1945. "The Broken Saber." Time 106 (August 25, 1975) 32. Fencing hero (Olympic gold medal in 1968) Jerzy Pawlowski was arrested for crimes against the state.

1946. Cesnulis, Petras. In the Shadow of the White Eagle: for Your Freedom and Ours: a Lithuanian's Memoirs of Political Captivity in Polish Prisons, 1936-1939. Hamilton, Ont.: Vilnius Region Lithuanian Association, 1983. 267. Poland occupied the Vilnius Region of Lithuania from 1919 to 1939. He was arrested in 1936 for "anti-state activities."

1947. Deming, Angus. "Walesa's Friends in the Dock." Newsweek 104 (July 23, 1984) 54. Four dissident intellectuals and members of Solidarity are on trial.

1948. Engelstein, Stanley. A Week in Warsaw. New York: U.S. Helsinki Watch Committee, 1986. 19. Appraises the repression in Poland in 1985, where criticism of the regime is a crime. There are about 400 prisoners in Poland.

1949. "Freedom Fallout." Time 124 (August 6, 1984) 45. U.S. response to Poland's amnesty for 652 political prisoners.

1950. Frons, Marc. "A Hollow Victory for Walesa?" Newsweek 100 (November 22, 1982) 92. On the release of Lech Walensa from house arrest and possible end of martial law.

1951. Harsch, Ernest. "Three Solidarity Leaders Jailed." Intercontinental Press 23.13 (July 8, 1985) 416. Three former prisoners were again imprisoned for criticizing the government of General Jaruzelski and for membership in an illegal trade union: Lis, Fresyniuk, and Michnik.

1952. Human Rights Violations in the Polish People's Republic, January 1984 - January 1985, With Particular Reference to Human Rights Violations Following the Amnesty Act of July 22, 1984: a Report. New York: Committee in Support of Solidarity, 1985. 82. Lists killed and prisoners. Describes arbitrary arrests, beatings, torture, degrading treatment, arbitrary dismissals from employment.

1953. "In From the Cold." Time 123 (June 25, 1984) 49. Police capture Solidarity leader Bogdan Lis.

1954. "In Investigation Prison." New York Review of Books 30 (November 10, 1983) 56-8. Interview of Adam Michnik, advisor of Solidarity, arrested in 1981 during the coup for attempting to overthrow the state, and still awaiting trial.

1955. Karsov, Nina, and Szymon Szechter. In the Name of Tomorrow: Life Underground in Poland. London: Hodder & Stoughton, 1970; New York: Schocken, 1971. 285. Karsov was imprisoned for preparing and distributing dissident literature. She married Szechter while she was in prison.

1956. Kelly, J. "An Unwinnable Game." Time 120 (November 22, 1982) 76-7. Walesa to be freed.

1957. Kopvillen, Peetes. "Solidarity in Shawdow." Macleans 99 (June 16, 1986) 18-19. The president of the banned Provisional Co-ordinating Committee and a Solidarity leader, Zbigniew Bujak, was arrested after six years of evasion.

1958. Kowalska, Anka. "Poems from an Internment Camp." Tr. Adam Czerniawski. Index on Censorship 12.2 (April 1983) 16-18. Polish poet held in detention centers from the beginning of martial law in 1981 until May 1982.

1959. Kuron, Jacek. "'We Must Move to Resistance.'" Nation 234 (May 8, 1982) 549. The author, an adviser to Walesa's Solidarity, has been in prison since December 1981.

1960. "Letting Up." Time 128.12 (September 22, 1986) 46. Over 200 political prisoners to be released by the Jaruzelski government, including Zbigniew Bujak.

1961. List of Political Prisoners in Poland: 22/07/86. Paris: Coordinating Office Abroad of Solidarnosc, 1986. Irreg. pag.

1962. "The Long Night of Martial Law." Time 119 (March 22, 1982) 45-6. An excerpt from an account of a Solidarity member in Bialoleka prison--imprisoned during General Jaruselski's martial law.

1963. Michnik, Adam. Letters From Prison and Other Essays. Berkeley, CA: U of California P, 1985. 354. Often arrested since 1965, sentenced in 1968 to three years in prison, and again in 1981, constantly harassed by the police, the author wrote a series of books promulgating liberalism, tolerance, and international brotherhood.

1964. Mikolajska, Halina. "Letter from Prison." Index on Censorship 12.2 (April 1983) 15-16. This renowned Polish actress explains why she will not sign a loyalty oath.

1965. MK/JB. "Czezlaw Bielecki." Index On Censorship 14.4 (August 1985) 49. The founder of one of the largest underground publishing houses was arrested.

1966. Moody, John and Roger Boyes. The Priest and the Policeman: The Courageous Life and Cruel Murder of Father Jerzy Popieluzko. New York: Summit, 1987. 251. Tells the story of Father Jerzy, "Solidarity's chaplain and champion," his murder at the hands of government assassins, and the resulting public trial--the first of secret policemen in the Communist world.

1967. Moszcz, Gustaw. "From the Prisons of Poland." Dissent 30.1 (Winter 1983) 56. Interviews with two unnamed political prisoners; one tells of being arrested and held on false charges for ten days; the other describes life for women in prison.

1968. No Mention of Solidarity: U.N. Report on Human Rights in Poland. New York: U.S. Helsinki Watch Committee, 1984. 34. Reports by the U.N. and the

Helsinki Committee in Poland regarding the degree of human rights abuses in Poland. Whereas the U.N. report had played down abuses, the Helsinki Committee emphasized the arbitrary searches and arrests, the cruel, inhuman and degrading use of force, the ill treatment of sick and disabled prisoners, and killings.

1969. Partial List of Political Prisoners and Arrested in Poland: with Appendix Sentenced and Charged Under Violations of the Decree of Martial Law, the Special Emergency Powers, and Articles of the Polish Penal Code Since December 13, 1981. New York: The Committee in Support of Solidarity in New York, 1983. No pagination, 255 leaves. 1781 listed.

1970. Poland Under Martial Law: A Report on Human Rights By the U.S. Helsinki Watch Committee. New York: Helsinki Watch, 1983. 325. An account of "political murder, torture, arbitrary mass arrests, blackmail" under martial law. "Lawlessness is a natural feature of the system," the "accuser, the judge, the prosecutor, the police and the executioner are united in one."

1971. "A Polish Amnesty." Newsweek 104 (July 30, 1984) 76. Over 600 dissidents given amnesty by Gen. Jaruzelski.

1972. Political Prisoners in Poland; An Exposure of the Persecution of Political, Racial and Religious Minorities Today in Poland, from Documentary Sources. New York: International Committee for Political Prisoners, 1927. 70. Hundreds of Orthodox churches have been confiscatied for the Roman Catholic faith and Orthodox bishops imprisoned or exiled; the Communist party was banned in 1919 and members prosecuted; etc.

1973. Prison Conditions in Poland: A Helsinki Watch Report. New York: Human Rights Watch, 1988. 76. Prison conditions "remain dreadful." Summaries of interviews with former prisoners pp. 43-65.

1974. "Prisoner of the Year." Newsweek 73 (January 6, 1969) 33. Amnesty International has named Nina Karsow one of its prisoners of the year, and she has gained at least temporary asylum in Britain.

1975. "A Proud and Special Moment." Time 119 (April 12, 1982) 41. Lech Walesa permitted to leave his place of internment to visit his infant daughter.

1976. Repression in Poland, September 1986-October 1987: A List of 810 Victims. New York: Committee in Support of Solidarity, 1987. 76. Lists the individual victims, mostly activists in Solidarity and other organizations, and describes the measures taken against each: detention, fines and confiscations, dismissal from work, beatings, and even killings.

1977. Roth, Kenneth. Repression Disguised as Law: Human Rights in Poland. New York: Lawyers Committee for Human Rights, 1987. 110. On the status of human rights in Poland on the fifth anniversary of the declaration of martial law: repression continues--official tolerance of police violence, draconian fines for demonstrating, etc.

1978. Ryan, William. "Amnesty Alters the Political Landscape." Guardian 36.41 (Aug 8, 1984) 14. 35,000 people have been freed, including 650 solidarity members and other political prisoners.

1979. Singer, Daniel. "Gdansk Showdown." Nation 240 (June 8, 1985) 693. On the trial of three men who advocated a strike to protest food price hike.

1980. Slodowski, Wojelech. "Curriculum Vitae of Jósef Sreniowski." Index On Censorship 14.6 (December 1985) 13. Biographical sketch of an often jailed intellectual, political dissident, editor of the newspaper Robotnik. He is in prison now charged with transporting material insulting to Poland.

1981. Smolowe, Jill. "Nails for Solidarity's Coffin." Time 127.24 (June 16, 1986) 20. Zbigniew Bujak, fugitive leader of the banned Solidarity trade-union, has been arrested.

1982. Special Action Update, Prisoners of Conscience and Events Leading Up to the Banning of the Independent Trade Union Organization, Solidarity. New York: Amnesty International USA, 1982. 4. Summary of arrests and imprisonments in 1982. Several case histories are presented.

1983. "Tadeusz Wypych." Index On Censorship 14.6 (December 1985) 54, 19. Wypych was sentenced to 2-and-a-half years for printing the Solidarity underground weekly in Warsaw.

1984. Turner, Henry. International Incident. London: Wingate, 1956. 205. Turner, an attaché of the British Foreign Office in Warsaw following WWII arrested for his involvment in a failed defection of a Polish citizen, describes his arrest by the secret police and the subseqent years of imprisonment and brainwashing.

1985. The Use of Political Imprisonment in the polish People's Republic : A Partial List of Political prisoners, August 1984-August 1985. Prepared by the Committee in Support of Solidarity in New York. New York: The Committee, 1985. 61. Most of these prisoners were arrested for distributing or printing publications, others for trade union activities, conscientious objection, and other "crimes."

1986. "U.S. Requests Repatriation of Noel, Herta, and Hermann Field; Note to Hungary; Note to Poland." United States Department of State Bulletin 31 (October 18, 1954) 586-7. Protests the arrest and disappearance of Hermann Field in Poland.

1987. Walsh, John. "American Scientists Protest Polish Actions." Science 215 (January 8, 1982) 145. Support for arrested scientists accused of being active in Solidarity.

1988. "Why Reagan Eased Up on Poland." U.S. News and World Report 97 (August 13, 1984) 8. General Jaruzelski gave amnesty to 40 percent of Poland's prison population, including 652 political prisoners.

1989. Willey, F. "Warsaw's Walesa Factor." Newsweek 99 (March 22, 1982) 40+. On political alternatives being considered by imprisoned Solidarity leaders.

1990. Wyszynski, Stefan. A Freedom Within: The Prison Notes of Stefan, Cardinal Wyszynski. Trans. Barbara Kryzwicki-Herburt and Walter Ziemba. London: Hodder and Stoughton, 1985. 270. His prison journal written 1953-1956.

PORTUGAL

1991. Amnesty International Report 1 June 1975-31 May 1976. London: Amnesty International, 1976. 164-65. Approximately 1,600 political prisoners need better trial procedures. Praises the new Constitution.

1992. Amnesty International Report 1980. London: Amnesty International, 1980. 288-290. The extreme slowness of some trials of a political nature and the lack of conformity to international norms are problems.

1993. "Free Portugal's New Political Prisoners." Militant 39.26 (July 11, 1975) 22. On the attempts to suppress the Maoist MRPP party, including jailings and torture.

1994. Kramer, Jane. "Letter from Europe." New Yorker 63 (Nov 30, 1987) 105-20. An account of Otelo Nieno Romano Saraiva de Carvalho, who led the peaceable overthrow in 1974 of the oldest Fascist regime in Europe, still in prison for "terrorist" actions during the revolution.

1995. Portuguese Poltical Prisoners: A British National Protest. 5th and enl. ed. London: L.U. Gill, 1913. 103. A British protest against the treatment of prisoners in a country "ground down by tyranny and oppression."

1996. "Portuguese Prisoners." Peace News 21.21 (May 30, 1980) 5. Contrasts the heavy sentences against Proletarian Revolutionary Party members and right wing bombers.

1997. Prison Conditions in Portugal: Conditions of Detention of Political Prisoners. London: Amnesty International, 1965. 36. Surveys illegal framework (political police and courts), brutal methods of interrogation, and prison conditions.

1998. Russell of Liverpool, Edward Frederick Langley Russell, Baron. Prisons and Prisoners in Portugal: an Independent Investigation. London: Waterlow, 1963. 16. An account of the author's inspection of prisons with several case studies of individual prisoners.

1999. Vieira, José. "From The Real Life of Domingos Xavier." Practice 4.3 (Winter 1986) 110. The author was imprisoned by the Portuguese Colonial authorities in Angola from 1961 to 1972. This section from his novel tells of the death of a poet prisoner on the morning in 1961 when the armed revolt against Portugal began.

RHODESIA (also see ZIMBABWE)

2000. Amnesty International Report 1 June 1975-31 May 1976. London: Amnesty International, 1976. 70-72. Condemns the rising number of political prisoners, the death penalty, the forced settlement of large numbers of Africans to concentration camps ("protected villages"), etc.

2001. "I Gave Them Names of my Children." Black Panther 17.25 (December 10, 1977) 2, 22. Narrative of one political prisoner's torture by Rhodesian security police who forced him to give names of people supposedly recruited for guerrilla warfare.

2002. Ian Smith's Hostages: Political Prisoners in Rhodesia. London: International Defence and Aid Fund for Southern Africa, 1976. 38. Of the two thousand in prison for a political offense, 1,839 are named.

2003. "Making of a Nonperson." Time 101 (March 19, 1973) 63. Reporter Peter Niesewand has been imprisoned by the government of Ian Smith for writing about its white-supremacist policies.

2004. Musa, Omari. "Rhodesia Jails Hundreds of Black Activists." Militant 42.36 (Sept 29, 1978) 26. Members of the Zimbabwe African People's Union and the Zimbabwe African National Union were arrested after Rhodesian Prime Minister Ian Smith declared his intention to "liquidate the internal workings" of Patriotic Front supporters.

2005. Mutasa, Didymus. Black Behind Bars: Rhodesia, 1959-1974. Harare: Longman, 1983. 150. Imprisoned for his opposition to Ian Smith's regime, the author describes his prison life.

2006. Niesewand, Peter. In Camera; Secret Justice in Rhodesia. London: Weidenfeld & Nicolson, 1973. 209. Rhodesian Broadcasting Corporation newsman Niesewand was sentenced in 1972 to two years in prison for violation of the Official Secrets Act (i.e. reporting the government's military actions in Mozambique). This is his account of arrest, detention, secret trial, and eventual release on appeal.

2007. Political Prisoners in Rhodesia in 1979. London: International Defence and Aid Fund, 1980. 57. On political trials, prison conditions, preventive detention (without charge or trial), executions, and other illegalities of the government under martial law. Includes list of persons sentenced to death.

2008. Political Repression in Rhodesia: Briefing Notes. London: International Defence and Aid Fund for Southern Africa, 1980. 17. At a time of transition of power to the Zimbabwe people, martial law still rules the country. Although political prisoners are being released, more than 10,000 remain confined.

2009. Prison Conditions in Rhodesia: Conditions for Poltical Prisoners and Restrictees. London: Amnesty International, 1966. 58. On the detention system, use of violence during interrogation, families, etc. Demands an end to the state of emergency and the release or trial of all detained.

2010. Report on the Education Scheme for Detainees, Restrictees and Convicted Political Prisoners in Rhodesia. London: International Defence and Aid Fund for Southern Africa, 1969. 7. Correspondence courses paid for by Swedish and Danish governments.

2011. "Rhodesia: Tactics of Terror; Zimbabwe: Three Reports." Matchbox (Fall 1977) 2-4. Testimonies of three political prisoners in detention without trial describe their arrest and the brutal torture received at the hands of the Rhodesian security police.

2012. Sithole, Ndabaningi. Letters from Salisbury Prison. Nairobi: Transafrica, 1976. 186. The author was imprisoned in 1962-1975 when the Zimbabwe African Peoples Union (ZAPU), of which he was National Chairman, was banned.

2013. Todd, Judith. The Right to Say No. London: Sidgwick & Jackson, 1972. 200. She was jailed briefly in 1972 under the Emergency Powers Regulations of 1970 on suspicion of being dangerous to public safety. She went on a hunger strike and was forcibly fed. (Her father, a former Rhodesian prime minister, was also jailed for the same charge.)

ROMANIA

2014. Amnesty International Report 1980. London: Amnesty International, 1980. 290-295. Those who have asserted their human rights have been subjected to forced labor, imprisonment, confinement in psychiatric hospitals, arbitrary arrests, and unfair trials for such "crimes" as "anti-social behavior," "parasitical conduct," and "anti-state propaganda" (the latter punishable by from five to fifteen years imprisonment). Also, emigration attempts risk reprisal; religious dissenters and union leaders are harassed; and detention is often brutal.

2015. Amnesty International Report 1990. New York: Amnesty International, 1990. 199-201. All political prisoners under the former government of President Ceausescu were released in December, 1989. During the uprising that overthrew him, hundreds of people were killed by troops and police.

2016. Craciunas, Silviu. The Lost Footsteps. Torrance, CA: Diana Books, 1974. 318. An account of the author's underground work in Romania, his arrest and imprisonment, and his escape.

2017. Dascalu, Nicolae. "The Human Rights Struggle in Romania: 'Hundreds of Explosions of Discontent.'" Matchbox (May 1981) 1,8. Interview with Dascalu, Romanian dissident who briefly headed the free trade union movement in his country and who was subsequently imprisoned for 10 months.

2018. Dima, Nicholas. Journey to Freedom. Washington, DC: Selous Foundation, 1990. 399. Describes his imprisonment and the techniques he and others used to survive.

2019. Kirschen, Leonard. Prisoner of Red Justice: An Account of Ten Years' Captivity in Communist Romania. London: Barker, 1963. 223. Kirschen, an AP reporter stationed in Bucharest, recounts his arrest in 1950 on charges of "spying for Anglo-American Imperialist Agencies," and the atrocities committed by his captors during his ten years imprisonment.

2020. Petrassevich, Cornel H. "A Papal Audience." National Review 35 (May 27, 1983) 621-2. The author was imprisoned and tortured for two years, 1948-50, without charge, then in 1950 sentenced to life imprisonment for treason.

2021. Poems From Communist Prisons. Collected by Zahu Pana. Trans. Mother Alexandra Ileana, Princess of Romania. Ellwood City, Pa.: Orthodox Monastery of the Transfiguration, 1985. 47. Includes works written by political prisoners.

2022. Prison Conditions in Rumania: Conditions for Political Prisoners, 1955-64: A Factual Report. London: Amnesty International, 1965. 28. Covers fifteen topics from administration and interrogation to forced labor.

2023. "Romania: Forced Labor Camps and Ethnic Minorities." Matchbox (Autumn 1978) 17,21. Notes a distinct pattern of persecution of political dissidents, and a significant increase in the number of persons confined to forced labor camps or psychiatric hospitals, or imprisoned for political reasons from 1970-1978, especially for ethnic Hungarians.

2024. Romania: Forced Labor, Psychiatric Repression of Dissent, Persecution of Religious Believers, Ethnic Discrimination and Persecution, Law and Suppression of Human Rights in Romania. New York: Amnesty International, 1978. 45. Contains about two dozen prisoner profiles and additional lists.

2025. Romania: Human Rights Violations in the Eighties. New York: Amnesty International, 1987. A pattern of human rights abuses, including the torture or imprisonment of government critics after unfair trials and the jailing of people for wanting to leave the country.

2026. Romania : Violations of Human Rights, Cases of Religious and Political Imprisonment. New York: Amnesty International, 1985. About unfair trials, ill-treatment following arrest, use of psychiatric hospitals for punishment, and other abuses.

2027. Samuelli, Annie. The Wall Between. Washington, DC: Robert B. Luce, 1967. 227. A Romanian Jewish woman imprisoned for espionage in Communist Romania from 1949 to 1961 writes about how women endured imprisonment without defeat.

2028. Scarfe, Alan. "Church Unity Cracks under Regime Pressure." Christianity Today 23 (May 25, 1979) 47-9. The Romanian government targets Christians in a wave of arrests. Individual cases are briefly discussed.

2029. Valéry, Nicole. Prisoner, Rejoice. London: Hodder and Stoughton, 1982. 238. (Benie sois-tu, prison, 1976). Imprisoned for four years because the state had not "been able to prove that you are guilty" (232)

2030. Wurmbrand, Richard. How Are You, Jesus? Audiotape, 60 min., 1967. Lecture on labor camps for political prisoners.

2031. Wurmbrand, Sabina. The Pastor's Wife. Ed. Charles Foley. London: Hodder & Stoughton, 1970. 218. Her husband was imprisoned as a counterrevolutionary in

1948, and she was sent to a labor camp until 1953 (her husband was not released until 1962).

RUSSIA (PRE-REVOLUTION)*

2032. Breshko-Breshkovskaya, Ekaterina Constantinovna (Katerina Breshkovskaia). The Little Grandmother of the Russian Revolution: Reminiscences and Letters of Catherine Breshkovsky. Ed. Alice Stone Blackwell. Boston: Little, Brown, 1918. 348. The author was a revolutionary against the Czarist government; the letters were written to her son from prison and from Siberia.

2033. Desind, Philip. Jewish and Russian Revolutionaries Exiled to Siberia, 1901-1917. Lewiston, NY: Edwin Mellen, 1990. 204. Part I is a translation of the Yiddish text of Israel Pressman's autobiography of becoming part of the Russian revolution movement, his arrest and exile to Siberia, and then conscription into the Russian army. Part II is the story of two sisters, daughters of a general and Socialists, who endured extreme hardships under both Tsarist and Soviet Dictatorships.

2034. Dzerzhinskii, Feliks Edmundovich. Prison Diary And Letters. Moscow: Foreign Languages Pub. House, 1959. 305. The author spent eleven years in Tsarist prisons.

2035. Figner, Vera. "When the Clock of Life Stopped." In Memoirs of a Revolutionist. Tr. Camilla Daniels, et al., Book 2, pp. 179-318. New York: International, 1927; rpt. Westport, CT: Greenwood, 1968. Describes her imprisonment in the Schlüsselburg Fortress from 1884 to 1904 for terrorist activities.

2036. Prelooker, Jaakoff. Heroes and Heroines of Russia; Builders of a New Commonweath. London: Simpkin, Marshall, Hamilton, Kent, 1908. 329. Stories of "Russian martyrs for freedom" who opposed "the tyranny of Autocratic Czarism.

2037. Steinberg, I. Spiridonova: Revolutionary Terrorist, Tr. and ed. by Gwenda David and Eric Mosbacher. London: Methuen, 1935. 313. The assassinator of General Luzhenovsky in 1906 because of his devastations in her home region tells of her imprisonments.

2038. Sukloff, Marie. The Life-Story of a Russian Exile: The Remarkable Experience of a Young Girl: Being an Account of Her Pleasant Childhood, Her Girlhood in Prison, Her Exile to Siberia, and Escape from There. London: Heinemann, 1915. 251. Imprisoned in 1905 for trade union and anti-government activites, she escaped and fled abroad in 1910.

2039. Tortures of Political Prisoners in Russia. Manchester, England: National Labour Press, 1913. 52. On the sufferings of criminals and political prisoners between the Revolution of 1905 and the Bolshevik Revolution.

**A diligent search has not uncovered any published work in English on political prisoners or trials in modern Russia (January 1, 1991, through December 31, 1993).*

RWANDA

2040. Amnesty International Report 1990. New York: Amnesty International, 1990. 201-202. Several individual political prisoners are disscussed.

2041. Rwanda: Persecution of Tutsi Minority and Repression of Government Critics, 1990 - 1992. New York: Amnesty International, 1992. 33. Extrajudicial execution, torture, "disappearances," political imprisonment, and efforts to silence government critics.

SÃO TOMÉ AND PRINCIPE

2042. Amnesty International Report 1980. London: Amnesty International, 1980. 69-70. Several people, including the former Prime Minister are in prison accused of plotting against the state. The death penalty was applied in 1979 to the crimes of "economic sabotage" and "colluding with imperialism."

2043. Amnesty International Report 1990. New York: Amnesty International, 1990. 202-203. In 1989 forty-three members of an opposition party were sentenced to long terms for allegedly trying to overthrow the government.

SAUDI ARABIA

2044. Amnesty International Report 1980. London: Amnesty International, 1980. 351-52. Lengthy pre-trial detention, frequent summary trials, and ill-treatment of prisoners are some of the problems in this country without a constitution.

2045. Amnesty International Report 1990. New York: Amnesty International, 1990. Dozens of political prisoners were imprisoned in 1989, some held incommunicado for prolonged periods, and torture was "reportedly common." At least 16 political executions took place.

2046. Saudi Arabia : Detention Without Trial of Suspected Political Opponents. New York: Amnesty International, 1990. 27. Arrest without warrant and detention for long periods are of "grave concern" especially since detention is routinely accompanied by solitary confinement and torture or ill-treatment.

2047. Shame in the House of Saud: Contempt for Human Rights in Saudi Arabia. Minneapolis: Minnesota Lawyers International Human Rights Committee, 1992. 170. Virtually all confessions are obtained by torture, and arbitrary arrest is common.

SENEGAL

2048. Amnesty International Report 1990. New York: Amnesty International, 1990. Several supporters of independence for the Casamance region arrested in 1988 remained confined without trial, and more were detained in 1989.

2049. Senegal: An Escalation in Human Rights Violations in Casamance Region. New York: Amnesty International, 1991. 8. Execution and torture by the armed forces as punishment. Includes the government's latest response.

SERBIA

2050. Gutman, Roy. "Serb Officials Remain Vague on Details of 'Disappearances.'" Morning News [Springdale, AR] (November 8, 1992) 12A. On the imprisonment, murder, and disappearance of prominent Muslims and Croats under Serb domination.

2051. War Crimes in Bosnia-Hercegovina: Volume II. New York: Human Rights Watch, 1993. 460. Helsinki Watch has covered the conflict since it began and continues to report atrocities done by those committed to ethnic cleansing.

SEYCHELLES

2052. Amnesty International Report 1980. London: Amnesty International, 1980. 70-71. Seventy-eight men and women were detained for alleged plotting against the government, but most were freed in 1980, though the remaining remained under indefinite detention without trial in poor prison conditions.

SIERRA LEONE

2053. Amnesty International Report 1990. New York: Amnesty International, 1990. 207-208. Twelve prisoners were executed for treason without fair trial. Detention without charge or trial continued in practice. The brutal prisons had high mortality rates.

2054. Maddy, Yulisa Amadu. "His Supreme Exellency's Guest." Index On Censorship 17.5 (May 1988) 88. The author was arrested in 1977 for his play Big Berrin, which criticized the dictator Siaka Stevens and his govenment's corruption. Extracts from his writings are quoted.

2055/56. Sierra Leone The Extrajudicial Execution of Suspected Rebels and Collaborators. New York: Amnesty International, 1992. 14. Human rights abuses by government forces and rebel forces including torture, ill-treatment, and arbitrary killings.

SINGAPORE

2057. "The 16 Detained Under the Internal Security Act." Index On Censorship 16.8 (September 1987) 24. Description of each of these dissenters from government policies through church principle, plays, and political party.

2058. Amnesty International Report 1980. London: Amnesty International, 1980. 228-29. Systematic preventive detention without charge or trial, and widespread physical and psychological ill-treatment of detainees.

2059. Amnesty International Report 1990. New York: Amnesty International, 1990. 208-210. Some long-term prisoners (one after 23 years of untried detention) were released, but others remained.

2060. Chandler, Ted. "Singapore Represses Opposition." Guardian 24.15 (January 19, 1977) 17. Focuses on the case of Wah Piow, who was imprisoned on false charges of incitement to riot. Piow was able to escape to Britain.

2061. Har, Tang Fong. "'I Stand By the Joint Statement.'" Index On Censorship 17.6 (June 1988) 28. Reaffirms her allegation of physical and psychological abuse that forced her to confess to something untrue.

2062. Report of an Amnesty International Mission to Singapore, 30 November to 5 December 1978. New York: Amnesty International, 1980. 60. Concerning detentions without trial, coerced public confessions, and psychological and physical ill-treatment, in some cases amounting to torture, under the Internal Security Act (1960), and the Banishment Act (1959). Dr. Lim Hock Siew, Ho Piao, and Lee Tse Tong have been in detention without trial for 17 years.

2063. Singapore. London: Amnesty International, 1976. 10. Condemns repression of political opposition by banishment, detention without fair trial, unfair trials, caning, and other abuses.

2064. Singapore. 2nd ed. Amnesty International briefing 1. London: Amnesty International, 1978. 12. Conditions have worsened since the first edition of 1976, an increased number of opponents to the government arrested without charge or trial, and former detainees have been re-arrested without trial.

2065. Singapore, Detentions Without Trial Under the Internal Security Act: Report of an Amnesty International Mission to the Republic of Singapore, 14-22 June 1987. New York: Amnesty International, 1987. 27. On the twenty-two prisoners arrested in May-June 1987 for their legitimate non-violent activities.

2066. "Singapore's Veteran Political Prisoner." Inside Asia 7 (February 1986) 46. Chia Thye Poh, former university lecturer and member of parliament, was detained without trial in 1966 and has yet to be released.

2067. Tan, Lek Hor. "The 'Communist Conspirators'." Index On Censorship 16.8 (September 1987) 21-26. Twenty-two people have been arrested, detained, or served with restriction orders under the Internal Security Act for involvment in a "clandestine Communist network" supposedly led by Tan Wah Piow, a law student at Oxford.

2068. Tan, Lek Hor. "Declaration of Innocence and Ill-Treatment." Index On Censorship 17.6 (June 1988) 26-29. Twenty-two opponents of the government were arrested in 1987. When nine of them after release protested their incarceration, all except one (abroad) were re-arrested. The statement of the nine, alleging severe abuse in prison, is printed in full.

2069. Tan, Lek Hor. "An Interview With Tan Wah Piow." Index On Censorship 16.8 (September 1987) 22-23. Former prisoner Piow (now in England) along with 16 others, who have been arrested, has been accused of a communist conspiracy.

SLOVAKIA (*see* CZECHOSLOVAKIA)

SOMALIA

2070. Amnesty International Report 1980. London: Amnesty International, 1980. 71-73. Under the dictator Siyad Barre over 100 people are in prison without charge or trial for opposing the government, some for over 10 years and in harsh conditions. Four students were sentenced to death in 1979 for demonstrating against the government. Attempts to visit the country by Amnesty International have been denied.

2071. Amnesty International Report 1990. New York: Amnesty International, 1990. 210-213. Hundreds of prisoners were released, but hundreds remained incarcerated, and more were arrested in 1989, some tortured, and hundreds were reportedly killed during anti-government demonstrations. Prison conditions were harsh.

2072. Scientists and Human Rights in Somalia: Report of a Delegation. Washington, D.C.: National Academy Press, Committee on Human Rights, National Academy of Sciences, 1988. 84. Report by the National Academy of Sciences Committee on Human Rights and the Institute of Medicine Committee on Health and Human Rights regarding eleven imprisoned scientific colleagues.

2073. Somalia: A Long-Term Human Rights Crisis. London: Amnesty International, 1988. 52. Human rights violations have persisted since 1969 and increased during the 1980s, including arbitrary detention, unfair trials, and torture.

2074. Somalia: Torture: Summary. New York: Amnesty International, 1988. 8. "Torture is part of a persistent pattern of gross human rights violations."

2075. "Stay Of Execution." Africa News 29.6 (March 21, 1988) 8-9. Suleiman Nuh Ali and Abdi Ismail Yunis have been sentenced to death charged with belonging to a subversive organization, part of President Siad Barre's purge of intellectuals and proponents of democracy.

SOUTH AFRICA

2076. 11 October Day of Solidarity with South African Political Prisoners. New York: United Nations Centre against Apartheid, 1990. 5. On October 11, 1963, the UN called on South Africa to release all political prisoners.

2077. Aberdeen City Anti-Apartheid Movement. Nelson & Winnie Mandela: Freemen of the City of Aberdeen. Aberdeen: City of Aberdeen District Council, 1986. 28. The city of Aberdeen conferred the title of "Freeman" on Nelson and Winifred Mandela and published these brief biographies of each and "The Freedom Charter," adopted in South Africa in 1955.

2078. Administration of Security Legislation in South Africa, 1976. Johannesburg: South African Institute of Race Relations, 1977. 43. Lists of people detained without charges, deaths in prison, and related matters.

2079. Administration of Security Legislation in South Africa, January 1976- March 1977. Johannesburg: South African Institute of Race Relations, 1977. 74. Lists of people detained, re-detained, released, and died in prison.

2080. Amnesty International Report 1980. London: Amnesty International, 1980. 74-79. In 1979 and 1980 new waves of political arrests, detentions, trials, and bannings occurred, and restrictions on the press tightened. Also in 1980 nine African National Congress (ANC) members were charged with treason, such a serious charge not employed since the late 1950s. Leaders of various black organizations were harassed and detained, and some held incommunicado. Police tortured some detainees. Execution of political prisoners increased.

2081. Amnesty International Report 1990. New York: Amnesty International, 1990. 213-216. At least 1,000 opponents of the government were held without charge at the beginning of 1989. A few long-term prisoners were released, but many more people were arrested in 1989. Reports of torture continued.

2082. Apartheid is Built on Torture. Helsinki: World Peace Council Information Centre, 1972. 37. Two cases illustrate the brutal repression of house arrests, banishments, arbitrary and incommunicado arrests, detention without trial, torture, and deaths in custody, all widespread and frequent. An entire chapter gives profiles of people who died in detention.

2083. "Apartheid Persecution." Christian Century 104 (January 21, 1987) 49-50. On imprisonment of clergy critical of the Government.

2084. "Appeal From Death Row." Sechaba 23.12 (Dec. 1989) 14. Political prisoners facing capital punishment appeal to world on U.N. Day of Solidarity with South African political prisoners.

2085. Askin, S. "Ex-South African Prisoner Exposes Destabilization." In These Times 12.7 (Dec. 23, 1987) 5. Ex-prisoner, Patricia Hanekom, gives "an inside look at the day-to-day activities of the secretive Directorate of Special Tasks (DST), the South African Defense Force (SADF) unit that supervises covert wars."

2086. Baard, Frances, as told to Barbie Schreiner. My Spirit is Not Banned. Harare: Zimbabwe Publishing House, 1986. 92. Biography of Baard, a black South African trade unionist, political activist, and leader of women's movements. She describes the treason trial of 156 people in 1956, and the many killings and arrests from 1960 when a State of Emergency was declared. She spent eight years in prison and four more in banishment, including a year in solitary confinement.

2087. Barad, Elizabeth. "Banned, But Not Bitter." Ms 17 (October 1988) 70. Albertina Sisulu was banned for eighteen years following an interview with Barad.

2088. Benson, Mary. Nelson Mandela: the Man and the Movement. Foreward by Bishop Desmond M. Tutu. New York: Norton, 1989. 273. The author is a South African white who was banned and house-arrested. Bishop Tutu in his foreward praises this "story of a people's struggle within the story of one [great] man's struggle."

2089. Benson, Mary, ed. The Sun Will Rise: Statements From the Dock By Southern African Prisoners. Rev. ed. London: International Defence and Aid Fund for Southern Africa, 1976. 56. Nineteen trial statements united by the struggle against oppression.

2090. Bernstein, Hilda. No. 46- Steve Biko. London: International Defence and Aid Fund, 1978. 150. Biko was the forty-sixth person to die in security police detention. This is an examination of his death and the inquest that exonerated the police but shocked the world.

2091. Bernstein, Hilda. The World That Was Ours: The Story of the Rivonia Trial. London: SAWriters, 1989. 309. Nelson Mandela and seven others were sentenced to life imprisonment in 1964, marking "the first time since the State of Emergency of 1960 and the banning of the ANC the whole story of black oppression and black struggle and aspirations was told."

2092. Bham, Thamsanga Enoch. The Will to Live. 1st ed. New York: Vantage, 1980. 115.

2093. Biko: Breaking the Silence. Videocassette. Nar. Mike Munyati. Dir. Edwina Spicer. Prod. Olley Maruma. New York: Filmakers Library, 1987; San Fransico: California Newsreel, 1988. 55 min. Presents the story of Stephen Biko, using interviews with other South African anti-apartheid activists. Parts of the motion picture Cry Freedom directed by Richard Attenborough, based on the novel Biko by Donald Woods, are shown along with interviews of Attenborough and Woods.

2094. "The Biko Case; a Slap on the Wrist." Newsweek 106 (July 15, 1985) 34. On the weak judicial response to the apparent murder in prison of Steve Biko.

2095. Bolnick, Joel. "After Biko, Montsitsi?" Nation 226 (January 28, 1978) 68. A white student briefly detained along with black students still in jail tells about prison conditions and about the prisoner Sechaba Daniel Montsitsi, president of the Soweto Students Council.

2096. Boyle, Kevin. "The Plight of Zwelakhe Sisulu." Index On Censorship 16.5 (May 1987) 28, 36. Sisulu, editor of New Nation, is held in solitary confinement without charge or trial.

2097. "Breaking Rules." Time 127.15 (April 14, 1986) 44. Winnie Mandela allowed to enter her home for the first time in nine years.

2098. Breytenbach, Breyten. The True Confessions of an Albino Terrorist. London: Faber, 1985. 396. A writer confined for his opposition to apartheid.

2099. Brittain, Victoria, and Abdul S. Minty, eds. Children of Resistance: Statements from the Harare Conference on Children, Repression and the Law in Apartheid South Africa. London: Kliptown, 1988. 146. The international conference in Harare, Zimbabwe in 1987 brought together 300 South Africans and over 200 representatives of more than 150 organizations throughout the world to focus on the "apartheid regime's brutal repression of children"--beatings, shootings, killings, torture, and imprisonment.

2100. Brown, Frank D. "Nelson Mandela Emerges Steadfast and Unbowed." Black Enterprise 20 (April 1990) 17. After 27 years in prison, Mandela is freed and resolves to continue the struggle.

2101. Brown, Frank D. "Sisulu Freed : the ANC Steps up the Pressure." Black Enterprise 20 (January 1990) 17. After 26 years in prison, former ANC Secretary General Walter Sisulu is freed.

2102. Bull, Chris. "South Arican Gay Activist Simon Nkoli." Advocate 542 (January 16, 1990) 44. Nkoli has been denied basic human rights and harassed because of his political and sexual views.

2103. "Campaign to Save Their Lives! End Apartheid Executions!" Sechaba (March 1988) 18-19. Concerns the Sharpeville 6 sentenced to death accused of killing an official who had fired on demonstrators, though the appeal judge declared the evidence very weak. Lists 45 political prisoners in death cells.

2104. Carroll, R. and Peter Younghusband. "A No-fault Verdict." Newsweek 90 (December 12, 1977) 67, 69. Prison jailers and doctors absolved by a judge of causing Steve Biko's death.

2105. Carroll, Raymond and Peter Younghusband. "'Steve Biko is Dead.'" Newsweek 90 (September 26, 1977) 41-2. "South Africa's Martin Luther King" died in custody, the twentieth black to die in detention during the past year.

2106. "Catalogue of Racist Oppression." Sechaba 11.1 (Winter 1977) 13-16. On the thousands of arrests since June 16, 1976, many of whom died in prison probably from torture or disappeared.

2107. "Children Behind Bars: Physician's Reports Document Abuse of Detainees." Health Pac Bulletin 17.4 (August 1987) 9-12. Reports on the far-reaching and psychologically devastating effects of detention, torture and intimidation on young people, and includes many individual case studies.

2108. Congress. House Committee on Foreign Affairs. Legislation Urging the South African Government to Engage in Meaningful Negotiations With That Country's Black Majority. Hearing and Markup Before the Committee on Foreign Affairs, Ninety-Ninth Congress, Second Session, on H. Res. 373, June 24 and August 6, 1986. Washington, D.C.: U.S. G.P.O., 1987. 68.

2109. Cooper, Nancy, et al. "Conditions for Freedom." Newsweek 106 (December 2, 1985) 57. Nelson Mandela's release seems to be approaching.

2110. Cries of Freedom: Women in Detention in South Africa. London: Catholic Institute for International Relations, 1989. 51. Discusses the 3,000+ women detained without trial during 1988, giving case studies of individuals; details such as sanitation, pregnancy, sexual assault and other forms of torture; and an overview of South African apartheid legislation concerning detention and women.

2111. Cronje, Suzanne. Witness in the Dark: Police Torture and Brutality in South Africa. London: Christian Action, 1964. 32. "African protest is now almost completely suppressed" by methods of extreme brutality.

2112. Cummings, Peter. "South Africa: A Double Bind for Black Gays." Advocate 488 (December 22, 1987) 28. Black gays are victimized by police murders, arrests, bomb threats, interrogations, mail seizures, phone taps, and HIV positive blacks are threatened with deportation.

2113. "Death Nearer For Six." Guardian 40.38 (June 22, 1988) 1. The Sharpeville 6 await execution despite the lack of evidence they killed anyone and despite evidence two witnesses gave false testimony under force.

2114. "Death of a Prisoner." Time 110 (September 26, 1977) 35. Black leader Steven Biko, founding member of the all- black South African Students' Organization, died in security detention. Officials claim he died from fasting.

2115. "Deaths in Detention." Southern Africa 10.8 (October 1977) 18. List compiled from March 1976 to September 1977 of known deaths of men held under terms of security laws giving names, ages, dates of death and the "official" cause of death.

2116. Deaths in Detention and South Africa's Security Laws. Washington: Southern Africa Project, 1983. 192. Sixty case histories.

2117. Denenberg, Barry. Nelson Mandela : "No Easy Walk to Freedom," a Biography. New York: Scholastic, 1991. 164. From boyhood to his release from prison in 1990, in popular style. Many photos.

2118. Detention and Detente in Southern Africa. Braamfontein, South Africa: Christian Institute of Southern Africa, 1976. 27. A summary of the many arrests and trials, many cases and statistics.

2119. Detention Without Trial in South Africa 1976-1977. Johannesburg: S.A. Institute of Race Relations, 1977. 68. Lists people in detention recently released, summarizes events leading to the deaths in detention of twenty people.

2120. Dingake, Michael. My Fight against Apartheid. London: Kliptown, 1987. 241. The author's autobiography of becoming aware of the effects of apartheid, joining the ANC and becoming a leader, kidnapped in Rhodesia, arrested, tortured, tried and imprisoned on Robben Island 1966-1981.

2121. "The Disease of Apartheid." Socialist Affairs 4 (1986) 53. Problems faced by women under apartheid because of the systematic detention and torture of children and other reasons.

2122. Dlamini, Moses. Hell-Hole: Robben Island, Reminiscences of a Political Prisoner. Nottingham: Spokesman, 1984. 202. Robben Island is 11 kilometers off Cape Town. Its prison "is a place where you are stripped of every vestige of human dignity," but the prison duplicates everyday life for blacks.

2123. Ebert-Minor, A. "A Disgrace to the American People." Guardian 37.3 (Oct. 17, 1984) 11. Six opposition leaders, the Durban six, confronted with arrest for demonstrating took refuge in the British Consulate. The U.S. refused refuge. Three left the Consulate and were arrested.

2124. Ellmann, Stephen. In a Time of Trouble: Law and Liberty in South Africa's State of Emergency. New York: Oxford UP, 1992. 304. On the failure of the legal framework and the courts to restrain the emergency abuses; repeatedly the judges vindicated the emergency powers that permitted arbitrary arrests and other violations of human rights.

2125. "Ex-officer Admits 4 Slain in S. African Custody." Arkansas Democrat-Gazette (January 26, 1993) 6A. "A black former police officer has confessed to assaulting and burying four black political activists while they were in custody on an isolated farm...The farm was used by police to interrogate, torture and assassinate detainees."

2126. Falk, Richard. "South Africa's War on Children." Nation 245 (November 7, 1987) 516-17. Tells about the International Conference on Children, Repression, and the law in Apartheid South Africa.

2127. Farisani, Tshenuwani Simon. Diary From a South African Prison. Philadelphia: Fortress Press, 1987. 93. An account of his first three detentions. The now deputy bishop of the Evangelical Lutheran Church in South Africa for preaching love, justice, and equality was imprisoned and tortured almost to death.

2128. Feinberg, Brian. Nelson Mandela. New York: Chelsea Juniors, 1992. 76. A biography for young people.

2129. First, Ruth. 117 Days. New York: Stein & Day, 1965; Penguin, 1982. 142. New York: Monthly Review Press, 1989. 170. A prison memoir. South African journalist First was imprisoned without trial in 1963 and held in solitary confinement, her term longer than any white woman in South Africa before her. (She was the wife of Joe Slovo, anti-apartheid activist. In 1982 she was killed by a letter bomb in Mozambique.) BBC made a film of the book entitle A World Apart with Barara Hershey as First.

2130. Fleshman, M. "Swapos Fiery Founder." Guardian 36.23 (March 14, 1984) 1, 13. Namibian nationalist Herman Toivo Ja Toivo has been released from Robben Island Prison after serving 16 years of a 20-year sentence for protesting colonialism by helping to create the Southwest Africa Peoples Organization (SWAPO).

2131. Forbes, Delysia. "South African Prisoners Demand Prisoner of War Status." Spare Rib 202 (June 1989) 44. Report on the Lawyers Against Apartheid campaign "calling for Prisoner of War status to be accorded to combatants who take up arms against the violence perpetrated by the racist South African Regime on the exploited and oppressed."

2132. Foster, Dan, ed. Detention & Torture in South Africa: Psychological, Legal, and Historical Studies. Ed. Don Foster; with Dennis Davis & Diane Sandler. Capetown: David Philip, 1987. 250. Study on security legislation and detention "developed for the purpose of maintaining white hegemony in South Africa." Chapter 5 contains statistical data and charts on pre-detention harassment, interrogation, physical and psychological torture. Chapter 7 records the testimonies of former detainees.

2133. Fourie, Enid. "The UN Convention on the Rights of the Child and the Crisis for Children in South Africa: Apartheid and Detention." Human Rights Quarterly 12 (1990) 106-114. Focuses on education and the state of emergency, which under the latter, beginning in 1986, has resulted in the brutal detention of thousands of youths.

2134. Frankel, David. "Racist Justice in South Africa." Militant 41.47 (Dec. 16, 1977) 32. Steve Biko died in police custody; blows to the head were reported.

2135. "Free But Gagged." Index On Censorship 18.1 (Jan. 1989) 4. Gives the extremely restrictive rules under which Zwelakhe Sisulu must live following his release from prison where he was kept without charge or trial 1986-1988.

2136. "Free South Africa's Children: A Symposium on Children in Detention." Human Rights Quarterly 10 (1988) 1-108. Witnesses and panelists "focus urgently needed attention on a particularly odious aspect of the abhorrent system of apartheid"--the detention and abuse of children. Sponsored by the South African Project of the Lawyers' Committee for Civil Rights Under Law.

2137. Harwood, Ronald. Mandela. London: Boxtree Limited, 1987. 133. Based on the TVS production for Channel 4. Danny Glover played Mandela.

2138. Hinds, L. "Apartheid in South Africa and the Universal Declaration of Human Rights." Crime and Social Justice 24 (1985) 5-34. "This article provides a very few samples of the voluminous documentation of apartheid and of South Africa's record as an international criminal whose continuing lawlessness is a danger not only to the majority people of South Africa but to the people of the world."

2139. Hoobler, Dorothy, and Thomas Hoobler. Mandela: The Man, The Struggle, The Triumph. New York: F. Watts, 1992. 143. A biography for young people, covering Mandela's life from his childhood to his release from prison and the beginnings of dismantling of apartheid, including background of South African history.

2140. Houser, George. "Treason in South Africa?" Christian Century 74 (March 6, 1957) 288-9. On the arrest of over 100 leaders of some forty-eight organizations that oppose apartheid.

2141. Hughes, Libby. Nelson Mandela: Voice of Freedom. New York: Toronto: New York: Dillon; Toronto: Maxwell Macmillan Canada; Maxwell Macmillan International, 1992. Examines the life and career of the South African civil rights leader and his impact on peace relations in his country. Written for young people.

2142. Hunke, Father Heinz, ed. Torture: A Cancer in Our Society. London: Catholic Institute for International Relations, 1978. 67. Detailed account of the methods of torture used by authorities in South Africa and includes many case studies.

2143. "Inquest into a Curious Death." Time 110 (November 28, 1977) 53. Describes the public inquest into the death of Black Consciousness leader Steven Biko.

2144. International Defense and Aid Fund. To Honor Women's Day: Profiles of Leading Women in the South African and Namibian Liberation Struggles. London: IDAF, 1981. 56. Collection of biographies of women who have suffered under apartheid in South Africa and Namibia. Includes a short list of women political prisoners.

2145. "Interview with Dean Molale." Sechaba 12.4 (Winter 1978) 28-30. Dean of the Anglican Church in Botswana, Dean Mokhasi Michael Molale was detained in violation of international law by South African security police and interrogated for thirteen days, ten hours a day, without being allowed to wash, change clothes, or remove his handcuffs.

2146. Jacobsen, Quentin. Solitary in Johannesburg. London: Joseph, 1973. 256. An account of his imprisonment, trial, and acquittal of charges of terrorism and aiding communists.

2147. Javers, Ron. "In a South African Prison." Commonweal 104 (December 23, 1977) 808-9. Percy Qoboza, editor of The World, South Africa's largest black newspaper (now closed), is in prison for criticizing apartheid.

2148. Jenkin, Tim. Escape From Pretoria. London: Kliptown, 1987. 240. Story of Jenkin, a white South African, in Part I joining the ANC, his arrest, and trial, in Part II his experiences as a political prisoner and his escape.

2149. Jenkin, Tim. "Welcome Home Dorothy Nyembe, Women's Leader!" Sechaba (March 1984) 18-19. Dorothy Nyembe was sentenced in 1969 to fifteen years imprisonment for "harbouring" ANC freedom fighters--the longest prison term ever imposed on a woman for a political "offence" in South Africa.

2150. Jones, Jeff. "'Subversive' Churchman Released." Guardian 38.1 (October 2, 1985) 12. Rev. Allan Boesak was released from prison and ordered to be tried for subversion, because he had planned a rally for Nelson Mandela and had urged an economic boycott. He faces a maximum of 25 years for each of three counts. Boesak is founder of the United Democratic Front and president of the World Alliance of Reformed Churches.

2151. Joseph, Helen. Side by Side: The Autobiography of Helen Joseph. New York: William Morrow, 1986. 249. Joseph's life, detention and banning as a white anti-apartheid activist in South Africa.

2152. Kalley, Jacqueline A. South Africa Under Apartheid: A Select and Annotated Bibiography. Pietermaritzburg, South Africa: Shuter & Shooter, 1987. 544. Over 1,100 alphabetically arranged entries with subject and author indexes.

2153. Khatami, James. "Charges of Torture in South Africa." Guardian 34.22 (Mar. 3, 1982) 6. Thozamile Gqweta, trade union leader, was admitted to a psychiatric hospital after solitary detention and interrogation. One week later another trade unionist, Dr. Neil Aggett, died in detention.

2154. Khatami, James. "SWAPO Founder: 'I Never Gave Up; I Never Will.'" Guardian 37.10 (Dec. 5, 1984) 16. Discusses the Namibian independence leader Herman Toivo ja Toivo's imprisonment in Robben Island Prison.

2155. Kitson, Norma. Where Sixpence Lives. London: Chatto and Windus, 1986. 326. Kitson and her husband worked for the ANC against apartheid. Her daughter was detained and tortured and her son-in-law was sentenced to 20 years' imprisonment.

2156. Konrat, Georg von. Passport to Truth: Inside South West Africa: An Astounding Story of Oppression. Nairobi: East African Pub. House, 1975. 241. The author, an engineer working on a water project, was harrassed, imprisoned, and beaten for defending his African workers.

2157. "Lady at Home." Newsweek 70 (December 25, 1967) 35-6. Helen Joseph, critic of apartheid, placed under house arrest for "sabotage."

2158. Lambert, R.E. "A Priest in Prison." America 150 (January 7-14, 1984) 4. Rev. Smangaliso Mkhatshiva detained at Fort Hare in the Ciskei region. He is secretary-general of the South African Catholic Bishops Conference.

2159. Lawyers Committee for Human Rights (U.S.) Deaths in Custody: 7 Recent Cases in South Africa. New York: The Committee, 1986. 61. Each case is discussed.

2160. "Letter From South African Prison." Militant 40.45 (Nov. 26, 1976) 26. Letter from a Namibian political prisoner telling of life-threatning working conditions and mental torture in Robben Island Prison.

2161. "Letter Smuggled From a South African Prison." Index On Censorship 15.2 (February 1986) 42. The writer describes his arrest and detention without trial, harsh prison conditions, the detention of many youth including a nine-year-old child, and urges readers to take action.

2162. Lewin, Hugh. Bandiet: Seven Years in a South African Prison. 2nd ed. London; Exeter: Heinemann Educational Books, 1981. 228. (London: Barrie & Jenkins, 1974). The title means convict. Lewin served seven years in prison for his opposition to the government, convicted of sabotage.

2163. "Lilian Ngoyi, AIUSA Adoptee, Dies in South Africa." Matchbox (May 1980) 12. Lilian Ngoyi died of a heart attack at the age of 68 in her home, where she had been restricted under house arrest for fifteen years.

2164. "Lutheran Pastor Arrested [T.S. Farisani]." Christian Century 103 (December 17, 1986) 1144. No charge specified for the arrest. Concern great because he was tortured five years while imprisoned by Venda security police.

2165. Lutz, Larry. "South African's Caeser's Trials in Rendering to God..." Christianity Today 24 (April 18, 1980) 48. The article discusses Caesar Molebatsi's arrest and harrassment by South African police because of his involvement with Youth Alive, a youth ministry in Soweto.

2166. Maduna, Penuell. "A Legal Analysis of de Klerk's Address to the Racist Parliament in February." Sechaba 24.5 (May 1990) 11-15. Since the expectation raised by de Klerk's speech of the speedy removal of all obstacles to free political activity was not realized, close analysis is necessary.

2167. Makhoere, Caesarina Kona. No Child's Play: In Prison Under Apartheid. London: Women's Press, 1988. 121. Imprisoned six years in 1976 for resistance to Bantu education.

2168. Maltreatment and Torture of Prisoners in South Africa: Report of the Special Committee on Apartheid. New York: United Nations, 1973, 136. "All known cases" involving "assaults, torture and other acts of brutality" are profiled pp. 44-118.

2169. "Mandela Demands Unitary State." Africa News 24.9 (May 6, 1985) 6. An interview of Nelson Mandela by Samuel Dash, former chief counsel of the Senate's Watergate Committee, in Pollsmoor Prison.

2170. Mandela, Nelson. I Have Done My Duty to My People and To South Africa: Statement From the Dock, 7 November 1962. New York; United Nations Centre against apartheid, 1982. 14. Mandela's statements during his two trials in 1962 and 1963-64 are "among the greatest documents in humanity's struggle for freedom and racial equality.'

2171. Mandela, Nelson. Nelson Mandela Speaks: Speeches, Statements, and Articles. London: African National Congress, 1970. 128. Seven writings: "Programme of Action," "Spectre of Belsen and Buchenwald," "No Easy Walk to Freedom," etc.

2172. Mandela, Nelson. Nelson Mandela, the Struggle is My Life: His Speeches and Writings Brought Together With Historical Documents and Accounts of Mandela in Prison by Fellow-prisoners. 3rd ed. New York: Pathfinder, 1990. 281. This third edition was published eight weeks after Mandela's release from twenty-seven years of imprisonment. It contains all of the second edition (with the exception of the elimination of the list of his honors and awards) plus additional documents and updated photographs.

2173. Mandela, Nelson. The Struggle is My Life : His Speeches and Writings brought Together with Historical Documents and Accounts of Mandela in Prison by Fellow-Prisoners. Rev. of 1978 ed. New York: Pathfinder Press, 1986. 249. Chaps. on the treason trial 1956-60, the Rivonia trial 1963-64, Robben Island Prison, and Pollsmoor Prison.

2174. "Mandela Urges Defiance, Despite Government Restraints." Jet 70 (April 14, 1986) 9. On Winnie Mandela.

2175. Mandela, Winnie. "Winnie Mandela in Exile." Ms 14 (November 1985) 98-100. Excerpt from Part of My Soul Went with Him.

2176. "Mandela's Defiant Message." Guardian 37.21 (Feb. 27, 1985) 16. Nelson Mandela's statement from prison in reply to the government's offer of release if he will renounce violence: armed conflict was the last resort.

2177. "Mandela's Release Brings Praise, Apprehension." Christianity Today 34 (March 19, 1990) 47-8. Different South African leaders--Nico Smith (director of Koinonia South Africa), Michael Cassidy (founder of Africa Enterprise) and Caesar Molebatsi (pastor of Concerned Evangelicals)--discuss the release of Nelson Mandela.

2178. Manegold, C.S. "Teatime in Pretoria." Newsweek 114 (July 24, 1989) 24. Negotiations over release of Mandela.

2179. Manning, Richard. "Winnie Mandela: 'Enough.'" Newsweek 106 (December 30, 1985) 28. Winnie Mandela defies exile and speaking ban.

2180. Marx, Anthony W. Lessons of Struggle: South African Internal Opposition, 1960-1990. New York: Oxford, 1992. 347. Covers the years from the banning of the ANC and PAC to the lifting of the ban; studies the dynamics that shaped the opposition and "the conflict even among the oppressed."

2181. Mashinini, Emma. Strikes Have Followed Me All My Life: A South African Autobiography. New York: Routledge, 1991. 142. She was Secretary of one of South Africa's biggest trade unions when she was arrested without charge and detained incommunicado six months mostly in solitary. The damage not only to her body but to her mind is described.

2182. Mbeki, Govan. South Africa: The Peasant's Revolt. Preface by Ruth First. Harmondsworth: Penguin, 1964. 159. Mbeki, sentenced to life imprisonment for his political activities, describes the government of South Africa's campaign to divide Black South Africans on tribal grounds, and in chapter nine the resistance and repression of the peasants.

2183. Meer, Fatima. Higher Than Hope: the Authorized Biography of Nelson Mandela. New York: Harper Perennial, 1990. 426. (Reprint of 1988 ed.). (Higher Than Hope: Rolihlahla We Love You. Johannesburg: Skotaville, 1988. 328.). The life of one of the best known political prisoners of the time is told through letters and reminiscences from Mandela and his family. Mandela is depicted sympathetically as an ordinary man who sacrificed his personal life and promising career for his cause; it is an interpretation "through Mandela's eyes" (xvi). The biography is 279 pp. and his letters are reprinted pp. 331-412. The account is limited by the strict censorship endured by Mandela in prison, and the full story of Mandela's underground days was pruned to avoid endangering participants. The author herself was banned three times; she was detained without trial for five months with Winnie Mandela; her husband was a fellow-accused with Mandela in the 1956 treason trial.

2184. A Memorandum On Children Under Repression. Johannesburg: Detainee's Parents Support Committee, 1986. 212. From June 12 through November 1986, 8,800 childern under the age of 18 were detained, beaten and tortured irrespective of their involvement in any political organizations. An examination of 500 released detainees revealed that 83% showed evidence of physical abuse, 60% were severely injured.

2185. Middleton, Jean. "Attacks on Democratic Forces: Injustice and the Courts." Sechaba (April 1987) 26-28. Describes the massive violence by the State: 21 people awaiting execution, an estimated 25,000 facing "public violence" trials (i.e. for demonstrating and being injured by the police), 5 tried for murder on very slim evidence.

2186. Middleton, Jean. "Murders in Gaol--The Case of Barberton." Sechaba (January 1984) 22-29. Report on the violent killings and work-related deaths of political prisoners in the maximum security farm prison of Barberton.

2187. Middleton, Jean. "Testimony of Her Imprisonment in Barberton, South Africa in 1968." South Africa: The Imprisoned Society. Ed. Allen Cook. London: International Defence and Aid Fund, 1974; from Anti-Apartheid News (June 1973). 71-72. Describes prison conditions; she was held from 1965 to 1968 for opposing apartheid.

2188. Mitchell, Elvis. "What's Wrong With this Picture?" Rolling Stone (Dec. 3, 1987) 31-2. Criticizes Richard Attenborough's film Cry Freedom for focusing on Donald Woods (played by Kevin Kline) instead of Steve Biko (Denzel Washington).

2189. Moss, Glenn. Political Trials: South Africa, 1976-1979. Johannesburg: Development Studies Group; U of Witwatersrand, 1979. 279. Thirty trials are analyzed.

2190. Moss, Glenn. The Wheels Turn: South African Political Trials, 1976-1979. Geneva: Southern African Information Programme of the International University Exchange Fund, 1979. 77. Documents the injustice of thirty trials mainly of young people and uses the trials to affirm the opposition to apartheid.

2191. Motala, Shireen. Behind Closed Doors: A study of Deaths in Detention in South Africa Between August 1963 and 1984, and of Further Deaths Between June 1984 and September 1985. Braamfontein, Johannesburg: South African Institute of Race Relations, 1987. 126. Examines 63 cases and the general features and conditions of such deaths.

2192. Mufson, S. "Why Free Mbeki?" Nation 245 (December 5, 1987) 670-1. Analyzes motives for releasing ANC leader Govan Mbeki.

2193. Murphy, Jamie. "Mandela Declines Offer of Freedom." Time 125.8 (February 25, 1985) 39. Mandela refuses the government's conditions and makes demands of his own.

2194. Musa, Omari. "Koka Tour Will Defend Prisoners." Militant 42.36 (Sept. 29, 1978) 26. Drake Koka, indicted by the South African government as a co-conspirator in the trial of eleven black student leaders, tours the U.S. for support and to publicize the trial.

2195. Musa, Omari. "South African Rebels Face Trial." Militant 42.34 (Sept. 15, 1978) 3-4. Opponents of apartheid call for massive demonstrations "to show their solidarity" in the support of eleven black South African students scheduled to stand trial.

2196. Naidoo, Indres. Robben Island: Ten Years as a Political Prisoner in South Africa's Most Notorious Penitentiary, as Told to Albie Sachs. New York: Vintage, 1983. 278. On his ten years in prison and the struggle for liberation within the prison.

2197. "NEC Statement on the Release of Political Prisoners." Sechaba 23.11 (Nov. 1989) 2. ANC demands following the release of some of their leaders after 25 years of incarceration.

2198. Nelan, B.W. "Two Voices That Will Not Be Stilled." Time 129 (January 5, 1987) 37. Nelson Mandela, in prison since 1962, and his wife, Winnie, also at times jailed, are leading anti-apartheid voices.

2199. Nelson Mandela. Videocassette. Prod. Jose Pretlow, et al. Dir. Bryan Russo. Princeton, N.J.: Multimedia Entertainment; Films for the Humanities, 1990. 53 min. One-on-one interview with Phil Donahue via satellite from Lusaka, Zambia in February, 1990. Mandela retraces his journey from insurrectionist to statesman, analyzing the psychological and political effects of his long imprisonment.

2200. Nelson Mandela: Free At Last. Videocassette. Prod. Rory O'Conner and Danny Schechter. Woodland Hills, CA: Globalvison; JCI, 1990. 79 min. Contains rare clandestine footage smuggled out of South Africa, insightful interviews with the principal players, plus the uncensored and unedited first speech Mandela gave upon his release from prison.

2201. Nelson Mandela, His Life in the Struggle: A Pictorial History. London: International Defence & Aid Fund for Southern Africa, 1988. 18. Publication in honor of his seventieth birthday and twenty-fifth year in prison.

2202. Nelson Mandela: The Long Walk to Freedom. Videocassette. Prod. Chris Sheridan. Falls Church, VA: Landmark Films, 1990. 28 min. Covers both the events in South Africa before and during Mandela's incarceration, and also those leading to his release.

2203. Nelson Mandela: The Man and His Country. Videocassette. Nar. Morton Dean. New York: ABC News; MPI Home Video, 1990. 50 min. Chronicles the life of Nelson Mandela against the backdrop of South African politics.

2204. "Nelson Mandela, We Salute You!" Sechaba (July 1983) 1-2. Update on Mandela in his 21st year of imprisonment, specifically his transfer to Pollsmoor prison.

2205. "New Hunger Strikes Possible." Africa News 31.5 (March 6, 1989) 8. Widespread hunger strikes challenge detention without trial.

2206. Newman, Anne. "Alberta Sisulu: A Small Step Toward Freedom." Ms 14 (April 1986) 19. Sisulu was acquited of treason when a key witness testified unexpectedly on her behalf. Sisulu was held for a year before trial.

2207. No Neutral Ground: South Africa's Confrontation with the Activist Churches, an African Watch Report. New York: Human Rights Watch, 1989. 145. On the government's and right-wing groups' war on religious opponents of apartheid.

2208. Nordland, Rod. "Out of Jail and on His Feet." Newsweek 110 (November 16, 1987) 81. Govan Mbeki, ANC leader, released after almost 25 years in prison.

2209. North, James. "Blacks and Whites Together." New Republic 187 (November 1, 1982) 14-16. Black and white cooperation and imprisonment in resistance to apartheid.

2210. "Notes and Comment." New Yorker 62 (Sept. 8, 1986) 27-8. An interview with evasive Louis Le Grange, South Africa's Law and Order Minister, about whether the detainees under the state emergency, ruled unconstitutional by the Supreme Court, would be released.

2211. One Union's Fight Against Apartheid: The Story of the Free Dave Kitson Campaign. Richmond: AUEW-TASS, 1980. 28. Kitson was sentenced in 1963 to twenty years for membership in the African National Congress's militant wing, Umkonto we Sizwe (Spear of the People).

2212. Orr, Wendy. First Applicant's Founding Affidavit: In the Supreme Court of South Africa (South Eastern Cape Local Division) in the Matter Between Wendy Orr & Others and the Minister of Law and Order and Others. s.l.: s.n., 1985. 41.

2213. Otfinoski, Steven. Nelson Mandela: the Fight Against Apartheid. Brookfield, Conn.: Millbrook, 1992. 128. A biography set in the context of S. African history, written for young adults.

2214. "Out of Prison But Not Yet Free." Sechaba (June 1984) 27. Reports on the release from prison of Herman Toivo Ja Toivo, Billy Nair, Curnick Ndlouv, and David Kitson.

2215. Over Two Thousand Mayors From Fifty-Six Countries Call For the Release of Nelson Mandela and Other South African Political Prisoners. Ed. International Solidarity with Political Prisoners in South Africa. New York: United Nations Centre against Apartheid, 1982. 31. Note on Mandela, text of the Declaration, and list of signatures.

2216. Pheto, Molefe. And Night Fell: Memoirs of a Political Prisoner in South Africa. London; Portsmouth, N.H.: Heinemann, 1985. 218. The author, director of Music, Drama, Art and Literature Institute was arrested as an alleged communist in 1975 and spent 281 days in jail, 271 in solitary confinement, awaiting trial.

2217. Poggi, Stephanie. "South Africa Releases Simon Nkoli On Bail." Gay Community News 15.5 (August 9, 1987) 1. Black gay anti-apartheid activist Simon Nkoli and nine co-defendants were freed on bail after three years in jail awaiting trial on capital charges.

2218. Pogrund, Benjamin. How Can Man Die Better: Sobukwe and Apartheid. London: Halban, 1989. 403. On Robert Mangaliso Sobukwe's and the Pan-Africanist Congress's campaign against the pass laws.

2219. Pogrund, Benjamin. Nelson Mandela : Strength and Spirit of a Free South Africa. Milwaukee: Stevens Children's Books, 1991. 68. Life and career for juveniles.

2220. Political Imprisonment in South Africa. Johannesburg: Human Rights Commission and IDAF Publications, 1991. 67.

2221. Political Imprisonment in South Africa: An Amnesty International Report. London: Amnesty International, 1978. 105. Includes a history, an appraisal of the legal situation, trials, bannings, number and type of prisoners, treatment (including torture), and profiles of selected prisoners.

2222. Political Imprisonment in South Africa: An Amnesty International Report. London; New York: Amnesty International, 1979. 108. Comprehensive analysis of political background, legal system, kind of prisoners, statistics, profiles of 7 prisoners, and treatment of prisoners.

2223. Political Imprisonment in South Africa : An Update to an Amnesty International Report. London: New York: Amnesty International, 1979. 34. Events and conditions since 1978.

2224. Political Prisoners and Banned Persons in Apartheid South Africa. New York: United Nations, Center Against Apartheid, 1978. 56.

2225. "Political Prisoners: Numbers Rising." Southern Africa 12.6 (July 1979) 17. Notes the continuous growth and abuses of political trials and convictions.

2226. "Pretoria Reneges On Promise, Detainees Fast Again.". Guardian 41.26 (March 29, 1989) 15. The hunger strike protests failure to release all the 800 prisoners promised and the harshness of prison conditions.

2227. "Prison Remembered." Sechaba 23.10 (Oct. 1989) 26-28. A former political prisoner describes her time in prison (1985-89) and the conditions for women political prisoners.

2228. Prisoner 885\63. Island in Chains: Ten Years on Robben Island. Harmondsworth: Penguin, 1982. 278. The struggle for freedom continued in Robben Island Prison.

2229. Prisoners of Apartheid. London: Christian Action Publications, 1965. 41. The large numbers imprisoned, the severe sentences, the brutal conditions in the prisons, which are not inspected by any independent commission, etc.

2230. Prisoners of Apartheid: A Biographical List of Political Prisoners and Banned Persons in South Africa. London: International Defence and Aid Fund for Southern Africa, 1978. 180. An incomplete list of 415 prisoners.

2231. "Prisoners Prepare for Freedom." Africa News 33.8 (May 28, 1990) 10. On the 300+ political prisoners waiting to be freed as a result of negotiations between F.W. de Clerk and Nelson Mandela.

2232. Program of Action for Banned People in South Africa 1985-86: South Africa, Banning and Banishment. London: Amnesty International, International Secretariat, 1985. Discusses individual cases: Abel Dube, Johnny Issel, et al.

2233. Rabkin, David. "Newly Released Political Prisoner Speaks." Sechaba (February 1984) 19. A speech given to an ANC members' meeting by Rabkin, recently released from Pretoria Security Prison after serving seven years.

2234. Randall, M. "Ruth First's Potent Words From Prison." Guardian 42.6 (November 29, 1989) 7. Discusses First's prison diary. She and her husband Joe Slovo, both white, were central members of South Africa's liberation struggle.

2235. Rayner, Mary. Turning a Blind Eye: Medical Accountability and the Prevention of Torture in South Africa. Washington, DC: American Association for the Advancement of Science (AAAS), Committee on Scientific Freedom and Responsibility, 1987. 96. On the role played by health professionals in torture in South Africa, including the professional misconduct in the death of Steve Biko.

2236. "Resistance and Repression." Southern Africa 11.7 (October 1978) 18. A general survey of arrests, trials, imprisonments, bannings, and the struggle for freedom.

2237. "Resistance and Repression." Southern Africa 12.5 (June 1979) 8. Eleven Soweto students were sentenced to prison for sedition during the Soweto uprising, one for 11 years, even though none had been armed.

2238. Riveles, Susanne. "Diplomatic Asylum as a Human Right: The Case of the Durban Six." Human Rights Quarterly 11 (1989) 139-159. Seven leading opposition party members were detained in prison but gained release by appeal to the Supreme Court. About to be re-arrested, 5 of them and another person took refuge in the British Consulate. Forced out of the Consulate, 5 were charged with high treason.

2239. Robben Island: Our University. Videocassette. Prod. and Dir. Lindy Wilson. 1988. 53 min. Kwedi Mkalipi and Neville Alexander meet to share their experiences after serving prison terms in Robben Island, the maximum security prison in South Africa.

2240. Robinson, Randall. "A Tale of Two Tragedies." Essence 15 (Oct 1984) 160. Nelson Mandela has been in prison 20 years yet few people in the U.S. know about him. Also indicts Reagan administration support of the regime.

2241. Russell, Diane E.H. Lives of Courage: Women for a New South Africa. New York: Basic, 1989. 375. Part 1, "Women in South African Prisons," details the brutality faced by incarcerated black South African women: detention without trial, solitary confinement, severe physical and psychological torture, sexual harrasment, rape, etc.

2242. Sachs, Albie. The Jail Diary of Albie Sachs. London: Grafton, 1990. 288. (Orig. pub. London: Harvill, 1966). An account of his first imprisonment for taking part in the Passive Resistance Campaign.

2243. Sampson, Anthony. "18 Days: A South African Journal." New York Times Magazine (March 18, 1990) 38-40+. Sampson's journal focuses on the recent changes in South Africa: official recognition of the ANC, the release of Nelson Mandela, etc.

2244. Sampson, Anthony. "The Invisible Leader." Newsweek 106 (September 9, 1985) 32. On the extraordinary influence of a man imprisoned twenty years--Nelson Mandela.

2245. Sansevere-Dreher, Diane. Changing Our World: Stephen Biko. New York: Bantam Skylark, 1991. 102. Biography for young readers.

2246. Save Robert McBride: No Apartheid Executions. London: SATIS, 1988. 23.

2247. Seminar on the Legal Aspects of Apartheid, July 6-7, 1985. Washington, D.C.: Lawyers' Committee for Civil Rights Under Law, 1985. Papers presented at the Seminar.

2248. The Sharpeville Six. Ed. The United Nations Centre Against Apartheid. New York: United Nations, 1988. 5.

2249. Sikakane, Joyce. A Window on Soweto. London: International Defence and Aid Fund, 1977. 80. A black journalist describes her imprisonment for membership in the African National Congress and various conspiracies under the Terrorism Act.

2250. Sisulu, Zwelake. "The View from Soweto." Africa News 25.3 (August 12, 1985) 4-6. Describes the mass arrests following the state of emergency.

2251. Slovo, Gillian. Ties of Blood. London: Michael Joseph, 1989. 568. This novel includes accounts of a trial for sabotage and prison life among its pictures of apartheid.

2252. Slovo, Shawn. A World Apart. London: Faber & Faber, 1988. 113. Screenplay of the movie which depicts middle-class whites involved in the struggle against apartheid, based on the lives of Joe Slovo, the only white member of the National Executive of the African National Congress, who was forced into exile, and his wife Ruth First, who was detained 117 days in solitary confinement--the first white woman to be detained under the Ninety-Day Detention Act--and later assassinated by a parcel bomb.

2253. Smith, W.E. "Apartheid with a Smiling Face." Time 127.6 (February 10, 1986) 60. President Botha offers to release Mandela if Angola will release a South African officer captured in a commando raid and if the Soviet Union will release two Soviet dissidents.

2254. Smith, W.E. "His Eloquent Silence Speaks to the Future." Time 127.1 (January 6, 1986) 68. On the confrontation between Mandela and the government.

2255. "Solomon Mahlangu Executed." Southern Africa 12.4 (May 1979) 1. ANC activist was hanged for being present when two white men were shot and killed.

2256. Somers, Sheila. "Michael Lapsley Tour: Still Prisoners." Briarpatch 19.4 (May 1990) 32-33. Lapsley, exiled member and Anglican chaplain for the ANC, toured Canada to increase awareness of the continued struggle.

2257. South Africa: A Compilation of Five Documents. New York: Amnesty International, 1991. 22. Human rights violations and the security forces--killings, whippings, etc.

2258. South Africa: Amnesty International Briefing. New York: Amnesty International, 1986. 17. Human rights violations have escalated in the wake of black protest against apartheid--detention without trial, banning, torture.

2259. South Africa: Briefing. New York: Amensty International, 1986. Prisoners of conscience, detention without trial, banning and banishment, torture and ill-treatment, abduction and murder of government political opponents, deaths in detention and the death penalty.

2260. South Africa Dept. of Information. Amnesty for Terrorism. N'Dabeni: Simondium Publishers on Behalf of the Department of Information, 1978. 76. The government's reply to an AI brochure entitled "Political Imprisonment in South Africa."

2261. "South Africa: Detention, Banning, Fatima Meer." Matchbox (Fall 1976) 3, 13. Includes a list of 33 people known to be detained at the time (out of thousands of others imprisoned), five case studies of house arrest, and a report on Fatima Meer, the first citizen to be charged under the Internal Security Act.

2262. "South Africa: How Many Will Die For How Long?" Matchbox (Winter 1978) 9-12. A review of South African apartheid repression sparked by Steve Biko's death in security police custody, "a system built upon detention without trial, maltreatment of convicted political prisoners, banning and banishment, widespread and systematic torture and frequent judicial and extra-judicial killing."

2263. South Africa : Imprisonment and Ill-treatment of Children and Young People. New York: Amnesty International, 1986. 14. Since the July 1985 state of emergency, more than 2,000 children under 16 have been detained without trial, some for long periods, and some were assaulted upon arrest and tortured during detention. More than 1,000 have been killed since late 1984.

2264. South Africa : Prisoners of Conscience Detained Under the State of Emergency. New York: Amnesty International, 1987. 14. "Since the imposition of a nationwide state of emergency on 12 June 1986, as many as 30,000 people are estimated to have been detained without charge or trial in South Africa." Many of these people have been tortured, including children.

2265. South Africa: State of Fear: Security Force Complicity in Torture and Political Killings 1990-1991. New York: Amnesty International, 1992. 100. Documents the continuing involvement of the security forces in torture and killings.

2266. "South Africa Tightens Press Restrictions." Black Panther 16.17 (March 5, 1977) 19, 24. Seventeen reporters have been detained recently. The entire detention system is off-limits to the press.

2267. South African Communists Speak: Documents from the History of the South African Communist Party 1915-1980. London: Inkululeko, 1981. 469. A collection of documents commemorating the 60th aniversary of the South African Communist Party (July 30, 1921) and its struggle against apartheid. Document 87 deals with the sedition of 1946-48; Document 98 protests bannings under the Suppression of Communism Act; Document 117 is a statement on the Rivonia arrests; etc.

2268. "South African Lutheran Pastor Tortured for Antiracist Views." Christianity Today 27 (Mar. 18, 1983) 34. Dean T. Simon Farisani, a black Lutheran pastor, suffered brutal torture by South African police because of unsubstantiated charges linking him to a bombing incident.

2269. "South African Symbol of Soul Power." U.S. News and World Report 100 (January 13, 1986) 8. A sketch of Winnie Mandela's life of political resistance and imprisonment.

2270. "Soweto Student Speaks Out: Interview with Nkosazana Dlamini, Vice President of SASO." Southern Africa 10.2 (March 1977) 5-7. Dlamini is a member of the ANC underground inside South Africa and the only SASO executive not in detention (South African Student Organization).

2271. Sparks, Allister. "Death in Dark Places." Macleans 95 (AUG 23, 1982) 27. Louis le Grange was the 52nd political prisoner to die in the government's custody in two decades.

2272. Stefoff, Rebecca. Nelson Mandela: a Voice Set Free. New York: Ballatine, 1990. 135. A biography for young adults.

2273. SWAPO Information on Namibian Political Prisoners. Lusaka, Zambia: SWAPO, Department of Information and Publicity, 1978. 42. South Africa's illegal occupation of Namibia resulted in numerous Namibian prisoners, especially through the Sabotage and Terrorism Acts, both of which cover an extraordinarily wide range of behavior and carry the death penalty.

2274. Tames, Richard. Nelson Mandela. Franklin Watts, 1991. 32. The life and accomplishments of Mandela to his release from prison; for young readers.

2275. Taylor, Susan L. and Elsie Washington. "Word From South Africa." Essence 20 (July 1989) 42-44+. Interview of Zenani Mandela Dlamini, daughter of Nelson and Winnie.

2276. Torture in South Africa? Cape Town: Christian Institute of Southern Africa, 1977. 56. Protests arrest without warrant, detention without trial, incommunicado detention, and torture, all common police practices. Many case studies.

2277. Torture of Detainees in South Africa. Washington, D.C.: Lawyers' Committee for Civil rights Under Law, 1985. 30. Abuse and torture are "systematic,' and at least 7,509 people have been detained since the beginning of this year (1985).

2278. "The Torture of Stephen Dlamini." Sechaba 11.3 (Summer 1977) 16-19. Sworn statement of the SACTU leader and Robben Island veteran who was again detained and brutally tortured for six-and-a-half months for having been visited by a trade unionist.

2279. Transit Camps in South Africa: Reports Submitted to the Special Committee on the Policies of Apartheid of the Government of the Republic of South Africa. New York: Unit on Aparthied, Department of Political and Security Council Affairs, United Nations, 1968. 22. Transit camps are impoverished rural areas to which released prisoners from urban areas are exiled. One, "Welcome Valley," is described.

2280. United Nations. Office of Public Information. Apartheid and the Treatment of Prisoners in South Africa; Statements and Affidavits. New York: United Nations, 1967. 112. Evidence of "continuing torture and ill-treatment" of prisoners.

2281. United States. Congress. House. Committee on Foreign Affairs. Calls for the Immediate Release of Detained Children Under Emergency Regulations in South Africa: Hearing and Markup Before the Subcommittee on Africa of the Committee on Foreign Affairs, House of Representatives, One Hundredth Congress, First Session on House Resolution 141 and House Resolution 214, July 29, 1987. Washington D.C.: U.S. G.P.O., 1988. 90. Denunciations of detentions without charge or trial, often with brutal treatment. An estimated 10,000 children have suffered detention.

2282. "U.S. Regrets South African Arrests and Trials." United States Department of State Bulletin 85 (June 1985) 39. Arrests for treason of "a significant number of opposition leaders."

2283. "The Use of Banning in South Africa." Matchbox (May 1980) 12. A person "banned" is neither charged nor tried before a court, nor can that person question the order, sometimes even prohibited from leaving their own home.

2284. van Es, Adrian and Marijke van Grup. Health Professionals and Human Rights in South Africa. Leiden, Netherlands: Dutch Foundation for Health and Human Rights, 1987. 86. "The report deals with: 1) the effects of apartheid regulations and the new constitution on health, including violations of medical ethics; 2) the rapidly increasing number of detainees, frequently exposed to mental and physical torture and abuse; and 3) the limitations and violations of professional integrity.

2285. "Victims of Torture Speak." Southern Africa 11.4 (May 1978) 21-22. Provides an account of the use of torture by authorities throughout South Africa, including several case studies.

2286. "We Will Punish Criminals." Sechaba 12.2 (Summer 1978) 1. Denounces the deaths of ANC members in prison and by execution. Calls for protests against the upcoming execution of Solomon Mahlangu.

2287. Whipple, Christopher. "Mother of Revolt." Life 9 (Aug. 1986) 30-32. On the great prestige of Winnie Mandela, wife of imprisoned ANC leader Nelson Mandela.

2288. "White Detainee Dies." Christian Century 99 (March 3, 1982) 232-3. A white physician employed by a Black union died in security police custody, allegedly by suicide. He is the first White to die under such circumstances (more than 40 Blacks have in their custody--Steve Biko, et al.)

2289. Woods, Donald. Biko. 3rd rev. ed. New York, London: Paddington, 1991. 288. (Orig. pub. Paddington, 1978). A biography of Steve Biko, who was South Africa's leading Black Consciousness spokesman, including an account of the torture and killing of Biko by the Security Police in 1977.

2290. Woods, Donald. Filming with Attenborough: the Making of "Cry Freedom." New York: Holt, 1987. 163. About the friendship between Woods and Steve Biko, who was murdered by the police while in custody. Woods' protests resulted in detention, which caused him to leave South Africa.

2291. "Yes, Again." Time 112 (July 24, 1978) 40. Another black prisoner dies mysteriously in the Port Elizabeth police building where Stephen Biko died.

2292. "Zwelakhe Sisulu: A Year Behind Bars." Guardian 40.15 (January 13, 1988) 12. Walter Sisulu's son and internationally praised journalist remains in prison without charge or trial.

SPAIN

2293. Alvarez de Toledo y Maura, Isabel, Duchess of Medina Sidonia. "Eight Months in Franco's Jail." Nation 210 (April 6, 1970) 396-99. A selection from her book on her experience.

2294. Alvarez do Toledo y Maura, Isabel, Duchess of Medina Sidonia. My Prison. Trans. Herma Briffault. New York: Harper & Row, 1972. 169. The author's account of her imprisonment in 1969 in the women's prison at Alcalá for publicly demonstrating in support of peasants in Palomares who sought redress for environmental damage done to their village by the crash of a U.S. B-52 bomber in 1966.

2295. Amnesty International Report 1980. London: Amnesty International, 1980. 296-99. Anti-terrorist legislation has been used to limit rights, incommunicado detention is common, ill-treatment and torture have occurred during detention, and political prosecutions have increased.

2296. Amnesty International Report 1990. New York: Amnesty International, 1990. 216-218. Scores of opponents were arrested, and some were tortured in 1989.

2297. "Appeal from Spanish Political Prisoners." Militant 39.13 (April 11, 1975) 22. A call for international solidarity for political prisoners suffering "physical and mental destruction" at the hands of "the regime born under the protection of Hitler and Mussolini."

2298. "Basque Nationalists' Death Sentence Sparks Protests." Militant 39.34 (September 19, 1975) 20. The Franco regime's military court sentenced two Basques to death for killing a policeman, partly based upon a dubious confession.

2299. Blunk, Tim. "Spanish Prisoners in Eighth Month of Strike." Guardian 42.37 (July 18, 1990) 18. Thirty-nine prisoners continue a hunger strike for better conditions. One died.

2300. Bredero, Bart. Detour to Freedom. Willemstad: Self-pub., 1989. 166. The Dutch author was detained a few months as an escapee from the Nazis, but was released and made his way to Gibraltar.

2301. "Carrillo: In from the Cold." Time 109 (January 10, 1977) 20+. Arrest and release of Santiago Carrillo, exiled head of outlawed Spanish Communist Party.

2302. Clark, Steve. "Spanish Workers, Students Demand Rights." Militant 39.47 (December 19, 1975) 18. The new government of King Juan Carlos continues the ban on trade unions and opposition political parties, and is rearresting opponents freed under a limited amnesty.

2303. Davidon, Ann Morrissett. "International War Resisters." Progressive 40 (October 1976) 8-9. A group of seven young men organized a war resistance group dedicated to civil service as opposed to military conscription and were subsequently seized in the middle of the night and locked away in a prison.

2304. Dear, Ruth. "The Lot of Radical Women in Spain." WIN 11.6 (February 20, 1975) 20. On the arrest of leading intellectuals charged with terrorism after the bombing of a cafe.

2305. "Dismantling the Dictatorship." Time 108 (August 16, 1976) 28. As a step toward a democratic Spain, King Carlos granted amnesty to political prisoners.

2306. Escobal, Patricio (Pedro). Death Row: Spain 1936. Trans. Tanade de Gámez. Indianapolis: Bobbs-Merrill, 1968. 277. The prison memoirs of one of thousands of political prisoners taken by the fascist rebels at the outbreak of the Spanish Civil War in 1936. He was released in 1940 and left Spain.

2307. Forest, Eva (Genoveva). From a Spanish Prison. Trans. Rosemary Sheed. New York: Moon Books/Random House, 1976. 191. Journal and letters 1974-75; she was imprisoned on charges of terrorist activity against Franco's government.

2308. Franco's Prisoners Speak. London: Spanish Ex-Servicemen's Association, 1960. 35. Protest letters and names and sentences of prisoners in Burgos Central Prison.

2309. From Burgos Jail : Poems and Drawings. London: Appeal for Amnesty in Spain, 1964. 30. The poems of two prisoners and the art of a third.

2310. Garcia, Miguel. Franco's Prisoner. London: Hart-Davis, 1972. 171. Imprisoned for twenty years for fighting against Franco, 1939-1941, 1952-1968. This memoir recounts his opposition outside and inside prison from 1937 to 1972.

2311. Garcia, Miguel. Looking Back after 20 Years in Jail. S.l: s.n., 1970. 12. One of Franco's prisoners describes some of his experiences.

2312. Ibarruri, Dolores. They Shall Not Pass: The Autobiography of La Pasionaria. Tr. 1962 Spanish Edition. New York: International, 1966. 351. A Communist, she was imprisoned from 1931 to 1933 for helping a fugitive.

2313. Koestler, Arthur. Dialogue With Death. London: Macmillan, 1983. 206. (Orig. pub. London: Hutchinson, 1966). An account of his prison experiences under Franco's regime beginning in 1937. It is "possibly the wisest in the literature of political captivity" (Laffin p.16.)

2314. Koestler, Arthur. Spanish Testament. London: Victor Gollancz, 1937. 384. Koestler was arrested by the Falangists at the defeat of the Republican city of Malaga. Part II gives an account of his experiences in the prisons of Malaga and Seville under sentence of death.

2315. Lombardo, Joe. "S.F. March Condemns Spanish Executions." Militant 39.41 (November 7, 1975) 27. A protest march against the recent execution of five political prisoners and the arrest of hundreds more.

2316. Mackay, Ruth. "The Death of Jose Arregui." Progressive 45 (July 1981) 18. Arregui, a suspected member of ETA, the Basque separatist organization, was arrested without charge and tortured to death.

2317. Meisler, Stanley. "How Democratic is Spain? A Mime Troupe Tests the Regime." Nation 226 (June 17, 1978) 724-7. Four imprisoned actors known as Els Joglars have been imprisoned for insulting the army by their play La Torna about the execution of two men during the Franco era.

2318. "Our Friend Franco." Nation 219 (December 14, 1974) 613. On the torture of Genoveva Forest.

2319. Political Imprisonment in Spain. London: Amnesty International, 1973. 35. Legal issues, prison conditions, case histories, list of prisons, etc. "Spanish prisoners are continually deprived of their basic human rights."

2320. Report of an Amnesty International Mission to Spain, 3-28 October 1979. London: Amnesty International, 1980. 64. Medical reports of abuse of 14 prisoners.

2321. Rosenthal, David. "Spanish Prisoner: An Interview." Nation 221 (September 20, 1975) 233-5. Eliseo Bayo, journalist, imprisoned and beaten on false charges, is released.

2322. Sanchez-Mazas, Miguel. Spain in Chains : A Report on Political Repressions in Franco Spain. New York: Veterans of the Abraham Lincoln Brigade, 1987. 32. Addressed to President Eisenhower.

2323. Shelton, Sharon. "Woman Brutalized in Franco Dungeons." Workers World 17.16 (April 18, 1975) 10. Maria Luz Fernandez Alvarez and other women have been tortured.

2324. "Spain in Prison." Nation 152 (February 15, 1941) 181-3. Describes typical prison life for the "two to three million" people in Spanish prisons, most of them victims of the Franco tyranny.

2325. Spain, the Question of Torture: Documents Exchanged by Amnesty International and the Government of Spain. London: Amnesty International, 1985. 60. Incommunicado detention and torture continued in Spain throughout 1983, and constitutional safeguards helped little.

2326. "Spain's 'Amnesty.'" Peace News 20.41 (April 8, 1977) 6. Statement from Basque prisoners in Puerto de Santa Maria Prison protesting inhumane conditions and treatment.

2327. Spanish Committee for the Relief of the Political Prisoners in Spain. Report on the Variations of the Human Rights In Spain: Documents From the Jails. Mexico: The Spanish Committee for the Relief of the Political Prisoners in Spain, 1963. 22.

SRI LANKA

2328. Amnesty International Report 1980. London: Amnesty International, 1980. 231-235. The Tamil separatist rebellion has produced repressive laws, wide police powers of arrest and detention, suspension of legal safeguards, and reports of torture and deaths while in custody.

2329. Amnesty International Report 1990. New York: Amnesty International, 1990. 218-221. Thousands disappeared, died in custody or were victims of extrajudicial executions carried out by security forces and their death squads. The fate of 800 people who disappeared in previous years was still not clarified. Thousands more were detained without trial, and allegations of torture were widespread.

2330. Hyde, Douglas Arnold. Punarutthapanaya. Rehabilitation; A Critical Evaluation of the Rehabilitation Effort of the Government of Sri Lanka. Sri Lanka: Dept. of Rehabilitation, Sri Lanka, 1972. 15.

2331. Report of an Amnesty International Mission to Sri Lanka, 9-15 January 1975. 2d ed. London: Amnesty International, 1976. 50. Some 18,000 people were arrested following the 1971 insurrection, and judicial standards were degraded especially regarding political prisoners.

2332. Rupesinghe, Kumar and Marit Haug. The Negotiations Process in Sri Lanka 1983-1986: A Select Annotated Bibliography. Olso, Norway: International Peace Research Institute, 1987. 103. Government negotiations to resolve Tamil conflict include human rights, terrorism, self-determination, refugees and genocide.

2333. Sri Lanka: Allegations of Extrajudicial Killings by Army Personnel: Details of Some Cases Reported During December 1984 and January 1985. New York: Amnesty International, 1985. 13. Two clergymen in one incident, twenty-seven (and five missing) in another.

2334. Sri Lanka "Disappearances." New York: Amnesty International, 1986. 35. Analyzes the mechanisms and process of disappearances--denial, disclaiming responsibility, torture, murder, etc. A list of 272 people who disappeared between June 1983 and April 1986. Also a special report on extrajudicial killings 1985-1986.

2335. Sri Lanka\The North East: Human Rights Violations in a Context of Armed Conflict. New York: Amnesty International, 1991. 44. Evidence of large scale extrajudicial executions in the North East Region, and human rights violations by the Liberations Tigers of Tamil Eelam and government security forces.

2336. Sri Lanka: Recent Reports of "Disappearances" and Torture. New York: Amnesty International, 1987. 63. Case data followed by list of 216 additional disappearances.

2337. Sri Lanka: Reports of Extrajudicial Executions. New York: Amnesty International, National Office, 1989. 19.

SUDAN

2338. Amnesty International Report 1980. London: Amnesty International, 1980. 79-81. Opposition political parties were banned in 1979 and several hundred people detained without charge or trial, particularly members of the Sudan Communist Party.

2339/40. Amnesty International Report 1990. New York: Amnesty International, 1990. 221-225. Hundreds were detained without charge following a coup in June 1989, hundreds were murdered, many disappeared, and dozens were tortured. Numerous harsh laws were instituted--e.g. organizing a strike became punishable by death.

2341. Breen, Frank. "Persecution in Sudan." Maryknoll 86.5 (May 1992) 51-53. The Muslim fundamentalist government is waging war against Catholics.

2342. The Copts: Passive Survivors Under Threat. New York: Human Rights Watch, 1993. 9. The Sudanese Copts, a prominent minority, are being driven out of their country by the current Islamic fundamentalist government.

2343. McLaughlin, Janice. "Reign of Terror in Juba." Maryknoll (December 1992) 20-23. A report on the expulsion of all foreign missioners as "Sudan government troops detain, torture and kill innocent civilians."

2344. Sudan: A Continuing Human Rights Crisis. New York: Amnesty International, 1992. 18. The use of torture continues to be routine, while the previous policy of detaining opponents in prisons has been partially replaced by the use of short-term incommunicado detention.

2345. "Sudan: A Human Rights Tragedy in the Making." Amnesty Action (Winter 1993) 5. Hundreds of people are being killed, arrested, tortured, and disappeared in Juba.

2346. "Sudan: Journalists Arrested." Index on Censorship (March 1990) 25. Two journalists were arrested in Khartoum in December 1989 without charge.

SURINAME

2347. Suriname: Violations of Human Rights. New York: Amnesty International, 1987. 17. Accounts of indiscriminate killings of unarmed civilians and other human rights violations from Surinamese refugees and other sources.

SWAZILAND

2348. Amnesty International Report 1980. London: Amnesty International, 1980. 81-82. Several opposition party leaders have been detained since 1978.

2349. Amnesty International Report 1990. New York: Amnesty International, 1990. 235-6. A few people were held under administrative detention without charge or trial.

SWEDEN

2350. Amnesty International Report 1990. New York: Amnesty International, 1990. 226. Nine Kurdish refugees suspected of being terrorists had some restrictions on movement.

SWITZERLAND

2351. Amnesty International Report 1990. New York: Amnesty International, 1990. 226-227. Several hundred people were sentenced to prison for refusing military service, most of them of religious, ethical, and political groups; they were not allowed alternative civilian service.

SYRIA

2352. Amnesty International Report 1980. London: Amnesty International, 1980. 352-355. Long-term detention without trial, abductions, torture to extract confessions, and death for some political crimes are some of the abuses by the government of President Hafez-al-Assad. Numerous arrests in northern Syria involved torture and summary executions. Eighteen members of the former government remain in prison since 1970.

2353. Amnesty International Report 1990. New York: Amnesty International, 1990. 227-230. Thousands continued in prison under 1963 state of emergency laws, the majority without charge or trial, and some very long-term. Torture was reported "widespread and routine."

2354. Dowd, Siobhan. "A Writer Detained: Khalil Burayez." Center: The Magazine of PEN Center USA West (Winter 1993) 7, 20. "One of the longest-held prisoners in Syria--and also the longest-serving writer in prison known to PEN--is Khalil Mustafa Burayez." He was sentence to death, then to life, then to fifteen years, but has never been released. He opposed the Ba'ath party.

2355. The Genocide from Hama to Lebanon. West Covina, CA: The Committee for the Defence of Freedoms and Political Prisoners in Syria, 1981. On the massacres perpetrated in Hama in 1980-1981 and related repression.

2356. Syria: An Amnesty International Briefing. London: Amnesty International, 1979. 16. Summarizes available information on detention without trial, abduction, torture, and deaths.

2357. "Syria: Appeal for Political Prisoners." Militant 42.41 (November 3, 1978) 25. Calls for an end to torture, for the freedom of some 1,000 political prisoners, and to stop the dozens of arrests that occur daily.

2358. Syria: Indefinite Political Imprisonment. New York: Amnesty International, 1992. 48. When President Hafez al-Assad unexpectedly released some 2,000 prisoners recently, hopes were raised of a new Syria in which human rights would be respected. But arrests of political suspects have continued, and some prisoners of conscience remain in jail--some after more than two decades. Nothing has been done to change the laws and practices which allow forgrave violations of human rights.

2359. Syria: Torture By the Security Forces. New York: Amnesty International, 1987. 44. Torture is "a regular experience for thousands of political prisoners in Syria."

2360. Syria Unmasked: The Suppression of Human Rights by the Asad Regime. New Haven: Yale UP/Human Rights Watch, 1991. 215. Describes the legal system, security services, prisons, torture, censorship, etc.

2361. "Syrians in Prison." Index On Censorship 19.2 (Feb. 1990) 21. Four Syrian journalists have been arrested for membership in prohibited political organizations and detained without charge or trial."

TAIWAN

2362. Amnesty International Report 1980. London: Amnesty International, 1980. 235-38. Problems include the continued detention of political opponents on charges of sedition, trials by military courts, and torture during interrogation.

2363. Amnesty International Report 1990. New York: Amnesty International, 1990. 230-231. Several prisoners remained incarcerated, a few released, a few added. Political parties allowed for the first time in 40 years.

2364. Clark, Ramsey. "The Government Stands Accused." Nation 230 (March 22, 1980) 327-8. Condemns the trial of the "Kaohsiung Seven," former employees of Formosa magazine, on charges arising out of a demonstration against the ruling Kuomintang Party.

2365. Knippers, Jan, et al. "Sentenced For Feminism: 12 Years to Life." Ms 10 (December 1981) 27. More than 200 people were arrested at a human rights rally; eight were convicted and face 12 years to life.

2366. Leary, Mary E. "The Formosa Affair." Nation 230 (March 22, 1980) 328-30. On the intensifying campaign by the government to stifle speech.

2367. Satomi, K. "The Awakening." Connexions 14 (Fall 1984) 10-11. Feminist Lii Hsiu-lien was imprisoned in 1979 and sentenced to 12 years in prison in 1980 for making a human rights speech.

2368. Taiwan (Republic of China). London: Amnesty International, 1976. 11. "Violations of human rights have been prevailing practice in Taiwan"--detention of political opponents for "sedition," unfair trials by military tribunals, torture, death penalty.

2369. Taiwan (Republic of China). 2d ed. London: Amnesty International, 1980. 15. Critical of detention of political opponents on charges of sedition, unfair trials, torture, and death penalty.

2370. "Taiwan: The Repression Mounts." Christian Century 97.20 (May 28, 1980) 605. On the arrest of Chun Ming Kao, general secretary of the Presbyterian Church, following the sentencing of others involved in a human rights rally.

TANZANIA

2371. Amnesty International Report 1980. London: Amnesty International, 1980. 82-83. More than half of the over 100 people held under preventive detention were released (perhaps several hundred people were tortured and one died in 1975).

2372. Amnesty International Report 1990. New York: Amnesty International, 1990. 231-3. More than 100 opponents of the government were jailed for varying periods. Some Burundi refugees are detained.

THAILAND

2373. Amnesty International Report 1980. London: Amnesty International, 1980. 239-41. Detention without trial has been a major abuse of power, but Parliament repealed one particularly abusive law. Kampuchean refugees have been forcibly returned.

2374. Amnesty International Report 1990. New York: Amnesty International, 1990. 233-5. Almost 100 people were detained for varying periods of time or were standing trial in 1989 for opposing the government.

2375. Arrowsmith, Pat, ed. To Asia in Peace: The Story of a Non-Violent Action Mission to Indochina. London: Sidgwick & Jackson, 1972. 188. The first draft was written in 1969 while in prison for protesting the Vietnam War. Arrowsmith and Rachel Blake in "Thailand" (127-56) describe being imprisoned at Udon, following an attempted demonstration at the U.S. base there. They were subsequently transferred to the "monkey house" (prison) in Bangkok.

2376. Porter, D. Gareth. "Bloody Wednesday in Bangkok: CIA Responsible for Growth of Fascism in Thailand." CounterSpy 3.2 (December 1976) 49-52. Focuses on the events of October 6, 1976: the massacre and mass arrests of students following the seizure of power by the military junta, and the events leading up to the coup.

2377. Shenon, Philip. "4 Weeks after Protest for Democracy Anguish Grows Over Missing Thais." New York Times International (June 14, 1992) Y3. Possibly 700 people have disappeared after troops attacked a peaceful demonstration in Bangkok demanding democracy.

2378. Ward, Richard. "No Prisoner Amnesty." Guardian 30.11 (December 21, 1977) 12. The Thai government granted amnesty to "several thousand prisoners" but excluded political prisoners. The case of 18 student leaders is discussed.

TIBET (*see* CHINA, PEOPLE'S REPUBLIC OF)

TOGO

2379. "15 Imprisoned Protesters Die in Togo." Arkansas Democrat-Gazette (August 28, 1993) 6A. The government says "friends of the detainees poisoned them to discredit the government."

2380. Amnesty International Report 1980. London: Amnesty International, 1980. 84-86. About 40 people including children were arrested for allegedly participating in a plot to overthrow President Eyadema. A few were convicted in unfair trials. Detention without trial of political opponents is fairly common.

2381. Amnesty International Report 1990. New York: Amnesty International, 1990. 235-6. Three government opponents were held incommunicado throughout 1989, and fifteen others were confined in harsh conditions.

2382. Maja-Pearce, Adewale. "In Trouble in Togo." Index On Censorship 15.9 (October 1986) 4. Many people in prison without trial.

2383. Togo: Political Imprisonment and Torture. London: Amnesty International, 1986. 88. Details on the "substantial" abuses of human rights--long term detention without trial, etc.

TUNISIA

2384. Amnesty International Report 1980. London: Amnesty International, 1980. 355-358. Prisoners of conscience were given unfair trials, torture, and ill-treatment in prison. Trade unionists have been particularly persecuted.

2385. Amnesty International Report 1990. New York: Amnesty International, 1990. 236-8. Amnesties released 90 prisoners in 1989, but perhaps dozens more were arrested.

2386. Bini, Obi. "Tunisia: Prisoners Tortured." Guardian 31.38 (June 27, 1979) 12. Responding to a 1-day general strike in January 1978 the army and police killed over 200 strikers and jailed several hundred more activists who have since been tortured.

2387. "Fourth International: 'Free All Prisoners.'" Militant 42.8 (March 3, 1978) 22. Letter from the United Secretariat of the Fourth International that asks for liberation from the Novira-Bourguiba regime. (See accompaning article.)

2388. "Tunisia Denied Defendants' Legal Rights, Report Says." Arkansas Democrat-Gazette (October 17, 1992) 8A. The trial of 279 Islamic activists was unfair and the accused were tortured.

2389. Tunisia: Human Rights Crisis of 1987. Minneapolis: Minnesota Lawyers International Human Rights Committee, 1988. 70. Surveys political trials, illegal and prolonged detention, torture, and other human rights violations.

2390. Tunisia Imprisonment of Trade Unionists in 1978. London: Amnesty International, 1979. 24. On three trials of over one hundred trade unionists for demonstrating against the government. Some were threatened with capital punishment and many alleged they had been tortured.

2391. Tunisia: Prolonged Incommunicado Detention and Torture. New York: Amnesty International, 1992. 33. Reports of incommunicado detention, unfair trials, torture, and deaths in detention. A focus on abuses against members of the al-Nahda and left-wing political movements.

2392. Tunisia: Trade Unionists Jailed. New York: Amnesty International, 1979. 8. Arrests resulting from the one-day general strike in 1978.

TURKEY

2393. 16 Deaths in Detention in 1992. New York: Human Rights Watch, 1993. 5. Reports on the deaths in police stations and the irregularly high number of those reported as suicides.

2394. Amnesty International Report 1980. London: Amnesty International, 1980. 300-301. Martial law has been used to stifle criticism by closing publications and arresting journalists, writers, and trade unionists, by torture, and by unfair trials.

2395. Amnesty International Report 1990. New York: Amnesty International, 1990. 238-240. Thousands of people were arrested for political reasons during 1989, trials were unfair, "torture continued to be widespread and systematic," sometimes causing death. There were approximately 5,000 political prisoners at the end of 1989.

2396. Balian, Hrair. Turkey: Coninued Violations of International Human Rights and Humanitarian Law. Berkeley, CA: Human Rights Advocates, 1987. 43. Despite a transition to a "parliamentary democracy" torture is still widespread, prison conditions are abominable, and democratic freedoms remain severely curtailed.

2397. Borowiec, Andrew. "The High Price of Stability." Macleans 95 (July 19, 1982) 20-21. Former premier Bülent Ecevit was jaile for "denigrating Turkey abroad, criticizing his country's planned constitution, and spreading false information.

2398. Corbin, Sam. "Torture Chambers and Repression Still Thrive, Despite Reform." Guardian 40.9 (November 25, 1987) 15. Widespread imprisonment for dissent and systematic torture continues unabated. Demonstrations by relatives have been ended by police violence.

2399. Cousins, Jane. Turkey: Torture and Political Persection. London: Pluto, 1973. 106. Covers 1971-1972, the twelve thousand persons detained for political "crimes," the systematic torture of detainees, the unfair trials, the destruction of the Constitution. Many individual cases are described and affidavits of torture are reproduced.

2400. Demir, Mehmet. "Repression Tightens Grip." Guardian 36.44 (September 12, 1984) 15. Since Turgut Ozal was elected prime minister last year, 18 prisoners have died in hunger strikes over brutal prison conditions, 138 have been sentenced to death, and 695 are slated to be tried on capital charges.

2401. Demir, Semra and Mehmet Demir. "Güney: Rebel with a Cause." Guardian 37.1 (Oct. 3, 1984) 19. Film director Yilmaz Güney died. For films on harsh realities in Turkey he was forced into exile. Earlier he had been imprisoned three times--in 1961 for a novel deemed "communist propaganda"--in all ten years in prison.

2402. "Discontent Boils Over in Turkey." Spare Rib 183 (October 1987) 13. Report on the "March of the White Scarves," August 31, 1987, a march of mothers, wives and sisters of political prisoners inspired by the women of Argentina.

2403. Four Deaths in Detention. New York: Human Rights Watch, 1993. 3. An addition to the February 1993 Helsinki Watch report on the 16 deaths in Turkish police stations, covers 4 other deaths.

2404. Furtado, Jean. "Playwrights Protest at Imprisonment." End Journal of European Nuclear Disarmament 16-17 (Summer 1985) 11. Arthur Miller and Harold Pinter visited Istanbul and reported on repression of writers by prison and torture.

2405. Human Rights Abuses in Cyprus. Washington, DC: Commission on Security and Cooperation in Europe, 1985. 152. Transcript of a public hearing on human rights violations in Cyprus: 1,600 missing, desecration and looting of homes and churches, displacement of Greek Cypriots, etc.

2406. Kazan, Elia. "View from a Turkish Prison." New York Times Magazine (February 4, 1979) 33-5+. Account of Kazan's tour of a Turkish prison guided by political prisoner and film director Yilmaz Güney.

2407. Kurds of Turkey: Killings, Disappearances and Torture. New York: Human Rights Watch, 1993. 64. Details the mistreatment of Kurds in Turkey after the Demirel government took office.

2408. Laber, Jeri. "Cruel and Usual Punishment." New York Review of Books 36 (July 20, 1989) 34-5. Torture "is still being used by the Turkish police in nearly every case of arrest," and "hundreds of thousands of political activists have been in prison."

2409. Margaronis, Maria. "The Crackdown Goes On." Nation 238 (April 21, 1984) 480. About 55,000 political prisoners suffer abuse; focuses on the twenty-three imprisoned leaders of the Turkish Peace Association.

2410. Miller, Arthur. "Dinner with the Ambassador." Nation 240 (May 18, 1985) 577+. An account of Miller's and Harold Pinter's trip to Turkey on behalf of the International PEN Club "to demonstrate to the country's writers and artists and to its political prisoners that the outside world cares about what is happening to them," despite the support of the military regime by the U.S.

2411. Turkey. London: Amnesty International, 1977. 12. Criticizes violations of the U.N. Declaration of Human Rights--torture, execution, etc.

2412. Turkey. London: Amnesty International, 1988. 18. "Over a quarter of a million people have been arrested in Turkey since 1980 on political grounds and almost all of them have been tortured." There are "more than 600 prisoners in Turkey" today.

2413. Turkey: Brutal and Systematic Abuse of Human Rights. New York: Amnesty International, 1989. 73. Since the military coup in 1980 "some 250,000 prisoners were detained and almost all of them were tortured." Over 60,000 of these were convicted "after unfair trials."

2414. Turkey: Continuing Violations of Human Rights. New York: Amnesty International U.S.A., 1990. 36. Gross abuses continue; thousands remain imprisoned for political reasons, and torture "continues to be widespread and systematic."

2415. "Turkey: Ozal to Visit UK." End Journal of European Nuclear Disarmament 20 (February/March 1986) 4. The Prime Minister is visiting Britain seeking arms and denying the existence of political prisoners, but there are possibly as many as 70,000.

2416. Turkey: Peace on Trial. Ed. Jean Furtado. London: European Nuclear Disarmament, 1983. 53. Account of the unfair trial of the leaders of the Turkish Peace Association.

2417. Turkey: Still Waiting for Change: Information on Continuing Human Rights Violations. New York: Amnesty International, 1991. 14. Although the Turkish authorities declared in 1989 their intention to make legal changes to improve safeguards against torture for detainees, and to abolish or amend articles of the penal code under which most prisoners of conscience are held, there has been no legislative or fundamental improvement in the human rights situation.

2418. Turkey: Testimony on Torture. London: Amnesty International, 1985. 76. "Torture is widespread and systematic in Turkey."

2419. Turkey : Torture and Unfair Trials of Political Prisoners: Case Studies Between August 1988 and August 1989. New York: Amnesty International, 1989. 31. Torture for political detainees is widespread despite Turkey's ratification of the European Convention for the Prevention of Torture. Also, statements extracted under torture deny fair trials.

2420. Turkey: Torture, Extrajudicial Executions, "Disappearances". New York: Amnesty International, 1992. 32. Deaths in custody, "disappearances," extrajudicial executions, and death squad killings.

2421. "Turkish Defenders Under Attack." Human Rights Internet Reporter 14.1 (Spring 1991) 49-50. Human rights leaders and lawyers suffer persecution.

2422. United States Congress. Implementation of the Helsinki Accords: Human Rights Abuses in Cyprus. 99th Cong. 1st Session, 1985. Washington: GPO, 1986. 152. On the Turkish invasion, killings, occupation, and repression of Cyprus.

2423. Violations of Human Rights by Turkey in Cyprus. Nicosia, Cyprus: International Association for the Protection of Human Rights in Cyprus, 1992. 17. The invasion of Cyprus by Turkey produced large-scale killings, murders of noncombatants, rapes, and torture.

2424. Violations of Human Rights in Turkey. London: Amnesty International, 1983. 7. Since the imposition of martial law in 1978, 30,000 people had been imprisoned for political offences, many of them tortured, and some have been killed in custody.

2425. Whitman, Lois. "Gross Violations in Turkey." Human Rights Watch 11.3 (Summer 1993) 2. Documented cases of torture, extra-judicial executions, killings of peaceful demonstrators, death-squad attacks on government opponents, dreadful abuse of government opponents and of the Kurdish minority in southeastern Turkey, and major restrictions on free expression.

TURKEY (ARMENIAN PERSECUTION)

2426. A.R.F. Youth Organization of Canada. The Armenian Genocide in the Canadian Press, 1915-1916. Vol 1. Montreal: Armenian National Committee of Canada, 1985. 159. Comprised of 134 articles about the Armenian genocide published in the Canadian press during 1915-1916.

2427. The Armenian Case. Videocassette. Thousand Oaks, CA: Armenian Film Foundation, n.d. 43 min. Documentary of the atrocities committed during the Armenian genocide by the Turks.

2428. An Armenian Journey. Videocassette. Chicago: Films, Inc., n.d. 60 min. Profiles an Armenian survivor's personal story.

2429. Back to Ararat: A Forgotten Genocide--A Dream of Return. Videocassette. New York: First Run Features, n.d. 100 min. Documentary examines the Armenian genocide and traces the lives of four survivors.

2430. Avakian, Asdghig. "Stranger" No More: An Armenian Nurse From Lebanon Tells Her Story. Beirut: Antelias, 1968. 200. Avakian tells of the round-up and arrest of all the men in her childhood village and the subsequent deportation of all the women and children.

2431. Bedrossyan, Mark D. The First Genocide of the 20th Century: The Perpetrators and the Victims. Flushing, NY: Voskedar, 1983. 480. Contains first-person accounts and entire texts by survivors and other witnesses.

2432. Boyajian, Dickran H. Armenia: The Case for a Forgotten Genocide. Westwood, NJ: Educational Book Crafters, 1972. 498. Contains excerpts of first-person accounts concerning the slaughter, and disputes the Turkish contention that the Armenians were guilty as a whole of rebellion.

2433. A Crime of Silence: The Armenian Genocide. London: Zed, 1985. 245. Text of the Permanent People's Tribunal's hearing on the Armenian genocide, April 13-16, 1984, at the Sorbonne in Paris includes testimony of Armenian survivors.

2434. Davidson, Khoren K. Odyessey of an Armenian of Zeitoun. New York: Vantage, 1985. 257. Davidson's memoirs of his years spent as a prisoner-deportee.

2435. Davis, Leslie A. The Slaughterhouse Province: An American Diplomat's Report on the Armenian Genocide of 1915-1917. Ed. Susan Blair. New Rochelle, NY: Aristide D. Caratzas, 1988. 224. Davis, U.S. counsul in Harput in eastern Asia Minor from 1915-1917, gives an eyewitness account.

2436. Hartunian, Abraham. Neither to Laugh nor to Weep: A Memoir of the Armenian Genocide. Trans. Vartan Hartunian. Boston: Beacon, 1968. 206. Hartunian witnessed the Armenian massacres of 1895-96 and 1906 and was a victim of the deportations and massacres of 1915.

2437. Jernazian, Ephraim K. Judgement Unto Truth: Witnessing the Armenian Genocide. Trans. Alice Haig. Cambridge, MA: Zoryan Institute, 1990. 235. Jernazian witnessed the "protracted genocidal process" that the Armenians were subjected to by the Turks.

2438. Kerr, Stanley E. The Lions of Marash: Personal Experiences With American Near East Relief, 1919-1922. Albany, NY: State U of New York P, 1973. 318. Kerr, an American Near East Relief official based in central Anatolia from 1919-1922, gives his eyewitness account.

2439. Kloian, Richard D., ed. The Armenian Genocide: News Accounts From the American Press (1915-1922). 3rd Ed. Richmond, CA: AAC, 1985. 388. A compilation of hundreds of American newspaper and magazine articles.

2440. Martin, Ramela. Out of Darkness. Cambridge, MA: Zoryan, 1988. 220. Martin, born in Ottoman Armenia just prior to the genocide of 1915-1917, recounts her experiences during this period.

2441. Minassian, John. Many Hills to Climb: Memoirs of an Armenian Deportee. Santa Barbara, CA: Jim Cook, 1986. 255. Minassian describes the destruction of his home and family, his deportation to Aleppo and subsequent escape into the Syrian desert.

2442. Totten, Samuel, comp. "The Ottoman Genocide of the Armenians." First Person Accounts of Genocidal Acts Committed in the Twentieth Century: An

Annotated Bibliography. Westport, CT: Greenwood, 1991. 7-43. 135 entries including bibliography and films/videos about the Tukish governments attempt to annihilate the Armenian people, 1915-1923. Many entries describe imprisonment and torture.

2443. Toynbee, Arnold J., ed. Armenian Atrocities: The Murder of a Nation. With a Speech Delivered by Lord Bryce in the House of Lords. New York: Hodder and Stoughton, 1915. 117. Compilation of eyewitness accounts from religious missionaries, consuls based in Turkey, numerous private and public letters, and newspaper articles.

2444. The Treatment of the Armenians in the Ottoman Empire: Documents Presented to Viscount Grey of Fallodon, Secretary of State for Foreign Affairs. London: J. Causton, 1916. 684. "Contains all the evidence that could be obtained up till July 1916 as to the massacres and deportations of the Armenian and other Eastern Christians dwelling in Asia Minor, Armenia and the northwest corner of Russia."

2445. Ussher, Clarence D. and Grace H. Knapp. An American Physician in Turkey. Boston: Houghton Mifflin, 1917. 339. Ussher recounts the slaughter he witnessed of the Armenians by the Turks from 1888 to August 3, 1915.

UGANDA

2446. "Amin's Horror Chamber." Time 113 (April 30, 1979) 45. The torture and murders systematically perpetrated by Amin's secret police, the SRB.

2447. "Amin's Legacy: Torture Still a Fact of Life in Uganda." Amnesty Action (Winter 1993) 7. Amin murdered between 100,000 and 500,000; under the new ruler, Milton Obote, abuses continued: by 1985 thousands more had been killed; and under the present ruler, Yoweri Museveni, serious human rights violations continue.

2448. Amnesty International Report 1980. London: Amnesty International, 1980. 86-88. The brutal dictator Idi Amin was overthrown in 1979 ("estimated one million widows and orphans of those tortured to death or otherwise murdered by Amin's security forces"). Considerable improvement resulted under the new President Binaisa, but detention of opponents is occurring under the new secret National Security Service, including the editor of the government-owned Uganda Times.

2449. Amnesty International Report 1990. New York: Amnesty International, 1990. 241-243. Some 2,300 political detainees were released in 1989, but more than 1000 others were added, and more than 2000 were in prison without charge or trial at the end of the year. Torture and murder by armed forces were reported. Some police and soldiers were tried for murder.

2450. "The Black Hole of Kampala." Time 100 (October 2, 1972) 32-34. Following an attempted invasion by opponents of dictator Idi Amin, security forces began arresting Europeans and Asians.

2451. "Chamber of Horrors." Newsweek 93 (April 23, 1979) 42. Torture in Amin's "Research Bureau" (the SRB).

2452. "Death Comes to the Archbishop." Matchbox (Spring 1977) 1-2. Report on the death and secret burial of Anglican Archbishop Dr. Janani Luwum, "just one more in an endless series of deaths" under the Amin regime, with estimates ranging between 50,000 and 300,000 killed from 1971 to 1977.

2453. Dring, S. "Sit on the Floor and Die." Newsweek 80 (October 2, 1972) 38. On foreigners jailed without charge by the army.

2454. The Human Rights Situation in Uganda: Amnesty International Submission to the United Nations Commission on Human Rights. London: Amnesty International, 1977. 6. Summary of terrible repression 1971-1976 following coup by General Amin.

2455. Human Rights Violations in Uganda: Extrajudicial Executions, Torture, and Political Imprisonment. London: Amnesty International, British Section, 1982. 23. Widespread killings and torture have resumed three years following the overthrow of Idi Amin.

2456. "Is Idi Amin Alive and Well in Kampala?" Guardian 36.43 (September 5, 1984) 16. On the massacres and torture under President Milton Obote that may equal dictator Idi Amin's atrocities.

2457. Kato, Wycliffe. Escape from Idi Amin's Slaughterhouse. London; New York: Quartet Books, 1989. 172. An account of his imprisonment, torture, and escape from Nakasero Prison, Idi Amin's torture center and headquarters of his State Research Bureau, whose job was to eliminate all of Amin's enemies real or imaginary.

2458. Keymba, Henry. A State of Blood: The Inside Story of Idi Amin. New York: Grosset & Dunlap, 1977. 288. Keymba, a former Ugandan cabinet minister under Amin, calls for international action against the genocide being waged.

2459. Lule, Yusef. Human Rights Violations in Uganda Under Obote. Pasadena: California Institute of Technology, 1982. 31. Briefly President of Uganda succeeding Idi Amin, Lule examines Milton Obote's two "murderous and dictatorial regimes."

2460. Summary of Amnesty International's Concerns in the Republic of Uganda. London: Amnesty Intrnational, 1987. 16.

2461. Totten, Samuel. "Ugandan Genocides Under Idi Amin and Milton Obote." First-Person Accounts of Genocidal Acts Committed in the Twentieth Century: An Annotated Bibliography. Westport, CT: Greenwood, 1991. 275-76. Four entries.

2462. Uganda: Human Rights Violations by the National Resistance Army. New York: Amnesty International, 1991. 21. Persistent human rights violations in 1991 by both the rebels and the Ugandan army in the northern districts of Uganda. Violations by authorities include imprisonment of prisoners of conscience, the screening of thousands of people, and general ill treatment of prisoners.

2463. Uganda and Human Rights: Reports to the UN Commission on Human Rights. Geneva, Switzerland: International Commission of Jurists, 1977. 167. Regarding the illegal arrests, detention, torture, and murder of civilians.

UNION OF SOVIET SOCIALIST REPUBLICS *

2464. 1917-1977: Sixty Years of Communism, The Age of the Gulag. N.p.: Aims for Freedom and Enterprise, [1977?]. 13. In "celebration" of 60 years of incalculable "human pain, misery, death and starvation" in the U.S.S.R., this pamphlet gives a month-by-month synopsis of human rights violations inflicted on the people of the Soviet Union by their government.

2465. Abuse of Psychiatry in the Soviet Union: Hearing before the Subcommittee on Human Rights and International Organizations of the Committee on Foreign Affairs and the Commission on Security and Cooperation in Europe, House of Representatives, Ninety-eighth Congress, first session, September 20, 1983. Washington, D.C.: U.S. G.P.O., 1983. 106.

**A diligent search has not uncovered any published work in English on political prisoners or trials in modern Russia (January 1, 1991, through December 31, 1993).*

2466. Adler, Thomas S. Psychoprisons: A Psychiatrist Exposes the Misuse of Psychiatry in Today's Soviet Union. Penrith, N.S.W., Australia: Christian Mission to the Communist World, The Voice of the Martyrs, 1985. 84.

2467. Alekseeva, Liudmila. Nyeformaly Civil Society in the USSR. New York: Human Rights Watch, 1990. 142. Focuses on civic clubs and movements with sections on "Arrests and Detentions" and "Defending Political Prisoners."

2468. Alexander, Edward. "Shcharansky's Secret." Commentary 82 (October 1986) 52-6. On the anti-Semitic arrest, trial, and imprisonment of Anatoly Shcharansky, now in Israel.

2469. "Alexandr Ogorodnikov." Index On Censorship 16.1 (January 1987) 46. Ogorodnikov has spent the last eight years of his life in prisons and camps for "parasitism" and "anit-Soviet propaganda," and he has now been sentenced to three more years.

2470. "Alexi Magarik." Index On Censorship 16.5 (May 1987) 4. Magarik, cellist, teacher of Hebrew, and emigration applicant, was sentenced to three years in a labor camp charged with drug possession, most likely trumped up by the KGB.

2471. Altmann, Hans. Shop Floors and Prisons: The Recollections of a German Engineer in Stalin's Russia of the 1930s. Edmonton, Canada: Central & East European Studies Society, 1987.

2472. Amalrik, Andrei. Involuntary Journey To Siberia. Trans. Manya Harari and Max Hayward. London: Collins and Harvill 1970. 282. (New York: HBJ. 297). Abrigement of original. The story of the author's exile to Siberia for "parasitism."

2473. Amalrik, Andrei. Notes of a Revolutionary. London: Weidenfeld and Nicolson, 1982. 343. Exiled to Siberia in 1965 as a "parasite," and again in 1966. In 1970 he was sentenced to three years in a labor camp for spreading "falsehoods derogatory to the Soviet state," and then resentenced in camp for three more years, which was commuted to exile in farthest Siberia. He emigrated in 1976. A leading dissident 1965-1976.

2474. Amerisov, A. "Soviet Dissident Deaths Point Up Moral Decline." In These Times 11.8 (Jan 14, 1987) 16. Details the political lives of dissidents Marchenko and Morozov and their deaths in prison.

2475. Amnesty International Report 1980. London: Amnesty International, 1980. 302-310. During the period May 1, 1979 to April 30, 1980, Amnesty International worked on 350 cases ranging from arrest and imprisonment and unfair trials to detention in mental hospitals and other abuses. Many more prisoners probably exist, but the real number is obscured by secrecy and threat of reprisal against those who speak out. Prison inmates are subjected to chronic hunger, inadequate medical care, and often dangerous labour. Political inmates of psychiatric hospitals are "deprived of virtually every right," and their number is increasing. Arrests of dissenters have increased often under false or fake charges ("hooliganism"). Attempt to emigrate is punishable as is writing considered anti-state, trade union activism, conscientious objection, religious activism, and defense of human rights. Some sentences have been extremely severe.

2476. Amnesty International Report 1990. New York: Amnesty International, 1990. 243-246. More than 2,000 people were put in prisons or psychiatric hospitals during 1989 for a variety of political protests. Some 20 people were killed and many injured when police broke up peaceful demonstrations. But under President Gorbachev many legal reforms have improved human rights.

2477. Anatoly and Avital Shcharansky: The Journey Home. San Diego: Harcourt Brace Jovanovich, 1986. 317. The story of their marriage and separation by his nine year imprisonment, and their efforts to gain his release in 1986.

2478. Andics, Hellmut. Rule of Terror: Russia Under Lenin and Stalin. Trans. Alexander Lieven. New York: Holt, Rinehart and Winston, 1969. 208. An account of the Great Purge detailing prisons, work camps, deportations, induced famine, etc, including many first-hand accounts from survivors.

2479. Antonov, Boris. "Prisoners of Conscience" in the USSR and Their Patrons. Moscow: Novosti Press Agency, 1988. 60. Defends the Soviet Union against accusations of having imprisoned millions or even thousands of political prisoners.

2480. Avinov, Maria. "Scheherazade." Ed. Paul Chavchavadze. New Yorker 44 (May 11, 1968) 41-5. An episode in the prison life of Avinov, arrested as the wife of an "enemy of the people," who was shot. She was sent to prison at Alma-Ata where she gained the nickname of Scheherazade for telling stories to entertain her fellow prisoners.

2481. "Back From Russia." Time 72 (July 21, 1958) 14. U.S. pilots shot down while flying over Soviet territory are released after ten days.

2482. Barinov, Valeri. Jailhouse Rock. ed. Valeri Barinov with Danny Smith. London: Hodder and Stoughton, 1990. 313.

2483. Barnathan, Joyce. "Inside a Mind Jail." Newsweek 108 (August 11, 1986) 26-7. On the abuse of psychiatry and mental hospitals to suppress dissent: the ease of Serafim Yevsyukov.

2484. Barry, Hugh. "The Ordeal of Joseph Begun." Human Rights Internet Reporter 11.5-6 (Winter 1987) 48-49. Begun was exiled to Siberia in 1977 and imprisoned in 1982 for teaching Hebrew. Persecution of Begun began in 1971 when he applied for emigration.

2485. Beamish, Tufton, and Guy Hadley. The Kremlin Dilemma: The Struggle of Human Rights in Eastern Europe. San Rafael: Presidio, 1979. 285. An account of the tragic situation in Eastern Europe where brave men and women are challenging the denial of human rights and suffering harsh penalties, this book expresses the opinion that the Soviet satellites are becoming more of a liability than an asset to the U.S.S.R.

2486. Beasley, Edwin L. "Political Dissent in the Soviet Union: An Analysis of the Neo-Bolshevik Faction of the Democratic Movement in the U.S.S.R." Thesis (M.A.). George Mason U, 1978. 71. Studies one of the three democratic factions, represented by Pyotr Grigorenko, Ivan Yakhimovich, and Alexei Kosterin, the first two incarcerated in psychiatric hospitals, the latter imprisoned seventeen years.

2487. Beausobre, Iulia de. The Woman Who Could Not Die. New York: Viking, 1938. 301. (London: Chatto & Windus, 1938; London: Gollancz, 1948.) Imprisoned in 1932 by the GPU, the Soviet Secret Police, for complicity in the alleged treason of her husband (who was later shot). This book is her prison memoirs.

2488. Beck, F. and W. Godin. Russian Purge and the Extraction of Confession. Trans. Eric Mosbacher and David Porter. New York: Viking, 1951. 277. Deals with the great purge of the Yezhov period, 1936-1939. Chapter 4 on interrogation, chapter 5 on prison life, Chapter 6 on types of prisoners (Old Bolsheviks, army officers, etc.), Chapter 7 on three cases.

2489. Beeson, Trevor. "Russia Tightens Squeeze on Religious Dissidents." Christian Century 97.17 (May 7, 1980) 510-512. "Carrying out its harshest antireligious campaign in several years."

2490. Begin, Menachem. White Nights; the Story of a Prisoner in Russia. New York: Harper & Row, 1957. 240. The former prime minister of Israel tells of his arrest, trial, and imprisonment by the NKVD in Lithuania in 1940 and his sentence of eight years to a Soviet prison. He includes stories of many other political prisoners.

2491. Bellow, Yuri. Prisoners of Conscience in the Soviet Union. Lexington, VA: Washington and Lee School of Law, 1987. Audiovisual, 60 min.

2492. Berger, Joseph. Nothing But The Truth. New York: John Day, 1971. 286. (Shipwreck of a Generation: the Memoirs of Joseph Berger. London, Harvill, 1971.) A leading communist in the 1930's, he was stripped of his posts and imprisoned in 1935 for being a Trotskyite. In 1941 he was sentenced to death, but only his sentenced was lengthened. He was released in 1951 but sentenced to Siberian exile. He was rehabilitated in 1956 and emigrated to Israel.

2493. Bierman, John. "A Pain Filled Mystery." Macleans 102 (October 30, 1989) 47. The continuing investigation to find out what really happened to Raoul Wallenberg, who saved some 20,000 Jews from Nazi gas chambers.

2494. Blake, P. and others. "Killing the spirit of Helsinki." Time 116 (December 1, 1980) 45. Crackdown on dissidents.

2495. Bloch, Sidney. Soviet Psychiatry Vs. Dissidents. Audiotape. Vital History Cassettes, No. 2. New York: Encyclopedia Americana; CBS News Audio Resource Library, 1977. 18 min. In an interview with CBS News, Bloch comments on the tendency of Soviet psychiatrists to equate social deviance with insanity.

2496. Bloch, Sidney, and Peter Reddaway. Psychiatric Terror: How Soviet Psychiatry Is Used to Suppress Dissent. New York: Basic Books, 1977. 510. (Russian's Political Hospitals: the Abuse of Psychiatry in the Soviet Union. London: Gollancz, 1977.) An account of the development of Soviet psychiatric abuse and of worldwide efforts to rescue the victims. Appendix I, pp. 347-398, gives a register of people who have been forciby interned in a psychiatric hospital since 1962.

2497. Bloch, Sidney and Peter Reddaway. Soviet Psychiatric Abuse: the Shadow Over World Psychiatry. London: Gollancz, 1984. 288. A continuation of the authors' study of political psychiatry. Focuses on the struggle of the World Psychiatric Association to abolish political psychiatry, culminating with the resignation of the Soviet Psychiatric Society. Lists victims 1977-1983.

2498. B'nai B'rith. Anti-defamation League. A Uniquely Jewish List: The Refuseniks of Russia. New York: Anti-Defamation League, 1987. 931. An alphabetical geographical listing of Jewish dissents. From the day they file their applications, aspiring emigrants lose their jobs and their friends.

2499. Bonner, Elena. Alone Together. New York: Knopf, 1986. 269. Account of her life and her husband, Andrei Sakharov, during 1983-1985 in exile in Gorky.

2500. Bonner, Elena. "At War with the KGB." Time 128.15 (October 13, 1986) 82-6+. Excerpts from Bonner's book Alone Together, which she wrote during her visit to the West.

2501. "Book Community Protests Internal Exile of Sakharov." Publishers Weekly 217 (February 15, 1980) 38. The Association of American Publishers, the Authors League of America, P.E.N., and prominent writers have joined in a formal complaint.

2502. Bowers, Mark. "Trust-Busting Soviet Style." Nuclear Times 1.8 (June 1983) 18-19. On the arrest and conviction of Alexander Shatravka and arrest and disappearance of Vladimir Mishenko, members of the Soviet Group to Establish Trust between the U.S.S.R. and the U.S. Shatravka has been confined in a psychiatric hospital and his wife constantly harassed.

2503. Bowne, Alan. "Soviet Director Remains in Jail for 'Homosexualism.'" Gay Community News 4.28 (January 8, 1977) 3. Film director Sergei Paradjanov was sentenced to five years for several trumped up charges, but behind them is his defence of freedom in the Ukraine.

2504. Bridges, Linda. "Psychiatry, KGB Style." National Review 26 (July 19, 1974) 815-16, 831. General survey of the types of political hospitals, drugs used, etc.

2505. "Brief Respite." Time 126.24 (December 16, 1985) 39. Elena Bonner allowed to leave the Soviet Union for medical treatment.

2506. Broad, William J. "Soviets Sentence Scientist to 5 Years in Exile." Science 213 (July 10, 1981) 186-7. Viktor Brailovsky, underground journal editor and emigration applicant, was convicted of "defaming" the state.

2507. Brown, Janice. "Gleb Yakunin, Unquenched Spirit." Commonweal 111 (September 7, 1984) 460-2. On the long imprisonment of this Russian Orthodox priest and the continuing campaign against the church in the Soviet Union.

2508. Brown, Michael. Witness, & the Apparitions & Persecutions in the USSR: Autobiography of Josyp Terelya. S.l.: Riehle Foundation, n.d. 352. Terelya at age 18 began the first of 23 years in prisons for defending the Ukrainian Catholic Church.

2509. Brunovsky, Vladimir. The Methods of the OGPU(1931). Westport, CT.: Hyperion, 1977. 255. Memoir of his four years in trials and prison, 1923-26, his death sentence, and release to Latvia.

2510. Buber, Margarete (Margarete Buber-Neumann). Under Two Dictators. Trans. Edward Fitzgerald. London: Gollancz, 1949. 331. She and her husband, German Communists in Moscow employed as translators, were imprisoned before being sent to Siberia. She was then sent to the Nazi concentration camp at Ravensbrück, which she survived.

2511. Buca, Edward. Vorkuta. Tr. Michal Lisinski and Kennedy Wells. London: Constable, 1981. 352. A Pole, he was imprisoned by the Nazis twice and twice escaped, then imprisoned by the Soviets in the labor complex called Vorkuta (approx. a million prisoners in 1953). He led a strike in 1953 for which he was sentenced to ten more years added to the ten remaining of his original sentence. Repatriated to Poland in 1958 and sentenced again but not imprisoned. Escaped to Sweden in 1970.

2512. Buckley, William F., jr. "Heroes of the Soviet Union." National Review 31 (June 8, 1979) 762-3. On the exchange of two Soviet spies imprisoned in the U.S. for several imprisoned dissidents.

2513. "The Bukovsky Papers: Note from Soviet Asylums." National Review 24 (June 9, 1972) 633-6. Anecdotes about and statements from victims.

2514. Bukovsky, Vladimir. A Manual on Psychiatry for Dissidents. Arlington, Va.: Keuffel and Esser, 1977. 18. Written by two dissidents in a labor camp, discussing laws, the psychology of the psychiatrist, behavior while incarcerated, etc.

2515. Bukovsky, Vladimir. "The Serbsky Treatment." Psychology Today 11 (June 1977) 38-44. Interview of Bukovsky, who was judged insane and committed to a mental hospital--for defending dissidents and civil liberties. Then he was sentenced to prison for three years, and then for twelve years for revealing case records to the World Psychiatric Association.

2516. Bukovsky, Vladimir. A Soviet Dissident Tells Why. Audiotape. Interviewed by Mike Wallace. New York: Encylopedia Americana; CBS News, 1977. 13 min. Discusses the role of dissidents like himself and the necessity for support in the West for political dissidents within the Soviet Union.

2517. Bukovsky, Vladimir. To Build a Castle: My Life as a Dissenter. Washington, D.C.: Ethics and Public Policy Center, 1988. 438. Orig. pub. New York: Viking, 1979. An account of the author's life as a dissident in and out of prison.

2518. Bukovsky, Vladimir. To Choose Freedom. Stanford, CA: Hoover Institution, 1987. 188. The author spent nearly one-third of his first 33 years in Soviet prisons, labor camps, and psychiatric hospitals. This book contains four essays.

2519. Bunyan, James. The Origin of Forced Labor in the Soviet State 1917-1921: Documents and Materials. Stanford, CA: Hoover Institute; Baltimore: Johns Hopkins, 1967. 276. The process of gradual militarization of work (and transportation) from the original concept of workers' control of industry to the introduction of labor compulsion for the bourgeoisie and finally to the working class, with consequent misery, tyranny, and cruelty.

2520. Butman, Hilel. From Leningrad to Jerusalem: the Gulag Way. Berkeley, Calif.: Benmir, 1990. 353. For his efforts to enable Soviet Jews to emigrate to Israel and to awaken Jewish consciousness of Soviet Jews, Butman spent nine years in prison.

2521. Butman, Hilel. "Statement by Prisoner H.I. Butman to the Chief of the Perm Admininstration of Corrective Labor Establishments (ITK-35)." National Review 29 (July 22, 1977) 822-5. Butman was sentenced to 10 years in prison in 1970 in the Second Leningrad Trial of Jewish activists. Here he protests prison conditions.

2522. "The Caged Cartoonist in the Andropov Era." Newsweek 101 (March 7, 1983) 48. Artist and cartoonist dissident Vyacheslav Sysoyev arrested.

2523. Care and Help for Expellees, Refugees, Immigrants, Evacuees, War Victims, Returnees, Prisoners of War, Homeless Foreigners, Political Refugees from Abroad, Repatriated Persons, Emigrants. Bonn: Federal Ministry for Expellees, Refugees, and War Victims, 1959. 68. One chapter on assistance by West Germany to former Soviet political prisoners.

2524. Cederholm, Boris. In the Clutches of the Tcheka. Trans. F.H. Lyon. Boston; New York: Houghton Mifflin, 1929. 349. The author was confined without trial in several prisons and the Solovetsky concentration camp from 1924 to 1926 even though he was a foreigner and was innocent. Intense protests by the Finnish government effected his release.

2525. Celmina, Helena. Women in Soviet Prisons. New York: Paragon House, 1985. 238. The author was imprisoned for "anti-Soviet agitation," like her mother. Chapter 11 describes political prisoners. Chapter 12 deals with Jehovah's Witnesses; Chapter 13 with religious prisoners, nuns.

2526. "Censuring the Soviets." Time 110 (September 12, 1977) 36. The World Psychiatric Association censured Soviet psychiatry for its political abuses.

2527. Charles, Keith. "Sakharov's Torment." Maclean's 94 (December 14, 1981) 39. Sakharov and his wife are fasting to protest the denial of a visa to their daughter-in-law; their son is already living in the United States.

2528. "A Christian Musician Awaits Trial in the Soviet Union." Christianity Today 28 (October 19, 1984) 39. Valeri Barinov was arrested for attempting to cross the Soviet-Norwegian border; he faces up to three years in a labor camp. Barinov has also been held in a psychiatric hospital for "expressing his religious views in public."

2529. Christian Prisoners in the USSR, 1979. 2nd rev. ed. Keston, Kent, England: Keston College, 1979. 39. These profiles are only the "tip of the iceberg" of the estimated 2000 religious prisoners.

2530. Chyz, Martha. Women and Child in the Modern System of Slavery--U.S.S.R.. Toronto: Suzero; New York: Dobrus, 1962. 176. On "the fate of women and children in the USSR" sentenced to slavery by arrest and exile."

2531. Clark, H.R. "Not Even an Ironic Smile." Time 124 (July 2, 1984) 28. On French President Mitterand's efforts in behalf of Sakharov.

2532. Cockburn, Alexander. "Cockburn Replies." Nation 242 (April 12, 1986) 506. Contrasts the different attitudes of the U.S. government and press toward our "criminals" Ronald Humphrey and David Truong and the Soviet Union's "victim" Shcharansky.

2533. Cohen, David. Soviet Psychiatry. London: Paladin, 1989. 160. Based upon a first-hand investigation, allowed by the new spirit of perestroika and glasnost. A film also resulted: Dispatches: Gorbachev's Asylums.

2534. Cohen, Stephen F. Social Dimensions of De-Stalinization, 1953-64: Final Report to the National Council for Soviet and East European Research. Washington: The Council, 1983. 45. On the release, return, and reintegration of approximately ten million Soviet political prisoners from Stalin's Gulag archipelago during the first years of Kruschev's reign following Stalin's death, 1953-1958.

2535. Coleman, Fred. "Human Right's Widows." Newsweek 91 (January 2, 1978) 28-9. On the mistreatment of prisoners' families.

2536. Commission on Security and Cooperation in Europe, Congress of the United States. Reports of Helsinki Accord: Monitors in the Soviet Union. Vol. 3. Washington: U.S.G.P.O., 1978. 183. Documents from the Moscow, Ukrainian, Lithuanian, and Armenian Helsinki Groups.

2537. Conquest, Robert. The Great Terror: A Reassessment. New York; Oxford: Oxford UP, 1990. 570. A confirmation and extention of the author's The Great Terror (1968).

2538. Conquest, Robert. The Great Terror: Stalin's Purge of the Thirties. New York: Macmillan, 1968. 633. The purges by which Stalin established his absolute power had three particular ingredients: 1) they snared millions; 2) they employed the confession trial and 3) secrecy. By supressing information about the trials, imprisonments and executions, and by coercing defendants to denounce themselves, millions were killed and incarcerated, and the Soviet public was convinced of a gigantic conspiracy against the nation.

2539. Conquest, Robert. Kolyma: The Arctic Death Camps. New York: Viking, 1978. 254; Oxford: Oxford UP, 1979. 256. A "history and the conditions of the huge labour camp complex of Kolyma," the "great archetype"- the "deadliest" Stalin prison system. Based mainly on seventeen first-hand accounts.

2540. Conquest, Robert. Tyrants & Typewriters: Communiqués from the Struggle for Truth. Lexington, MA: Lexington Books/D.C. Heath, 1989. 208. Miscellaneous writings on the struggle by Soviet writers to destroy "the huge edifice of falsehood." Heavy toll in suffering in trials and imprisonment--Solzhenitsyn, Djilas, Sakharov, and others.

2541. "Crackdown on Dissent." Time 100 (December 18, 1972) 31-32. Repression of dissent is hardening.

2542. Dallin, David J. and Nicolaevsky, Boris I. Forced Labor in Soviet Russia. New Haven, CT: Yale UP, 1947. 331. Compiles various first-hand accounts of Soviet labor camps "written by men and women who have had a record of sad personal experience."

2543. Daniloff, N. "'Living in the Soviet Union Deforms You as a Person.'" U.S. News and World Report 101 (October 21, 1986) 23. A statement by Yuri Orlov, a founder of the Soviet human rights movement, after his release from nearly ten years of imprisonment.

2544. Danylo Shumuk Life Sentence. Videocassette. New York: Amnesty International, 1987. 27 min. Shumuk spent more than 42 years in detention for the non-violent expression of his political opinions. This is his life story, including AI's efforts to sustain him.

2545. Darel, Sylva. A Sparrow in the Snow. Harmondsworth: Penguin, 1977. 186. Orig. pub. New York: Stein and Day, 1973. This prisoner's autobiography.

2546. "Death of a Soviet Dissident: True Grit" U.S. News and World Report 101 (December 22, 1986) 6. On Anatoly Marchenko.

2547. "Defending Yuri Orlov." New Yorker 53 (September 19, 1977) 29-31. Describes barrister John Macdonald's efforts to represent Orlov in Moscow.

2548. "Dehumanization in Soviet Concentration Camps." Intellect 106 (January 1978) 263+. Tells abut Dr. Mikhail Stern's trial and imprisonment and the successful international effort to bring his release.

2549. Deutscher, Isaac. The Great Purges. Oxford and New York: Blackwell, 1984. 176. Report on Stalin's genocide in his own country includes first-hand accounts of trials, executions, concentration camps, torture, etc.

2550. Deyneka, Anita. "God in the Gulag." Christianity Today 29 (August 9, 1985) 28-31. Christian prisoners subjected to horrible conditions and denied medical care.

2551. "The Disease is Dissent." Matchbox (Summer 1976) 6-8. On the use of psychiatric torture and hospitalization as punishment, including an interview with a survivor and other case studies.

2552. Dobczansky, Jury. "A Plea From Under the Gun." America 140 (May 19, 1979) 414-15. On Rev. Vasyl Romanyuk's long prison sufferings.

2553. Documents of the Helsinki Monitoring Groups in the USSR and Lithuania (1976-1986). Vol 3. Washington, D.C., 1987. 322. Topics range from individual persecution to broader human rights violations: psychiatric torture, religious persecution, etc. 37 of the Group's 38 members have been imprisoned, and 3 have died in camps.

2554. Documents of the Public Groups to Promote Observance of the Helsinki Agreements in the USSR. Washington: Commission on Security and Cooperation in Europe, 1977. 5. Describes repression of Helsinki Watchers and presents appeals by Andrei Sakharov and others in their support.

2555. Dolgun, Alexander. Dolgun. London: Fontana, 1976. 448. U.S. citizen Dolgun was imprisoned from 1948 to 1956 and then kept under surveillance for fifteen more years, until allowed to emigrate in 1971.

2556. Dolgun, Alexander. "Story Behind the Book: 'Alexander Dolgun's Story: An American in the Gulag'." Publisher's Weekly 207 (May 26, 1975) 45. Summarizes his hardships.

2557. Dong, Stella. "Poet Speaks Out for Silenced Dissident." Publisher's Weekly 217 (February 15, 1980) 38. Bella Akhmadulina denounces the internal exile of Andrei Sakharov.

2558. Dubasova, Irina Fedorovna. Ten Months in Bolshevik Prisons. Edinburgh: Blackwood, 1926. 308. The author was sentenced to ten years in prison because her father was a leader in the Czar's government and she was Maid of Honor of the Empress. During parole she fled to Finland.

2559. Eisner, T. "Bioprofile: Sergei Kovalev." BioScience 32 (April 1982) 297. Deplores the persecution of Kovalev and his family.

2560. Elliot, Laurence. "The Haunting Riddle of Raoul Wallenberg." Reader's Digest 138 (January 1991) 114-18. Wallenberg "saved tens of thousands of Jews" during World War II, then disappeared in prisons in the USSR because the Soviets thought he was a spy. A chronology of his life, exploits, imprisonment, and death.

2561. Emiot, Isreal. The Birobidzhan Affair: A Yiddish Writer in Siberia. Trans. Max Rosenfeld. Philadelphia: Jewish Publication Society of America, 1981. 205. Chronicle of the persecution of Jews during the last years of Stalin's rule. Birobidzhan was the Jewish Autonomous Region of the U.S.S.R. on the border with Manchuria until a decree by Stalin prevented it in 1936 and his purges further undermined it.

2562. "End of Fast." Time 118 (December 21, 1981) 39. Sakharov's hunger strike to protest refusal to allow his wife, N. Alexeyeva, to emigrate to the U.S.

2563. Evangelista, Matthew. "Sakharov and Gorky." Bulletin of Atomic Scientists 43 (April 1987) 21. On Gorvbachev's glasnost and hope for political prisoners.

2564. "An Exile." New Yorker 62 (April 7, 1986) 27-31. On the plight of Yuri Orlov, scientist and human rights advocate exiled to Siberia, and efforts to rescue him.

2565. Fabian, Béla. "Khrushchev's Broken Promise on Slave Labor in Russia." U.S. News and World Report 47 (September 7, 1959) 84-5. Accuses the Soviet Union of holding "hundreds of thousands" in labor camps, and many thousands in other European countries.

2566. A Family Torn Apart. Toronto: Human Rights Commission, World Congress of Free Ukranians, 1981. 43. Vasyl (son) and Petro (father) Sichko were sentenced to three years in prison in 1979 for protesting against Soviet lies and crimes. A second son, Volodymyr, was sentenced to three years in 1981 for protesting.

2567. "A Fast to the Finish." Newsweek 98 (December 14, 1981) 45. Sakharov and Bonner are in their third week of a hunger strike.

2568. Fireside, Harvey. Soviet Psychoprisons. New York: Norton, 1979. 201. Some thousand persons are confined in special psychiatric hospitals for their political or religious convictions. Discusses the patients, the doctors, and the resisters.

2569. Fireside, Harvey. "The Trial of Sergei Kovalev." Commonweal 103 (July 16, 1976) 459-60. Eminent biologist and human rights activist is in prison for "anti-Soviet propaganda" (i.e., authoring reports on repression in Lithuania under Soviet rule).

2570. Fireside, Harvey, and Bryna Fireside. "Unlicensed Doves." New Republic 187 (December 27, 1982) 11-12. The silencing of the few remaining human rights representatives.

2571. Fischer, Louis. "Political Prisoners under Bolshevism." Nation 120 (March 4, 1925) 237-8. Discussion: Nation 120 (March 18, May 20, 1925) 293-4. General appraisal of repression in early 1920s by a writer sympathetic to the Communist experiment.

2572. Fischer, W. "German Scientist tells what he found in Soviet Union." U.S. News and World Report 44 (March 21 1958) 88-9. Account of German scientists and engineers seized at close of World War II.

2573. Fitzpatrick, Catherine A. Soviet Abuse of Psychiatry for Political Purposes: A Helsinki Watch Report Update. New York: U.S. Helsinki Watch Committee, 1987. 21. Lists and discusses 95 cases of political incarceration in psychiatric hospitals, the criminal code, Soviet psychiatrists, recent releases, Soviet press coverage, proposed remedial legislation, etc.

2574. Frankel, D. "Plyushch Answers Jackson." Militant 40.15 (April 16, 1976) 18. Leonid Plyushch asks for support from Senator Henry Jackson for political prisoners.

2575. Frantzell, L. "Alive or Dead? The Last of the Pimpernels." National Review 31 (August 17, 1979) 1019. On Raoul Wallenberg's struggles to rescue Jews, his conflict with Eichmann, arrest by the new Soviet commander as a spy, and Soviet cover-up.

2576. "Free at last." Time 118 (September 28, 1981) 43. Association of American Publishers boycott of the Moscow book fair because of Soviet mistreatment of Sakharov and others.

2577. "Freedom Fast." Time 118 (December 7, 1981) 45. Sakharov refuses food to protest the government's denial of permission for his daughter's husband to join her in the United States.

2578. "Freedom for a Refusenik." Macleans 100 (April 27, 1987) 6+ Josef Begun, sentenced to 12 years for distributing anti-Soviet literature, was released after serving three-and-a-half years. Begun discusses anti-Semitism in the USSR.

2579. From, D. "Who's Crazy Now?" National Review 35 (January 21, 1983) 44. Proposal to expel the Soviet Union from the World Psychiatric Association.

2580. "From Gulag to Gotham." Time 113. (May 7, 1979) 20. U.S. trades two Soviet spies for five Soviet dissidents.

2581. Garvey, John. "The Trial of V. Poresh." Commonweal 110 (March 11, 1983) 136-8. Poresh was imprisoned not for "anti-Soviet agitation" as accused but for membership in the Christian Seminar.

2582. "Georgy Mikhailov." Index On Censorship 16.6 (June 1987) 11. Mikhailov, who has been imprisoned twice for his support of unofficial art, tells about the continued repression despite glasnost.

2583. Gilbert, Martin. Shcharansky, Hero of Our Time. New York: Viking, 1986. 467. Shcharansky was sentenced to 13 years in prison in 1978 for leading the refuseniks of the Helsinki Watchdog human rights group in Moscow, and for trying to gain an exit visa to emigrate to Israel. He was released in 1986.

2584. Gilboa, Jehoshua. The Black Years of Soviet Jewry, 1939-1953. Trans. Yosef Shachter and Dov Ben-Aba. Boston: Little, Brown, 1971. 418. Gilboa deals mainly with the final years of Stalin's rule, 1948-1953, but includes material on the Jewish Anti-Fascist Committee and other aspects of the Holocaust years.

2585. Gilboa, Jehoshua. Confess! Confess! Eight Years in Soviet Prisons. Trans. Dov Ben-Aba. Boston: Little, Brown, 1968. Personal narratives of Jews in Soviet Prisons during World War II.

2586. Ginzburg, Eugenia. Journey into the Whirlwind. Tr. Paul Stevenson and Max Hayward. New York: Harcourt Brace Jovanovich, 1967. 418. Describes her eighteen years in prisons after being arrested in 1937 during Stalin's purges despite her dedication to communism.

2587. Ginzburg, Eugenia. Within the Whirlwind. Tr. Ian Boland. Intro. Heinrich Böll. New York: Harcourt Brace Jovanovich, 1981. 423 Deals with her Siberian camp experiences that followed eighteen years in prison.

2588. Gorbanevskaya, Natalya. "Fourteen Poems." Index on Censorship 1.1 (Spring 1972) 107-115. Written 1964-1970 concerning her trial and detention in a prison psychiatric hospital.

2589. Gorbanevskaya, Natalya. Selected Poems by Natalya Gorbanevskaya, With a Transcript of Her Trial and Papers Relating to Her Detention in a Prison Psychiatric Hospital. Ed. and tr. Daniel Weissbort. Oxford: Carcanet, 1972. 156. This leading dissident intellectual in Moscow was incarcerated in several mental hospitals from 1968.

2590. Gorbatov, A.V. Years Off My Life: The Memoir of General of the Soviet Army A.V. Gorbatov. Trans. Gordon Clough and Anthony Cash. New York: Norton, 1964. 222. Gorbatov's account, the first of its kind to be published in the Soviet Union, of his arrest and imprisonment during Stalin's "Great Purge."

2591. Gorodetzky, Benjamin. Light in the Darkness: 60 Years of Activity in Russia and Throughout the World. New York: Shengold, 1986. 270. The author's diary in two parts, the first includes prison in the Soviet Union until 1946, the second his international work for Jews.

2592. Grigorenko, Petr Grigor'evich. The Grigorenko Papers: Writings By General P.G. Grigorenko and Documents on His Case. London: Hurst, 1976. 187.

2593. Grigrenko, Petro (Petr) G. Memoirs. Trans. Thomas Whitney. New York: Norton, 1982. 462. Imprisoned 1968-1972 for his human rights activities and "exposing government lies and tyranny." To avoid trial, the KGB had him committed to a psychiatric hospital for forty-nine months. The special psychiatric hospitals and the psychiatric experts were part of "a single organ of political terror."

2594. "Gulag III." Newsweek 87 (March 8, 1976) 44. On Solzhenitsyn's third and final volume of Gulag Archipelago, completing his history of the Soviet Union's forced-labor camps.

2595. "Gulag and the Zek." Newsweek 83 (January 7, 1974) 36-7. On the publication of Solzhenitsyn's The Gulag Archipelago, 1918-1956.

2596. "Gulag Avenger." Time 113 (April 30, 1979) 51. A French citizen wrongly imprisoned for treason is suing the Soviet Union for reparations.

2597. "Gulag Eyewitness: Daring Photographs by a Soviet Prisoner." Life 10 (September 1987) 73-5. Georgi Mikhailov, physicist at Leningrad University, was sentenced to four years in prison and exile in Siberia for exhibliting unsanctioned works of art. He secretly photographed prison life at the Kolyma labor camp.

2598. Henryk Erlich and Victor Alter: Two Heroes and Martyrs for Jewish Socialism. Hoboken, NJ; New York: Ktav; Jewish Labor Bund, 1990. 386. Erlich and Alter were leaders of Poland's Jewish Labor Bund, a militant social democratic socialist movement. Stalin imprisoned and murdered them.

2599. Herling-Grudzinski, Gustaw. A World Apart. New York: Arbor House, 1986. 262. During 1940-1942 he was first in prison and then in a forced labor camp near Archangel, convicted of trying to leave the Soviet Union, which had signed a non-aggression pact with Hitler, to fight the Nazis. Describes life in the prison and camp.

2600. Herman, Victor. Coming Out of the Ice: an Unexpected Life. Oklahoma City, Okla.: Freedom Press, 1979. 369. The author, a U.S. citizen, accompanied his parents to the Soviet Union, his father sent there by the Ford Motor Company. He was imprisoned in 1938 for 18 years, finally allowed to return to the U.S. in 1976.

2601. Herman, Victor. The Gray People: Hundreds of Americans Murdered in the Gulag: Sexual Abuse of Political Prisoners. Pittsburgh: Independent Publishing House, 1981. 106. Tells the story of the 300 U.S. Ford Motor Co. employees who went to the Soviet Union in the 1930's to build an auto plant and who died in prisons and labor camps.

2602. Herman, Victor and Fred Dohrs. "The True Horror of Soviet Internal Exile." National Review 32 (July 25, 1980) 883-6. On the unfair trials of dissidents and exile to a village under strict restraint.

2603. Hirsh, Sherry, et al., eds. Madness Network News Reader. San Fransico: Glide, 1974. 192. Dedicated to ending injustices in the psychiatric system. Includes Solzhenitsyn's protest of the psychiatric confinement of Zhores Medvedev. Also see Madness News Network 4.6 (Spring 1978) 17 and 7.5 (Winter 1985) 17 on psychiatric control of dissent.

2604. Holden, Constance. "Emigrés Express Caution on Soviet Human Rights." Science 235 (February 13, 1987) 738-40. Despite recent releases of scientists from prisons and hospitals, optimism about a genuine change under Gorbachev is premature.

2605. Holden, Constance. "Is Soviet Psychiatry Changing its Ways?" Science 242 (October 28, 1988) 505-6. Hopeful signs: U.S. delegation to visit prisoners in mental hospitals, and the Soviets plan to reapply for membership in the World Psychiatric Association.

2606. Honerkamp, P. "Mind Destruction in the USSR." National Review 31 (October 26, 1979) 47-8. On the incarceration of Sister Valeria Makeyeva in the Kazan Special Psychiatric Hospital for selling religious belts to raise money for convents.

2607. "How Soviets Make Psychiatry a Weapon." U.S. News and World Report 97 (July 23, 1984) 12. On the use of mental hospitals and psychotropic drugs to control dissidents.

2608. Hrytsiak, Ievhen (Hrycyak, Yevhen). An Open Letter to Mykola V. Pidhorny. New York: Ukrainian Information Center, 1977. 15.

2609. Hrytsiak, Ievhen. The Norilsk Uprising : Short Memoire. Munich: Ukrainisches Institüt für Bildungspolitik, 1984. 63. Account of the 1953 uprising in the Norilsk Prison camp.

2610. Human Rights Activists in the Soviet Union. United States Department of State Bulletin 83 (December 1983) 31-2. On a new campaign of repression: the trials ofIosif Begun, Father Sigitas Temkevicius, and Oleg Radzinskiy.

2611. Human Rights and the Detention of Andrei Sakharov, Update: Hearing Before the Subcommittee on International Organizations of the Committee on Foreign Affairs, House of Representatives, Ninety-sixth Congress, second session, April 24, 1980. Washington: U.S.G.P.O., 1980. 35. Statements and articles by and about Sakharov.

2612. "Imprisonment: Sergei Kovalev." BioScience 32 (December 1982) 874. A profile of this persecuted dissident.

2613. The Increased Arrests of Soviet Jews in 1981. London: Institute of Jewish Affairs Report No. 21, 1981. 6. On Jewish dissidents.

2614. Inside Soviet Prisons: Documents of the Struggle for Human and National Rights in the USSR. New York: Committee for the Defence of Soviet Political Prisoners, 1976. 72. Individual appeals, excerpts from autobiographies, maps, prisoner profiles, bibliographies, etc.

2615. International Sakharov Hearings. Fifth International Sakharov Hearing: Proceedings, April 1985. London: A. Deutsch, 1986. 214. Thirty-three essays and three appendices cover a wide range of topics related to Sakharov and political prisoners in the Soviet Union: e.g. the Helsinki movement, changes in prisoner categories, deterioration of prisoners, abuse of psychiatry.

2616. International Sakharov Hearings: Testimony. Christianborg, Copenhagen, Denmark: October 17-19, 1975. 250. Sample testimonies: "Persecution of Nationalists in the USSR: The Case of the Ukrainian SSR," "Concerning the Question of the Persecution of the Lithuanian Nation."

2617. An Interview with Political Prisoners in a Soviet Perm Camp. Trans Taras Drozd. Baltimore: Smoloskyp, 1975. 30. A samizdat of replies to questions smuggled into and out of a labor camp. Clandestine interviews of eleven prisoners.

2618. "Intolerance." Newsweek 79 (January 17, 1972) 39. On Vladimir Bukovsky and Andrei Amalrik sentenced for criticizing the system.

2619. Invincible Spirit: Art and Poetry of Ukrainian Women Political Prisoners in the U.S.S.R. Tr. Bodhan Yasen. Baltimore: Smoloskyp, 1977. 136. Contains poetry, letters, and photographs of designs created by women who have been imprisoned in Soviet labor camps for defending Ukrainian nationalism and human rights.

2620. "Involuntary Journey." Time 102 (August 6, 1973) 33. Writer Andrei Amalrik has been resentenced to prison for "defaming the Soviet state."

2621. "Islands of Slavery." Time 103 (June 24, 1974) 48+. Alexander Solzhenitsyn's The Gulag Archipelago, Vol. 2, is published; an account of the forced-labor system under Stalin.

2622. Ivanov-Ruzumnik, R.V. The Memoirs of Ivanov-Ruzumnik. Trans. P.S. Squire. London: Oxford UP, 1965. 348. Literary critic and sociologist Ivanov-Ruzumnik's memoirs include numerous arrests and long periods of imprisonment.

2623. Jackson, James O. "A Day in the Depths of the Gulag." Time 129 (March 9, 1987) 52. Iosif Begun and other prisoners released.

2624. Jakobson, Michael. Origins of the Gulag: The Soviet Prison Camp System, 1917-1934. Lexington, KY: U of Kentucky P, 1992. 192. Examines the most crucial period in the history of the Soviet prison camps: from the October Revolution of 1917, when the tsarist prison system was destroyed, to October 1934, when all places of confinement were consolidated under one agency--the infamous GULAG. Focuses on the structure and interrelations of prison agencies, the Bolshevik views of crime and punishment and inmate reeducation, and prison self-suffiency.

2625. Jenness, Linda. "Women In Revolt: Communist Party and Women Political Prisoners." Militant 39.23 (June 20, 1975) 11. Jenness's criticism of the U.S. Communist party for overlooking examples of "courageous women imprisoned and tortured in Soviet prisons" includes case studies.

2626. Joffe, Maria. One Long Night: A Tale of Truth. Tr. Vera Dixon. Clapham, Eng.: New Park, 1978. 248. An opponent of Stalin tells of her long years (1929-1957) in prisons and labor camps for protesting the expulsion of Trotsky from the country and other criticisms. This is her prison memoir.

2627. Kaminska, Ruth Turkow. Mink Coats and Barbed Wire. London: Collins, Harvill, 1979. 255. (Orig. I Don't Want to Be Brave Anymore. Washington, DC: New Republic, 1978). An account of her years in Stalin's prisons and camps. She was a singer and actress, and Jewish.

2628. Kandyba, Ivan. Russian Unlawfulness in Ukraine: The Life of a Martyr. Munich: Ukrainisches Institüt für Bildungspolitik, 1980. 40. Sentenced along with six others to ten to fifteen years in prison, 1961-1976, for raising the issue of Ukrainian secession from the Soviet Union.

2629. Karklins, Rasma. The Organization of Power in Soviet Labor Camps. Urbana-Champaign, IL: Soviet Interview Project, U of Illinois, 1988. 42. Analyzes the main political features of the labor camp system, from coercion to co-opting inmates, incentives, and self-policing, to prisoner protest.

2630. "The KGB Admits a Mistake." Newsweek 109 (January 19, 1987) 32. A KGB official is fired for ordering the arrest of a journalist who told the truth--a reflection of Gorbachev's glasnost.

2631. Khodorovich, Tatiana Sergeevna. The Case of Leonid Plyushch. Trans. Marite Sapiets, et al. London; Boulder, Colo.: Hurst; Westview, 1976. 152. An account of his persecution in psychiatric hospitals 1972-1976 accompanied by letters and other writings by Plyushch. Plyushch has become "a symbol of resistance" to the crime of dissent. He was imprisoned in 1972 for "anti-Soviet activities," then declared insane, and then in a secret trial sentenced to treatment in a special psychiatric hospital. He was released and allowed to emigrate in 1976.

2632. Khorev, Mikhail. Letters From a Soviet Prison Camp. Grand Rapids, Mich.: Baker Book House, 1989. 222. Account of the trials and imprisonment of a popular pastor, one of the leaders of the Evangelical Baptists. One of Khorev's sons has also been imprisoned for his faith.

2633. Khrushchev's Crimes in Ukraine: Mass-Murders of Ukrainian Political Prisoners. London: Ukranian, 1962. 93. "Some of the foulest mass murders of Ukrainian political prisoners took place" during Nikita Khrushchev's period in office as "the virtual Governor-General and viceroy in Ukraine."

2634. Kitchin, George. Prisoner of the OGPU. New York: Longmans, Green, 1935. Rpt. New York: Arno, 1970. 336. Memoir of his four years in prison, mainly in penal camps in Siberian areas of Archangel and Vologda, 1928-1932.

2635. Kmiecik, Jerzy. A Boy in the Gulag. New York: Quartet Books, 1983. 248. The story of a Polish citizen's imprisonment in a labor camp from 1939 to 1941, until he was released to join the Polish Army.

2636. Kohan, John. "Battening down the Hatches." Time 123 (June 4, 1984) 32-5. On the persecution of Sakharov and his wife Elena Bonner.

2637. Kopelev, Lev. Ease my Sorrows: A Memior. Trans. Antonina Bovis. New York: Random House, 1983. 256. The third of three volumes of memoirs deals with the years 1947-1954 he spent in a special prison camp for scientists, where they could continue to conduct research. Kopelev was convicted of "bourgeois humanism" after World War II because he tried to prevent troops under his command from pillaging and raping on their advance through Prussia.

2638. Kopelev, Lev. No Jail For Thought. Trans. Anthony Austin. London: Secker & Warburg, 1977. 268. Harmondsworth: Penguin, 1979. 319. (To Be Preserved Forever. Philadelphia: Lippincott, 1977. 268.) Account of the author's prosecution 1945-47 for "crimes against the state" (i.e. protesting against Soviet military outrages against the German population in the closing days of WW II). This is an abridged translation of Khranit vechno.

2639. Koppers, Andre. A Biographical Dictionary on the Political Abuse of Psychiatry in the USSR. Amsterdam: International Association on the Political Use of Psychiatry, 1990. 180.

2640. Koryagin, Dr. Anatoly. "An Appeal From a Soviet Labor Camp." Matchbox (May 1982) 5. By a Soviet psychiatrist who was sentenced to twelve years for his opposition to the use of political psychiatry to lock up and torture dissidents.

2641. Koryagin: A Man Struggling for Human Dignity. Ed. Robert van Voren; with contributions by Dutch Parliamentarian Group in Defence of Koryagin. Amsterdam: Second World Press, 1987. 112. On Koryagin's trial, receiving the alternative Nobel Peace Prize, the campaign for his release, etc.

2642. Krasin, Victor. "How I Was Broken by the KGB." Trans. Antonina W. Bovis." New York Times Magazine (March 18, 1984) 54-5+. Victor Krasin, arrested for supporting "anti-Soviet agitation and propaganda," describes how the KGB forced him to publicly confess guilt.

2643. "Kremlin Silences its Foremost Critic." U.S. News and World Report 88 (February 4, 1980) 7. Sakharov exiled to Gorky.

2644. Krickus, Richard. "Case of Vytautas Skuodis, U.S. Citizen." Commonweal 108 (September 25, 1981) 525. Skuodis was hounded by the KGB and then imprisoned for defending human rights and joining the Lithuanian Helsinki Watch Group.

2645. Krickus, Richard. "Hostages in their Homeland." Commonweal 107 (February 15, 1980) 75-80. About Lithuanian human rights dissidents, particularly Viktoras Petkus and Balys Gajauskas.

2646. Krickus, Richard. "To the Finland Border." Commonweal 108 (September 25, 1981) 523-6. Vladys Sakalys escaped from a Soviet prison camp.

2647. Kudirka, Simas and Larry Eichel. For Those Still at Sea. New York: Dial, 1978. 226. The author was imprisoned four years for trying to defect to the U.S. He was finally allowed to emigrate.

2648. Kudirka, Simas. Testimony of Simas Kudirka at Bicentennial Convocation on Global Justice, Convened by the National Conference on Catholic Bishops, Committee for the Bicentennial. Maryknoll, New York, July 14,1976. Maspeth, N.Y.: Lithuanian Roman Catholic Religious Aid, 1976. 24. Served three and three-fourths years in alabor camp for attempting to leave the country. Discusses how the Soviet Union has trampled on the Lithuanian people and the United Nation's Declaration of Human Rights

2649. Kuznetsov, Eduard. "Flight from the Gulag." Trans. L. Thorne. New York Times Magazine (April 27, 1980) 36-41+. An account of Eduard Kuznetsov's last three days in a Soviet prison before he and others were released to the U.S. in exchange for two Soviet spies.

2650. Kuznetsov, Eduard. Prison Diaries. 1st Scarborough Books ed. Briarcliff Manor, N.Y.: Stein and Day, 1980. 254. (Orig. Russian ed. 1973; orig. English ed. 1975). Along with ten others the author was tried on the charge of treason for planning to highjack an airplane to leave the country. Kuznetsov and one other were sentenced to death, which was commuted to fifteen years. The author had already served seven years for his writings and poetry readings.

2651. Kwak, Byong-Kyu. The Land of Eternal Darkness: Memories of Siberian Labor Camps. Tr. Paul White, et al. New York: Vantage, 1978. 384. The author was accused of being a U.S. spy in N. Korea in 1946 and was sent to a Soviet Siberian prison for 13 years. Many stories of the sex lives of prisoners.

2652. Laird, Sally. "Diary of Russian Enlightenment." Index On Censorship 17.4 (April 1988) 17-23, 28. Extracts from her diary of her visit to Moscow with the International Helsinki Federation to talk with Soviet officials and private rights groups about human rights--Sakharov, psychiatric hospitals, religious persecution, etc.

2653. Langone, J. "A Profession Under Stress." Time 133 (April 10, 1989) 94-5. On efforts by Soviet Psychiatrists to regain international respectability.

2654. Laquer, Walter. Stalin: The Glasnost Revelations. New York: Scribners, 1990. 382. On the war against the peasants, the great purges of the 1930's killing "millions of people," including the old guard of the Bolshevik party and the Red Army Command.

2655. Larina, Anna. This I Cannot Forget: The Memoirs of Nikolai Bukharin's Widow. Trans. Gary Kern. New York: Norton, 1993. 384. On Stalin's destruction 1936-1938 of the "old Bolsheviks" who had helped create the Soviet state, and their relatives and friends (Bukharin was the principal defendant in the third trial), and an account of her twenty years in prisons and camps.

2656. Latvian Dissent: Case Histories of the 1983 Soviet Campaign to Silence Political Dissidents in Occupied Latvia. Rockville, MD.: World Federation of Free Latvians, 1985. 101. About the "wave of terror" in 1983 against religious and human rights leaders.

2657. Lawton, Kim A. "Glasnost in Perm 35?" Christianity Today 33 (October 20, 1989) 37-8. Discusses Soviet prison camps in the wake of glasnost--few changes have occured; many changes are needed.

2658. Lawton, Kim A. "I Did Not Compromise, Says Released Evangelist." Christianity Today 32 (February 19, 1988) 40-1. Vladmir Khailo emigrated with his wife and eighteen family members to escape the severe persecution they received after Vladmir spoke openly of his beliefs as a Christian.

2659. Lawton, Kim A. "Soviet Believers: Still Paying a High Cost for Commitment." Christianity Today 31 (June 12, 1987) 40-2. Some political prisoners have been released (about 120) but plenty still remain behind bars.

2660. Leipman, Flora. The Long Journey Home: the Memoirs of Flora Leipman. London, Bantam, 1987. 443. The author's mother took her children back to her native Russia after the death of their father, where they were arrested and sent to a labour camp. Her sisters and brother perished in the camps.

2661. Lermolo, Elizabeth. Face of a Victim. Tr. I.D.W. Talmadge; Foreword Alexandra Tolstoy. New York: Harper, 1955. 311. The author was imprisoned for eight years beginning in 1934 for alleged counterrevolutionary activities and complicity in an assassination. Stalin himself aided in questioning her.

2662. Letters from Russian Prisons, Consisting of Reprints of Documents by Political Prisoners in Soviet Prisons, Prison Camps and Exile, and Reprints of Affidavits Concerning Political Persecution in Soviet Russia, Official Statements by Soviet Authorities, Excerpts from Soviet Laws Pertaining to Civil Liberties, and Other Documents. London: C.W. Daniel; New York: Boni, 1925. 317. (New York: Hyperion, 1977.) Published for the International Committee for Political Prisoners. Includes supporting letters by twenty-two distinguished European and American authors.

2663. Letters of Love: Women Political Prisoners in Exile and the Camps. Comp. & ed. Julia Voznesenskaya. Trans. Roger and Angela Keys. London: Quartet, 1989. 119. The editor of the collection was herself a prisoner. The letters focus upon love--for children, husbands, lovers, friends, love for poetry, etc.

2664. Lewis, Jonathan, and Phillip Whitehead. Stalin: A Time For Judgement. New York: Pantheon; London: Methuen, 1990. 254. On Stalin's ruthless exploitation of the national security state.

2665. Linke, Maria Zeitner. East Wind: the Story of Maria Zeitner Linke. Ed. Ruth Hunt. Grand Rapids, Mich.: Zondervan Publishing, House, 1987. 240. (Orig. 1976). Linke's account of nine years in Soviet prisons as told to Hunt.

2666. Lipper, Elinor. Eleven Years in Soviet Prison Camps. Tr. Richard and Clara Winston. Chicago: Henry Regnery, 1951. 310 p. This Dutch Socialist working for a Moscow publisher was imprisoned 1937-48 in ten different prisons, convicted of counterrevolutionary activities.

2667. List of Political Prisoners in the USSR. 8th ed. Munich: Das Land und die Welt, 1986. 268. (Orig. pub. 1978). 745 prisoners in detention, psychiatric hospitals, exile, or labor camps are annotated.

2668. Lubarsky, Cronid. "The Human Rights Movement and Perestroika." Index On Censorship 17.5 (May 1988) 16. Former prisoner Lubarsky now in exile in Munich edits the USSR News Brief on human rights and publishes an annual List of Political Prisoners in the USSR. This article discusses the continued repression.

2669. Luryi, Yuri. "On the 35-year Old Trail of a Missing War Hero." Macleans 94 (March 2, 1981) 16-18. Interview with Yuri Luryi on Raoul Wallenberg, who is credited with saving 100,000 Jews from death during World War II.

2670. Lyons, Paul J. "Torture in the USSR." National Review 21 (Dec 16, 1969) 1259-60. Focuses on Yuli Daniel's experiences, based upon Amnesty International reports.

2671. "Making Up For Lost Time." Index On Censorship 14.5 (October 1985) 40-41. A account of physicist and poet Irina Ratushinskaya, sentenced to 12 years in prison and exile, accompanied by six of her poems.

2672. Malsagoff, S.A. An Island Hell: A Soviet Prison in the Far North. Trans. F.H. Lyon. London: Philpot, 1926. 223. An account of the conditions in the Soviet prisons in the Solovetsky Islands by former soldier of the Caucasus and escapee from Solovetsky. Chapter 9 deals specifically with the fate of women in Soviet political prisons.

2673. Mandelshtam, Nadezhda. Hope Abandoned. Tr. Max Hayward. New York: Atheneum, 1974. 687. New York: Penguin, 1976. 767. Volume two of the life of her husband, Osip Mandelshtam. This book complements the first by filling in biographical gaps from their first meeting in 1919 up to the present, and by providing interpretive contexts for her husband's defiance of Stalin.

2674. Mandelshtam, Nadezhda. Hope Against Hope. New York: Atheneum, 1970. 431. Narrates the last four years (1934-38) of the life of her husband, Osip Mandelshtam, from his first arrest to his death in transit camp near Vladivostock, for criticizing Stalin.

2675. Manning, R.A. "One Free, Many Left Behind." U.S. News and World Report 100 (Feb. 24, 1986) 41. On the release of Anatoly Shcharansky after nine years in labor camps for alleged espionage.

2676. Marchenko, Anatoly. From Tarusa to Siberia. Royal Oak, MI: Strathcona, 1980. 139. The author was repeatedly sentenced to prison and exile and his wife was subjected to many searches and constant harrassment for their criticism of the government and desire to emigrate. This book recounts his experiences during 1975-1977.

2677. Marchenko, Anatoly. My Testimony. Trans. Michael Scammell. New York: E.P. Dutton, 1969. 415. An account of his six years' hard labor 1961-66, focusing on the 3 main groups of political prisoners: intellectuals accused of anti-Soviet propaganda, nationalists (advocating autonomy for non-Russian parts of the USSR), and religious believers. The author was first arrested over a fight, then for escaping from prison and trying to flee the country, again in 1968 for writing letters critical of the prison camps and in praise of freedom and democracy, and that sentence was extended when this book was published abroad.

2678. Marchenko, Anatoly. To Live Like Every One. Trans. Paul Goldberg. New York: Holt, 1989. 227. Memoir that fits chronologically between My Testimony and From Terusa to Siberia, about his life in post Stalin prisons--20 of his 48 years.

2679. Marshall, Eliot. "U.S. Scientists Protest Punishment of Sakharov." Science 207 (February 8, 1980) 625. U.S. scientific organizations oppose Sakharov's exile to Gorki.

2680. Martin, Andre. Buried Alive in Soviet Hospital-Prisons. Tongerlo, Belgium: Staf Vermeulen, 1972. 48. An appeal for the release of Vladimir Bukovsky from a psychiatric prison hospital.

2681. Marton, K. "The Wallenberg Mystery." Atlantic Monthly 246 (November 1980) 33-40. Raoul Wallenberg, savior of tens of thousands of Jews, has not been heard of since 1945.

2682. "Martyrdom of Soviet Political Offenders." Literary Digest 104 (January 4, 1930) 14-15. An account of the escaped political prisoners from the Solovyetsky prison into Finland.

2683. Martz, Larry, et al. "A Hard Bargain." Newsweek 109 (January 5, 1987) 12-13. Gorbachev frees Sakharov.

2684. Maryniak, Irena. "Oles Shevchenko et al. in the Botanical Gardens." Index On Censorship 18.5 (May 1989) 32-35. "Index's USSR researcher interviews an ex-political prisoner (and some others...) in Kiev."

2685. McKenzie, J. The White Terror. London: British Section of the International Class War Prisoners Aid, 1925. 88. Violations by the counterrevolutionary forces.

2686. Medvedev, Roy, ed. The Samizdat Register I. London: Merlin; New York: Norton, 1977. 316. The Samizdat Register II. London: Merlin; New York: Norton, 1981. 323. Translations of dissident writings published in the clandestine journal XXth Century. From 1977 the editor and contributors were increasingly harrassed by authorities and some arrested.

2687. Medvedev, Roy, and Giulietto Chiesa. "Some Glimpses into Recent Soviet Events." Dissent 37.3 (Summer 1990) 315. On the rehabilitation of prisoners under de-Stalinization.

2688. Medvedev, Zhores, and Roy Medvedev. A Question of Madness. Tr. Ellen de Kadt. New York: Knopf, 1971. 223. An account by Zhores Medvedev of his incarceration in a mental hospital (Aug.-Sept. 1970), interspersed with commentary by his brother Roy to "complete the picture." "My brother's case clearly marked a new phase in the abuse of psychiatry for political purposes. There was no criminal charge against him, he was neither brought to court nor put under arrest. The only pretext for his committal was some anonymous criticism of his writings on the problem of science" (220). A strong warning against the political use of psychiatric hospitals.

2689. Medvedev, Zhores A. and Roy A. Medvedev. "Question of Madness." New York Times Magazine (November 7, 1971) 34-5. Excerpt from the Medvedevs' book A Question of Madness recounting authorities seizing Zhores from his home, 19 days of intense "psychiatric examinations," and his provisional release.

2690. Medvedev, Zhores. "Russia Under Brezhnev." New Left Review 17 (September 1979) 3-33. Part IV "Oppositions," deals with repression of dissent as compared to that of the Kruschev regime.

2691. Mee, Cornelia. The Internment of Soviet Dissenters in Mental Hospitals. 2nd augm. ed. Cambridge, Eng: John Arliss, 1971. 22. Examines the use of psychiatric hospitals to silence dissenters, e.g. General Grigorenko.

2692. Melgounov, Sergey Petrovich. The Red Terror in Russia. Westport, CT: Hyperion, 1975. 271. (Orig. pub. 1926). Memoirs of Melgounov, opponent of Bolshevism, arrested eight times before receiving a death sentence in 1920 (commuted to 10 years solitary confinement), and finally exiled for life. Chapter 6 explicitly details the many brutal methods of prison torture and other atrocities: mass executions, mock executions, starvation, rape, mutilation, etc.

2693. Memorandum from the Committee for the Defence of Ukrainian Political Prisoners in the USSR to the Right Honourable James Callaghan, M.P., Secretary of State for Foreign and Commonwealth Affairs. London: The Committee, 1974. 8. An appeal to the British government and people to intervene for the prisoners, several of whom are profiled.

2694. Meshko, Oksana. Between Death and Life. New York: Women's Association for the Defense of Four Freedoms for Ukraine, 1981. 176. First sentenced to ten years of hard labor then in 1980 to a psychiatric hospital for her work with the Kiev Helsinki Accords Group, and then in 1981 to six months incarceration and five years exile for anti-Soviet propaganda. This book describes her life from 1917 to 1977.

2695. Mintz, Israel. White Prison. Ed. & trans. Shira Twersky-Cassel. Israel: Israeli Center for Public Libraries, 1990. 179. Prison life and conditions.

2696. "Missing Person." Time 123 (May 28, 1984) 58. On Sakharov's hunger strike and disappearance.

2697. Mitchell, Jared. "Keeping the Pressure On." Macleans 96 (February 7, 1983) 27. The Kremlin feels the pressure as Western activists push for the release of Anatoly Shcharansky, who is steadily being subjected to worse living conditions.

2698. Moody, John. "Homeward Bound, Reluctantly." Time 127.23 (June 9, 1986) 44. On Yelena Bonner's visit to the United States; she is soon to return to her exiled husband Andrei Sakharov in Gorki.

2699. Moroz, Valentyn. Among the Snows: Protest Writings from Ukraine. London: Ukrainian Information Service, 1971. 64. Author sentenced to 14 years in prison for protesting the "terror regime." List of other persecuted Ukrainians, and other documents.

2700. Moroz, Valentyn. Boomerang: the Works of Valentyn Moroz. Baltimore; Toronto: Smoloskyp, 1974. 272. For his dissent against the Soviet system, this history instructor in the Ukraine was imprisoned a total of 18 years between 1965 and 1984. This book contains accounts of his trials, imprisonment, and appeals.

2701. Moroz, Valentyn. Instead of a Final Statement. Munich: Press Bureau of the Anti-Bolshevik Bloc of Nations, 1979. 121.

2702. Moroz, Valentyn. Report From the Beria Reserve: the Protest Writings of Valentyn Moroz. Chicago: Cataract, 1974. 162. Imprisoned 1966-1969 accused of "anti-Soviet agitation" for the secession of the Ukraine from the USSR. The title essay (pp. 1-51) was written in solitary confinement and smuggled out. He was re-imprisoned in 1970 for the writings gathered together here, and treated harshly. "Perhaps the most important political prisoner in the USSR today."

2703. Moshinsky, Efim. Raoul Wallenberg is Alive!: The Amazing Autobiography of the KGB Officer Who Arrested Him in 1945. Jerusalem: Rescue; Good Times, 1987. 172. Working through the Swedish Embassy, Wallenberg saved thousands of Jews. He was arrested and imprisoned by the Soviets in Moscow, and disappeared.

2704. Netzach, Avraham. "Subbota": My Twenty Years in Soviet Prisons: Experiences of a Russian Jew, Who Survived Twenty Years of Captivity in the Prisons and Slave-Labor Camps of the Soviet Union. Brooklyn: Moriah Offset, 1979. 375.

2705. Noble, John H. I Was a Slave in Russia: an American Tells His Story. Broadview, IL.: Cicero Bible, 1969. 182. (Orig. pub. 1958, this is the 14th printing of the paper ed.). (Amerikanetz. Muncy, Pa: Faith and Freedom Forum, 1986. 117.). A U.S. citizen interned in Dresden during WWII was imprisoned by the Soviet Union from 1945 to 1955.

2706. "Not Quiet on the Russian Front." Matchbox (Winter 1977) 4-5, 13. Four case studies of dissidents, three of whom are still in prison: Alexander Argentov, Sergei Kovalyov, Vladimir Bukovsky, and Andre Amalrik.

2707. "Notes and Comment." New Yorker 54 (June 12, 1978) 23-4. On the bravery of Alexander and Kyril Podrabinek.

2708. Olenko, George. I Was a Slave and a Beggar. New York: Pageant, 1969. 165. The Ukrainian author was falsely accused in 1940 in order to fill a quota of slave laborers in Siberia. This is his story of starvation, filth, torture, death, and eventual release and emigration to the U.S.

2709. Olhovych, Orest, ed. An Interview with Political Prisoners in a Soviet Perm Camp. Trans. Taras Drozd. 2nd Ed. Ellicott City, MD: Smoloskyp, 1978. 30. The 1974 undertaking of smuggling questions into a Soviet prison camp and conducting interviews with political prisoners representing several generations of Ukrainian dissidents.

2710. On Speaking Terms: An Unprecedented Human Rights Mission to the Soviet Union, January 25-31, 1988. Vienna, Austria: International Helsinki Federation for Human Rights, 1988. 55. The Federation visited at the invitation of the Soviet Union, but they were not allowed to visit the Soviet Helsinki monitors, who were imprisoned in Perm labor camp. The IHF estimated "approximately 360 known political prisoners remained in prison."

2711. Orlov, Yuri. "My Life in Exile." Trans. Catherine A. Fitzpatrick. New York Times Magazine (March 15, 1987) 26-8+. "A Soviet physicist looks back on his years in Siberia--the hardships, the cold, the fear, the lies."

2712. Osadchyi, Mykhailo Hyrhorovych. Cataract: An Autobiographical Outline in Two Parts. London: Ukrainian Publishers, 1975. 111. An underground publication from Ukraine ("samvydav" in Ukrainian) re-published in the West in the magazine Liberation Path, 1972. This book was written in 1968 after its author returned from two years severe regime in Mordovia for "ideological subversion." He was again imprisoned in 1972 this time for seven years.

2713. Osipova, Tatyana. "It's Wrong to Kill People." Trans. Cathy Fitzpatrick. Kick It Over 21 (Summer 1988) 10. Report on Leonid Gromov, who sabotaged armored vehicles produced for the Afghanistan campaign, and who was sentenced to a psychiatric prison.

2714. Panin, Dimitrii Mikhailovich. The Notebooks of Sologdin. Trans. John Moore. New York: Harcourt Brace Jovanovich, 1973. 320. The real-life model of the character Sologdin in Solzhenitsyn's novel The First Circle gives his account of thirteen years spent in prisons and labor camps.

2715. Parchomenko, Walter. "Ukrainian Dissidents, Waiting in Hope." America 141 (August 11, 1979) 54-5. Ukrainian prisoners need more attention from the West. From 1965 to 1978 massive arrests occurred, and the severe repression continues, in fact it is worse than in Russia.

2716. Parchomenko, Walter. "Vladimir Shelkov." Commonweal 107 (September 26, 1980) 517-519. Shelkov of Tashkent, Uzbekistan, 83 years old, was sentenced to five years hard labor for his leadership as a Seventh Day Adventist. He died in a few months.

2717. Parvilahti, Unto. Beria's Gardens: A Slave Laborer's Experiences in the Soviet Utopia. Trans. Alan Blair. London: Hutchinson, 1959. 286. The author, who fought for the Nazis, was kidnapped from his native Finland in 1944, flown to Moscow and imprisoned, then in 1950 transfered to Siberia for 10 more years.

2718. Pasternak, Grigory I. To Reach This Season: A Russian's Odyssey to the West. Berkeley: Judah L. Magnes Museum, 1983. 241. The author's experiences in Soviet Labor camps.

2719. "Patients' Rights" Time 131 (January 18, 1988) 33. Gorbachev reforming misuse of psychiatry to control dissidents.

2720. The Persecution of the Ukranian Helsinki Group: Fifth Anniversary Update, November 9, 1981. Toronto: Human Rights Commission, World Congress of Free Ukranians, 1981. 36. On trials, sentences, and new arrests. Thiry-one of the persecuted are discussed.

2721. Petrov, Vladimir. It Happens in Russia: Seven Years Forced Labour in the Siberian Goldfields. London: Eyre & Spottiswoode, 1951. 470. Russian defector Petrov describes life in a Siberian labor camp.

2722. "Plea for Kuznetsov." Index On Censorship 19.1 (Jan. 1990) 32. Sergei Kuznetsov is held in isolation after his trial. "Neither his family, friends, lawyer nor doctor are being permitted to see him."

2723. Plyushch, Leonid. History's Carnival: A Dissident's Autobiography. Trans. Marco Carynnyk. New York: Harcourt Brace Jovanovich; London: Collins and Harvill, 1979. 429. An active dissident imprisoned in 1972 for criticizing the government, he was subjected to repeated psychiatric examinations, diagnosed psychopathic and schizophrenic and sentenced to a psychiatric hospital after an illegal trial even by Soviet law in which he was convicted of "anti-Soviet agitation and propaganda." A vociferous international protest persuaded the government to release him and allow him and his family to emigrate in 1976.

2724. Plyuschch, Leonid. "Statement by Leonid Plyuschch." Militant 40.7 (February 20, 1976) 19. Plyuschch is released from a Soviet psychiatric hospital after being arrested for holding anti-communist views, and later labled schizophrenic.

2725. Podrabinek, Aleksander. Punitive Medicine. Ann Arbor, Mich.: Karoma, 1980. 223. The author was arrested in 1978 for his opposition to the use of psychiatric hospitals for political purposes. The original full manuscript of the book was confiscated by the KGB. He then reconstructed the text. Includes lists of prisoners in hospitals.

2726. Podrabinek, Aleksander. "Soviet Psychiatry: a Message From Moscow." New York Review of Books 35 (December 8, 1988) 40-2. About the perversion of psychiatry for political purposes.

2727. Pogrebin, Letty Cottin. "A Communist Plot." Ms. 17 (October 1988) 28-9. Interview with Ida Nudel, who was arrested and sent to Siberia for three years for hanging a banner that said, "KGB, Give Me My Visa!"

2728. Political Abuse of Psychiatry in the USSR. New York: Amnesty International USA, 1983. 17. Documents Soviet political misuse of psychiatry over the last five years.

2729. "Political Imprisonment in the USSR." Matchbox (May 1980) 5. Overview of punishments used by Soviet authorities on political dissenters: imprisonment, forced labor, dangerous drug therapy, exile, starvation, etc.

2730. Popoff, George. The Tcheka: The Red Inquisition. London: Philpot, 1925. 308. Popoff's memoirs of the horrors of imprisonment and torture at the hands of the political secret police (later the KGB), and a history of the Tcheka.

2731. Priess, Anita. Exiled to Siberia. Steinbach, Manitoba, Canada: Derksen, 1972. 82. Imprisoned 1946-1953 for refusing to divorce her German husband.

2732. "Prison Conditions on Solovetsky." Nation 120 (March 4, 1925) 248-52. Letters from political prisoners followed by a government report on conditions there.

2733. Prisoners of Conscience in the USSR: Their Treatment and Conditions. 2nd ed. London: Amnesty International, 1980. 213. Updated and revised edition of the 1975 report. "During the past four years the abuses documented in the first edition...have remained part of official practice in the USSR"--imprisonment for non-violent exercise of human rights, etc.

2734. Profiles: The Helsinki Monitors. Washington: Commission on Security and Cooperation in Europe, 1979. 50. Eighty-three Helsinki monitors are profiled, most of them accompanied by photos. Many of them are in prison or have been in prison.

2735. "Prolonged Visits to the Soviet Gulag." Whole Earth Review 54 (Spring 1987) 20-26. Describes known religious prisoners--at least 398, of whom 333 are Christians. Some are profiled, many are listed.

2736. "Protesting Spiritual Murder." Time 95 (June 29, 1970) 30-1. Scientists and intellectuals protest confinement of dissidents in mental institutions.

2737. Prychodko, Nicholas. One of the Fifteen Million. Boston: Little, Brown; London: Dent, 1952. 236. The author, a university lecturer, was imprisoned in a Siberian forced labor camp in 1938 for three years on unknown charges. After his release, he escaped from the country.

2738. Psychiatric Abuse of Political Prisoners in the Soviet Union: Testimony by Leonid Plyushch: Hearing Before the Subcommittee on International Relations, House of Representatives, Ninety-Fourth Congress, Second Session, March 30, 1976. Washington: U.S.G.P.O., 1976. 82. And many other documents-"Inside Soviet Prisons," "A Chronicle of Human Rights in the U.S.S.R," "Women Political Prisoners in the U.S.S.R."

2739. "Psychoadaption; or How to Handle Dissenters." Time 98 (September 27, 1971) 44-5. Tells of scientist and dissident Zhores Medvedev's incarceration in a mental institution.

2740. Pulerevitch, Yechezkel (pen name: Yechezkel Avishabi Maor). Short Stories of the Long Death. Tel Aviv: Former Zion Prisoners from the U.S.S.R., 1974. 291. The author was a prisoner for seventeen years (1940-1957) in Siberian slave camps. This book gives vignettes and profiles of prison life and prisoners.

2741. "Punitive Medicine" by Alexander Podrabinek: A Summary. London: Amnesty International, 1977. 26. Podrabinek's 265 page Samizdat monograph on political abuses of psychiatry. The KGB confiscated his final version on which he had worked three years and threatened him with seven years imprisonment for "anti-soviet agitation."

2742. Rapoport, Yakov. The Doctors' plot of 1953. Cambridge, MA: Harvard UP, 1991. 280. The author, a pathologist, and other doctors were arrested and accused of membership in an "anti-Soviet terrorist organization," spying, and murdering political figures and generals. Most of the accused were Jews alleged to have been directed by capitalist intelligence services and by a U.S. Jewish organization. The author was released after a hearing by a commission set up to investigate false plot allegations by the MGB as part of efforts by the new Soviet government to do away with the Stalinist terror.

2743. Ratushinskaia, Irina. Grey is the Color of Hope. New York: Knopf, 1988. 355. When she was 28, this rising poet and human rights activist was sentenced in 1983 to seven years hard labor plus five years internal exile for "anti-Soviet agitation and propaganda." This is her account of four years under strict regime for "dangerous" political prisoners.

2744. Ratushinskaia, Irina. Grey is the Color of Hope. 12 Audiocassettes. Oxford: Oasis Audio Books, 1989. 960 min. A reading of Ratushinskaya's autobiography.

2745. Ratushinskaya, Irina. In the Beginning. London: Hodder and Stoughton, 1990. 320. The author's autobiography from childhood to prison to release from prison and emigration to England in 1986. She was sentenced in 1982 to seven years hard labor and five years internal exile for her poetry, but released in 1986.

2746. Ratushinskaia, Irina. Irina Ratushhinskaya Christian Poetess. Audiotape. Wheaton, Ill.: Communication Resources Dept., Wheaton College, 1987. Ratushinskaya, now free in the U.S., reads her poems.

2747. Ratushinskaia, Irina. No, I'm Not Afraid. Trans. David McDuff. Newcastle upon Tyne, Eng.: Bloodaxe, 1986. 142. A selection of her poems (pp. 75-142) accompainied by accounts of her arrest and life in a labor camp, an Amnesty International report on women prisoners, and statements by Ratushinskaia.

2748. Rayfield, Donald. "The Killing of Paolo Lashvili." Index On Censorship 19.6 (June 1990) 9-14. "The most devastating event in Georgia's cultural history was the purge of about one third of its writers, artists and intellectuals in 1924, 1931 and 1937."

2749. Reddaway, Peter. "The Attack on Anatoly Koryagin." New York Review of Books 30 (March 3, 1983) 39. On psychiatrist Koryagin's imprisonment for revealing Soviet use of mental hospitals to "cure" dissidents.

2750. Reddaway, Peter. "More Psychiatric Terror." New York Review of Books 25 (Febuary 23, 1978) 44. On the abuse of psychiatry hospitals to intern dissidents.

2751. Reddaway, Peter. "New Purge." New York Review of Books 27 (March 20, 1980) 7-8. Current assault on dissent.

2752. Reddaway, Peter. "Should World Psychiatry Readmit the Soviets?" New York Review of Books 36 (October 12, 1989) 54-8. The use of psychiatry to silence dissidents, though decreased in scope, continues.

2753. Reich, Walter. "Grigorenko Gets a Second Opinion." New York Times Magazine (May 13, 1979) 18+. Dissident General Grigorenko, twice declared mentally ill, twice committed to prison hospitals, was reexamined on a visit to the United States and deemed perfectly healthy.

2754. Reich, Walter. "Soviet Psychiatry on Trial." Commentary 65 (January 1978) 40-8. A detailed account of the process by which the World Psychiatric Association condemned Soviet political psychology.

2755. "Release of Georgi Vins." Christianity Today 23 (June 29, 1979) 10. Protestant leader Georgi Vins was "stripped of his citizenship, ousted from the land he loved, and removed from direct contact with the churches he ably served."

2756. Removsky, Semion. 29 Years Among Prisoners. [s.l.: s.n.], 1976. 288. The extraordinary prison life of Lova Leon Rouell, 1927-1956.

2757. Reuter, Madalynne. "Moscow Book Event in Exile Salutes 21 Russian Writers." Publishers Weekly 220 (October 2, 1981) 40,44. The exiled writers met in the New York Public Library for the third Moscow Book Fair reception.

2758. Rodgers, Dick. Irina. Tring: Lion, 1987. 180. In 1983, Irina Ratushinskaya, one of Russia's leading poets, was sentenced to twelve years in a strict regime prison camp for "anti-Soviet agitation in the form of poetry." This is the story of the struggle to gain her release by the author of this book and by others.

2759. Roeder, Bernhard. Katorga: An Aspect of Modern Slavery. Trans. Lionel Kochan. London: Heinemann, 1958. 271. The author spent 6 years in Soviet Prison camps from 1950 to the ascendancy of Krushchev. From this vantage point he analyzes the slavery of the "machine" of the tyranny by terror.

2760. Romanyuk, Vasyl Omelyanovych. A Ukranian Priest's Appeals from a Soviet Labor Camp. Baltimore: Smoloskyp, 1976. 12. Two letters by Rev. Romanyuk, who was imprisoned in 1972 for "anti-Soviet agitation."

2761. Romanyuk, Vasyl Omelyanovych. Vasyl Romanyuk, A Voice in the Wilderness: Letters, Appeals, Essays. Trans. Jurij Dobczansky. Wheaton, IL: Society for the Study of Religion Under Communism, 1980. 126. Writings of a priest of the Orthodox Church in the Ukraine imprisoned since 1970 and at a time of publication of this book in exile in Siberia.

2762. Rosenberg, Suzanne. A Soviet Odyssey. Toronto; New York: Oxford UP, 1988. 212. Autobiography that includes arrest and imprisonment on false charges of treason/espionage and anti-Soviet agitation, repeated interrogations, solitary confinement, Siberian (Taishet) labor camp, hard labor, hunger, and other hardships.

2763. Rupert, Raphael. A Hidden World. New York: World, 1963. 224. Rupert describes his arrest in 1947 falsely accused of espionage and of surviving nine years of a Soviet labor camp before escaping to freedom in 1956.

2764. Rupert, Raphael. Red Wire and the Lubianka. Whitegate, Co. Clare, Ireland: Ballinakella, 1991. 196. An account of his years in Soviet concentration camps, on a trumped-up charge of espionage.

2765. "Russia's 'Gift' to the West." Christianity Today 31 (June 12, 1987) 41. Interview with Irina Ratushinskaya, who reflects on her experiences in prison.

2766. "Russian Mystery: An American's Death." U.S. News and World Report 60 (February 7, 1966) 12. Newcomb Mott was killed on a prison train after he had crossed the border from Norway. The Russians claim suicide.

2767. "Sakharov's Painful Triumph." U.S. News and World Report 100 (March 3, 1986) 34-38. Describes a number of Andrei Sakharov's letters from the 1980's regarding his exile to Gorky beginning in 1980 and the persecution of himself and his wife, Yelena.

2768. Sakharov, Andrei. Memoirs. Trans. Richard Lourie. New York: Knopf, 1990. 773. Creator of the Soviet H-Bomb and Nobel laureate, Sakharov gave up his positions to become the leader of the Soviet dissident movement and a world-renowned human rights activist. Part One (18 chaps.) tell about his life as a scientist; Part Two (chaps 19-50) about his life of opposition on behalf of victims of persecution and the government's attempts to silence him and his wife Yelena Bonner. In 1975 he received the Nobel Prize for Peace. In 1980 he denounced the invasion of Afghanistan, and a few days later he was seized by the KGB in Moscow and exiled to Gorky, until freed by Gorbachev.

2769. Sakharov, Andrei. "My KGB Ordeal." U.S. News and World Report 100 (February 24, 1986) 29-36. Account of Andrei Sakharov's letters written in 1984 while exiled in Gorky. The letters were smuggled out of the USSR.

2770. Sakharov, Andrei. "A Message from Gorky." Bulletin of Atomic Scientists 39 (June/July 1983) 2-3. Response to his receiving the Szilard Award.

2771. Salisbury, Harrison. "'A Great Writer Is a Second Government': Why the Kremlin Fears Solzhenitsyn." Atlantic Monthly 233 (April 1974) 41-6. Tells how Solzhenitsyn stands in a tradition of Russian writers who exposed government crimes. Solzhenitsyn was arrested and deported instead of imprisoned because the government was afraid of him.

2772. The Sanest Men in Russia. Cheltenham, Eng: Ringrone Newspapers, 1972. 26. A sweeping indictment of Stalinism, focusing on internment in mental hospitals.

2773. Sattin, A., et al. "Ilya Glezer's Struggle." Science 187 (March 14, 1975) 902. On neuropathologist Gleser's imprisonment for possessing Zionist literature.

2774. Saunders, George. Samizdat: Voices of the Soviet Opposition. New York: Monad, 1974. 464. On protest movements 1930-1973, dedicated to "all those Soviet Communists and Marxists who have given their lives or sacrificed their well-being in the fight against Stalinism."

2775. Schwarz, Soloman. The Jews in the Soviet Union. New York: Syracuse UP, 1951. 380. A history of anti-Semitism in the USSR. The second part emphasizes anti-Semitism during and after the Nazi occupation.

2776. Senate Committee on the Judiciary. Subcommittee to Investigate the Administration of the Internal Security Act and Other Internal Security Laws. Abuse of Psychiatry for Political Repression in the Soviet Union. Washington, D.C.: GPO, 1972; New York: Arno, 1973 (reprint). 257. Testimonies and documents from the victims.

2777. "Sergei Kovalyov Sentenced." Matchbox (Winter 1976) 1. Kovalyov, founding member of the Initiative Group for the Defense of Human Rights and of the first Amnmesty International Group in the USSR, was sentenced to seven years in a labor camp followed by three years in exile.

2778. Sgovio, Thomas. Dear America: Why I Turned Against Communism. Kenmore, N.Y.: Partners' P, 1979. 287. The author, a U.S. citizen, was arrested in 1938 for seeking to leave the Soviet Union and spent many years in the Kolyma labor camp. (His father had been imprisoned in the U.S., deported for his communist activities, and then imprisoned in Moscow until his death.) This book is his story of his life, particularly of the Kolyma prison.

2779. Shabad, S. "Death of a Dissident." Newsweek 108 (December 22, 1986) 39. Anatoly Marchenko, long-time dissident and prisoner, died in prison.

2780. "Shatravka Released--But Repression Continues." End Journal 22-23 (Summer 1986) 6. Discusses several prisoners--Annetta Fedeyeva, et al.

2781. Shcharansky, Natan (Anatoly). Fear No Evil. New York: Random House, 1988. 437. The author was charged with espionage and treason in 1977, imprisoned for nine years, including more than 400 days in punishment cells and more than 200 on hunger strikes. During all this time his captors tried to make him confess to crimes he never committed.

2782. Shentalinsky, Vitaly. "Babel: Lies, Confessions and Denials." Index On Censorship 20.8 (Aug./Sept. 1991) 32-37. "The case against Babel was a fabrication from start to finish. It relied on anonymous 'sources' and shady 'informers', but it took 15 years to unmask the fraud and rehabilitate the writer."

2783. Shentalinsky, Vitaly. "The Case Against Mandelshtam, Poet." Index On Censorship 20.8 (Aug./Sept. 1991) 18-25. In May 1938, Osip Mandelshtam was sentenced to five years' exile in a labour camp for counter-revolutionary activity. He never returned, and his poetry was suppressed.

2784. Shentalinsky, Vitaly. "The Case of Nikolai Kluyev, prophet." Index On Censorship 20.8 (Aug./Sept. 1991) 26-31. Kluyev was arrested in 1934, his poetry confiscated, and he was confined in an isolation cell in the Lubianka Prison.

2785. Shifrin, Avraham. The First Guidebook to Prisons and Concentration Camps of the Soviet Union. Toronto, New York: Bantam, 1982. 390. A tour of the shocking worlds of modern-day Soviet prison camps--where men, women, and children are imprisoned for such crimes as reading forbidden books, believing in God, or merely thinking differently.

2786. Shimanov, Gennadii Mikhailovich. Notes from the Red House. Montreal: Russian Orthodox Church Outside of Russia in Canada, 1971. 52. An account of the author's incarceration in psychiatric hospitals for political reasons. Part of the author's Before Death, which was published by Samizdat.

2787. Shingarev, Andrei Ivanovich. The Shingarev Diary: How it Was: The Peter and Paul Fortress, 27-XI-17-5-I-18. Royal Oak, MI: Strathcona, 1978. 120. Minister of the government and a deputy to the Constituent Assembly after the February 1917 Revolution, the author was imprisoned and murdered by Red Guards.

2788. Shumuk, Danylo. Life Sentence : Memoirs of a Ukranian Political Prisoner. Edmonton: Canadian Institute on Ukrainian Studies, U of Alberta, 1984. 401. Amnesty International's most senior political prisoner, Shumuk has been imprisoned by the Poles (in the 1930s) for being a communist, by the Nazis, and then by the Soviets as an "enemy of the people."

2789. Shymko, Yuri R., comp. For This Was I Born: The Human Conditions in USSR Slave Labor Camps: Photographs, Testimonies, Readings, Petitions, Letters and Other Documents. Toronto: Ucrainica Research Institute, 1973. 188. Documents to support the compiler's call for world protest against the Nazism in Siberia.

2790. "A Siberian Exile Gets a Phone Call." Newsweek 104 (December 10, 1984) 57. News of Yuri Orlov in exile in Siberia after serving seven years in prison for his human rights activities as founder of the Moscow Helsinki Watch Group.

2791. Smith, Danny. Wallenberg: Lost Hero. Springfield, IL: Templegate, 1987. 192. The story of Raoul Wallenberg, a Protestant Swede who saved tens of thousands of Hungarian Jews from extermination by the Nazis, and who was then imprisoned by the Soviet Union, where he died.

2792. Smith, R. Jeffrey. "Brailovsky Arrested." Science 210 (December 5, 1980) 1106. Victor Brailovsky, founder of Moscow Sunday Scientific Seminars for scientists fired after applying for emigration, is charged with "defaming" the state.

2793. Smith, R. Jeffrey. "Scientists' Boycott Grows." Science 210 (October 31, 1980) 513. U.S. effort, including 32 Nobel laureates, to free dissident Soviet scientists.

2794. Smolowe, Jill. "Picking Up Where He Left Off." Time 129 (January 5, 1987) 53-4. Back home in Moscow, Sakharov speaks out on human rights.

2795. Solomon, Michael. Magadan. Montreal: Chateau Books; New York: Vertex, 1971. 243. The author spent seventeen years in prisons, eight of them in Siberia followed by nine years in Romania, his native country. Magadan is a transit prison on the way to the Kolyma labor complex.

2796. Solzhenitsyn, Aleksandr. "Brezhnev Cannot Look a Priest Straight in the Eye." Christianity Today 24 (June 6, 1980) 13. Statement by Solzhenitsyn concerning two priests fighting repression by the government: Father Dimitri Dudko and Father Gleb Yakunin.

2797. Solzhenitsyn, Aleksandr Isaevich. The Gulag Archipelago, 1918-1956: An Experiment in Literary Investigation. 3 vols. Parts I-II (Vol. 1) and III-IV (Vol. 2) trans. Thomas Whitney; Parts V-VII (Vol. 3) trans. Harry Willetts. New York: Harper and Row, 1973-1978. I: 660; II: 712; III: 558. A massive account of the Soviet prison system based upon the author's own experience and the reports, memoirs, and letters of 227 other witnesses. Extensive Glossaries and Indexes.

2798. Solzhenitsyn, Aleksandr Isaevich. The Gulag Archipelago, 1918-1956; an Experiment in Literary Investigation. Vol. 1. Trans. Thomas Whitney. New York: Harper, 1976. 660. (Orig. Russian language edition, 1973). Volume I of the author's eleven years in prison camps, supplemented by the reports, memoirs, and letters of 227 other witnesses. The archipelago is "the enormous network of penal institutions and all the rest of the web of machinery for police oppression and terror imposed on Soviet life. Gulag is the acronym for the Chief Administration of Corrective Labor Camps which supervised the larger part of this system." The original work consists of seven parts in three volumes. Vol. one contains two parts, or about one-third of the whole. A glossary identifies persons, institutions, etc. mentioned in the text.

2799. Solzhenitsyn, Aleksandr Isaevich. The Gulag Archipelago Audiocassette. Ashland, OR: Classics on Tape, 1989. 52 sound cassettes in four containers read by Frederick Davidson.

2800. Solzhenitsyn, Aleksandr Isaevich. "Solzhenitsyn Speaks Out." National Review 27 (June 6, 1975) 603-9. Interview in Stockholm on a wide range of subjects--Raoul Wallenberg, Amnesty International, etc.

2801. Solzhenitsyn, Natalya. "Fate of Families." Time 109 (February 21, 1977) 30. Wife of the famous writer dissident writes about the families of dissidents and urges the West to support them.

2802. Soviet Christian Prisoner List 1981. Orange; Keston, England: SSRC; Keston College, 1981. 59. Updated 1982.

2803. "A Soviet Dissenter: Visit From the KGB." Newsweek 75 (June 1, 1970) 43-4. On Andrei Amalrik's arrest.

2804. Soviet Forced Labor Practices. Washington, DC: Commission on Security and Cooperation in Europe, 1986. 85. Testimony from former political prisoners on many issues, from personal experience to the US forced labor import ban.

2805. Soviet Psychiatric Abuse in the Gorbachev Era. Ed. Robert van Voren. Amsterdam: International Association on the Political Use of Psychiatry, 1989. 112. Eight essays and Voren's Introduction on the history of psychiatry in the Soviet Union, Snezhnevskyism, the media, etc.

2806. Soviet Psychiatry Today. Boston: Boston U, Institute for the Study of Conflict, Ideology and Policy, 1991. 33. Interview with Semyon Gluzman and essay by Mark Field.

2807. "Soviet Severity." Christian Century 97.29 (September 24, 1980) 871. On suppression of religious groups.

2808. The Soviet Union's Vast Network of Slave Labor Camps: An Eyewitness Account Given in Sworn Testimony to the U.S. Government. (Orig. U.S.S.R. Labor Camps. Washington, DC: GPO, 1973). Wheaton, Ill.: Church League of America, 1976. 128.

2809. "Soviets Arrest Dudko in Try at Suppressing Orthodox Dissent." Christianity Today 24 (February 22, 1980) 50. Dimitri Dudko, a Russian Orthodox priest, suffers continual threats and harrassment at the hands of the Soviet government with help from the church leadership.

2810. "A Spokesman Muffled." Time 100 (July 3, 1972) 21. Historian and dissident Pyotr Yakir is arrested.

2811. Stahel, T.H. "Trees Planted by the Water." America 130 (February 9, 1974) inside back cover. Discusses Fr. Walter Ciszek's account of fifteen years in prison, He Leadeth Me.

2812. Stajner, Karlo. Seven Thousand Days in Siberia. New York: Farrar/Straus/Giroux, 1988. 400. After 20 years of Soviet prison and camp, this Yugoslavian was then condemned to internal exile for life, until Tito intervened through Kruschev in 1956. Two copies of the manuscript disappeared at publishers in Yugoslavia, but finally published in 1971, when it won the Book of the Year prize. The author treats Soviet history under Stalin as a counter-revolution against socialism.

2813. Starlinger, W. "My Six Years with Russia's Political Prisoners." U.S. News and World Report 39 (November 4, 1955) 136-151. Dr. Wilhelm Starlinger, a German physician, tells of six years spent in a Soviet concentration camp.

2814. Steele, Richard, et al. "Swapping Spies for Dissidents." Newsweek 93 (May 7, 1979) 49. Five dissidents are exchanged for two Soviet spies.

2815. Steinberg, I. "For the Imprisoned of the Revolution." Nation 126 (June 20, 1928) 701-2. On the prison sufferings of members of the Left Social Revolutionary and Maximalist parties who participated in the October Revolution and the creation of the Soviet Republic, but who were imprisoned by the Communists (the Cheka) over differences. Five prisoners are described: Maria Spiridonova, et al.

2816. Stetsko, Slava, ed. Revolutionary Voices. Ukrainian Political Prisoners Condemn Russian Colonialism. Munich: Anti-Bolshevik Bloc of Nations, 1971. 269. 2d rev. ed. 1971. Encyclopedic coverage of Soviet repression of the Ukraine and sustained protest against the persecution of dissidents.

2817. Strimaityte-Meliene, Matilda. Crosses in the Arctic: A Lithuanian Woman Survives the Gulag. Detroit, MI: Lithuanian National Guard in Exile, Stasys Butkus Chapter, 1987. 179. A victim of Stalin's first mass deportation from Soviet-occupied Lithuania, she spent 15 years in a Siberian labor camp.

2818. Strokata, Nina. Ukrainian Women in the Soviet Union: Documented Persecution 1975-1980. Baltimore: Smoloskyp, 1980. 63. Twenty case studies.

2819. Strong, Anna Louise. "Jailed in Moscow." New York Harold Tribune (March 27-April 11, 1949). Six articles describing her imprisonment charged with spying (she sympathized with the Chinese Revolution).

2820. Stypulkowski, Zbigniew. Invitation to Moscow. New York: Walker, 1950. 359. This distinguished politician narrates his life in and out of Soviet and German internment before WW II, then member of the Polish Resistance, finally imprisoned by Soviets again at the end of the war, charged with treason during a trial in which he defended himself. (On a larger level a history of Polish politics 1939-1945).

2821. "A Survivor's Tour of Triumph." U.S. News and World Report 100 (May 19, 1986) 35-8. Shcharansky's visit to the U.S., including an account of his incarceration in the USSR and an interview about political prisoners there.

2822. Swift, M.G. "Moscow's Catherine of Sienna." America 155 (July 19-26, 1986) 29-32. Persecution of Dominican nun Anna I. Abrikosova, imprisoned from 1923 to 1936, when she died in Butyrka Prison.

2823. Taagepera, Rein. Softening Without Liberalization in the Soviet Union: The Case of Juri Kukk. Lanham: UP of America, 1984. 244. On the arrest and imprisonment in 1980 of this Estonian chemist at Tartu University, who had resigned from the Communist party. He died three months after incarceration.

2824. "Televised Samizdat." Newsweek 76 (August 10, 1970) 43. On CBS film on dissident Soviet intellectuals smuggled out of the country.

2825. "There is No Return." Newsweek 80 (July 3, 1972) 33. Historian Pyotr Yakir rearrested for criticizing the regime (he had earlier spent fourteen years in Siberian prison camps).

2826. Thiessen, C.R. "From Russia, with Love." Christianity Today 29 (November 8, 1985) 94+. The founder of a Christian rock group in the Soviet Union is being held in prison for attempting to get officially recognized.

2827. "This year in Jerusalem?" U.S. News and World Report 100 (February 17, 1986) 10. A sketch of the life of Anatoly Sharansky, Jewish dissident and originator of the Moscow Helsinki Group who was charged with treason and sentenced to ten years in prison and labor camp.

2828. Thomsen, Alexander. In the Name of Humanity. New York: Dutton, 1963. 230. Thomsen, a volunter Red Cross doctor helping victims of the Nazis, unwittingly gave aid to a group of "fascists," and was sentenced to ten years imprisonment in the Soviet Union.

2829. Thorne, Ludmilla. "Inside Russia's Psychiatric Jails." New York Times Magazine (June 12, 1977) 26-30+. Report on the use of psychiatry in the Soviet Union to punish dissidents: ten percent of the patients in psychiatric hospitals are political prisoners.

2830. Thorne, Ludmilla. "Mother Courage: How Vladimir Bukovsky was Saved." New York Times Magazine (February 27, 1977) 38-40+. Account of Bukovsky's incarcerations in labor camps, prisons, and psychiatric wards, and of his mother Nina Ivanova's campaign to rescue her son.

2831. Three Philosophers-Political Prisoners in the Soviet Union. Baltimore: Smoloskyp, 1976. 18. Three young philosophers--Lisovy, Pronyuk, Bondar--are in prison for long terms for criticizing the Communist Party and demanding respect for human rights.

2832. "'To Communists of Europe & the USA:' An Open Letter From Soviet Political Prisoners." Militant 39.33 (September 12, 1975) 13. Text of letter sent to European and U.S. Communist Parties in hope of solidarity, depicting brutal repression at the hands of the KGB.

2833. To the United Nations General Assembly, a Resolution with Appended Documents Concerning the Decolonization of the Union of Soviet Socialist Republics. Toronto: [s.n.], 1978. 148. Includes a section on genocide in various political subdivisions of the U.S.S.R. (Ukraine, Lithuania, etc.).

2834. Tomlinson, Kenneth Y. "Man Called Simas." Reader's Digest 107 (August 1975) 138-44. Simas Kudirka jumped aboard a U.S. Coast Guard ship from his own Russian boat seeking political asylum, but was refused and ordered back.

2835. "Torture by Diet." Time 119 (February 1, 1982) 53. Anatoly Shcharansky, sentenced to 13 years incarceration in 1978, is being harassed in prison.

2836. Toth, Zoltan, Dr. Prisoner of the Soviet Union. Tr. George Unwin. Old Woking: Gresham, 1978. 202. Year by year (1945-1955) account of his prison experiences which began as a prisoner of war but lasted eleven years.

2837. Totten, Samuel, comp. "The Soviet's 'Great Purge'," and "Soviet Deportation of Whole Nations." First-Person Accounts of Genocidal Acts Committed in the Twentieth Century: An Annotated Bibliography. Westport, CT: Greenwood, 1991. 65-71 and 72-90. 102 entries.

2838. Townsend, Alison. "Free Spirit." Women's Review of Books 6.8 (May 1989) 18. Review of Irina Ratushinskaya's Grey Is the Color of Hope, an account of her four years in a Soviet strict regime camp.

2839. Trautmann, Emilie. "Inside a Soviet Psychiatric Ward--Protecting a 'Patient' from Thorns." Matchbox (November 1982) 1,3. Documents the case of Sergei Batovrin, confined to a psychiatric hospital and sedated for the "crime" of contributing some of his paintings to an art exhibit in commemoration of the anniversary of the U.S. bombing of Hiroshima.

2840. Trimple, J. and M. Horn. "Siberian Exile Yuri Orlov Punches his Ticket to the West." U.S. News and World Report 101 (October 13, 1986) 20. Orlov is freed after ten years in prison.

2841. Tucker, Robert C. Stalin in Power: The Revolution From Above, 1928-1941. New York: Norton, 1990. 707. Study of the motives and methods of Stalin, especially in regard to the mass murders of the 1930s.

2842. Turkow Kaminska, Ruth. I Don't Want to Be Brave Anymore. Washington, D.C.: New Republic, 1978. 255. This notable singer and actress and her musician husband, Adi Rosner, both Polish Jews, were imprisoned by Stalin's police in 1946, charged with illegal border crossing. She was first sent to Lvov Prison, then to Siberian camps, and released in 1952.

2843. U., Ruta. Dear God, I Wanted to Live. Brooklyn, N.Y.· Gramatu Draugs, 1978. 141. The author when age fourteen, her sisters, mother, and grandmother were exiled from Riga, Latvia, to Siberia in 1941 as "the people's enemies." After five years the girls were allowed to return (their mother and grandmother dead), but a few years later they were again deported to Siberia along with their father, who was charged with treason.

2844. Ukrainian Political Prisoners in the Soviet Union: A Biographical List. Toronto: Canadian League for the Liberation of Ukraine and Studium Research Institute, 1979, 128. Several hundred prisoners are described.

2845. United States. Congress. Implementation of the Helsinki Accords: Soviet Violations of the Helsinki Accords in Afghanistan. 99th Cong., 1st Session. Washington: GPO, 1986. 95. On Soviet "brutal, pervasive, and massive" violations (Richard Schifter).

2846. United States. Congress. Implementation of the Helsinki Accords: The Situation of Andrei Sakharov and Unofficial Peace Groups in the U.S.S.R. and Eastern Europe. 98th Cong., 2nd session. Washington: GPO, 1984-87. Testimony and discussion of Soviet repression.

2847. United States. Congress. Implementation of the Helsinki Accords: Soviet Forced Labor Practices. 99th Cong., 1st Session, 1985. Washington: GPO, 1986. 85. Consideration of how to prevent importation of goods made by political prisoners.

2848. U.S. Congress Commission on Security and Cooperation in Europe. Implementation of the Helsinki Accords, Hearing Before the Commission on Security and Cooperation in Europe. Washington: U.S. G.P.O. 1988. 99. Two Ukrainian and two Georgian human rights activists recently released from Soviet prisons give testimony, including Danylo Shumuk, who was the "longest-serving prisoner of conscience" known in the U.S.S.R.

2849. United States. Congress. Commission on Security and Cooperation in Europe. Implementation of the Helsinki Accords Hearing before the Commission on Security and Cooperation in Europe, One Hundredth Congress, First Session, Dr. Anatoly Koryagin and Alexander Shatravka on the Abuse of Psychiatry in the U.S.S.R., May 15, 1987. Washington, D.C.: U.S. G.P.O., 29.

2850. United States. Congress. Commission on Security and Cooperation in Europe. Implementation of the Helsinki Accords Hearing Before the Commission on Security and Cooperation in Europe, One Hundredth Congress, First Session, Irina Ratushinskaya, March 31, 1987. Washington, D.C.: U.S. G.P.O., 1988. 23. Testimony of poet Irina Ratushinskaya and her husband Igor Gerashchenko.

2851. United States. Congress. House. Committee on Energy and Commerce. US and USSR Psychiatric Care Practices: Hearing Before the Subcommittee on Health and the Environment of the Committee on Energy and Commerce, House of Representatives, One Hundred First Congress, First Session, October 2, 1989. Washington, D.C.: U.S. G.P.O., 1989. 61. On Soviet psychiatric practices and future U.S. policy options.

2852. United States. Congress. Senate. Committee on the Judiciary. Subcommitte to Investigate the Administration of the Internal Security Act and Other Internal Security Laws. Abuse of Psychiatry for Political Repression in the Soviet Union, v.2: Hearing Testimony of Dr. Norman B. Hirt. Washington: U.S.G.P.O., 1975. 101. Also about sixty pages of documents and publications.

2853. U.S.S.R: Conditions for Women Prisoners of Conscience in the "Small Zone." London: Amnesty International, 1985. 15. Describes Zone 4 of the Mordovian corrective labour colony No. 3, focusing on 10 women prisoners of conscience kept on harsh regime, all convicted of "anti-Soviet agitation and propaganda."

2854. U.S.S.R.: Human Rights in a Time of Change. New York: Amnesty International, 1989. 29. Political arrests and prisoners have declined, and laws are being improved, yet at the same time repressive laws have been added, and there are at least 90 people in prison for exercising their rights of expression and association.

2855. U.S.S.R. Labor Camps: Hearings Before the Subcommittee to Investigate the Administration of the Internal Security Act and Other Internal Security Laws of the Committee on the Judiciary, United States Senate, Ninety Third Congress. Bartlesville, OK: Living Sacrifice, 1987. 282. (Rpt. Feb. 1-2, 1973, Hearings by the Christian Mission to the Communist World). Primarily the testimony of Avraham Shifrin millions of political prisoners remain in concentration camps and prisons. Committee Staff summary, Shifrin's testimony, Appendices containing letters from prisoners, biographies of prisoners, trial accounts, and other materials. Shifrin eventually was allowed to emigrate to Israel.

2856. USSR News Brief=Vest iz SSSR. Bruxelles: Cahiers du Samizdat, 1980. No. 1 (April 30, 1980). Lists and discusses prisoners.

2857. Urwich, John. Inside the Soviet Union Without a Passport. Vol. 1. Flushing, NY: Transdacia, 1989. 258. Arrested at age 20 in 1947 and imprisoned for 9 years for accidentally being in a secret zone of uranium mines.

2858. Vaghin, Evgenii. "Dostoevsky Behind Barbed Wire." Trans. Nadja Jernakoff. National Review 35 (August 5, 1983) 938+. The author draws some parallels between his and Dostoevsky's imprisonment.

2859. Vaksberg, Arkady. The Prosecutor and the Prey: Vyshinsky and the 1930's Moscow Show Trials. Tr. Jan Butler. London: Weidenfeld & Nicolson, 1990. 374. Life and deeds of the lawyer Stalin used to destroy his erstwhile comrades, to purge the army, academic, and professional institutions, and extract confessions by torture.

2860. van Voren, Robert, ed. Soviet Psychiatric Abuse in the Gorbachev Era. Amsterdam, Netherlands: International Association on the Political Use of Psychiatry, 1989. 112. Eight essays and Voren's Introduction on the history of psychiatry in the SU, Snezhnevskyism, psychiatry in the Soviet press and other topics.

2861. van Voren, Robert, ed. Koryagin--A Man Stuggling for Human Dignity. Amsterdam: n.p., 1987. 112. Anatoly Koryagin spent six years in a Soviet prison camp for his activities in the Working Commission to Investigate the Use of Psychiatry for Political Purposes.

2862. Vitzthum, Hilda. Torn Out by the Roots: The Recollections of a Former Communist. Trans. Paul Schach. Lincoln: U of Nebraska P, 1993. 273. Reminiscence of her nearly ten years in Soviet labor camps.

2863. "Vladas Lapienis." Index On Censorship 14.3 (June 1985) 43-4. A former prisoner has again been arrested for "slandering" the state.

2864. Vogt, Marilyn. "Stalinists Continue to Harass Dzhemilev." Militant 42.48 (December 22, 1978) 23. Crimean Tatar leader Mustafa Dzhemilev served four terms in prison and is again threatened with confinement.

2865. Vogt, Marilyn. "Kremlin Jails Worker--Dissident in Mental Hospital." Militant 43.11 (March 23, 1979) 14. Vladimir Klebanov, the Ukranian coal miner who organized a trade union, is confined to a psychiatric hospital.

2866. Von Meck, Galina. As I Remember Them. London: Dennis Dobson, 1973. 448. Accounts of her imprisonments between 1923 and 1931, when she was transferred to Siberian labor camps until 1935. Charges against her including attempted escape into Poland and espionage for the western powers.

2867. Wade, Nicholas. "Kronid Lyubarsky: the Soviet State Tries to Unmake a Scientist." Science 193 (September 3, 1976) 863-4. Astrophysicist and Mars expert sentenced to a five year sentence for distributing civil rights literature.

2868. Walsh, John. "Soviets Take Tougher Line on Human Rights." Science 221 (July 22, 1983) 347. On Sakharov and other dissident scientists.

2869. Ward, H.F. "Civil Liberties in Russia." Nation 120 (March 4, 1925) 234-7. The author travelled to the Soviet Union to try to ascertain the number and treatment of political prisoners.

2870. Wat, Aleksander. "Proust in Lubyanka." New York Review of Books 35 (December 8, 1988) 29-30. On the impact of literature (Proust, Machiavelli) on the author while in prison.

2871. Watson, Russell, et al. "Better, but Not Enough." Newsweek 112 (November 7, 1988) 70. Gobachev promises to release all political prisoners.

2872. Watson, Russell, et al. "Scoring at Will." Newsweek 108 (December 29, 1986) 24-5. The Soviet Union's increasing leniency toward dissidents under Gorbachev.

2873. Weissberg, Alexander. The Accused. New York: Simon & Schuster, 1951. 518. Weissberg was imprisoned without trial in the Kharkiv GPU prison for three years.

2874. Where Are They Now?: Human Rights Monitors in the USSR: Ten Years after Helsinki. New York: U.S. Helsinki Watch Committee; Human Rights Watch, 1985. 7. Tells about former Helsinki Watch prisoners in the USSR, Helsinki monitors who have died, monitors forced to emigrate, and monitors in prison or internal exile. Their "crime" was reporting abuses of the human rights provisions of the Helsinki Final Act signed by the USSR and 34 nations in 1975.

2875. Wierzynski, G.H. and Robert Kroon. "Vladimir's Voice." Time 109 (January 3, 1976) 54. Interview of just-released dissident Vladimir Bukovsky.

2876. Willey, Fay, et al. "In the Psychiatric Ward." Newsweek 99 (January 11, 1982) 31-2. Indicts use of psychiatry against dissidents--e.g., Anatoly Koryagin.

2877. Wilson-Smith, Anthony. "The Wasted Years." Macleans 102 (May 15, 1989) 24. Asir Sandler, originally arrested in 1941 for having two anti-Stalin poems in his possession, tells of his prison hardships.

2878. Woal, Ralph. "Solzhenitsyn as Latter-Day Prophet." Christian Century 93 (May 19, 1976) 480-3. Review of Solzhenitsyn's The Gulag Archipelago Vol. II on the labor camps (Vol. I on prisons). The two volumes "will stand as his great prophetic judgment" against totalitarianism.

2879. Wolfe, Bertram. "The Government of Dr. Caligari; Soviet Mental Hospitals." National Review 23 (December 31, 1971) 1461-2. Text of an address giving the general facts about the police use of psychiatric hospitals to punish dissidents.

2880. Wolfer, Barbara. "Five Poems that Spelled Danger." Commonweal 114 (February 27, 1987) 107-11. Poet Irina Ratushinskaya released from prison: an account of her life and work.

2881. Women Political Prisoners in the USSR. New York: Ukrainian National Women's League of America, 1975. 20. Includes selected profile and lists of prisoners arranged by type (Baptist, Ukraine, Russian, and Jewish).

2882. Women's Voices from Soviet Labor Camps. Trans. Lesya Jones. Ed. Bohdan Yasen. Smoloskyp Samvydav Series: Documents of Ukranian Samvydav. Baltimore: Smoloskyp, 1975. 12. Includes letters protesting violations of human rights in Soviet prison camps; the women were sentenced 1972-73 for "anti-Soviet agitation and propaganda."

2883. Yakir, Pyotr. A Chilhood in Prison. Ed. Robert Conquest. London: Macmillan, 1972. 155. A possibly unique first-hand record of the experiences of an orphaned boy in Stalin's prison camps 1937-1942. During Krushchev's regime he was rehabilitated, but later he became a leader in the democratic movement and was again imprisoned in 1972.

2884. Yancey, P. "Frozen Fire." Christianity Today 28 (October 5, 1984) 108+. A comparison of Feodor Dostoevsky and Alexander Solzhenitsyn and how they coped with being in prison by finding religion.

2885. Yasen, Bohdan. A Ukrainian Priest's Appeals from a Soviet Labor Camp. Baltimore; Toronto: Smoloskyp, 1976. 12. Two letters by Rev. Vasyl Romanyuk, serving a 10-year sentence for "anti-Soviet agitation."

2886. Yasen, Bohdan. Ukrainian Women in Soviet Prisons. Baltimore, MD: Smoloskyp, 1975. 26. An appeal for amnesty, specifically for seven women, and a eulogy for one woman who was murdered.

2887. Zawodny, Janusz. Death in the Forest: The Story of the Katyn Forest Massacre. New York: Hippocrene, 1988. 235. (5th printing). The story of the execution of over 15,000 Polish officers by Soviet forces in 1940.

UNITED ARAB EMIRATES

2888. Amnesty International Report 1990. New York: Amnesty International, 1990. 246-247. One or two prisoners were held without charge or trial.

2889. Khamees, Dhabiya. "My Detention in Abu Dhabi." Index On Censorship 17.5 (May 1988) 70-72. Journalist, poet, and short story writer, she was detained and interrogated for three months in 1987 without charge or trial.

UNITED KINGDOM

2890. Ackroyd, Carol, et al. The Technology of Political Control. New York: Penguin, 1977. 320. Examines the application of science and technology to the suppression of the state's internal enemies, mainly civilian. Part one describes the "maximum repression" in Northern Ireland. Part four presents the various technologies.

2891. Adams, Gerry. Cage Eleven. Dingle, Co. Kerry, Ireland: Brandon, 1990. 156. Mainly composed of articles written during imprisonment in Long Kesh/Maze Prison. The author perceives himself as a prisoner of war in a country occupied by foreign power.

2892. Ajemian, R. "Ready to Die in the Maze." Time 118 (August 17, 1981) 46-8. On the IRA hunger strikers, what starving is like, and why the IRA do it. Tom McElwee died last weekend after fasting 62 days.

2893. Amnesty International Report 1980. London: Amnesty International, 1980. 310-312. Focuses on Northern Ireland where incommunicado detention, forced confession, and harsh prison conditions exist.

2894. Amnesty International Report 1990. New York: Amnesty International, 1990. 247-50. The long-term IRA prisoners, the Guildford Four, were released when police malpractice was proven. The IRA Birmingham Six convictions were under examination. Asylum-seekers from Turkey were forcibly returned.

2895. Amnesty International. Report of an Enquiry into Allegations of Ill-treatment in Northern Ireland. London: Amnesty International, 1972. 46. The Amnesty Commission of Enquiry heard evidence of brutal assault during arrest and transportation and ill-treatment in detention (hoods, threats, etc.).

2896. Amnesty International. Report on an Enquiry into Allegations of Ill-treatment in Northern Ireland. London: Amnesty International, 1972. 46. On brutal treatment of persons during interrogation under the Special Powers Act between August 9 and November 18, 1971.

2897. Amnesty International. United Kingdom: Human Rights Concerns. New York: Amnesty International, 1991. 66. Despite the U.K.'s ratification of international treaties against such abuse, ill-treatment of detainees, unfair trials and unlawful killings by security forces continue, particularly in Northern Ireland.

2898. Arrowsmith, Pat. Jericho. London: Cresset, 1965. 322. A novel abut people demonstrating nonviolently against nuclear weapons and the personal consequences, written during her six-month term in Holloway Prison. Arrowsmith was imprisoned six times for protesting.

2899. Beeson, Trevor. "Northern Ireland's Ordeal: No Easy Solution." Christian Century 98.20 (June 3-10, 1981) 629-30. An overall explanation of the deaths of the hunger strikers in Maze Prison [British point of view].

2900. "Behind IRA Prison Break: Desperation." U.S. News and World Report 95 (October 10, 1983) 10. Mainly about the use of informers to prosecute IRA members.

2901. Bell, J. Bowyer. The Irish Troubles: A Generation of Violence, 1967-1992. New York: St. Martin's, 1993. 872. This political history mainly of recent Northern Ireland (he goes back to the 1920s) offers an overview and summing up of the old and new Irish Republican Army, the Protestant militias (the A, B, and C Specials), the Ulster Defense Regiment, the repression, trials, imprisonments, etc.

2902. Beresford, David. Ten Men Dead: the Story of the 1981 Irish Hunger Strike. London: Grafton Books, 1987; New York: Atlantic Monthly, 1989. 334. An account of the ten men in Maze\Long Kesh Prison who starved themselves to death in support of independence from Great Britain.

2903. Bernard, Margie. Daughter of Derry: The Story of Brigid Sheils Makowski. London: Pluto, 1989. 200. Based on Makowski's experiences as a Republican Socialist fighting for a united Ireland freed from British Control. Chapter 11 describes the experience of internment: severe beatings, mock executions, starvation, sleep deprevation, etc.; Chapter 18 details Amnesty International's concerns about human rights violations.

2904. Berry, Steve. To the Bitter Climax of Death if Necessary: The H-Block Hunger Strike and the Struggle for Political Status. London: Socialists Unlimited for the SWP, 1980. 21.

2906. Boyer, Sandy. "Paid Perjuers, Juryless Courts." Changes: Socialist Monthly 6.5 (May 1984) 4, 27. Describes the use of informers, agent provocateurs, and juryless courts to convict members of proscribed groups.

2907. Boyer, Sandy. "Torture and Resistance in Northern Ireland." Changes: Socialist Monthly 1.5 (June 1979) 26-28, 30. On the routine torture of prisoners.

2908. Brady, Brian J. Internment 1971-1975. Dungannon (St. Patrick's academy, Dungannon, Co. Tyrone): Fr. Denis Faul, 1975. Imprisoned suspected terrorists.

2909. Brecher, John and Lea Donosky. "An Election with a Difference." Newsweek 97 (June 15, 1981) 51-2. Joe McDonnell, in prison for IRA activities and in his fifth week of a hunger strike, is running for Parliament.

2910. Brecher, John and Lea Donosky. "The Hunger Strike Ends." Newsweek 96 (December 29, 1980) 24. The 40 IRA prisoners ended their self-starvation, Sean McKenna close to death after 53 days.

2911. British Army and Special Branch RUC Brutalities, December, 1971 - February, 1972. Ed. Denis Faul and Raymond Murray. Dungannon: Denis Faul and Raymond Murray, 1972. 78. Torture by the Royal Ulster Constabulary and British armed forces.

2912. Brown, Myra Sadd. Papers. Suffragette Fellowship Collection, Museum of London (50.82/1136). Letters and statement describing and protesting her experience of forcible feeding.

2913. Buxton, Jane and Margaret Turner. Gate Fever. London: Cresset, 1962. 197. Tells about their experience in Holloway Prison in 1960 for civil disobedience against nuclear arms.

2914. Catalfio, Maria. "Repression in Northern Ireland: H- Block Struggle Grows." Changes: Socialist Monthly 1.11-12 (December-January 1979-1980) 9-10. On the 360 prisoners in Long Kesh Prison, their struggle to attain political status, and abominable conditions in the prison.

2915. Caveeshar, Sardul Singh, ed. The Lahore Fort Torture Camp: Being the First Hand Account of Physical and Mental Torture and Persecuton of Political Detenues Kept in the Lahore Fort Under the Defence of India Rules During the War. Lahore: Hero, 1946. 136. Thirteen accounts of incarceration and torture by British officials during WWII.

2916. Clarke, Thomas James. Glimpses of an Irish Felon's Prison Life. Dublin, Maunsel and Roberts, 1922 (first published 1912-13 in Irish Freedom). 103. He was the first signatory to the Proclamation of the Irish Republic and was shot in 1916, aged 59 years, following the Fenian Insurrection of Easter week. He had earlier served 15 years in prison, which this book is about.

2917. Collins, Tom. The Irish Hunger Strike. Dublin: White Island, 1987. 626. A recounting of what members of their families felt about the ten prisoners (Bobby Sands et al.) who died in Long Kesh Prison after fasting. Photos.

2918. Conlon, Gerry. Proved Innocent: the Story of Gerry Conlon of the Guildford Four. London: Hamish Hamilton, 1990. 233. The author was sent to prison for fifteen years for bombing a pub, of which he was innocent. The pub had been bombed by the IRA.

2919. Coogan, Tim Pat. On the Blanket: The H Block Story. Dublin: Ward River, 1980. 271. Focuses on the section of Maze prison (formerly Long Kesh) which houses political prisoners, who protested the refusal of authorities to designate them political prisons by remaining naked (going "on the blanket") and by rubbing dirt and faeces on the walls.

2920. Cook, Alice and Gwyn Kirk. Greenham Women Everywhere: Dreams, Ideas, and Actions from the Women's Peace Movement. London: Pluto, 1983. 127. Discusses the nonviolent civil disobedience of members of the Greenham Common women's peace camp and the methods authorities have used to deal with them--charging protestors with various offences ranging from a £50 fine for "obstruction" to 14 years to life for violations of the "Official Secrets Act."

2921. Coulter, Carol. Web of Punishment: An Investigation. Dublin: Attic, 1991. 157. A study of the impact of imprisonment on the families of the prisoner. In 1990 1,802 people were in prison most of them for "violence against the person"; since 1973, 14,220 people have been charged with a "terrorist" type of offence. Thus there are many more thousands "women and children in the main, who are experiencing separation, stress, poverty and the disruption of their lives because of imprisonment." (The author won the 1990 National Media Award for her coverage of the Birmingham Six and the Guildford Four.)

2922. Cronin, Sean. "Everyone but the Terrorists." Commonweal 94 (September 17, 1971) 470-1. Some 300 violently arrested and interned, but apparently none were terrorists and the Unionist right-wing terror groups escaped.

2923. Crozier, A. "Frame-up Exposed, Four 'IRA Bombers' Free after 14 Years." Guardian 42.4 (November 15, 1989) 15. The Guildford Four have been released after the exposure of systematic police and prosecutorial misconduct.

2924. D'Arcy, Margaretta. Tell Them Everthing: A Sojourn in the Prison of Her Majesty Queen Elizabeth II at Ard Macha (Armagh). London: Pluto Press, 1981. 127. Irish playwright D'Arcy was imprisoned as the result of her protest against Armagh Prison conditions. She and thirty Republican prisoners made a "no-wash protest" for thirty days.

2925. "A Daring Escape from the Maze." Macleans 96 (October 10, 1983) 34. Thirty-eight IRA prisoners excaped from the Maze Prison in Northern Ireland; 19 were recaptured.

2926. "Death Cycle." Time 117 (June 1, 1981) 36. Raymond McCreesh and Patrick O'Hara are the 3rd and 4th IRA hunger strikers to die in Maze Prison.

2927. The Death of Thomas Ashe; Full Report of the Inquest. Dublin: J.M. Butler, 1917. 84. Fighter for Irish independence, Ashe died in prison following hunger strike and forced feeding.

2928. "Deathlock in Northern Ireland." America 144 (May 9, 1981) 376. On Bobby Sands, critical of both sides.

2929. De Brun, B. "Women and Imperialism in Ireland." Women's Studies International Forum 11.4 (1988) 323. On the oppression of women prisoners in the six counties of Northern Ireland.

2930. "Disaffection." Time 118 (August 3, 1981) 43. On popular attitudes toward the hunger strikers in Maze Prison. Kieran Doherty and Kevin Lynch are near death.

2931. Duval, Elsie. Papers. Fawcett Library, City of London Polytechnic, London. Prison diaries and correspondence (1911-1918) by this suffragette, who was forcibly fed.

2932. "End to a Dangerous Fast." Time 116 (December 29, 1980) 39. Fast ended in response to Prime Ministes Thatcher's promise of prison reforms, but requested political status was not granted.

2933. Fairweather, Elaine, et al. Only the Rivers Run Free: Northern Ireland, The Women's War. London: Pluto, 1984. 343. On the politicization of women in Northern Ireland in the face of harsh repression, political and economic exploitation of the working-class. Chapter 4 deals specifically with Armagh women's prisons.

2934. Faul, Denis, and Raymond Murray. The Castlereagh File: Allegations of RUC Brutality 1976\1977. Dungannon, County Tyrone, Ireland: The Authors, 1978. 195. On torture and brutality by the Royal Ulster Constabulory in the Castlereagh RUC Interrogation Centre and other places.

2935. Feehan, John M. Bobby Sands and the Tragedy of Northern Ireland. Sag Harbor, NY: Permanent Press, 1985. 152. Story of an IRA leader and member of Parliament who died as the result of a hunger strike in Long Kesh Prison.

2936. Feldman, Allen. Formations of Violence: the Narrative of the Body and Political Terror in Northern Ireland. Chicago: U of Chicago P, 1991. 319. Presents oral histories with commentary on the violence from the intercommunal rioting of 1969 to the 1981 Hunger Strike in Maze Prison. Focuses on the symbolic forms, material practices, and narrative strategies of political construction.

2937. Flatman, Ada. "Reminiscences of a Suffragette." Typescript. Suffragette Fellowship Collection, Museum of London (Group C, vol. 2: 58.87/67). Account of her imprisonment in Holloway in 1908.

2938. Gakaara wa Wanjau. Mau Mau Author in Detention. trans. from the Gikuyu by Paul Ngigi. Nairobi: Heinemann Kenya, 1988. 252. Arrested in 1952 by British Colonial rulers and imprisoned for eight years for advocating Mau Mau nationalism. This is his diary of those years, which won the 1984 Noma Award for Publishing in Africa.

2939. Gardiner, Gerald Austein Gardiner, Baron. Report by Lord Gardiner on Procedures for the Interrogation of Persons Suspected of Terrorism. Dublin: Amnesty International, Irish Section, 1974. 12. Orig. the minority report in "Report of the Committee of Privy Counsellors...Persons Suspected of Terrorism."

2940. Gordon, Helen. The Prisoner: A Sketch. An Experience of Forcible Feeding by a Suffragette. Letchworth, Eng.: Garden City, 1912. She was imprisoned a month in 1907 for a suffrage protest and forcibly fed when she demanded to be treated as a political prisoner.

2941. Haverty, Anne. Constance Markievicz: An Independent Life. London: Pandora, 1988. 251. Recounts Markievicz's development from an upper class aristocrat to an Irish nationalist and member of Parliament committed to socialism and the suffrage movement. Chapter 11 describes her imprisonment and the executions of her comrades in the wake of the Easter Rebellion.

2942. Hill, Paul and Ronan Bennett. Stolen Years: Before and After Guildford. New York: Doubleday, 1990. 287. An account of his 15 years in prison for IRA bombings he did not commit. One of the innocent Guildford 4.

2943. Hitchens, Christopher. "Human Rights in Ulster: 'Without Identifiable Culprits.'" Nation 229 (September 8, 1979) 173-4. The Bennett committee has affirmed Amnesty International's accusations that British soldiers had tortured political detainees.

2944. Holland, Jack. "The Secret Torturers." Nation 229 (September 8, 1979) 174-5. On the five reports documenting violations of human rights by British forces in Northern Ireland since 1971, particularly the Strasbourg Commission Report.

2945. In the Government's Arsenal: the "Supergrass." Belfast: Concerned Community Organizations, 1984. 50. On informers.

2946. "The Internees: 'No Nonsense.'" Newsweek 79 (April 10, 1972) 30-1. On John Curry and some 900 others jailed as terrorists with trial.

2947. Jennings, Anthony, ed. Justice under Fire: The Abuse of Civil Liberties in Northern Ireland. London: Pluto, 1988. 297. Collection of essays examining the political and economic policies enforced in Northern Ireland by England and the resultant systematic abuse of Irish Civil Liberties.

2948. Johns, Stephen. Tory Torture in Ulster. London: Socialist Labor League, 1971. 29. Cases.

2949. Joshua, Harris, Tina Wallace, and Heather Booth. To Ride the Storm: The 1980 Bristol "Riot" and the State. London: Heinemann, 1983. 221. Examines the 'Bristol Riot' from a political perspective: "crowd violence as an expression of the political struggles and aspirations of black communities settled in Britain" and injustice faced by the sixteen defendants that were pulled randomly from a crowd to stand trial for the actions of a community.

2950. Karunatilake, H.N.S. Life and Times of Edward Henry Pedris, National Hero. s.l.: Gangodagedera, 1978. 24. Pedris was executed by the British in 1915 on the false charge of instigating a riot in Sri Lanka.

2951. Kearney, Peadar. My Dear Eva: Letters Written from Ballykinlar Internment Camp (1921). Dublin: P.J. Bourke, 1976. 43. Kearney was a leader of the Irish Republican Brotherhood, the Fenien Revolutionary organization.

2952. Kelley, Kevin. The Longest War: Northern Ireland and the IRA. Rev. ed. London: Zed, 1988. 395. Chapter 4, part 11 details the internment, "Operation Demetrius," of 1971 when the British army stormed into nationalist areas of Belfast arresting many innocent civilians without charges, a prelude to the suspension of habeus corpus and 2,000+ orders of internment.

2953. Kenney, Annie. Memoires of a Militant. London: Edward Arnold, 1924. 308. Describes her imprisonments for suffragette protests, beginning in Strangeways Gaol, Manchester (1905).

2954. The Last Hunger Strike? Videocassette. Prod. James Gaffney, et al. New York: Irish Northern Aid, 1991. 56 min. Highlights the political and social agony of Northern Ireland through a biographical sketch of Michael James Devine, an Irish Republican Army supporter who died in a hunger strike in 1981.

2955. LeMoyne, James. "The IRA breaks the Maze." Newsweek 102 (October 10, 1983) 53. IRA prisoners escape from Maze Prison.

2956. Levenson, Samuel. Maud Gonne. New York: Reader's Digest, 1976. 436. Gonne went to prison many times for the cause of Irish independence. After incarceration in 1918 she strove to aid prisoners suffering from inhumane conditions under long terms. E.g., she published a monthly called Prison Bars, and she visited prisoners.

2957. Lowe, Ben. "Tory Frame-Up Finally Unraveled." Guardian 43.20 (March 13, 1991) 17. The British government is preparing to release the Birmingham Six, who were wrongly convicted of an IRA bombing 16 years ago.

2958. Lytton, Constance. Papers. Suffragette Fellowship Collection, Museum of London (50.82/119). Letters and notes by a suffragette leader.

2959. Lytton, Constance. Prisons and Prisoners. New York: Doran, 1914. 337. (London: Heinemann; East Ardsley, Yorkshire: E.P. Publishing, 1914; reprint, Wakefield, Eng.: EP, 1976; Boston: Charles River, 1977.) Lytton posed as Jane Warton, a working class suffragette, to expose the inequality of treatment by class; she suffered forced feeding.

2960. Maitra, Apurba. We Cried Together: Memories of Our Martyrs and Freedom Fighters. Calcutta: Firma KLM, 1982. 192. Reminiscences of a prison official and the freedom fighters and terrorists he supervised.

2961. Marion, Kitty. Papers. Suffragette Fellowship Collection. Museum of London (50.82/1120.1121). Typescript account of her suffragette activities and imprisonments in Holloway Prison from 1909 to 1914.

2962. Markievicz, Countess Constance de. Prison Letters of Countess Markievicz. London: Longmans, Green, 1934; rpt., Millwood, NY: Kraus, 1970. 135 p. Imprisoned between 1916 and 1921 for her Irish revolutionary activities.

2963. McAuley Chrissie. Women in a War Zone: Twenty Years of Resistance. Dublin: AP/RN, 1989. 88. Women's involvement in the past 20 years in occupied North Ireland.

2964. McCafferty, Nell. The Armagh Women. Dublin: Co-op Books, 1981. 90. Investigates over 30 Republican women in Armagh Women's Prison for ten months in unsanitary conditions.

2965. McGeever, Jenny. "A Woman's Place Is in the Struggle: An Interview with Mairead Farrelll." Spare Rib 204 (Aug. 1989) 16-20. At 19 Farrell was imprisoned in Armagh Women's Prison for 10 years, where she participated in a hunger strike and refused to be strip-searched, and was treated harshly.

2966. McGuffin, John. Internment. Tralee, Ire.: Anvil, 1973. 228. On the brutal treatment of political internees in Northern and Southern Ireland during the past fifty years, especially working-class men and women imprisoned for their beliefs, 1916-1973.

2967. McGuffin, John. The Guinea Pigs. San Francisco: Irish Northern Aid, 1980. 75. Ill treatment by sensory deprivation of 14 Irishmen by British security forces in 1971.

2968. McKee, Grant, and Ros Franey. Time Bomb: Irish Bombers, English Justice, and the Guildford Four. London: Bloomsbury, 1988. 495. An account of the arrest and imprisonment of four people accused of bombing two public houses in Guildford. They were sentenced to life, and in 1988 had been in prison for 14 years, though innocent.

2969. Mitchell, Hanna Maria. The Hard Way Up: The Autobiography of Hannah Mitchell, Suffragette and Rebel. Ed. Geoffrey Mitchell, with a Preface by George Ewart Evans. London: Faber & Faber, 1968. 260. A working class suffragette imprisoned in 1926 charged with obstruction.

2970. Nevinson, Evelyn Sharp. Papers. Bodleian Library, Oxford University. Writings by suffragette who went on a hunger strike in prison.

2971. Nic Giolla Easpaig, Aine and Eibhlín . Sisters in Cells: Two Republican Prisoners in England. Westport, County Mayo, Ireland: Foilseachain Naisiunta Teoranta, 1987. 169. They were imprisoned from 1974 to 1983 on a bombing conspiracy charge.

2972. "No Bail for British Plowshare Activist." The Nuclear Resister No.88 (April 2, 1993) 1,4. Chris Cole entered a British Aerospace factory to protest bomb manufactury, pouring blood on documents, painting slogans, etc.

2973. Northern Ireland: Alleged Torture and Ill-Treatment of Paul Caruana. New York: Amnesty International, 1985. 28. Amnesty International investigation confirms Caruana's claim he was tortured by the police in 1984.

2974. Northern Ireland: Human Rights Abuses by All Sides. New York: Human Rights Watch, 1993. 9. Abuses by paramilitary and security force in detention, unfair trials, etc.

2975. Northern Ireland, the Mailed Fist: a Record of Army & Police Brutality from August 9 - November 9, 1971; with a foreword by Tony Smythe. Castlefields, Dungannon: Campaign for Social Justice in Northern Ireland in Collaboration with the Association for Legal Justice, 1971. 71. Almost a thousand people have been arrested, many interned without trial, and many abused physically and psychologically.

2976. O'Malley, Padraig. Biting at the Grave: the Irish Hunger Strikes and the Politics of Despair. Boston: Beacon Press, 1990. 330 During 1980-1981 many IRA prisoners refused food at the Maze/Long Kesh prison outside Belfast in a campaign for political status. Ten died of starvation in the summer of 1981. The author sees no end to the class and religious war between Catholics and Protestants until British troops withdraw.

2977. "On Trial for Being on Strike." Guardian 37.19 (Feb. 13, 1985) 15. Ten miners face a possible life sentence for "unlawful assembly."

2978. Pankhurst, Dame Christabel. Unshackled: The Story of How We Won the Vote. Ed. Lord Fredrick Pethick-Lawrence. London: Hutchinson, 1959. 312. Published after her death in 1958. Christabel, a leader with her mother in the struggle for women's suffrage, writes of her imprisonments for organizing protests from 1905 to 1908.

2979. Pankhurst, E. Sylvia. Papers. Suffragette Fellowship Collection, Museum of London. Daughter of Emmeline writes about hunger strikes, forcible feeding, and other abuses suffered in prison.

2980. Pankhurst, E. Sylvia. The Suffragette: The History of the Women's Militant Suffrage Movement 1905-1910. London: Gay & Hancock, 1911; rpt. New York: Source Book Press, 1970. 517. Includes her account of her imprisonment in Holloway (1906).

2981. Pankhurst, E. Sylvia. The Suffragette Movement: An Intimate Account of Persons and Ideals. London: Longmans, Green, 1931; rpt. New York: Kraus, 1971. 631. An account of her several imprisonments for protests; she continued protesting in prison by thirst and hunger strikes, and was forcibly fed.

2982. Pankhurst, Emmeline. My Own Story. London: Eveleigh Nash, New York: Hearst's International Library, 1914; rpt. New York: Kraus, 1971. 364. This leader of the militant women's suffrage movement writes of her imprisonments for demonstrating and for conspiring to destroy the Prime Minister's country house. She protested in prison by thirst and hunger strikes.

2983. Pethick-Lawrence, Emmeline [Pankhurst]. My Part in a Changing World. London: Gollancz, 1938. 367. A leader in the Women's Social and Political Union, she was imprisoned six times in Holloway for her suffrage activism, including attempts to break into the House of Commons in 1906 and 1909. She and her husband were imprisoned and forcibly fed in 1912 for allegedly conspiring to damage property.

2984. Randle, Michael, and Pat Pottle. The Blake Escape. London: Harrap, 1989. 298. The authors helped George Blake, a convicted spy, escape form prison. Blake had received the longest sentence imposed by a British court in modern times.

2985. Rault, Caroline. "Voices from Broadwater Farm." Spare Rib 178 (May 1987) 10. Three young black men were convicted on little evidence and given long prison sentences for their involvement in an uprising.

2986. Report of an Enquiry into Allegations of Ill-treatment in Northern Ireland.. London: Amnesty International, 1972. 46. On brutal treatment of persons during arrest and transport to interrogation under the Special Powers Act between Aug. 9 and Nov. 18, 1971.

2987. Richardson, Mary R. Laugh a Defiance. London: Weidenfeld & Nicolson, 1953. 194. Memoirs of a militant suffragette imprisoned several times for protesting, including her slashing of the Rokeby Venus in the National Gallery to protest the imprisonment of Emmeline Pankhurst.

2988. Richardson, Mary R. "Tortured Women: What Forcible Feeding Means--a Prisoner's Testimony." Typed extracts from The Woman's Dreadnought, ed. Sylvia Pankhurst, August 8, 1914. Suffragette Fellowship Collection, Museum of London. (Group A: 57.116/52). Accounts of several individual cases.

2989. Robbins, Keith. The Abolition of War: The "Peace Movement" in Britain, 1914-1919. Cardif, Wales: U of Wales P, 1976. 255. Sporadic accounts of imprisonment of war protestors--Lord Clifford Allen, Bertrand Russell, Stephen Hobhouse, and others.

2990. Rosen, Andrew. Rise Up Women!: The Militant Campaign of the Women's Social and Political Union 1903-1914. London: Routledge & Kegan Paul, 1974. 312. Chap. 10, "Violence Begins," and subsequent chapters describe confrontations with the police, mass arrests, imprisonments, hunger strikes, forced feeding, window breaking, physical attacks on political leaders, arson, etc.

2991. Roy, M. N. Fragments of a Prisoner's Diary: India's Message. New Delhi, India: Ajanta, 1982. 184. (Rpt. rev. ed. 1950). Collection of essays written during the author's six years in an Indian prison for "conspiracy to overthrow the British Government."

2992. Roy, M. N. Letters from Jail. Dehra Dun: Indian Renaissance Assoc., 1943. 228. Former member of the Comintern and independent Marxist, Roy served over five years in prison 1932-36 for his revolutionary activities. These letters were written to his future wife, Ellen Gottschalk.

2993. Roy, M. N. The Memoirs of a Cat. Dehra Dun: Indian Renaissance Assoc., 1940. 96. Fragments of his prison diary (1932-36) by the eminent Marxist politician and scholar.

2994. Russell, George. "Shadow of a Gunman." Time 117 (May 18, 1981) 52-4. IRA leader and member of Parliament Bobby Sands starved himself to death in Maze Prison.

2995. Sands, Bobby. Bobby Sands, Irish Rebel: a Self-Portrait in Poetry and Polemics, Issued on the 10th Anniversary of His Death. San Francisco: Mellen Research UP, 1991. 140. Sands was the first of IRA prisoners to die of a hunger strike.

2996. Sands, Bobby. One Day in My Life. Cork (Ireland) and Dublin: Mercier, 1989. 118. Written on sheets of toilet paper and smuggled out of Long Kesh Prison. Sands spent almost the last nine years of his life in prison. He began a hunger strike in March 1981 and died sixty-six days later. This is the record of a single day in Long Kesh.

2997. Sands, Bobby. The Writings of Bobby Sands: A Collection of Prison Writings. Dublin: Sinn Fein POW Dept., 1981. 35. Sands wrote these essays in 1978-79.

2998. Sharp, Evelyn. Unfinished Adventure: Selected Reminiscences from an Englishman's Life. London: John Lane, 1933. 316. Contains a chapter on her participation in militant suffrage demonstrations in 1911-1913 which led to brief imprisonments, the second involving a hunger strike.

2999. Sinha, Bejoy Kumar. In Andamans, the Indian Bastille. 1st. ed. 1939. New Delhi: Peoples Pub. House, 1988. 160. Account of his incarceration by the British in Andamans Prison from 1929 to 1938 in the Lahore Conspiracy Case for opposing British rule. The book was banned by the government and some 500 copies seized. He was later imprisoned again for the duration of the war.

3000. Smith, Beverly A. The Irish Prison System, 1854-1914: Prisons and Political Prisoners. Miami U, 1977. 396. DAI 38.9 (March 1978) 5644-A. Imprisoned nationalist opposition leaders (Parnell, O'Brien, Dillon, and others) demanded special treatment as political prisoners and disrupted changes in prison administration throughout Ireland.

3001. Special Category 'A' : Irish Political Prisoners in England: A Account of Prison Life in England Based on the Experiences of Irish Republican John Higgins, Imprisoned Between 1976 and 1979. Dublin: Sinn Fein POW Department, 1980. 100.

3002. Stalker, John. The Stalker Affair. New York: Viking, 1988. 288. An account of his investigation of several killings of unarmed suspects by the Royal Ulster Constabulary, and the attempt by higher officials to suppress his findings.

3003. Stetler, Russell. The Battle of Bogside: The Politics of Violence in Northern Ireland. London and Sydney: Sheed and Ward, 1970. 212. Denounces the use of the military technology CS against the residents of Bogside.

3004. "Strike ends." Time 118 (October 12, 1981) 58. IRA prisoners have abandoned their seven-month fast that has left ten dead since it began last March.

3005. Strip Searching: an Inquiry Into the Strip Searching of Women Remand Prisoners at Armagh Prison Between 1982 and 1985. London: National Council for Civil Liberties, 1986. 36. The report opposes such searches as basically punitive in motive.

3006. Swart, Betsy. "Ireland's Targeted Generation." Covert Action 45 (Summer 1993) 46-53. The British army deliberately harasses young people for screening purposes to "determine whom they will imprison and whom they will kill."

3007. Taylor, Mary Ellen. Letters. Fawcett Library, City of London Polytechnic, London. Accounts of her prison experiences, the result of her suffrage work.

3008. United Kingdom: Human Rights Concerns. New York: Amnesty International, 1991. 66. Despite the U.K.'s ratification of international treaties against such abuse, ill-treatment of detainees, unfair trials, and unlawful killings by security forces continue, particularly in Northern Ireland.

3009. United Kingdom: Killings by Security Forces in Northern Ireland. New York: Amnesty International, 1986. 14. Security forces shot dead 34 people from 1982 to 1986 in circumstances that suggest premeditation.

3010. Van Slyke, Leslie. "Information for Sale." This Magazine 17.6 (Jan. 1984) 15-17. Describes how the law has become a political pawn in N. Ireland--show trials without juries, detention without trial, convictions on non-corroborated evidence supplied by informers, etc.

3011. Walsh, Louis J. "On My Keeping" and in Theirs. Dublin: Talbot, 1921. 112. Account of prison life by an Irish Sinn Feiner fighter for Irish independence.

3012. Walton, Olive. Diary during imprisonment in Aylesbury Prison, 1912 (typescript). Suffragette Fellowship Collection, Museum of London (Group C, vol. 2: 50.82/1131). On her brief imprisonment for breaking windows, hunger striking, and forced feeding.

3013. Ward, Margaret. Maud Gonne: Ireland's Joan of Arc. London: Pandora, 1990. 211. Gonne endured prison life and hunger strikes on behalf of Irish independence and all those in prison.

3014. Webb, P. and T. Clifton. "Politics of Suicide." Newsweek 97 (May 25, 1981) 59. Patrick Hughes dies by hunger strike.

3015. Wilkinson, R. and T. Clifton. "An IRA Man Wins a Seat in Commons." Newsweek 97 (April 20, 1981) 59. Prisoner Bobby Sands is elected to Parliament in the middle of a hunger strike.

UNITED STATES OF AMERICA

3016. Abernathy, Ralph, John Abt, and Paul Miller. On Trial: Angela Davis or America?. New York: Angela Davis Legal Defense Fund, 1971. 15. Two speeches and an article supporting Davis against government persecution.

3017. "Activist Gives Refugees a Lift on Freedom Train." Guardian 36.39 (July 11, 1984) 7. Interview of Jack Elder, a Catholic, who awaits trial and faces up to fifteen years in prison for helping Central American refugees.

3018. Adams, Frank T. James A. Dombrowski: An American Heretic, 1897-1983. Knoxville: U of Tennessee P, 1992. 368. Victim of red-baiting, racist attacks, arrests, and jailings as a subversive, Dombrowski ultimately helped establish a landmark Supreme Court decision (Dombrowski v. Pfister) in defense of civil liberties.

3019. "AI Asks Inquiry into Possible Abuses by FBI Agents." Matchbox (November 1981) 6. On the "production of false evidence, misstatements about FBI action, harassment, infiltration of defense teams by informants and failure to make available information which the defense might have used" in regard to the cases of Elmer Pratt, a leader of the Black Panther Party, and Richard Marshal, of the American Indian Movement.

3020. Alisberg, Nancy. "Guild & NCBL Focus on U.S. Political Prisoners." Guild Notes 14.5 (November 1990) 10. Report on the National Lawyers Guild and National Conference of Black Lawyers joint project to improve their political prisoner and anti-repression work, including the creation of a database.

3021. Allen, Charles, Jr. Concentration Camps U.S.A.. Citizens Committee for Constitutional Liberties, 1966. 60. Authorized by Title II of the McCarran Internal Security Act of 1950, concentration camps were established at Allenwood, PA, El Reno, OK, Florence, AZ, Wickenberg, AZ, and Tule Lake, CA.

3022. Aloisi-Nally, Jon. "Hundreds of US Prisoners Fast in Solidarity." Guardian 41.26 (March 29, 1989) 4. Resistance Conspiracy, Puerto Rican, and Black prisoners initiated the fast to support South African and West German prisoners.

3023. Alpert, Jane. Growing Up Underground. New York: William Morrow, 1981. 372. Antiwar activist Alpert describes her stay in 1969 in the Women's House of Detention, NYC, awaiting trial on charges of conspiracy to destroy government property. Also a brief account of her incarceration in the State Correctional Institute at Muncy, Penn., 1975-77.

3024. Amana, Harry. "US Political Prisoners Interviewed." Guardian 31.44 (August 22, 1979) 7. Report on the 1979 convention of the National Conference of Black Lawyers, especially the workshop around the 128-page petition presented to the UN outlining the racist history of the US, and the conditions of political prisoners in the US.

3025. "American Military Aid May Perpetuate Abuse of Rights, Report Says." Arkansas Democrat-Gazette (June 9, 1993) 3A. The U.S. supports military training to repressive countries -Guatemala, Turkey, Egypt ($3.1 billion), Israel ($1.8 billion), contrary to U.S. law.

3026. "America's Oubliette." Nation 224 (May 7, 1977) 548. A critique of the harsh sentences of possibly the "longest incarcerated political prisoners in the Western Hemisphere: the five Puerto Rican nationalists" who attacked Blair House and Congress.

3027. Ameringer, Oscar. "If You Don't Weaken": The Autobiography of Oscar Ameringer. Norman: U of Oklahoma P, 1983. 465. (Orig. 1940). Includes an account of the arrest for treason during WWI of all Socialist congressional candidates and Ameringer, publisher of the American Guardian.

3028. Amnesty For Political Prisoners. New York: American Civil Liberties Union, 1920. 12. On the status of 400-500 people imprisoned for expressing their views in wartime.

3029. "Amnesty for War Objectors." Christian Century 51 (January 3, 1934) 7. On the release in 1933 of COs imprisoned in 1917.

3030. Amnesty International Report 1980. London: Amnesty International, 1980. 162-65. More than 600 prisoners were on death row. Four prisoners of conscience were released on parole: James Grant and T.J. Reddy of the Charlotte Three, Ben Chavis of the Wilmington Ten, and Imari Obadele. Geronimo Pratt, former Black Panther and object of COINTELPRO, will be retried for his murder conviction.

3031. Amnesty International Report 1990. New York: Amnesty International, 1990. 250-253. Eight convicted members of the Sanctuary Movement lost their appeals. Leonard Peltier was again denied a new trial.

3032. Anderson, Jack. "Will It Be Human Rights or Hypocrisy?" Arkansas Democrat-Gazette (February 17, 1993) 3F. The U.S. supports 18 countries that violate human rights with impunity. Turkey and Morocco, for example, receive hundreds of millions of dollars yet are torture states.

3033. Anderson, Johnathan. "No Peace for the 'L.A. Eight'--Or the Constitution." Civil Liberties 377 (Summer-Fall 1992) 8. The INS continues to press for the deportation of seven Palestinians and one Kenyan who engaged in completely legal activities.

3034. Andrews, Joan. You Reject Them, You Reject Me: The Prison Letters of Joan Andrews. Ed. Richard Cowden-Guido. Manassas, Va.: Trinity Communications,

1988. 222. Experiences of an anti-abortion protester, including solitary confinement, 1986-88.

3035. Archer, Peter. "Carter Urged to Free P.R. Nationalists." Militant 43.6 (Feb. 16, 1979) 12. The three prisoners are "the longest held political prisoners in the Western Hemisphere," jailed in the 1950's for armed action.

3036. Armor, John, and Peter Wright. Manzanar. New York: Times; London: Secker and Warburg, 1989. 167. The story of America's most notorious experiment with concentration camps, focusing on everyday life in one relocation center in Nevada where up to 10,000 U.S. citizens of Japanese descent were interned during WW II. Commentary by John Hersey and photographs by Ansel Adams.

3037. Avrich, Paul. Sacco and Vanzetti: The Anarchist Background. Princeton: Princeton UP, 1991. 265. Dispenses with the image of innocent immigrants brutalized by the state, but does show that Sacco and Vanzetti were "clearly victimized."

3038. Bach, John M. Political Prisoner's View of Prison. St. Paul: Minnesota Public Radio, 1973. 1 sound cassette. 60 min. Bach spent 35 months in seven federal prisons for refusing induction into military service during the Vietnam War. Speech delivered at Moorehead State College.

3039. Backiel, Linda, et al. "Ties That Bind: Left Mustn't Abandon Political Prisoners." Guardian 40.37 (June 15, 1988) 10-11. A general article and a list of 115 prisoners.

3040. Bader, E. "Prison Control Unit Exposed in New Documentary." Guardian 42.10 (December 27, 1989) 19. Discusses Nina Rosenblum's film about the Lexington (KY) Control Unit, "Through the Wire," and focuses on three women prisoners--Baraldini, Rosenberg, and Torres.

3041. Baez, Joan. Daybreak. New York: Dial Press, 1968. 159. Singer Baez recalls her imprisonment for nonviolent resistance to the Vietnam War. She and her mother were incarcerated at California's Santa Rita Prison. She describes their friendly relations with the prisoners and their resistance to prison authority.

3042. Baker, Scott. "Activists Attack New Women's Control Unit." Guardian 40.25 (March 23, 1988) 6. On the campaign to close the control unit for women political prisoners in Lexington, KY.

3043. Balagoon, Kuwasi, et al. Look For Me in the Whirlwind: The Collective Autobiography of the New York 21. New York: Random House, 1971. 364. Twenty-one Black Panthers tell their life stories. They were arrested in 1969 on various charges, and all were acquitted in 1971.

3044. Balber, Susanrachel, and Joshua Greenspan. The Book of Joshua: An Historical Biography. Brooklyn: Galen Press, 1988. 130. Joshua Greenspan was incarcerated (in a mental hospital) in 1920 for an anarchist bombing he had nothing to do with.

3045. Baldwin, Roger W. "Mr. Roosevelt's Amnesty." Christian Century 51 (January 17, 1934) 92. The Director of the ACLU explains of the amnesty for war objectors.

3046. Barber, James David. "Never Say Die!" Matchbox (February 1982) 4-6. Dr. James Barber's appeal for an end to capital punishment.

3047. Barkan, Steven. Protesters on Trial: Criminal Justice in the Southern Civil Rights and Vietnam Antiwar Movements. New Brunswick, NJ: Rutgers UP, 1985. 198. Analyzes the use of political trials in these two movements and how they differed. Local and state officials used the legal system to thwart civil rights goals, forcing defendants to spend enormous amounts of money and energy and closing out issues.

The trials of the antiwar movement were not as harassing or closed to issues. Bibliography, pp. 159-190.

3048. Barricklow, Denise. "Jailed Four Years Without a Trial." Guardian 39.41 (July 29, 1987) 2. IRA member Joe Doherty has been held without trial for four years in a federal prison.

3049. Becker, Theodore and Vernon G. Murray, eds. Government Lawlessness in America. New York: Oxford UP, 1971. 411. A collection of material ranging from the Walker Report on the 1968 riot at the Democratic National Convention to the killing of Black Panther Fred Hampton.

3050. Belfrage, Cedric. The American Inquisition. Indianapolis: Bobbs-Merrill, 1973. 316. Drawing parallels between the Spanish Inquisition and the government's attempts to silence opposition, the book is a history of McCarthyism by one of its victims.

3051. Belfrage, Sally. Freedom Summer. New York: Viking, 1965. 246. Chapter 9 describes being jailed in Greenwood, Miss., for helping Blacks to register to vote as part of the 1964 Mississippi Summer Project organized by the Student Nonviolent Coordinating Committee (SNCC).

3052. Belknap, Michal R., ed. American Political Trials. Westport, CT: Greenwood, 1981. 316. Political trials are an historical constant of Anglo-American law. Essays are chronologically arranged and cover the 19th-century trial for sedition of John Peter Zinger, the Pullman Strike cases, the Red-scare trials following WWI, and the Chicago conspiracy case against antiwar activists for allegedly inciting riots in the 1968 Democratic convention.

3053. Belknap, Michal R., ed. Cold War Political Justice: The Smith Act, the Communist Party, and American Civil Liberties. Contributions in American History, No. 66. Westport, CT: Greenwood, 1977. 322. The study on American political trials focuses on the Smith Act prosecutions of the Communist Party: "these radicals suffered unjustly, and the Bill of Rights suffered along with them."

3054. Benn, Ruth. "Cuban Prisoners: Detained Without Due Process." Nonviolent Activist 5.2 (March 1988) 6. On the Cubans in the Atlanta Federal Penitentiary under the "excludable alien" category.

3055. Berkman, Alexander. Prison Memoirs of an Anarchist. New York: Mother Earth, 1912; Schocken, 1970. 512. The author spent fourteen years in prison, and his book gives an account of his work preceding arrest, his trial, and mainly his life in prison. The book makes a case for the elimination of prisons for their corruption, brutality, stupidity, and demoralization. Berkman shot Henry Clay Frick during the Homestead strike when Carnegie Co. Pinkerton agents shot strikers including women and children.

3056. Berlet, Chip. "Forgotten But Not Gone: Violations of Civil and Political Rights in the U.S." Extra! (Summer 1989) 48-9. Summary of rights and abuses in the U.S.

3057. Berman, Nina and Colleen McGuire. "Anti-Apartheid Poet Fighting Deportation." Guardian 35.42 (August 24, 1983) 5. Dennis Brutus, South African poet, seeks asylum in the U.S. against INS efforts to deport him as a "subversive." [Brutus gained asylum later. Guardian 36.2 (October 12, 1983) 9.]

3058. Berrigan, Daniel. To Dwell in Peace: An Autobiography. San Francisco: Harper & Row, 1987. 416. His life as a dissident priest, anti-war activist, trials (Catonsville, Harrisburg), and prisoner. Chapter 8 on his first political activism and arrest at the Pentagon while his brother Philip was arrested for pouring blood on draft files in Baltimore in 1967. Chapter 9 tells the story of the burning of the draft files in Catonsville, MD by Daniel, Philip, and others in 1968, their trial, and sentencing. Chapter 10 recounts his experiences underground. Chapter 11 describes prison life. Chapter 12 is about the trial in Harrisburg, PA of Philip and Elizabeth McAlister, which exonerated them.

3059. Berrigan, Philip. "Leonard Peltier Hearing." Akwesasne Notes 16.05 (Fall 1984) 13-14, 20. After nearly seven years, Peltier finally had his say in court. The article describes the trial filled with inaccuracies by the prosecution and the worldwide support behind Peltier's cause.

3060. Berrigan, Philip. Prison Journals of a Priest Revolutionary. Ed. Vincent McGee. New York: Holt, Rinehart and Winston, 1970; Ballantine, 1971. 198. On the trial and sentencing for six years in prison for pouring blood on and burning Selective Service files as acts against the Vietnam War, perhaps the first priest imprisoned by the U.S. government for a political crime.

3061. Bingham, James. "Indiana Case Threatens Free Assembly." Rights 12.5-6 (October-November 1965) 31-32. The author is one of three students indicted at Indiana University for conspiring to overthrow the State of Indiana (i.e., he attended a meeting to hear a speech).

3062. Biskind, Peter. "Political Prisoners USA: Is the U.S. a Major Violater of Human Rights?" Sevendays 2.13 (September 8, 1978) 22. According to U.N. Ambassador Andy Young, "There are hundreds, perhaps thousands of political prisoners in the United States." Presents individual case studies.

3063. Biskind, Peter. "USA: Political Prisoners by any Other Name." Sevendays 1.8 (May 23, 1977) 23. A report on the 200 political prisoners "cooling their heels" in American jails, including individual case studies.

3064. Blackstock, Nelson. Cointelpro: The FBI's Secret War on Political Freedom. New York: Vintage, 1976. 216. Exposes the FBI's illegal, secret Counterintelligence Program organized to disrupt legal political activities of Blacks, socialists, peace advocates, teachers, and many other citizens.

3065. Blunk, Tim and Raymond Levasseur, eds. Hauling Up the Morning: Writings & Art by Political Prisoners of War in the U.S. Trenton, NJ: Red Sea, 1990. 408. Collection of writings and artwork of 65 political prisoners and anti-colonial prisoners of war formerly or currently held in U.S. federal and state prisons, assembled to debunk the U.S. government's assertion that it holds no political prisoners.

3066. Bonfield, Lynn A. Jailed for Survival: The Diary of an Anti-Nuclear Activist. San Francisco: Mother Courage Affinity Group, 1984. About her imprisonment in Santa Rita Prison, California, for demonstrating against nuclear weapons work at Lawrence Livermore Laboratory.

3067. Bosworth, Allan R. America's Concentration Camps. New York. W.W. Norton, 1967. 283. A story of "racist hysteria and abuse of government power"--the WWII relocation of over 100,000 West Coast Japanese-Americans to camps in Utah, Arkansas, and other locations, even though there was not one single instance of sabotage or espionage. (The laws and machinery remain ready for a repetition of another mass arrest for imagined national security.)

3068. "Boudin Pleads Guilty." New Women's Times 10.6 (June 1984) 1. Kathy Boudin was sentenced to 20 years to life for involvement in the robbery of a Brinks armored truck in which two officers were killed.

3069. Bourgeois, Roy, Fr. "Mission Among Prisoners." Maryknoll (June 1992) 42-3. Father Bourgeois is in prison for civil disobedience in protest against the training of Salvadoran troops at Ft. Benning, Ga., and generally against "the immorality of U.S. foreign policy in Latin America."

3070. Boyle, Kay. The Long Walk at San Francisco State. New York: Grove, 1970. 150. An account of the student and faculty strike against the Vietnam War at San Francisco State University and police violence. One essay covers the jury selection in the trial of Huey P. Newton, co-founder of the Black Panther Party.

3071. Boyle, Robert. "Tribunal Urges Freedom for U.S. Political Prisoners." Guild Notes 15.1 (Winter 1991) 8. An international tribunal, comprised of jurists and legal scholars from around the world, has found that many U.S. political activists jailed under criminal statutes are being illegally detained.

3072. Bradley, Ben, Nathan Hine, et al., eds. Por Amor al Pueblo: Not Guilty! Montpelier, VT: Front Porch, 1986. 176. The edited transcript of the trial of the Winooski 44, charged with illegal trespass after occupying United States Senator Robert Stafford's Vermont office in protest of the Reagan Administration sponsored war against the people of Central America. 26 people were acquitted on the basis of their necessity defense (trespassing justified to save lives).

3073. Bradley, Scott and Douglas Spalding. "Parole Nixed; 'Free Berkman' Effort Launched." Gaurdian 43.9 (Dec. 19, 1990) 5. Demands release of Dr. Alan Berkman, imprisoned for treating fugitive Marilyn Buck. He is ill and was eligible for parole in 1987.

3074. Braley, Scott. "Ex-Panther Leader Denied Parole." Guardian 44.9 (Dec. 18, 1991) 8. Geronimo ji Jaga Pratt again denied release, despite petitions with 10,000 signatures and letters of support from prominent political leaders.

3075. Brechtel, Judith A. and Robert M. Coughlin. Building the Beloved Community: Maurice McCrackin's Life for Peace and Civil Rights. Philadelphia, Temple U P, 1991. 288. Life of the pacifist's struggle for justice, several times imprisoned for his protests. The opening chapter describes a marshal's use of an electric cattle prod on the then seventy-nine-year-old Rev. McCrackin.

3076. A Brief History of Black Struggle in America: Which is a Reproduction of the Brief Submitted to an Ad Hoc Hearing in New York City, on Behalf of Black Prisoners-of-war & Political Prisoners Held Today in Prison Unlawfully by the United States Government, December 1990. Baton Rouge, La.: House of Songhay, Commission for Positive Education, 1991. 66. On the Black struggle in America, submitted to an ad hoc hearing in New York City.

3077. Brown, Archie. "Militant Unionist Wins over Bill of Attainder." Rights 12.5-6 (October-November 1965) 12-14. A union officer is guilty of the crime of membership in the Communist Party.

3078. Bryan, Helen. Inside. Boston: Houghton Mifflin, 1953. 305. She was sentenced to the Federal Reformatory for Women at Alderson, WV, 1950-51, for refusing to cooperate with the House Committee on Un-American Activities.

3079. Buhle, Mari Jo, Paul Buhle, and Dan Georgakas, eds. Encyclopedia of the American Left. New York; London: Garland, 1990. 928. See Subject Index: Rapp-Coudert Inquiry, Red Scare, Rosenberg Case, etc.

3080. Burkhalter, Holly J. "How We Bring the Bad News Home to Congress." Human Rights Watch 10.2 (Spring 1992) 2. Human Rights Watch's opposition to the government's aid to torture states.

3081. Burns, James MacGregor and Stewart Burns. A People's Charter: The Pursuit of Rights in America. New York: Knopf, 1992. 577. On the struggles for political and civil rights by American laborers, blacks, and women since the 18th century.

3082. Bushell, Agnes. Local Deities. Willimantic, CT: Curbstone, 1990. 306. Dedicated to Pat and Ray Levasseur, members of the Ohio 7, this novel includes the trial of a radical group convicted of conspiracy.

3083. Butz, Tim. "COINTELPRO: Psychological Warfare and Magnum Justice." CounterSpy 3.1 (Spring 1976) 24-31. Overview of 15 years of officially sanctioned FBI vigilante terrorism against dissidents and minorities who challenged the policies of the US government. Focuses especially on the FBI's decimation of the Black Panther Party, including the assassinations of Bunchy Carter, John Huggins, Mark Clark, and Fred Hampton.

3084. Cadrain, Diane L. The Literature of Civil Disobedience in Thoreau, the Berrigan Brothers, and King. M.A. Thesis, Ohio State U, 1973. 93.

3085. Can't Jail the Spirit : Political Prisoners in the U.S., a Collection of Biographies. Chicago: Editorial El Coqúi, 1988. 214. (Washington D.C.: Center for Constitutional Rights, 1989). Produced by the National Commission to Free Puerto Rican Prisoners of War, as a contribution to Freedom Now: The National Campaign for Amnesty and Human Rights for Political Prisoners in the United States.

3086. "Can't Kill the Spirit." Breakthrough 9.1 (Spring 1985) 47. Protests the arrest and harsh treatment of seven anti-imperialists accused of conspiracy and bombings.

3087. Cantine, Holley, and Dachine Rainer, eds. Prison Etiquette: The Convict's Compendium of Useful Information. Pref. Christopher Isherwood; illust Lowell Naeve. Bearsville, NY: Retort, 1950. A miscellany of memoirs, poems, and sketches by WWII COs.

3088. Carroll, Peter. "Steve Nelson: Good Fight Fighter." In These Times 16.25 (May 20-26, 1992) 4-5. From 1950 to 1956 Nelson was jailed while being tried under state sedition laws and the Smith Act, until all convictions were overturned by the Supreme Court.

3089. "The Case of Elizam Escobar, Prisoner of War, and the Struggle for Puerto Rican Independence." Left Curve 11 (1986) 55-56. Escobar, a "painter, poet, illustrator, and theoretician on the relation of art and politics," and a Puerto Rican dedicated to Puerto Rican independence, was arrested on charges of seditious conspiracy, dubbed a "terrorist" by the US media, and given a 68 year sentence.

3090. Chambliss, William. "State-Organized Crime--The American Society of Criminology, 1988 Presidential Address." Criminology 27.2 (1989) 183-208. Defines criminality organized by the state as acts defined by law as criminal and committed by state officials in the pursuit of their job as representatives of the state. Thus, for example, torture and random violence by the police in numerous countries are state crimes because they are both state policy and in violation of existing laws. The author focuses upon U.S. state crimes.

3091. Chaplin, Ralph. Bars and Shadows: The Prison Poems of Ralph Chaplin. New York: Leonard, 1922. 48. (2nd rev. ed. [Ridgewood, NJ: Nellie Seeds Nearing, 1923. 63.] contains nine poems not in 1st edition.) Chaplin was a leading IWW organizer.

3092. Chevigny, Paul. Cops and Rebels : A Study of Provocation. New York: Curtis, 1972. 332. An account of the criminal conspiracy case against Black Panther Party members Alfred Cain, Jr., Ricardo de Leon, and Jerome West in 1969.

3093. Christgau, John. Enemies: World War II Alien Internment. Ames: Iowa State UP, 1985. 187. These internees were ordinary people victimized by the politics of global war and the Enemy Alien Internment Program, 1941-46. A total of 31,275 enemy aliens (Japanese, Germans, Italians) were imprisoned in camps like the one described in this book--Ft. Lincoln, just south of Bismarck, North Dakota.

3094. Churchill, Ward and James Vander Wall. Agents of Repression: The FBI's Secret War Against the American Indian Movement and the Black Panther Party. Boston: South End, 1988. 325. On the FBI as political police, focusing on its war against the American Indian Movement (AIM) particularly at the Pine Ridge Sioux Reservation. Extensive notes and index.

3095. Churchill, Ward and Jim Vander Wall. "COINTELPRO Against the Black Panthers: The Case of Geronimo Pratt." Covert Action Information Bulletin 31 (Winter 1989) 35-39. As part of its racist campaign against the Panthers, the FBI targeted Pratt, who was head of the Los Angeles Black Panther Party, for neutralization by armed assault, false indictments, and other violations of justice. Pratt has spent nearly 20 years in prison, 8 of them in solitary confinement.

3096. Churchill, Ward. "Due Process Be Damned." Z Magazine 1.1 (January 1988) 77-83. On the twelve-year effort by the federal government to prosecute the Portland Four (American Indian Movement leader Dennis Banks and three other members) for alleged illegal transportation of weapons, a "travesty of justice" that is part of the extensive effort by the FBI to destroy AIM.

3097. Churchill, Ward. "Semantic Masturbation." Z Magazine 2.12 (December 1989) 29-30. Discusses the meaning of "political prisoner" and related terms.

3098. Clavir, Judy and John Spitzer, eds. The Conspiracy Trial. Indianapolis: Bobbs Merrill, 1970. 615. Proceedings of 1969 trial against David T. Dellinger and others of the Chicago Seven.

3099. Cleaver, Eldridge. Soul On Ice. New York: McGraw-Hill, 1967. 210. Written in prison about the colonization of Blacks by an oppressive White society.

3100. Clifton, T. "The Bloody War in Belfast Spills into the U.S. Courts." Newsweek 114 (December 11, 1989) 96, 98. IRA's Joe Doherty has been held in a New York jail for over six years while he fights deportation to England and possible life imprisonment for murder.

3101. Cohen, Dan. "'Framing the Panthers': How to Destroy a Movement." Guardian 42.35 (June 27, 1990) 19. Review of a PBS film about how the FBI's COINTELPRO (counterintelligence program) killed, imprisoned, or exiled all of the Black Panther leaders.

3102. Cohen, Jeff and Norman Solomon. Adventures in Medialand. Monroe, ME: Common Courage, 1993. 259. Brett Kimberlin was placed in solitary confinement prior to the 1988 presidential election to silence him for claiming to have sold marijuana to Vice-Presidental candidate Dan Quayle.

3103. "The Cointelpro Papers." Militant (1975). Series of articles on the FBI's covert, illegal efforts to destroy radical organizations and ideas.

3104. Cole, Nancy. "Kentucky Judge Jails 11 Stearns Miners." Militant 41.42 (November 11, 1977) 27. Circuit Judge J.B. Johnson, Jr. sentenced eleven miners to jail for violating his orders "limiting the number of pickets allowed at the mine entrance."

3105. Coleman, McAlister. Eugene V. Debs: A Man Unafraid. New York: Greenberg, 1930. 345. Includes accounts of the many times Debs was jailed for defending working people (charged with conspiracy, contempt of court, etc.) beginning in 1894 and for opposing war (sentenced to ten years in 1918). Chapters 14 and 15 deal with his trial and imprisonment for opposing U.S. participation in WWI.

3106. Colhoun, Jack. "A Resisters's Victory Fuels the Movement." Guardian 37.6 (November 7, 1984) 9. A federal judge dismissed the Justice Department's case against draft resister Gillam Kerley.

3107. Conference on Human Rights. International Tribunal on Human Rights Violations of Political/POW Prisoners in the United States. Ed. Luis Nieves Falcon, coordinator. Chicago: Editorial El Coque, 1990. 53. Hunter College, New York, 1990.

3108. Cook, Fred J. The FBI Nobody Knows. New York: Macmillan, 1964. 436. On the danger of a police state resulting from Hoover's creation of a sacrosanct national police of unchecked power. Political arrests and trials are described.

3109. Cook, Jack. Rags of Time: A Season in Prison. Boston: Beacon, 1972. 192. The author, an editor of the pacifist-anarchist monthly, The Catholic Worker, and draft refuser, was tried and sentenced to 3 years in prison in 1969. This book narrates events occurring in the Lewisburg and Allenwood prisons during less than a two-week period in the spring of 1970, one year into his jail time.

3110. Cover, Robert. "A Year of Harassment." Nation 210 (February 2, 1970) 110-113. On judicial misconduct toward twenty-two Black Panthers in New York City by effective denial of bail.

3111. Coy, Patrick, ed. A Revolution of the Heart: Essays on the Catholic Worker. Philadelphia: Temple UP, 1988. 388. (Rpt. New Society, 1993). Essays on the notable individuals and events in the history of the pacifist Catholic Workers Movement.

3112. Craine, Steve. "North Carolina High Court Rejects Appeal." Militant 42.2 (Jan. 20, 1978) 5. Wilmington 10 exhaust appeals in state courts.

3113. Crane, Margaret. "Five Vignettes from the Tennessee Prison for Women." Prison Writing Review 8.2 (Winter-Spring 1985) 10-22. Crane claims she was prosecuted for concealing stolen goods because of her social activism.

3114. Crittenden, Ann. Sanctuary: A Story of American Conscience and the Law in Collision. New York: Weidenfeld and Nicolson, 1988. 410. An account of the clergy and lay people of Arizona, and then of the nation, who offered legal guidance and physical protection to political refugees from Central America despite the hostility of the Reagan administration that made such assistance illegal. The book includes accounts of the arrest and trials of sanctuary leaders by the INS.

3115. Curry, Richard. An Uncertain Future: Thought Control and Repression During the Reagan-Bush Era. Los Angeles: First Amendment Foundation, 1992. 97. Various accounts of political trials and imprisonment--e.g., the Arizona Five Earth First! members.

3116. Davidson, Joe. "Trial May Turn on Whether Aliens Share the Rights of U.S. Citizens." Wall Street Journal (August 14, 1992) B4. The government is trying to deport eight resident aliens as terrorists for distributing a magazine legally available in the U.S. and for holding fund-raisers for Palestinian causes.

3117. Davidson, Miriam. Convictions of the Heart: Jim Corbett and the Sanctuary Movement. Tucson: U of Arizona P, 1988. 187. On Jim Corbett's and others' attempts to help Latin American refugees' struggles to find political asylum in the

United States, and the trial and conviction of eleven members of the Sanctuary Movement.

3118. Davis, Angela. If They Come in the Morning: Voices of Resistance. New York: Okpaku; Third Press, 1971. 281. An anthology of writings about the black liberation movement which Davis worked on while in prison; the book contains prison interviews. "Political repression...has reached monstrous proportions"--thousands in jails, tens of thousands under surveillance, 13,000 recently arrested for protesting the Vietnam War and placed in stadiums converted into detention centers.

3119. Davis, Angela. "The Soledad Brothers." Black Scholar 2 (April-May 1971) 2-7. A defense of the Soledad Brothers, including George Jackson, written in the Marin County Jail, Calif.

3120. Davis, Angela. "Walls." An Autobiography. New York: Random House, 1974. 283-346. Describes her imprisonment in Marin County Jail and Santa Clara Jail, California, 1970-71, on false charges of murder, kidnapping, and criminal conspiracy. (She was later acquitted.)

3121. Day, Dorothy. The Eleventh Virgin. New York: Albert and Charles Boni, 1924. 312. Autobiographical novel part of which describes June Henreddy's (Dorothy Day) prison experiences. After Henreddy is arrested with a group of suffragists demonstrating for the rights of political prisoners, the suffragists stage a hunger strike in prison.

3122. Day, Dorothy. From Union Square to Rome. Silver Spring, MD: Preservation of the Faith Press, 1938; rpt., New York: Arno, 1978. 173 p. Autobiography that includes details of her confinement in Occoquan Workhouse and the Washington city jail in 1917 for suffrage activity (pp. 81-87).

3123. Day, Dorothy. "Jail." The Long Loneliness. New York: Harper & Row, 1952. 72-83. Describes her experience in a Washington jail after picketing in front of the White House in support of suffragists. She went on a hunger strike while incarcerated.

3124. Day, Dorothy. "Thoughts After Prison." Liberation: An Independent Monthly 2.6 (September 1957) 5-7. Day and others of the Catholic Workers movement were jailed for picketing instead of taking shelter during an air-raid drill.

3125. Day, Samuel H., Jr. Crossing the Line: From Editor, to Activist, to Inmate--A Writers Journey. Baltimore, MD: Fortkamp, 1991. 280. Chapters 16-20 give an account of the author's resistance to U.S. nuclearism and his imprisonments as the result.

3126. Day, Samuel H., Jr., ed. Nuclear Heartland: A Guide to the 1,000 Missile Silos of the United States. Madison, WI: Progressive Foundation, 1988. 96. Maps and details on each silo prepared by former prisoners.

3127. Day, Samuel H., Jr., ed. Prisoners on Purpose: A Peacemakers' Guide to Jails and Prisons. Madison, WI: Progressive Foundation, 1989. 145. From the people who demonstrated at missile silos as the Missouri Peace Planting Project, fifteen of whom were sent to prison, some for twenty-six months.

3128. Day, Susie. "Three Defendants Plead Guilty in 'Conspiracy' Case." Gay Community News 18.15 (October 7, 1990) 1. Marilyn Buck, Linda Evans and Laura Whitehorn pleaded guilty to a series of eight protest bombings in an effort to free Alan Berkman, who suffers from Hodgkin's disease.

3129. DeBenedetti, Charles, with Charles Chatfield. An American Ordeal: The Antiwar Movement of the Vietnam Era, 1961-1975. Syracuse, NY: Syracuse UP, 1990. 495. Scattered details about arrests.

3130. "De Ple Y En Guerra." Breakthrough 9.1 (Spring 1985) 23-34. Interview with Puerto Rican Ocar Lopez Rivera, sentenced to 75 years for seditious conspiracy.

3131. Debs, Eugene V. Eugene V. Debs Speaks. Ed. Jean Y. Tussey. New York: Pathfinder, 1970. 320. Chapter 28 is Debs' address to the jury of his trial for espionage (discouraging enlistment) in 1918. Debs was sentenced to 10 years and ran for the presidency behind bars as the Socialist candidate for the fifth time.

3132. Dellinger, Dave. From Yale to Jail: The Life Story of a Moral Dissenter. New York: Pantheon, 1993. 501. The author served two prison terms for refusing to register for the draft in WWII and was arrested numerous times later in pacifist protests. As one of the Chicago Eight Defendents for the 1963 Democratic Convention protests, he was again sent to prison.

3133. Deming, Barbara. "In the Birmingham Jail." Nation 25 (May 1963) 436-37. About her imprisonment for peacefully demonstrating for racial equality.

3134. Deming, Barbara. Prison Notes. New York: Grossman, 1966. 185. Describes her 1964 imprisonment in Albany, GA, for a civil rights demonstration, lists her 35 fellow prisoners, and defends her theory of nonviolent protest.

3135. Deming, Barbara. We Are All Part of One Another: A Barbara Deming Reader. Ed. Jane Meyerding. Philadelphia: New Society, 1984. 295. Includes "In the Birmingham Jail" and selections from Prison Notes.

3136. Deutsch, M. "Political Prisoners in the United States." Social Justice 18.3 (Fall 1991) 92-106. The author describes who U.S. political prisoners are and how the government uses its power to detain them. Includes five personal stories.

3137. Dietrich, Jeff. Reluctant Resister. Greensboro, N.C.: Unicorn, 1983. 165. The author's prison letters. He was incarcerated for protesting the 1979 Arms Bazaar in Anaheim, CA.

3138. Ditz, Jeff. "Sentenced to Jail Indefinitely." Guardian 37.15 (January 16, 1985) 4. Continuing arrests of protesters at the Williams International war plant. Some ninty people have been arrested during two years of vigils.

3139. Dolph, George. "Wilmington 10: Still No Justice." Militant 42.4 (Feb. 3, 1978) 1. Governor Hunt of North Carolina refuses to pardon the defendants despite recantations by three major prosecution witnesses.

3140. Donner, Frank. The Age of Surveillance: The Aims and Methods of America's Political Intelligence System. New York: Knopf, 1980. 554. Details the "secret war waged continuously for over fifty years against all shades of dissenting politics by the domestic intelligence community, a virtually autonomous network of executive agencies dominated by the FBI and supported and protected by a powerful congressional constituency."

3141. Donner, Frank. Protectors of Privilege: Red Squads and Police Repression in Urban America. Berkeley: U of California Press, 1990. 503. During "the past hundred years [specialized] urban police ['red squads'] have served as the protective arm of the economic and political interests of the capitalist system." At their peak in the 1960s, they numbered in the hundreds and employed possibly 300,000 people in the pursuit of "subversion," that is, political dissent.

3142. Donner, Frank J. The Un-Americans. New York: Ballantine, 1961. 313. Documents the House Un-American Activities Committee as an Orwellian "Big Brother" that keeps millions of records of "subversives," subjects many innocent people to unfair hearings, and sends some innocent people to prison.

3143. Doremus, Andrea. "Jailed Seneca Protesters End Month-long Hunger Strike." Guardian 36.23 (March 14, 1984) 7. Three women sentenced to jail for three months for throwing paint on a recruiting office in protest of militarism protested by a thirty-day hunger strike.

3144. Douglass, James. The Non-Violent Coming of God. Maryknoll, NY: Orbis, 1991. 250. (Adaptation of one chapter appeared in Ground Zero 9.3-4 [Winter 1991] 6-7.) On the author's philosophy, trials, imprisonment, and activism against nuclear weapons. At one trial in 1985, the judge dismissed the conspiracy charge, and the jury voted acquittal of trespassing after he was allowed to explain his reasons for civil disobedience.

3145. "Dr. Alan Berkman, Fighting For His Life." Breakthrough 5.2 (Fall 1990) 46. On the harsh treatment of Dr. Berkman, seriously ill in prison with lymphatic cancer.

3146. "Drop the Charges! Real Crime is Colonialism." Breakthrough 11.2 (Fall 1987) 22. Indicts the government's determination to destroy the Puerto Rican independence movement and defends the seven defendants charged with conspiracy to liberate two prisoners from Leavenworth Federal Prison.

3147. Duberman, Martin. Paul Robeson. New York: Knopf, 1988. 804. Biography of Robeson--actor, singer and advocate for racial justice; his story of internal exile and persecution during the Truman era.

3148. DuBois, W.E.B. The Autobiography of W.E.B. DuBois: A Soliloquy on Viewing My Life from the Last Decade of its First Century. New York: International, 1968. 448. DuBois' third autobiography, written in his 90th year, is an overview of his entire life, including the 1906 Atlanta Riot, "pogrom would be more accurate," of organized violence against blacks, and his indictment and trial on the charge of being an "unregistered foreign agent" in connection with his leadership of the Peace Information Center.

3149. Dworkin, Ronald. Taking Rights Seriously. Cambridge, MA.: Harvard UP, 1977. 295. Chapter eight, "Civil Disobedience," examines the principles and arguments pro and con for disobeying laws believed to be immoral.

3150. Eby, Kermit. "The Refiner's Fire." Christian Century 79 (February 14, 1962) 199-200. Interview of Willard Uphaus, jailed a year for contempt of court, explains his Christian pacifism and socialism.

3151. Eller, Cynthia. Conscientious Objectors and the Second World War: Moral and Religious Arguments in Support of Pacifism. New York: Praeger, 1991. 218. Based upon oral interviews with sixty WWII conscientious objectors who were imprisoned as a result, or performed alternative or noncombatant service.

3152. "Environmental Objector Challenges Navy." Nonviolent Activist 10.5 (September-October 1993) 17. Aaron Ahearn is being courtmartialed by the Navy for refusing to dump toxic materials in the ocean.

3153. Epstein, Barbara. Political Protest and Cultural Revolution: Nonviolent Direct Action in the 1970's and 1980's. Berkeley: U of California P, 1991. 327. On the Clamshell Alliance's opposition to the Seabrook nuclear energy plant and the many arrests.

3154. Epstein, Jason. The Great Conspiracy Trial: An Essay on Law, Liberty and the Constitution. New York: Random House, 1970. 433. An account of the trial of the Chicago Eight, another effort by the state to repress free speech during the Vietnam War.

3155. Farewell to Manzanar. TV film, dir. John Korty, NBC, 1976. Story of Japanese-American internment during World War II.

3156. Farley, Gay. "Banks, Peltier and the 'Spirit of Crazy Horse.'" Guardian 35.37 (June 15, 1983) 7. About Peter Matthiessen's book on the American Indian Movement (AIM) and subsequent struggles of Dennis Banks and Leonard Peltier

3157. Fawcett, James W., ed. Jailed for Birth Control: The Trial of William Sanger, Sept. 10, 1915. New York: Birth Control Review, 1917. 15 Newspaper articles on trial and Sanger's statement.

3158. Fernandez, Ronald. Los Macheteros: The Wells Fargo Robbery and the Violent Struggle for Puerto Rican Independence. New York: Prentice Hall, 1987. 272. On the September 12, 1983 robbery of $7 million from the Wells Fargo depot in West Hartford, Connecticut and its connection with the Puerto Rican militant group Los Macheteros, whose fervent belief in Puerto Rican independence brings into question their status as terrorists as opposed to patriots.

3159. Ferris, Timothy. "Hometown Folks: Letters from American Political Prisoners." The Rolling Stone Reader. Ed. editors of Rolling Stone. New York: Warner, 1974. 108-147. Mainly by white middle-class males whose alleged crimes were political or whose due process was warped because of their social or political background.

3160. Fiedler, Leslie. Being Busted. New York: Stein and Day, 1969. 255. A book about "the endless war," 1933-1967, "sometimes cold, sometimes hot, between the dissenter and his imperfect society," especially the government's war against privacy. The author, a notable dissident, was arrested in 1967 for smoking marijuana in his home.

3161. Findley, Tim. "George Jackson: Death on the Yard." The Rolling Stone Reader. Ed. editors of Rolling Stone. New York: Warner, 1974. 85-107. On California prison conditions, Soledad prison, and George Jackson, who was killed in prison by guards.

3162. Fink, Elizabeth. "Two-Year Sedition Trial Ends in Defense Victory." Guild Notes 14.1 (January 1990) 18. Reports on the trial on charges of sedition, "thought crime," against three of the Ohio Seven.

3163. Finkel, David. "Defend Elias Ayoub and Ziad Abu Em!" Changes 1.10 (November 1979) 10. Opposes efforts to deport these two Palestinians.

3164. Fitzgerald, Tamsin. Tamsin. Ed. Richard A. Condon. New York: Dial, 1973. 180. Eighteen-year-old Tamsin was imprisoned in 1969-1970 for helping her boyfriend attempt to hijack an airplane from New York to Havana in order for him to avoid the draft.

3165. Flanders, Laura. "Parents Fight Draconian Sentence." New Directions For Women 19.2 (March 1990) 7. The parents of Susan Rosenberg struggle against her harsh sentence and prison treatment for possessing explosives.

3166. Flynn, Edith. "Political Prisoners and Terrorism in American Correctional Institutions." Terrorism and Criminal Justice. Ed. Ronald Crelinsten, et al. Lexington, MA: Heath, 1978. 87-92. Urges reforms in the treatment of political prisoners.

3167. Flynn, Elizabeth Gurley. The Alderson Story: My Life as a Political Prisoner. New York: International, 1963. Imprisoned 1955-57 under the Smith Act for allegedly teaching and advocating the violent overthrow of the government. Flynn had worked for the IWW, was a founder of the ACLU, and later a communist.

3168. Ford, Linda G. Iron-Jawed Angels: The Suffrage Militancy of the National Woman's Party 1912-1920. Lanham, NY: UP of America, 1991. 299. The story of the 168 suffrage women who chose jail rather than comply with law that forbade their suffrage demonstrations, a militancy based on non-violent principles.

3169. "Forgiving War-offenders." Literary Digest 67 (October 2, 1920) 18-19. The debate over freeing conscientious objectors and other opponents of the war jailed under the Espionage Law.

3170. Fornaro, Carlos de. A Modern Purgatory. New York: Kennerley, 1917. 178. A record of the prison experiences of Carlos de Fornaro, artist, writer, editor, revolutionary in the famous Tomb's prison, in New York City, and in the N.Y.C. penitentiary on Blackwell's Island.

3171. Fraker, Susan, et al. "U.S. Political Prisoners?" Newsweek 92 (July 31, 1978) 23-4. The Wilmington Ten, the Charlotte Three, Imari Obadele, Johnny Harris, Ben Chavis.

3172. Frankel, David. "'People in the Streets...That's How We Can Win Victories': Interview with Ben Chavis." Militant 42.5 (Feb.10, 1978) 6-7. One of the Wilmington 10 held in prison on trumped up charges discusses the trial, prison conditions, and efforts to gain exoneration. (See accompanying article.)

3173. Franklin, H. Bruce. Prison Literature in America: The Victim as Criminal and Artist. Expanded ed. New York: Oxford UP, 1989. 352. (The Victim as Criminal and Artist: Literature from the American Prison. 2nd ed. New York: Oxford UP, 1978. 337.). Scattered references (see index) streching in time from the Anti-Renters of 1839 and the abolitionists prior to the Civil War to Alexander Berkman's Prison Memoirs of an Anarchist(1912) to Malcolm X.

3174. Frantz, Laurent. "Junius Scales." Nation 193 (December 30, 1961) 528-530. Protests six-year imprisonment of Scales under the Smith Act for membership in the Communist Party.

3175. Free Pennsylvania's Political Prisoners. New York: American Civil Liberties Union, 1979. 11. Milan Resetar, Tom Zima, and Peter Muselin, were each convicted under the sedition law to five years of hard labor in the Allegheny County Workhouse for being members of the Communist Party and for distributing Communist literature.

3176. "Free Speech and Jailed Speakers." Literary Digest 77 (June 16, 1923) 10-12. Describes a petition signed by forty-eight prominent men and women for the release of all espionage-act prisoners, most of them guilty of voicing unorthodox opinions or of joining some organization disapproved of by the government.

3177. Freed, Donald. Agony in New Haven: The Trial of Bobby Seale and Ericka Huggins and the Black Panther Party. New York: Simon & Schuster, 1973. 347. On the trial of Black Panther members on murder charges as part of a nationwide government effort to eradicate the Panthers. Seale, Chairman of the Party, and Huggins were acquitted.

3178. Freedom Now!. Chicago, IL: Campaign for Amnesty and Human Rights for Political Prisoners in the U.S., 1990. A periodical.

3179. Freeman, Harrop Arthur. An Historical Justification and Legal Basis for Amnesty Today. Tempe, AZ; Louisville, KY: Arizona SU College of Law; Distributed by Southern Conference Educational Fund, 1971. Reprinted from Law and Social Order (Arizona SU law journal) 5.3 (1971). Amnesty for Vietnam War protesters.

3180. French, Peter. Conscientious Actions: The Revelation of the Pentagon Papers.

Cambridge, MA: Schenkman, 1974. 176. On Daniel Ellsberg's civil disobedience in blowing the whistle on secret papers about the Vietnam War.

3181. From Women in Prison Here to Women of Vietnam: We are Sisters. San Francisco: Peoples Press, 1975. 23. Letters written from the California Institution for Women (Frontera) to women political prisoners in South Vietnam expressing solidarity.

3182. Frontier Injustice: Human Rights Abuses Along the U.S. Border with Mexico Persist Amid Climate of Impunity. New York: Human Rights Watch, 1993. 46. U.S. immigration law enforcement agents continue to abuse the human rights of Mexicans along the border, and efforts to regulate their actions are inadequate.

3183. Gannett, Betty. Papers 1929-1970. Madison, Wis.: State Historical Society of Wisconsin. An active member of the Communist Party, she was imprisoned 1955-57 in the Federal Reformatory for Women in West Virginia charged under the Smith Act with conspiracy against the government.

3184. Gans, Donna. "The New York Eight Plus: A Question of Conspiracy, but Whose?" Overthrow 7.2 (Summer 1985) 10, 15. The article gives the background of the incident involving the New York 8+ and an interview with Lateefah Carter, Robert Taylor, and Jose (Pepe) Rios.

3185. Garry, Charles and Art Goldberg. Streetfighter in the Courtroom: The People's Advocate. New York: Dutton, 1977. 268. Autobiography of Charles Garry, controversial trial lawyer whose clients included Huey Newton, Bobby Seale, Inez Garcia, the Oakland Seven, and other politically oppressed.

3186. Gavzer, Bernard. "Held Without Hope" Parade (March 21, 1993) 4-5. More than 1800 Cubans have been detained in prisons--some as long as ten years without charges--the last of the 125,000 people Castro allowed to leave in 1980.

3187. Gaylin, Willard. In the Service of Their Country: War Resisters in Prison. New York: Viking, 1970. 344. A psychoanalyst studies draft resisters who chose prison instead of participation in the Vietnam war, based upon interviews recorded in prison of a representative sample. These are war resisters who out of belief opposed the war.

3188. Gesensway, Deborah and Mindy Roseman. Beyond Words: Images from America's Concentration Camps. Ithaca; London: Cornell UP, 1987. 176. An account of the WWII Japanese-American relocation camps through their art and artists, particularly in conveying what it was like to be interned.

3189. Gibney, Mark. "A 'Well-Founded Fear' of Persecution." Human Rights Quarterly 10 (1988) 109-121. Analyzes contradictions between U.S. law and U.S. politics regarding refugees from state terrorism and calls for an emphasis upon the plight of the people rather than where they came from (Cubans get in, Haitians and Guatemalans do not).

3190. Ginger, Ray. The Bending Cross: A Biography of Eugene Victor Debs. New Brunswick: Rutgers UP, 1949. 516. Brief sections on his imprisonment under the Espionage Act for opposing WWI, pp. 354ff.

3191. Gioglio, Gerald R. Days of Decision: An Oral History of Conscientious Objectors in the Military During the Vietnam War. Trenton, NJ: Broken Rifle, 1989. 338. Accounts by twenty-four in-service conscientious objectors plus the record of one court martial. There are three main categories: in-service, imprisoned COs; noncombatant service COs, those who entered the military as 1-A-O; and in-service, discharged COs. Chapter 1 gives the development of a personal belief system that led to opposition to war; Chapter 4 reports on antiwar activities, including court-martial and imprisonment; etc.

3192. Glick, Brian. War at Home: Covert Action Against U.S. Activists and What We Can Do About It. Edison, NJ: South End, 1989. 92. History of government repression of activists and movements.

3193. Golden, Renney and Michael McConnell. Sactuary: The New Underground Railroad. Maryknoll, N.Y.: Orbis, 1986. 214. The story of the US sanctuary movement. Brutal counterrevolutionary repression in Central America has driven many thousands to flee to refugee camps and to the U.S. and Canada. The U.S. government seeks to prevent legal sanctuary of political refugees from selected countries by prosecuting supporters of sanctuary, because the refugees have witnessed U.S. complicity with murderous dictatorships.

3194. Goldman, Emma. A Fragment of the Prison Experiences of Emma Goldman and Alexander Berkman: In the State Prison at Jefferson City, MO., and the U.S. Penitentiary at Atlanta, GA., February, 1918-October 1919. New York: Stella Comyn, 1919. 25. They describe the terrible conditions in their prisons and the special discriminations and persecutions of politicals.

3195. Goldman, Emma. "Letters from Prison." Little Review 3.3 (May 1916) 17-18. Reprinted in The Little Review Anthology, ed. Margaret Anderson. New York: Horizon Press, 1953. 62-63. Written during April 1916 after being arrested for lecturing on birth control.

3196. Goldman, Emma. Living My Life. 2 vols. New York: Knopf, 1931; reprint, Dover, 1970. 993. Vol. I, Chapter 12 describes her imprisonment in 1893 in Blackwell's Island Penitentiary, NY, for inciting to riot, and Vol. II, Chapters 45-49 describe her imprisonment 1917-19 in the Missouri State Penitentiary for conspiracy against the draft.

3197. Goldstein, Robert. Political Repression in Modern America From 1870 to the Present. Cambridge, MA: Schenkman, 1978. 682. The purpose of this study is to demonstrate that political repression has frequently interfered with the free market of ideas in modern American history. Numerous political trials and prisoners are discussed.

3198. "Good News Plowshares Strike USS Tucson." Nuclear Resister 89 (June 23, 1993) 1, 5. Three Plowshares activists were fined for boarding a nuclear submarine, hammering on it, pouring blood, and raising banners.

3199. Goodell, Charles. Political Prisoners in America. New York: Random House, 1973. 400. A history from the 18th century to the 1960's. Lawbreaking for reform has occured frequently in US history. "Those in political power, frightened and confused by dissent and unorthodoxy, have just as frequently tried to use the criminal process to control American political life and to repress dissent." Essays on "Political Prisoners in American History" (Part I), "How Does Repression Survive in America?" (Part II), and "Living with Civil Disobedients" (Part III). The author was a Republican U.S. Senator from New York. "I have come to see that our legal and political institutions are dangerously unresponsive and unyielding to the impassioned grievances of our own people."

3200. Gornik, Vivian. The Romance of American Communism. New York: Basic Books, 1977. 265. Several of the subjects of this book--e.g., Eric Lanzetti, Anthony Ehrenpreis--suffered imprisonment.

3201. Gray, Ian and Moira Stanley. A Punishment in Search of a Crime: Americans Speak Out Against the Death Penalty. New York: Avon, 1989. 379. Contains 48 interviews, challenging all of the traditional arguments in support of capital punishment.

3202. Green, Gil. Cold War Fugitive: A Personal Story of the McCarthy Years. New York: International, 1974. 275. Green was one of the U.S. Communist Party leaders sentenced to prison under the Smith Act who chose to go underground. His book gives an account of the FBI hunt for him and its consequences for him, his family, and his friends

3203. Gwattney, John, ed. The Dissenters: Voices from Contemporary America. New York: Random House, 1986. 321. First person accounts by people who have suffered the consequences of taking unpopular stands, even to going to jail for some.

3204. "Haitians Denied Justice in U.S." Guardian 29.35 (June 8, 1977) 8. Hatians seeking political asylum in the U.S. are being arrested and then denied the right to asylum.

3205. Halperin, Morton H. and Daniel Hoffman. Freedom Vs. National Security: Secrecy and Surveillance. New York: Chelsea House, 1977. 594. Explains how the courts have attempted to satisfy the requirements of national security against perceived threats from abroad or from internal subversion "by constricting the freedoms guaranteed by the Bill of Rights."

3206. Halsted, Fred. Out Now! A Participant's Account of the American Movement Against the Vietnam War. New York: Monad, 1978. 759. The resistance to the Vietnam War from 1960 to 1975, a movement that involved millions of Americans, hundreds of organizations, and the trials and jailings of many people.

3207. Hariman, Robert, ed. Popular Trials--Rhetoric, Mass Media, and the Law. Tuscaloosa: U of Alabama P, 1990. 257. Includes the Chicago 7 and Catonsville 9 trials.

3208. Harris, David. Goliath. New York: R.W. Baron, 1970. 134. Goliath is the nation-state, America, who "is currently crushing lives more efficiently and in greater numbers than any other country on earth." David Harris, an honor student, eagle scout, football player and former president of the Stanford student body, served three-years in federal prison for refusing induction into the armed forces in 1968.

3209. Harris, Emily. "On the Open Road." Fortune News (June 1981) 4. Written while she was in the California Institution for Women, Frontera, for robbery, assault, and kidnapping (Patricia Hearst) while a member of the Symbionese Liberation Army (SLA).

3210. Harth, Erica. "Concentration and Memory." In These Times 16.28 (June 24-July 7, 1992) 22, 24. On Feb. 19, 1992, the Manzanar, CA, "relocation camp" for Japanese- Americans during WWII was declared a national historical landmark; almost nothing remains of the one square mile of 36 blocks of barracks.

3211. Hawk, David. "Genocide: Will the U.S. Senate Say 'Never Again'?" Matchbox (Feb. 1982) 7. Analyzes past failures to ratify the Genocide Treaty.

3212. Hellman, Lillian. Scoundrel Time. Boston: Little, Brown, 1976. 155. Memoirs of the McCarthy period, including her defiant testimony in front of the House Committee on Un-American Activities in 1952.

3213. Herngren, Per. Path of Resistance: The Practice of Civil Disobedience. Philadelphia: New Society, 1993. 256. He spent 18 months in Danbury Federal Prison for his dissent. This is a practical handbook for nonviolent civil disobedience.

3214. Herrick, Brad. "Ramsey, Tax Protester, Jailed for Following His Pacifist Beliefs." St. Louis Journalism Review 22.159 (Sept. 1993) 1, 8. Ramsey refused to pay his income taxes in protest of US militarism.

3215. Hoeffel, Paul, and Phil Garber. "Seduced and Abandoned." Z Magazine 1.2 (Feb. 1988) 75-78. On the approaching trial for conspiracy to overthrow the government of the Ohio 7, who are already serving long terms for violent acts committed in opposition to racism, militarism, and injustice.

3216. "Huey P. Newton: 'The Power of the People Freed Me.'" Black Panther 18.24 (Nov. 4, 1978) 1. Newton gains freedom on bail pending his appeal of two illegal convictions.

3217. Huggins, Ericka. "A Letter from Sister Ericka Huggins." Movement 5.8 (Sept. 1969) 7. Supports political prisoners in their fight against government oppression.

3218. Incident at Oglala. Film, dir. Robert Redford. 1992. Documentary on the shootout in 1975 which led to the imprisonment of Leonard Peltier.

3219. "Interview with Puerto Rican patriot Rafael Cancel Miranda." Breakthrough 11.1 (Winter 1987) 31. One of the armed attackers on the U.S. House of Representatives. He received an 81-year sentence.

3220. Jackson, Bruce, and Diane Christian. Death Row. Boston: Beacon, 1980. 292. On US slowly cruel method of killing death row inmates.

3221. Jackson, George. Soledad Brother: The Prison Letters of George Jackson. New York: Coward-McGann, 1970. 330. Written 1964-1970. Introduction by Jean Genet.

3222. Jailed for Freedom: Some Phases in the Front Line of a War for Democracy Not Quite Won. Washington, DC: s.n., 1919. 15. Account of incidents in Washington, DC 1917-19 in the fight for women's suffrage.

3223. "Jail Too Small for Persistent ELF Resisters." The Nuclear Resister No.88 (April 2, 1993) 3. One hundred thirty-seven arrests in the latest of a two-year campaign against the Navy's ELF (extremely low frequency) facility in Wisconsin.

3224. Jaimes, M.A. "The Trial of the 'Columbus Day Four.'" Lies of Our Times 3.9 (Sept. 1992) 8-9. The four co-directors of the Colorado chapter of the American Indian Movement were found not guilty on all 12 criminal charges filed by the City of Denver for obstructing a parade commemorating Columbus.

3225. Jenness, Doug. "Carl Skoglund: Example for Communist Workers." Militant 48.29 (Aug. 3, 1984) 7-14. Skoglund was "among eighteen socialist workers railroaded to jail under the Smith Act."

3226. Jezer, Marty. Abbie Hoffman: American Rebel. New Brunswick, NJ: Rutgers UP, 1992. 345. Hoffman, master organizer, political actor, humorist, and idealist spent time in jails, trials (one of the Chicago 7 in 1969, vs. CIA in 1987), and under ground (seven years).

3227. "Jill Raymond Still in Jail." Lesbian Tide 5.4 (March 1976) 6. She was imprisoned for refusing to testify to a grand jury investigating fugitives Susan Saxe and Katherine Power.

3228. Johnson, Diane. Dashiell Hammett: A Life. New York: Random House, 1983. 344. Chapters 18-20 tell of Hammett's arrest and imprisonment for refusing to testify regarding a fugitive convicted under the Smith Act, the subsequent tax lien for

$100,629 against him, and Senator McCarthy's questioning him regarding his "subversive" books.

3229. Jones, Jeff. "Government Moves to Stage 'Antiterrorist' Show Trial." Guardian 41.41 (Aug. 2, 1989) 5. An overview of the various trials of the Resistance conspiracy case--Berkman, Blunk, Rosenberg, Whitehorn, et al.

3230. Jones, Mary H. Autobiography of Mother Jones. Ed. Mary Field Parton. Chicago: Kerr, 1925; rpt. Kerr for Illinois Labor Historical Society, 1972. 242. A major force in the American labor movement from 1880, Mother Jones describes her several arrests and imprisonments for supporting striking miners and railroad workers.

3231. Joyce, Lynda. "Cops Riot Against Ohio Nuclear Workers Strike." Militant 43.33 (Aug. 31, 1979) 14. Police arrest 25 peaceful strikers.

3232. Judd, Gordon. "Voices From Prison." Ground Zero 9.3-4 (Winter 1991) 11. Sentenced thirty days for demonstrating at Wurtsmith AFB, Michigan.

3233. "Juries Refuse to Convict Antiwar Activists." Guardian 39.30 (April 29, 1987) 7. Two of three cases of protests against the US war in Central America resulted in mistrials.

3234. Kane, H.F. Why Eleven Members of the I.W.W., Imprisoned at Leavenworth, Refused Conditional Pardon. Philadelphia: s.n., 1974. Statement given to Kane by the I.W.W. prisoners

3235. Karagueuzian, Dikran. Blow It Up! Boston, MA: Gambit, 1971. 196. On the black student revolt at San Francisco State College and the arrest of hundreds of students participating in peaceful demonstrations (over 450 on one day), in which some students were beaten.

3236. Katz, Sanford. "New York City Officials Stifle Dissent." Rights 12.5-6 (Oct.-Nov. 1965) 34-36. Analyzes the succession of criminal contempt trials against members of the Progressive Labor Pary and others for refusal to testify.

3237. Kaufman, Natalie Hevener, and David Whiteman. Human Rights Treaties and the Senate: A History of Opposition. Chapel Hill: U of North Carolina P, 1990. 256. Argues that current opposition in the Senate to human rights treaties is a legacy of the 1950's assumptions that the treaties threaten the sovereignty of the "American way of life." Chapter two discusses the Genocide Convention, a UN backed international response to Nazi atrocities that took 35 years for Senate approval. Chapter four discusses the Bricker Amendment, the Senate's argument in opposition to human rights treaties.

3238. Kaufman, Natalie Hevener, and David Whiteman. "Opposition to Human Rights Treaties in the United States Senate: The Legacy of the Bricker Amendment." Human Rights Quarterly 10 (1988) 309-337. Explains why the U.S. Senate has not ratified the covenants and most other human rights treaties.

3239. Kempton, Murray. The Briar Patch: The People of the State of New York v. Lumumba Shakur et al. New York: Dutton, 1973. 282. On the arrest of a group of Black Panthers in New York City in 1969 on trumped-up charges, their trial, and acquittal.

3240. Kempton, Murray, ed. Trials of the Resistance. New York: Random House, 1970. 246. Essays on accused people who respond to charges "by bringing the state to trial"--Captain Howard Levy, Bobby Seale, et al.

3241. Kennedy, Jane. "Detroit Jail Abuse." Health Rights News 4.3 (May-June 1971) 10-11. She was sentenced to four years for the destruction of computer tapes at the Dow Chemical Research Center, Midland, MI, in opposition to the Vietnam War.

3242. Kennedy, Jane. "Letters from Prison." Health Rights News 4.1 (January 1971) 14. Written while awaiting trial for an alleged raid on an Indianapolis draft board.

3243. Kentucky Alliance Against Racist and Political Repression. Newsletter. Louisville, KY: The Alliance, 1975.

3244. Keyser, Christine. "Earth First! Trial Shows FBI Flair for Deception." In These Times 15.34 (Sept. 1991) 18-24. On the set-up of an environmental group by the FBI.

3245. Kinoy, Arthur. Rights on Trial: The Odyssey of a People's Lawyer. Cambridge: Harvard UP, 1983. 340. First-person narration by the lawyer who defended persons blacklisted as communist-sympathizers, leftist unions, helped with Rosenbergs' appeals, supported civil rights efforts including the Willie Seals case, etc.

3246. Kittrie, Nicholas and Eldon Wedlock, Jr., eds. The Tree of Liberty: A Documentary History of Rebellion and Political Crime in America. Baltimore: Johns Hopkins UP, 1986. 714. A history through documents of "two unorthodoxies--unorthodox politics and unorthodox crimes"--people who deviate from authorized political procedures often in the name of values transcending particular laws.

3247. Kleffner, Heike. "Ex-Panther on Death Row Leads Strike." Guardian 42.4 (Nov. 15, 1989) 4. Mumia Abu-Jamal, former member of the Black Panther Party, exemplifies the persection of a generation of political Black activists.

3248. The "Knights of Liberty" Mob and the I.W.W. Prisoners at Tulsa Oklahoma (November 9, 1917). New York: National Civil Liberties Bureau, 1979. 16. On November 9, 1917 the police department of Tulsa, Oklahoma arrested on false charges of vagrancy 10 members of the I.W.W. and turned them over to the Knights of Liberty, who whipped, tarred and feathered them.

3249. Kohn, Stephen M. Jailed For Peace: The History of American Draft Law Violaters, 1658-1985. Contributions in Military Studies, No. 49. Westport, CT: Greenwood, 1986. 169. Covers resistance from the "earliest colonial days, when American conscientious objectors refused to fight against Native American tribes, until the early 1980s when 500,000 youths refused to register for the draft."

3250. Kunstler, William. "The Harsh Government Prosecution of Military Resisters." War Crimes: A Report on United States War Crimes Against Iraq. Ramsey Clark et al. Washington, DC: Maisonneuve, 1992. 201-203. Defends the conscientious objectors in the Gulf War, who are being court-martialed.

3251. Kuntsler, William. "A Time for Amnesty." Nation 193 (December 30, 1961) 526-8. Calls for clemency for Frank Wilkinson and Carl Braden, unjustly imprisoned because of the anti-communist witch-hunt.

3252. Kunstler, William. Trials and Tribulations. New York: Grove, 1985. 201. Stories of people accompanied by poetic commentary on such prisoners as the Chicago Eight, Bobby Seale, Jerry Rubin and Abbie Hoffman, the Catonsville Nine, Martin Luther King, Jr., Freedom Riders, and many others.

3253. Kurshan, Nancy. "Supermax: Control" Breakthrough (Summer 1992) 40-45. Denounces the "super maximum security prisons" modeled after the Federal Penitentiary of Marion, IL, where some political prisoners have been incarcerated.

3254. Kutler, Stanley. The American Inquisition: Justice and Injustice in the Cold War. New York: Hill and Wang, 1982. 285. Case studies of government repression: Tokyo Rose, Beatrice Braude, Ezra Pound, et al. The essays in this book depict events largely dictated by the loyalty and security demands of the post-World War II period.

3255. Lamont, Corliss. Freedom is as Freedom Does: Civil Liberties Today. New York: Horizon, 1956. 322. Surveys the police state machinery of the 1950s with chapters on HUAC, Senator McCarthy, unconstitutional laws, the loyalty-security program, the assault on academic freedom, etc.

3256. Lebrón, Lolita. Poems. Tr. Gloria Waldman. Rpt. Voices of Women: Poetry By and About Third World Women. New York: Women's International Resource Exchange (WIRE), 1982. Also rpt. Doris Myer and Marguerite Fernandez Olmos, Contemporary Women Authors of Latin America, New Translations. Brooklyn College Humanities Series. Brooklyn, N.Y.: Brooklyn College Press, 1983. Puerto Rican Nationalist imprisoned for twenty-five years in the Federal Reformatory for Women at Alerson, WV, for participating in a 1954 armed demonstration in the U.S. House of Representatives. Released in 1979.

3257. Lederer, Bob. "Activist Jailed For 'Contempt.'" Guardian 40.40 (July 6, 1988) 4. FBI harassment of Puerto Rican independentistas has culminated in the jailing of Nelson Ramirez, who believes the U.S. is illegally occupying Puerto Rico.

3258. Lederer, Bob. "U.S. Indicted for Imprisonment and Abuse of Activist." Guardian 42.31 (May 30, 1990) 4. A symposium sponsored by Freedom Now! prepares for the International Tribunal in December. Freedom Now! has adopted 96 political prisoners in U.S. jails, some long term.

3259. Lederer, Bob. "U.S. Political Prisoners Face Media Silence." Extra 5 (September 1992) 18-19. Media coverage of political prisoners of color is particularly distorted--criminalized or made invisible.

3260. Lemke-Santangelo, Gretchen. "The Radical Conscientious Objectors of World War II: Wartime Experiences and Postwar Activism." Radical History Review 45 (1989). 5-29. On how conscientious objectors were radicalized by their wartime experiences.

3261. Leone, Bruno, et al., eds. Police Brutality. Current Controversies series. San Diego, CA: Greenhaven, 1991. 160. Debate whether police brutality is a national crisis, probes the causes of police brutality and remedies.

3262. Lernoux, Penny. Cry of the People: United States Involvement in the Rise of Fascism, Torture and Murder and the Persecution of the Catholic Church in Latin America. Garden City, NY: Doubleday, 1980. 535. Documents the political and economic linkages that undergird the repression in many Latin American countries.

3263. Levinson, Nan. "Silvia Baraldini: Political Prisoner." In These Times 16.39 (October 14-27, 1992) 6. Serving a forty-three year sentence under the RICO act.

3264. Levy, Howard, and David Miller. Going to Jail; the Political Prisoner. New York: Grove P, 1970. 243. The authors employ twenty-two topics to analyze the experience of being a political prisoner. Levy, a physician in the U.S. Army, was imprisoned twenty-six months 1967-69 for disobeying a direct order to train Special Forces Medics for Vietnam. Miller was sentenced to twenty-two months for burning his draft card.

3265. The Light from Another Country: Poetry from American Prisons. Ed. Joseph Bruchac. Greenfield Center, NY: Greenfield Review, 1984. 326. Includes poems by male and female political prisoners.

3266. Linfield, Michael. Freedom Under Fire: U.S. Civil Liberties in Times of War. Boston: South End, 1990. 282. Details on the violation of civil liberties and the repression of dissident voices since the founding of the nation.

3267. List, Dave. "N.Y. Nonregistrant Sentenced." Guardian 37.23 (March 13, 1985) 4. Andy Mager was sentenced to prison for draft refusal based upon the illegal war the U.S. was waging in Nicaragua.

3268. Litwak, Leo and Herbert Wilner. College days in Earthquake Country: Ordeal at San Francisco State, a Personal Record. New York: Random House, 1971. 235. An account of the strike initiated by the Black Students Union in 1968 and subsequent arrests.

3269. Liveright, Betty and Herman. "Laaman: Don't Judge Armed Struggle." Guardian (May 15, 1975) 7-8. Describes a visit with one of the Ohio 7 revolutionaries imprisoned for bombing military recruiting centers and other buildings.

3270. Liveright, Betty and Herman. "Prisoners Look to a Free and Independent Homeland." Guardian 43.17 (Feb. 20, 1991) 9. U.S. black nationalists speak from prison.

3271. Lockwood, Lee. Daniel Berrigan: Absurd Convictions, Modest Hopes: Conversations after Prison with Lee Lockwood. New York: Random House, 1973. 227. Dedicated to "all resisters in American prisons--Prisoners of War in their own country." An account of Berrigan's incarceration for 17 months 1970-1972 accused of plotting to kidnap a government official.

3272. Lofland, John. Polite Protesters: The American Peace Movement of the 1980s. Syracuse, NY: Syracuse UP, 1993. 320. Although unusually restrained, these campaigns against the Reagan-Bush military buildup produced arrests, trials, and jailings. Emphasis upon philosophy, organizations, and evolution.

3273. López, Alfredo. Doña Licha's Island: Modern Colonialism in Puerto Rico. Boston: South End, 1987. 178. Details a large span of Puerto Rican history, from the ravages of Spanish colonialism to present day exploitation by the United States, covering the extermination of the native Taino population, slavery, ongoing repression, cultural marginalization, forced sterilization, etc.

3274. Lowenthal, Max. The Federal Bureau of Investigation. New York: Sloane, 1950. 559. On how the FBI developed into a political police.

3275. Lukas, J. Anthony. The Barnyard Epithet and other Obscenities: Notes on the Chicago Conspiracy Trial. New York: Harper & Row, 1970. 107. Focuses on aspects of the trial which "are least understood."

3276. Magnes, Judah Leon. Amnesty for Political prisoners: Address Delivered in Washington, D.C. on April 17, 1919. New York: National Civil Liberties Bureau, 1979. 23. Defends WWI conscientious objectors.

3277. Magnes, Judah Leon. War-Time Adresses, 1917-1921. New York: Seltzer, 1923. 114. "Amnesty for Political Prisoners" (1919) calls for release of all imprisoned as "political heretics". As of June 30, 1918, there were approximately 363 prisoners and 499 prosecutions pending on the basis of beliefs, but these are incomplete figures (e.g. I.W.W. prisoners were incompletely counted).

3278. Magno, P. "No Jails for Plowshares Eight!" Nonviolent Activist 7.5 (July 1990) 12. The eight members of Plowshares (led by the Berrigan brothers) have been resentenced to lesser terms for the 1980 blood and hammer demonstration against General Electric's King of Prussia (Pa.) aerospace plant where first-strike MK12A warheads were made.

3279. Major, John. The Oppenheimer Hearing. New York: Stein & Day, 1971; London: Batsford, 1971. 336. On the 1953 Cold War purge trial of J. Robert Oppenheimer, father of the atomic bomb, who tried to stop the creation of the hydrogen bomb.

3280. Malinowitz, Harriet. "Sanctuary Defendant to Put U.S. Policy on Trial." Guardian 37.2 (Oct. 10, 1984) 7. On the trial of Jack Elder, who has assisted refugees from El Salvador and Guatemala.

3281. "'The Man Who Had No Papers': Case of Carl Skoglund." Militant 42.2 (Jan. 20, 1978) 16-17. The government tried to deport Skoglund in 1944 when he was one of the eighteen Socialist Worker Party and teamster leaders jailed in the Smith Act trial. The government tried again in the 1950's and jailed him again in 1959.

3282. Manchester, Leonard. "FBI Frames Adelita Medina." Militant 42.39 (October 20, 1978) 7. A sympathizer with Puerto Rican independence, she is accused of mailing a gun in 1975.

3283. Marion, George. The Communist Trial: An American Crossroads. 2nd Ed. New York: Fairplay, 1950. 192. The trial under the Smith Act of the leaders of the Communist Party U.S.A. for allegedly advocating the overthrow of the government.

3284. Marzani, Carl. The Education of a Reluctant Radical. New York: Topical. The general title of several autobiographical volumes by one of the first political prisoners of the Cold War. In 1947 Marzani was indicted for his Communist Party membership, and he spent three years in prison.

3285. McElwain, Max. "Practicing Christian Anarchy." Progressive 57.5 (May 1993) 15. Story of Father Frank Cordaro, arrested some thirty times for protesting the arms race and unequal society.

3286. McGee, Doug. Slow Coming Dark. New York: Pilgrim, 1980. 181. Interviews with eleven men and one woman on death row.

3287. McMahon, B. "Chavis Imprisonment Denounced." Guardian 31.19 (February 14, 1979) 6. Two U.S. Congressmen denounced the jailing of Ben Chavis, one of the Wilmington 10 and the only one still in prison.

3288. McMahon, B. "North Carolina Prison Support." Guardian 31.20 (February 21, 1979) 6. On the movement supporting the release of the Charlotte Three.

3289. McWilliams, Carey. Witch Hunt: The Revival of Heresy. Boston: Little, Brown, 1950. 361. Describes the "grotesque regression to witch hunting and the ways of the Inquisition," and the use of heresy as an instrument of social control by government, colleges, and other institutions during the late 1940s.

3290. Melish, William Howard, Rev. "Congressional Committees Conspire Against Civil Rights." Rights 12.5-6 (October-November 1965) 37-38. On the police raid, theft of records, and arrest of officers of the Southern Conference Educational Fund to convict the organization of sedition.

3291. Melville, Samuel. Letters from Attica. New York: Morrow, 1972. 181. Letters written by Melville, who while serving a 13-18 year sentence in Attica for politically motivated bombings became an advocate for prisoner justice and humane treatment and helped lead the prisoners' rebellion of September 9, 1971, during which he was shot to death by state police. The introduction argues that Melville was deliberately executed by the state for his political activity.

3292. Meyer, Matt. "Freedom Now." Nonviolent Activist 10.6 (Nov.-Dec. 1993) 10-16. Survey accompanied by seven case studies.

3293. Miller, Shelly. "Political Prisoners." Gay Community News 15.7 (August 23, 1987) 4. A Puerto Rican independence former prisoner reports on the living conditions of women political prisoners in Alderson as well as in the "state-of-the-art" isolation unit in Lexington, KY.

3294. Miller, William D. A Harsh and Dreadful Love: Dorothy Day and the Catholic Worker Movement. New York: Liveright, 1973. 370. Their anti-war and anti-conscription activities and consequent jailings are described.

3295. Mirandé, Alfredo. Gringo Justice. Notre Dame, IN: U of Notre Dame P, 1987. 261. Ever since the end of the war between Mexico and the U.S., displaced Mexicans, or Chicanos, have been subjected to a prejudicial, discriminatory, double-standard legal system.

3296. Moore, Howard W. Plowing My Own Furrow. New York: Norton, 1985; Syracuse: Syracuse Studies on Peace and Conflict Resolution. 225. Because the author refused to serve in the armed forces in WWI, as an absolutist objector to war and to the militarization of the U.S., he was court-martialed and sentenced to twenty-five years of hard labor at Fort Leavenworth, KS, where he was tortured with solitary confinement, bread and water, and forced to stand, shackled to the bars of his cell for fourteen days.

3297. Morales, F. "Jury Acquits Puerto Rican Activists." Guardian 35.5 (November 3, 1982) 9. Vicente Alba freed after a four-and-a-half year struggle over a false 1978 arms possession charge, part of a larger repression of the Puerto Rican independence movement.

3298. Morrow, Lance. "Who (and What) Is a Political Prisoner?" Time 98 (September 6, 1971) 18-19. Analyzes whether George Jackson was a political prisoner.

3299. Mutnick, Deborah. "Fort Benning Three: 'Paupers' Who Won't Stop Protesting." Guardian 36.7 (November 16, 1983) 5. Father Roy Bourgeois and two others have been imprisoned for protesting the training of Salvadoran soldiers.

3300. Naeve, Lowell, and David Wieck. A Field of Broken Stones. Glen Gardner, NJ: Libertarian, 1950. (Denver: Swallow, 1959). Prison memoir by a conscientious objector to WWII, who refused to kill and who carried on a relentless campaign against prison authorities.

3301. Nathenson, Nathaniel. "Freedom of Association and the Quest for Internal Security: Conspiracy from Dennis to Dr. Spock." Northwestern University Law Review 65.2 (May-June 1970) 153-192. Questions the application of the conspiracy charge for the "possible chilling effect of such essentially 'political' trials upon freedom of association and public debate, to say nothing of the danger of discrediting the judicial process itself."

3302. Nation, Carry. The Use and Need of the Life of Carry A. Nation. Written by Herself. Topeka: Steves, 1904. 184. An account of her numerous jailings for destroying taverns to protest the sale of alcohol.

3303. "Navstar Satellite Smashers Sentenced." Nuclear Resister 86 (October 7, 1992) 1. Recounts the trial of two men who damaged nuclear missile equipment at the Rockwell plant in California.

3304. Neier, Aryeh. "Global Human Rights Work Includes U.S. Too." Human Rights Watch 10.3 (Summer 1992) 1, 7. Guidelines followed by Human Rights Watch.

3305. Nelson, Lars-Erik. "Stun Guns Put U.S. on Torture List." Arkansas Gazette (May 8, 1985) 17A. The use of electric stun guns to interrogate prisoners by the Queens, NY, police has drawn attention of Amnesty International.

3306. New Studies on the Left (Boulder, CO: Saxifrage) 14.1-2 (Spring-Summer 1989). Special no. on prisons: articles on the federal penitentiary at Marion, IL, the Lexington Prison High Security Unit, Puerto Rican women prisoners, George Jackson, Leonard Peltier, Geronimo Pratt, COINTELPRO, Ray Luc Levasseur, etc.

3307. Nieves Falcón, Luis, ed. International Tribunal on Human Rights Violations of Political/POW Prisoners in the United States. Chicago: Editorial El Coquí, 1990. 53. Four essays examine types of sentences, treatment, and prison conditions of political prisoners. Includes a list of political prisoners and their addresses.

3308. Novick, Michael. "'De Donde' Pushes on the Borders." Guardian 42.35 (June 27, 1990) 18. Review of a play written by Mary Gallagher about the virtual state of siege by the INS against Central American refugees and the Sanctuary Movement.

3309. Novick, Michael. "Tale of an Anti-Palestinian Frame-up." Guardian 42.19 (March 7, 1990) 20. Discusses "Voices in Exile: Immigrants and the First Amendment," a video which follows the case of the arrest of nine Mideast activists.

3310. Nowlan, B. "A Strategy For Irish Solidarity." Against the Current 2.4 (Sept. 1987) 5-6. On Northern Ireland citizens held in prisons without being charged with a crime, and a new treaty with Britain which allows extradition.

3311. Nunnelley, William. Bull Connor. Tuscaloosa: U of Alabama P, 1991. 225. Biography of Birmingham's police commissioner during the height of the civil rights movement, when Martin Luther King, Jr., was jailed incommunicado in solitary confinement for more than 24 hours, and numerous other abuses.

3312. O'Brien, Sally. "New York 8 Defense Committee Formed." Guardian 37.23 (March 13, 1985) 4. United Church of Christ and other organizations and individuals are protesting the government's extremely severe charges against the eight black activists--not only conspiracy but RICO laws.

3313. Ogden, Don. "Government's Case Against Ohio 7 Activists Collapses." Guardian 42.8 (December 13, 1989) 5. The longest and perhaps most expensive sedition trial in U.S. history ended in a mistrial. All are already serving or have served sentences on other charges, four of them up to 45 years.

3314. Ogden, Don. "War-Tax Refusers Fight on after Feds Sell Home." Guardian (Feb. 26, 1992) 4. Anti-war tax refusers had their home sold by the IRS and were imprisoned.

3315. Ogden, Rose and Larry Seigle. "Miami Black Socialist Wins Support." Militant 42.34 (September 15, 1978) 4. Leo Harris, a black socialist, is publicly supported after being hit by a Miami police car while picketing and then charged with disorderly conduct and criminal mischief.

3316. O'Hare, Kate Richards (Cunningham). "Human Ostriches." Nation 120 (April 8, 1925) 377-78. Criticizes prison conditions she experienced during her incarceration for protesting against WWI in 1919.

3317. O'Hare, Kate Richards (Cunningham). In Prison. New York: Knopf, 1923; rpt. American Library, no. 30; Seattle: U of Washington P, 1976. 211. An account of her imprisonment in Missouri 1919-1920 for protests against U.S. participation in WWI and a study of the role of political prisoners in prison reform.

3318. O'Hare, Kate Richards (Cunningham). Kate O'Hare's Prison Letters. Modern Series no. 1. Girard, Kan.: Appeal to Reason, 1919. 125. Sixteen letters while in the penitentiary in 1919 for opposing the war.

3319. O'Hare, Kate Richards. Letters From Kate Richards O'Hare to Her Family From April 20, 1919 to May 27, 1920. Bowling Green, Ohio: Center for Archival Collections, 1989.

3320. Okubo, Miné. Citizen 13660. New York: Columbia UP, 1946. 209. First person account by a young person for young persons, accompanied by drawings on almost every page, of her internment as a Japanese-American during WWII.

3321. Ola, Akinshiju. "Cops Harass Black Activist Group." Guardian 36.14 (January 11, 1984) 6. Members of the African People's Socialist Party have been jailed in Florida and California for confronting city governments for the poor.

3322. Ola, Akinshiju. "FBI Raids: A Prelude to Another Witchhunt?" Guardian 37.5 (Oct. 31, 1984) 7. Nine people have been arrested in suspicion of planning to rob an armored car. They are members of the New Afrikan Freedom Fighters organization.

3323. Ola, Akinshiju. "Grand Jury Spreads New Dragnet." Guardian 37.13 (December 26, 1984) 5. Possibly up to 30 persons will appear before the jury charged with conspiracy to commit armed robbery.

3324. Ola, Akinshiju. "Kunstler: Using the System Against Itself." Guardian 37.22 (March 6, 1985) 5. William Kunstler is honored for 35 years of defending jailed dissidents.

3325. Ola, Akinshiju. "Native Americans: 'It is the People Who Have Brought Justice, Not the System.'" Guardian 41.5 (October 26, 1988) 3. A federal jury voted not guilty in the hostage-taking trial of two Tuscarora Indians, who sought to draw attention to police corruption in the county.

3326. Ola, Akinshiju. "N.C. Indian Activist Fights Extradition." Guardian 41.31 (May 3, 1989) 4. On the continuing efforts of the government to persecute Eddie Hatcher and Timothy Jacobs.

3327. Ola, Akinshiju. "U.S. Convicted: People Imprisoned for Politics." Guardian 43.9 (Dec. 19, 1990) 5. (Also see 43.17 [Feb. 20, 1991)] 9). Describes the Special International Tribunal on the Violation of Human Rights of Political Prisoners of War in U.S. prisons, held in New York City. Over 100 political prisoners were identified, many of whom had received harsh sentences.

3328. An Open Letter to President Harding. Chicago: Industrial Workers of the World, 1922. 28. From 52 members of the I.W.W. in Leavenworth Penitentiary.

3329. O'Reilly, Kenneth. "Racial Matters:" The FBI's Secret File on Black America, 1960-1972. New York: Free Press, 1989. 456. "The story of the FBI and black America is part of the larger history of a government that has been at odds, more often than not over the past two hundred years, with its own nonwhite citizens and its own professed values."

3330. Orrick, William H., Jr. Shut it Down! A College in Crisis: A Report to the National Commission on Causes and Prevention of Violence. Washington, D.C.: GPO, 1969. 172. An inquiry into the events which led to the eight month student and faculty strike at San Francisco State College, resulting in 731 arrests.

3331. "The Outlaw Editor." American Atheist 30.1 (January 1988) 11. Robin Murray-O'Hair was jailed for refusing to affirm God in the oath for jury duty.

3332. "Over 2 Years in Atlanta Dungeon's Hole." Worker's World 18.11 (March 12, 1976) 11. A call for letters of support on behalf of Jerry Mack Dorrough and Jesse Evans, two prisoners who have been subjected to brutal treatment due to their religious and political beliefs.

3333. Parenti, Christian. "Torture in Chicago and the Silent Press." Z Magazine 6.5 (May 1993) 43-45. Police brutality is more widespread than the media report.

3334. Payne, Robert. "Come See the Paradise: The Color of Paradise." Jump Cut 37 (July 1992) 51-55. Hollywood's first theatrical film about the Japanese-American internment during World War II, "an act of legalized racism which... violated their Fourteenth Amendment rights."

3335. "Peltier Warriors Bid for Freedom." Akwesasne Notes 11.3 (Summer 1979) 14. Details the escape of Leonard Peltier from Federal hands and his struggle to stay free only to be once again captured and sent to Marion Prison in Illinois.

3336. Pendás, Miguel. "Chicano Cointelpro: The Government's War Against la Raza." Militant 41.40 (October 28, 1977) 15-19. Evidence points to the existence of a coordinated "Counterintelligence Program" to disrupt the struggles of the la Raza chicano movement.

3337. Penner, Steve. "International Defense Campaign Backs Jailed Political Activist." Canadian Dimension 23.1 (January 1989) 42. Mark Curtis, a 29 year old union and political activist, and a member of the Socialist Workers Party, has been sentenced to 25 years in what many believe was a frame-up trial.

3338. Pérez, José G. "CAIFI 6 Charges Dropped." Militant 42.9 (March 10, 1978) 32. Trumped up charges against six members of CAIFI (Committee for Artistic and Intellectual Freedom in Iran) filed by the Jersey City State College were dropped.

3339. Pérez, José G. "Cordero Devoted Life to P.R. Independence." Militant 43.11 (March 23, 1979) 14. Andrés Figueros Cordero died. He and three compatriots were imprisoned in 1954 for an armed attack on the House of Representatives.

3340. Pérez, José G. "Okla. Iranians Framed Up." Militant 42.10 (March 17, 1978) 18. 21 Iranian students charged with disruption during a demonstration at Southwestern College in Oklahoma City are threatened with deportation.

3341. Pérez, José G. "Puerto Rico: The Face of U.S. Colonialism." Militant 43.28 (July 20, 1979) 22. Protests of Navy bombing practice resulted in the death of two and the arrest of 13 people.

3342. Pérez, José G. "Victory! U.S. Grants Visa to Hugo Blanco." Militant 41.38 (October 14, 1977) 5. Peruvian writer and peasant leader is to be allowed into the U.S. for a speaking tour, barred since 1975 because of his socialist views.

3343. Perkins, Pete. "Free Juan Haro." Worker's World 18.6 (February 6, 1976) 11. Haro, Chicano activist in Denver, has apparently been framed on a bombing conspiracy charge.

3344. Perotti, John. "John Perotti: An Appeal from Lucasville." Independent Worker 87.1 (January 1990) 1. Letter from Perotti, a 34 year old activist in maximum securty prison.

3345. A Personal Matter. Film. PBS, 1992. Japanese American Gordon Hirabayashi's fight against WWII internment of West coast Nisei and Isei. In 1942 he was illegally prosecuted, and his innocence was not confirmed until over 40 years later.

3346. Peters, Charles, and Taylor Branch, eds. Blowing the Whistle: Dissent in the Public Interest. New York: Praeger, 1972. 305. Articles on A. Ernest Fitzgerald, Daniel Ellsberg, Otto Otepka, Charles Pettis, John McGee, Jacqueline Verrett, Terry Lenzner, Frank Jones, and others, all from Washington Monthly, which has made whistleblowers a chief subject.

3347. Phillips, Glen S. "Choctaw With a Mission." Progressive 53.7 (July 1989) 14-15. Report on Native American and ex-convict Ben Carnes, and his activism on behalf of Native American inmates and prison reform.

3348. Phillips, Margaret B. "Eleven Days in the Cage." Focus/Midwest 10.64 (1974) 24-5. Imprisoned briefly for her demonstration against racial discrimination by a St. Louis military contractor.

3349. Polenberg, Richard. Fighting Faiths: The Abrams Case, the Supreme Court, and Free Speech. New York: Viking Penguin, 1987. 431. On 23 August 1918, five Russian Jewish anarchists (and immigrants) were arrested for distributing leaflets protesting the U.S. intervention in the Russian revolution. One died in prison. The others were convicted of violating the Sedition Act of 1918, sentenced to prison terms of fifteen to twenty years, and finally deported to Russia at their own expense in 1921.

3350. "Police Abroad Gain a Shield in Abuse Suits." Arkansas Democrat-Gazette (March 24, 1993) 10A. The Supreme Court ruled that U.S. citizens abused and tortured abroad cannot sue in the U.S. courts.

3351. "Political Grand Juries Must Be Stopped." Guardian 36.14 (January 11, 1984) 9. Protests incarceration of Puerto Rican independence supporters for refusing to testify before a grand jury. Also see 36.16 (January 25, 1993) 7.

3352. "Political Prisoners." Workers World 17.11 (March 14, 1975) 10. On the Smyrna 4 and San Quentin 6.

3353. "Political Prisoners." Workers World 17.12 (March 21, 1975) 10. Repression of dissident prisoners in Oklahoma and Alabama.

3354. Political Prisoners by States. New York: American Civil Liberties Union, 1924. 3. Imprisoned for their opinions under sedition and criminal syndicalism laws.

3355. Political Prisoners: The Cases of Angela Davis, Ruchell Magee, and the Soledad Brothers. Memphis: Southern Committee to Free Angela Davis and All Political Prisoners, 1971. 11. All are in prison for protesting the established order of discrimination, wars, and low wages.

3356. "Political Prisoners: Herb Powless." Akwesasne Notes 9.3 (Summer 1977) 30. Powless, a gadfly for justice for Native Americans, was sentenced to prison on a gun charge.

3357. Political Prisoners in Federal Military Prisons. New York: National Civil Liberties Bureau, 1918. 21. Documents inhumane prison practices used against conscientious objectors at Fort Jay, Governors Island, New York, and Fort Leavenworth, Kansas, including solitary confinement in dark unsanitary cells, manacling, beatings, and bread and water diets.

3358. "Political Prisoners in the U.S.: Breaking the Silence." Breakthrough 13.1 (Spring 1989) 3. Over 150 political prisoners remain locked up in conditions that violate recognized international laws.

3359. Political Prisoners: Racism and the Politics of Imprisonment: A Report by the National Advisory Council on Criminal Justice. D.C.: The Council, 1981. 60. Section one details history of political prisoners especially as it impacts minorities. Section two links historical persons to today's realities.

3360. "Politics of Repression." Nation 221 (October 25, 1975) 386. On dictatorships supported by the U.S.: Spain, South Korea, and Chile.

3361. "Press Releases." Z Magazine 3.11 (Nov. 1990) 10-11. Three women were convicted of bombings at the Capitol and other sites in protest of the U.S. invasion of Grenada and other "unjust practices."

3362. Preston, William. Aliens and Dissenters: Federal Suppression of Radicals, 1903-1933. Cambridge: Harvard UP, 1963. 352. Describes an era of mounting fear of the radical and the foreign, blaming so-called heretics and strangers for national problems, with severe consequences of restraints on liberty. A part of the history of bigotry in the U.S.--the jailing and deportation of aliens and radicals during the first third of the twentieth century.

3363. Price, Lucien. "Witchcraft: Then and Now." Nation 115 (October 4, 1922) 331-33. Compares the persecution of "witches" in Massachusetts in 1692 with the persecution of opponents of war in 1917-1922. Focuses on the seventy-one I.W.W. anti-war protesters incarcerated in Leavenworth.

3364. Prison Etiquette. Sound recording, 52 min. Berkeley, CA: Pacifica Tape Library, 1970. Interviews of Decise Bertolucci and Richard Chandler about their experiences serving time for draft offenses in seven federal prisons.

3365. Prisoners on Purpose: A Peacemakers' Guide to Jails and Prisons. Ed. Samuel H. Day, Jr.; illus. Bonnie Urfer. Madison, WI: Nukewatch, 1989. 145. Stories of fifteen peace activists, the Missouri Peace Planters, who entered nuclear missile launch sites in Missouri and were imprisoned for terms up to 26 months. Sixteen jails and prisons are discussed.

3366. Ray, James Earl. Tennessee Waltz: The Making of a Political Prisoner. Saint Andrews, Tenn.: Saint Andrew's, 322. 1987. 322. Although Ray pleaded guilty to murdering Martin Luther King, Jr., he repudiated the confession; this is his denial of guilt in the case.

3367. Reasonable Fear: Human Rights and the United States Refugee Policy. New York: Amnesty International, 1990. 30. Documents "patterns of bias and obstruction" against asylum seekers from El Salvador, Guatemala, and Haiti, where refugees were threatened with becoming prisoners, victims of torture, or with execution. Despite the Humanitarian Refugee Act of 1980, the U.S. "has not met its responsibilities to refugees."

3368. Reed, L. "Native American Prisoners Rehabilitation Project." Akwesasne Notes 21.6 (Winter 1989) 24. Focuses on the denial of Native American religious freedom in prisons.

3369. Rein, David. "McCarran Act Establishes Guilt by Association." Rights 12.5-6 (Oct.-Nov. 1965) 8-12. Crushing the Communist Party without evidence of a crime.

3370. "Report on the High Security Unit for Women, Federal Correctional Institution, Lexington, Kentucky." Social Justice 15.1 (Spring 1988) 1-7. A report by the ACLU on Lexington Prison, briefly discusses prisoners treated unfairly due to their political beliefs.

3371. "Resisters Observe Christian Holidays." The Nuclear Resister No.88 (April 2, 1993) 5. Demonstrations against militarism around the country resulting in arrests.

3372. Reweaving the Web of Life: Feminism and Nonviolence. Ed. Pam McAllister. Philadelphia: New Society, 1982. 440. Feminist pacifists and opponents of discrimination tell of their imprisonment for civil disobedience.

3373. Rice, Jim. "On the Front Lines of Resistance." Sojourners 20.3 (April 1991) 26-29. Discusses Bryan Centa and other COs to the Gulf War.

3374. Rights. Journal founded in 1951 by the National Emergency Civil Liberties Commmittee to defend the Bill of Rights. A storehouse of cases of unfair trials and imprisonments.

3375. Rizzo, Renata, and Patrick Crawford. "Activists Jailed Indefinitely." Nuclear Times 3.4 (March 1985) 13-14. Thirteen protesters against cruise missiles and arms sales were arrested in Michigan, and all have applied to Amnesty International for political status.

3376. Roebuck, Julian, and Stanley Weeber. Political Crime in the United States: Analyzing Crime by and against Government. New York: Praeger, 1978. 244. Divides political crime into two categories: crimes by government and corporations against the people, and crimes by the people against government and corporations. Corporations and government are treated as one because government is an extension of the economic system.

3377. Rogge, O. John. Our Vanishing Civil Liberties. New York: Gaer, 1949. 187. Circumstantial indictment of the anti-communist repression by the House Committee to Investigate un-American Activities (HUAC): the Joint Anti-Fascist Refugee Committee, Frank Coe, Harry White, et al.

3378. Rosenbaum, Rebecca. "Sick of SAC." Guardian 36.16 (Jan. 25, 1984) 7. For the fifth year nuclear opponents have been arrested at Offut Air Force Base.

3379. Rosenberg, Ethel. Letters. In We Are Your Sons: The Legacy of Ethel and Julius Rosenberg, by Robert Meeropol and Michael Meeropol. Boston: Houghton Mifflin, 1975; rpt., Champaign: U. of Illinois P., 1986. 419. Written during the three years preceding her execution for alleged conspiracy to give atomic secrets to the Soviets.

3380. Rosenberg, Ethel. The Testament of Ethel and Julius Rosenberg. 2d ed. New York: Cameron & Kahn, 1954. 222. Revised and enlarged edition of The Death House Letters (New York: Jero, 1953), published during their imprisonment to raise money for their children.

3381. Rosenberg, Susan. "Existence of Political Prisoners Denied." Kinesis (June 1987) 13. Report on the over 100 political prisoners and the abuse they endure.

3382. Ross, Charles G. Sacramento Political Prisoners Not Guilty of Overt Acts. Washington, D.C.: Joint Amnesty Committee, 1923. 8.

3383. Roth, Michael. "California Cop Critic Cleared." Guardian 35.40 (July 27, 1983) 13. Michael Zinzun was acquitted of five felony counts for protesting police violence.

3384. Rothschild, Matthew. "Contemptible Punishment." Progressive 48 (April 1984) 29. The government's use of "criminal contempt" to repress Puerto Rican activists.

3385. Rothschild, Matthew. "The Crime of Politics." Progressive 53 (May 1989) 28-30. Deals with a variety of political prisoner issues.

3386. Rout, Kathleen. Eldridge Cleaver. Boston: Twayne, 1991. 303. Author of best-selling Soul on Ice and Black Panther leader, Cleaver was jailed following a shoot-out with police in Oakland in 1968, and later fled to Algeria.

3387. Ruchell Magee: $10 Argument = Life Sentence; the Courage to be a Man = Death Sentence. San Jose, CA: Committee to Free Angela Davis and All Political Prisoners, 1971. 6. On Magee's efforts to gain freedom from prison.

3388. Salmon, Ben. An Open Letter to President Wilson. Baltimore, Md.: Baltimore Amnesty League, 1920. 16. Appeal for release of opponents of the war still in prison.

3389. Salter, Kenneth. The Pentagon Papers Trial. Berkeley: Justa, 1975. 123. Basic information and documents.

3390. Salvatore, Nick. Eugene V. Debs: Citizen and Socialist. Urbana, IL; Chicago: U of Illinois P, 1982. 437. Socialist presidential candidate Debs was imprisoned in 1919 for opposing the war (Chap. 9). Chap. 10 describes his prison experiences.

3391. Sanger, Margaret. Margaret Sanger; An Autobiography. New York: Norton, 1938; rpt, Dover, 1971. 504. Chapters 17-19 describe her imprisonment in 1916-17 in Long Island for distributing birth-control information.

3392. Sanger, Margaret. My Fight for Birth Control. New York: Farrar & Rinehart, 1931; rpt, New York: Maxwell, 1969. 360. Chapter 14 describes her imprisonment after distributing pamphlets at the Brownsville Clinic in Brooklyn.

3393. Saxe, Susan. "To My Friends." Off Our Backs: A Women's News Journal 7.2 (March 1977) 5. She pled guilty to charges of armed robbery and destruction of government property, which she states were expressions of her opposition to sexism, racism, and the Vietnam War.

3394. Schultz, Bud, and Ruth Schultz. It Did Happen Here: Recollections of Political Repression in America. Berkeley, CA: U of California P, 1989. 427. Stories of persons "who have been grossly discriminated against because they challenged existing power relationships or government policie"s.

3395. Seager, Moe. "America's Secret: Political Prisoners." Z Magazine 4.3 (March 1991) 101-106. An account of the Special International Tribunal on the Violation of Human Rights of Political Prisoners and Prisoners of War in the U.S., held at Hunter College, NYC.

3396. Seale, Bobby. A Lonely Rage: The Autobiography of Bobby Seale. New York: Times Books, 1978. 238. Seale was Chairman of the Black Panther Party and often imprisoned and ill-treated, experiences described in detail.

3397. Seale, Bobby. Seize the Time. New York: Random House, 1968. 429. (New York: Vintage, 1970). Written in the San Francisco County Jail at a time when "nearly 100 of us are political prisoners." The story of the Black Panther Party.

3398. Seigle, Larry. "U.S. Orders Socialist Deported." Militant 46.2 (Jan. 22, 1982) 3. Student Mojgan Hariri-Vijeh was ordered deported to Iran after she joined the Young Socialist Alliance.

3399. Shakur, Afeni. "Prison Women." Ann Arbor Argus 37 (February 1-14, 1971) 8-9. A member of the Black Panthers New York 21 condemns the legal system's violation of the rights of poor women. She was imprisoned for conspiracy to bomb a New York department store.

3400. Shakur, Afeni. "The Prisons and Jails are Filled with Political Prisoners." Black Panther 5.2 (July 18, 1970) 11. Denounces the inadequate legal counsel given to political prisoners.

3401. Shakur, Assata. Assata: An Autobiography. Westport, CT: Hill, 1987. 274. Assata, a leader of the Black Panthers, was incarcerated four years awaiting trial as an accomplice to the murder of a state trooper, convicted in 1977 despite heavy evidence to the contrary and prosecution witnesses that were proven to have lied in their testimony, and then confined in prison under constant surveillance, without medical attention and exercise, before finally escaping two years later and finding political asylum in Cuba.

3402. Shakur, Assata (Joanne Chesimard). "Women in Prison: How We Are." Black Scholar 9.7 (April 1, 1978) 8-15; reprint 12.6 (November-December 1981) 50-57. A member of the Black Liberation Army imprisoned on charge of murder describes how prisoners' dependency is encouraged.

3403. Sibley, Mulford and Ada Wardlaw. Conscientious Objectors in Prison, 1940-1945. Philadelphia: Pacifist Research Bureau, 1945. 68. About the over five thousand conscientious objectors imprisoned during World War II--laws, trials, prison life, etc.

3404. Sibley, Mulford, and Ada Wardlaw. "The Jehovah's Witnesses in Prison, 1940-1945." American Anti-War Movements. Ed. Joseph R. Conlin. Beverly Hills, CA: Glencoe Press; London: Collier-Macmillan, 1968. 37-44. The Witnesses, who refused to cooperate with conscription in any way, were the largest single group of religious objectors to military service during WWII.

3405. Sibley, Mulford, and Philip E. Jacob. Conscription and Conscience: The American State and the Conscientious Objector, 1940-1947. Ithaca: Cornell UP, 1952. 580. Tells the story and analyzes the problems of the conscientious objector in WWII.

3406. Simons, Donald L. I Refuse: Memories of a Vietnam War Objector. Trenton, NJ: Broken Rifle, 1992. 184. Focuses on his experiences of resisting the war and induction.

3407. Sinclair, John. Guitar Army: Street Writings/Prison Writings. New York: Douglass, 1972. 366. Part III contains fifteen essays on his imprisonment on trumped-up charges over two marijuana cigarettes.

3408. Skolnick, Jerome H. The Politics of Protest. U.S. National Commission on the Causes and Prevention of Violence, Task Force on Demonstrations, Protests, and Group Violence. Washington, DC: GPO, 1969. 276. (New York: Balantine, 1969). Urges awareness of the political significance of protest and argues for less force against protest and more reform. A democratic society cannot depend upon force as its recurrent answer to long-standing and legitimate grievances.

3409. Smedley, Agnes. "Cell Mates." Call Magazine, (Sunday Supplement to the New York Call) (February 15, 22, 29 and March 14, 1920). She was imprisoned in New York charged under the Espionage Act for involvement with Indian nationalists.

3410. Smith, Lee. "Protests Say: 'Drop Charges Against Leo Harris!'" Militant 42.39 (Oct. 20, 1978) 5. Harris protested racist language, was injured by a police car, and then arrested.

3411. Smith, Robert, Richard Axen, and De Vere Pentowy. By Any Means Necessary. San Francisco, CA: Josey-Bass, 1970. 370. An account of the student strike at San Francisco State College in 1968.

3412. Sobell, Morton. On Doing Time. New York: Scribner, 1974. 525. Sobell was sentenced to thirty years in prison in 1951 for "conspiracy to commit espionage," for which the Rozenbergs were executed. He was released in 1969. This is an account of his trial and imprisonment.

3413. Spector, Mordecai. "'Silo Pruning Hooks' Found Guilty." Guardian 37.23 (March 13, 1985) 4. Four disarmament activists who hammered a Minuteman missile silo were convictied of four charges that could bring a 25-year sentence.

3414. Speeches from the Soledad Brothers Rally, Central Hall, Westminster 20/4/71. Ed. John Thorne, James Baldwin, et al. London: Friends of Soledad, 1971. 36. In support of George Jackson, John Cluchette, and Fleeta Drumgo, who await trial for the alleged murder of a guard in Soledad Prison, Calif.

3415. Stafford, William E. Down in My Heart. 2nd ed. Swarthmore, PN: Bench, 1985. 94. Orig. pub. 1947. Compiled from letters and diary notes, this memoir tells of his four years (1942-1946) interned as a conscientious objector during WW II. (Some 12,000 went into the Civilian Public Service, some 5,000 to prison, and many thousands more into noncombatant service in the armed services.)

3416. Stark, Rodney. Police Riots: Collective Violence and Law Enforcement. Belmont, CA: Wadsworth, 1972. 250. A study of incidents when police beat, gassed, and shot "helpless and nonprovocative persons"--at the Democratic National Convention in 1968 and elsewhere earlier and later. The author seeks to understand why policemen are so angry, fearful, and prejudiced.

3417. State Poltical Prisoners. The Facts About Political Prisoners Held Under Sedition and Criminal Syndicalism Laws. New York: American Civil Liberties Union, 1924. 8. Over one hundred men in prison for their opinions.

3418. Steif, William. "Justice, American Style." Progressive 49.9 (Sept. 1985) 17. Carlos Noya Murati arrested and convicted on charges of contempt because of his role in the struggle for the independence of Puerto Rico.

3419. Stern, Susan. With the Weathermen: The Personal Journal of a Revolutionary Woman. Garden City, NY: Doubleday, 1975. 374. One chapter describes her prison experiences, the result of conviction for conspiracy as a member of the Seattle 7 in 1970. Her book is mainly about her growing involvement in radical politics.

3420. Stevens, Doris. Jailed for Freedom. New York: Boni & Liveright, 1920; rpt. Freeport, NY: Books for Libraries Press, 1971. 388. An account of the U.S. woman suffrage movement (1913-1919) and the imprisonment of its participants. Includes a list of suffrage prisoners.

3421. Struik, Dirk. "The Struik Case of 1951." Monthly Review 44.8 (January 1993) 31-48. An account of his persecution by HUAC and the FBI from 1951 to 1955 on indictments for conspiracy to overthrow the government.

3422. Suarez, Manuel. Requiem on Cerro Maravilla: The Police Murders in Puerto Rico and the United States Government Coverup. Maplewood, NJ: Waterfront, 1987. 378. On Carlos Enrique Soto Arrivi and Arnaldo Dario Rosudo, two young men lured in 1978 by an undercover agent into an ambush of heavily armed police.

3423. The Suffragist: Official Weekly Organ of the National Woman's Party. Articles on demonstrations, jailings, etc. The July-Dec. 1917 issue focuses on Washington, DC.

3424. Sunshine, Alice. "Gulf Resister May Face New Charges." Guardian (Feb. 26, 1992) 4. Tahan Jones, who refused to go to the Gulf War, has been jailed since May 1991 and faces seven years in prison if convicted of desertion. Other dissenters remain in prison.

3425. Sunshine, Cathy. "First She's Toppled, Then She's Arrested." Guardian 37.6 (Nov. 7, 1984) 5. Grenada's former ambassador to the OAS, Dessima Williams, strong critic of the U.S. invasion, was arrested following a speech on the first anniversary of the invasion.

3426. Swede, Shirley. "Who Is Jean Gump?" Z Magazine 2.10 (Oct. 1989) 95-96. As a Plowshares Witness, Gump is in federal prison for pouring her blood on a missile site, along with her husband, who was placed in solitary confinement for non-cooperation.

3427. Tannenbaum, Frank. Wall Shadows: A Study in American Prisons. New York: Putnam's, 1922. 168. Includes an account of a prisoner who served a year for unlawful assembly 1913-14 and then worked on prison reform.

3428. Taylor, John F. "Conspiracy: Handy Tool for Judicial Murder." Human Quest 207.5 (Sept.-Oct. 1993) 15. Denounces the execution of the Rosenbergs and the prosecution of others under Espionage Law which makes it a heavy crime to conspire to commit espionage.

3429. Teepen, Tom. "A Death Chase We Can't Win." Arkansas Democrat-Gazette (June 29, 1991) 7B. On the "wild expansion of crimes on the federal death-penalty list." At the end of 1990 there were 2,400 people on death row, far more than international norms.

3430. Theoharis, Athan G., ed. Beyond the Hiss Case: The FBI, Congress, and the Cold War. Philadelphia: Temple UP, 1982. 423. Collection of essays dealing with the FBI's disdain for individual rights, citing cases from Hiss to Reagan's unleasing of the intelligence agencies, all in the name of national security.

3431. Theoharis, Athan G. Spying on Americans: Political Surveillance from Hoover to the Huston Plan. Philadelphia: Temple UP, 1978. 331. Focuses on internal security policy and the anti-democratic history of the FBI--break-ins, wiretapping, politically-motivated investigations, and preventive detention programs.

3432. Thiers, Naomi. "Designed to Intimidate." Sojourners 20.4 (May 1991) 16-23. General survey of political prisoners--from Native Americans to the Black Liberation Army. The government "has abused its legal system to get them behind bars," and "once incarcerated, they are singled out for brutal treatment."

3433. Thomas, Norman. The Conscientious Objector in America. New York: Huebsch, 1923. 299. Deals with WWI.

3434. "Through the Wire." Film, PBS, "P.O.V.," June 26, 1990. Dir. Nina Rosenblum. On the incarceration of three women in a subterranean prison with a prison, the High Security Unit in Lexington, KY. They were sentenced for non-violent, political offenses.

3435. Tilsen, Ken. "There Are Thousands of Political Prisoners in the United States." Akwesasne Notes 10.3 (Summer 1978) 18. Tilsen, a lawyer, defended the American Indian Movement people against indictments arising out of the 1973 occupation of Wounded Knee.

3436. Tollefson, James. The Strength Not to Fight. Waltham, MA: Little, Brown, 1993. 272. Interviews with 40 conscientious objectors to the Vietnam War, some of whom experienced criminal trials and imprisonment.

3437. Tomsho, Robert. The American Sanctuary Movement. Austin: Texas Monthly, 1987. 214. An account of the movement to provide political asylum to Central American refugees and the government's crackdown.

3438. Trial Bulletin of National United Committee to Free Angela Davis and All Political Prisoners. San Francisco: The Committee, 1972. A weekly serial.

3439. Trinkl, John. "Blockade Accompanies Trial of Nuke Bomb Bashers." Guardian 36.35 (June 6, 1984) 9. On the trial of the Griffiss Plowshares 8, who hammered and poured blood on a B52-G bomber.

3440. Trinkl, John. "The Bomb Stops Here." Guardian 35.36 (June 8, 1983) 12-13. On the nationwide protests against the nuclear buildup. Over 4,000 protesters were arrested in 1982.

3441. Trinkl, John. "Nuke Train Harried En Route to Nuclear 'Auschwitz.'" Guardian 36.22 (March 7, 1984) 5. Fifty-one protesters were arrested near Portland, OR, trying to stop a train carrying nuclear weapons materials for the Trident base in Bangor, WA.

3442. Trinkl, John. "On the Line Against the War." Guardian 36.37 (June 20, 1984) 10-11. 350 protesters against the U.S. war in Central America and the caribbean were arrested.

3443. Trowbridge, Elizabeth D. Political Prisoners Held in the United States, Refugees Imprisoned at the Request of a Foreign Government. Los Angeles: Mission Press, 1900. 12. About imprisoned members of the Mexican Liberal Party.

3444. The Truth About the I.W.W. Prisoners. New York: American Civil Liberties Union, 1979. 47. About the imprisonment of 96 members of the Industrial Workers of the World (I.W.W.), on charges of conspiracy to obstruct the war and violation of the Draft Act, though their "conspiracy" amounted to nothing more than speaking out against WWI.

3445. Tunnell, Kenneth, ed. Political Crime in Contemporary America: A Critical Approach. New York: Garland, 1993. 233. Defines political crime as the social harms committed or tolerated by the managers of political and economic forces--"inequality, racism, sexism, homelessness, and unemployment"--and political prisoners as the victims of these conditions. Nine essays.

3446. Turner, William W. Hoover's FBI: The Men and the Myth. Los Angeles: Sherbourne, 1970. 363. A critique of J. Edgar Hoover's national police force fiefdom and of Hoover's authoritarian, conspiracy-obsessed personality. Chapter 10, "The Red Hunter," probes Hoover and the FBI as thought police.

3447. "The Unamericans." Time Machine video, Jack Perkins Commentator (March 26, 1993). On the repression of the Communist Party USA, none of whom had violated laws. Some 50,000 people and 16,000 federal employees lost their jobs as the result of the witch-hunt. Over 1,000,000 people were placed under surveillance by the FBI.

3448. United States. Congress. House of Representatives. Committee on the Judiciary. Amnesty for Political Prisoners: Hearing Before the Committee on the Judiciary, House of Representatives, Sixty-seventh Congress, Second Session on H.J. Res. 60, March 16, 1922. Washington, D.C.: G.P.O., 1922. 85. Concerns especially 113 prisoners, 95 of whom had been convicted in three I.W.W. conspiracy trials.

3449. United States. Congress. Senate. Committee on the Judiciary. Amnesty and pardon for Political Prisoners. Washington, D.C.: GPO, 1921. 198. Hearings on a resolution to free prisoners sentenced during WWI for a wide range of crimes under the Espionage Act but actually only for expressing opinions. Amnesty is recommended under the First Amendment bar against prosecution for beliefs.

3450. United States. National Minority Advisory Council on Criminal Justice. Political Prisoners: Racism and the Politics of Imprisonment. Washington, D.C.: The Council, 1981. 48. The relationship between racial discrimination and imprisonment.

3451. United States of America: The Death Penalty. London: Amnesty International, 1987. 245. Over-view of issues surrounding the renewed use of the death penalty.

3452. Van Buren, Cassandra. "'Family Gathering': Release From Emotional Internment." Jump Cut 37 (July 1992) 57-63. Family Gathering (1988) is a documentary by Japanese-American filmmaker Lise Yasui about her family's imprisonment during World War II.

3453. Van Buskirk, I.C. "Bob Canney Freed in Florida." Guardian 28.29 (April 28, 1976) 7. The article discusses the case against Bob Canney, "jailed for his role in an April 1970 antiwar rally in St. Petersburg, Fla.," the support that helped secure his release, and the civil liberties questions that were raised by the case--including the right to resist an illegal arrest," and prison conditions.

3454. Van Dyck, Harry R. Exercise of Conscience: a World War II Objector Remembers. Buffalo: Prometheus Books, 1990. 250. Of the three types of Conscientious Objectors (COs)--noncombatants in the armed forces, prisoners, and those assigned to civilian service--the author was among the latter (some 12,000). A member of the Mennonite community in Nebraska, he was assigned first to the Civilian Public Service Program camp at Fort Collins, later to a mental hospital and other work, serving almost four years from 1942 to 1946.

3455. Vavrina, Vernon Joseph. "Human Rights and American Foreign Policy: Violations of the Integrity of the Person, Selected Cases, 1969-1980." Thesis (Ph.D.) Georgetown U, 1984. 534. U.S. policy regarding torture and other abuses has been inconsistent, based upon comparison of Brazil, Chile, Cuba, Ethiopia, Iran, North Korea, South Africa, South Korea, and the Soviet Union. The chief cause was its national security\anti-communist bias.

3456. "Veteran Socialist: 'I'm Glad to have Worked for a Better World.'" Militant 41.42 (November 11, 1977) 20. Socialist Worker Party members Lil Curtiss and Max Geldman spent their lives fighting for the cause of socialism. Geldman was indicted under the Smith Act.

3457. Wald, Karen. "A Fugitive Stephen Bingham Surfaces at Last." Guardian 36.44 (September 12, 1984) 7. George Jackson's lawyer, who went underground in 1971, says he wants a trial and is innocent of Jackson's "escape attempt" when Jackson was killed.

3458. Walker, Annette. "Feds To Go All Out To Convict Independentistas." Guardian 40.44 (August 31, 1988) 11. On the trials of sixteen Puerto Rican independentistas. The trial for seven of them is beginning in Hartford (the Hartford 7).

3459. Wang, Diane. "The 7-Year Fight of Prof. Morris Starsky." Militant 41.48 (December 23, 1977) 21. Professor Morris Starsky, who taught philosophy at Arizona State University was fired for his political views. As an outspoken socialist who organized a protest against the Vietnam War, Starsky was marked by the school, the state, and the FBI, and was forced to leave Arizona.

3460. Warrior: The Life of Leonard Peltier Film. Wesport, CT: Cinammon Prod., 1992. The American Indian leader is serving a life term for actions at Wounded Knee and Pine Ridge.

3461. Watner, Carl. "Voluntaryist Insights from Prison." Frying Pan (July 1984) 30. A tax protester discusses his sentence.

3462. Weglyn, Michi. Years of Infamy: The Untold Story of America's Concentration Camps. New York: Morrow, 1976. 351. A history and protest of the "unjust and unconstitutional" internment of 110,000 Japanese Americans in prison camps during WWII. Warns that it can happen again.

3463. Weinstein, Corey and Eric Cummins. "The Crime of Punishment at Pelican Bay Maximum Security Prison." CovertAction 45 (Summer 1993) 38-45. Report on disturbing developments in U.S. maximum security prisons, especially the Security Housing Unit (SHU) specifically designed to minimize all human contact and maximize sensory deprivation--a clear repudiation of any rehabilitation: "SHU will drive men mad, predispose them to violence, and thus legitimize their solitary confinement.

3464. Weisbord, Vera Buch. A Radical Life. Bloomington, Ind.: Indiana UP, 1977. 330. An active communist in the 1920s, she was jailed in North Carolina on charges of murder and conspiracy in connection with a strike.

3465. Weisburd, Abe. "Harlem Hails Indian Fugitive." Guardian 35.25 (March 23, 1983) 11. Dennis Banks has sanctuary from the FBI at the Onondega Indian Reservation.

3466. Weisburd, Abe. "Political Prisoners: Demand Extradition." Guardian 30.44 (August 23, 1978) 8. Richard Armstrong and other Lucasville (Ohio) State Penitentiary inmates who "claim their rights under the Universal Declaration of Human Rights and the Helsinki Accords" demand extradition to a third world country.

3467. Weisburd, Abe. "Uncertain Fate Awaits Banks in S. Dakota." Guardian 39.45 (Sept. 19, 1984) 7. The ongoing case of Native American Dennis Banks, convicted in 1975 over a "police riot."

3468. Weissberg, Arnold. "100 Arrested in Antinuclear Protests." Militant 42.39 (October 20, 1978) 7. Protests against nuclear power.

3469. Weissberg, Arnold. "The FBI's Mexican Cointelpro." Militant 42.2 (January 20, 1978) 15-16. The FBI conducted years of harassment and violence in Mexico with the coop of the Mexican government against "subversive" students, workers, etc.

3470. Weissberg, Arnold. "Thousands Hail Puerto Rican Nationalists." Militant 43.36 (September 21, 1979) 32. Oscar Collazo, Irving Flores, Lolita Lebrón, and Rafael Cancel Miranda were the longest held political prisoners in the Western Hemisphere, in jail since the early 1950s when they took up arms to protest U.S. domination of Puerto Rico.

3471. "When 2,300 Soldier-Prisoners Struck at Ft. Leavenworth." Literary Digest 60 (March 1, 1919) 50-57. Mainly an account of the role conscientious objector prisoners played in resolving a prisoner strike at Fort Leavenworth.

3472. Wieck, David Thoreau. Woman from Spillerton: A Memoir of Agnes Burns Wieck. Carbondale, IL: Southern Illinois UP, 1992. 280. Wieck spent her adult life struggling to organize unions. The book includes stories of arrests and imprisonments of organizers and strikers. The author, her son, was jailed as a conscientious objector during WWII.

3473. "Wife of Detained American Unionist Asks For Support." Philippine Human Rights Update 4 (April 15-May 14, 1989) 5. About Mark Curtis, union activist and socialist possibly framed on criminal charges.

3474. Wilcox, Clair, ed. Civil Liberties Under Attack. Philadelphia: U of Pennsylvania P, 1951. 155. An early collection of essays against the restraining of individual freedoms due to paranoid Cold War mentality. Chaffee's essay, "Investigations of Radicalism and Laws Against Subversion," especially relevant.

3475. Wilde, Margaret D. "Torture Prevention: Dragging Our Heels." Christian Century 104.21 (1987) 616-7. Due to U.S. government reluctance to ratify international agreements prohibiting torture and genocide, the Torture Victims Protection Act, recently introduced in the U.S. Senate, is needed.

3476. Williams, Lynora. "Republic of New Afrika: Demand Release." Guardian 31.20 (February 21, 1979) 10. Imari Obadele, AI prisoner of conscience and RNA head, was charged with murder in connection with the death of a policeman killed during the August 18, 1971 FBI raid on RNA headquarters in Jackson, MS. Obadele was not present during the assault.

3477. "The Wilmington 10." Nation 231.22 (Dec. 27, 1980) 691-92. These defendants, wrongly accused of shootings and arson in 1970, have at last had their conviction overturned. Amnesty International designated them prisoners of conscience in 1976.

3478. "Wilmington 10 Magistrate Criticized." Guardian 31.30 (May 2, 1979) 10. Federal magistrate Logan Howell was repremanded by the U.S. Department of Justice for recommending overturning the 1971 convictions of the Wilmington 10, who were framed on arson charges "because of their role in the self-defense of the Wilmington, NC black community...under seige from the Ku Klux Klan and police forces."

3479. Wilson, E. "American Political Prisoners." New Yorker 26 (May 13, 1950) 125-7. Review of Prison Etiquette, ed. Cantine and Rainer, and A Field of Broken Stones by Naeve and Wieck, about the over 10,000 violations of the Selective Service law during WWII.

3480. Wise, David. The American Police State: The Government Against the People. New York: Random House, 1976. 437. On the development of unconstitutional and illegal political police.

3481. Wiseberg, Laurie S. and Hazel Sirett. North American Human Rights Directory. Washington, DC: Human Rights Internet, 1984. 264. A guide to over 700 organizations based in the U.S. and Canada concerned with human rights and social justice.

3482. Wittner, Lawrence S. Rebels Against War: The American Peace Movement, 1941-1969. New York: Colombia UP, 1969. 339. A few pages on COs.

3483. "Woodson Paroled; Back in Again." Nuclear Resister 89 (June 23, 1993) 3. Helen Woodson was paroled from her 17-year sentence for anti-nuclear nonviolent action, but was re-incarcerated after burning money in a bank to make a symbolic point.

3484. Wyman, David S. The Abandonment of the Jews: America and the Holocaust, 1941-1945. New York: Pantheon, 1984. 444. Reports on the failure of the U.S. government and its people to respond to the extermination of the Jews during the Holocaust, citing anti-Semitism and anti-immigration attitudes in society and Congress; the supression of information by the mass media; the admittance of only 21,000 refugees, "10 percent of the number who could have been legally admitted" under existing immigration quotas, etc.

3485. Yàñez, Arturo Ramìrez. "103 Iranians arrested at Texas College." Militant 42.11 (March 24, 1978) 20. At Bee County College in Beeville, TX, 105 Iranian students were arrested and charged with trespassing after refusing to leave a meeting.

3486. Yeshitela, Omali. "Call Made for Black POW Exchange." Burning Spear 10.10 (January 1984) 2. Yeshitela, chairman of the African People's Socialist Party, in a letter to Syria's Ambassador to the U.N. calls for the exchange of Syrian-held

U.S. prisoner of war Robert Goodman for "any one of all the hundreds of African political prisoners and P.O.W.'s currently held by the U.S. government.

3487. Zahn, Franklin. Deserter from Violence: Experiments with Gandhi's Truth. New York: Philosophical Library, 1984. 272. Includes accounts of his three jailings for pacifist protest in Word War II and later.

3488. Zahn, Gordon C. Another Part of the War: The Camp Simon Story. Amherst: The U of Massachusetts, 1979. 273. During WWII opponents of war on religious grounds could serve in the Civilian Public Service without pay in isolated camps. This is an account of one of those, a forestry camp under Catholic auspices. Zahn argues that this was the first corporate Catholic initiative against war in the U.S.

3489. Zahn, Gordon. "Get Ready, I Feel a Draft." Commonweal 108 (September 25, 1981) 527-29. On Catholic principles and methods for electing conscientious objection.

3490. Zingaro, John. "'Greater Harm' Defense Upheld in Antinuke Cases." Guardian 36.28 (April 18, 1984) 7. Because judges refused to allow Plowshares 8 and Shippingport 6 defendants to call expert scientific witnesses to justify their protests, the Superior Court overturned their convictions.

3491. Zwerman, Gilda. "Special Incapacitation: The Emergence of a New Correctional Facility For Women Political Prisoners." Social Justice 15.1 (Spring 1988) 31-47. Focuses on the High Security Unit at Lexington, the purpose of which "is to contain and monitor primarily...women political prisoners."

URUGUAY

3492. Amnesty International Report 1980. London: Amnesty International, 1980. 165-170. The year 1979 was the sixth anniversary of the country's change to military rule, marked by a high number of political prisoners, unconstitutional detentions, unfair trials and torture, especially of trade union and human rights leaders. The military controls all stages of the legal system, and "torture has become routine."

3493. Amnesty International Report 1990. New York: Amnesty International, 1990. 253-255. Proceedings continue over several past human rights violations.

3494. Amnesty International Report on Human Rights Violations in Uruguay: Including a Memorandum Sent to the Government on 26 July 1983. London: Amnesty International, 1983. 34. Report of a 1983 delegation visit to Montevideo to investigate serious human rights violations since the coup in 1973--arbitrary detention, disappearances, torture, deaths in custody, unfair trials, etc.

3495. "And Now Uruguay." Christian Century 87 (August 26, 1970) 1009. Guerrilla and government kidnappings. (Reply E. M. Smith [Oct. 28, 1970] 1287).

3496. Andersen, M. "Exile's Return." Nation 238 (June 30, 1984)) 789. On the return from exile of opposition leader Wilson Ferreira Aldunate, who was immediately arrested.

3497. Aquirre, Luis Pérez. "Freely and Without Fear." Index on Censorship 14.5 (October 1985) 52-54. The founder of the Uruguayan Service for Peace and Justice (SERPAJ) describes the past work of his organization in defense of human rights and against torture, and present work to rehabilitate the nation under a democratic government.

3498. "Arismendi of Uruguay Relesed." Granma 10.11 (March 16, 1975) 5. Rodney Arismendi, General Secretary of the Communist Party of Uruguay, denounces the regime "which seizes universities and keeps thousands of people imprisoned."

3499. Breslin, Patrick, et al. Report on a Mission to Uruguay, August, 1984: A Special Report to the Human Rights Committee of the New York Academy of Sciences. New York: The Academy, 1984. 31. On the plight of victims from the sciences.

3500. "Campaign to Save Tupamaros." Guardian 31.19 (February 14, 1979) 13. A movement to save the Tupamaros leader, Raul Sendic, has been initiated; Sendic was arrested by Uruguay's military, and has since "been in solitary confinement without proper food, medical care, ventilation or sanitation."

3501. First Supplement (Dated January 1975) to the International Commission of Jurists Report on Uruguay of June 17, 1974. Geneva: International Commission of Jurists, 1975. 3. Worsening repression--purge of universities, increased arrests, etc.

3502. "Five Prisoners of Conscience." New York Review of Books 27 (May 15, 1980) 36. Case studies of five prisoners and incommunicado detention, prison brutality, etc.

3503. The Generals Give Back Uruguay: A Report on Human Rights. New York: Lawyers Committee for International Human Rights, 1985. 62. A summary of human rights abuses in the country on the eve of the country's return to democratic elections.

3504. Goytisolo, Juan. "Case of General Seregni." New York Review of Books 27 (May 15, 1980) 35. The "brutality of methods used by Uruguayan militarists to keep themselves in power emulates, perhaps goes beyond, that of their Argentine colleagues." Since 1971 the number of political prisoners has risen to 6000. In 1979 one percent of the population are in jails as political prisoners.

3505. "Inside a Uruguayan Torture Center: El Infierno (Hell)." Matchbox (Summer 1977) 7-10. Testimony from a Uruguayan detained and tortured for months.

3506. Jackson, Geoffrey, Sir. Surviving the Long Night: An Autobiographical Account of a Political Kidnapping. New York: Vanguard, 1974. 226. Pub. in Great Britain as People's Prison (1973). An account of the author's imprisonment for a year by the Tupamaros. He was Britain's ambassador.

3507. Mental Health Aspects of Political Imprisonment in Uruguay: An Amnesty International Special Briefing. New York: Amnesty International, 1983. 11. About 1000 political prisoners are being subjected to "cruel, inhuman and degrading treatment" in the two main military prisons and other military detention centers.

3508. Núñez, C. "Eleuterio Fernandez Huidobro." NACLA 20.5 (September 1986) 43-50. An interview of a founder of the revolutionary Tupamaros, Fernandez Huidobro, who served fifteen years in solitary confinement.

3509. Political Imprisonment in Uruguay. London: Amnesty International, 1979. (various pagings). Surveys the increasing repression since 1971 (a military coup in 1973). In 1976, for example, possibly one in every fifty citizens had been imprisoned and many of them tortured.

3510. Sayagues, Mercedes. "A Death in Uruguay." Progressive 49 (January 1985) 14-15. Doctor Vladimir Roslik, resident of San Javier, a small town of 1,000 founded by Russian immigrants and frequently terrorized by police in search of communist propoganda, was repeatedly arrested, tortured, and placed under house arrest since 1980 before a final abduction in 1985 in which he was tortured to death.

3511. Second Supplement (dated January 1976) to the International Commission of Jurists Report on Uruguay of June 17, 1974. Geneva: International Commission of Jurists, 1976. 9. Protests, mass arrests, deaths of political detainees caused by ill-treatment, and other violations of human rights.

3512. "Tortured to Death in Uruguay: 22 Cases." Matchbox (Winter 1976) 7-10. A detailed list of twenty-two verified cases of death by torture, methods of torture, a description of prison conditions, and a report on the political climate.

3513. Tortured to Death in Uruguay: 22 Known Cases. London: Amnesty International, 1976. 8. Profiles of each victim.

3514. Uruguay, an Amnesty International Briefing. London: Amnesty International, 1983. 8. On the serious human violations since 1973.

3515. Uruguay: Conditions in Punta de Rieles Prison. London: Amnesty International, 1984. 9. On the 99 women political prisoners held in this prison, some long term from 1972.

3516. Uruguay Deaths Under Torture, 1975-77. London: Amnesty International, 1978. 12. Twelve cases of people who died and five cases of people who disappeared following arrest or abduction.

3517. "Uruguayan Militants Are Victims of Savage Torture." Militant 39.37 (October 10, 1975) 20. Fourteen socialists were detained and tortured by police and military in Cavalry Regiment barracks. Twelve were sentenced to prison for conspiracy and other acts of speech and association.

3518. Uruguay, the Cases of Fourteen Prisoners of Conscience. London: Amnesty International, 1979. 21. Representative cases illustrating illegal arrests, long periods of incommunicado detention, maltreatment, torture, and disappearance.

3519. Weschler, Lawrence. "The Great Exception I." New Yorker 65 (April 3, 1989) 43-85. "The Great Exception II." 65 (April 10, 1989) 85-108. Tells about Uruguay's struggle over what to do with the former torturers.

UZBEKISTAN

3520. "Uzbek Chief Casts Fundamentalism as Villain." Arkansas Democrat-Gazette (5 Mar. 1993) 7A. "International human rights groups have accused Uzbekistan of some of the worst human rights abuses in the former Soviet Union."

3521. "Uzbekistan: Political Activist Detained for 'Calling for the Overthrow of the State and Social Order.'" Amnesty Action (Spring 1993) 2. Babur Shakirov, formerly imprisoned by the Soviets (1970-1980), suffers again for his advocacy of democratic reforms.

VENEZUELA

3522. Amnesty International Report 1980. London: Amnesty International, 1980. 170-172. The new government (1979) of Luis Herrera Campins set free some political prisoners, but some remain and more have been arbitrarily arrested, accompanied by torture and killings.

3523. Amnesty International Report 1990. New York: Amnesty International, 1990. 255-257. Demonstrations in 1989 against government economic measures resulted in hundreds of killings, some 80 students were held up to a week, and thirteen people were detained incommunicado for "incitement," and 10 tortured. Several long-term prisoners were released.

3524. Davila, F. de P. "Venezuela's Political Prisoners." Nation 120 (April 15, 1925) 416-17. Claims some 5,000 political prisoners and 75,000 exiles, victims of the despot Gomez.

3525. Marin, L.M. "Tyranny and Torture in Venezuela." Nation 120 (April 15, 1925) 412-14. Describes the regime of Juan Vicente Gomez, who for sixteen years has ruled by terror and corruption. He has intimidated, exiled, imprisoned, tortured, and killed his political opponents relentlessly.

3526. Political Prisoners in Venezuela. New York: Amnesty International, 1987. 9. At least thirty-six prisoners, some long term, are held under the charge of rebellion, their trials repeatedly delayed. Profiles are given.

VIETNAM (Socialist Republic of)

3527. Amnesty International Report 1980. London: Amnesty International, 1980. 241-6. Many thousands connected to the Thieu governmnet remain in "re-education" detention camps five years after the war ended, and new detainees have been added for criticizing the present government or for other political reasons.

3528. Amnesty International Report 1990. New York: Amnesty International, 1990. 257-259. Many people were held for their religious or political activities, some after unfair trials. Some prisoners had been detained without charge or trial in reeducation camps. Torture and ill-treatment was apparently widespread.

3529. Amnesty International's Concerns in the Socialist Republic of Viet Nam with Selected Case Histories of Prisoners of Conscience. New York: Amnesty International, 1983. 20. Report based on a delegation visit in 1979. Concerns include: compulsory reeducation camps, unfair trials, and ill-treatment in prison.

3530. Behr, Edward. "Camps of Despair." Newsweek 92 (July 3, 1978) 41. On "reeducation" camps.

3531. "Buddhist Booked." Peace News 20.78 (September 8, 1978) 5. "Thich Thien Minh, a former prisoner under Diem and Thieu, was arrested, bringing to seven the number of high officials of the Unified Buddhist Church to be detained in post-war Vietnam.

3532. Chen, Wilson. "I Learned the Hard Way, But I Learned." Christianity Today 26 (March 19, 1982) 22-4. A lieutenant in the South Vietnam army looks at the horrors of war and concentration camps.

3533. Denney, Stephen A. "Urgent Action For Prisoners In Vietnam." Reconciliation International 3.4 (November 1988) 29. "Hundreds of prominent writers, artists and religious leaders remain imprisoned, along with many arrested for such crimes as trying to leave the country."

3534. "Dissident's Appeal Highlights Vietnam's Human Rights Woes." The Morning News, Springdale, AR (January 3, 1993) 8A. On dissident intellectuals detained without trial.

3535. Doan-van-Toai. "A Lament for Vietnam." New York Times Magazine (March 29, 1981) 64. "A former South Vietnamese dissenter tells in a personal memoir of his disillusionment with the victorious communists, his imprisonment at their hands, and the new tyranny that North Vietnam has brought to his country."

3536. Duffey, Dan. "Terra Incognita?" Nation 256.14(April 12, 1993) 491-94. Reviews Duong Thu Huong's novel Paradise of the Blind. She is under heavy surveillance in Hanoi, after 7 months in prison.

3537. Forest, James. "The Parable of the Unresponsive Witness." Commonweal 105 (Dec. 22, 1978) 814-16. Thich Thien Minh, head of the Unified Buddhist Church, died in prison in Ho Chi Minh City. The S. Vietnam government had also persecuted him.

3538. Frame, R. "Canadians Question Vietnamese Government on Imprisoned Pastors." Christianity Today 30 (September 5, 1986) 50. The Vietnamese government has at least 17 inprisoned pastors and is continually closing churches, trying to rid the country of religion.

3539. Jenish, D'arcy. "Hanoi Opens the Jails." Maclean's 101 (February 29, 1988) 36. More than 1,000 political prisoners are released from North Vietnam prisons.

3540. Paul, Anthony. "Ly Tong's Long Trek to Freedom." Reader's Digest 124 (June 1984) 122-8. On Tong's prison life, escape, and seventeen month flight through five countries.

3541. Political Prisoners in South Vietnam. London: Amnesty International, 1983. 37. Thousands of prisoners are still held in terrible conditions in 41 main prisons for civilians.

3542. Report of an Amnesty International Mission to the Socialist Republic of Vietnam, 10-21 December 1979 Including Memoranda Exchanged Between the Government and Amnesty International. London: Amnesty International, 1981. 42.

3543. Report on the Violations of Human Rights in the Socialist Republic of Vietnam, April 1975-December 1988. Atherton, CA: Aurora Foundation, 1989. 158. "The brutalities in Vietnam against real or perceived political opponents have continued to the present day."

3544. Schwartz, Eric. Still Confined: Journalists in "Re-education" Camps and Prisons in Vietnam. Washington, DC: New York: Asia Watch Committee; Committee to Protect Journalists, 1987. 84. Twelve years after the Vietnam war, dozens of journalists remain in long-term detention without trial and in harsh conditions. Includes an annotated list of 48 documented detainees.

3545. Toai, Doan Van. "... and Baby Makes Three." National Review 34 (October 1, 1982) 1213-14. An account of the night the author was arrested, and then imprisoned for twenty-eight months without charge or trial.

3546. Tran, Da Tu. Writers and Artists in Vietnamese Gulags. Westminster, CA,: Century, 1990. 114. On the occasion of the exhibition "15 Years of Vietnamese Writers in Prison" sponsored by the National Press Club, Washington, DC, Sept. 11, 1990.

3547. Tran, Tri Vu (pseud.). "1632 Days of Re-Education." Index On Censorship 16.6 (June 1987) 31. An extract from the author's book on his more than 4 years of imprisonment for "re-education."

3548. Tran, Tri Vu (pseud.). Lost Years: My 1,632 days in Vietnamese Reeducation Camps. Berkeley, Calif.: Institute of East Asian Studies, University of California, 1988. 381. After the fall of Saigon in 1975, thousands of Vietnamese were imprisoned long-term for reeducation, including the author from 1975 to 1979.

3549. "Writers and Journalists in Prisons, or 'Re-education Camps,' in Vietnam Today." Index On Censorship 16.6 (June 1987) 34-35. Describes sixty-six prisoners and lists several more.

VIETNAM, NORTH (Democratic Republic of Vietnam)

3550. Amnesty International Report 1975-1976. London: Amnesty International, 1976. P. 149. Members of a music band imprisoned in 1971 are still incarcerated. A writer imprisoned in 1958 was released in 1974.

VIETNAM, SOUTH (Republic of South Vietnam)

3551. After the Signing of the Paris Agreements: Documents on South Vietnam's Political Prisoners. Philadelphia; Cambridge, Mass.: National Action/Research on the Military Industrial Complex; Vietnam Resource Center, 1973. 49. Deals with the more than 200,000 people held in Thieu's prisons for political purposes--personal letters, government documents, court records, excerpts from laws, etc. Chapters on the prison system, the families of prisoners, the legal framework, etc.

3552. Armstrong, James and John Conyers, Jr. "Vietnam: Sojourn and Sequel." Christian Century 86 (October 15, 1969) 1307-9. Two members of a team that visited South Vietnamese leaders in behalf of political prisoners complain of the indifference and lying by both the Thieu\Ky and the U.S. governments.

3553. Brown, Holmes, and Don Luce. Hostages of War, Saigon's Political Prisoners. Washington, DC: Indochina Mobile Education Project, 1973. 109. Documents the increasingly corrupt and brutal totalitarian regime of President Thieu, a government the Nixon administration supports in the name of democracy.

3554. Debris, Jean Pierre, and Andre Menras. We Accuse; Back from Saigon's Prisons. Washington: Indochina Mobile Education Project, 1973. 93. These French teachers were imprisoned 1970-1972 for their public protests in Saigon against the South Vietnam government and their U.S. allies. This is their account of their arrest and imprisonment. "Epilogue: The American Resposibility," by Don Luce.

3555. Drinan, R.F. "Political Freedom in Vietnam." America 120 (June 28, 1969) 731-3. On the imprisonment of 20,000 non-communist opponents of the Thieu-Ky government and what role the U.S. should play.

3556. Drinan, R.F. "Ultimate Form of Corruption." New Republic 161 (July 19, 1969) 15-16. Exposes the lies of the U.S. State Department regarding prisoners in South Vietnam, who are increasing instead of decreasing.

3557. Eleven Poems of Political Prisoners. Berkeley: Union of Vietnamese in the U.S., 1974. 75. Poems, prose and drawings protesting the Saigon government's "jungle laws."

3558. Floerke, Jill. "Vietnam Cease-Fire Will Not Bring Reconciliation: Don Luce." Christian Century 90 (February 28, 1973) 263-4. U.S. complicity in keeping an estimated 50,000 political prisoners in South Vietnam.

3559. The Forgotten Ones: The Political Prisoners of Vietnam. Singapore: Student Christian Movement, 1973. 34. Indicts the brutal treatment of some 200,000 imprisoned by the Thieu regime. Gives a calendar of key events, 1969-1973, a diagram of the prison system, etc.

3560. Forgotten Prisoners of Nguyen Van Thieu, The. Trans. John Atherton, et al. Paris: Front Solidarite Indochine, 1973. 47. Prepared by faculty members of the Académie de Paris under the direction of Professor Madeleine Rebérioux. The Thieu regime has ignored the Paris Accords for peace by refusing democratic freedoms to hundreds of thousands of political prisoners still being held, with U.S. complicity.

3561. Fox, Tom. "Devil's Island Off Vietnam; the Price of Political Dissent." Commonweal 90 (July 11, 1969) 432-5. Reports on the Con Son prison where torture is routine. Most inmates have been sentenced by military courts.

3562. Free Political Prisoners in South Vietnam. London: British Campaign for Peace in Vietnam, 1974. 46. The Paris Peace Agreement on Vietnam (Jan. 27, 1973) did not end the suffering of the tens of thousands of prisoners. Many cases are cited. Includes section on U.S. responsibility for these atrocities.

3563. Hamilton, Marianne. "A Red Cross Copout." Progressive 38 (October 1974) 7-8. The International Committee to Free South Vietnamese Political Prisoners' resolution to the Red Cross asking for aid and recognition of the 200,000 political prisoners in South Vietnam "encountered first a flurry of diplomatic rhetoric, and finally a stony refusal."

3564. Herman, Edward. "Thieu's South Vietnam; or How We Built and Learned to Love a Charnel House." Commonweal 98 (April 20, 1973) 160-1. The lies and myths rationalizing the war are again exposed and refuted by the study of Hostages of War, Saigon's Political Prisoners by Holmes Brown and Don Luce. South Vietnam is no democracy but an "exceptionally brutal police state."

3565. Hong, Nguyen Thi (pseud.). "A Prison Memoir." Indochina Chronicle 40 (April 1975) 3. Tells of how women helped each other.

3566. Hung, Truong Dinh. "Whose Running the Show in Saigon's Prisons?" Christian Century 90 (April 25, 1973) 470-1. An account of the imprisonment since 1967 of Troung Dinh Dzu, former candidate for S. Vietnam's presidency, and others, by the Thieu regime.

3567. In Thieu's Prisons. Hanoi: Foreign Languages Publishing House, 1973. 154. Describes the "Nixon-Thieu regime of terror": liquidating militants, jailing all opponents real or supposed, terrorizing the population, torture, despite the Paris peace accord.

3568. Minh Nguyêt, Thich. "Memoirs." Trans. Paul Quinn-Judge. Bulletin of Concerned Asian Scholars 10.4 (October 1978) 49. Minh Nguyêt, Buddhist monk and resistance "fighter," gives an account of his fifteen years of imprisonment during the U.S. and Diem regime, including description of torture and severe prison conditions.

3569. Nguyen, thi Hong (pseud.). "A Prison Memoir." Indochina Chronicle 40 (April 1975) 3-5. She was imprisoned on suspicion of being a Communist; describes bad prison conditions.

3570. Political Prisoners in South Vietnam. London: Amnesty International, 1973. 37. Some 100,000 civilians are still detained despite the January 1973 cessation of hostilities. Explains who they are, conditions of their imprisonment, and the tortures they have experienced.

3571. Political Prisoners in South Vietnam. London: Amnesty International, 1974. 36. Some 100,000 civilians remain detained by the Saigon government despite the end of hostilities, in "appalling conditions."

3572. Political Prisoners in South Vietnam and the Philippines: Hearings before the Subcommittee on Asian and Pacific Affairs of the Committee on Foreign Affairs,

House of Representatives, Ninety-third Congress, second session, May 1 and June 5, 1974. Washington: U.S.G.P.O., 1974. 127. Diverse testimony mainly from U.S. officials and experts.

3573. Proffitt, Nicholas. "Thieu's Political Prisoners." Newsweek 80 (December 18, 1972) 61. On the approximately 150,000 in prisons.

3574. Que, Phuong. "We Do Not Lose Heart." Indochina Chronicle 40 (April 1975) 11-15. Que recounts one experience in a detention camp of brutal punishment and prison resistance.

3575. Rojas, Marta. "An Interview with 'The Girl With the Smile of Victory.'" Granma 10.11 (March 16, 1975) 10. Vo Thi Thang was sentenced to 20 years for participating in revolutionary activities in 1968: "They sentenced me to 20 years, but they didn't know they wouldn't last that long...That's why I smiled."

3576. "School of Hard Knocks." Newsweek 82 (July 23, 1973) 35. On the 40,000 to 60,000 prisoners held by the Thieu regime, most without trial, and many tortured.

3577. Sdarner, Francis. "Tiger Cage Victims Describe Horrors." Guardian 27.36 (June 18, 1975) 13. "Prisoners from the infamous Con Son Island internment complex--freed when liberation forces defeated the facist government of Nguyen Van Thieu." This article shares some of the horrors encountered by the political prisoners inside.

3578. The South Viet Nam Committee of Struggle for the Release of Patriotic and Peace Loving People Detained by the Saigon Administration. Cairo, Egypt: Permanent Secretariat of the Afro-Asian Peoples' Solidarity Organization, 1975. 46. On the "barbarous regime of arrest, torture, and imprisonment" maintained by the U.S., despite the Paris Agreement. The system of prisons and torture is set forth. Lists of prisoners.

3579. "South Vietnamese Prisoners Speak." Women: A Journal of Liberation 3.3 (1972) 40-43. Female prisoners describe their brutal treatment.

3580. "Spotlight on Vietnam; Findings of U.S. Interreligous Study Team." Nation 209 (July 7, 1969) 2-3. On the arbitrary arrests and imprisonments by the Thieu-Ky regime, which now holds perhaps 25,000 political prisoners.

3581. Study of Terror; Documents on Political Imprisonment. Torture and Repression in South Vietnam. Stockholm: Committe for the Release of the Political Prisoners in South Vietnam, 1973. 44.

3582. "Thieu's Political Prisoners of War." Time 100 (December 25, 1972) 18+. Some 200 to 300 people suspected of being Viet Cong are arrested every night under martial law.

3583. "Those Political Prisoners." Nation 217 (August 13, 1973) 101. Denounces U.S. financial support of South Vietnam National Police, which operates the Con Son Prison and other prisons for political prisoners.

3584. The Treatment of Political Prisoners in South Vietnam by the Government of the Republic of South Vietnam. Washington: U.S.G.P.O., 1973. 62. Concerned with the release of the 100,000 to 200,000 prisoners and their present mistreatment despite the ceasefire.

3585. Van Minh, Nguyen. "Jail Notes of a Young Vietnamese." Nation 208 (March 24, 1969) 359-62. An account of prison life by a man imprisoned in 1966 for protesting government policies.

YEMEN ARAB REPUBLIC (North)

3586. Amnesty International Report 1990. New York: Amnesty International, 1990. 259-261. Over 100 prisoners were held in 1989 without charge, some of them tortured, one of whom died.

YEMEN (People's Democratic Republic of)

3587. Amnesty International Report 1980. London: Amnesty International, 1980. 325. AI recognizes 43 prisoners of conscience, and more are in prison for political opposition. Trials have often been summary, prison conditions are brutal, including torture and death.

3588. Amnesty International Report 1990. New York: Amnesty International, 1990. 261-262. At least 31 government opponents were held without charge in 1989, and about 17 others detained in previous years continued in confinement. Some torture was reported.

3589. People's Democratic Republic of Yemen. London: Amnesty International, 1976. 12. Criticizes widespread arrests, disappearrances, detention without trial, torture, extra-judicial execution, and other rights violations. Prisoners fluctuate between 2,000 and 10,000.

YUGOSLAVIA

3590. Amnesty Fact-finding Team Back from Yugoslavia. Amnesty Action (Winter 1993) 10. Massive human right abuses are being documented--massacres, murders, arbitrary arrest, torture--especially by Serbian forces.

3591. Amnesty International Report 1980. London: Amnesty International, 1980. 313-317. Most of the prisoners adopted by AI during 1979-80 were convicted of "hostile propaganda," punishable up to 10 years imprisonment. Numerous Albanians in Kosovo were arrested for protesting against discrimination. Some political prisoners of all kinds have been beaten, and prison conditions are harsh.

3592. Amnesty International Report 1990. New York: Amnesty International, 1990. 263-265. At least 4,500 people were detained for political reasons, mainly Albanians in Kosovo. Unfair trials and ill-treatment were apparently common.

3593. Amnesty International's Work With Political Prisoners. Audiotape. St. Paul, MN: Minnesota Public Radio, 1979. 1 Cassette. Recording of a phone call sponsored by the Fargo-Moorehead chapter of Amnesty International with Vladmir Soliyhu(?), supposedly held in Zenitsa Prison, Yugoslavia.

3594. Busic, Bruno. A Report on the Prison Situation in Croatia. Arcadia, CA: Croation Information Service, 1975. 11. Critique of poor conditions in two prisons and profiles of nine prisoners.

3595. Djilas, Milovan. "From a Prison Diary." Dissent 22.3 (Summer 1975) 269-275. [From "Jail Diary," reprinted from Parts of a Lifetime.] Djilas, Tito's comrade in the partisan resistance against the Nazis, was imprisoned by Tito for his criticism of the government.

3596. Djilas, Milovan. Of Prisons and Ideas. San Diego: Harcourt Brace Jovanovich, 1986. 166. A meditation on his 12 years in prison under two dictatorships and many more years under Tito's Communist regime, of which he had been a Vice-President.

3597. Fleming, Thomas. "The Meaning of Mihajlov." America 137 (September 17, 1977) 145-7. Mihajlo Mihajlov, imprisoned for criticizing the government and communism, represents the new spirituality growing underground in the communist countries.

3598. For Amnesty in Yugoslavia. Hamburg: Ost-Dienst, 1987. 133. An account of the first petition in Yugoslavia drafted in Zagreb demanding amnesty for all political prisoners and an end to arrests for a multitude of insignificant behavior. All of the initiators of the petition were arrested. Particular attention to the case of Dobroslav Paraga.

3599. Kardelj, Edvard. Struggle. New York: Tomorrow, 1935. 26.

3600. Mihajlov, Mihajlo. "Belgrade Jails its Dissenters." Nation 233 (October 17, 1981) 373-4. Demands for greater freedom following the death of Tito have resulted in more arrests and trials.

3601. Parker, Mushtak. Muslims in Yugoslavia: The Quest for Justice. Toronto: Croation Islamic Center, 1986. 55. On the persecution of Muslims "because of their quest for religious and national freedom." Biographies of prisoners in "the Yugoslav Gulag system" are presented.

3602. The Petition, Amnesty For All Political Prisoners in Yugoslavia. Sudbury (Ont.): Northern Tribune, 1987. 133. An elaborated and updated translation of the German text Die Petition (1986) about efforts to free political prisoners and the arrest of the signatories.

3603. Qira, Zijadin. Cell Number 31. New York: Vantage, 1970. 269. The author was imprisoned ten years for his support of Albanian rights, but accused of spying for the U.S. and other false charges. Upon release he escaped to the U.S. just ahead of another arrest. This is his autobiography and prison memoirs.

3604. "Sop to the Soviets." Time 105 (March 10, 1975) 52+. Dissident Mihajlo Mihajlov sentenced to prison for disseminating anti-Yugoslavian and Soviet propaganda.

3605. Sudar, Drago. Coming of Age in Tito's Prisons. Los Angeles: Mosor, 1987. 128. Original Croatian version 1985.

3606. Willey, Fay. "Tito's Last Roundup?" Newsweek 86 (December 15, 1975) 62. Tito has jailed more than 200 Yugoslavs recently for political crimes.

3607. Yugoslavia: Amnesty International Briefing. London: Amnesty International, 1985. 13. Summary of political prosecutions--over 500 people a year since 1980.

3608. Yugoslavia: Conditions of Imprisonment of Prisoners of Conscience. New York: Amnesty International, 1987. 50. Eye-witness accounts 1982-1986 of conditions in eight prisons used for political prisoners.

3609. Yugoslavia: Prisoners of Conscience. London: Amnesty International Publications, 1985. 95. Since 1980 more then 500 people a year have been prosecuted for political offences, particularly ethnic Albanians, but also students, teachers, and members of religious organizations.

3610. Yugoslavia, Prisoners of Conscience: An Amnesty International Report. London: Amnesty International, 1982. 50. Historical background, overall situation at present, laws, arrests, detention, trials, prisons, death penalty, and many case studies.

3611. Yugoslavia: Torture and Deliberate and Arbitrary Killings in the War Zones. New York: Amnesty International, 1991. 14. Reports from the war zones showing that all sides have blatantly flouted international human rights standards, regarding treatment of captured combatants and civilians, hundreds of whom have been murdered or tortured.

ZAIRE

3612. "AI Launches Campaign on Zaire." Matchbox (May 1980) 10. From 1978-1980, human rights abuses noted include the dentention without charge or trial of suspected opponents of the government for long periods; the frequent "disappearance" of those detained; the use of torture; the frequency of deaths in detention resulting from torture, ill-treatment, and harsh prison conditions; and the use of the death penalty in political cases and extrajudicial executions.

3613. Amnesty International Report 1980. London: Amnesty International, 1980. 88-92. Detention without trial for criticizing the government, long-term prisoners, harsh prison conditions, torture, high prison mortality rate, frequent death penalty. Strikes and protests have resulted in many arrests, and several have reportedly died in custody.

3614. Amnesty International Report 1990. New York: Amnesty International, 1990. 266-268. At least 100 people were imprisoned in 1989 for their political or religious beliefs, some incommunicado, few brought to trial. Beatings occurred frequently especially at time of arrest.

3615. Bisikisi, Tandundu E.A. "My Theatre is My Freedom." Index On Censorship 14.1 (February 1985) 20. The dramatist author was imprisoned for his criticism of corruption in his plays.

3616. Inciting Hatred: Violence Against Kasaiens in Shaba. New York: Human Rights Watch, 1993. 25. "President Mobutu's actions blocking a movement toward democratic change have created ethnic and regional violence in the country.

3617. Political Imprisonment in Zaire: An Amnesty International Special Briefing. New York: Amnesty International, 1983. 16. Concerned with detention without charge or trial, unfair trials, internal banishment, torture, harsh prison conditions, and extrajudicial executions.

3618. "Zairean Students Arrested, Tortured." Matchbox (November 1980) 6. Over 100 students arrested in Zaire during the first six months of 1980 have been subject to many human rights abuses: detention without charge or trial, "trial" before rigged courts, house arrest, expulsion of the university, violent beatings and other forms of torture, execution, etc, with no chance to appeal.

ZAMBIA

3619. Amnesty International Report 1980. London: Amnesty International, 1980. 92-93. Many people were detained in 1979 and 1980 under administrative detention laws that hold people indefinitely and cannot be challenged in court. Some long-term prisoners were amnestied by President Kaunda in 1979 and 1980.

3620. Amnesty International Report 1990. New York: Amnesty International, 1990. 268-269. A dozen or so political prisoners were held at the beginning of 1989, most eventually released.

3621. Hamalengwa, Munyonzwe. Thoughts Are Free: Prison Experience and Reflections on Law and Politics in General. Don Mills, Ont.: Africa in Canada Press, 1991. 390. Tells about the consequences in his life stemming from his detention without trial in 1976, accused falsely of inciting revolution, i.e., expressing his own ideas on foreign policy as a student. He was expelled and made his way to Canada.

3622. Manifesto of ZANU Political Prisoners in Zambia: An Open Letter. London: Zimbabwe Solidarity Front, 1975. 13. ZANU is the Zimbabwean revolutionary movement. This is an account of Zambia's repression of the movement in its borders.

3623. Model for Democracy Declares State of Emergency. New York: Human Rights Watch, 1995. 7. A state of emergency was declared on March 4, 1993 by President Chiluba, who claimed there was a plot to overthrow the government, and twenty-six people were detained by the government.

3624. Mwaanga, Vernon J. The Other Society: a Detainee's Diary. Lusaka, Zambia: Fleetfoot, 1986. 327. Diary kept 1985-1986 from arrest to detention without trial. The author had been a high official of the government.

ZIMBABWE (also see RHODESIA)

3625. Amnesty International Report 1980. London: Amnesty International, 1980. 93-99. Independence and black majority rule under Robert Mugabe came in 1980. Up until the end of 1979 considerable political repression prevailed under a state of emergency by the governments of Ian Smith and Bishop Muzorewa. Perhaps 8000 to 15000 were detained by August 1979. Torture "increased drastically" under martial law since 1978. Military courts were not subject to review, including the death penalty, which was frequent.

3626. Amnesty International Report 1990. New York: Amnesty International, 1990. 269-271. At least 15 people were held without charge for short periods. A few of the long-term prisoners were released.

3627. "Court Overruled." Time 122 (September 12, 1983) 38. White officers accused of sabotage declared innocent because confessions forced by torture.

3628. LeMoyne, J. "Mugabe's New Justice." Newsweek 102 (September 12, 1983) 53. White Air Force officers are redetained despite a court's innocent verdict.

3629. Nyagumbo, Maurice. With the people: An Autobiography from the Zimbabwe Struggle. New York: Schocken, 1982. 248. (London: Allison & Busby, 1980). Imprisoned 1959-1963 and again 1966-1979 in various prisons for opposition to the government and for national liberation.

3630. "'Operation Scorpion' Stings the Bishop." Newsweek 102 (November 14, 1983) 75. Bishop and former Prime Minister Abel Muzorewa imprisoned as a subversive by the Mugabe regime.

3631. Rhodesia \ Zimbabwe. London: Amnesty International, 1976. 13. Analyzes the legal structures within which detention without charge or trial, unfair trials, death penalty, and torture occur. Almost all the prisoners are Africans who support the nationalist struggle.

3632. Rodriques, Sara. "Zimbabwe Ceasefire Talks Stalled." Guardian 32.9 (December 5, 1979) 24. As many as 15,000 political prisoners are being held without charges, according to an International Defense Aid Fund report.

3633. Willey, Fay, et al. "Nkomo's Bitter Homecoming." Newsweek 102 (August 29, 1983) 33. On PM Robert Mugabe's repressions against Joshua Nkomo and his ZAPU party supporters.

INDEX

References are to entry numbers. A notation of (p) following a name identifies that person as a political prisoner.

This is an index not only to the bibliography itself but to the books, articles and other materials that it lists. If a name or subject that appears in the index is not found in the annotation of the entry cited, it is discussed in the actual article (or other item) listed.

AAA (Triple A) *see* Argentine Anti-Communist Alliance
AAAS Clearinghouse on Science and Human Rights 269
Aabed, Abdel Wali Abdel Hafes (p) 972
Abakay, Ahmet (p) 2412
Abancay Prison (Peru) 1855
Abdallahi, Ghalia (p) 1759
Abdel-Karim, Omar (p) 1524
Abdel-Wahend Nijim, Fawzi (p) 1524
Abdeli Intelligence Service Prison (Jordan) 1587
Abdennour, Maitre Ali Yahia (p) 331
abduction 81, 236, 341, 342, 347, 349, 350, 362, 367, 370, 376, 399, 402, 519, 529, 545, 554, 556, 590, 1318; El Salvador 879
Abdul Rohman, Sheik Omar 856
Abdullah, Ayed (p) 1539
Abdurachman, Emeng (p) 1394
Abeba Tesfagiorgas (p) 911
Abernathy, Ralph 3016
Abokor, Aden Yusuf (p) 2071
aboriginals *see* indigenous people
abortion 3034
Abourisade, Femi (p) 1807
Abrams, Elliott 901
Abrams, Floyd 1590
Abrams, Jacob (p) 3028
Abrikosova, Anna I. (p) 2822
Abrutiene, Edita (p) 2853
Abu Ghraid Prison (Iraq) 1496
Abu Salim Prison (Libya) 1690, 1692
Abu Za'abal Prison (Egypt) 876
Abu-Ghabiyes (p) 1524
Abu-Jamal, Mumia (p) 3247, 3395
academia *see* teachers 215
academic freedom (Africa) 125; US 3255
Acan, Ibrahim (p) 2421
Acevedo Movement Against Torture 513
Aché Indians 1838
Achiron, Marilyn 600
Achour, Habib Ben (p) 2386
Ackerly, John 601
Ackroyd, Carol 2890
ACLU 3180, 3255
AÇÑO Popular 457
Acoli, Sundiata (p) 3270
Acre Prison (Israel) 1540
actors 530, 1106, 2317, 2627
actresses 530
Adams, Frank T. 3018
Adams, Gerry (p) 2891
Adams, Lois 1804
Adams, Virginia 511
Adana Prison (Turkey) 2411
Adel-Abbad Prison (Iran) 1448
Adelson, Alan 979
Adilman, Mona 2
Adjei, Mike (p) 1215
Adler, Thomas S. 2466
administrative detention 623, 856, 860; *see also* detention without charge
Adra Civil Prison (Syria) 2353
Advani, Lal K. (p) 1345
aeroplane, torture 1759
Afghanistan 69, 125, 317–323; and USSR 2845
Africa 3–5, 14, 106, 125, 215, 303, 314
African Americans 278
African People's Socialist Party 3321, 3486
agent provocateur 2906, 3092, 3094, 3397; UK 2947; US 3064
Agetua, John 1805
Aggett, Dr. Neil (p) 2153, 2288
Aghbari, Said (p) 3588
agitprop theater 1019
Agosin, Marjorie 6, 513, 514
Agudo Escudero, Felix José (p) 736, 771
Aguilab, Fidel (p) 1922
Aguilar, Delia 1873
Aguilar, Mila (p) 1873, 1874, 1882, 1887, 1927, 1940
Aguilar, Socorro (p) 3117
Aguirre, Juan Sequiere (p) 1800
Aguirre, Luis Pérez 3495
Ahmad, Abu (p) 1533
Ahmad, Dr. Eqbal (p) 3271
Ahmad, Kassim (p) 1715
Ahmed, Abukar Hassan (p) 2071
Ahmed, Basir (p) 1821
Ahmed Qandil, Emad Yussef (p) 876
Ahvaz Prison (Iran) 1448
Aikenhead, Sherri 1423
Aikman, David 854
AIM *see* American Indian Movement
Ain Boya Prison (Morocco) 1756
Ainsztein, Reuben 980
Aiud Prison (Romania) 2014

Ajemian, R. 2892
Ajiveh, Isma'il (p) 1545
Akaraipattu STF Camp (Sri Lanka) 2334
Akatui Prison (Russia) 2036, 2038
Akhmadulina, Bella 2557
Alagoon, Kuwasi (p) 3043
al-Ajaji, Yusif 429
al Akrami, Ali Muhammad (p) 1692
Alarcón, Alejandro (p) 530
Alata, Jean-Paul (p) 1304
Alba, Vicente (p) 3297
Albania 324–330
Albanians, Yugoslavia 3591, 3603, 3609
al-Barquti, Bashir (p) 1533
al-Beraat, Abdallah (p) 1533
Alberto Corvalon, Luis (p) 585
Alcalá-Meco Prison (Spain) 2296
Alcorta, Alfredo (p) 1847
Alderson Prison (US) 3127
al-Dibi, Zudhir (p) 1524
al-Disi, Walid (p) 1534
Alegría, Claribel (pseud.: Eugenia) 878
Alegria, Fernando (p) 6
Alekseeva, Liudmila 2467
Aleksic, Zarko (p) 3591
Alex 5 (p) 2131
Alexander, Edward 2468
Alexander, Dr. Neville (p) 2221, 2222
Alexander, Noble (p) 733
al-Fara'a Prison (Israel) 1551
Alfoni, Luigi (p) 1571
Alfonsín, Raúl (p) 350
Algeria 220, 331–334
Algeria, French 926, 929
Algerian War of Independence 931
al-Hammati, Saleh (p) 3588
Ali, David Addawe (p) 299
Ali, Khalid Abdel Rahim (p) 1540
Ali, Mustafa (p) 299
Ali, Suleiman Nuh (p) 2071, 2075
Ali, Dr. Syed Husin (p) 1715
Ali, Tariq 1819
Ali Yahya Mu'ammar, Hassan (p) 1692
Alien Tort Claims Court 1853
aliens, US 3093, 3362
Alisberg, Nancy 3020
Aljube Prison (Portugal) 1997, 1998
al-Khalil, Samír 1485
al-Khatib, Ahmad Fares (p) 1588
al-Kurdi, Ali (p) 2360
Alleg, Henri (p) 926
Allen, Charles, Jr. 3021
Allen, Lord Clifford (p) 2989
Allende, Isabel 515, 516
Allende, Laura (p) 585
Allende Gossens, Salvador (p) 524, 578
Allenwood Federal Correctional Institution (US) 3060, 3075, 3109
Alma-Ata Prison (USSR) 2479
al-Mahatta Prison (Jordan) 1587
al-Mahmud, Izzat (p) 2360
al-Mansura Prison (Yemen, PDRY) 3587–3589
al Maskoubyah Prison (Israel) 1539
Almeida, Luciano (p) 460
Almeyda, Clodomiro (p) 530
Almeyda, Manuel (p) 588
al-Mezze Military Prison (Syria) 2352, 2353
al-Muhalwas, Nabil (p) 1534
al Musaiwi, Sayyid Muhammed Baquir (p) 1674
al-Mutawa', Ahmad Hassan (p) 2046
al-Nasser, Zahra' Habib Mansur (p) 2045, 2046
Aloisi-Nally, Jon 3022
Alonso, Fr. Carlos Perez (p) 1287
Alpert, Jane (p) 3023, 3291
al-Qala'a Prison (Bahrain) 429
al Qasbi, Salih Omar (p) 1692
al-Rahman, Amir Abdur 323
al-Sadat Prison (Syria) 2353
al-Sadda, Sayyid Fadhil (p) 2045
al-Saghin, Hassan (p) 1540
al-Sitebi, Shekh Muhammed (p) 2045
Altamirano, Amanda (p) 559
Alter, Victor (p) 2598
Altesor, Alberto (p) 3502
Altmann, Hans 2471
Altunyan, Genrikh (p) 183
al-Turbi, 'Umran 'Umar (p) 1690
al-'Urfiyah, Rashid (p) 1690
Alvarado Delgado, Jose (p) 736
Alvarado Rivera, Pedro Daniel 905
Alvares Santibáñez, Federico (p) 517
Alvarez de Toledo y Maura, Isabel (p) 2293, 2294
Alvariza, Carlos (p) 3513
al-Wathba Central Prison (UAE) 2888
al-Zarrow, Nawaf (p) 1540
Amado, Guillermo Márquez (p) 1832
Amalrik, Andrei (p) 2620, 2742, 2743
Aman, Oumarou (p) 493
Amana, Harry 3024
Amara, Mary (p) 2053
Amaya, José 905
Amaya, Mario (p) 408
Ament, Susan 1186
America, Latin *see* Latin America
America, Rocio (p) 884
American Indian *see* Native American
American Indian Movement (AIM) 3094, 3224, 3435, 3460
Americas Watch 248, 353, 376, 377, 556; criticism 775
Ameringer, Oscar (p) 3027
Amerisov, A. 2474
Améry, Jean (p) 981, 982
Amiel, Barbara (p) 1762
Amin, Idi 106, 2446, 2447, 2450–2452, 2454
Amine, Tahini (p) 1761
Amira, Bassam Abdul Razzak (p) 1539
Amira, Hanna (p) 1534
Amn al-Dawla Prison (Kuwait) 1674
amnesty 285; of torturers 901; US 3176, 3177; USSR 2534
Amnesty International 7, 8, 11–13, 18–24, 42–46, 55, 59, 66, 75, 104, 105, 107, 111–113, 133, 207, 222, 226, 230–233, 240, 247, 248, 275, 277, 286, 287, 291, 298, 300, 306, 317–319, 331, 358, 363, 399, 409, 531, 548, 565, 617, 621, 623, 624, 675, 676, 736, 737, 773, 780, 860–863; country reports 3, 10, 14–17, 25–41, 49, 53, 258, 320, 321, 324, 326, 327, 332, 334–336, 342, 343, 426, 428–430, 432, 433, 443–445, 447–449, 455, 456, 482–484, 487–489, 492, 493, 504–507, 517, 518, 528–533, 602, 603, 618, 620, 677, 691, 709–713, 717–720, 723, 724, 726, 727, 789, 790, 793, 794, 797, 840–843, 850, 851, 855, 856, 864, 865, 1324, 1325, 1331,

1333, 1334, 1346, 1347, 1382, 1486, 1487, 1491, 1499-1503, 1518, 1519; criticism 315
Amora, Vincent (p) 1835
An Kang Military Prison (Taiwan) 2369
Ana, Marcos (p) 2309
anarchism, US 3055
anarchist 2662
Anaya Montes, Melida (p) 884
ANC (African National Congress) 2080, 2088, 2091, 2149, 2180, 2196
Anchayoa, Victor (p) 1865
Andamans Prison (UK) 2999
Anderson, G.M. 46
Anderson, Harry 604
Anderson, Jack 3032
Anderson, Jonathan 3033
Anderson, Martin E. 344
Andics, Hellmut 2478
Andreis, Sergio (p) 1569
Andrews, J.A. 47
Andrews, Joan (p) 3034
Andropov, Yury 2668
Angola 335-339
Anh, Vu van (p) 3529
animals, rape 68
Ankara Police Headquarters (Turkey) 2414
Ansar Prison (Israel) 1528, 1549
Antalya E-type Prison (Turkey) 2414
Antanimora Prison (Madagascar) 1696
anthology 62, 129, 1053, 1054, 1061, 1068, 1072, 1076, 1100, 1101, 1105, 1124, 1367
anti-communism 56, 130, 209, 297, 343, 344, 347, 350, 370, 399, 432, 453, 466, 499, 500, 517, 518, 524, 534, 536, 543, 544, 547, 558, 562, 578, 582, 586, 590, 596, 597, 760, 775, 821, 849, 855, 856, 926, 938, 1019, 1132, 1142, 1255, 1273, 1348, 1349, 1351, 1354, 1359, 1365, 1381, 1386, 1476, 1689, 1707, 1748; Guatemala 1281; Indonesia 1395, 1399; Iran 1424, 1425, 1436, 1437, 1446, 1459; Italy 1572; Japan 1585; Jordan 1587, 1588; Mexico 1726; Paraguay 1836, 1843, 1847; Philippines 1875, 1876, 1879, 1886, 1917, 1926-1928; Poland 1972; Portugal 1993-1998; Singapore 2057, 2059, 2062-2065, 2067-2069; S. Africa 2146, 2216, 2267; S. Korea 1632, 1651, 1654-1656, 1662, 1663, 1672; S. Vietnam 3551, 3560-3562, 3567, 3569, 3578; Spain 2301, 2305, 2312, 2314; Sudan 2338; Syria 2352, 2353, 2356, 2357; Taiwan 2362, 2363, 2369; Thailand 2373, 2374; Tunisia 2385; Turkey 2399, 2401, 2412-2414, 2419, 2421; UK 2984; US 3018, 3053, 3061, 3077-3079, 3089, 3108, 3141, 3148, 3150, 3167, 3174, 3179, 3183, 3197, 3199, 3206, 3245, 3251, 3255, 3283, 3284, 3289, 3369, 3377, 3394, 3421, 3430, 3446, 3447, 3455, 3464, 3474, 3200, 3202, 3212, 3225, 3228; Uruguay 3498, 3513, 3517; Venezuela 3522
Anti-Defamation League of B'nai B'rith 422
anti-radicalism, US 3197, 3199
anti-Semitism 278, 279, 347, 350, 360, 387, 389, 411, 413, 414, 816; USSR 2768, 2775; *see also* Jews
anti-socialism, US 3197
anti-Soviet activity 2733, 2743, 2760, 2777
anti-Soviet propaganda 2469, 2484
Anti-Terrorist Law 517; *see also* terrorism
anti-war 498, 3023; *see also* pacifism; peace protest; war
Antigua Prison (Guatemala) 1274
Antonov, Boris 2480
Antonyuk, Zinoviy (p) 2709
Anyona, George (p) 1609, 1613
Aparicio, Julián (p) 2320
apartheid 278, 282; *see* S. Africa
Apaydin, Orhan (p) 2416
Apenszlak, Jacob 983
Apostolou, Electra (p) 1242
Apparnu, M.P. (p) 1382
Appiah, Joe 1219
Applegate, Richard (p) 644, 645
April, James (p) 2089
April Fifth Forum 706
Aqri, Diyya (p) 1534
Aquino, Benigno (p) 1919, 1927, 1931
Aquino, Pres. Corazon 1876, 1933
Arad, Yitzhak (p) 984, 985
Arak Prison (Iran) 1448
Aranda, Severo (p) 1836
arbitrary arrest or detention 136, 342, 455, 517, 603, 618, 624, 625, 752, 793, 1590, 1594, 1598, 1599, 1692; Kenya 1607-1611; Poland 1952, 1977; Saudi Arabia 2047; *see also* detention
arbitrary execution, Sierra Leone 2055
arbitrary firing 269
Arce, Santiago (p) 1910, 1911
Arce Gómez, Luís 449
Archer, Peter 3055
Arcos Bergnes, Gustavo (p) 736, 771, 785
Arcos Bergnes, Sebastian (p) 736, 771
Aredon, John 605
ARENA Party 880, 896; *see also* Nationalist Republican Alliance, El Salvador
Arens, Richard 1838, 3251
Arévalo Gonzalez, R. (p) 3525
Argentina 10, 65, 68, 69, 72, 121, 125, 152, 153, 177, 192, 246, 256, 257, 260, 262, 269, 278, 297, 340-425
Argentine Anti-Communist Alliance (AAA), death squad 297, 347, 349, 378, 408
Argentov, Alexander (p) 2706
Arifin, Zainal (p) 1394
Arikan, Hatice (p) 2421
Arismendi, Rodney (p) 3498
Aristide, Jean-Bertrand 1322
Arizona Five (p), Earth First 3115
Armagh Prison (UK) 2919, 2924, 2933, 2964, 3005
armed forces *see* military
Armenia 194, 196, 262, 278, 279, 292, 2426-2445; *see also* mass killings, Armenia
Armor, John 3036
arms race, US 3285
arms trade 226
Armstrong, James 3552

Armstrong, Patrick (p) 2942, 2968
Armstrong, Richard (p) 3466
army 413, 711; *see also* military
Arniel, Annie (p) 3168
Arregui, José (p) 2296, 2316
Arriagada, Ramón (p) 542
Arrowsmith, Pat (p) 2375, 2898
Arroyo, Patricio (p) 588
Arruda, Marcos (p) 291
Arseni, Katerina (Ekaterini) (p) 1230, 1261
art 232, 286, 1081; USSR 2619; US 3188
artists 230, 347, 727; Vietnam 3546
Asahi, Dalou (p) 3065
Ashe, Thomas (p) 2928
Asia 15, 49, 50, 140, 223, 303; Southeastern 223
Asia Watch 641, 652, 656, 678
Askin, S. 2085
Asphalia, torture 1246
asphyxiation, El Salvador 880
Assad, Hafez-al 2352–2361
assassination 161, 349, 556, 571, 1512; El Salvador 877, 896, 900; Russia 2036, 2037; *see also* killings
assault 772
Association for Free Art (Cuba) 727
Astiz, Alfredo, torturer 424
Aston, Clive C. 52
Astra, Gunars (p) 2656
Asunción Prison (Paraguay) 1840
Atabek, Dr. Erdal (p) 2416
Atienza, Monica (p) 1922
Atlanta Federal Penitentiary (US) 3054, 3332
Attademo, Abigail (p) 399
Attenborough, Richard 2188
Attica Prison (US) 3291
Attock Fort Prison (Pakistan) 1819
Audi, Rasmeya (p) 1540
Auguste, Carl (p) 1318
Auguste, Yves (p) 1318
Aung, Sein Hla (p) 1777
Auschwitz (Oswieçim) Extermination Camp (Nazi Germany) 201, 279, 981, 996, 1000, 1015, 1017, 1018, 1023, 1031, 1038, 1049, 1056, 1067, 1069–1071, 1074, 1078, 1079, 1081, 1092, 1093, 1101, 1104, 1111, 1113, 1118, 1121, 1130, 1134, 1138, 1145, 1147, 1149, 1150, 1152, 1158, 1163, 1183–1185, 1190, 1192, 1204; revolt 980
Auschwitz-Monowitz Prison 1019
Austin, Hudson (p) 1268
Australia 279, 292, 426, 427
Austria 428
Avakian, Asdghig 2430
Averof Prison (Greece) 1231
Avilés, Mario Baldizón (p) 1797
Avinov, Maria (p) 2479
Avni, Haim 987
Avrich, Paul 3037
Avril, Prosper 1320
Awwori, Horace 1609
Axelsson, Sun 582
Ayala, Carlos (p) 408
Ayden Eleven 3063
Aydin Prison (Turkey) 2395, 2419
Aylesbury Prison (UK) 2962
Ayoub, Elias (p) 3163
Azudi, Dr., torturer 1429, 1432

Baader-Meinhof 226
Baard, Frances (p) 2086, 2144
Babalis, Greek torturer 1259
Babatope, Biola 1808
Babatope, Ebenezer (p) 1808
Babel (p) 2782
Bach, John (p) 3038
Bachelet, Alberto (p) 524
Backiel, Lina 3039
Backiri, Siavoush (p) 1433
Bader, E. 881, 3040
Baez, Carlos (p) 3526
Baez, Joan (p) 3041
Bago Bantay Detention Century (Philippines) 1883
Baha bin Mohammed (p) 482
Baha'i 278, 284, 1424, 1435, 1439, 1443, 1452, 1480, 1481
Bahintasi, Claude (p) 2040
Bahrain 225, 429–431
Bahro, Rudolf (p) 947, 951, 956, 962
Bai-shun, Stanislaus Shen (p) 668
Bailey, George 54
Bailey, Melvin (p) 745
Bakary, Djibo (p) 3
Baker, Eric 55
Baker, Scott 3042
Baker, Theodore 3049
Bakhmin, Vyacheslav (p) 2728
Balafreij, Anis (p) 1756
Balais-Serrano, Evelyn 1877
Balakhonov, Vladimir (p) 2709
Balan, C.A. (p) 1348
Balber, Susanrachel 3044
Baldwin, Roger 3045
Balfour, Ngconde (p) 2081
Balian, Hrair 2396
Ballah, Vedi (p) 1724
Ballykinlar Internment Camp (UK) 2951, 3011
Baltazar, Marcos Juan (p) 1274
Baltimore Four 3060, 3240
Baluch, Akhtar (p) 1822, 1823
Bam, Fiks (p) 2239
Banda, Dr. Hastings 1699
Bandar-Abbas Prison (Iran) 1448
Bandiola, Amy 1878
Bangalore Prison (India) 1345
Bangladesh 72, 253, 262, 280, 432–443, 1829
Bangoura, Mohamed Ali (p) 1306
banishment, Singapore 2063; *see also* banning; exile
banking 362
Banks, Dennis (p) 3094, 3096, 3465, 3467
banning 483, 517; S. Africa 2080, 2086, 2087, 2180, 2232, 2258, 2259, 2261, 2283; *see also* banishment; exile
Bantzen Prison (USSR) 2857
Banzer, Hugo 453/54
Bao, Ruo-Wang (Jean Pasqualini) (p) 607
Baraheni, Dr. Reza (p) 1429–1432, 1462, 1468
Baraldini, Silvia (p) 3042, 3263
Barad, Elizabeth 2087
Baranov, Vikolai (p) 2735
Barbara, Joe 756
Barber, James D. 3046
Barberton Prison (S. Africa) 2144, 2187; deaths 2186
Barbie, Klaus 1003
Barbosa, Roberto 457, 1839
Barczewo Prison (Poland) 1943

Bareiro, Virgilio (p) 1836
Barghouti, Abdel (p) 1539
Barinov, Valeri (p) 2482, 2528, 2826
Barkan, Steven 3047
Barkans, Janis (p) 2656
Barnathan, Joyce 2483
Barnouw, David 988
Barrantes Lingán, Alfonso (p) 1865
Barraqué, Dr. Martha (p) 726
Barre, Siyad, Somalia 2070-2072
Barricklow, Denise 3048
Barrilla Muñoz, Captain Hernán (torturer) 562
Barro, Carlos (p) 399
Barro, Oumou Kalsoum (p) 1722
Barron, John 1593
Bartoszcze, Piotr (p) 1952
Basauri Prison (Spain) 2319
Basavapunniah, M. (p) 1359
Baser, Eyuphan (p) 2414
Basisu, Mu'in 56
Basque 2296, 2298, 2315, 2316, 2326
Bastian, Father Mary (p) 2333, 2334
Basu, Jyotirmoy (p) 1359
Batalla, Luis (p) 3512, 3513
Batallón de Seguridad Prison (Paraguay) 1847
Batallón Sinchi 1854
Ba'th regime 1495
Batoum, Frédéric (p) 493
Batovrin, Sergei (p) 2570, 2839
Battek, Rudolf (p) 183, 831
Battle, Hellen (p) 946
Batu Gajah Detention Camp (Malaysia) 1706, 1715, 1717
Bauer, Yehuda 990
Baumann, Michael 608, 970
Bautzen Prison (GDR) 951, 958, 960
Bayildiran, Cengiz (p) 2413
Baylosis, Rafael (p) 1879, 1890
Bayo, Eliseo (p) 2321
Bayotlang, Fortunato (p) 1910, 1911
Bazoft, Farzad (p) 1488
Bazze, Hugo de (p) 362
Beamish, Tufton 2485
beating 318, 320, 413, 547, 601, 623, 652, 674, 709, 841, 851; El Salvador 880; Poland 1952, 1973, 1977; S. Africa 2257; USSR 2733, 2743, 2855, 2857; UK 2986
Beausobre, Iulia de (p) 184, 2487
Beauvoir, Simone de 929
Beaver 55 3241
Becerra, Euduardo and Natasha (p) 114
Becerra, Jorge de (p) 362
Becerra, Violeta de (p) 362
Beck, F. 2488
Beck, Julian 475
Becker, Theodore 57
Beckett, James 1230
Bedau, Hugo 58
Bednarova, Otta (p) 793, 802, 824
Bedrossyan, Mark 2431
Beeson, Trevor 2489, 2899
Begin, Menachem (p) 184, 2490
Begun, Josef (p) 2578, 2484
beheadings: El Salvador 879
Behr, Edward 3530
Beijing Prison No. 1 706
Beilin, Yosef (p) 2477
Beirut 282
Belene Prison (Bulgaria) 483
Belfrage, Cedric (p) 3050
Belfrage, Sally (p) 3051
Belgium, WWII Resistance 1164
Belgrade Central Prison (Yugo.) 3608
Belknap, Michal 3052, 3053
Bell, J. Bowyer 2901
Bella Yalla Prison (Liberia) 1688
Bellow, Yuri (p) 2491
Belorussians 1209
Belov, Sergei (p) 2533
Belsen Trial 1153
Belyak, Sofya (p) 309
Belzec 1015
Belzec Prison (Nazi) 984
ben Bella, Ahmed (p) 334
Ben Chebroun, Abdelali (p) 231
Benario, Olga (p) 1142
Benavides, Consuelo (p) 309
Benavides Cevallos, Consuelo (p) 851
Benda, Dr. Vaclav (p) 793, 802, 824, 826
Benedetti, Mario (p) 6
Benedetti, Osualdo Sigrido de (p) 346
Benenson, Peter 59
Bengalis 115
Benha Prison (Egypt) 860
Benin 444-446
Benn, Ruth 3054
Bennahmias, Daniel (p) 1056
Bennett, Alison 290
Bennett, Amanda 686
Bennett, Ralph K. 1433
Bennett, Ronan 2942
Bennett Committee Report 2943, 2944
Bennour, Neji (p) 1496
Benny, Edmond (p) 1834
Benson, Mary (p) 2088, 2089
Bentall, Jacob (p) 3225
Benzekri, Driss (p) 1749
Beran, Josef (p) 247
Beresford, David 2902
Bergen-Belsen concentration camp (Nazi Germany) 91, 981, 1085, 1120, 1153, 2799
Berger, Joseph (p) 2492
Bergman, Gregory 1727
Beria, Lavrenti 2537, 2538, 2855
Berkman, Dr. Alan (p) 3065, 3073, 3145
Berkman, Alexander (p) 3055, 3194
Berkowitz, Sarah (p) 991
Berlet, Chip 3056
Berman, Claudio (p) 173
Berman, Nina 3057
Bernadac, Christian 992
Bernard, Margie 2903
Bernstein, Dennis 519
Bernstein, Hilda 2090, 2091
Berrigan, Daniel (p) 3047, 3084, 3271, 3278, 3958
Berrigan, Philip (p) 3047, 3058-3060, 3084, 3126, 3199, 3271
Berrouaghia Prison (Algeria) 331
Berry, Steve 2904
Bertolucci, Decise (p) 3365
Besikci, Dr. Ismail (p) 2424, 2394
Bestic, Alan 1204
Betencourt Ramos, Pablo (p) 736
Bethal 18 (p) 2225
Bethge, Eberhard (p) 993
Bettelheim, Bruno (p) 184, 994
Betto, Frei (Carlos Alberto Libanio Christo) (p) 458
Beunza, Pepe (p) 2303
Beyer, Gail (p) 3127
Beyer, Gunter (p) 944
Beyrodt Pavia, Rubens (p) 462; *see also* Pavia
Bezwinska, Jadwiga 995
Bham, Thamsanga 2092
Bhatti, Muhammad Ejaz (p) 1827
Bhutan 447
Bhutto, Begum 1820
Bhutto, Benazir 1820
Bhutto, Zulfikar Ali (p) 1824, 1825
Bialoleka Prison 1954, 1962, 1963
Bible 212
bibliography 47, 61, 74, 102,

110, 234, 290, 1065, 1080, 1088, 1089, 1107, 1144; Jews 1005; Kampuchea 1600
Bicutan Prison (Philippines) 1875, 1915
Bielecki, Czeslaw (p) 1944, 1965
Bieliauskiene, Jadvyga (p) 2853
Bierman, John 2493
bigotry, Indonesia 1395; Poland 1972; US 3255; *see also* anti-communism, racism
Biko, Stephen (p) 2080, 2090, 2093, 2094, 2104, 2105, 2134, 2143, 2188, 2235, 2262; biography 2245, 2289
Bilgin, Siddik (p) 2413
Bill of Attainder 3077
Bilski, Andrew 882
Bin, Xiao (p) 603
Bin-Wahad, Dhoruba (p) 3258
Bingham, James (p) 3061
Binh, Nguyen Si (p) 3534
Binh, Nugen Thi (p) 3551
Bini, Obi 1610, 1636, 1728, 2386
Binzhang, Father Huo (p) 620
biographies 1110
Birenbaum, Halina (p) 996
Birkenau concentration camp (Nazi Germany) 1146, 1152, 1160, 1195
Birmingham City Jail (US) 3133
Birmingham Six 2894, 2921
Birni-Nkonni New Prison (Niger) 1803
birth control, US 3195
Birtles, Dorothy 60
Bishara, Suha (p) 1512
Bishop, Maurice 1264–1271
Bisikisi, Tandundu E.A. (p) 3615
Biskind, Peter 3062, 3063
Bislimi, Rexhep (p) 3592
Bismilla, Goolam (p) 2159
Black, George 609, 1275
Black Liberation Army, US 3402
Black Panthers 178, 3019, 3043, 3064, 3083, 3092, 3094, 3095, 3110, 3175, 3185, 3197, 3199, 3239, 3247, 3386, 3396, 3397, 3399, 3400, 3432; film 3101
Black September 52, 282
Black Slave (torture) 2359
blacklist 253, 813, 872; US 3245, 3255, 3394
blacks, UK 2949, 2985
Blackstock, Nelson 3064
Blackwell's Island Penitentiary (US) 3196
Blady Szwajger, Adina 997
Blake, P. 2494
Blake, Patricia 352
Blake, Rachel (p) 2375
Blanco, Hugo (p) 392, 393, 1865, 3342
Blanco, Miguel (p) 3526
Blantyre Central Prison (Malawi) 1699
blasphemy 1418
Blaustein, Albert P. 61
Blease, Walter Lyon 2905
Blida Prison (Algeria) 331
Blidaru, Dumitru (p) 2024
blindfold 6
Blitt, Connie 519
Bloch, Sidney 2495–2497
Bloemfontein trial 2118
Blunk, Tim (p) 2299, 3065
Boardman, Rick (p) 3199
Boas, Jacob 998
Bobrowska, Barbara (p) 1984
Bodian, Ansoumane (p) 2048
Boehm, Erich 999
Boesak, The Rev. Allan (p) 2150
Boetsch, Jąacques 1231
Bofill, Ricardo (p) 248
Bofill Pages, Ricardo (p) 736, 771, 785
Bogoraz, Larisa (p) 2676
Bogside 3003
Bohra, Bhola (p) 1791
Boiro Prison (Guinea) 1305
Boix, Eduardo (p) 726
Bokassa, Jean-Bedel 106
Bolivia 448–453
Bolnick, Joel (p) 2095
Bolsheviks 2655
Bomani Sababu, Kojo (p) 3146
Bomay, Saul (p) 1402
bombing 1250; El Salvador 878; UK 2971, 3128; US 3361
Bona, Alita (p) 1903
Bondar, Mykola (p) 2831
Bondhus, Barry (p) 3240
Bone, Edith (p) 184, 1335
Bonfield, Lynn (p) 3066
Bongco, Washington (p) 2280
Bonhoeffer, Dietrich (p) 993, 1002, 1109
Bonhoeffer, Klaus (p) 1109
Boniato Prison (Cuba) 726, 737, 765, 770–772, 785
Bonner, Elena (Yelena) (p) 2499, 2500, 2768
Boodhoo, Harish (p) 1724
book-burning 536
Bookholane, Feziwe (p) 2241
Booshenir Prison (Iran) 1448
Booth, Marilyn 857
Boqiao, Tang (p) 656, 657
Borazjan Prison (Iran) 1448
Bordewich, Fergus M. 610
Borin, Igino (p) 1571
Borkova, Anna A. 2525
Borowiec, Andrew 2397
Boscawen Jail (US) 3150
Bose, Dwijendra Nath (p) 2915
Bose, Souren (p) 1383
Boston Eight (p) 3240
Boston Five (p) 3199
Boston Two (p) 3240
Bosworth, Allan 3067
Botez, Mihail (p) 2014
Bouabid, Abderrahim (p) 1760
Bouboulinas Station, torture 1243
Boudin, Kathy (p) 3068
Bouillard, Thomas 1316
Bould, Geoffrey 62
Boulesbaa, Ahcene 63
Boupacha, Djamila (p) 929
Bourgeois, Fr. Roy (p) 3069, 3299
Bourguiba, Pres. Habib 2384
Bourj Er-Roumi Prison (Tunisia) 2384
Boussa, Boudra (p) 1749
Bowen, Gordon 1276
Bowers, Mark 2502
Bowker, Michael 611
Bowne, Alan 2503
Boyajian, Dickran 2432
Boyer, Sandy 2906, 2907
Boyle, Francis 64
Boyle, Kay (p) 3070
Boyle, Robert 3071
Bozhilov, Grigor Simov (p) 486
Braden, Carl (p) 3251
Bradley, Ben 3072
Bradley, Scott 3073
Bradshaw, Homer (p) 628
Bradshaw, Wilda (p) 628
Brady, Brian J. 2908
Brady, Diane 1768
Braham, Randolph 1006
Brailovsky, Viktor (p) 2506, 2792
brainwashing 614, 627, 664, 677, 688, 698
Brajder, Ernest (p) 3598
Braley, Scott 3074
Brandenburg Prison (GDR) 951, 953, 957, 958, 960
Brandenburg-Gorden Prison (Nazi Germany) 1019

Braniewo Prison (Poland) 1943
Braselli, Selva (p) 3515
Brasfield, Phil (p) 3286
Bravo, Gabriela 520
Brazil 125, 226, 253, 278, 280, 291, 295, 1142
Brazilian Communist Party (PCB) 460
Brecher, John 728, 858, 1434, 1594, 2909
Brechtel, Judith 3075
Bredero, Bart (p) 2300
Breen, Frank 2341
Breitowicz, Jacob (p) 1007
Bremer, Michael (p) 3127
Brenni, Lenni 66
Breshko-Breshkovskaya, Ekaterina (Katerina Breshkovskaia) (p) 2032
Breslau Prison 939, 940
Breslin, Patrick 3499
Breytenbach, Breyten (p) 2098
Breytenbach trial 2118
Briceño, Senén (p) 1832
Bricker Amendment, US 3237
Bridges, Linda 2504
Bridges, S. 1841
Brieba, Juan (p) 3493
Brill, Julie 1637
Bristol Riot 2949
Broad, William J. 2506
Brother Deuch, Kaing Kech Ieu 1594
Brown, Archie (p) 3077
Brown, Dr. Charles 729
Brown, Frank D. 2100, 2101
Brown, H. Rap (p) 3118, 3252
Brown, Holmes 3553
Brown, Janice 2507
Brown, Michael 2508
Brown, Myra (p) 2912
Brown Tribunal, UK 2966
Browning, Christopher 1008
Brownlie, Ian 67
Brunei Darussalam 482
Brunovsky, Vladimir (p) 2509
Brutus, Dennis (p) 3057
Bryan, Helen (p) 3978
Bu Gia Map Camp (Vietnam) 3548
Bu-yong, Lee (p) 1656
Buber, Margarete (Buber-Neumann) (p) 1009, 1010, 2510
Buca, Edward (p) 2511
Buca Prison (Turkey) 2411, 2418
Buchenwald Prison (Nazi Germany) 279, 941, 993, 1011, 1070, 1157; and USSR 2665
Buck, Marilyn (p) 255, 3128
Buckley, William F., Jr. 1824, 2512
Buddhists, Vietnam 3529, 3537, 3568
Buen Pastor Prison (Chile) 559
Buffalo Range Prison (Rhodesia) 2005
Bugajski, Janusz 795
Buhle, Mari Jo 3079
Bujak, Zbigniew (p) 1957, 1960, 1981
Bukharin, Nikolai (p) 2538, 2655
Bukit Duri Women's Prison (Indonesia) 231, 1399
Bukovsky, Vladimir (p) 108, 2496, 2513–2517, 2680, 2706, 2830
Bulgaria 483–486
Bull, Chris 2102
Bunster-Burotto, Ximena 68
Bunyan, James 2519
Buol, Laurence (p) 669
Burayez, Khalil (p) 2352, 2354
Burchalter, Holly 3080
Burgos Central Prison (Spain) 2308
Burkhalter, Holly 353, 1858
Burkino Faso 487
Burmeisters, Juris (p) 183
Burney, Christopher (p) 184, 1011, 1012
Burnier, Father Joao (p) 468, 474
burning 709, 1424, 1922
Burns, James MacGregor 3081
Burns, Lucy (p) 3168
Burreli Prison (Albania) 324, 326
Buru Island labor camp (Indonesia) 75, 173, 1395, 1399–1401, 1406, 1411
Burundi 72, 488–491
Buscayno, Bernabe (p) 1926
Bush, George 571; administration 171
Bushell, Agnes 3082
Bushnell, P. Timothy 69
Busic, Bruno (p) 3594
Bustillo, Ovidio (p) 2303
Butler, Judy 521
Butler, William Jack 1638
Butman, Hillel (p) 2477, 2520, 2521
Butt, Mam Teeda (p) 1596
Butterworth, Joseph (p) 3289
Butyrki Prison (USSR) 2472, 2476, 2479, 2589, 2637, 2666, 2714, 2762, 2822, 2855, 2866
Butz, Tim 3083
Buxton, Jane (p) 2913
Byelorussians 2833
Byron, John 612
Cabieses, Manuel (p) 574
Cabo, Dardo (p) 347
Cabral, Amilcar (p) 1311
Cabrera, Fatima (p) 399
Cacayorin-Tayag, Jean (p) 1922
Cadraine, Diane 3084
Cai-jun, Stephen Chen (p) 668
Caíca, Fernando (p) 337
Cain, Alfred, Jr. (p) 3092
Calciu, Father (p) 2014
Calderon, Melvyn (p) 1922
California Institution for Women (US) 3181, 3209
Calitis, Ints (p) 2656
Camacho, Marcelino (p) 2302
Camara, Abdul Karim (p) 1719, 1720
Camarda, Renato 883
Cambiaso, Osvaldo (p) 385
Cambodia 69, 72, 256, 262, 279; *see also* Kampuchea
Came, Barry 522, 1881
Camejo, Mary Jane 730
Cameroon 492–494
Camp Crame Prison (Philippines) 1890, 1923, 1931
Camp Murphy Army Prison (Philippines) 1910
Camp Simon (US) 3488
Campbell, Patrick (p) 2934
Campo Militar No. 1 (Mexico) 1725
Campos Mendoza, Antonio (p) 903
Campos, C. (p) 1859
Cana, Dr. (p) 2014
Canada 139, 305, 495–503, 1064
Cancel Miranda, Rafael (p) 3026, 3219, 3395
Cannakhale Prison (Turkey) 2412
Canney, Bob (p) 3453
Canto Grande Prison (Peru) 1864, 1872
Canwell Committee 3289
Capetillo, Luisa (p) 3273
capital punishment 39, 97, 104, 105, 162, 193, 226, 227, 244, 298, 300, 301, 573, 737, 917, 921, 1266, 1475; Jamaica 1582; S. Africa 2084; S. Korea 1642; Turkey 2400; US 3030, 3046, 3201, 3220, 3286, 3380, 3429, 3451; *see also* executions; extrajudicial killings
capitalism 107
capucha, torture 1287
Cárcel Model Prison (Nicaragua) 1795, 1801; (Venezuela) 3522

Cargas, Harry J. 1014, 1015
Caribbean 303
Carlos, Benigno (p) 1922
Carlos, King Juan 2305
Carlos, Sixto Jr. (p) 1875
Carmarck, Robert 1277
Carnes, Ben (p) 3347
Carole, Jerome 1472
Carrasco, Rolando (p) 524
Carrillo, Santiago (p) 2301
Carrillo Cubas, Jose Rugen 906
Carrión, Natacha (p) 530
Carroll, Peter 3088
Carroll, R. 2104
Carroll, Raymond 1395
Carter, Brenda 884
Carter, Pres. Jimmie 629
Carter, Lateefah (p) 3184
cartoonist 2522
Caruana, Paul (p) 2973
Carvalán, Luis (p) 568
Carvalho, Rene de (p) 477
Casa Grimaldi Prison (Chile) 525
Caseros Prison (Argentina) 342
Casolo, Jennifer (p) 881, 898
Cassese, Antonio 70
Cassidy, Dr. Sheila (p) 525–527, 539, 591/92
Castello Branco, Marshal Humberto 466
Castillo, Carmen (p) 547, 559
Castillo, Fernando (p) 3526
Castillo, Mario (p) 1797
Castillo, Pedro (p) 588
Castillo, Ramón (p) 350
Castlereagh RUC Interrogation Centre (UK) 2934, 2943
Castro, Carmen de Lara (p) 1852
Castro, Fidel 734, 761–763, 767
Castro, Oscar (p) 524
Catalfio, Maria 2914
Catarama, Dorel (p) 2026
Catete Road Prison (Luanda) 336
Catholic Worker 3109, 3111, 3285, 3294
Catholic Worker Movement 3121–3124, 3137
Catholics 189, 326, 457, 458, 613, 617, 620, 626, 627, 636, 647, 655, 661, 668, 699, 880, 1114, 1182, 3047; priests and nuns, El Salvador 879, 880, 896, 897, 902; UK 2975; US 3111, 3488, 3489
Catonsville Nine, US 3058, 3060, 3199, 3207, 3152
Caudill, Dr. Herbert (p) 742
Cavanagh, Joan (p) 3372
Caveeshar, Sardul Singh (p) 2915
Caxias Prison (Portugal) 1994, 1997, 1998
Ccahua, Alejandra (p) 255
Ccahua, Ubaldina (p) 255
Ceausescu, Pres. Nicolae 2015, 2018
Cederholm, Boris (p) 2524
Cekanavicius, Arvydas (p) 2728
cells 184
Celmina, Helena 2525
censorship 6, 80, 215, 275, 324, 349, 375, 464, 499, 602, 652, 794, 825, 837, 872, 934, 1390, 1479, 1681; books 828; Kenya 1608, 1620; N. Korea 1625–1627; Pakistan 1820; Paraguay 1845; Philippines 1874, 1879; Poland 1944, 1970, 1980, 1983 Rhodesia 2003, 2006; Singapore 2063; S. Africa 2091, 2135, 2147, 2266; S. Korea 1671; S. Vietnam 3552; Syria 2360, 2361; Taiwan 2366, 2367; Turkey 2410, 2412, 2413; UK 2999; US 3028; Yugoslavia 3597, 3600; Zaire 3615
Centa, Bryan (p) 3373
Centeno, Jaime (p) 899
Centeno, José Vladimir (p) 899
Center for Victims of Torture (Minneapolis) 153
Central African Republic 226, 504, 505
Central America 64, 69, 226; sanctuary 3193; US 3069, 3072, 3233, 3308, 3437, 3442
Central Intelligence Agency 161, 236, 257, 297, 322, 571, 679, 1259, 1329; Indonesia 1413; Morocco 1755; SAVAK 1456; S. Korea 1656, 1661, 1669, 1672, 1673; Thailand 2376
Central Jail (Haripur, India) 1391
Central Nacional de Informaciones (CNI) *see* National Center for Information
Central Prison (Ethiopia) 915
Central (Nkondengui) Prison (Cameroon) 132, 493
Cerezo, Pres. Vinicio 1274, 1294
Cervelló, Josep Maria (p) 2325
Cesnulis, Petras (p) 1946
Cha-hun, Lee (p) 1663
Chacabuco Prison (Chile) 524, 585
Chad 152, 506–510
Chadudhuri, Kalyan 436
Chakpori Prison (Lhasa) 603
Chalidze, Valery (p) 2768
Chalk, Frank 72
Chambliss, William 3090
Chan, Connie 1882
Chandler, Richard (p) 3365
Chandler, Ted 2060
Chang-pyo, Koh (p) 1664
Changi Prison (Singapore) 2063
Chao-lin, Chen (p) 663
Chaoui, Abdel Kader (p) 1750
Chaplin, Ralph (p) 3091
Charles, Keith 2527
Charles, Pearnel (p) 1581
Charlotte Three (p) 3171, 3288
Charney, Israel 74
Charter 77, Czechoslovakia 792, 795, 802, 804, 818, 822, 826, 839
Chary, Frederick 1016
Chase-Sardi, Prof. Miguel (p) 1847
Chavez, Irma Leticia (p) 1280
Chavis, Ben (p) 3030, 3172, 3287
Chee, Heng Leng (p) 1716
Chekhanavichius, Arvidus (p) 2729
Chelminski, Rudolph (p) 606, 796
Chen, Theodore 614
Chen, Wilson (p) 3532
Cheng, Nien (p) 615, 616, 696
Cheng, Vincent (p) 2057, 2059, 2065
Chengxun, Luo (p) 687
Chernikhov, Vasili (p) 2680
Chernyakhovsk Special Psychiatric Hospital (USSR) 2728
Chevigny, Paul 3092
Chi, Buu (p) 3557
Chi Ha, Kim (p) 1632, 1640, 1656, 1666–1668
Chi Hoa Prison (S. Vietnam) 3552, 3554, 3557, 3559, 3562, 3570, 3573, 3584
Chia-wen, Yao (p) 2366
Chiapas, Mexico 1736
Chiba, Laloo (p) 2211
Chicago City Jail (US) 3125
Chicago conspiracy trial 3052
Chicago Eight 3132, 3154, 3199, 3226, 3252, 3275
Chicago Fifteen 3240
Chicago Seven 3098, 3207
Chicanos, 3295, 3336

Chichaoui, Jamal (p) 1748
Chiesa, Giulietto 2687
Chikurubi Maximum Security Prison (Rhodesia) 2008
children 3, 19, 75, 102, 158, 217, 226, 238, 243, 278, 291, 316, 342, 350, 362, 372a, 384, 564, 580, 1052, 1057, 1058, 1079, 1094, 1205, 1318, 1364; Guatemala 1283; Holocaust 1013, 1033, 1043; Jewish 997, 1172; Nazis 1179, 1191; Peru 1855; S. Africa 2099, 2107, 2121, 2126, 2133, 2136, 2161, 2184, 2263, 2281; USSR 2530, 2883; UK 3006
Chile 10, 65, 68, 125, 153, 177, 208, 246, 253, 257, 260, 262, 276, 278, 291, 511–594; secret police 522, 531; torture 153
Chilean Air Force Intelligence Service 548
Chilean Resistance 546
Chimerenga, Coltrame (p) 3322, 3323
China 142, 226, 278, 291; Nationalist 595–597; People's Republic of 598–708; *see also* Taiwan
Ching Mei Prison (Taiwan) 2369
Ching-jung, Li (p) 2362
Ching-kuo, Pres. Chiang, Taiwan 2362
Chirwa, Fumbani (p) 1700
Chirwa, Orton (p) 1697
Chirwa, Vera (p) 1697
Chistopol Prison (USSR) 2484, 2678, 2733
Chitive, Constantino (p) 337
Chomsky, Noam (p) 58
Chong-chol, Park (p) 1637
Chong-sam, Kim (p) 1667
Chong-wan, Kim (p) 1657
Chongju Protective Custody Prison (S. Korea) 1637
Chongxi, Liu (p) 674
Chornovil, Vyacheslav (p) 2614
Christ 37
Christgau, John 3093
Christians/Christianity 212, 370, 593, 760, 854, 869, 993 1002, 1025, 1155; Guatemala 1299; Holocaust 1015
Christie, Renfrew (p) 2209
Christoffel, Harold (p) 3377
Chu, Chen (p) 2366
Chubar, Vlas (p) 2538
Chukayeva, Larissa (p) 2780
Chul, Lee (p) 1655, 1672
Chul-ho, Shin (p) 1637
Chul-hyon, Kim (p) 1655
Chumakova, Aleksandra (p) 2774
Chung Hee, Park 1640, 1649, 1651
Chungju Prison (S. Korea) 1652, 1655
Churchill, Ward 3094–3097
Churn, Arn (p) 1604
Chyz, Martha 2530
CIA *see* Central Intelligence Agency
Cid de la Paz, Horacio (p) 367
Cinderella Prison (S. Africa) 2218
Cisneros, Evengelina (p) 732
Ciszek, Fr. Walter (p) 184, 2811
civil disobedience 58, 64, 179, 251, 252, 1513, 3149; US 3084, 3213
civil rights 39, 42; US 3047, 3051, 3133–3135, 3245, 3348
civil war 335
Clamshell Alliance 3153
clandestine military operations 500, 528, 529
clandestine prisons 412
Clare, Anthony 76
Clark, H.R. 2531
Clark, Mark (p) 3397
Clark, Ramsey 2364
Clark, Steve 2302
Clarke, Gerald 540
Clarke, Joan 427
Clarke, Thomas J. (p) 2916
Claude, Sylvio (p) 1314
Claustre, Françoise (p) 509
Clavir, Judy 3098
Clayton, R.M. 77
Cleaver, Eldridge (p) 3099, 3386
Clements, Alan 1771, 1772
Clemina, Helena (p) 2525
Clifton, T. 3100
Clifton, Tony 1435
Club Atletico 367
Clutchette, John (p) 3355
Coard, Bernard (p) 1266, 1268
Coard, Phyllis (p) 1266
Coche, Benita Tale (p) 1276
Code of Military Justice 349
Códoba Penitentiary (Argentina) 399
Coe, Frank (p) 3377
Coffin, William Sloane (p) 3199
Cohen, Dan 3101
Cohen, David 2533
Cohen, Elie A. (p) 1017, 1018
Cohen, John (p) 3291
Cohen, Stanley 1503
Cohen, Stephen 2534
Coillie, Father Dries van (p) 627
COINTELPRO 3064, 3083, 3094, 3103, 3192, 3431, 3432
Coker, Joseph (p) 2053
Colas, Gustave (p) 1314
Cold Comfort Farm 2005
Cold War 3053; US 3255, 3289
cold water torture 413, 601
Cole, Chris (p) 2972
Cole, Nancy 3104
Coleman, Fred 2535
Coleman, McAlister 3105
Colhoun, Jack 3106
Collar, Hugh (p) 1584
Collazo, Oscar (p) 3026
collectivization 279
Colman, Louis 595
Colombia 246, 709–716
Colonia Dignidad torture camp (Chile) 550
colonialism 494, 1311, 1616; UK 2938, 2960, 2999
Columbus Day Four 3224
Co-Madres 886
Comando Libertadores de America 349
Comas-Diaz, Lillian 570
Combinado del Este Prison (Cuba) 726, 727, 737, 740, 759, 770–772, 782, 785
Comité (Komite, Committee) Prison (Iran) 1429, 1432, 1448
Commission for Defense of Human Rights, Paraguay 1852
communist 246, 401, 429, 939, 1259, 2991; S. Africa 2267 *see also* anti-communism
Communist Control Act 1954, US 3255
Communist Party USA 3255, 3183, 3283
Communist Party, Indonesia (PKI) 1395, 1399–1401, 1406, 1411, 1413; *see also* anti-communism
Comoros 717, 718
Compton Commission 193
Compton Report, UK 2966

Con Son Prison (S. Vietnam) 3551, 3552, 3557, 3559, 3561, 3570, 3571, 3573, 3577
Conaway, Janelle 733
concentration camps 203, 204, 296, 311, 376, 725, 1047; resistance 254; Soviet 1024; US 3021, 3036, 3067, 3462; US, film 3155, 3334, 3452
Concepcion, Efron (p) 1903
confession, forced 49, 184, 244, 245, 627, 688, 698, 840, 1585, 1654, 1661, 1664, 1672, 1731, 1830, 2419, 2781; Singapore 2061, 2064; S. Africa 2119; torture 318, 322; USSR 2655; UK 2893
Cong-sik, Yu (p) 1663, 1664
Conger, Dr. Amy (p) 541
Congo 719–721
Conlon, Gerry (p) 2917, 2942, 2968
Connor, Bull 3311
Conquest, Robert 80, 2537–2540
conscientious objection 179, 206, 229, 265, 291, 301, 501, 790, 791, 794, 925, 927, 928, 930, 933, 951, 953, 1212, 1228, 1229, 1339, 1340, 3109; audio 3038; Italy 1569, 1570; Spain 2303; Switzerland 2351; USSR 2476, 2529, 2733; UK 2989; US 3029, 3038, 3045, 3151, 3169, 3187, 3191, 3208, 3249, 3250, 3260, 3264, 3276, 3296, 3300, 3365, 3373, 3433; Vietnam War 3436; WWII, US 3403–3405, 3415, 3424
conscription 723
conspiracy 331; S. Africa 2249; US 3098, 3154, 3162, 3301, 3421, 3428, 3464; *see also* sedition
Conti, Haroldo (p) 368
contraception 3391, 3392
Contras 161, 884, 1797, 1798
Contreras, Equidio (p) 530
Contreras Maluje, Carlos Humberto (p) 536, 544
Convention Against Torture (1987) 63
Cook, Alice 2920
Cook, Fred J. 3108
Cook, Jack (p) 3109
Cook County Jail (US) 3397
Cooper, Nancy 2109
Copa, Victorio M. 734, 735
Copek, Karel (p) 814
Copts 866, 869
Coraud, Alain (p) 927
Corbacho Astorga, Carlos (p) 530
Corbett, Jim (p) 3114, 3193
Corbin, Sam 2398
Cordaro, Fr. Frank (p) 3285
Corillon, Carol 542
Cork Prison (UK) 2962
Cormbatore Central Jail (India) 1348
Cornea, Doina (p) 2015
Cornell, Angela 1860
Corona, Norma (p) 1738
Coronado Vargas, Carlos (p) 722
Coronel, Constantino (p) 1836
Coronel, Florencio (p) 1741
Coronel, Irma (p) 1741
Coronodo, Daniel (p) 577
corporal punishment 244
Corpus, Victor (p) 1883
Corradi, Juan 81
corrective labor 677
Correia Terruta, Antonio (p) 1998
Corrigan, Edward 1504
Cortázar, Julio (p) 341
Corvalán, Luis (p) 524, 543
Corwin, Charles 673
Cossali, Paul 1505
Costa Rica 722
Costello, Mary 82
Côte d'Ivoire (Ivory Coast) 723, 724
Coti Martínez Prison (Argentina) 413
Cotonou Prison (Benin) 444
Cottbus Prison (GDR) 951, 960
Coulter, Carol 2921
counterinsurgency 149; Guatemala 1288, 1293
counterrevolution 643, 2031, 2666; USSR 2685
country reports 84–96, 170–172, 199; comparative 140–147, 197; U.S. 180
coup d'état 190, 362, 551, 552, 1218, 1226, 1255; Thailand 2376
courts 366; S. Africa 2124
Cover, Rogert 3110
coverup, S. Africa 2104; UK 3002
Cox, Larry 97
Cox, Robert 355
Cox, Stephanie 1506
Coy, Patrick 3111
Craciunas, Silviu (p) 2016
Craine, Steve 3112
Crane, Margaret (p) 3113
Crawford, James 99
Crawford, Kathryn Lee 356
Crelinsten, Ronald 100
crematory 1152, 1158
Crespi, Robert 1729
crimes against humanity 64
criminal contempt, US 3384
Crittenden, Ann 3114
Croatia 725
Crockett, George (p) 3053
Crome, Len 1019
Cronin, Sean 2922
Croy, Norma Jean (p) 3292
Crozier, A. 2923
Cruz, Maria Elena (p) 730
Cry Freedom, film 2093, 2188, 2290
Cuadra, Angel (p) 750
Cuatro Alamos Prison (Chile) 525, 585
Cuba 57, 291, 726–788; security police 727, 737, 785
Cuban Human Rights Party 727
Cubans, US 3054, 3186
Cuellar, Daniel (p) 903
Cuello, Juan José (p) 364
Cuernavaca Prison (Mexico) 1725
Cul-soon, Kang (p) 1663
Cultural Revolution (PRC) 69, 615, 616, 651, 658, 705
Curry, Jane L. 101
Curry, John (p) 2946
Curry, Richard 3115
Curtis, Mark (p) 3337
Cyprus 789–791
Cyprus, Turkey 2405, 2422, 2423
Czarist Russia 2032–2039
Czech, Danuta 995
Czechoslovakia 53, 253, 792–839, 1051
Czerniakow, Adam (p) 1073

Dacca Central Jail (Bangladesh) 432
Dachau concentration camp

(Nazi Germany) 279, 1146, 1155, 1181, 1189, 1203
Dadoo, Yusuf (p) 2267
Dae Jung, Kim (p) 1639, 1643, 1646, 1648, 1656, 1658
Dafni, Reuven 1020
Dahgani, Ashraf (Iran) (p) 225
Dahinten, John (p) 1273
dairy 1374
Dallin, David 2542
D'Amico, Alicia (p) 341
Dammam Prison (Saudi Arabia) 2044
Dan, Wang (p) 610, 674
Danane Army Prison (Somalia) 2073
Danang Prison (S. Vietnam) 3584
Danbury Federal Correctional Institution (US) 3058, 3213, 3271
Dandala, The Rev. Hamilton (p) 2277
Danesh, Ahmad (p) 1459
Danhash, Mahmoud Abud (p) 1540
Daniel, Yuli (p) 184, 2670
Daniloff, N. 2543
Danquah, J.B. (Joseph Boakye) (p) 1219, 1223, 1225, 1226
Daoud, Abdulqadir (p) 841
Daoud, Hassan Jasim (p) 2046
Daraj, Saudi (p) 2338
D'Arcy, Margaretta (p) 2924
Darel, Sylva (p) 2545
Darío Rosado, Arnaldo (p) 3341, 3422
Darlowék Detention Center (Poland) 1958
Darlowék Women's Internment Center (Poland) 1964
Darwish, Adel 1508
Dasagupta, Sudhamsu (p) 1349
Dascalu, Nicolae (p) 2017
Dassa, Robert (p) 867
Daundi, Soleman (p) 1402
Davadi, Hassan Nic (Iran) (p) 225
Davidoff, Victor (p) 2851
Davidson, Ann M. 2303
Davidson, Joe 3116
Davidson, Karen 1350
Davidson, Khoren (p) 2434
Davidson, Miriam 3117
Davies, Miranda 103
Dávila, José Antonio (p) 1800
Davis, Angela (p) 1730, 3016, 3118-3120, 3355, 3438
Davis, Benjamin (p) 3053
Davis, Leslie 2435
Dawa (p) 605, 652
Dawidowicz, Lucy 1021, 1022
Dawli, T. 1508
Dawson Island Prison (Chile) 543, 564, 585
Day, Dorothy (p) 301, 3109, 3111, 3121-3124, 3294
Day, Samuel H., Jr. (p) 3125-3127, 3364
Day, Susie 3128
Dayer, Augusta 844
Dayya, Alia Abu (p) 1540
de Klerk, Venetia (p) 2110, 2166
de Leon, Oliverio Castaneda (p) 1289
de Leon, Ricardo (p) 3092
de Piedra, Jesús (p) 1740
de Piedra, Rosario 1737, 1747
de Vera, Benjamin (p) 1879
Dear, Ruth 2304
death camps 984, 1047; construction 1022
death in detention 463; Kampuchea 1599; S. Africa 2090, 2106, 2115, 2116, 2119, 2125, 2159, 2191, 2291; Sri Lanka 2328, 2329; Turkey 2393, 2399, 2403, 2412, 2420; *see also* death in prison
death in prison 184, 822, 829, 973; S. Africa 2078, 2082; Togo 2379, 2383; USSR 2539, 2549, 2634, 2654, 2660, 2673, 2674, 2708, 2823; UK 2954; Uruguay 3494, 3503, 3510/11; *see also* death in detention
death penalty *see* capital punishment
death squads 38, 157, 161, 173, 347, 375, 408, 516, 533, 566, 711, 712, 1329, 1735, 1924; El Salvador 878, 884, 885, 887-889, 893, 894, 896, 900, 903; Guatemala 1273, 1274, 1289; Philippines 1886, 1907, 1924; S. Africa 2081, 2257; Turkey 2420
DeBenedetti, Charles 3129
Debray, Régis (p) 184, 450
Debris, Jean P. (p) 3554, 3559
DeBrun, B. 2929
Debs, Eugene V. (p) 3105, 3131, 3190, 3390
Decalo, Samuel 106
Decker, Karl 732
DeCormis, Anna 1220-1222, 1611
"Decree 50," torture, El Salvador 903
Dedijer, Vladimir 725
Defence of Canada Regulations 500
DeFreitas, Nick 357
Dehghani, Behrouz (p) 1436
Dehqani, Ashraf (p) 1431
Dejmal, Ivan (p) 173
Delbo, Charlotte (p) 186, 1023
Delbruck, Justus (p) 1109
Delfina Magliero, Ana Lia (p) 399
Delgado, Jaime (p) 3146
Delgado Fernandez, Dr. Domingo (p) 736
Dellinger, Dave (p) 301, 3132, 3226, 3098
Delmas Four (p) 2131
DeMelo, Marcela Maria (p) 460
Deming, Angus 1510, 1883, 1947
Deming, Barbara (p) 301, 3133-3135, 3372
Demir, Mehmet 2400, 2401
democracy movement, China 609, 618, 625, 633, 637, 638, 670
demonstrating 675
Denney, Stephen 3533
Dennis, Eugene (p) 3053
deportation 1515, 1567, 1575, 3629; FBI 3274; Jews 1008, 1016; UK 2956; US 3033, 3116, 3349; *see also* exile
Derb Moulay Cherif Prison (Morocco) 1759
Dérésil, Kador (p) 1318
Derry Gaol (UK) 3011
Des Pres, Terrence 1024
Desai, Shri Morarji (p) 1387
Desind, Philip 2033
Désiré, Ulrich (p) 1314
Desmond, Cosmas (p) 107
Dessalines, Casernes (p) 1318
de-Stalinization 2534
Detention House No. 1 (Shanghai) 615, 616
detention without charge 412, 500, 566, 603, 621, 624, 675, 718, 860; S. Africa 2076, 2078, 2080-2082, 2132; Thailand 2373, 2374; Togo 2380-2383; *see also* incommunicado detention

detention without trial 3, 49, 202, 314, 337, 355, 408, 421, 456, 594, 681, 717, 860, 913, 916, 1318, 1531, 1808, 3617; indefinite 49; Malawi 1702; Malaysia 1706–1710; North Africa 202; Rhodesia 2009, 2011; Singapore 2065; Somalia 2070, 2073, 2074; S. Africa 2258, 2259, 2261, 2262, 2276; Tunisia 2389; USSR 2873; US 3067, 3155; *see also* incommunicado detention
Detroit House of Correction (US) 3241
Detwiler, Donald S. 1131
Deutsch, M. 3136
Deutscher, Isaac 2549
Deutscher, Tamara 108
Devine, Michael (p) 2954, 2976
Devine, Mickey (p) 2917
Devoto Prison (Argentina) 417
Deyneka, Anita 2550
Dgaies, Amer Taher (p) 1691
D'Harcourt, Pierre (p) 1025
Dhondup, Tsering (p) 602
Di Chiro, Giovanna 109
diaries of victims 995, 1055, 1073, 1082, 1130, 1375, 1377
Diaz, Gladys (p) 546, 547
Diaz, Nidia (p) 890
Diaz, Victor (p) 544, 562, 590
Diaz Lestrem, Guillermo 372
dictatorships, US 3360
Dienstbier, Jiri (p) 793, 824, 826
Dietrich, Jeff 3137
Diez de Carrera, Carmen (p) 562
Dihgani (Dehghani), Ashraf (p) 1436, 1442
Dikerdem, Mahmut (p) 2409, 2416
Dima, Nicholas (p) 2018
Dimaranam, Sister Mariana (p) 1925
DINA 276, 512, 524, 536, 544, 547, 548, 562, 567, 571, 590, 591/92; *see also* Chile
Dingake, Michael (p) 2120
Dinh, Mai Kim (p) 3529
Diokno, Jose (p) 1931
Dionysus Prison (Greece) 1259
Diori, Hamani (p) 3
Direction Nacional de Investigation (Honduras) 1329
directory 303, 304, 304a, 305
disaparecidos *see* disappearance
disappearance 6, 10, 19, 49, 75, 81, 111–113, 161, 163, 173, 231, 241, 257, 320, 337, 341, 342, 344, 346–350, 355, 358–364, 367, 368, 370, 371, 373, 374, 376, 379, 381, 382, 384, 385, 392, 395, 396, 399, 401, 402, 410, 412, 418, 421, 457, 460, 465, 512, 514, 516, 517, 519, 528, 530, 540, 542, 544, 545, 548, 560, 562, 566, 572, 579, 582, 584, 589, 710–712, 851, 852, 912, 915, 1326, 1764, 1783, 1786; El Salvador 877, 879, 880, 885, 888, 889, 894–896; Guatemala 1272–1303; Guinea 1305, 1309; Mexico 1728, 1732, 1733, 1739–1741; Morocco 1759; Nepal 1792, 1793; Nicaragua 1795, 1800; Paraguay 1836, 1837, 1842; Peru 1855, 1856, 1862, 1867, 1868; Philippines 1875–1877, 1884, 1896, 1900, 1901, 1910, 1918, 1934; Rwanda 2041; Serbia 2050, 2051; Sri Lanka 2328, 2334, 2336; Thailand 2377; Turkey 2405, 2407, 2413, 2420; Uruguay 3492, 3494, 3502, 3518; *see also* salvaging
disappeared *see* disappearance
disarmament *see* nuclear war; war
discrimination 278
disease 184, 2634
displacement, El Salvador 877; *see also* exile
dissent, US 3203, 3213, 3408
dissident writings 1955
District Jail (Abbottabad, India) 1391
Ditz, Jeff 3138
Dixon, Don (p) 644, 645
Diyarbakir Military Prison (Iraq) 248
Diyarbakir Prison (Turkey) 2413, 2418, 2424
Djajus, Dr. (p) 1399
Djibouti 840, 841
Djilas, Milovan (p) 3595, 3596
Djodan, Dr. Sime (p) 3594
Dlamini, Clemens (p) 3
Dlamini, Moses (p) 2122
Dlamini, Nkosazana (p) 2144, 2270
Dlamini, Stephen (p) 2278
Dlamini, Zenani Mandela 2275
Dnipropetrovsk Special Psychiatric Hospital (USSR) 2631, 2723–2726, 2733
Do Socarro Vigevani, Maria (p) 477
Dobczansky, Jury 2552
Dobkowski, Michael 292
Dobrin, Arthur 114
doctors *see* medical: doctors
doctors' plot, USSR 2742
Doctrine of National Security 350; *see also* national security
Doe, Sgt. Samuel 1685–1687
Doherty, Joe 3048
Doherty, Kieran (p) 2917
Dohnanyi, Christine (Bonhoeffer) von (p) 1002
Dohnanyi, Hans von (p) 993, 1002, 1109
Dolgun, Alexander (p) 2555, 2556
Dolph, George 3139
Dombrowski v. Pfister 3018
Dombrowski, James (p) 3018
Domínguez, Jorge I. 115
Dominican Order 458
Dominican Republic 842–849
Don-oon, Park (p) 1664
Donat, Alexander (p) 1028, 1029
Donato Avendo, Jaime (p) 590
Donfang, Han (p) 610
Dong, Stella 2557
Dongen, Toine van 852
Dongping, Bai (p) 674
Donnelly, Jack 116, 117
Donnelly, Joan (p) 2963
Donner, Frank J. 3140–3142
Donnet, Pierre-Antoine 635
Donohue, J.W. 636
Donosky, Lea 1909, 1910
Doremus, Andrea 3143
Dorfman, Ariel 118, 549
Dorfman, Ron 637
Dorian, Emil 1030
Dorrough, Jerry M. (p) 3332
Dors, Traian (p) 2024
Dougherty, M. 359

Douglass, James (p) 3144
Dow Chemical 3241
Dowden, Richard 1437
Dowty, Alan 119
Doyle, Mary (p) 2964
Dr. Marinescu Hospital 2014
draft, US 3132; resistance 3196, 3199, 3206, 3240, 3249, 3264, 3267
draft files 3047, 3058, 3060
draft refusal 785
drama 255a, 827, 1137
dramatists 658
Drapchi Prison (China/Tibet) 606, 652, 678
Drda, Milos (p) 808
Drda, Vlastimil (p) 808
Dreifus, Claudia 360
Dribben, Judith Strick (p) 1031
Drinan, R.F. 120, 3555, 3556
Dring, S. 2453
drugs 709; psychiatry 65; USSR 2691; US 3407
Drumbo, Fleeta (p) 3118, 3355
Drumm, Maire (p) 2963
Du, Pa (p) 1767
Duarte 890, 899
Dubasova, Irina (p) 2558
Dubcek, Alexander (p) 820
Duberman, Martin 3147
DuBois, W.E.B. 3148
Dubrovlag Labor Camp complex (USSR) 2712
Dudek, Andrzej (p) 1982
Dudko, Dimitri (p) 2809
Duffy, Dan 3536
Dufournier, Denise (p) 1032
Dun, U Saw Ne (p) 1782
Dunn, James 1396
Dupré, Peter (p) 1336
Durban 6 2238
Durban Six (p), S. Africa 2123
Duval, Elsie (p) 2931
Duvalier, "Papa Doc" 190
Duvalier, Jean-Claude, "Baby Doc" 1321
Dwork, Debórah 1033
Dworkin, Ronald 3149
Dwyer, Cynthia (p) 1434
Dylag, Stanislaw (p) 1982
Dzerjinski, Felix, mass murderer 2034, 2509
Dzhemilev, Mustafa (p) 2536, 2864
Dzu, Truong Dinh (p) 3566
E-type Prison (Turkey) 2418
Eagle, James T. "Jimmy" (p) 3094
Eain, Ziad Abu (p) 1528
East Timor 72, 262, 279, 291, 1393, 1394, 1396–1398, 1403, 1407, 1410, 1412, 1416, 1417, 1420; *see also* Chomsky, Noam
Easter Rebellion, UK 2941, 2952
Eastern Europe, USSR 2485
Eber, Dorothy (p) 3125
Eberhardt, David (p) 3060
Ebert-Miner, A. 2123
Ebrahimi, Anoushirvan (p) 1459
Eby, Kermit 3150
Ecevit, Bülent (p) 2397
Echaniz, Randal (p) 1917
ecology 498, 1834, 3152; *see also* environmentalism
economic exploitation 586
economics and dictatorship 362
Ecuador 850–853
Edelheit, Abraham 1035–1037
Edelheit, Hershel 1035–1037
Edelstein, Dov (p) 1038
Edling, Joyce 1752
education/teaching 134, 138
Education through Labor (Lao Jiao) 607, 621, 702
educators *see* teachers
Effendi, Basuki (p) 1401, 1406
Ege, Konrad 550, 972
Egypt 56, 291, 854–876
Egyptian Communist Party 855
Ehrenburg, Ilya 1039
Ehrenpreis, Anthony (p) 3200
Ehud, Ya'ar 1568
Eichmann, Adolf 252, 279
Eight-Day War 282
Eisenberg, Azriel 1040, 1041
Eisenstein, Raymond (p) 2162
Eisner, Jack (p) 1042
Eisner, T. 2559
Eitinger, Leo 1043
Ekafera Prison (Zaire) 3, 3613
Ekart, Antoni (p) 184
Elam, F. 1642
Elansari, Ibrahim (p) 1753
Elansari, Nour al-Din 1753
El Banco 367
Elder, Jack (p) 3017, 3280
electric shock 342, 370, 405, 413, 517, 524, 547, 585, 591, 601, 623, 675, 709, 874, 1246, 1304, 1490, 1761, 1795, 1893, 1922; El Salvador 880, 895
Elkins, Stanley 1044
El Kouki, Houcine (p) 2386
Ellacunia, Ignacio (p) 897
Eller, Cynthia 3151
Elliot, L. 639
Elliott, Lawrence 2560
Ellis, R.E. 942
Ellmann, Stephen 2124
Ellsberg, Daniel (p) 3178
Elmi, Saida Botan (p) 307
El Mozote Massacre 887
El Olimpo concentration camp (Argentina) 350
El Renacer Prison (Panama) 1832
El Salvador 10, 125, 161, 246, 256, 278, 291, 877–907
Elungat, August Pampilio (p) 2449
Elvia Alavarado (p) 1330
Embassy hostages (Iran) 1477
Emboscado Prison (Paraguay) 1841, 1842
emigration 324, 326, 945; denial 944, 946, 948, 951, 952; Romania 2025; USSR 2470, 2475, 2498, 2520, 2604, 2615, 2675, 2676
Emiot, Israel (pseud. of Israel Yanovsky-Goldwasser) 2561
Encarnaeión, Alcides (p) 848
encyclopedia 1066, 1127, 1131
Endara, Guillermo (p) 1832
Enders, Tom 901
Eng, Lim Guan (p) 1712
Engelmann, Larry (p) 611
England 174; *see also* UK
Engs, Phillip (p) 1423
Enríquez, Cirilo Torres (p) 1737
Enriquez, Edgardo (p) 375, 536
enslavement 154
environmentalism 355, 502–531; Malaysia 1713; US 3244; *see also* ecology
Enzo Villanueva, William (p) 530
Epiphany 4 (p), US 3233
Epstein, Barbara 3153

Epstein, Jason 3154
Equatorial Guinea 908–910
Erdogan, Bektas (p) 2412
Erdost, Ilhan (p) 2418
Eritrea 911
Erjin, Chen (p) 620
Erlich, Henryk (p) 2598
Erwin, Lorenzo (p) 3062
Erzurum Prison (Turkey) 2418
escape 782, 946, 981, 1251, 1575, 1939, 2016, 2148, 2457, 2891; Auschwitz 1204; Russia 2038; Treblinka 1028; USSR 2682; UK 2925; US 3401; Vietnam 3540
Escharcha, Bernardo (p) 1922
Escobal, Patricio (Pedro) (p) 2306
Escobar, Elizam (p) 3089
Escobar Salgado, Jose Carlos 906
Esenin-Volpin, Alexander (p) 2676
Eskisehir Prison (Turkey) 2395
Esmail, Sami (p) 1547, 1556
espionage 628, 680, 818, 956, 1673, 2027; USSR 2763, 2764; US 3067, 3131
Espionage Act, US 3027, 3028, 3169, 3180, 3190, 3277, 3390, 3409, 3449
Essagayyer, Mohammed (p) 1691
Essop, Mahomed (p) 2082
Estadio Nacional 524
Estado Prison (Mexico) 1731
Estonia 279, 2833
Estradet, Luis (p) 3503
Estrella, Miguel Angel (p) 378
Etale Camp (Namibia) 1786
Etemadzadeh (Beh-Azin), Mahmoud (p) 1473
Ethel, Garland (p) 3289
Ethiopia 911–922
ethnic cleansing, Serbia 2051
ethnic conflict 490, 491, 507
ethnic groups 720; Myanmar 1779, 1780; Pakistan 1821; Yugoslavia 3592
ethnocentrism 278
Etienne, Marino (p) 1320
Europe 16, 122, 123
Europe, Eastern 98, 101, 108, 304a; Western 304
euthanasia 1182
Evangelista, Matthew 2563
Evans, Jesse (p) 3332
Evans, Linda (p) 255, 3361
Everett Massacre, US 3394
Evin Prison (Iran) 291, 1426, 1431, 1433, 1436, 1437, 1448, 1451, 1452, 1454, 1462, 1465, 1467
executions 225, 244, 256, 323, 337, 370, 566, 753, 2008, 2055, 2314; El Salvador 878, 894; firing squad 1433; mock 1424, 1484, 1498; without trial 1694; *see also* capital punishment; extrajudicial killings; summary executions
Executive Order 9066 3067
exhumations 159, 374
exile 2, 136, 154, 225, 257, 269, 279, 282, 314, 327, 517, 522, 542, 884, 885, 889, 1646, 2279; USSR 2500, 2676, 2692, 2843; Uruguay 3503; Venezuela 3524, 3525; *see also* banishment; banning; deportation; refugees
extrajudicial killings 244, 256, 337, 753, 1694; Myanmar 1769, 1780; Philippines 1905; Sri Lanka 2333, 2335, 2337; Sudan 2339/40; Turkey 2420; *see also* executions, killings

Fabian, Béla 2565
Fabian, Dora (p) 942
Fabre, Jean (p) 933
Fadoul, Sidik (p) 507
Fainberg, Victor (p) 2680, 2852
Fainlight, Ruth 1731
Fairweather, Elaine 2933
Fajabi, Afsaneh (p) 1424
falaqa, Saudi Arabia 2045; Syria 2353; torture (falage, falanga, falaka) 1246, 1259, 1261, 1759, 2395, 2419
Falcon, Lidia (p) 2304
Falcón, Nieves 3307
Falginano, Lisa 125
Falk, Richard 2126
Falklands War 424, 425
Fallahi, Fatima (p) 1428
false evidence 2742
Falstein, Louis 1046
families 350, 511, 514, 520, 577, 1877, 2402; Iran 1454
family, Romania 2022; USSR 2535; UK 2917, 2921
Family Gathering, film 3452
famine 278
Far'a Detention Camp (Israel) 1542, 1544
Farabundo Martí Liberation Front 878–880, 884, 887, 903
Farber, Samuel 740
Farhi, Moris 1754
Farisani, Dean T. Simon (p) 2083, 2164, 2268
Farisani, Tshenuwani (p) 2127
Farley, Gay 3156
Farrell, Mairend (p) 2964
Fascism 1571, 1577
Faul, Denis 2911, 2934
Faulk, John (p) 3394
Favali, Father Tullio (p) 1929
Fawaz, Turki (p) 282
Fawcett, J.E.S. 126
Fawcett, James W. 3157
Fawehinmi, Gani (p) 1807
Fazzie, Ethesia Buyiswa (p) 2081
Fazzie, Mutile Henry (p) 2081
FBI 3019, 3053, 3058, 3064, 3083, 3094, 3095, 3108, 3140, 3175, 3192, 3197, 3199, 3202, 3244, 3274, 3322, 3329, 3376, 3394, 3421, 3430, 3431, 3435, 3446; Mexico 3469
Fecteau, Richard (p) 679
Fedchenko, Yuri (p) 2735
Federal Reformatory for Women (Alderson, US) 3167, 3183, 3256
Fedeyeva, Annetta (p) 2780
Feehan, John 2935
Fehervary, Istvan (p) 1337
Feig, Konnilyn 1047
Fein, Helen 127, 134, 1048
Feinberg, Brian 2128
Feldman, Allen 2936
Feldman, F. 741
feminism 271, 502, 503, 872; Taiwan 2367
Fenelon, Fania 1049
Feng, Hu (p) 677
Fenian Insurrection 2916
Ferdowsi, Faran (p) 1439
Ferencz, Benjamin 1050
Fernandez, George (p) 1351, 1386

Fernandez, Ronald 3158
Fernandez Alvarez, Maria Luz (p) 2323
Fernández Cabrelli, Alfonso (p) 3502
Fernandez Huidobro, Eleuterio (p) 3508
Fernández Meijide, Graciela (p) 361
Ferner, Mike (p) 3191
Ferrari, Enrico (p) 1571
Ferreira, Silvio (p) 1837
Ferreira Aldunate, Wilson (p) 3496
Ferris, Timothy 3159
Ferro Estrada, Carmela (p) 1855
fiction *see* novels
Fiedler, Leslie (p) 3160
Field, Hermann (p) 1986
Fife, John (p) 3114, 3117
Figner, Vera (p) 2035
Figueroa, Julio (p) 1273
Figueroa Cordero, Andrés (p) 3026
Fiji 923, 924
Filartiga, Dr. Joel (p) 75, 1846
Filipek, Jan (p) 1051
Filipescu, Radu (p) 2026
Fillizola, Carlos (p) 1837
film 78, 118, 133, 161, 235, 372a, 464, 540, 554, 560, 578, 655, 961, 1069, 1880, 1886; psychiatry 2533; S. Africa, Biko 2093; USSR 2824; UK 2954
film guide, human rights 148
filmmaker 2401, 2503
Final Solution *see* Holocaust
Findley, Tim 3161
fingernails, torture 320
fingers, broken 1429
Fink, Elizabeth 3162
Finkel, David 1511, 3163
Finland 925
Fiori, Giuseppe 1571
Fireside, Harvey 2569, 2570
First, Ruth (p) 2129, 2234, 2252
First Amendment 64
Fischer, Bram (p) 2089, 2120
Fischer, Louis 938, 2571
Fischer, Werner (p) 954
Fischer, Wilhelm 2572
Fisher, Jo 362
Fite, Clifton Edgar 742
Fite, David (p) 742
Fitzgerald, Tamsin (p) 3164
Fitzpatrick, Catherine 2573
Flanders, Laura 3165
Flatman, Ada (p) 2937
Fleener, Terre (p) 1540
Fleming, Lady Amalia (p) 1232, 1234, 1256
Fleming, Thomas 3597
Fleshman, M. 2130
Floerke, Jill 3558
flogging 1764, 1765; *see also* beating
Flores, Fernando (p) 594
Flores, Irvin (p) 3026
Flores, Lila (p) 512
Flossenburg concentration camp (Nazi Germany) 993, 1002, 1109
Flynn, Edith 3166
Flynn, Elizabeth Gurley (p) 3053, 3167
FMLN *see* Farabundo Martí Liberation Front
Foca Prison (Yugo.) 3608
Folon, Jean-Michel 286
Folsom Prison (US) 3099
football 402, 404; torture 1438
Foppa de Solorzano, Alaida (p) 309, 1291
Forbes, Delysia 2131
forced feeding 1526, 1973, 2013, 2593; UK 2912, 2928, 2931, 2940, 2959, 2961, 2981, 2988, 2990, 3012
forced labor 819, 1050, 1096; Indonesia 1399, 1401; Myanmar 1770; Romania 2014, 2022, 2023; USSR 2519, 2539, 2542, 2634, 2708, 2709, 2721, 2737, 2785, 2797, 2798, 2804, 2808, 2817, 2847; *see also* labor camp; slave labor
forced repatriation 505
Forché, Carolyn 129, 1887
Ford, Linda G. 3168
Ford Motor Company 362
Foreman, Dave (p) 3244
forensics 159, 193, 374
Forest, Eva (Genoveva) (p) 2307, 2318
Forest, James 3537
Fornaro, Carlos de (p) 3170
Forsythe, David P. 130
Fort Benning, GA 3069, 3299
Fort Bonifacio Prison (Philippines) 1928, 1931, 1939
Fort Breendonk Prison (Nazi, Holland) 981
Fort Dimanche Prison (Haiti) 1318
Fort Glamorgan Prison (S. Africa) 2264
Fort Leavenworth *see* Leavenworth Penitentiary
Fort Lincoln, NB, Internment Camp (US) 3093
Foster, Don 2132
Foster, William Z. (p) 3053
Foucault, Michel 370
Fourie, Enid 2133
Fourtouni, Eleni 1242
Fox, Richard (p) 3159
Fox, Tom 3561
Fraczak, Lech (p) 1952
Fraker, Susan 3171
frame-up, US 3297
France 174, 926–934, 1119, 1127a; Jews 1194; torture 220
Francis, Desmond (p) 291
Franco, General 2308, 2310, 2314, 2322
Franey, Ros 2968
Frank, Anne (p) 279, 988
Frankel, David 715, 1441, 2134, 2574, 3172
Frankel, Jennifer 150
Frankl, Viktor (p) 184
Franklin, A. 973
Franklin, H. Bruce 3173
Franklin, Linus (p) 2334
Franks, C.E.S. 131
Frantz, Laurent 3174
Frantzell, L. 2575
Frantzeskakis, Costas (p) 1230
Frasca, Tim 365
Fraser, Antonia 132
Frasyniuk, Wladyslaw (p) 1948, 1951, 1963, 1982
Fratti, Rolando (p) 477
Fredericton Internment Camp (Canada) 496
free market economics 362
Freed, Donald 3175
Freedman-Apsel, Joyce 134
Freedom Riders, US 3252
Freeman, Harrop 3177
Freimanis, Gunars (p) 2656
Freistadt, Hans 3289
Frelimo 1765
French, Peter 3178
Freney, Denis 1397
Fretilin 1394
Fried, Jonathan 1279
Friedman, Ina R. 1052
Friedman, Julian R. 138
Friedman, Philip 1053
Friedman, Mrs. Philip 1167
Friedman, Saul 1054, 1055
From, D. 2579
Fromer, Rebecca 1056
Frondizi, Silvio (p) 400
Frongoch Prison (UK) 2966
Fu'ad Najm, Ahmad (p) 857
Fuad Qassim, Tal'at (p) 876

Fucik, Julius (p) 1009
Fuente, Danilo dela (p) 1883
Fuentes Romero, Ricardo (p) 542
Fuenteseca, Douglas (p) 542
Fuerzas de Seguridad (security forces, Honduras) 1329
Fujimori, Pres. Alberto 1858, 1862, 1869
Fulbright Scholars 654, 685
Fuller, Elaine 744
Furen, Mai (p) 684
Fuyuan, Hao (p) 674

Gabeira, Fernando (p) 477
Gabon 935, 936
Gabori, George 1332
Gaddafi, Col. Mu'ammar 509, 1689-1691
Gaga, Negeni (p) 2116
Gaitov, Bajram (p) 483
Gajauskas, Balys (p) 2645
Galindo, Rodolfo (p) 714
Gamarra, Remigio Gímenez (p) 1837
Gamba de Negrotti, Isabel (p) 399
Gambia 937
Gandhi, Indira (p) 1352, 1385
Gandhi, Mahatma (p) 2960
Gandia, Angel (p) 845
Gang, Liu (p) 622
Gang of Four 615, 616
Gannett, Betty (p) 3183
Gans, Donna 3184
Ganyile, Anderson (p) 2182
Gara, Larry 139
Garcés Parra, Alvaro (p) 711
Garcia, Miguel (p) 2310, 2311
García, Gen. Romero Lucas 1273
García Alarcia, Juan (p) 2325
García Meza, General Luís 449
Garcia Salve, The Rev. Francisco (p) 2302
Garcia Vilas (p) 307
García Villegas, Judge René 583
garde à vue *see* incommunicado detention
Gardiner, Gerald A. 2939
Garmaroudi, Mousavi (p) 173
Garmendía Artola, Antonio (p) 2298
Garrastazú Médici, General Emilio 476
Garrett-Schesch, Adam (p) 552
Garrett-Schesch, Patricia (p) 552
Garry, Charles 3185
Garvey, John 2581
gas chambers 1158
Gaspar, Karl (p) 1889
Gastil, Raymond D. 140-147
Gathitu, Kariuki 1614
Gatt, Jorge (p) 530
Gatti, Gerardo (p) 297
Gavalas, Petros (p) 1230
Gavzer, Bernard 3186
Gaylin, Willard 3187
Gaza 1505
Gazis, Emmanuel (p) 1228
Gazmere, Ratan (p) 447
Gazzar, Dr. Hilmy (p) 873
Gcina, Ivy Cikiswa (p) 309
Gdansk Prison (Poland) 1963
Geisel, President Ernesto 465
Geldman, Max (p) 3456
Gellen, K. 1442
Gellen, Karen 1398
Gelman, Anne 148
Gelman family (p) 399
Gemmeker, Albert K. 998
Genefke, Dr. Inge Kemp 260
General Electric 3278
General Intelligence Prison (Saudi Arabia) 2045
Genet, Harry 745
Geneva convention 64
genocide 64, 69, 72, 74, 115, 127, 151, 161, 196, 255a, 256, 262, 264, 278, 279, 292, 341, 435-442, 490, 491, 612, 1366, 1476, 1480, 1481, 1489, 1498; Armenia 2426-2445; East Timor 1393, 1394, 1396-1398, 1403; Holocaust 1048; Indonesia 1417; Kampuchea 1593-1597, 1600-1602, 1604-1606; Pakistan 1829; Paraguay 1838; teaching about 134; USSR 2478, 2549, 2837, 2841; *see also* mass killings; state terrorism; purges
Genocide Convention 3237; United States 72
Genocide Treaty 3211
George, Alexander 149
George, Nicholas 1238
Georgia, USSR 2748
Gerchun, Vladimir (p) 2680
Gerena Ortiz, Victor (p) 3158
German Democratic Republic (East) 259, 943-965
Germany 174, 278, 938-942; *see also* German Democratic Republic; Germany, Federal Republic of; Germany, Nazi
Germany, Federal Republic of (West) 550, 966-978
Germany, Nazi 69, 196, 204, 268, 278, 725, 979-1214; Foreign Office 1008
Gesensway, Deborah 3188
Gestapo 279, 1003
Geussenhainer, Frederick (p) 1177
Geve, Thomas (p) 1057, 1058
Ghana 53, 190, 1215-1227
Gharaybah, Hashem (p) 1588
Ghasr Prison (Iran) 1426
ghetto 1027, 1033; revolts, Jewish 980
Ghezel-Hezar Prison (Iran) 1426, 1437, 1451
Ghose, Aurobindo (p) 1352
Ghosh, Ajoy (p) 1354
Ghotbzadeh, Foreign Minister Sadegh (p) 1457, 1469, 1471
Gibney, Mark 3189
Gil, Mieczyslaw (p) 1982
Gilbert, Margaret (p) 3421
Gilbert, Martin 1059
Gilboa, Jehoshua 2584
Gill, Anton 1060
Ginger, Ann Fagan 150
Ginger, Ray (p) 3190
Ginzburg, Alexander (p) 2768
Ginzburg, Eugenia (p) 2586
Gioglio, Gerald 3191
Girder, William 366
Glaser, Sylke (p) 945
glasnost 2657
Glass, Charles 870
Glatstein, Jacob 1061
Glezer, Ilya (p) 2773
Glick, Brian 3192
Glick, J. Theodore (p) 3271

Globocnik, Odilo 984
Gloria Quintana, Carmen (p) 566
Glusman, J.A. 800
Gluzman, Semen (p) 2709
Gobabis Prison (Namibia) 1783
Godin, W. 2488
Godka NSS Prison (Somalia) 2073, 2075
Godoy, Carlos (p) 518
Godoy, Dr. Ricardo (p) 542
Goering, Curt 1443
Gohar Dasht Prison (Iran) 1451, 1452
Golan, Aviezer 867
Gold, Donna 1280
Goldap Detention Center (Poland) 1958
Goldberg, Denis (p) 2209
Goldbloom, Maurice 1239, 1240
Golden, Renny 3192
Goldman, Emma (p) 301, 3055, 3194–3196
Goldman, Robert 1733
Goldshtein, Grigory (p) 2734
Goldstein, Robert 3028, 3197
Golendorf, Pierre (p) 757
Goli Otok Prison (Yugoslavia) 3602, 3608, 3609
Gollwitzer, Hellmut 1034
Gollwitzórah 1033
Gomes Catassalo, Adriano (p) 337
Gomez, Filomeno (p) 1394
Gomez, Juan Vicente, dictator of Venezuela 3524, 3525
Gómez López, José (p) 530
Gonakudzingwa Prison (Rhodesia) 2010
Gong Pinmei, Bishop Ignatius (p) 701
Gonne, Maud (p) 2956, 3013
Gonzales, Oscar Alfredo (p) 367
Gonzalez, Clarita (p) 765
González, Jean Luis (p) 208
González Flores, Libardo (p) 715, 716
González González, Manuel (p) 727
Goodell, Charles 3199
Gorbachev 2871, 2872
Gorbanevskaya, Natalia (p) 301, 2588, 2589, 2691
Gorbatov, Alexander (p) 2478, 2590
Gorchoff, George (p) 3377
Gordon, Eric (p) 646
Gordon, Helen (p) 2940
Gorgzadeh, Mustafa (p) 1441, 1445
Gornick, Vivian 3200
Gorodetzky, Benjamin (p) 2591
Gospic Prison (Yugo.) 3608
Gotovac, Vlado (p) 3594
Gover, Yerach 1513
Goytisolo, Juan 3504
Gqweta, Thozamile (p) 2153
Graf, Wilhelm (p) 1177
Graft, Dr. Joseph de (p) 1218
Graham-Youll, Andrew 152, 368, 369
Gramajo, Hector 1296, 1303
Gramsci, Antonio (p) 1571, 1572, 1579
grand jury, US 3351, 3394
Grandman, William (p) 3488
Grant, James (p) 3030
Grassi, Gustavo (p) 364
Gray, Ian 3201
Gray, Martin (p) 1062
Graziano, Frank 370
Great Leap Forward 673
Great Purge, Soviet Union 69
Greece 53, 253, 291, 1056, 1146, 1228–1263
Green, Gil (p) 3053, 3202, 3394
Green Island (Lu Tao) Prison (Taiwan) 2369
Greenberg, Peter 554
Greene, Robert W. (p) 647
Greenfield, Charles 746
Greenham Common Peace Camp 2920
Greens, USSR 2467
Greenspan, Joshua (p) 3044
Grenada 1264–1271
Grenada 17 1269; invasion 3425; invasion, US 3361
Grey, Anthony (p) 640, 648, 651, 683
Grey, Ian Douglas (p) 1764
Grieco, Ruggero (p) 1579
Griffiss Plowhsares Eight 3439
Griffith, Aline 1755
Grigorenko, Gen. Pyotr (p) 56, 108, 291, 2486, 2592, 2593, 2691, 2723, 2753, 2772, 2774
Grimaux, Christian (p) 927
Gromov, Leonid (p) 2713
Gross, Leonard 1063
Grossman, Patricia 1355, 1356
Grossman, Vasily 1039
Gruschow, Janet 153
Guadelupe Martinez, Ana (p) 884
Guanajay Prison (Cuba) 754, 759, 765, 785, 3526
Guangdong, Liu (p) 621
Guardia Nacional, Nicaragua 1795–1797, 1799
Guatemala 10, 46, 125, 161, 278–288, 290, 291, 781, 1272–1303
Gubanov, Leonid (p) 2517
Gudava, Eduard (p) 2848
Gudava, Tengiz (p) 2848
Guernsey, Isabel Russell (p) 1064
Guerro, Manuel (p) 529
Guest, Iain 371
Guevara, Che 450
Guha, Archena (p) 1382
Guildford Four, UK 2894, 2918, 2921, 2942, 2968
Guillermo Recabarren, Manuel (p) 520
guilt 370
guilt by association, US 3369
guilty until proven innocent 517
Guinea 1304–1309
Guinea-Bissau 1310, 1311
GULAG 2624, 2629
Gulag, Yugoslavia 3601
Gulag Archipelago 2797, 2798
Gulf War 125, 206, 1491, 1492, 3424; US 3373
Gulton (p) 1399
Gump, Jean (p) 3126, 3364, 3426
Gump, Joe (p) 3126
Gun Court Detention Centre (Jamaica) 1581
Gundlach, Ralph (p) 3289
Güney, Yilmaz (p) 2401, 2406
Guoqi, Wang (p) 670
Guoxing, Xu (p) 621
Gurs Prison (Nazi) 981
Gurung, Gopal (p) 1791
Gusmao, Xanana (p) 1410, 1416

Gutierrez, Carlos Orlando, warden 1801
Gutiérrez, Cortéz (p) 1739
Gutierrez Menoyo, Eloy (p) 765
Gutman, Israel 1065
Gutsa Prison (China/Tibet) 601, 675, 678
Guyana 1312, 1313
Guzman, Luis Armando (p) 1795
Gwaltney, John 3203
Gwelo Prison (Rhodesia) 2005, 2010
Gyatso, Palden 599
Gyatso, Panden (p) 605, 652
gypsies 125, 154, 278, 279, 984, 1052, 1090, 1199, 1209; (Nazi) 1160

H Block *see* Long Kesh Prison
Haas, Albert (p) 1067
Habash, Henry (p) 1534
habeas corpus 350, 372, 399, 1217, 1836; Peru 1854; Philippines 1876, 1930; Singapore 2059
Hadad, Husni (p) 1533
Hadda Detention Center (Yemen, Arab Rep.) 3586
Haddad, Rida (p) 2360
Hadley, Guy 2485
Hae-dong, Lee (p) 1657
Hagad, Primo (p) 1931
Hagen, Dick (p) 1178
Hague Conventions 64
Haig, Alexander 901
Haile-Mariam, Mengistu 912, 920
Haiphong Road Camp (Shanghai) 1584
Haiti 190, 1314–1323; film 1319; US 1319, 1323, 3204
Hajdarowicz, Grzegorz (p) 1942
Hak Soun, Bishop Tju (p) 1669
Halawi, Rassim Mohammed (p) 1526
Hales, Carmen (p) 529
Halimi, Gisele 929
Halliday, Fred 1456
Halperin, Morton 3205
Halsted, Fred (p) 3206
Hamad, Seif Shariff (p) 2372
Hamakwayo, James (p) 2116
Hamalengwa, Munyonzwe (p) 3621
Hamid Kishk, Sheik Abdel (p) 875
Hamide, Khader Musa (p) 3033
Hamilton, Marianne 3563
Hammarberg, Thomas 748
Hammer, Dean (p) 3278
Hammett, Dashiell (p) 219, 3212, 3228
Hampton, Fred (p) 3049, 3397
Han, Hooi Chin (p) 1706
Hancock, Ian 154
Handler, Andrew 1068
Handler, Yuri (p) 114
Hanekom, Patricia (p) 2085
Hannibal, Kari 153
Hannum, Hurst 155
Happe, Manuela (p) 968
Har, Tang Fong (p) 2061
Harare Conference on Children 2099
Harare Prison (Rhodesia) 2005
Harb, Ghassan (p) 1524, 1539
Harb, Sheikh Raghib (p) 1557
Harbert, Mary Ann (p) 649, 679
Hardwari Lal (p) 1357
Hargeisa Group (p) 2075
Hariman, Robert 3207
Hariri-Vijeh, Mojgan (p) 3398
Harlow, Barbara 156
Haro, Juan (p) 3343
Haron, Imam (p) 2082
Haroun, Shehata (p) 865
Harris, David (p) 3208
Harris, Emily (p) 3209
Harris, Leo (p) 3314, 3410
Harrisburg Eight 3118
Harsch, Ernest 1358, 1359
Hart, Kitty Felix (p) 1069, 1163
Hartford Seven 3458
Harth, Erica 3210
Hartunian, Abraham (p) 2436
Harvey, Pharis 1644
Harwood, Ronald 2137
Hasanat, Abul 437
Hashe, Robert (p) 2279
Hashemi, Mahsa (p) 1428, 1441
Hashemi, Mehdi (p) 1472
Hashim, Nashir (p) 1716
Hassett, John 897
Hassler, Alfred (p) 301
Hatcher, Eddie (p) 3325, 3326
Haug, Marit 2332
Hauptman, Petr (p) 818
Hauser, Leo (p) 1019
Havana Prison (Cuba) 765
Havel, Vaclav (p) 792, 793, 801–804, 824, 826, 827, 839
Haverty, Anne 2941
Hawk, David 3211
Haworth, Neil (p) 301
Hayakawa, S.I. 3070, 3268
Hayes, John 157
Haz-Haz Prison (Ethiopia) 915
Hazaribagh Jail (India) 1388
Hearst, Patricia 3209
Hebron Prison (Israel) 1533
Héctor Suárez, Hubo (p) 362
Hee-nam, Kang (p) 1632
Heimler, Eugene (p) 184, 1070
Hein, Moe (p) 1767, 1779
Heissmeyer, Dr. Kurt, murderer 1179
Hellinas, Enas (pseud.) 1243
Hellman, Lillian (p) 219, 3212
Hellman, Peter 1071
Helsinki Accords, USSR 2710
Helsinki Committee, Poland 1968, 1970
Helsinki Groups, USSR 2536, 2553, 2554, 2768, 2874
Helsinki Monitoring Groups 2733, 2734
Helsinki Watch 248, 818; Lithuania 2644; Turkey 2425
Hemmi, Mohamad Faraj (p) 1691
Hennacy, Ammon (p) 3111
Henríquez Barra, Pedro (p) 530
Hereros 72
heresy, US 3289; trials, US 3394
Hergert, Kerstin (p) 943
Herling-Grudzinski, Gustaw (p) 2599
Herman, Edward 1844, 3564
Herman, Victor (p) 2600–2602
Hermanice Prison (Czechoslovakia) 802
Hernandez, Delfino Pascual, murderer 1292

Hernandez, Israel Gutierrez (p) 1731
Hernandez Calderon, Jorge Alberto (p) 895
Hernández Cortez, Daniel Antonio 905
Hernandez Doctrine, Philippines 1916
Herngren, Per (p)
hero 370
Herrera Campins, Luis 3522
Herrera, Fidelia (p) 562
Herrick, Brad 3214
Herz, Dr. Max (p) 427
Herzog, Valdimir (p) 460, 469, 481
Hesse, Lutz (p) 943
Heydrich, Reinhard 984
Hidalgo Guillen, Ariel (p) 740, 749, 770, 771, 785
Hien, Yap Thiam (p) 1399
highjacking 2650
Highlander Folk School 3018, 3075
Hikmet, Nazim (p) 2416
Hilal, Muhammad (p) 1690
Hilao, Liliosa (p) 1910, 1911
Hilberg, Raul 1072, 1073
Hill, P. 1645
Hill, Paul (p) 2942, 2968
Hillesum, Esther ("Etty") (p) 998
Hiltermann, Joost 1515
Himidi, Salim (p) 717
Hin, Tan Hock (p) 1712, 1715
Hinds, L. 2138
Hindus 433
Hines, W.D. 47
Hirabayashi, Gordon (p) 3067, 3345
Hirsch, Sherry 2603
Hirson, Baruch (p) 2162
Hitchens, Christopher 2943
Hitler, Adolph 279, 311
Ho, Chi Minh (p) 932
Hoat, Doan Viet (p) 3534
Hobhouse, Stephen (p) 2989
Hoch, Nancy 158
Hochman, Jirí (p) 805, 813, 836
Hock, Teo Leong (p) 1707
Hoefer, Reiner (p) 944
Hoeffel, Paul 373, 3215
Hoess, Rudolf 1074
Hoffman, Abbie (p) 3226
Hoheneck Women's Prison (GDR) 951, 960
Hohenschoenhausen Prison (USSR) 2665
Hoi, Kong (p) 1706
Holden, Constance 374, 2604, 2605
Holder, Mark (p) 3062
Holguin Prison (Cuba) 771
Holiday, David 159
Holland, Jack 2944
Holloway Prison (UK) 2898, 2913, 2937, 2953, 2956, 2959, 2961, 2962, 2980, 2987, 2990, 2998
Hollywood Ten (p) 3289, 3394
Holmes, Judith 974
Holocaust 134, 204, 279, 292, 311, 316, 979–1214; audio video collections, 1166; bibliography 1013, 1026, 1035, 1036, 1043, 1167, 1168, 1173, 1196, 1200, 1214; children 1013, 1033, 1040, 1043, 1168, 1179, 1191; Christians 1015; chronology 1210; countries 1187; dictionary 1037; France 934, 1194; historians 1021; Holland 1159; Hungary 1038, 1174; industry 1190; Jewish doctors 1046; letters 1020, 1041; medical 1040; non–Jews 1209; Nuremberg Trials 1168, 1201, 1202; organizations 1026; pedagogy 1045; personal narratives 1180, 1193, 1200, 1214; philosophical 1169; psychology 1014, 1018, 1024, 1025, 1043; rehabilitation 1043; rescue 1197; Romania 1030; scholarly journal 1188; Soviet Union 1039; testimony 1170; textbook 1186; Württemburg 1193
Homestead Strike 3055
homosexual (Nazi) 1162; S. Africa 2102, 2112; USSR 2503
homosexuality 235, 1052, 2014, 2795; S. Africa 2217
Hon Bom, Shin (p) 1671
Hon-chi, Lee (p) 1664
Honduras 1324–1330
Honecker, Erich 945
Honerkamp, P. 2606
Hong, Nguyen Thi (pseud.) (p) 3565
Hong Kong 1331
Hong-sheng, Vincent Zhu (p) 668
Honglin, Li (p) 674
Hontz, Craig 1444
Hoobler, Dorothy 2139
Hoobler, Thomas 2139
hood, torture 895
hooliganism, USSR 2475
Hoover, J. Edgar 3108, 3329; *see also* FBI
Horman, Charles (p) 118, 540, 554, 555, 560, 578
Horn, Camilla (p) 2795
Horn, E.M. 1244
Horowitz, Gordon 1075
Höss, Rudolf, mass murderer 1190
Hosseinzadeh, Dr., torturer 1432
hostages 52; Iran 1425
Hotze, William (p) 3028
house arrest 1774, 271, 334, 640; S. Africa 2163
House Committee on Un-American Activities 3078, 3124, 3212, 3251, 3255, 3377, 3394, 3421, 3431
House of Bells prison (Chile) 585
Houser, George 2140
Houston, Diana (p) 114
Howard, Rhoda E. 116
Hoye, Pongoloshe (p) 2116
Hradec Kralove Prison (Czechoslovakia) 822
Hrubieszow Prison (Poland) 1969, 1982
Hrytsiak, Ievhen (Yevhen Hrycyak) (p) 2608, 2609
Hsiu-lien, Lu (p) 307, 309, 2366, 2367
Hua, Liew Yet (p) 1715
Hua-min, Chang (p) 2362
HUAC *see* House Committee on Un-American Activities
Huanwen, Liu (p) 621
Huber, Kurt (p) 1177
Huberband, Simon (p) 1076
Hubl, Dr. Milan (p) 173, 813
Hüble, Milan (p) 820
Huda, Noorul (p) 1359
Huertas Tapi, Pedro (p) 585
Huessy, Mark (p) 963
Huggins, Ericka (p) 3175, 3217, 3397
Huggins, John (p) 3397
Hughes, Francis (p) 2899, 2917
Hughes, Patrick (p) 3014
Hull Prison (Quebec, Canada) 500
human rights 115, 259, 266, 328, activist 1738; bibliography 164; convention 126;

declarations 312, 313; documents 61, 67, 162; film guide 148; monitors, USSR 2874; organizations 303-305, 3481; teaching syllabi 138; theory 117; treaties, US 3237; U.S. 189; U.S. security aid 165
Human Rights Internet Reporter 164
Human Rights Watch 5, 9, 46, 168, 638, 656, 678
Human Rights Watch Quarterly Newsletter 169
Human Rights Watch World Report 170
Humana, Charles 172
Hun, Hahm Suk (p) 1651
Hunat, Cestmir (p) 808
Hung, Truong Dinh 3566
Hungary 69, 268, 279, 1070, 1174, 1332-1344; Jews 1004-1006
hunger 278; in prison, USSR 2539, 2667, 2785
hunger strike 76, 193, 335, 432, 460, 523, 584, 727, 782, 967, 974, 1376, 1483, 1508, 1522, 1526, 1748, 2469; Paraguay 1841; Poland 1943, 1944; S. Africa 2205, 2226; Spain 2299; UK 2892, 2899, 2902, 2909, 2910, 2917, 2935, 2936, 2952, 2954, 2970, 2976, 2979, 2981, 2982, 2990, 2995, 3012; US 3058, 3123; USSR 2593, 2662, 2676, 2781
Hunke, Father Heinz 2142
Hunt, Antonia 1077
Hunt, Paul 1516
Huong, Duong Thu (p) 3536
Hurson, Martin (p) 2917
Hurtado, María Elena 557
Husák, Gustan (p) 836
Hussain, Muhammad Sabir (p) 1827
Hussein, King bin Talal 1588
Husyak, Darka (p) 2818
Hüttner, Jonny (p) 1019
Hutton, Bobby (p) 3397
Hutus 490, 491
Huyen, Tran Tu (p) 3544
Hwan, General Chun Doo 1646
Hyde, Douglas A. 2330
Hyon-jang, Kim (p) 1655
Hyon-su, Park (p) 1655
Hyong-sung, Hwang (p) 1672
Hyung-kyu, The Rev. Park (p) 1667
I.G. Farbenindustrie 1190
Ibarrola, Agustin (p) 2309
Ibarruri, Dolores 2312
Iblacker, Reinhold 185
Ibrahim el Nur, Dr. Farouk (p) 215
ideology and torture 931
Idil Prison (Turkey) 2413
Ignotus, Paul (p) 184, 1338
Ihle, Siegfried 958
Ik-hwan, The Rev. Moon (Timothy Moon) (p) 1633, 1648, 1652
Ikeye, Damase (p) 720
Iko Andaur, Roberto (p) 518
Ikoku, Sam (p) 1810
Ilagan, Bonifacio (p) 1922
Ilic, Jovo (p) 3609
illegal arrest 460; *see also* arbitrary
illegal detention 187, 623; *see also* detention without charge
illegal executions *see* executions
illegal trial 829
illness, USSR 2670
Ilopango Women's Prison (El Salvador) 881, 884, 903, 907
Imam Issa, Sheikh (p) 857
immigration, US 3182
Immigration Act, US 3362
imperialism 292, 606, 635, 1266; US 578, 3086
imprisonment without trial *see* detention without charge
in camera trials *see* secret trial
Incident at Oglala, film 3218
incitement 818
incommunicado 49
incommunicado detention 342, 347, 350, 362, 363, 409, 517, 529, 537, 538, 623, 649, 652, 718, 845; El Salvador 895, 903; Guatemala 1278; Indonesia 1405; Morocco 1749, 1753, 1758-1760; Myanmar 1779; Pakistan 1827, 1830; Spain 2295, 2325; Syria 2359, 2361; Tunisia 2391; Turkey 2419; Uruguay 3492, 3494, 3502, 3518
India 125, 204, 259, 276, 291, 1345-1391; untouchables 204
Indians 455, 709, 711; (Amazon) 72; *see also* indigenous people; Native Americans
indigenous people 279, 280, 426, 440, 455, 851; Guatemala 1273, 1277, 1290
Indonesia 72, 149, 253, 256, 1392-1421; genocide 72
infants 342; *see also* children
informers 2906, 3108; US 3114, 3394
Ingraham, Barton L. 174
Ingram, Norman 930
inquisition, US 3050, 3254, 3255, 3289
insecticide Gamezán, torture 1273
Insein Prison (Myanmar) 1767, 1779
insulin shock treatment 2728
insulting head of state 1393
intellectuals 614
intelligence system, US 3140-3142
Inter-American Commission for Human Rights 402
internal exile 327; *see also* exile
Internal Security Act: Malaysia 1706-1716; Singapore 2058, 2062-2065, 2067-2069; S. Africa 2078, 2080, 2116, 2258; US 3255, 3362
International Civil Liberties Report 175
International Court of Justice 64
International Labor Organization 67
international law 64, 244
International Military Education and Training Program (US-sponsored counterinsurgency training) 382
International Workers of the World (IWW) 3091, 3180, 3199, 3234, 3248, 3274, 3328, 3362, 3363, 3444, 3448
internment camps 496, 497, 500; interrogation 184, 349, 370; US 3093
interrogation 1503; USSR 2488
interviews 1060, 1505
intifada 1504, 1568
IRA 2891-2897, 2899-2904, 2907-2911, 2914, 2917-2919, 2921; hunger strike 2892
Iran 53, 225, 238, 276, 278, 291, 1422-1484

Irangate 1472
Iranian Socialist Workers Party 1425, 1428, 1440, 1441, 1445, 1455
Iraq 191, 291, 1485–1498
Iratperiyakulam Army Camp (Sri Lanka) 2334
Irbid Prison (Jordan) 1587
Ireland 291, 3000; Northern 125; Republic of 1499, 1500; UK 2916, 2941; *see also* UK
Iriarte Iriarte, Alfredo (p) 542
Irish Republican Army *see* IRA
Irish Republican Brotherhood 2951
Irwin, Dr. Robert 2943
Isabel, Reina (p) 884
Ishak, Abdul Aziz (p) 1711
Islada Pinos Prison (Cuba) 782, 785
Islamic fundamentalism 856, 869, 870, 875, 1437
Islamic Revolutionary Tribunals 1425
Ismail, Samad (p) 1706, 1715
isolation cell *see* solitary confinement
Israel 56, 125, 279, 282, 291, 1501–1568; Occupied Territories 271
Issa, Namat 916
Issel, Shahieda (p) 2241
Isti'naf Prison (Egypt) 855
Isvan, Ahmet (p) 2416
Isvan, Reha (p) 2416
Italy 1086, 1153, 1569–1579
Itsundzu Prison (Comoros) 718
Itta, Dominic (p) 1835
Ivanov-Rusumnik, R.V. (p) 2622
IWW *see* International Workers of the World
Iyayi, Festus (p) 1811
Izetbegovic, Dr. Alija (p) 3607
Izmailovich, Alexandre (Sanya) (p) 2033

Jaafri, Mohammed Shahada (p) 1526
Jaber, Abdel Rahim (p) 1540
Jabora, Abdeen 1528
Jacinto, José Luis (El Salvador) (p) 231
Jackson, Bruce 3220
Jackson, C.S. (p) 499
Jackson, Sir Geoffrey (p) 3506
Jackson, George (p) 3119, 3161, 3221, 3298, 3414
Jackson, James 2623
Jackson, Jesse 754, 768
Jackson, Livia E. Bitton 1079
Jacobs, Timothy (p) 3325, 3326
Jacobsen, Quentin (p) 2146
Jacoby, Daniel 1733
Jae-mun, Lee (p) 1657
Jae-oh, Lee (p) 1657
Jae-won, Ha (p) 1672
Jägerstätter, Franz (p) 201, 1212
Jahn, Roland (p) 943
Jaimes, M.A. 3224
Jakobson, Michael 2624
Jama, Fahima Dahir (p) 2071
Jamaica 1580–1582
Jamal, Mumia Abu (p) 3258
James, Francis (p) 619
Jammal, Laila 1529
Jamyang (p) 605, 652
Jana, Priscilla (p) 2080
Janabi, Nabil (p) 1493
Jang-hyong, Lee (p) 1664
Janowska concentration camp (Nazi) 1176, 1206
Jansen, Ludvina (p) 1540
Jantjies, Moses (p) 2185
Japan 1583–1586
Japanese Americans 320, 3036, 3067, 3155, 3188, 3462; film 3334, 3345, 3452
Jaquith, Cindy 1455
Jara, Pedro (p) 562
Jara, Victor (p) 536
Jaramillo, Victor Hugo Rodríguez (p) 1274
Jaruzelski, General 1988
Jashari, Liman (p) 3592
Jasmines, Alan (p) 1922
Javers, Ron 2147
Jaworski, Seweryn (p) 1973
Jayeyarajasingham, The Rev. G (p) 2333
Jazani, Bizhan (p) 1431
Jazz Section (Czechoslovakia) 800, 806, 808, 823, 830, 833, 834
Jean-Louis, Sénèque (p) 1318
Jedda Island Prison (Bahrain) 429
Jeddah Prison (Saudi Arabia) 2044
Jehovah's Witnesses 122, 493, 771, 790, 927, 928, 1052, 1228, 1229, 1569, 1698, 1702; USSR 2476, 2525; US 3403, 3404; Yugoslavia 3592; Zaire 3614
Jele, Sylvia (p) 2110
Jendrzejczyk, Mike 1407
Jeng-sheng (Jing-sheng), Wei (p) 600, 602, 604, 610, 633, 637, 643
Jenkin, Tim (p) 2148, 2149
Jenkins, Lyll Becerra de 176
Jenness, Doug 3225
Jenness, Linda 2625
Jennings, Anthony 2947
Jernazian, Ephraim 2437
Jerudong Place of Detention (Brunei Darussalam) 482
Jesenská, Milena (p) 1009
Jesuits: El Salvador 897
Jeu Eon, Kim (p) 1671
Jewish Autonomous Region, USSR 2561
Jewish Councils 998, 1022
Jews 194, 278, 279, 316, 352, 389, 411–414, 979–1214; Bulgarian 1016; children 316; USSR 2033, 2470, 2477, 2484, 2506, 2520, 2561, 2583–2585, 2591, 2598, 2626, 2627, 2654, 2675, 2718, 2723, 2733, 2740, 2742, 2773, 2775, 2781, 2795, 2842, 2855; US 3484
Jezer, Marty 3226
Jharna, Abdul Razzaq (p) 1830
Jiang, Yeng (p) 658
Jihad 864
Jilava Prison (Romania) 2022
Jimmy, Ida (p) 1788
Jirous, Ivan Martin (p) 810
Jnaid Prison (Israel) 1508
Jo-hsi, Chen (p) 629
Joe Prison (Bahrain) 429
Joffe, Maria (p) 2626
Johannes, Axel (p) 1783, 1788
Johannesburg Fort No. 4 Prison (S. Africa) 2120
John Vorster Square Police Station (S. Africa) 2080, 2227
Johns, Stephen 2948
Johnson, Alexandra 1530
Johnson, Diane 3228
Johnson, L.B. 1629
Johnson, Lee Otis (p) 3062
Johnson, William O. 952
Johnson-Sirleaf, Ellen (p) 1687
Johnstone, Diana 1573
Joksimovic, Milorad (p) 3591
Jonas, Cecilia (p) 577
Jonas, Susanne 1290
Jonassohn, Kurt 72
Jones, Jeff 2150, 3229
Jones, Mary H. (Mother Jones) (p) 3230
Jones, Sidney 656, 657
Jones, Tahan (p) 3424
Jones, Ted 496
Jong Hwan, Lee (p) 1641
Jong-hon, Kan (p) 1655
Jong-in, Yu (p) 1663

Jong-kil, Choi (p) 1672
Jong-kon, Kang (p) 1655, 1667
Jong-kwan, Lee (p) 209
Joon-Shik, Soh (p) 1637, 1655, 1657, 1667
Jordan 1587–1589
Jorquera, Carlos (p) 530
Joseph, Helen (p) 2144, 2151, 2157
Joseph, Lafontant (p) 1315
Joseph, Sharon 1080
Joshua, Harris 2949
journalists/journalism 176, 347, 350, 360, 404, 411, 412, 418, 425, 460, 469, 481, 530, 574, 644–646, 651, 683, 751, 869, 1009, 1215, 1263, 1220, 1221, 1317, 1343, 1377, 1484, 1488, 1504, 1507, 1689, 1701; Nigeria 1807, 1818; Paraguay 1845, 1851; Philippines 1878, 1899, 1928; Poland 1944; Rhodesia 2003, 2006; Romania 2019; S. Africa 2096; S. Korea 1671; Spain 2321; Sudan 2346; Taiwan 2364; Togo 2382; Vietnam 3544, 3547, 3549
Joy, Cain 1809
Joyce, Lynda 3231
Judd, Gordon (p) 3232
Judenräte 1073; *see also* Jewish Councils
judges 583
judicial remedies: Latin America 200
Jung Hi, Pak 1661
Jungsheng, Zhang (p) 656
Jungwirth, Barbara 975
junta 370
Juntao, Wang (p) 610
Jurczak, Stefan (p) 1952
Juretzko, Werner (p) 953

Kabat, Carl (p) 3278
Kabui, Joseph (p) 1834
Kachovskaia, Irina (p) 2815
Kaggia, Bildad (p) 1615
Kai, Dr. Poh Soo (p) 2062
Kaitouni, Ali Idrissi (p) 1749, 1754
Kaitouni, Mohamed Idrissi (p) 1749
Kalandra, Závia (p) 1009
Kalden (p) 605, 652
Kalemba, Robert (p) 1701
Kaliisa, John (p) 2455
Kalisosok Prison (Indonesia) 1402
Kalnyshevsky, Petro (p) 2844
Kalp, Malcolm (p) 1477
Kalsang, Jampa (p) 605, 652
Kaluga Mental Hospital (USSR) 2496
Kamal, Ghassan (p) 1540
Kamalarajah, Thambimuthu (p) 2334
Kamenev, Lev (p) 2538, 2655
Kamhawi, Wajdi (p) 1539
Kaminska, Ruth T. (p) 2627
Kamiti Maximum Security Prison (Kenya) 1613, 1617, 1623
Kampuchea 279, 1590–1606
Kamunting Detention and Rehabilitation Camp (Malaysia) 1712, 1717
Kamyshlag Concentration Camp (USSR) 2855
Kananasbis Prison (Alberta, Canada) 500
Kandanga, Gertrude (p) 1788
kandooya, torture 2449
Kandyba, Ivan (p) 2628
Kane, H.F. 3234
Kanja, Waruru (p) 1615
Kantor, Alfred 1081
Kao, Chun Ming (p) 2370
Kaohsiung Seven (p), Taiwan 2364–2366
Kaplan, Carl 1456
Kaplan, Chaim A. (p) 1082
Kaplan, Karel (p) 836
Karaganda Prison Camp (USSR) 2759
Karagoz, Enver (p) 2418
Karagoz, Isilay (p) 2418
Karagueuzian, Dikran 3235
Karameh 282
Karapanayotis, torturer 1259
Karasulski, Leonard (p) 1982
Karavansky, Svyatoslav (p) 2712
Kardelj, Edvard 3599
Kareth, Nixon Robert (p) 1402
Karikari, Kwame (p) 1221, 1222
Kariseb, Hendrik (p) 1788
Kariuki, Josiah Mwangi (p) 1612
Kariuki, Mirugi (p) 1607
Kariuki, Ngotho (p) 1613
Kariuki, Wang'ondu (p) 1615
Karklins, Rasma 2629
Karpen Moffitt, Ronni (p) 571
Karski, Jan 1083
Karsow, Nina (p) 1955, 1974
Karunatilake, H.N.S. 2950
Käsemann, Elisabeth (p) 114, 382
Kashchenko Mental Hospital (USSR) 2589
Kateka, Markus (p) 1788
Kato, Wycliffe (p) 2457
Katsiaficas, George 178
Katt, Barb (p) 3126
Katyn Forest Massacre 279, 2887
Katz, Esther 1084, 1166
Katz, Joseph (p) 1085
Katz, Robert 1086, 1087
Katz, Sanford 3236
Kaufman, Edy 179
Kaufman, Natalie H. 3237, 3238
Kaura, Peter (p) 1835
Kavan, J. 809
Kavan, Jan (p) 837, 954
Kavuna, Clement (p) 1835
Kay, Regiwalda 490
Kayseri Closed Prison (Turkey) 2395, 2411
Kazan, Elia 2406
Kazan Special Psychiatric Hospital (USSR) 2568, 2733
Kazandris, Vanghelis 324
Kazim, Raza (p) 1828
Keane, Mairend (p) 2963
Kearney, Peadar (p) 2951
Kebd, Abdallahi Ould (p) 1722
Kebede, Kongit (p) 307
Keene, Beverly 380
Kehler, Randy (p) 3315
Kehr, Helen 1088, 1089
Kekchi Indians 1289
Kekilova, Annasultan (p) 2881
Kelley, Kevin 2952
Kelly, Mike (p) 1866
Kelsang Thalutsogentsang, Thubten (p) 605
Kempton, Murray 3239, 3240
Kenitra Central Prison (Morocco) 1749, 1756, 1760
Kennedy, Jane (p) 3241, 3242
Kennedy, Kit 559
Kenney, Annie (p) 2953
Kenrick, Donald 1090
Kentucky Prison (Zimbabwe) 3629
Kenya 4, 69, 125, 1607–1624
Kenyatta, Jomo 1612
Kepler, Roy (p) 3260
Kérékou, President Mathieu 445
Kerley, Gillan (p) 3106
Kermish, Joseph 1091
Kerr, Bob (p) 499
Kerr, Stanley E. 2438
Keryile Labor Reform Detachment (Xinjiang) 702
Kesse-Adu (p) 1225
Kessel, Sim (p) 1092
Ketsiot Detention Camp (Israel) 1536, 1541, 1542
Keun-tae, Kim (p) 1647, 1655
Key Agitator Index, FBI 3094

Keymba, Henry (p) 2458
Keyser, Christine 3244
Kgogung, Jairus (p) 2225
Khadour, Mohammed Ait (p) 1751
Khailo, Vladmir (p) 2658
Khaled, Leila (p) 1531
Khalil Ibrahim, Kamal (p) 876
Khamees, Dhabiya (p) 2889
Khami Prison (Rhodesia/Zimbabwe) 2012, 3629
Khan, Abdul Ghaffar (p) 247, 291
Khan, Asghan 1820
Khan, Jehangir Ahmed (p) 1830
Khatami, James 2153, 2154
Kheng, Tan Ka (p) 1716
Khiam detention center (Israel) 1532
Khin, U Aung (p) 1779
Khmer Rouge 279, 1590, 1591, 1593–1597
Khodorovich, Tatiana (p) 2631
Khomeini, Ayatolla Ruhollah 1425, 1426
Khonje, Thoza (p) 1699
Khorev, Mikhail (p) 2632
Khoury, Sam'an (p) 1507
Khrushchev, Nikita 2633
Khumalo, Duma (p) 2113
Khumalo, Sipho (p) 2092
Kidal Prison (Mali) 1719
Kidane, Meg 150
kidnapping *see* abduction
Kielar, Wieslaw (p) 1093
Kienas, Bernhard (p) 960
Kiev Helsinki Accords Group 2694
Kigali Prison (Rwanda) 2040
Kihoro, Wanyiri (p) 1607, 1611, 1614
Kilic, Sevgi (p) 2418
Killiber Frers, Alfredo A. (p) 347
killings 10, 38, 39, 161, 222, 257, 309, 318, 337, 342, 344, 346, 347, 349, 350, 353, 355, 367, 370, 371, 373, 375, 376, 379, 382, 385, 386, 399, 400, 402, 418, 421, 434, 453, 456, 459–461, 463, 469, 504, 508, 517, 524, 529, 530, 536, 554, 556, 571, 582, 589, 601, 618, 711, 712, 781, 851–853, 877, 879, 880, 896, 900, 1273, 1512, 2036, 2037; El Salvador 879, 880, 888, 896, 897; Guatemala 1281; Haiti 1314–1323; Mexico 1738; Poland 1966; S. Africa 2090, 2125; Suriname 2347; Uganda 2446–2463; UK 3002, 3008, 3009; US 3422; Uruguay 3513; Yugoslavia 3611; *see also* death squads; mass killings; torture
Kilo 7 Prison (Cuba) 771, 772
Kim Chi Ha (p) 301
Kimberlin, Brett (p) 3102
King, Dwight 1408
King, Martin Luther, Jr. (p) 68, 3047, 3084, 3311
K'ing-hsan, Teng (p) 694
Kinoy, Arthur 3245
Kinyatti, Maina wa (p) 1613, 1617
Kiraly, Karoly (p) 2023
Kirbas, Dr. Dursun (p) 2394
Kirberg, Enrique (p) 585
Kiri Kiri Prison (Nigeria) 1809, 1810
Kirk, Gwyn 2920
Kirkpatrick, Jeanne 901
Kirov, Sergei (p) 2538
Kirschen, Leonard (p) 2019
Kis, Danilo 181
Kissinger, Henry 578
Kissinger Commission 905
Kistemaker, Peter (p) 1368
Kiszely, Karoly (p) 1339, 1340
Kit, Chan Kok (p) 1715
Kitchin, George (p) 2634
Kitson, Dave (p) 2148, 2209, 2211
Kitson, Norma (p) 2155
Kittrie, Nicholas 3246
Kittson, Doris 1270
Klarsfeld, Serge 1094, 1095
Klebanov, Vladimir (p) 2865
Kleffner, Heike 3247
Kleg, Milton 278
Kleiman, Yehudit 1020
Klein, Gerda (p) 1096
Klein, Dr. Hans (p) 483
Klodzko Prison (Poland) 1969
Kloian, Richard 2439
Kluyev, Nikolai (p) 2784
Kmiecik, Jerzy (p) 2635
Knapp, Grace 2445
Knippers, Jan 2365
Knoll, Erwin 182
Knowles, Christopher 381
Koazo, Thomas (p) 505
Kober Prison (Sudan) 2338, 2339
Koch, S.S.-Sturmbannführer 1011
Koepke, Bettina (p) 884
Koeprue, Seviye (p) 2421
Koestler, Arthur (p) 80, 1097, 2313, 2314
Kogan, Eugen 1098
Kohan, John 2636
Kohn, Stephen 3249
Kohner, Hanna (p) 1099
Kohner, Walter (p) 1099
Koirala, B.P. (p) 1794
Koka, Drake (p) 2194
Kokchetau Camp (USSR) 2842
Kokkalis, Daniel (p) 1229
Kolb, Suzanne 519
Kolev, Dimiter (p) 483
Kolyma Labor Camp (USSR) 2539, 2778, 2795
Komisaruk, Katya (p) 3065
Kon-ho, Song (p) 1657
Kondofersky, Dr. Peter (p) 483
Konrad, George 183
Konrat, Georg von (p) 2156
Koon, Lim Hock (p) 2062
Kopelev, Lev (p) 2637, 2638
Koppers, Andre 2639
Kopru, Seviye (p) 2413
Kopvillen, Peeter 1957
Korchari, Abas (Jen Shan-hsueh) (p) 329, 659
Kordon, Diana R. 395
Korea, North 291, 1625–1631
Korea, South 1632–1673
Korea Christian Academy 1657, 1673
Korelava, John (p) 1835
Korematsu, Fred (p) 3067
Korman, Gerd 1100
Kornfeld, Paul (p) 1009
Koroveses, Perikles (p) 1246, 1261
Koryagin, Anatoly (p) 65, 2640, 2641, 2748, 2849, 2861
Kosík, Milan (p) 836
Kosma Utca Prison (Hungary) 1336
Kosmowski, Patrycjusz (p) 1982
Kossy, Daniel (p) 337
Kostava, Merab (p) 2734
Kosterin, Alexei (p) 2486, 2774
Kotan, Mumtaz (p) 2418
Kotane, Moses (p) 2267
Kouril, Vladimir (p) 808, 830
Kovalev, Sergei (p) 269, 2559, 2569
Kovalyov, Sergei (p) 2777
Kovno Ghetto 1139
Kowalska, Anka (p) 1958
Koykind, Andrew 560
Kpoleh, Gabriel William (p) 1686
Krama, Mohamed (p) 493
Kramer, Jane 1994
Kramer, Jesef 1153
Krasin, Victor (p) 2642
Krasnaya Presnya Transit Prison (USSR) 2472
Krasnov, Levitin (p) 2680
Kraus, Ota 1101

Krausnick, Helmut 1102
Kravchuk, Petro (p) 497
Kren, George M. 1103
Krickus, Richard 2644–2646
Krisher, Bernard 1649
Kristof, Nicholas D. 660
Kristol, Irving 352
Krivanck, Tomas (p) 808
Krokovay, Zsolt 1341
Kroonstad Prison (S. Africa) 2080, 2144, 2167
Kropiwnicki, Jerzy (p) 1973
Krugovikh, Aleksandr (p) 2847
Kua, Kla Soong (p) 1712
Kudayr, Muhammad Hasan Abu (p) 1534
Kudirka, Simas (p) 2647, 2648, 2834
Kuhn, Kathe 1034
Kui-yong, Shin (p) 1664
Kukk, Juri (p) 2823
Kulka, Erick 1101
Kumar, Dileep (p) 1382
Kumara, Santa (p) 1369
Kumsa, Martha (p) 132, 913
Kunsang-tse (p) 605, 652
Kunstler, William 3250–3252, 3324
Kuntui, Paulus (p) 1402
Kuomintang 595
Kuomintang Party, Taiwan 2364
Kurds 248, 1424, 1426, 1476, 1489, 1498; Syria 2352, 2356; Turkey 2394, 2395, 2398, 2402, 2407, 2411–2413, 2424
Kuria, Gibson (p) 1618
Kuron, Jacek (p) 1941, 1959, 1963
Kurshan, Nancy 3253
Kuti, Fela Anikulapo (p) 1812
Kutler, Stanley 3254
Kutumela, Lucky (p) 2159
Kuwait 1492, 1674
Kuweifiya Prison (Libya) 1689, 1694
Kuznetsov, Eduard (p) 2649, 2650
Kuznetsov, Sergei (p) 2721
Kwak, Byong-Kyu (p) 2651
Kwan, Ying (p) 663
Kwangju Massacre 1672
Kwanuka, Benedito (p) 2454
Kyi, Aung San Suu (p) 1767, 1768, 1773, 1774, 1776, 1777, 1779, 1781, 1782
Kyncl, Karel (p) 183, 810, 813, 838
Kyung-won, Suh (p) 1633
La, Nan Zing (p) 1779
Laabdi, Mohamed Zakaria (p) 1761
Laalou Prison (Morocco) 1760
Labatan Jirow Prison (Somalia) 2070, 2073
Laber, Jeri 811, 2408
Laber-King, Sharon (p) 1436
labor camp 73, 329, 702, 2539; *see also* slave labor
labor movement 457, 3197, 3199; *see also* unions
Lacaba, José (p) 1922
Lacaba-Echaniz, Erlinda (p) 1917
La Cabaña Prison (Cuba) 726, 757, 759, 776, 782, 785
Lacan, Jacques 370
Lacey, Hugh 897
La Escuelita (the Little School torture center) 391, 396
La Esperanza Prison (Mariona, El Salvador) 895, 899, 903, 905, 906
Laffin, John 184
LaForge, John (p) 3126
Lagos, Ricardo (p) 536, 590
Lahore Fort Prison (UK) 2915
Lai, Ying 661
Laird, Eileen 1929
Laird, Sally 2652
Lajejardi, Kambiz (p) 1445
Lake, Christopher 1247
Laks, Szymon 1104
Lama, Aang Dorje (p) 1792
Lamaan, Juan (p) 3065
Lambert, R.E. 2158
Lambrou, Vasilipos, torturer 1259
Lameda, Ali (p) 1627, 1630
Lamont, Corliss 3255
Lance, Christopher (p) 184
Landa, Malva (p) 2818
Landau, Saul 464
landowners 1287
Landrove, Angel (p) 726
Lange, Martin 185
Langer, Felicia 1533, 1534
Langer, Jo (p) 812
Langer, Lawrence 186, 1105
Langer, Oscar (p) 812
Langhoff, Wolfgang (p) 1106
Langmaid, Helen 1088
Langone, J. 2653
Lankapura, Charitha (p) 2329
Lanta Bur Prison (Somalia) 2070, 2073
Lanza Lopez, Rafael (p) 736
Lanzetti, Eric (p) 3200
laogai (laogaidui, labor reform camps) 702
Laos 1675–1679
La Perla Concentration Camp (Argentina) 367
La Pica Prison (Venezuela) 3526
Lapienis, Vlada (p) 2863
La Prensa 1798
Lapsley, Michael (p) 2256
Laquer, Walter 2654
Larca Tobar, Carlos (p) 536
Lardner, Ring, Jr. 3394
Larina, Anna (p) 2655
Larkin, Brian (p) 3375
Larrínga Prison (Spain) 2312
Larue-Langlois, Jacques (p) 495
Lashvili, Paolo (p) 2748
Laska, Vera (p) 1107, 1108
Lasocki, Wojciech (p) 1982
Lasota, Irena (p) 114
Lastuvka, Vladimir (p) 809
Latin America 6, 10, 46, 48, 81, 115, 118, 163, 185, 187, 189, 200, 237, 239, 246, 263, 274, 303; and US 3262
Latin American Political Prisoners Report 188
Latorre, Alejandro (p) 1851
Latvia 279, 1983, 2656, 2833
law 64, 162, 244, 829; S. Africa 2124, 2247
Law 209, "Defence of Public Peace and Liberty" 1837
Law 294, "Defence of Democracy" 1837
Lawasia conference 49
Lawrence Livermore Laboratory 3066
Lawton, Kim 2657–2659
lawyers 350, 530, 711; defence 943
Lazar, Edward 1774
Lazareva, Natalya (p) 2853
Lazim, Ebibi (p) 3609
Lean, Heng Boon (p) 1707
Leander, Birgitta 582
Leary, Mary E. 2366
Leavenworth Penitentiary (US) 3125, 3146, 3234, 3296, 3471
Lebanon 1680, 1681
Leber, Annedore 1110
Lebrón, Lolita (p) 3026, 3256
Lebu Prison (Chile) 585
Lecaille, Suzanne (p) 493
Lecumberri Prison (Mexico) 1737, 1742, 1744
Leczyca Prison (Poland) 1943, 1973
Lederer, Bob 3257–3259
Lederer, Jiri (p) 839
Ledien, Curt (p) 1177
Lee, Robert (p) 322
Lee, Stephen (p) 2148

Leeuwkop Prison (S. Africa) 2122
Lefever, Ernest 352
Lefortovo Prison (USSR) 2477, 2555, 2583, 2593, 2626, 2742, 2762, 2781, 2855
left, US 3079
legal structure, Zimbabwe 3631
legal system, Syria 2361
Leghari, Wazir (p) 1821
Legion of Mary 627
Le Grange, Louis (p) 2210, 2271
Lehter Street Prison (Nazi Germany) 1109
Leipelt, Hans (p) 1177
Leipman, Flora (p) 2660
Leisner, Father Karl (p) 184, 1155
Leitner, Isabella (p) 1111, 1112
Lekas, Theodosios (p) 324
Lekovac Prison (Yugoslavi, 3601a) 3592
Leloudas, Yiannis (p) 1230, 1251
LeMaire, Kerstin 125
Lemer, Calel (p) 1019
Lemke, Udo (p) 948
Lemke-Santangelo, Gretchen 3260
Lemmé, Janet E. (p) 1342
LeMoyne, James 2955
Lengyel, Olga (p) 1113
Leningrad Jail (USSR) 2661
Leningrad Psychiatric Prison Hospital (USSR) 2691
Lenkoe, James (p) 2082
Lenz, John M. (p) 1114
Leo, Ambrose (p) 1834, 1835
Leone, Bruno 3261
Leong, Lim Choo (p) 1715
Leonidas, Felipe "Wilson" (p) 1903
Lepoglava Prison (Yugo.) 3602, 3607-3609
Lermolo, Elizabeth (p) 2661
Lernoux, Penny 845, 1891, 3262
Lesotho 1682-1684
Letelier, Orlando (p) 530, 564, 571
letters 1094, 1115; Holocaust 1020; Nazi victims 1034
Letulle, Claude J. (p) 1116
Levasseur, Pat (p) 3082
Levasseur, Raymond (p) 3065, 3082, 3162
Levendokaterini (p) 1242
Levenson, Samuel 2956
Levi, Jefferey 757
Levi, Primo (p) 184, 1117, 1118
Levin, John (p) 3235
Levinson, Nan 3263
Levy, Claude 1119
Levy, Capt. Howard (p) 813-815, 3240, 3264
Levy, Victor (p) 867
Lévy-Hass, Hanna (p) 1120
Lewin, Hugh (p) 2162
Lewinska, Pelagia (p) 1121
Lewis, Fulton, Jr. 3289
Lewis, Jonathan 2664
Lewis, Primila (p) 1370
Lewis, Tom (p) 3058, 3060
Lewisburg Federal Correctional Institution (US) 3060, 3109, 3174, 3199, 3284
Lexington Federal Prison (US) 3263
Lexington High Security Unit (US) 3040, 3043, 3062, 3491; film 3434
Leyte 26 1936
Li, Fu-jen 663
Li-I-Chi 598
Libanio Christo, Carlos Alberto (p) *see* Frei Betto
Liberia 1685-1688
Libertad Men's Prison (Uruguay) 3503, 3507
Libo, Yang (p) 621
Libya 1689-1694
Licha, Doña (p) 3273
Liebknecht, Karl (p) 940
Lifton, Robert Jay 664, 1122
Light, J. 1799
Lilongive Prison (Malawi) 1699
Liman, Dr. Hilla (p) 1218
Lindorff, Dave 1291
Linfield, Michael 3266
Linke, Maria Zeitner (p) 2665
Lipper, Elinor (p) 184, 2666
Lippert, Ronald P. 758
Lis, Bogdan (p) 1948, 1951, 1953, 1963, 1979
Lisbon Penitentiary (Portugal) 1998
Lisovy, Vasyl (p) 2831
List, Dave 3267
list of names 184, 1095
literature 62, 129
Lithuania 279, 2553, 2644-2648, 2733, 2734, 2818
Litwak, Leo 3268
Litynski, Jan (p) 1941, 1982
Livanos, Dionysios (p) 1230
Liveright, Betty 3269, 3270
Liveright, Herman 3269, 3270
Lobsang, Chamba (p) 677
Lobsang Dhondup 601
Lobsang Wangchuk, Geshe (p) 652
Lodronio, Rosario (p) 1903
Lodz ghetto 279, 979, 1027
Loebl, Eugen (p) 816
Loest, Erich 958
Lofland, John 3272
Lohia, Dr. Ram Manohar (p) 2915
Lok, Po 665
Lombardo, Joe 2315
Long Kesh/Maze Prison (UK) 2891, 2914, 2917, 2919, 2921, 2966, 2997
long term: Indonesia 1393, 1399; Iran 1426; Laos 1675-1678; Malawi 1697; Malaysia 1715, 1717; Morocco 1751; Paraguay 1847; Portugal 1994; Romania 2031; Saudi Arabia 2046, 2047; Singapore 2059, 2062, 2066; S. Korea 1654, 1663; S. Vietnam 3562; Spain 2310; Syria 2352, 2353, 2356, 2358; USSR 2508, 2544, 2552, 2555, 2586, 2587, 2600, 2626, 2629, 2655, 2660, 2661, 2665, 2666, 2699, 2700, 2704, 2712, 2714, 2717, 2721, 2739, 2756, 2763, 2788, 2812, 2822, 2836; UK 2968, 2984; US 3026, 3031, 3035, 3385, 3470 (*see also* Puerto Rico); Uruguay 3503; Vietnam 3528, 3529, 3544, 3548
long term prisoners 209, 231, 337, 603, 618, 625, 630, 636, 663, 667, 668, 701, 746-748, 772, 774, 785, 786, 788
Loon, Albert ("Red") (p) 2601
Lopes, Dr. Humberto (p) 1998
Lopez Castillo, Edmigio (p) 736, 770, 771, 785
López Rivera, Oscar (p) 3130, 3146
López Vila, Carlos (p) 522
López, Alfredo 3273
López, Eugenio, Jr. (p) 1939
Lopez, George A. 262, 263
López, L. 1864
Lorant, Stefan (p) 1123
Lorca Tobar, Carlos (p) 520, 590
Lornes, Isabel (p) 714
Lorscht, Lucy (p) 559
Los Angeles Eight (p) 3033, 3116, 3309
Lousman, Bohumil (p) 821
Lovegren, Levi (p) 680
Lowe, Ben 2957
Lowell, Robert (p) 301
Lowenthal, Max 3274
Lowrie, Dr. Howard (p) 499
loyalty oath/test: Poland 1964; US 3255, 3289, 3377, 3394

Lozáno, Armando (p) 1737
Lu, Chen (p) 602
Lubarsky, Cronid (p) 2668
Lubarsky, Kronic (p) 2867
Lubyanka Prison (USSR) 2509, 2510, 2560, 2666, 2742, 2762, 2764, 2784, 2819, 2820, 2822, 2855, 2866, 2870
Lucero, Mireya (p) 884
Luel, Steven A. 1124
Lugo, Olmedo (p) 3522
Luis Boitel, Pedro (p) 765
Lukas, J. Anthony 3275
Lukman, Salihu Mohammed (p) 1807
Lukyanenko, Levko (p) 2715, 2844
Lule, Yusef 2459
Luli, Father Ndoc 327
Luneto, Ernesto (p) 1922
Lung, Teo Soh (p) 2059, 2068
Lunt, Lawrence K. (p) 759
Luntz, Prof. D.R. 2691
Lunyou, Zhou (p) 621
Lurigancho Prison (Peru) 1855
Luryi, Yuri 2669
Lussu, Emilio (p) 1575
Luttwak, Edward 190
Lutuli, Chief Albert 2088
Lutz, Larry 2165
Luwum, Dr. Janani (p) 2452
Luxemburg, Rosa (p) 301, 939, 940
Luzira Prison (Uganda) 2449
Lvov Ghetto 1176
Lwin, Aye (p) 1767
Lynch, Kevin (p) 2917
Lynn, J. 1458
Lyons, Paul 2670
Lysak, Pyotr (p) 2691
Lytton, Constance (p) 301, 2958, 2959

Mabahith al-'Amma Prison (Saudi Arabia) 2046
Mabhida, Moses (p) 2267
Mabilangan, Soledad (p) 1903
Mabuza, Obert Mpangele (p) 2348
Macchi Torres, Yessie (p) 3515
Macedonia 1236
Machacek, Ales (p) 809
Machava Prison (Mozambique) 1762
Machira, Blaise (p) 1699
machismo 68
Machlejd, Wanda 1125
Macias Nguema, Francisco 106
Mack, Myrna (p) 1298
Mackay, Ruth 2316
Madagascar 1695, 1696
Maddy, Yulisa Amadu (p) 2054
Madisson, Tiit (p) 2823
MADRES 884
Maduna, Penuell 2166
Magadan Transit Prison (USSR) 2795
Magalhaes, Vera Silva Araujo (p) 291
Magalis, Elaine 382
Magarik, Alexei (p) 2470
Magee, Ruchell (p) 3118, 3387
Mager, Andy (p) 3267
maggots 1963
Magilligan Prison (UK) 2946, 2966
Magnes, Judah 3276, 3277
Magno, P 3278
Maguire, Dorothy (p) 2963
Maguire Seven 2942
Mahabad Prison (Iran) 1448
Maharaj, Mac (p) 2211
Mahlangu, Solomon (p) 2236, 2255, 2286
Mahmoudi, Ashraf (p) 1461
Maidana, Dr. Antonio (p) 1843, 1847
Maidanek (Majdanek) Concentration Camp (Nazi) 996, 1015, 1204
Maidstone (Ship) Prison (UK) 2966
Maitra, Apurba 2960
Maja-Pearce, Adewale 1811
Majid, Datuk Abdullah (p) 1715
Major, John 3279
Makeyeva, Sister Valeria (p) 2606
Makhoere, Caesarina Kona (p) 2167
Makindye Prison (Uganda) 2459
Makiya, Kanan (pseud. of Samir Khalil) 191, 1494
Mak'Onyango, Otieno (p) 1613
Makowski, Brigid Sheils (p) 2903
Makris, Thanasis (p) 1229
Makronisos Prison (Greece) 1242
Mal Ja, Kwon (p) 1661
Malamud, Liliana (p) 399
Malamud-Goti, Jaime 192
Malatya Prison (Turkey) 2418
Malawi 152, 1697–1705
Malaysia 1706–1717
Maldives 1718
Mali 1719, 1720
Malianga, Moton (p) 3629
Malik, Amita 439
Malina, Judith (p) 301, 475
Malinowitz, Harriet 3280
Maliqi, Nexhat (p) 3592
Malkani, K.R. (p) 1371
Malmaison Prison (Romania) 2029
Malsagoff, S.A. (p) 184, 2672
Malvinas Concentration Camp (Argentina) 367
Mama Dorothy (p) 2167
Mamak Military Prison (Turkey) 2411, 2412
Mampe, Bellington (p) 2116
Man, John 1606
Manandhar, Bishnu Bahadur (p) 1792
Manchester, Leonard 3282
Mandela, Nelson (p) 2077, 2088, 2089, 2117, 2169–2174; biography 2128, 2139, 2183, 2272, 2274; film 2137, 2141, 2199, 2200, 2202, 2203; letters 2183; Pollsmoor Prison 2204; Robben Island 2196; speeches 2170–2172, 2175
Mandela, Winnie 307, 2077, 2088, 2097, 2151, 2175, 2179, 2287
Mandelshtam, Nadezhda 2673, 2674
Mandelshtam, Osip (p) 2673, 2783
Mandera Prison (Somalia) 2073
Mangakis, George (p) 1233, 1249
Mango, Paul (p) 3065
Manjaca Camp Prison (Yugoslavia) 3590
Manning, Carol (p) 3162
Manning, R.A. 2675
Manning, Richard 2179
Manning, Thomas (p) 3162
Mansilla, Ariel (p) 562
Manz, Beatriz 1293
Mao, Tse-tung 615, 616, 632, 651, 673
Maoist MRPP, Portugal 1993
Mapalala, James (p) 2372
Mapanje, Jack (p) 1699
maps 197, 198
Mar del Plata Naval Base (Argentina) 367
Marakalla, Deborah (p) 2110
Maran, Rita 931
Marange, Valerie 193
Marchant, Charlotte (p) 3372
Marchenko, Anatoly (p) 2474, 2546, 2676–2678, 2779
Marchesini, Victor Carlos 342
Marcos, Pres. Ferdinand 1875, 1881, 1891, 1897, 1925
Marcus, Paul 1124
Marek, Vlastimil (p) 808
Margaronis, Maria 2409
Marian, Tiberiu (p) 2026
marijuana 3407

Marin, Edison (p) 3513
Marin, L.M. 3525
Marinetti, Roseta (p) 585
Mario, Mencia 761
Marion, George 3283
Marion, Kitty (p) 2961
Marion Prison (US) 3026
Mariona Prison *see* La Esperanza
Markievicz, Countess Constance de (p) 2941, 2956, 2962, 2966
Marko Prison (Hungary) 1342
marriage, forced 121
Marroquín, Hector (p) 1735, 1739, 1746
Marrus, Michael R. 194, 1126, 1127, 1127a
Marsh, Dave 1812
Marshall, Eliot 2679
Marston, John 1600
Martí, Ana (p) 342
martial law 443, 601, 603, 606, 674, 675; Jordan 1588; Philippines 1873–1876, 1894, 1898, 1900, 1915, 1922, 1923, 1925, 1927, 1929, 1931; Poland 1944, 1962, 1970, 1977; Rhodesia 2008, 2009; S. Korea 1652; S. Vietnam 3582; Taiwan 2362, 2367, 2369; Turkey 2394, 2399, 2424; UK 2947; Zimbabwe 3625, 3626; *see also* state of emergency; state of siege
Martin, Andre 2680
Martin, Gilbert 2583
Martin, Ramela 2440
Martín-Baró, Ignacio (p) 897
Martinez, Gabriel (Argentina's ambassador to the U.N.) 371
Martínez Lara, Dr. Alfredo Samuel (p) 727, 905
Marton, K. 2681
Maryniak, Irena 2684
Marzani, Carl (p) 3284
Mascarenhas, Dom José (p) 1995
Mashabane, Jacob (p) 2078
Mashed Prison (Iran) 1448
Mashego, Johannes (p) 2159
Mashinini, Emma (p) 2181
mass arrests 529, 536, 853, 856, 858, 859, 862, 870, 871; Poland 1941; S. Africa 2106, 2140, 2250; Thailand 2376; Turkey 2408, 2412, 2413; US 3067; Uruguay 3511
mass imprisonment 375; Indonesia 1393–1395, 1399–1401; USSR 2511
mass killings 38, 39, 149, 257, 264, 278, 349, 359, 362, 367, 421, 452, 524, 528, 612, 674, 710, 896, 1293; Armenia 2426–2445; East Timor 1396, 1400, 1407; El Salvador 887–889; Indonesia 1404, 1405; Myanmar 1771, 1772, 1780; Namibia 1788; Nazi 979–1214; Peru 1855, 1856, 1871; Serbia 2051; Somalia 2071; Spain 2314; Sri Lanka 2329; Sudan 2343; Syria 2355; Tunisia 2386; USSR 2633, 2654, 2887; *see also* killings
Massera, Admiral Emilio 370
Massera, José-Luis 269
Masykur, Haji Abdul Ghani (p) 1394
Matchbox (Amnesty International) 195
Mateu Martinez, Juan (p) 2320
Mathausen concentration camp (Nazi Germany) 1138
Mathlaka, Martha (p) 2151
Mato Fagiani, Miguel (p) 3494
Matos, Huber (p) 741, 765, 774, 785
Matson, Charles O. (p) 3377
Matthews, Adam 465
Matthews, John (p) 2148, 2211
Matthiessen, Peter 3156
Matusevych, Olha (p) 2853
Matyunjwa, Vangine (p) 255
Mau Mau rebellion, Kenya 1612, 1616, 2938
Maumbe-Mukwana, Jack (p) 2455
Maung, General Saw 1767, 1780
Maurel, Micheline (p) 1128
Maurin, Peter (p) 3111
Mauritania 1721–1723
Mauritius 1724
Mauthausen concentration camp (Nazi Germany, Austria) 1018, 1075
May, Someth (p) 1601
Mayan Indians 1277
Mayekiso, Khola (p) 2110
Mayer, Arno J. 1129
Maysar, Ziyad Abu (p) 1534
Maze Prison *see* Long Kesh/Maze
Mazian, Florence 196
Mazumdar, Charu (p) 1380
Mazwembe, Luke (p) 2078, 2119
Mbanda, Hornisdas (p) 3
Mbatha, Dumisani (p) 2078, 2119
Mbeki, Govan (p) 2182, 2192
McAlister, Sister Elizabeth (p) 3058, 3271
McAuley, Chrissie 2963
McBride, Robert (p) 2246
McBroom, Marie (p) 1808
McCafferty, Nell 2964
McCarran-Walter Act, US 3033, 3362, 3369
McCarthy, Senator Joseph 3255, 3289
McCarthyism 3050, 3078, 3147, 3185, 3237, 3474
McCaughan, Ed 383
McColm, R. Bruce 197, 198
McCrackin, The Rev. Maurice (p) 3075
McCreesh, Raymond (p) 2899, 2917
McDonnell, Joe (p) 2909, 2910, 2917
McDonough, Roisín 2933
McElwain, Max 3285
McElwee, Thomas (p) 2917
McFadden, Robert 1775
McFadyean, Melanie 2933
McGeary, Johanna 1536
McGee, Doug 3286
McGeever, Jenny 2965
McGlynn, B. 817
McGuffin, John 2967
McKee, Grant 2968
McKenna, Sean (p) 2910
Mckenzie, J. 2685
McLaughlin, Sister Janice (p) 114, 2343
McLaughlin, Fr. Neil (p) 3271
McLennan, Barbara N. 199
McLoughlin, Pauline (p) 2964
McMahon, B. 3287, 3288
McNamara, Cynthia (p) 1864
McNamara, Robert 350
McWhirter, William 401
McWilliams, Carey 3289
Mdluli, Joseph (p) 2078, 2119
Means, Russell (p) 3094
Mechanicus, Philip (p) 998, 1130
Meckel, Thea (p) 2857
Meda, Luigi (p) 1574
Medea, Benjamin 1330
media 258, 349, 464; medical: doctors 68, 76, 193, 244, 469, 517, 525, 526, 530, 539, 569, 1067, 1122, 1125, 1140, 1146, 1150, 1179, 2090; (S. Africa) 2235; (USSR) 2733, 2763; (UK) 2934; (Uruguay) 3505; ethics (S. Africa) 2284; experiments 279, 941, (Nazi) 992, (Nazi) 1040, 1078, 1116, 1122, 1125,

1138, 1140, 1150, 1157, 1168, 1190, 1192; malpractice 455
medicine 76, 208, 542
Medina, Adelita (p) 3282
Medina, Reinaldo (p) 760
Medvedev, Roy (p) 80, 2686–2689
Medvedev, Zhores (p) 2496, 2688–2690
Mee, Cornelia 2691
Meehan, Maura (p) 2963
Meenan, Rosemary (p) 2934
Meer, Fatima (p) 2183
Mehta, Ved 1372
Meinhof, Ulrike 977, 978
Meins, Holger (p) 978
Meisler, Stanley 2317
Mejia, José Reyes (El Salvador) (p) 231
Mejía Egocheaga, Fernando (p) 1855
Meknes Civil Prison (Morocco) 1748, 1756
Meletis, Constantine (p) 1230
Melgar, Hugo (p) 1273
Melgarejo Ponce, Aladino (p) 1855
Melgovnov, Sergey Petrovich (p) 2692
Melish, The Rev. William 3290
Melville, Samuel (p) 3291
Menchú, Rigoberta (p) 6, 468, 1295
Mendelevich, Yosef (p) 2477
Mendelsohn, John 1131
Méndez, Juan (p) 46, 353
Méndez, Juan E. 200
Méndez, Sara (p) 3493
Menebhi, Abdelaziz (p) 1756
Meneses, Juan (p) 536
Mengel, Jim (p) 3060
Mengele, Josef 279, 1150
Menina, 'Abdullah (p) 1692
Mennonite 3454
Menoyo, Eloy (p) 726
Menras, Andre (p) 3554, 3559
Mensah, Joseph (p) 1217
mental asylum 203; *see also* psychiatry
Merkt, Stacey (p) 3193
Merson, Allen 1132
Merton, Thomas 201
Meshko, Oksana (p) 2694
Mesyeux, Jean-August (p) 1320
Metrinko, Michael (p) 1477
Metris Prison (Turkey) 2418
Metzger, Max Josef (p) 201
Mexico 125, 1725–1747
Mey, Wolfgang 440
Meyer, Karl (p) 3159
Meyer, Matt 3292
Meyer, Reinhold (p) 1177
Meyerding, Jane (p) 3372
Mhango, Goodluck (p) 1699
Michaelis, Meir 1133
Michalski, Andrzej (p) 1982
Micheels, Louis J. (p) 1134
Michel, Jean 1135
Michelini, Zelmar (p) 375
Michillanca, Joel (p) 530
Michnik, Adam (p) 1941, 1948, 1951, 1954, 1979, 1982
Middle East 17, 191, 202, 225, 303
Middleton, Dorothy (p) 680
Middleton, Jean 2185–2187
Miedzyrzecze Prison (Poland) 1973
Mielies, Mlamli (p) 2185
Mielke, Fred 1140
Mignone, Emilo (p) 350
Mignone, Monica (p) 173, 371
Mihajlov, Mihajlo (p) 3597, 3600
Miká, Primo José Esono 909
Mikes, George 203
Mikhailov, Georgy (p) 2582, 2597
Mikhel'son, Frida (p) 1136
Mikolajska, Halina (p) 1964
Mikuyu Prison (Malawi) 1699
Mile II Prison (Gambia) 937
Milgrom, Ida (p) 2477
militarism 262, 263; Japan 1585; US 3143, 3371, 3375; *see also* Cold War; war
military 192, 349, 367, 528; courts 432, 594, 709, 710, 927, 1516, 1521, 1551, 1827, 1830; (Peru) 1854; (UK) 2947; crime 551; prisoners 548; prisons (US) 3357; torture 709; tribunals 342
military-industrial complex 3121–3129, 3131, 3132, 3137
military service 122; alternative 122; *see also* conscientious objectors
Miller, Arthur 1137, 2410
Miller, David (p) 3264
Miller, John M. 1410
Miller, Shelly (p) 3293
Miller, William D. 3294
Milwaukee Twelve (p) 3047, 3240
Min, Nay (p) 1777
Minassian, John (p) 2441
Minawa, Lt. Col. Farouk 2446
Mindszenty, Josef Cardinal (p) 2836
miners 819; UK 2977; US 3104, 3230
Ming, Shih 596
Mingdao, Wang (p) 677
Minh Nguyet, Thich (p) 3533, 3537, 3568
mining 324, 452
Minis, Anastassios (p) 1250
Minitong, Aloysius (p) 1834, 1835
Minkovice Prison (Czechoslovakia) 818
Minnou, Paul (p) 1834
Mintz, Israel (p) 2695
Miranda, Salvador Suarez (p) 1800
Mirandé, Alfredo 3295
Mirante, Edith 1776
Mirchuk, Petro (p) 1138
Mirek, Erich (p) 1019
Mirga, Roman (p) 1160
Miringtoro, Steven (p) 1835
Mirlo, Anita (p) 524
Mirov Prison (Czechoslovakia) 231, 814
Mirzazadeh, Nemat (p) 1473
Mishell, William M. (p) 1139
Mishenko, Vladimir (p) 2502
missionaries 613, 626, 628, 647, 655, 680
Missouri State Penitentiary (US) 3196, 3316
Mitchell, Elvis 2188
Mitchell, Hanna (p) 2969
Mitchell, Jared 2697
Mitchell, Richard H. 1585
Mitrovica Prison (Yugo.) 3607
Mitscherlich, Alexander 1140
Mityero, Ben Masaba (p) 2449
Mkalipi, Kwedi (p) 2239
Mkhatshwa, The Rev. Smangaliso (p) 2207, 2158
Mkwayi, Wilton (p) 2089, 2211
Mlangeni, June (p) 2089, 2110
Mncina, David (p) 2349
Moabit Prison (FRG) 967
Mobutu, General 3615, 3616
Mocuta, Ion (p) 2024
Moczulski, Leszek (p) 1973
Modelo Prison (Panama) 1832
Modzelewski, Karol (p) 1963
Moeng, Isaiah (p) 2080
Mofokeng, Connie (p) 2241
Mogale, Miriam (p) 2110
Moghadam, Val 1459
Mohamed, Datuk Seri Mahathir 1716
Mohamed, Elaine (p) 2241
Mohamed, Nasreen (p) 121
Mohamed Samara, Ahmad (p) 1539
Mohammad Ershad, President Hossain 433
Mohan, Jaq 441

Mohapi, Mapetla (p) 2078, 2119
Moi, Daniel arap 1611, 1622
Moise, Eddy (p) 1318
Mokesi, Francis Don (p) 2113
Mokotow Prison (Poland) 1941, 1973
Molale, Dean (p) 2145
Molebatsi, Caesar (p) 2165
Molekwa, Godfrey (p) 2081
Molobi trial 2118
Mommsen, Hans 1141
monitors 151, 167
monks 603, 606, 617, 675, 678
Monmondjo, Lecas Atondi (p) 720
Monrovia Central Prison (Liberia) 1686
Montague, Elizabeth (p) 1477
Montaluo, Juan 373
Montane Oropesa, Jesus 762
Montazeri, Ayatollah H. (p) 173
Montenegro, Miguel Angel (p) 903
Montes, Segundo (p) 897
Montevideo (Assembly and Declaration) 400
Montoneros 404
Montsitsi, Sechaba Daniel (p) 2080, 2095, 2195, 2237
Moodley, Strinivasa Rajoo (p) 2221, 2222
Moody, John 2698
Moon Crescent Detention Center (Singapore) 2058, 2062, 2063
Mooney, Tom (p) 3225
Moore, Barrington, Jr. 204
Moore, Howard (p) 3296
Moquete, Plinio (p) 848
Morais, Fernando 1142
Morales, Danilo (p) 1276
Morales, F. 3297
Morales, Horacio (Boy) (p) 1883, 1920
Morán, Gustafo Hirales (p) 1737
Mordovian Camp Complex (USSR) 2614, 2650, 2733, 2844, 2853, 2874
Morefield, Richard (p) 1477
Moreillon, Jacques 205
Moreira Alves, Marcio (p) 466
Moreno, Nahvel (p) 473
Morey, Katherine (p) 3168
Morgan, Lawrence Cloud (p) 3413
Morocco 1748–1761
Morón Prison (Cuba) 765
Moroni Central Prison (Comoros) 717
Moroz, Valentyn (p) 2699, 2701
Morozov, Mark (p) 2474
Morris, Fred B. (p) 465, 467, 478
Morrow, Lance 3298
Moshinsky, Efim 2703
Mosissa, Mulugetta (p) 919
Moskos, Charles C. 206
Moslem 483; *see also* Muslim
Moss, Glenn 2189, 2190
MOSSAD (Israel) 972, 1546
Mostafa Ibrahim, Mohamed (p) 876
Moszcz, Gustaw 1967
Mothers of the Plaza de Mayo 341, 342, 348, 350, 355, 362, 370, 395, 398, 401, 410
Mothopeng, Zeph (p) 2189
Motsoaledi, Elias (p) 2089, 2091
Mott, Newcomb (p) 2766
Moufhe, Isaac Tshifhiwa (p) 2247
Moumbaris, Alex (p) 2148
Mountjoy Prison (UK) 2928, 2956, 2962, 2966
Mouru, Dr. Muhammad (p) 860
Movement of Revolutionary Youth (Czechoslovakia) 832
Movement of the Revolutionary Left (MIR) 534
Movimiento Revolucionario Febrerista 1840
Movimiento Todos por la Patria (MTP) 343
Moyers, Bill 389
Mozambique 1762–1765
Mrosek, Margarethe (p) 1177
Mtafu, Dr. George (p) 1699
Mtintso, Tenjiwe Ethel (p) 2221, 2222
Mu'askar al-Fatah Prison (Yemen, PDRY) 3587, 3588
Mubarak, President Hosni 856
Mucha, Jiri (p) 819
Muehsam, Erich (p) 942
Muffs, Judith Herschlag 1144
Mufson, F. 2192
Mugabe, Robert 3633
Muge, Alexander (p) 1618
Muhammad Aissa, Sheikh Imam (p) 865
Muhlenkamp, Sr. Diane (p) 3193
Muigai, Andrew (p) 1618
Mujahadeen (Mujahideen, Mohahedine) 321, 1437
Mukong, Albert (p) 493, 494
Mulhim, Imad (p) 1587, 1588
Muller, Filip (p) 1145
Muller, Jiri (p) 108
Munich Olympics (1972) 52
Muñoz, Carlos (p) 577
Muñoz, Viola (p) 530
Muñoz Marin, Luis (p) 3273
Muñoz Poutay, Jorge (p) 590
Munro, Robin 609
murder *see* killings
Murego, Donat (p) 2040
Murphy, F. 1865, 1866
Murphy, Fred 853, 1462
Murphy, Jamie 2193
Murray, Raymond 2934
Murray, Vernon 3049
Murray-O'Hair, Robin (p) 3331
Musa, Alhaji Balarabe (p) 1807
Musa, Omari 2004, 2194, 2195
Muselin, Peter (p) 3179, 3394
Museveni, Yoweri 2447
music 800, 806, 808, 823, 830, 833, 834, 857, 1049, 1104, 1137, 1156, 1231, 1341, 1812; USSR 2826
musicians 823, 830–834, 2470, 2842
Musisi, Daniel (p) 2455
Muslim Brotherhood 856, 869, 872
Muslims 1778, 1876; Indonesia 1404; Saudi Arabia 2045; Serbia 2051; Yugoslavia 3601
Musoke, Fr. Clement (p) 2454
Mussolini 1133, 1579
Muste, A.J. (p) 58
Mutai, Chelagat (p) 1615
Mutambara, Arthur (p) 3626
Mutasa, Didymus (p) 2005
mutilation 6; El Salvador 878, 884
Mutnick, Deborah 3299
Muzaffar, Chawdra (p) 1708
Muzorewa, Abel (p) 3630
MVD, USSR 2795
Mwaanga, Vernon (p) 3624
Mwithaga, Mark (p) 1615
Mxenge, Griffiths (p) 2081
Myanmar (Burma) 1766–1782
Myers, Gerald E. 1169
Myint, Aye (p) 1777
Myint, Dr. Zaw (p) 1782
Mylonas, George (p) 1238, 1251, 1253
Myoung Guk, Chang (p) 1641
mythology 370

NAACP 3148
Nabdel, Alireza (p) 1436
Nabi, Muhammad Hassan (p) 2046
Nablus Prison (Israel) 1524, 1539
Naddaf, Imad (p) 2360
Nadler, Eric 1846

Naeve, Lowell (p) 301, 3300
Nafha Prison 1527, 1528
Nagad Prison (Djibouti) 841
Nahon, Marco (p) 1146
Nai-fu, Pu (p) 705
Naidoo, Indres (p) 2196, 2228
Naimski, Piotr (p) 1941
Naipaul, V.S. 386
Nair, Vijayan (p) 1382
Najaf, Parvin 1463, 1465
Nak Chung, Paik (p) 1670
Nakasero Prison (Uganda) 2457
Namibia 53, 314, 1783-1789, 2273
Nammary, Kamal (p) 1540
Namo, Dalle (p) 1373
Namvar, Majid 1465
Nanabhai, Shirish (p) 2111
Nangoloh, Phil Ya (p) 1786
Nanziri, Theresa (p) 2446
Napso, Azat (p) 1558
Napsu, Izat (p) 1552
Naqqash, Farida (p) 865
Naraghi, Ehsan (p) 1466
Narain, Jai Prakash (p) 1375
Narayan, Shri Jayaprakash (p) 1362, 1374, 1387
Narayan, V.S. (p) 1382
Narcisse, Daniel (p) 1318
Nargolkar, Vasant (p) 1376
Nasta, Liviv (p) 2019
Nasution, Adnan Buyong (p) 1399, 1414
Natanson, Philip (p) 867
Nateg, Dr. Homa (p) 1473
Nathanson, Nathaniel 3301
Nation, Carry (p) 3302
National Liberation Army (ELN) 453/54
National Penitentiary (Paraguay) 1847
national security 257, 350, 472; US 3205, 3430; *see also* anti-communism
National Security Council: Turkey 2412, 2413; Uruguay 3509
National Security Court, Somalia 2071
national security doctrine 81, 262, 263; Uruguay 3495
National Security Law: S. Korea 1632, 1633, 1656, 1663, 1664; Taiwan 2363
National Security Office, Nicaragua 1795
National Security Service, Somalis 2073
national security state, USSR 2664
Native Americans, US 278, 3094, 3224, 3356, 3368, 3432, 3435, 3460
Natteno, Santiago (p) 529
Naumann, Bernd 1147
Naumberg Prison (GDR) 960
Navas, Maximiliano Castro (p) 903
Navy Engineering Institute (Argentina) 367
Nayar, Kuldip (p) 1377
NAYO trial, S. Africa 2118
Nazi Germany *see* Germany, Nazi
Nchabeleng, Peter (p) 2159
Ndayambaye, Innocent (p) 2040
Ndlovu, Stanley (p) 2225
Ndongmo, Bishop (p) 494
Necessity defense 64
Nefolovhodwe, Pandelani (p) 2223
Negga, Col. Belay 916
Neier, Aryeh 209, 210, 376, 387, 763, 868, 901, 3304
Nekipelov, V.A. (p) 2852
Nekipelov, Victor (p) 2723
Nelson, A. 764
Nelson, Juanita (p) 3372
Nelson, Lars-Erik 3305
Nelson, Steve (p) 3088
Nemcova, Dana (p) 824
Nemeth, Mary 902
Nepal 1790-1794
Nestor, Stelios (p) 291, 1230, 1251
Netherlands 1143; Jews 1017, 1018
Netzach, Avraham (p) 2704
Neuberg Prison (Germany) 942
Neubrandburg concentration camp (Nazi Germany) 1128
Neve Tertza (Tirzeh) Prison (Israel) 1506, 1562
Nevinson, Evelyn (p) 2970
New Castle Prison (UK) 2959
New Left 178
New York Eight (p) 3184, 3312, 3323, 3240
New York Times 1844
New York Twenty-One (p) 3397, 3399, 3400
Newman, Anne 2206
Newman, Frank C. 565
Newton, Huey (p) 3070, 3185, 3216, 3386
Ng, Cecilia (p) 1716
Ng'ang'a, Mukaru (p) 1607
Ngaragba Prison (Central African Republic) 504, 505
Ngau, Harrison (p) 1716
Ngoli, Jacques (p) 505
Ngomane, Eric (p) 2159
Ngor, Haing (p) 1602
Ngoyi, Lilian Mazediba (p) 2151, 2163, 2221, 2222
Ngudle, Looksmart (p) 2082, 2111, 2116
Nguyen, Thi Hong (pseud.) (p) 3569
Nhuan, Thich Duc (p) 3528
Nic Giolla Easpaig, Aine (p) 2971
Nic Giolla Easpaig, Eibhlin (p) 2971
Nicaragua 64, 161, 246, 1795-1802
Niccolls, S. Thomas 212
Nicgorski, Sister Darlene (p) 3114, 3117
Nickel, James W. 213
Nicolas, Vidal de (p) 2309
Niesewand, Peter (p) 2003, 2006
Niewyk, Donald L. 1148
Nigde Prison (Turkey) 2411
Niger 1803
Nigeria 4, 1804-1818
Night and Fog decree 370
Niitsoo, Nictor (p) 2823
Nikitin, Alexei (p) 65
Niklus, Mart (p) 132
Ninio, Marcelle (p) 867
Niño, Alvaro (p) 714
Nino, Carlos Santiago 214
Nitti, Francesco Fausto (p) 1575
Nixon, Richard 3480, 3553
Nkoli, Simon (p) 2102, 2217
Nkomo, Joshua 3633
Nkosi, Stanley (p) 2189
Nkrumah, Kwame 1227
NKVD 2488, 2490, 2828
Nobel Peace Prize 380, 1768
Noble, John H. (p) 2705
Noel, Emmanuel (p) 1314
Nolasco, Cynthia (p) 1927
Noman, Taha al (p) 2346
Nomberg-Przytyk, Sara (p) 1149
noncooperation 301; *see also* resistance
nonviolence 301, 606
nonviolent resistance 201
Noriega, General Manuel 1832
Norilsk Prison Camp uprising 2609, 2795
Norman, Colin 388
North Africa 202
North America 305
North End Prison (S. Africa) 2264
Northern Ireland 149, 2890-2897, 2899-2904, 2906-2911, 2914, 2917-2919, 2921-2927, 2929, 2930,

2932-2936, 2939, 2942-2948, 2952, 2954, 2955, 2957, 2963-2965, 2967, 2968, 2973-2976, 2986, 2994-2997, 3002-3006, 3008-3010, 3014, 3015; women 2933
Notaras, Gerassimos (p) 1230, 1251
Novakovic, Nikola (Yugoslavia) (p) 231
novels, fiction writing 6, 176, 216, 235, 515, 516
Novick, Michael 3308, 3309
Novoa Ponce, Carlos (p) 727
Novodvorskaya, Valeriya (p) 2513
Nowlan, B. 3310
Noya Murati, Carlos (p) 3418
Nsawam Prison (Ghana) 1216-1219, 1223, 1224, 1226
N'Sunda, Kisunga (p) 3612
Nu, U (p) 1767
nuclear: 502, 503; energy, US 3153; missile sites, US 3364; power, US 3468; protest, UK 2920; silos 3125-3127; war 3198, 3426, 3439-3442; war, US 3125, 3126, 3144, 3232, 3278, 3303, 3307, 3364, 3413, 3490; weapons 64, 1513, 1561, 1563, 1565, 3066; weapons, UK 2898, 2913; weapons, US 3378
Nudel, Ida (p) 2727
Nugent, Ciaran (p) 2919
Nugent, Mairend (p) 2964, 2965
Nughes, Juan Angel (p) 346
Nugroho, Bamban "Isti" (p) 1394
Nukewatch 3127
No. 2 Labor Reform Detachment (Qinghai) 702
Núñez, C. 3508
Nunez, Gilberto (p) 585
Nunez, Osiel (p) 536
Nunnelley, William 3311
Núñoz Alarcón, Juan Rene (torturer) 567
Nuoera, Louis 1135
nuns 601; Tibet 603, 606, 621, 675, 678
Nurdy, Julian 869
Nuremberg defense 1538
Nuremberg Principles 64, 3267
Nuremberg War Trials 1201
Nusa, Pandu (p) 1411
Nusa Kambangan prison island (Indonesia) 1411
Nusrat, Mirza Ahmad (p) 1821
Nwana, Olivier (p) 493
Nyagumbo, Maurice (p) 3629
Nyakato, Evelyn (p) 2459
Nyembe, Dorothy (p) 2149
Nyiszli, Miklós (p) 1150
Nylstroom Prison (S. Africa) 2249
Nyoike, Kimani wa (p) 1607
Nyunt, U Than (p) 1779

Oakely, R.B. 1412
Oakland Seven (p) 3185, 3240
OAS Convention against Torture 244
Oaxaca State Prison (Mexico) 1737
Obadele, Imari Abubakari (p) 3030, 3076, 3476
Obama, Bishop Ildefonso 908
Oberski, Jona (p) 1151
Obote, Milton 2447, 2456, 2459
Obregón, Alejandro (p) 1800
O'Brien, S. 1538
O'Brien, Sally 3312
Ocampo, Saturnino (p) 1899, 1928
Ocana Prison (Spain) 2319
Occoquan Workhouse (US) 3122, 3420, 3423
Occupied Territories (Israel) 271
O'Connor, Bernard (p) 2934
Odinga, Raila (p) 1613
Odinga, Sekou (p) 3270
O'Donnell, Barry (p) 3006
O'Donovan, Rose 2966
O'Farrell, Sean (p) 3006
Official Secrets Act, Rhodesia 2006
Ogden, Don 3313, 3315
Ogden, Rose 3314
Ogorodnikov, Aleksandr (p) 2469
O.G.P.U. (new Cheka) 2509
Oh, Chng Min (p) 2062
Oh, Tan Kim (p) 2062
O'Hara, Patrick (p) 2899, 2917
O'Hare, J.A. 668
O'Hare, Kate R. (p) 3316-3319
Ohio Seven 3082, 3086, 3162, 3215, 3269, 3313
Ojeda Rios, Filiberto (p) 3031, 3158
Ok-Kwan, Paik (p) 1655
Okubo, Miné (p) 3188, 3320
Okullo, Ambrose (p) 2455
Ola, Akinshiju 3321-3327
Olarra, José María (p) 2325
Olel, Odhiambo (p) 1607
Olenko, George (p) 2708
Olhovych, Orest 2709
Olimpo Prison (Argentina) 68, 367
Olite, Raphael (p) 1876
Oliver, April 1814
Olteanu, Ion (p) 2026
Omaar, Rakiya 215
O'Malley, Padraig 2976
Oman 225
Omega 367
Omidi, Behzad 1467
Onaindia, Dr. Xavier (p) 2295
Oneg Shabbat Archives 1165
Onganía, General 350
Opava Women's Prison (Czechoslovakia) 802
Operation Lypistarata 466
Operation Phoenix: El Salvador 878, 887
Oppenheimer, J. Robert (p) 54, 3279
Orangeburg Massacre, US 3394
ORDEN (El Salvadoran gov. terror organ) 879, 896
O'Reilly, Kenneth 3329
Orentlicher, Diane 1590
Organization of American States *see* OAS
Orive Velez, José (p) 2320
Orlov, Yuri (p) 2547, 2564, 2711
Ornest, Ota (p) 839
Oropos Prison (Greece) 1231
Orozco, Antonio (p) 1726
orphans 75
Orpheé, Elvira (p) 6
Orr, Wendy (p) 2212
Orrick, William, Jr. 3330
Ortega, Ines Beatriz (p) 346
Ortiz, Sr. Diana (p) 1274, 1296
Ortiz Hernandez, Oscar Alexander 906
Ortiz Letelier, Prof. Fernando (p) 536, 544
Orwell, George 216
Osadchyi, Mykhailo (p) 2712
Osipova, Tatyana (p) 2713
Osmeña, Sergio III (p) 1939
Ossobleh, Jumaale (p) 2071
Otaegui Echeverría, Angel (p) 2298
Otfinoski, Steven 2213
Otieno, Vincent (p) 1613
Otto, J. 1413
Ottoman empire 279
Otu, Igbuku (p) 1815
Oualata Prison (Mauritania) 1722
Ouandié, Ernest (p) 494
Oufkir, Fatima (p) 1751

Owolowo, Chief Obafemi (p) 1816
Oyugi, Edward (p) 1609
Özer, Feyzullah (p) 2412
Ozyurt, Fatma (p) 2414

Pachman, Ludek (p) 836
pacifism 303, 499, 501, 930; US 3109, 3111, 3150, 3214, 3225, 3285, 3372, 3415; *see also* conscientious objection
Pack, Robert 612
Paco 1287
Padilla, Amado 570
Pagác, Stefan (p) 821
Pailodze, Valentina (p) 2734
Paita Cardozo, Omar (p) 3494
Pajibo, Ezekiel (p) 1688
Pakistan 279, 291, 1819–1831
Pál, Béla (p) 2026
Palach, Jan (p) 792
Palestine Liberation Organization 56, 271, 282; *see also* Occupied Territories
Palestinian National Congress 282
Palestinians 56, 972; and US 3163, 3309
Pall, Ellen 1297
Palmer Raids, US 3108, 3362, 3446
Palo (p) 1879
Paloczi-Horvath, George (p) 1343
Palubicki, Janusz (p) 1943
Pan Chiao Prison (Taiwan) 2369
Panaghoulis, Alexandros (p) 1232, 1245, 1258
Panama 1832, 1833; U.S. invasion 1833
Panin, Dimitrii (p) 2714
Pankhurst, Christabel (p) 2953, 2978
Pankhurst, E. Sylvia (p) 2979–2981, 2990
Pankhurst, Emmeline (p) 2953, 2982, 2983, 2987, 2990
Pankrac Prison (Czechoslovakia) 814
Pantaleón, José Rolando (p) 1274
Panther Fourteen 3397
Panther Thirteen 3199
Panzos Massacre 1289
Papadopoulos, Col. George 1237, 1259, 1262
Papandreou, Andreas (p) 1248, 1254, 1259
Papua New Guinea 1834, 1835
Paquette Habana 64
Parada, José (p) 529
Paradjanov, Sergei (p) 2503
Paraga, Debroslav (p) 3598
Paraguay 10, 65, 276, 279, 280, 1836–1853
parasitism: Romania 2014, 2026; USSR 2469, 2472
Parchomenko, Walter 2715, 2716
pardon of torturers 343
Parenti, Christian 3333
Parker Commission 193
parliamentarians 548
Parlicek, Frantisek (p) 839
parrot (Le perroquet), torture 1759, 1761
Partnoy, Alicia (p) 6
Parvilahti, Unto (p) 184, 2717
Pasadena Three (p) 3240
pass laws, S. Africa 2218
Passive Resistance campaign, S. Africa 2242
Passtoors, Helene (p) 2227
Pasternak, Grigory (p) 2718
Pathi, A. Aparam Biksha (p) 1382
patriarchy 68
Patterson, Judy 217
pau de arara (parrot's perch torture) 46
Paul, Alice (p) 3168
Paul, Anthony 1593, 3540
Paul, Evans (p) 1320
Pavese, Cesare (p) 1576
Pavia family *see* Beyrodt Pavia
Pavón Prison (Guatemala) 1274
Pawelczynska, Anna (p) 1152
Pawiak Prison (Nazi) 1152
Pawlowski, Jerzy (p) 1945
Payer, Cheryl 1414
Payne, Robert 3334
Pazienza, Francesco (p) 1573
peace: activism 1511, 1537, 1555, 1561, 1563, 1565; groups, USSR 2467; movement, UK 2920; movement, US 3272; protest 3023; protest, UK 2972, 2989; protest, US 3105
Peace Planters 3125–3127
peasants (campesinos) 548, 709, 851, 1836, 1847; El Salvador 879; Guatemala 1301; Mexico 1726, 1736; Peru 1854; Philippines 1875
Pechora Prison (USSR) 2490
Peck, Jim (p) 301, 3260
Peck, Winslow 571
Pedris, Edward H. (p) 2950
Peerman, Dean 766
Peking 651
Pelican Bay Maximum Security Prison (US) 3463
Pellecer Faena, Luis Eduardo (p) 1300, 1302
Peltier, Leonard (p) 3059, 3094, 3218, 3335, 3460
P.E.N 71, 132, 218, 1940
Pena, George Washington (p) 536
Pena, Michelle (p) 536
Peña Delgado, Jorge (p) 530
Peña Estrabao, Gregorio (p) 770, 771
Peña Hermosa Concentration Camp (Paraguay) 1840
Pendás, Miguel 3336
Peniche Prison (Portugal) 1997, 1998
Penintaex, George 791
penitentiaries 203; *see also* prisons
Penner, Jake (p) 500
Penner, Steve 3337
Penselin, Ulla (p) 971
Penson, Boris (p) 2614
Pentagon Papers 3178, 3389
Pentecostals, USSR 2529
Pentecostels 483
Pentothal 547
Pereyra Rossi, Enrique (p) 385
Pérez, Armando (p) 726
Pérez, José 392, 393, 3338–3342
Pérez Castro, Dr. Carlos Hernán 542
Perez de Jacinto, Maria (El Salvador) (p) 231
Perez Dopico, Hilda (p) 765
Perez Esquivel, Adolfo (p) 380
Perez Tobar, Carlos (p) 530
periodical 5, 8, 9, 11, 13, 22, 50, 71, 73, 211, 233, 288, 290, 312, 313, 765
Perkins, Pete 3343
Perkins, Sarah (p) 680
Perm Camp No. 35 (USSR) 2614
Perm Complex 2733
Perm concentration camps (USSR) 2844, 2874
Perm 36/1 Prison 132
Perotti, John (p) 3344
Peroutka, Ferdinand (p) 1009
Peru 125, 246, 593, 1854–1872
Pétain 934
Petawawa Prison (Ontario, Canada) 499, 500
Peters, Charles 3346
Peters, Edward 220
Petkus, Viktoras (p) 2645

Petrassevich, Cornel (p) 2020
Petrov, Vladimir (p) 2721
Phala, John (p) 2189
phallus 370
Phan, Boi Chau (p) 932
Pheto, Molefe (p) 2216
Pheto trial 2118
Phildius, Nils (p) 2351
Philippines 153, 263, 276, 1873-1940
Phillips, Glen S. 3347
Phillips, Herbert P. (p) 3289
Phillips, Margaret B. (p) 3348
Phillips, Raymond 1153
Phnom Penh 279
Phoenix program, S. Vietnam 3567
Phoshoko, Joel (p) 2159
photographs 275, 1071; Kampuchea 1595
Phuong, Nguyen Ngoc (p) 3551
physicians *see* medical: doctors
Piao, Ho (p) 2058, 2062
picana electrica 370; *see also* electric
Pierce, K.M. 768
Pies, Otto (p) 1155
Pietmaritzburg Prison (S. Africa) 2238
Piffarretti, Anna Maria (p) 402
Pinar del Rió Prison (Cuba) 765
Pine Ridge Sioux Reservation 3094
Pingel, Roy 394
Pingying, Hsieh 597
Pinmei, Gong (p) 231
Pinochet, General Augusto 81, 276, 517, 522, 524, 534, 535, 571, 577; *see also* Chile
Pinter, Harold 2410
Piola, Susana (p) 173
Piow, Wah (p) 2060, 2063
Pisarev, S.P. (p) 2691
Pityana, Barney Nyameko (p) 2221, 2222
Plakhotnyuk, Dr. Mykola (p) 2715
Planas, Charito (p) 114
Plant, Roger 748
plantados 737, 768, 771, 772, 785, 786; *see also* long term prisoners
Plantungan Women's Prison (Indonesia) 1406
Platt, T. 769
plays 549; *see also* theatre
Pledge of Resistance (p), US 3233
Plot 29 (mass grave) 528
Ploughshares, UK 2972
Plowshares 3198, 3293
Plowshares Eight (p) 3278, 3490
Plummer, Viola (p) 3312
Plyushch, Leonid (p) 2496, 2574, 2631, 2723, 2724, 2738, 2852
Pnevmatikos, Anghelos (p) 1230, 1251
Po-sun, Yun (p) 1667
Poarta Alba Prison (Romania) 2014
Pocco Pachaconas, Juan (p) 1855
Podrabinek, Aleksander (p) 2533, 2707, 2725, 2726
Podrabinek, Kyril (p) 2707
poetry: poets 129, 581, 782, 783, 857, 942, 1243, 1259, 1367, 1430, 1624; Romania 2021; S. Vietnam 3557; Spain 2309; USSR 2619, 2673, 2674, 2743-2747, 2758, 2783, 2784; UK 2995; US 3057, 3065, 3089, 3091, 3256, 3265; *see also* writers
Poggi, Stephanie 2217
Pogrebin, Letty 2727
Pogrund, Benjamin 2218
Poh, Chia Thye (p) 209, 2059, 2062, 2066
Pol Pot 69, 279, 1590, 1594
Poland 125, 279, 291, 990, 1941-1990
Polenberg, Richard 3349
police brutality 10, 793; US 3261, 3305, 3333, 3376, 3416
police riot 182
Polisario Front 1748
Politica Obrera 364
political crime 174; defined 281; US 3376
political prisoner, definition 3097, 3137; US conference 3107
political prisons 203; *see also* prisons
Political Women's Penitentiary (Romania) 2027
Poller, Walter (p) 1157
Pollsmoor Prison (S. Africa) 2088, 2264
pollution 498
Polo, Orlando (p) 743
Pomaks 483
Ponce, Exequiel (p) 544, 590
Ponomaryov, Anatoly (p) 2750
Popieluszko, Father Jerzy (p) 1952, 1966
Popoff, George (p) 2738
Popov, Nikolai (p) 2847
Popovych, Oskana (p) 121
Poresh, V. (p) 2581
Port Elizabeth 6 (p) 2225, 2241
Porteous, Jeffrey (p) 3191
Porter, D. Gareth 2376
Portland Four, US 3096
Portland Prison (UK) 2956
Portnoy, Alicia (p) 391, 396
Portugal 1991-1999
Posner, Michael H. 1541
Pospichal, Petr (p) 817
Post Stockade Prison (Liberia) 1685
Potchefstroom Female Prison (S. Africa) 2144
Potima Camp (USSR) 2670
Potma Prison complex (USSR) 2677
Potulice Prison (Poland) 1969
Poulo-Condor Prison (S. Vietnam) 3560
Powell, John William (p) 3028, 3254
Power, Jonathan 226
Powless, Herb (p) 3356
Pradenas, Marcela (p) 529
Pradith, Khamphan (p) 1676
Prague Spring 815, 1963
Prague Springtime of Freedom 836
Prasos brothers 327
Pratt, Geronimo ji Jaga (p) 3074, 3094, 3306
Preda, Florin (p) 2014
pregnancy 384
Prejean, Helen 227
prejudice 278
Presidio Stockade (US) 3199
Pressac, Claude 1158
Presser, Jacob (p) 1159
Pressman, Israel (p) 2033
Preston, Frank (p) 3028
Preston, William 3362
Pretoria Central Prison (S. Africa) 2081, 2148, 2181, 2249
Pretoria Local Prison (S. Africa) 2218
Pretoria 12 (p) 2189
prevention of a crime defense 64
Prevention of Terrorism Act, UK 2894
preventive detention 860; Italy 1569; *see also* arbitrary arrest, detention without charge
Price, Lucien 3363
Priess, Anita (p) 2731
Priest, Roger (p) 3199

priests 326; *see also under* Catholics
Prime, Cecil (p) 1267
Principe Prison (Cuba) 757
Prinsen, Haji (p) 1414
prison brutality 342, 657
prison camp system, USSR *see* GULAG
prison conditions 237, 244, 351, 399, 667, 677, 700, 752, 799, 957, 1224, 1509, 1522, 1523, 1532, 1541, 1544, 1547, 1549, 1566, 1696, 1697, 1705; ill treatment 753–755; Kampuchea 1599; Morocco 1756; Mozambique 1762; Philippines 1909, 1915; Poland 1968, 1973; Portugal 1995; Rhodesia 2007; Romania 2018, 2019, 2022; Sierra Leone 2053; Somalia 2073, 2074; S. Africa 2187, 2229; S. Vietnam 3559, 3567–3571; Spain 2324; Sri Lanka 2331; Turkey 2396, 2400, 2406, 2412; USSR 2488, 2522, 2530, 2670, 2733, 2738, 2789, 2797–2799, 2808; UK 2964, 2966, 3000, 3001; US 3161, 3166, 3194, 3253, 3357, 3396, 3397, 3401, 3427, 3463; Uruguay 3507, 3512; Vietnam 3543, 3544; Yugoslavia 3591, 3594, 3608; Zaire 3612
prison farms 677
prison strikes 301; US 3471; *see also* strikes
prisoner(s): exchange 689, 690, 695; interviews 2617; letters 2663; release 666, 672, 728, 731, 734, 735, 741, 747, 756, 764, 768, 787, 834, 849, 866, 1462, 1510, 1528, 1547, 1554, 1558; types (USSR) 2677; women (USSR) 2881, 2882, 2886
prisoners of conscience 291; concept 179
prisoners list 184, 2363; Brazil 461, 463, 466, 468; Latvia 2656; Poland 1969, 1976, 1985; Rhodesia 2001, 2007; S. Africa 2079, 2103, 2115, 2116, 2118, 2119, 2168, 2182, 2230, 2258, 2259, 2261, 2264, 2273, 2276, 2277, 2279, 2280, 2303; S. Vietnam 3551, 3557–3561, 3570, 3571, 3578; Spain 2308, 2315, 2317, 2319, 2320, 2325; Sri Lanka 2331, 2333, 2334, 2336; Sudan 2339; Syria 2353, 2359; Thailand 2374, 2378, 2382; Togo 2381; Tunisia 2385, 2390–2392; Turkey 2393–2395, 2399, 2409, 2412–2414, 2416, 2418, 2421; Uganda 2449; USSR 2475, 2476, 2492, 2494, 2496–2498, 2513, 2520, 2529, 2536–2539, 2542, 2549, 2553, 2568, 2583–2585, 2614, 2616, 2639, 2654, 2662, 2667, 2668, 2673, 2709, 2726, 2728, 2734, 2735, 2776, 2798, 2802, 2816, 2818, 2844, 2847, 2848, 2874; UK 2941, 2966, 2976, 2990; US 3039, 3043, 3053, 3072, 3085, 3087, 3094, 3118, 3193, 3199, 3246, 3307, 3327, 3375, 3394, 3395, 3397, 3420, 3432, 3437, 3441–3444; Uruguay 3494, 3502, 3512, 3515–3518; Venezuela 3526; Vietnam 3527–3529, 3544, 3549, 3560; Yugoslavia 3594, 3598, 3599, 3602, 3607–3610; Zimbabwe 3626
prisons: medical care 208; Philippines 1912; USSR 2785, 2789, 2797–2799, 2808; Yugoslavia 3608–3610; *see also* medical
Prittie, Terence 958
Probst, Cristoph (p) 1177
Proffitt, Nicholas 3573
Progressive Labor Party, US 3236
Prokop, Peter (p) 499
Pronyuk, Yevhen (p) 2831
propaganda 402
Protestants 620
Prychodko, Nicholas (p) 2737
Przemyk, Grzegorz (p) 1952
psychiatry 65, 76, 193, 208, 221, 244, 267, 284, 291, 369, 395, 483, 729, 737, 793, 796, 818; rehabilitation of victims 153, 511; Romania 2014, 2023, 2024, 2026; USSR 2465, 2466, 2475, 2476, 2483, 2486, 2495–2497, 2502, 2504, 2513–2518, 2533, 2551, 2568, 2573, 2588, 2589, 2592, 2593, 2603, 2606, 2607, 2615, 2631, 2639–2641, 2653, 2680, 2688–2691, 2710, 2713, 2723, 2725, 2728, 2733, 2750, 2753, 2754, 2772, 2774, 2776, 2786, 2805, 2806, 2829, 2830, 2839, 2849, 2851, 2852, 2860, 2861, 2865; US 3044 Yugoslavia 3610
psychology: Holocaust 1014, 1018; of repression 81; of victims 994
Pu Ning *see* Pu Nai-fu
Public Prison (Santiago) 517
Public Security Act 1614, 1624; Nepal 1790–1792
Puchuncavi Prison (Chile) 524, 585
Puebla Prison (Mexico) 1725
Puello, Jorge (p) 848
Puenzo, Luis 372a
Puerto de Santa Maria Prison (Spain) 2310, 2319
Puerto Rico 3026, 3031, 3035, 3085, 3089, 3146, 3158, 3256, 3257, 3273, 3293, 3306, 3307, 3341, 3351, 3384, 3418, 3422, 3458, 3470
Puig, Manuel 235
Pujols, Castillo (p) 848
Pul-e Charkhi Prison (Afghanistan) 318, 320, 321
Pulerevitch, Yechezkel (Yechezkel Avishabi Maor) (p) 2739
Puletti, Guido (p) 364
Punamiya, Mohan (p) 1359
punishing security forces (state criminals) 356; *see also* pardon
punishment cells 737; USSR 2781
Punta de Rieles Women's Prison (Uruguay) 3503, 3504, 3507, 3515
purchasing prisoners 955, 959, 965
Purdy Institution for Women (US) 3419
purge 69, 2590, 2654; USSR 2488, 2538, 2549; *see also* state terrorism
Puxon, Grattan 1090
Puyallup 59 3118
Pyong Sik, Nah (p) 1671

Qabalani, Nabil (p) 1534
Qahwaji, Hind (p) 309
Qanater Prison (Egypt) 865
Qasr Prison (Iran) 1431, 1433, 1436, 1448
Qezel-Qale Prison (Iran) 225
Qiang, Liu (p) 674
Qincheng Prison (China) 622, 704
Qing, Dai (p) 674

Qing, Jiang (p) 632, 662
Qing, Liu (p) 604, 681
Qinghe Farm (Beijing) 702
Qinglin, Liu (p) 621
Qingshan, Deng (p) 677
Qira, Zijadin (p) 3603
Qoboza, Percy (p) 2147
Quaderi, Fazlul Quader 442
Que, Phuong (p) 3574
Que, Vo (p) 3557
Que Que Prison (Zimbabwe) 3629
Queens County Penitentiary (US) 3391
Quichang, Geng (p) 620
Quiché Indians 1295
Quigley, John 236
Quinn-Judge, P. 1920
Quiñones, Fr. Marón (p) 3117
Quintana, Carmen (p) 529
Quintanilla, Rodolfo (p) 529
Quintanilla, Virginio Canenguez 906
Quiriquina Island Prison (Chile) 585
Quynh, Dr. Truong van (p) 3529

Rabie Report, S. Africa 2132
Rabkin, David (p) 2148, 2233
Raceaunu, Mircea (p) 2015
Raciborz Prison (Poland) 1942
racism 64, 196, 227, 278, 299, 924; official 115; US 3018, 3359, 3372, 3397, 3401, 3445, 3450, 3462; *see also* S. Africa
Radek, Karl (p) 2538, 2655
radicalism, US 3079, 3362
Rafael Santo, June (p) 843
Rafael Videla, General Jorge 370
Ragal, Kim 869
Raggio, Lauro (p) 3513
Rahil, Mabrouka Houni (p) 507
Rahman, Asaad Abdel (p) 1543
Rajasak, Salat (p) 1676
Rakowiecka Prison (Poland) 1973
Raleigh Central Prison (US) 3139
Ram Sejda (p) 324
Ramahi, Mahmoud Mustafa (p) 1516
Ramallah Prison (Israel) 1533, 1539
Raman, G. (p) 2064
Ramati, Alexander 1160
Ramirez, José Ruiz (p) 1276
Ramirez, Nelson (p) 3257
Ramle Prison (Israel) 1540
Ramos, Dr. Orlando (p) 1998
Ramphele, Dr. Mamphela (p) 2221, 2222
Randall, M. 2234
Randle, Michael (p) 2984
Rangel, Oscar (p) 3526
ransom 650
Rao, Varavara (p) 1368
rape 6, 39, 68, 121, 217, 309, 348, 362, 1356, 1363, 1379, 1494, 1496, 1497, 1893; El Salvador 880, 884, 887, 889; Guatemala 1273, 1296; Myanmar 1770; Pakistan 1821, 1826, 1831; S. Africa 2241
Rapoport, Yakov (p) 2742
Rappoport, Leon 1103
Rasht Prison (Iran) 1448, 1454
Rasmawi, Atallah (p) 1533
Rassi, Reynold 574
rats 216
Ratushinskaia, Irina (p) 2671, 2743–2747, 2758, 2838, 2850, 2880
Rauda, Fermín (p) 899
Rault, Caroline 2985
Ravensbrück concentration camp (Nazi Germany) 1009, 1032, 1125, 1197, 1198, 2510
Ravera, Camilla (p) 1579
Ravi, Shri (p) 1387
Rawicz, Piotr 1161
Rawlings, Flt. Lt. Jerry 1218, 1220
Rawson Prison (Argentina) 342
Ray, James Earl 3366
Rayfield, Donald 2748
Raymond, Jill (p) 3227
Razvigor Street State Security Center (Sofia) 483
Reagan, Ronald 46, 64, 120, 901, 1266, 1798, 3268; administration 46, 352, 906; Doctrine 149
rebellion in US 3246
Recinos, Héctor Bernabe (p) 895, 904
recording 783
Rector, Frank 1162
Red Army Faction 967–970, 974, 975, 978
red-baiting *see* anti-communism
Red Brigades 1578
Red Cross 205, 1255
Red Guards 615, 616, 651
Red Rosa (Luxemburg) 940
red scare, US 3197; trials 3052
red squads, US 3141
Reddaway, Peter 183, 2496, 2497, 2749–2752
Reddy, Shri Narsimka (p) 1387
Reddy, Snehalatu (p) 1381
Reddy, T.J. (p) 3030
Reed, David 397, 721, 774, 959
Reed, L. 3368
re-education camps: Kampuchea 1598; Laos 1675–1679; Vietnam 3527–3530, 3543, 3544, 3547, 3548
Reese, Michael 870
Reform through Labor (Lao Gai) 607, 677
Refugee Act 1980, US 3189
refugees 10, 19, 194, 237, 345, 408, 436, 1402; El Salvador 883, 896; sanctuary, US 3367; US 3114, 3193, 3437; *see also* banishment; banning; deportation; exile
refuseniks 2498
Regelson, Lev Lvovich (p) 2489
rehabilitation, Sri Lanka 2330; *see also* psychiatry
Reich, Walter 2753, 2754
Reimers, Isolde 398
Rein, David 3369
Reissner, Will 904
Rejali, Darius 238, 1470
relatives 577
religion 184, 185, 266, 324, 326, 330, 347, 350, 457, 458, 483, 603, 627, 652, 653, 684, 696, 733, 742, 745, 760, 771, 793, 796, 856, 866, 1657, 2164, 2165, 2991; Indonesia 1409; Paraguay 1839; Philippines 1910; Poland 1972; Romania 2014, 2015, 2024, 2026, 2028; Singapore 2057; S. Africa 2127, 2150, 2158, 2207; Sudan 2341–2343; USSR 2467, 2475, 2476, 2489, 2528, 2529, 2507, 2508, 2550, 2552, 2581, 2583, 2632, 2658, 2659, 2665, 2710, 2733, 2735, 2755, 2760, 2796–2800, 2802, 2807, 2809; UK 2972, 2976; US 3114, 3127, 3151; Vietnam 3538
religious intolerance 631
religious persecution, Iran 1439; Myanmar 1770, 1782; Nepal 1791
religious prisoners 620
Remington, William (p) 3108
Remmer, Karen L. 239
Removsky, Semion 2756
RENAMO 1764

Rensburg, Ihron (p) 2277
Repka, William (p) 500
Resck, Prof. Luis (p) 1849
rescue (of Jews) 987, 989
Resha, Robert (p) 2151
Resistance against Nazis 81, 279, 993, 1152, 1175, 1177, 1213; Belgium 1164; France 1023; Greece 1242, 1250; Italy 1574; Japan 1586; Jewish 980; Netherlands 1178
Resistance Conspiracy trials, US 3145, 3229
resistance movements 252
Restelli Portuguez, Dr. Juan (p) 542
Restrepo, Andres (p) 852
Restrepo, Santiago (p) 852
restricted liberty 342
Retboll, Torben 1417
Reuter, Madalynne 2757
Reuter, Thomas (p) 1546
revocation of degrees 269
Revolutionary Guards, Iran 1438
Reyes, Adelina de (p) 231
Reyes Bazán, Alvaro (p) 530
Reyes Valenzuela, José Nazario (p) 517
Reynolds, Reginald 261
Reysio-Cruz, Amelita (p) 1923
Rezaia Prison (Iran) 1448
Rezvan, Dr., torturer 1429
Rhee, Syngman 1654
Rhodesia 53, 2000–2013; *see also* Zimbabwe
Ribeiro, Lazaro (p) 1394
Riboldi, Ezio (p) 1571
Rice, Jim 3373
Rice, Fr. Patrick (p) 399
Richardson, Carole (p) 2942, 2968
Richardson, Mary (p) 2987, 2988
Richmond Hill Prison (Grenada) 1268
Richter, Jurgen (p) 949
Rickett, Adele (p) 685
Rickett, Allyn (p) 685
Ridd, Karen (p) 882
Ridenour, Ron 241
Rifa'iy Abu 'Aita, Muhammad (p) 860
Riga Ghetto 1136
Rigaud, Claire-Lise (p) 1321
Rigaud, Lucien (p) 1321
Rigby, Françoise (p) 1164
right wing 517; *see also* martial law; military; state terrorism
rights, laws, Philippines 1894, 1895, 1901, 1914
Riker's Island Correctional Institution for Women (US) 3402
Ring, Harry 775
Ringelblum, Emmanuel (p) 1165
Ringelheim, Joan 1084, 1166
Riquelme, Samuel (p) 524
Risal, Bairav (p) 1792
Risley Remand Center (UK) 2971
Ritoque Prison (Chile) 524, 543, 585, 686
Ritterman, Michele 577
Rivabella, Omar (p) 6, 242
Rivard, Robert 905
Rivera, Jésus (p) 1735
Rivonia Trial, S. Africa 2091, 2120, 2172
Riyadh Prison (Saudi Arabia) 2044
Roballo, Americo (p) 3503
Robben Island Prison (S. Africa) 1785, 2080, 2088, 2111, 2120, 2122, 2160, 2172, 2196, 2218, 2228; film 2239
Robbins, Keith 2989
Robert Lapides 979
Roberts, Kenneth 1860
Robeson, Paul (p) 3147
Robideaux, Bob (p) 3395
Robinson, Jacob 1167, 1168
Robinson, Randall 2240
Robson, Clive 1505
Rocha, Ruth 243
Rodgers, Dick 2758
Rodley, Nigel S. 244
Rodrigues, Sara 3632
Rodriguez, Adrian (p) 884
Rodríguez, Angel (p) 3522
Rodriguez, José Antonio (p) 1280
Rodriguez, Juan Carlos 354
Rodriguez Alegria, Daniel (p) 577
Rodriguez Fernandez, Amado (p) 771
Rodriguez Quesada, Carlos 776
Rodríguez Sánchez, Francisco (p) 2296
Roebuck, Julian 3376
Roeder, Bernhard (p) 2759
Rogal, K. 687
Rogge, O. John 245, 3377
Rohwer (Ark.) Relocation Center (US) 3067
Roja, Clarita (Mila Aguilar) (p) 1908
Rojas, Marta 3575
Rojas, Rodrigo (p) 518, 529
Rojas Castañeda, Alfredo (p) 562
Rojas de Negri, Rodrigo (p) 566
Roland, Jane 1739
Rolando Garcia, Alfonso (p) 577
Romania 125, 2014–2031; Holocaust 1030
Romanova, Olga (p) 2662
Romanyuk, The Rev. Vasyl (p) 2552, 2715, 2760, 2761, 2885
Romas, Julio (p) 1847
Romaszewski, Zbigniew (p) 1942, 1982
Romer, Josef (p) 818
Romero, General Carlos 879
Romero, Francesca (p) 884
Romero, Archbishop Oscar 879, 896
Romo, Marcelo (p) 530
Romulus, Marc (p) 291
Rosa Mena, Nalvia (p) 520
Rosebaugh, Fr. Larry (p) 3299
Rosen, Andrew 2990
Rosenbaum, Rebecca 3378
Rosenberg, Alan 1169
Rosenberg, Ethel (p) 301, 3379, 3380
Rosenberg, Julius (p) 301
Rosenberg, Susan (p) 3065, 3165, 3381, 3434
Rosenberg, Suzanne (p) 2762
Rosenberg, Tina 246
Rosenbergs 3108, 3428
Rosenblum, Nina 3040
Rosenthal, David 2321
Roslik, Dr. Vladimir (p) 3503, 3510
Ross, Charles G. 3382
Ross, Irwin 247
Rosselli, Carlo (p) 1575
Roth, Andrew 1586
Roth, Kenneth 823, 1977
Roth, Michael 3383
Roth, Otavio 243
Rothchild, Sylvia 1170
Rothe, Greta (p) 1177
Rothenbacher, Wulf 960
Rothschild, Matthew 3384, 3385
Rouell, Lova Leon (p) 2756
Rousset, David (p) 1171
Rout, Kathleen 3386
Roveda, Giovanni (p) 1571
Roy, M.N. (p) 2991–2993
Royal Ulster Constabulary 2911
Rtskhiladze, Victor (p) 2734
Ruban, Petro (p) 2715
Ruban, Pyotr (p) 2554
Rubin, Humberto (p) 1851

Rubin, Jerry (p) 3226
Rubin, Robin 1546
Rudenstein, Roger 1740
Rudolf, Anthony 1172
Rudolfi, Elsa (Coca) (p) 530, 559
Ruhengeri Prison (Rwanda) 2040
Ruml, Jan (p) 838
Ruml, Jiri (p) 838
Rupert, Raphael (p) 184, 2763, 2764
Rupesinghe, Kumar 2332
Rusek, Antonin (p) 173
Rushdie, Salman (p) 1426, 1479
Russell, Bertrand (p) 58, 2989
Russell, Diane 2241
Russell, G. 1471
Russell, George 401, 2994
Russia (Pre-Revolutionary) 2032–2039
Russian Orthodox Church 2489, 2529
Rusu, Gheorghe (p) 2014
Ruzyne Prison (Czechoslovakia) 805, 821, 828
Rwanda 2040, 2041
Ryan, Sheila 1547, 1548
Ryan, William 824–826, 976, 1978
Rykov, Alexei (p) 2538

Saad, Aida (p) 1540
Saadawi, Dr. Naural el (p) 871, 872
Sabac Prison (Yugoslavia) 3592
Sabata, Dr. Jaroslav (p) 108, 173
Sábato, Ernest (p) 350
Sable, Martin 1173
sabotage, S. Africa 2162; Act 2111
Sacco and Vanzetti (p) 301, 3037
Sachs, Albie (p) 2196, 2242
Sachs, Henry 1168
Sachsen-Waldheim Prison (USSR) 2665
Sachsenhausen Prison (GDR) 958, 1019; concentration camp (Nazi Germany) 1109
Sackda, Khamtou (p) 1676
sacrifice 370
Sadat, President Anwar 429, 855, 858, 859, 866, 869, 873
Sadunaite, Nijole (p) 2648
Safo-Adu, Kwame 1226
Safra Camp (Bahrain) 429
Sagmalcilar Prison (Turkey) 2395, 2411, 2412
Sago, Mitch (p) 500
Saguier, Dr. Rafael Hermes 1850
Sahara 1748
Said, Dr. Al-Sayyid (p) 876
Saïd Cheikh, Moustoifa (p) 718
Sa'id Zahran, Ali (p) 865
Saidnaya Prison (Syria) 2353
St. Alban's Prison (S. Africa) 2277
Saint Giles Prison (Belgium, Nazis) 1164
Sakalys, Vladys (p) 2646
Sakharov, Andrei (p) 54, 80, 2499, 2500, 2615, 2679, 2846; letters 2769; memoirs 2768
Salawati, Charlotte (Ibu) (p) 1399
Salem, Amir (p) 876
Salemal-Nahhas, 'Ali (p) 1588
Salemba Men's Prison (Indonesia) 1399, 1406
salesmen 548
Salisbury, Harrison 2771
Salisbury Prison (Rhodesia/Zimbabwe) 2005, 2012, 3629
Sallah, Halifa 937
Salmon, Ben (p) 3388
Salomon, Ernst von 941
Saloojee, Suliman (p) 2116
Salosa, Mecky (p) 1402
Salter, Kenneth 3389
Salvador, David (p) 776
Salvadoran Human Rights Commission 879
salvaging (abduction and murder) 1875, 1898, 1918, 1925, 1929
Salvatore, Nick 3390
Sam, Cheah Swee (p) 1707
Samadien-Pour, General 1436
Samantar, Usuf Osman (p) 2071, 2073
Samba, Omene (p) 3614
Samghabadi, Raji (p) 1484
samizdat 2645, 2676, 2686, 2774
Samkhe Prison (Laos) 1675
Sampson, Anthony 2243
Samuelli, Annie (p) 2019, 2027
Samuelli, Norah (p) 2019
San Bernardo Infantry School 528
San Francisco State College 3330, 3411
San Juan, E., Jr. 1926, 1927
San Quentin Six 3352
San Severino Prison (Cuba) 765
San Vittore Prison (Italy) 1571
Sanabria, Ernesto Anaya (p) 900, 903
Sanbar, Moshe (p) 1174
Sanchez, Elizardo (p) 743
Sanchez, Fernando (p) 364
Sánchez-Galan, Brenda (p) 3193
Sanchez-Mazas, Miguel 2322
Sánchez Salgado, Domingo (p) 1800
sanctuary, US 3017, 3114, 3117, 3031, 3189, 3193, 3204, 3280, 3308, 3367, 3437
Sandinistas 1796
Sandler, Asir (p) 2877
Sands, Bobby (p) 2899, 2902, 2917, 2935, 2952, 2995–2997
Sané, Cheikh Kouressi (p) 2048
Sang-dok, Yu (p) 1655
Sang-nok, Cho (p) 1664
Sanger, Margaret (p) 3391, 3392
Sanger, William (p) 3157
Sanguinetti, Alicia (p) 341
Sangyip Prison (China/Tibet) 601, 675, 678
Santa Clara Prison (Cuba) 765
Santa Rita Prison (US) 3041
Santos, Alfonso (p) 2043
Santos, Jaime dos (p) 1394
Santos Mendoza, Hugo (p) 3512
Santucho, Amílcar (p) 1836
Sanyal, Kanu (p) 1383
São Paulo Prison (Angola) 335, 337
São Tomé & Principe 2042, 2043
Saqr, Youssef (p) 860
Sarafend Military Concentration Camp (Israel) 1543
Saraiva de Carvalho, Otelo (p) 1994
Sarfaty, Abraham (p) 1751
Sarin, Garish 1383
Sarkar, Barid Kantu (p) 1382
Sarpo, Sarponin bin (p) 482
Sartov, Paul (p) 3488
SASO/BPC trial, S. Africa 2118
Satchell, Michael 248
Satomi, K. 2367
Sattin, A. 2773
Saudi Arabia 225, 2044–2047
Saunders, Geore 2774
SAVAK (National Intelligence and Security Organization, Iran), Iran 276, 291, 1431, 1454, 1456, 1468

Savren, Shelley 579
Sax, Boria 249
Saxe, Susan (p) 3393
Sayagues, Mercedes 3510
Scales, Junius (p) 3053, 3174
Scanlon, Kevin 1472
scapegoats 370
Schaerer, Mario (p) 1837
Schear, Tracey (p) 884
Scheffler, Judith 250
Schein, Edgar 688
Scheveningen concentration camp 1197
Schirmer, Jennifer 580
schizophrenia 65, 2568; *see also* psychiatry; Snezhnevsky
Schlabrendorff, Fabian von 1175
Schleicher, Rudiger (p) 1109
Schlesinger, Kurt (p) 998
Schlüsselburg Fortress (Russia) 2035
Schmidt, Frank (p) 960
Schmidt, Lt. Peter (p) 2036
Schmidt, Wolfgang 952
Schmorell, Alexander (p) 1177
Schneider, Reinhold 1034
Schnookal, Deb 1928
Schoenfeld, Joachim (p) 1176
scholars 673
Scholl, Hans (p) 1177
Scholl, Inge 1177
Scholl, Sophie (p) 1177
Scholmer, Joseph (p) 184
Schonemann, Sybille (p) 961
School of the Americas (Ft. Benning) 888, 3069, 3299
Schreurs, J.J.M.H. (p) 1178
Schucht, Tatiana (p) 1579
Schultz, Brigit (p) 1540, 1546
Schultz, Bud (p) 3394
Schultz, Ruth (p) 3394
Schultz enterprises 984
Schumannstrasse Prison (GDR) 964
Schünemann, Peter (p) 943
Schütt, Thomas (p) 945
Schwarberg, Guenther 1179
Schwartz, Eric 3544
Schwartz, Leo 1180
Schwartzman, Prof. Mauricio (p) 1847
Schwarz, Oliver (p) 943
Schwarz, Solomon 2775
Schwarzheide concentration camp (Nazi Germany) 1081
Schwen, Marcia 1658
science 54, 208, 542
scientists: Guatemala 1298; Poland 1987; Somalia 2072
Scoble, Harry 303, 305
Scoccimarro, Mauro (p) 1571, 1579
Seager, Moe 3395
Seale, Bobby (p) 3175, 3240, 3396, 3397
searches, USSR 2676
Seattle City Jail (US) 3419
Seattle Seven 3419
secrecy 500
Secret Anti-Communist Army (ESA) 1273, 1287, 1289
secret detention 362; *see also* incommunicado detention
secret detention centers 363, 409
secret graves 517, 528
secret police 69, 276, 556, 571; El Salvador 887
secret trial 943
Security Act 20, 840
security and human rights, U.S. 165
security forces 356
Security Prison (Namibia) 1786
Security Statute (Colombia) 709
Sedillot, Jacques (p) 1627, 1630
sedition 495, 1617; Pakistan 1821; Taiwan 2362, 2364, 2368, 2369; UK 2916; US 3162, 3179, 3290, 3313, 3349, 3394, 3417
Seequeiros, David Alfaro (p) 301
Segundo Recabarren, Manuel (p) 520
Segura, Luisa (p) 121
Seiden, Matthew 1659
Seidman, Peter 1550
Seigle, Larry 3398
Seko, Isaac (p) 2189
self-censorship 6
Selic, Momcilo (p) 3600
Selukwe Prison (Zimbabwe) 3629
Selzer, Michael 1181
Sembel Prison (Ethiopia) 915
Sendic, Raul (p) 3500
Senegal 2048, 2049
Seng, Chua Kee (p) 2062
Seng, Goh Kean (p) 1715
sensory deprivation 969, 2967
Senyk, Iryna (p) 2619, 2881
Seong, Patrick (p) 2068
Seow, Francis (p) 2068
Sepah Military Prison (Iran) 1435
separatist movements 433
Sepulueda, José (p) 408
Serbia 2050, 2051
Serbsky Institute of Forensic Psychiatry (USSR) 2496, 2513–2518, 2533, 2593, 2631, 2691
Serebrov, Felix (p) 2728
Seregni, Liber (p) 3504
Sereny, Gitta 1182
Seroney, Jean-Marie (p) 1613
Serrano, Bruno 581
Servan-Schreiber, Jean-Jacques 1231
Seung-hon, Han (p) 1656, 1657
Seventh Day Adventists 771, 2475; Romania 2014, 2026; USSR 2529, 2716, 2733
Sevillano, Jose (p) 2299
Sevillias, Errikos (p) 1183
sex: 184, 370, 2763, (USSR) 2651, 2795; abuse 309, 1438; harassment 68, (UK) 2963; slavery 68
Sexwale, Mosima (p) 2189
Seychelles 2052
Sgovio, Thomas (p) 2778
Shabad, S. 2779
Shabalin, I.A. (p) 2662
Shabatura, Stefaniya (p) 2619
shackles 1590, 1598, 1599
Shafig, Habib (p) 1514
Shafooli, Kally (p) 1786
Shah of Iran 1431, 1432
Shaha, Shambynath (p) 1382
Shaheen, Abdel Aziz Ali ("Abu Ali") (p) 1567
Shahrabi, Hamid (p) 1441, 1445
Shakirov, Babur (p) 3521
Shakur, Afeni (p) 3399, 3400
Shakur, Assata (Joanne Chesimard) (p) 3401, 3402
Shakur, Lumumba (p) 3239
Shalla Prison (Sudan) 2339/40
Shambali, Yusif (p) 2346
Shamma, Geraldine (p) 777
Shanghai 1584
Shapell, Nathan (p) 1184
Shapiro, L. 827
Sharma, Balaram (p) 1791
Sharma, Pt. Ram Rup (p) 2915
Sharp, Evelyn (p) 2998
Sharp, Gene 251, 252
Sharpeville Six 2103, 2113, 2120, 2248
Shatravka, Alexander (p) 2502, 2849
Sha'ur, Zayid (p) 1534
Shcharansky, Anatoly (Natan Sharansky) (p) 2468, 2477, 2532, 2583, 2675, 2781
Shehadeh, Michel (p) 3033
Shehadeh, Raja 1551
Sheikh Nikman bin Sheikh Mahmud (p) 482
Shelkov, Vladimir (p) 2716
Shelly, Lore (p) 1185
Shelton, Robert 253
Shelton, Sharon 1661, 2323

Sheng, Kang ("The King of Hell") 612
Sheng, Ong Loong (p) 1715
Shengchang, Niu (p) 674
Shenon, Philip 1603
Shenouda III, Pope (p) 865, 866, 869
Shentalinsky, Vitaly 2782–2784
Shernock, Stanley 254
Sherwin, Byron 1186
Shevchenko, Oles (p) 2684
Shi'a Muslims 430, 1674
Shifrin, Avraham (p) 2855
Shikuku, Martin (p) 1613
Shimanov, Gennadii (p) 2786
Shingarev, Andrei (p) 2787
Shining Path (Sendero Luminoso), Peru 1856, 1860, 1864
Shipilov, Vasily (p) 2729
Shiraz Prison (Iran) 1448
Shirvani, Ali 1476
Shohat, Ella 1513
Shongwe, Musa (p) 2348
Shorris, Earl 778
Shorrock, Tim 1662
short stories 629
Shpalernaya Prison (USSR) 2634
Shu-teh, Father Francis Xavier Chu (p) 636, 653
Shu-tse, Peng 663
Shuang, Li (p) 639, 665
Shub, Boris 1187
Shufeng, Wang (p) 674
Shukhevych, Yuriy (p) 2789, 2844
Shumuk, Danylo (p) 2544, 2614, 2788, 2848
Shuzang, Guo (p) 602, 620
Shymko, Juri 2789
Siang, Lim Kit (p) 1707, 1712
Sibay, Generoso (p) 1910, 1911
Siberia *see* forced labor
Sibley, Mulford (p) 3403–3405
Sichko family (p) 2566
Sidarous, Father Louqa (p) 865
Siderman, Jose (p) 366
Siedman, Peter 1473
sieges 52
Siegrist, Roland 1255
Sierra Chica Prison (Argentina) 342, 399, 417
Sierra Leone 2053-2055
Sieu, Thich Tri (p) 3528
Siew, Dr. Lim Hock (p) 2062, 2063
Sik, Na Byung (p) 1653
Sikakane, Joyce (p) 2249
Sikivese, Fred 1699
Siklová, Jirina (p) 828, 838
Silberman, David (p) 590
Silhanova, L. 829
Silika, Ayanti (p) 2159
Silo Pruning Hooks, US 3413
Silva, Raul 582
Silver, Eric 1552
Silver Spring Three (p) 3240
Sim, Cecelia Ng Choon (p) 1709
Simbra rebellion (Congo) 721
Simecka, Milan (p) 838
Simon, Sinyetha (p) 2279
Simons, Donald L. (p) 3406
Sinclair, John k(p) 3407
Sindhi nationalism 1822, 1826
Singapore 2057-2069
Singer, Daniel 1979
Singh, Bhagat (p) 1354
Singh, Gulab (p) 1384
Singh, Karpal (p) 1707
Singh Talib, S. Narinjan (p) 2915
Sinha, Bejoy Kumar (p) 2999
Sinn Fein 2952, 2963
Sinyavski, Andrei (p) 2670, 2676
Siregar, Hariman (p) 1399
Sirett, Hazel 304
Sisaleumsak, Tiao Sisoumang (p) 1676
Sison, Jose Maria (p) 1888, 1922, 1926
Sisulu, Albertine (p) 2086, 2206
Sisulu, Walter (p) 2081, 2089, 2101, 2180
Sisulu, Zwelakhe (p) 2096, 2135, 2250, 2292
Sithole, Edson (p) 2000
Sithole, Ndabaningi (p) 2012
Situmorang, Sitor (p) 1399, 1406
Siwakoti, Radheshyam (p) 1792
Skalnik, Josef (p) 808
Skloot, Robert 255a
Skoglund, Carl (p) 3225, 3281
Skolnick, Jerome 3408
Skuodis, Vytautas (p) 2644
Skvorecky, Josef 830
slander 960, 963; USSR 2678, 2863
Slansky trial 816
slave labor 606, 1209; Holocaust 1033, 1044; USSR 2530, 2539, 2549; *see also* forced labor; Nazi Germany; Siberia
slavery 1044
Slepak, Vladimir (p) 2477
Slipie, Josef (p) 2836
Slobodyan, Mykola (p) 2729
Slodowski, Wojciech 1980
Slovo, Gillian 2251
Slovo, Joe 2129
Slovo, Shawn 2252
Smart, Betsy 3006
Smedley, Agnes (p) 3409
Smirnoff, Viktor (p) 2780
Smith, Beverly A. 3000
Smith, David 1553
Smith, Ian 3625
Smith, Lee 3410
Smith, Marcus J. 1189
Smith, Michal 583
Smith, Oscar 372
Smith, R. Jeffrey 2792, 2793
Smith, Robert 3411
Smith, W.E. 873, 1554, 2253, 2254
Smith Act 3053, 3094, 3167, 3174, 3183, 3202, 3228, 3251, 3281, 3289, 3456
Smolen, Kazimierz 1190
Smolensk Special Psychiatric Hospital (USSR) 2726
Smyrna Four 3352
SNCC 3047
Snezhnevsky, Andrei 2568, 2631, 2723, 2806
Snolowe, Jill 1981
Soames, Emma 874, 875
Sobadschiev, Ljuben (p) 483
Sobel, Lester 224
Sobell, Morton (p) 3412
Sobibór extermination camp (Nazi) 984, 1182; revolt 980
Sobrino, Eduardo (p) 726
Sobukwe, Robert Mangaliso (p) 2218
socialism 107, 586, 714–716, 832; US 3027, 3105, 3190, 3390; *see also* anticommunism
Socialist Workers Party, US 121, 473, 562, 3064, 3281, 3314
Socknat, Thomas P. 501
Soedjono, Roespanadi (p) 1399
Sogioka, Gene (p) 3188
Solares Teseiro, Andrés José (p) 771
Soledad brothers 3414, 3457
Soledad Prison (US) 3099, 3161
Soledad Three 3118, 3119
Soler, Miguel Angel (p) 1836, 1847
Solidarity 1943, 1947, 1952
solitary confinement 244, 623, 646, 740, 780, 782, 816, 829, 857, 860, 968, 969, 974, 975, 1012, 1246, 1353, 1436, 1646, 1654, 1874, 1918, 1931, 2035, 2242; Malaysia 1712, 1717; Poland 1984; S. Africa 2129, 2144-2146, 2216; USSR 2626, 2655, 2745, 2747, 2758, 2762,

2763, 2797; US 3253; Uruguay 3508
Sölle, Dorothee 402, 584
Solomon, Michael (p) 2795
Solovetsky Concentration Camp (USSR) 2524, 2682, 2732
Solovetsky Islands, prisons (USSR) 2672
Soltanpour, Saeed (p) 291
Solzhenitsyn, Alexander (p) 80, 186, 2540, 2771, 2796–2800, 2884
Solzhenitsyn, Natalya 2801
Somalia 2070–2075
Sombath, Meas (p) 114
Somers, Sheila 2256
Somo, Abu (p) 1615
Somoza Debayle, Anastasio 1795, 1800
Sonderkommando (crematoria workers) 995
Song-man, Kim (p) 1664
Song-u, Cho (p) 1633
Sopron-Kohida Prison (Hungary) 268
Soria, Carmelo (p) 545
Soroka, Mikhaylo (p) 2844
Sorong Prison (Indonesia) 1402
Sosnowski, Kiryl 1191
Sotiris, Angelos 1257
Soto, David 403
Soto Arriví, Carlos (p) 3341, 3422
Sousa, Alfonso de (p) 1992
South Africa 64, 65, 125, 208, 263, 278, 291, 314, 337, 1783, 2076–2292; torture 153
South African Communist Party 2267
South America 257
Southern Ohio Correctional Facility (US) 3344
Souza Soccas, Marlene de (p) 291
Soviet Union, Holocaust 1039
Sovietphobia, US 3141, 3197, 3379; *see also* anti-communism
Soyinka, Wole (p) 1804, 1805, 1814, 1817
Soylemezoglu, Haydar (p) 2414
Soztre, Martin (p) 114
Spac labor camp (Albania) 324
Spadafora, Dr. Hugo (p) 1832
Spain 53, 253, 291, 987, 2293–2327; civil war 2306; Communist Party 2301
Spaniola, Thomas 1556
Sparks, Allister 2271
Spector, Mordecai 3413
Speer, Albert (p) 966
Spencer, Miranda 258
spies 685, 687, 777
Spire, Antoine 804
Spiridonova, Maria (p) 2036, 2037, 2815
Spock, Dr. Benjamin (p) 301, 3240
sportsmen 548
Spoul, B.C. 831
Spriano, Paolo 1579
Spring, Beta 779
Sproul, Barbara 183
Spurling, Robert (p) 1496
spying 646, 649, 964, 3431; *see also* surveillance
Sremska Mitrovica Prison (Yugo.) 3597
Sreniowski, Jósef (p) 1980
Sri Lanka 223, 2328–2337; bibliography 2332
Srifi, Mohamed (p) 1749
Srp, Karel (p) 808, 823, 830, 834
SS 279, 1022, 1190
Ssebunnya, Enos (p) 2454
Stachel, Jack (p) 3053
Stackhouse, Max 259
Stadelheim Prison 942
Stafford, William (p) 3415
Stahel, T.H. 2811
Stajka, Nika (p) 330
Stajner, Karlo (p) 2812
Stalin, Josef 311, 2654, 2655, 2661, 2664, 2772, 2841, 2859; Stalinism vs. socialism 2812, 2815
Stalker, John 3002, 3009
Stamets, Bill 961
Stammheim Prison (FRG) 968
Stangle, Franz 1182
Stanski, Tadeusz (p) 1973
Stara Gradiska Prison (Yugo.) 3591, 3594, 3602, 3608, 3609
Stara Zagore Prison (Bulgaria) 483
Starakis, Jean (p) 1231
Stark, General Arrelano ("Butcher of the North") 536
Stark, Rodney 3416
Starlinger, Wilhelm (p) 2813
Starsky, Morris (p) 3459
Startup, Patricia 1929
starvation, Guinea 1308; Indonesia 1411; USSR 2670, 2672, 2708
Stasi 952
Stasiv-Kalynets, Iryna (p) 2619, 2881
state crime 192, 260; US 3090, 3445
State Department: country reports, criticism 744
state of emergency 482, 856, 860, 864, 1350, 1357, 1362, 1372, 1389; Guatemala 1272–1280, 1290–1303; Jamaica 1581; Peru 1865, 1871; S. Africa 2087, 2091; Zambia 3623; *see also* martial law; state of siege
state of siege 342, 343, 399, 517, 542, 709; El Salvador 879, 896; Paraguay 1836; *see also* martial law; state of emergency
State Penitentiary (Haiti) 1314
State Security Court 331, 1674
State Security Decree, Nigeria 1807
State Security Department (GDR) 960
State Security Intelligence 1674
State Security Intelligence Police (Egypt) 856
State Security Law, Sudan 2338
state terrorism 52, 69, 100, 115, 149, 192, 262, 263, 350, 355, 369, 370, 382, 385, 395, 402, 465, 1102, 1356, 1380, 1485, 1495; El Salvador 896; Guatemala 1272–1303; Turkey 2412–2414, 2416–2418; Uganda 2446–2463; USSR 2478, 2530, 2537, 2538; US 3032, 3080
Statkevicius, Dr. Algirda (p) 2728
STB (Czech Secret Police) 805
Steele, Richard 2814
Stefoff, Rebecca 2272
Stehlik, Milos 148
Steif, W. 3418
Steif, William 1851, 1852
Steinberg, I. 2815
Steinberg, Jon 404
Steine, Charles (p) 3028
Stella Gallego, Gloria (p) 716
Stentzel, Jim 1669
Stephens-Feria, Dolores (p) 1922
sterilization 154
Stern, Dr. Mikhail (p) 2548
Stern, Susan (p) 3419
Stetler, Russell 3003
Stevens, Doris (p) 3420
Stevens, Janet 1557
Stevens, Siaka 2054
Stiffel, Frank (p) 1192
Stock, A.G. 261
Stohl, Michael 262, 263
Stolypin vans 2763
Stone, Julie L. (p) 2963

Stoneyard Prison (S. Africa) 2218
Storr, Anthony 264
Strangeways Gaol (UK) 2953, 2969
Strasberg, Rita (p) 473
Strasbourg Commission Report 2944
Strasser, Steven 1385, 1477
Straus, Austin 217
Strauss, Walter 1193
Strausz-Hupe, Robert 2410
Strefilevich, Nora (p) 405
strikes/strikers 81, 178, 433, 529, 853; in prison 1454, 3403; Poland 1979; US 3230, 3231; Romania 2014, 2026
Strimaityte-Meliene, Matilda (p) 2817
strip search 309, 968, 2965; UK 3005
Strobl, Ingrid (p) 971
Stroessner, General Alfredo 1836, 1837
Strokata, Nina (p) 2881
Strokata-Karavanska, Dr. Nina (p) 2818
Strong, Anna Louise (p) 2819
Stroom, Jerrold van der 988
Struik, Dirk (p) 3421
Strzelin Prison (Poland) 1943, 1973
students 81, 362, 446, 505, 525, 526, 548, 552, 603, 620, 634, 654, 685, 690, 717, 723, 873, 923, 1273, 1274, 1393, 1418, 1686, 1688; Mali 1719, 1720; Mexico 1727, 1735, 1742, 1744; Morocco 1749, 1753, 1759, 1761; Nepal 1792; Nigeria 1807, 1811; Resistance 1177; Senegal 2048; S. Africa 2195, 2237, 2270; S. Korea 1645; S. Vietnam 3551, 3567, 3571; US 3070, 3235, 3268, 3330, 3338-3340, 3411, 3485; Venezuela 3522; Zaire 3614, 3618; Zimbabwe 3626
stun guns 3305
Stutthof concentration camp 1203
Stypulkowski, Zbigniew (p) 2820
Styron, Rose 585
Su Kyung (Su-kyong), Im (p) 1633, 1641
Suarez, Domiro (p) 365
Suarez, Jacinto (p) 1801
Suarez, Manuel 3422
Subadi, (p) 1399
Subono, Bambang (p) 1394
Subukwe, Robert (p) 1089
subversion 367, 370, 457, 711, 793, 838, 709; laws 1402; US 3140-3142, 3446, 3474; Zaire 3615; *see also* anti-communism
Sudan 2338-2346
Sudan Communist Party 2338
Sudar, Drago (p) 3605
Sudjinah (p) 231
suffocation 1759, 1761
suffragists (women): UK 2905, 2931, 2937, 2940, 2941, 2953, 2958, 2961, 2969, 2970, 2978-2983, 2987, 2990; US 316, 3121-3123, 3228, 3420, 3423
Sugijah, Jose Ricardo Vrteaga (p) 217
Sugimoto, Henry (p) 3188
Sugiyah (p) 1399, 1406
Suhaili bin Badas (p) 482
Suharto 1393-1397, 1399
suicide 1172
Suk Hon, Hahm (p) 1656, 1667, 1669
Sukhanovka Prison (USSR) 2555
Sukloff, Marie (p) 2038
summary execution 320, 399, 603, 618, 625, 912, 1318; *see also* executions; killings
Summersworth Armory 301
Sumpul River Massacre 887
Sun-Myong, Kim (p) 209, 1641
Sung, Soh (p) 1632, 1655, 1657, 1663, 1667
Sung Hyun, Chung (p) 1671
Suni Quispe, Porfirio (p) 1855
Sunshine, Alice 3424
Sunshine, Cathy 3425
Supardi (p) 1399
Supit, Karel (p) 1399, 1406
Suratih, Siti (p) 121, 1399, 1406
Suriname 2347
Suriwon Prison (N. Korea) 1625
surveillance 465; US 3205; *see also* spying
suspension, torture 623, 1438
Sutayasa, I. Made (p) 1399
Suttner, Raymond (p) 2209
Svarinskas, Fr. Alfonsas (p) 2507
Svitlychna, Nadiya (p) 2818, 2881
Swankey, Ben (p) 500
SWAPO 339, 1783, 1785, 1786, 2130, 2273
Swaqa Prison (Jordan) 1588
Swaziland 2348, 2349
Swede, Shirley 3426
Sweden 2350
Swedish Action Group 918
Swidler, Arlene 266
Swift, M.G. 2822
Switzerland 2351
Swomley, John, Jr. 1931
Sy, Doan Quoc (p) 3528, 3533
Sychyovka Special Psychiatric Hospital (USSR) 2733
Syed, G.M. (p) 1821
Symbionese Liberation Army, US 3209
Syria 125, 2352-2361
Sysoyev, Vyacheslav (p) 2522
Sywulka, S.R. 1300
Szajkowski, Zosa 1194
Szász, Béla 1344
Szasz, Thomas Stephen 267
Szechter, Szynon 1955
Szent-Miklosy, Istvan (p) 268
Szikszai, Jeno (p) 2023
Szmaglewska, Seweryna (p) 1195
Szonyi, David 1196

T3 Prison (Kampuchea) 1599
Taagepera, Rein (p) 2823
Tabriz Prison (Iran) 1448, 1451, 1454
Tabrizi, Vida Hajebi (p) 173, 1478, 1482
Taco Taco Prison (Cuba) 759
Tacumbu Prison (Paraguay) 1845
Tadmur Prison (Syria) 2359
Tae-bok, Lee (p) 1655
Tae-kwon, Hwang (p) 1664
Tae-woo, Roh 1633, 1641
Taejon Prison (S. Korea) 1646, 1654
Tai, Law Kam (p) 1715
Taiping Detention Camp (Malaysia) 1706, 1715
Taiwan 2362-2370
Takamura, Kango (p) 3188
Tal, David 833
Talamente, Olga (p) 357, 383, 406, 407
Tamari, Salah (p) 1549
Tambo, Oliver (p) 2088
Tames, Richard 2274
Tamil rebellion 2328, 2329, 2331
Tan, Lek Hor 2068
Tan Hiep Prison (S. Vietnam) 3551, 3562, 3570, 3574
Tanforan Assembly Center (US) 3067
Tanggerang Prison (Indonesia) 1399
Tangley, Laura 269
Tannenbaum, Frank 3427
Tannus, Rima (p) 1540
Tanzania 226, 253, 2371, 2372
Tao-lei, Yeh (p) 309

Taoudenit Prison (Mali) 1719
tapols, Indonesian prisoners 1400
Tarnopolsky family (p) 399
Tarnuto, Joseph (p) 1835
Tarsis, Valery (p) 2496
Tarupiu, Peter (p) 1835
Taseer, Salman (p) 1821
Taussig, Michael 270
Tavárez, Claudio (p) 849
Tawil, Raymonda 271
tax protest, US 3461
Tayag, Fernand (p) 1922
Taygun, Aly (p) 2404, 2410
Taylan, Orhan (p) 2404
Taylor, Deb 1478
Taylor, John 1419
Taylor, John F. 3428
Taylor, Mary E. (p) 3007
Taylor, Robin 272
Taylor, Susan 2275
Tazoult-Lambese Prison (Algeria) 331
Tcheka 2738; *see also* KGB
Tchidimbo, Archbishop Raymond-Marie (p) 3, 1305
Tchollire Prison (Cameroon) 492
teachers 215, 347, 548, 611, 658, 659, 673, 843, 1617, 1620, 1273, 1274; anti-Nazi resistance 1177; Morocco 1749, 1761; Nepal 1790, 1791; Peru 1854, 1855; Philippines 1932; USSR 2699, 2700
technology of mass murder 1158; of repression 2890
Teepen, Tom 3429
Tegel Prison (Nazi) 993
Tejas Verdes Prison (Chile) 585
Tel Zaatar 282
Tellez, Rene Nuñez (p) 1795
Telmissani, Omar (p) 873
Temniskovsky Prison (USSR) 2717
Temple of the Lotus Flower Prison (China) 604
ten Boom, Corrie (p) 1197
Terelya, Josyp (p) 2508, 2848
Terezin concentration camp (Nazi Germany) 1055, 1081
Terracini, Umberto (p) 1571, 1579
terrorism/terrorists 236, 517, 864
Terrorism Act, S. Africa 2078, 2080
terrorist state *see* state terrorism
Teruel Prison (Spain) 2319
Teso, Tenh (p) 1675
testimonies 1065, 1105
Teteh, Narh (p) 1217
Thailand 2373–2378
Thalutsogentsang, Thubten Kelsang (p) 684
Than, Daw Cho (p) 1767
Thang, Vo Thi (p) 3575
Thayer, Millie 1802
theatre 475, 2057
Theiner, George 273
Theingi, Ma (p) 1779
Thelesuma, Robert (p) 1314
Theodorakis, Mikis (p) 1231, 1235, 1254, 1259, 1260
Theodorou, Victoria (p) 1242
Theoharis, Athan 3430, 3431
Theresienstadt concentration camp (Nazi) 1001
Thiers, Naomi 274, 3432
Thiessen, C.R. 2826
Thieu, Nguyen Van, President 3552, 3553, 3564, 3567
Thiong'o, Ngugi wa (p) 1613, 1623
Third World 262
Thomas, Evan (p) 301
Thomas, Norman (p) 3433
Thompson, D.O. (p) 1227
Thomsen, Alexander (p) 184, 2828
Thoreau, Henry David (p) 3084
Thorne, Ludmilla 2829, 2830
Thornton, Lawrence 410
Thu Duc Prison (S. Vietnam) 3551, 3570
Thubten (p) 605, 652
Thuy, Hoang Hai (p) 3528
Tian, Oon Siew (p) 1715
Tiananmen Square (Beijing) massacre 603, 610, 622, 660, 674, 704
Tianxiang, Father Gabriel Chen (p) 620
Tibet 599, 603, 605, 606, 617, 618, 620, 621, 625, 635, 641, 652, 677, 684, 692, 693
Tichitt Prison (Mauritania) 1722
Tiflis Prison (USSR) 2672
tiger cage 291, 3560, 3562
Tihar Prison (India) 1352
Tillard, Paul 1119
Tilsen, Ken 3435
time 184
Timerman, Hector 411
Timerman, Jacobo (p) 6, 118, 350, 352, 360, 387, 389, 411–414, 416
Timisoara Prison (Romania) 2014
Timmermanns, Father (p) 1178
Timol, Ahmed (p) 2082
Tinggal bin Muhammed (p) 482
Tipitapa Prison (Nicaragua) 1800
Tiradentes Prison (Brazil) 458
Tirana Prison (Albania) 326
Tirgusor Prison (Romania) 2031
Titchy Prison (China/Tibet) 601
Titu, Ghejan (p) 2024
Tlatelolco massacre 1729
Toai, Doan Van (p) 3535, 3545
Többens enterprises 984
Todd, Judith (p) 2013
Todea, Dragos (p) 2026
Toer, Pramoedya Ananta (p) 1399
Togliatti, Palmiro (p) 1579
Togo 2379–2383
Toivo, Herman Toivo ja (p) 1785, 2089, 2130, 2154
Tokoin (barracks) Prison (Togo) 2381
Toledo Reyes, Juan (p) 3492
Tolento, Aurelio "Willy" (p) 1927
Tolio, Romeo (p) 1922
Tollefson, James 3436
Toller, Ernst (p) 942
Tombs Prison (US) 3170, 3409
Tomlinson, Kenneth 2834
Tomsho, Robert 3437
Tong, Lee Tze (p) 2058, 2062
Tong, Ly (p) 3540
Tong-Kyu, Im (p) 1657
tonton macoutes 1314, 1318
Topaz (Utah) Relocation Center (US) 3067
Toptasi Prison (Turkey) 2411
Tora Prison (Egypt) 855, 860, 865, 876
Torgau Prison (GDR) 958
Torok, Janos (p) 2023
Torrado, Horácio (p) 337
Torre, Father Edicio dela (p) 1883, 1902
Torres, Alejandrina (p) 3042, 3292
Torres, César (p) 714
Torres, Eric (p) 1932
torture 2, 3, 6–8, 10–43, 46, 49, 53, 55, 59, 60, 63–65, 68, 70, 75, 76, 81, 97, 104, 105, 107, 111–113, 133, 157, 184, 185, 193, 208, 216, 217, 220, 225, 226, 228, 231, 238, 242, 244, 253, 260, 264, 269, 276–278, 284, 291, 295, 307, 309, 314, 317–321, 323, 324, 337, 341, 342, 344, 347–351, 354, 355, 357, 360, 362, 365–367, 370, 371, 375, 376, 379, 380, 386, 399, 400, 402, 405–408, 412–415, 418, 434,

445, 453, 455, 456, 458, 460, 463-469, 471, 472, 477, 479, 480, 492-494, 504, 511, 513, 517, 522, 524-533, 536, 542, 545-547, 550, 556, 559, 562, 564, 566, 569, 570, 577, 582, 591, 594, 596, 601, 603, 604, 618, 621, 623, 652, 657, 675, 676, 678, 699, 700, 710, 711, 715, 716, 729, 760, 780-782, 785, 840, 847, 851, 852, 856, 860, 863, 864, 868, 908, 909, 912, 913, 915, 917, 926, 929, 931, 981, 1155, 1189, 1230, 1237, 1241, 1242, 1246, 1249, 1273, 1363, 1364, 1387, 1438, 1465, 1470, 1490, 1496, 1497, 1506, 1520, 1524, 1525, 1530, 1533, 1539, 1540, 1548, 1552, 1684, 1686, 1691, 1694, 1759, 1761; Argentina 160; children, S. Africa 2184; deaths 623; Egypt 876; El Salvador 877-879, 881, 883-885, 890, 891, 894, 895, 903, 905, 906; Guatemala 1273, 1282, 1296; Guinea 1304, 1306-1308; Haiti 1314-1323; Indonesia 1392, 1395, 1399, 1402, 1405, 1413, 1415; Iran 1422, 1424, 1429, 1430, 1438, 1447; Kampuchea 1590, 1598, 1601; Kenya 1613, 1616, 1618; Latin America 3262; Mali 1719, 1720; Mauritania 1722; Mexico 1725-1727, 1731, 1733-1735; modernization 238; Morocco 1753, 1756, 1758-1761; Mozambique 1765; Myanmar 1766, 1767, 1769-1772, 1779; N. Korea 1631; Namibia 1783, 1787-1789; Nazi 1178; Nepal 1792; Nicaragua 160, 1795, 1798, 1800, 1801; Nigeria 1815; Northern Ireland 160; Pakistan 1819-1821, 1826; Papua New Guinea 1834, 1835; Paraguay 1836, 1837, 1842, 1846-1848, 1851-1853; permanent effects 415; Peru 1855, 1856, 1862; Philippines 1875, 1876, 1884, 1886, 1887, 1891, 1893, 1898, 1900, 1901, 1910, 1911, 1917, 1918, 1922, 1927, 1929, 1937; photographs 1449; Poland 1952; Portugal 1993, 1997; rehabilitation 241, 260; Rehabilitation Center for Torture Victims 260; Rhodesia 2002, 2011; Romania 2019, 2020, 2025; Russia 2038; Rwanda 2041; Saudi Arabia 2046, 2047; Senegal 2049; Singapore 2062; Somalia 2072-2074; S. Africa 2076, 2080, 2082, 2090, 2099, 2105, 2111, 2122, 2127, 2132, 2136, 2143-2145, 2164, 2168, 2191, 2258, 2259, 2261, 2262, 2265, 2268, 2276-2278, 2280, 2284, 2285, 2289; S. Korea 1641, 1647, 1650, 1653, 1656, 1661, 1664, 1672; S. Vietnam 3551, 3553, 3554, 3557, 3560, 3561, 3564, 3567, 3568, 3578, 3581; Spain 2316, 2318, 2325; Sri Lanka 2328, 2329, 2336; Sudan 2344, 2345; Syria 2352, 2353, 2359, 2361; Taiwan 2362, 2368, 2369; techniques 477, 561, 623, 2359, 2395, 2418, 2419; technology 68, 173, 276, 2890; Togo 2383; trade unionists 187; treatment 153; Tunisia 2384, 2386, 2388-2391; Turkey 2395, 2396, 2398, 2399, 2407, 2408, 2412-2414, 2416-2421, 2424; Uganda 2446-2463; USSR 2593, 2672, 2692, 2723, 2738, 2756, 2763, 2797, 2820, 2859; UK 2903, 2907, 2911, 2915, 2934, 2935, 2939, 2944, 2948, 2967, 2973, 2975; US 3080, 3296, 3300, 3358, 3455; Uruguay 3492, 3494, 3502-3505, 3507, 3510-3513, 3517; Venezuela 3522; videocassette 160; water 3567; Yemen, Arab Rep. 3586; Yugoslavia 3603, 3611; Zaire 3612, 3617; *see also* torturers

Torture in the Eighties 46

Torture Victims Protection Act 3475

torturers 6, 192, 295, 403, 424, 562, 612; Greece 1230, 1237, 1246; Uruguay 3519

Totangay, Kalilu (p) 2053

Toth, Dr. Zoltan (p) 2836

Totten, Samuel 278-280, 1199, 1200, 1480, 1605, 2442, 2837

Touré, Sékou 1304

Tourón Landaburu, Alberto (p) 3494

Townsend, Alison 2838

toxic waste 3152

Toynbee, Arnold 2443

Trach, Le Khai (p) 3544

trade unions *see* unions

Tran, Tri Vu (p) 3547, 3548

Trang Lon Camp (Vietnam) 3548

transit camp (Nazi) 998

Traoré, Ladji (p) 1722

trauma treatment 153

Trautmann, Emilie 2839

travel, right of 155

treason 324, 1816, 2053; S. Africa 2087; USSR 2628

Treason Act, Nepal 1791

Treasury Police (El Salvador) 903

Treblinka concentration camp (Nazi) 279, 1028, 1062, 1182; revolt 980

Trejos, Carlos Huembes (p) 1797

Trembevilla, Helen (p) 1903

Tres Alamos Prison (Chile) 524, 525, 543, 546, 547, 562, 585, 587, 591/92

Trial Bay Gaol 427

trials 19, 53, 57, 1147; denial of 10; S. Africa 2189, 2190; secret 624; without appeal 860

Trident nuclear submarine 3441

Trikeri Prison (Greece) 1242

Trillion, Germaine (p) 1198

Trimple, J. 2840

Trinkl, John 3439-3442

Tripoli Central Prison (Libya) 1689, 1694

Troba, Martz (p) 6

Trotskyist 364, 608, 663, 697, 715, 832

Trotter, Desmond (p) 846

Trowbridge, Elizabeth 3443

Truman Doctrine 1242

Trung, Nguyen dan (p) 3557

Truong, David (p) 2532

Tsehai, Tolessa (p) 231

Tsele, Molefe (p) 2083

Tsemel, Lea 1509, 1550, 1562

Tsering, Lhakpa (p) 606

Tsering, Yulo Dawa (p) 603

Tshikangu, Musungayi (p) 337

Tsirka, Anastasia (p) 1261

Tucker, Robert C. 2841

Tuhadeleni, Eliaser (p) 2089

Tuka, John (p) 1835

Tula de Canales, Maria Teresa (p) 309

Tule Lake (Calif.) Relocation Center (US) 3067

Tumsa, Gudina (Ethiopia) (p) 231

Tun, Tin Nain (p) 1779

Tunis Civil Prison (Tunisia) 2384, 2390
Tunisia 2384–2392
Tunnell, Kenneth 3445
Tupamaros 3500, 3508, 3509
Tur, Pramoedya Ananta (p) 1401
Turbay, President 709
Turk, Austin T. 281
Turkey 279, 2393–2425; and Armenians 2426–2445; in Bulgaria 484, 485; and US 2425
Turki, Fawaz 282
Turkish Peace Association 2409, 2410, 2416, 2421
Turkow Kaminska, Ruth (p) 2842
Turner, Henry (p) 1984
Turner, Margaret (p) 2913
Turner, William W. 3446
Tutsi, Rwanda 2041
Tuzi-Ouzou Prison (Algeria) 332
Tweedale, Douglas 416
Tyita, James (p) 2116
Tyler, Mary (p) 1388
tyrannicide 1232, 1245
Tz'ong, Mi 694
Tzmailovich, Ekaterina (Katya) (p) 2033

U, Aung Thet (p) 1777
U, Tin (p) 1777, 1779
U., Ruta (p) 2843
U.S.S. Pueblo 1629
Uganda 4, 256, 291, 2446–2463
Ugarte, Marta (p) 562
Ugarte Roman, Maria (p) 545
UHA (Stasi prison, GDR) 952
Uhl, Petr (p) 231, 793, 824, 826, 832, 834
Uhlir, Frank (p) 835
Ukpong, Anthony (p) 1807
Ukraine 1209, 2566, 2609, 2614, 2616, 2628, 2633, 2693, 2694, 2699, 2709, 2712, 2715, 2733, 2737, 2761, 2816, 2831, 2833; prisoners 2844; women 2881, 2882, 2886
Ukrainian Catholic Church 2848
Ukrainian Helsinki Group 2720
Umaña, Luis (p) 711
underground (US) 3202
underground press, Poland 1944, 1965, 1983
unfair trials 49, 318, 337, 517, 625, 674, 698, 753, 864, 872, 1674; Kenya 1613, 1615; Pakistan 1830; Poland 1941, 1948, 1970; Tunisia 2388, 2389, 2390; Turkey 2416, 2419; USSR 2699, 2788; UK 3008; US 3052, 3115, 3207, 3377
Union of Soviet Socialist Republics 57, 65, 73, 80, 125, 208, 221, 226, 260, 268, 278, 279, 304a, 568, 2464–2887; genocide 72
unions: El Salvador 879, 880, 896, 899, 904; and FBI 3274; Guatemala 1273, 1281; Indonesia 1399; Jamaica 1581; Lesotho 1684; Nepal 1792; Nigeria 1807; Pakistan 1820; Peru 1854, 1855, 1861, 1865; Philippines 1876, 1904; Poland 1963; Romania 2017; Singapore 2062; S. Africa 2153, 2180, 2181, 2211, 2228; S. Korea 1632, 1633, 1641, 1645; Spain 2302; Thailand 2373; trade unions 81, 187, 204, 345, 347, 350, 354, 367, 420, 429, 455, 456, 499, 517, 518, 524, 530, 543, 544, 548, 562, 586, 590, 709, 711, 716, 724, 776, 800, 843, 853, 856, 927, 1317, 1706, 1715, 1837, 1847, 1969; Tunisia 2384, 2386, 2387, 2390–2392; Turkey 2413, 2414, 2416; USSR 2865; US 3077, 3105, 3225, 3230, 3245, 3464, 3472; Uruguay 3492, 3509; Venezuela 3522
UNITA 337
United Arab Emirates 2888, 2889
United Kingdom 2890–3015
United Nations 64, 107, 124, 278, 283, 312, 313, 371, 521
United Nations Convention Against Torture 244
United Nations Declaration Against Torture (1975) 55, 220
United Nations Declaration on Religious Intolerance 620
United Nations Human Rights Commission 781
United Nations resolutions on torture 244
United States: 57, 161, 255, 259, 263, 278, 279, 305, 1112, 3016–3491; anti-communist containment policy 130, 263; country reports: evaluation 180; El Salvador 878, 896; foreign policy, criticism 750; human rights policy 371; intervention 453; Latin America 189; military aid 173, 350; State Department 376
Universal Declaration of Human Rights 39, 243, 278, 286, 287; US 3466
universities, closed 453/54
Up Park Camp (Jamaica) 1581
Uphaus, Willard (p) 3150
uprisings 984
Urbina, María Rivas (p) 1797
Urdang, Stephanie 1311
Urfer, Bonnie (p) 3127
Urman, Jerzy Feliks 1172
Uruguay 10, 46, 68, 257, 260, 269, 276, 295, 297, 3492–3519
Urwich, John (p) 2857
Usior, Adrianus (p) 1402
Ussher, Clarence 2445
Ussher Fort Prison (Ghana) 1219, 1225, 1227
Utitod Prison (China/Tibet) 601
Uvira Prison (Zaire) 3613
Uzbekistan 3520, 3521
Uzun, Pasa (p) 248

Vaghin, Evgenii (p) 2858
Vakil Abad Prison (Iran) 1454
Vaksberg, Arkady 2859
Valda, Roberto 453/54
Valdes, Hernan (p) 586
Valdés, Mia 289, 781
Valdice Prison (Czechoslovakia) 818
Valer Munalla, Walter (p) 1855
Valéry, Nicole (p) 2029
Valladares Pérez, Armando F. (p) 739, 746, 747, 750, 766, 778–780, 782–784, 788
Valle, Mauricio (p) 3193
Valls, Jorge (p) 6, 785
Van Buren, Cassandra 3452
Vancouver Five 502, 503
Vancura, Vladislav (p) 1009
Vander Wall, Jim 3094, 3095
Van Dyck, Harry (p) 3454
Van Es, Adriaan 2284
van Grup, Marijke 2284
Van Minh, Nguyen (p) 3585
van Nieberk, Dr. B. (p) 215
Vannuchi Leme, Alexandre (p) 463
Van Slyke, Leslie 3010
Vanunu, Mordechai (p) 1513, 1561, 1563, 1565
van Vorem, Robert 2860, 2861
Vanzetti *see* Sacco and Vanzetti

Vara, Eric (p) 2279
Vargas Gomez, Andres (p) 750
Vaughn, Ellen Santilli 696
Vavrina, Vernon 3455
Vega, Christobal (p) 291
Vega Angel, Nicolas (p) 530
Veis, Frantisek (p) 818
Velikano, Tatyana (p) 307
Vemmer, Wilfried 960
Venezuela 3522-3526
Venkatrathnam, Sonny (p) 2223
Ventimiglia, Linda (p) 3299
Vera, Marta (pseudonym) 587
Verdi, Requiem 1001
Verkhne-Uralsk Isolation Prison (USSR) 2774
Vernau, Judi 290
Verwoerd, Hendrik 2111
Veselica, Marko (p) 3600
victims 370
Victor Verster Security Prison (S. Africa) 2122
Victoria, Dr. Maximo Pedro (p) 173, 399, 417
Videla, General Jorge R. 347, 382, 402, 423
video 277, 287, 298, 354, 389, 533, 552, 751, 1065, 1163
Vieira, José (p) 1999
Vietnam, France 932
Vietnam, North 141, 1675, 3550
Vietnam, Socialist Republic of 3527-3549
Vietnam, South 141, 253, 3551-3585
Vietnam Veterans Against the War 3394
Vietnam War 3038, 3041, 3047, 3058, 3060, 3129, 3154, 3164, 3178, 3241, 3264, 3271, 3372, 3393; conscientious objection 3406, 3436; protest (US) 2375, 3197, 3206, 3209; resisters 3187, 3191
vigilantes 1924; *see also* death squads
Vilardel, Raul del Valle (p) 771
Villa d'Ambouli (torture, Djibouti) 840
Villa Devoto Prison (Argentina) 342, 399
Villa Grimaldi Prison (torture center, Chile) 536, 546-548, 562, 585, 591/92
Villa Morista *see* Department of State Security Police
Villa Soldati Prison (Argentina) 399
Villar, Miguel (p) 1865
Vinas Cirera, Jesus (p) 2303
Vins, Georgi (p) 2755
Viola, General Roberto 363
Vishnevskaya, Yulia (p) 2517
Vitoriano, Jose (p) 184
Vitullo, Anita 1564
Vitzthum, Hilda (p) 2862
Vlachos, Helen (p) 1263
Vladimir Prison (USSR) 2477, 2484, 2517, 2560, 2733
Vlassis, Petros (p) 1230
Vogel, Wolfgang 959
Vogt, Marilyn 2864, 2865
Voikhanskaya, Marina (p) 2526
Volpin, Alik (p) 2517
Von Hassel, Fey (p) 1203
von Meck, Galina (p) 2866
VONS (Committee to Defend the Unjustly Prosecuted) 802, 811, 826
Voon, Chen Shek (p) 1715
Voravong, Chansamone (p) 1675
Vorenberg, Elizabeth 1415
Vorenberg, James 1415
Vorkuta Labor Complex (USSR) 2511, 2759, 2774
Vorkuta Prison Camp (USSR) 2714
Vorster, John 2104, 2105, 2147
Voznesenskaya, Julia (p) 2663
Vranje Prison (Yugoslavia) 3592
Vrba, Dr. Rudolph (p) 184, 1204
Vyatlag Prison Camp (USSR) 2714
Vyshinsky, Andrey 2859

Waal, Alex de 920
Wabunoha, Steven (p) 114
Wachira, Kamoji (p) 1609
Wade, Nicholas 413, 588, 2867
Wahad, Dhoruba Bin (p) 3395
Wahhab, Murad Abdul (p) 225
Wainggai, Dr. Thomas (p) 1394, 1402
Wakeman, Carolyn 703
Walczak, Boguslaw (p) 1952
Wald, Karen (p) 3457
Waldheim Prison (GDR) 958
Walesa, Lech (p) 1950, 1956, 1975
Walker, Annette 3458
Walker Report, 1968 riot 3049
Wall, James M. 478
Wallace, Joe (p) 500
Wallach, Erica (p) 964
Wallance, Gregory 786
Wallenberg, Raoul (p) 414, 2493, 2560, 2575, 2669, 2681, 2703, 2791
Walliman, Isidor 292
Walsh, Bishop James E. (p) 655
Walsh, John 1987, 2868
Walsh, Louis (p) 3011
Walsh, Rodolfo J. (p) 347, 418
Walton, Olive (p) 3012
Walton Jail (UK) 2959
Wamala, Bakulu Mpagi (p) 2459
Wamwere, Koigi wa (p) 1609, 1613, 1624
Wanding, Ren (p) 674
Wang, Diane 1482, 3459
Wangchuk, Geshe Lobsang (p) 605, 684
Wanjau, Gakaara wa (p) 2938
war 296, 942; and US 3128, 3129, 3132, 3137, 3143, 3162, 3190, 3192, 3223, 3225, 3233, 3266, 3277, 3303, 3315-3319, 3363, 3373, 3375, 3390, 3453, 3482; protest 976; resistance 3111; *see also* draft; conscientious objection; peace protest
war crimes 64, 115
War Resisters League 3260
Ward, Margaret 3013
Ward, Richard 419, 479, 589, 921, 1390, 1483, 1937, 2378
Ward Road Jail (Shanghai) 663
Ward 7 (Tarsis) 2496
Wardlaw, Ada 3403, 3404
Warner, Roger 1602
warrants 1930; *see also* habeas corpus
Warsaw Ghetto 279, 982, 997, 1042, 1062, 1073, 1076, 1082, 1091; archives 1165; uprising 980
Warschawsky, Michael (p) 1511, 1537, 1555
Washington, Albert (p) 3065
Wat, Aleksander (p) 2870
water torture 3567
Watner, Carl (p) 3461
Watson, Russell 2871, 2872
Watt, George (p) 698
Wattenmaker, Steve 1566
Way, Saul (p) 1402
weapons proliferation 3137; *see also* nuclear
Weathermen 3419
Webb, P. 3014
Webb, P.R. 591
Webster, Paul 934
Wedlock, Eldon, Jr. 3246
Weglyn, Michi 3462
Wei, Chen (p) 670
Wei, Yang (p) 707
Weibel, Jose (p) 536, 544

Weinstein, Corey 3463
Weinstock, Earl (p) 1205
Weiping, Zhang (p) 603
Weisbord, Vera (p) 3464
Weisburd, Abe 293, 3465–3467
Weiss, Renata 294
Weissberg, Alexander (p) 2478, 2873
Weissberg, Arnold 84, 722, 1745–1747, 3468–3470
Weissenborn, Hans (p) 948
Wells, Leon Weliczker (p) 184, 1206
Wenderoth, Fr. Joseph (p) 3271
Wenli, Xu (p) 603, 633, 706
Wenzel, D. 1673
Weschler, Lawrence 295, 480, 837, 3519
West, Lewis J. 296
West Bank 282
West Germany 226
Westerbork Prison (Nazi) 998
Westerkamp, José Gustavo (p) 342, 388
Wheaton, Philip 297
whipping 1424; *see also* beating
Whipple, Christopher 1939, 2287
whistleblower 2943; US 3346
Whitaker, M. 302
Whitcomb, Richard 751
White, Harry (p) 3377
White, Harry Dexter (p) 3108
White, Judy 420, 421, 849
White, Tom (p) 745
White Brigade (Brigada Blanca) 1725, 1727, 1734, 1739, 1741
white collar workers 548
White Rose, Resistance 1177
Whitehorn, Laura (p) 255
Whiteman, Kate 510
Whitley, Andrew 1498
Whitley Road Holding Center (Singapore) 2063
Whitman, Lois 2425
Wiechert, Ernst (p) 1207
Wiechert, Jurgen (p) 247
Wieck, Agnes (p) 3472
Wieck, David (p) 3472
Wierzynski, G.H. 2875
Wiesel, Elie (p) 1208
Wilcox, Clair 3474
Wilde, Margaret 3475
Wilde, Margaret 423
Wilkinson, Frank (p) 3251
Wilkinson, R. 858, 3015
Will, G.F. 788
Willenson, K. 591/92
Willenson, Kim 922
Willey, F. 1989
Willey, Fay 424, 481, 700, 2876, 3606
Williams, Dessima (p) 3425
Williams, Langdon (p) 3397
Williams, Lynora 3476
Williams, Suzi (p) 3240
Williamson, John (p) 3053
Willis-Conger, Philip (p) 3114, 3117
Wilmington Ten 3063, 3112, 3139, 3171, 3172, 3477, 3478
Wilner, Herbert 1205
Wilson, Edmund 3479
Wilson-Smith, Anthony 2877
Win, Ko Aung (p) 1767
Win, Ne 1771, 1772, 1776
Win, Dr. Tin Myo (p) 1779
Win, U Mya (p) 1782
Win, Zaw (p) 1777
Winchester, Simon 425
Windhoek Prison (Namibia) 1783, 1784, 1788
Winkler, Karl (p) 943
Winner, Harry (p) 3421
Winooski 44, US 3072
Winston, Henry (p) 3053
Wise, David 3480
Wiseburg, Laurie S. 138, 303–305, 3481
witch hunt, Indonesia 1400; US 3289, 3363, 3377, 3447, 3251
witnesses 38
Wittner, Lawrence 3482
Wolf, Jiri (p) 818
Wolfe, Bertram 2879
Wolfer, Barbara 2880
Wollin, A. 1567
women 6, 19, 68, 103, 109, 121, 125, 156, 242, 255, 271, 306–309, 314, 357, 381, 384, 396, 408, 514, 520, 532, 546, 547, 559, 579, 752, 754, 871, 872, 911, 929, 971, 1084, 1108, 1125, 1149, 1379, 1478, 1506, 1529, 1562, 1808; El Salvador 878, 884, 886, 907; Guinea-Bissau 1311; Indonesia 1401; Iran 1428; Japan 1586; Kenya 1616, 1619; Malaysia 1709; Pakistan 1822, 1831; Philippines 1877, 1917; pregnant 350; Ravensbrück 1032, 1198; Resistance, Greece 1242; rights 308; Romania 2027; Russia 2032; S. Africa 2110, 2121, 2144, 2151, 2167, 2181, 2227; S. Vietnam 3565, 3574, 3578; Spain 2294, 2323; suffrage (UK) 2905, 2912; Turkey 2402; USSR 2525, 2530, 2539, 2619, 2625, 2663, 2672, 2743, 2795, 2853, 2862, 2881, 2882, 2886; UK 2924, 2929, 2933, 2963, 2964, 2978; Uruguay 3515; US 3041, 3168, 3181, 3293, 3370, 3372, 3399, 3402; *see also* Ilopongo; suffrage
Women Against Daddy Warbucks 3240
Women's House of Detention (US) 3043
Women's Prison of Madrid (Spain) 2312
Won Yang, Kang (p) 1673
Wong, Father Aloysius (p) 653
Won-ho, Yu (p) 1633
Wonka, Pavel (p) 798, 818, 822, 829
Woo Jae, Lee (p) 1673
Woo Jung, Lee (p) 1669
Woods, Donald (p) 2118, 2289, 2290
Woodson, Helen (p) 3127, 3364, 3483
work/workers 184, 548
A World Apart, film 2129, 2252
World Court 64; *see also* International Court of Justice
World Cup 404
World Psychiatric Association 65; *see also* psychiatry
World War I 285; conscientious objection, US 3433
World War II, conscientious objection 3403–3405; internment 3188; US 3454, 3472, 3479, 3487, 3488
Wright, Paulo (p) 457
writers 2, 6, 80, 81, 132, 137, 156, 186, 219, 255a, 273, 275, 291, 310, 347, 368, 450, 515, 516, 536, 549, 581, 658, 705, 739, 740, 746, 747, 749, 766, 778–780, 782, 788, 804, 819, 827, 828, 871, 942, 1009, 1015, 1207, 1231, 1242, 1244, 1246, 1368, 1462, 1473, 1493, 1804; exile 2757; Iran 1429; Italy 1576; Kenya 1608, 1617; killed, USSR 2748; Mexico 1731; Morocco 1750, 1752, 1753; Nigeria 1804, 1805, 1810; Philippines 1873, 1874, 1887, 1927, 1940; Poland 1958, 1963, 1965, 1980; Portugal 1999; Sierra Leone 2054; S. Korea 1640; Turkey

2404, 2410, 2412, 2413, 2416; USSR 2619–2622, 2650, 2671, 2796–2800, 2816; UAE 2889; UK 2924; US 3065, 3173; Vietnam 3533, 3543, 3544, 3546, 3549; Zaire 3615
Wrobel, Brian 1446
Wroclaw-Kleczkowska Prison (Poland) 1969
Wronke Prison 939, 940
Wu, Hongda Harry (p) 702, 703
Wu-ming-shih (pseudonym) *see* Pu Nai-fu
WuDunn, Sheryl 704
Württemburg Jews 1193
Wujec, Henryk (p) 1941, 1982
Wulff-Tagoe, Franz (p) 1218
Wurmbrand, Michael (p) 745
Wurmbrand, Richard 2030
Wurmbrand, Sabina (p) 2031
Wyatt, Jiai 838
Wyeweera, Rohana (p) 2329
Wyman, David 3484
Wypych, Tadeusz (p) 1983
Wyszynski, Stefan Cardinal (p) 1990
Wytwycky, Bohdan 1209

Xenlin, Wang (p) 674
xenophobia 278; *see also* anti-communism; racism; war
Xiang, Liu (p) 660
Xiaobo, Liu (p) 610, 674
Xiaohuz, Li (p) 674
Xiaoping, Deng 602, 638
Xiling, Lin (p) 677
Xueyan, Bishop Fan (p) 620, 684

Yahil, Leni 1210
Yajee, Pt. Sheelbhadra (p) 2915
Yakhimovich, Ivan (p) 2486, 2688, 2774
Yakir, Pyotr (p) 2810, 2825, 2883
Yakunin, Gleb (p) 2489, 2507, 2807
Yaldoi, Nusrat (p) 1435
Yan, Xiong (p) 670
Yancey, P. 2884
Yancey, Phillip 311, 593
Yañez, Arturo 3485
Yankton Federal Prison Camp (US) 3125–3127
Yap, Salvador (p) 1922
Yasen, Bohdan (p) 2885
Yathay, Pin (p) 1606
Ye Kyi Aing Prison (Myanmar) 1767
Yemen, People's Democratic Republic of 3587–3589
Yemen Arab Republic (North) 3586
Yen, Luu Thi (Thuy An) 3550
Yeong-gon, Kim (p) 1663
Yeshitela, Omali (p) 3486
Yevsyukov, Serafim (p) 2483
Yew, Lee Kuan 2063
Yiaros Island Prison (Greece) 1239
Yijun, Wang (p) 621
Yildirim, Huseyin (p) 2418
Yildiz, Pamuk (p) 255
Yildiz, Usuf Ali (p) 2414
Ying, Lai (p) 708
Yinhan, Peng (p) 673
Yoko Prison (Cameroon) 492, 493
Yong, Kim (p) 1655
Yong-hee, Lee (p) 1633
Yong Hui, Lee (p) 1670
Young, Andrew 3062
Young, Jacob 965
Young, Richard J. 1211
Younghusband, Peter 2104
Yrigoyen, Hipólito (p) 350
Yu Bo, Song (p) 1656
Yude, Song (p) 603
Yudevitch, G.M. (p) 2662
Yuehua, Wei (p) 602
Yugoslavia 221, 3590–3611
Yumbel (mass grave) 528
Yun-tang, Joseph Chen (p) 668
Yunis, Abdi Ismail (p) 2071, 2075
Yunus, Mohammad (p) 1391
Yusefi, Aziz (p) 1454

Z 1259
Zabela Prison (Yugoslavia) 3608
Zadrozynski, Edmund (p) 1941
Zahari, Said (p) 2063
Zahedan Prison (Iran) 1448
Zahn, Curtis (p) 301
Zahn, Franklin (p) 3487
Zahn, Gordon (p) 1212, 3488, 3489
Zaire 291, 3612–3618
Zalaquet Daher, Jose (p) 594
Zaldaña, Angel 905
Zamarstynów Prison (USSR) 2870
Zambia 53, 3619–3624
Zamora Prison (Spain) 2319
Zamorano, Mario (p) 544, 590
Zana, Mehdi (p) 2418
ZANU, Zambia 3622
Zatouna Prison (Greece) 1231
Zawodny, Janusz 2887
Zazueta, Bertha (p) 1734
Zeeuw, Jan (p) 1178
Zehm, Guenter 958
zeks (prisoners) 2797
Zeller, David (p) 2795
Zeller, Eberhard 1213
Zenger, Peter (p) 3052
Zenica Prison (Yugoslavia) 3591, 3608, 3609
Zerwoual, Abdellatif (p) 1761
Zézé, Samuel (p) 493
Zhengtian, Li (p) 677
Zhimin, Su (p) 621
Zhixin, Jiao (p) 674
Zia ul-Haq, Pres. 1819
Zibakalam, Sadiq (p) 173
Zim Cheng Prison (China) 700
Zima, Tom (p) 3179
Zimbabwe 4, 314, 3625–3633
Zimbabwe African Peoples Union (ZAPU) 2012
Zimmermann, Matilde 839
Zingaro, John 3490
Zink, Larry (p) 3159
Zinoviev, Aleksandr (p) 2536
Zinoviev, Grigory (p) 2655
Zinzun, Michael (p) 3383
Zionism 2520
Zivs, Samuil 315
Zoff, Otto 316
Zomba Prison (Malawi) 1697, 1699
Zondi, Nonginkosi (p) 2081
Zubatsky, David 1214
Zubelevitch, Julia (p) 2662
Zuccolillo, Aldo (p) 1851
Zufriategui, Carlos (p) 3502
Zweibrucken Prison (FRG) 974
Zwerman, Gilda 3491